Communication Yearbook 39

Communication Yearbook 39

Edited by
Elisia L. Cohen

international
communication
association.

Published Annually for the
International Communication Association

Routledge
Taylor & Francis Group
NEW YORK AND LONDON

P
87
.C5974

V39

First published 2015
by Routledge
711 Third Avenue, New York, NY 10017

and by Routledge
2 Park Square, Milton Park, Abingdon, Oxon OX14 4RN

Routledge is an imprint of the Taylor & Francis Group, an informa business

ISSN: 0147-4642
ISSN: 1556-7429

ISBN: 978-1-138-85384-3 (hbk)
ISBN: 978-1-315-72253-5 (ebk)

Typeset in Times
by Apex CoVantage, LLC

Printed and bound in the United States of America by
Edwards Brothers Malloy on sustainably sourced paper

Contents

The International Communication Association

The International Communication Association (ICA) was formed in 1950, bringing together academics and other professionals whose interests focus on human communication. The Association maintains an active membership of more than 4,000 individuals, of whom some two-thirds teach and conduct research in colleges, universities, and schools around the world. Other members are in government, law, medicine, and other professions. The wide professional and geographic distribution of the membership provides the basic strength of the ICA. The Association serves as a meeting ground for sharing research and useful dialogue about communication interests.

Through its divisions and interest groups, publications, annual conferences, and relations with other associations around the world, the ICA promotes the systemic study of communication theories, processes, and skills. In addition to *Communication Yearbook*, the Association publishes the *Journal of Communication*, *Human Communication Research*, *Communication Theory*, *Journal of Computer-Mediated Communication*, *Communication, Culture & Critique*, *A Guide to Publishing in Scholarly Communication Journals*, and the *ICA Newsletter*.

For additional information about the ICA and its activities, visit online at www.icahdq.org or contact Michael L. Haley, Executive Director, International Communication Association, 1500 21st Ave. NW, Washington, DC 20036 USA; phone 202–955–1444; fax 202–955–1448; email ica@icahdq.org.

Editors of the *Communication Yearbook* series:

Volumes 1 and 2, Brent D. Ruben
Volumes 3 and 4, Dan Nimmo
Volumes 5 and 6, Michael Burgoon
Volumes 7 and 8, Robert N. Bostrom
Volumes 9 and 10, Margaret L. McLaughlin
Volumes 11, 12, 13, and 14, James A. Anderson
Volumes 15, 16, and 17, Stanley A. Deetz
Volumes 18, 19, and 20, Brant R. Burleson
Volumes 21, 22, and 23, Michael E. Roloff
Volumes 24, 25, and 26, William B. Gudykunst
Volumes 27, 28, and 29, Pamela J. Kalbfleisch
Volumes 30, 31, 32, and 33, Christina S. Beck
Volumes 34, 35, and 36, Charles T. Salmon
Volumes 37, 38, and 39, Elisia L. Cohen

James A. Danowski
Communication & Technology Div. Chair
U of Illinois at Chicago

Richard K. Popp
Communication History Div. Chair
U of Wisconsin–Milwaukee

Seamus Simpson
Communication Law & Policy Div. Chair
U of Salford

Richard J. Doherty
Environmental Communication Div. Chair
U of Leeds

Miyase Christensen
Ethnicity & Race in Communication Div. Chair
Stockholm University; Royal Institute of Technology (KTH)

Paula M Gardner
Feminist Scholarship Div. Chair
OCAD University

James D. Ivory
Game Studies IG Chair
Virginia Tech

Travers Scott
Gay, Lesbian, Bisexual & Transgender IG Chair
Clemson U

Adrienne Shaw
Gay, Lesbian, Bisexual & Transgender IG Chair
Temple U

Rashmi Luthra
Global Comm/Social Change Div. Chair
U of Michigan–Dearborn

Kevin B. Wright
Health Communication Div. Chair
George Mason University

Prabu David
Information Systems Div. Chair
Washington State U

Aaron R. Boyson
Instructional/Developmental Div. Chair
U of Minnesota–Duluth

Hee Sun Park
Intercultural Communication Div. Chair
Korea University

Howard Giles
Intergroup Communication IG Chair
U of California–Santa Barbara

Timothy R. Levine
Interpersonal Communication Div. Chair
Korea University

Matt Carlson
Journalism Studies Div. Chair
Saint Louis U

Theresa R. Castor
Language & Social Interaction Div. Chair
U of Wisconsin–Parkside

Rene Weber
Mass Communication Div. Chair
U of California–Santa Barbara

Craig R. Scott
Organizational Communication Div. Chair
Rutgers U

Amit Pinchevski
Philosophy, Theory and Critique Div. Chair
Hebrew U

Jesper Stromback
Political Communication Div. Chair
Mid Sweden U

Melissa A. Click
Popular Communication Div. Chair
U of Missouri–Columbia

Jennifer L. Bartlett
Public Relations Div. Chair
Queensland U of Technology

Andrew C. Billings
Sports Communication IG Chair
U of Alabama

Jana Holsanova
*Visual Communication Studies
Div. Chair*
Lund U

Michael L. Haley
Executive Director (ex-officio)
International Communication
Association

DIVISION CHAIRS

Erica L. Scharrer
*Children, Adolescents & the Media
Div. Chair*
U of Massachusetts–Amherst

Sahara Byrne
*Children, Adolescents & the Media
Div. Vice-Chair*
Cornell U

James A. Danowski
*Communication & Technology
Div. Chair*
U of Illinois at Chicago

Lee Humphreys
*Communication & Technology
Div. Vice-Chair*
Cornell University

Richard K. Popp
Communication History Div. Chair
U of Wisconsin–Milwaukee

David W. Park
*Communication History
Div. Vice-Chair*
Lake Forest College

Seamus Simpson
*Communication Law & Policy
Div. Chair*
U of Salford

Katharine Sarikakis
*Communication Law & Policy
Div. Vice-Chair*
University of Vienna

Richard J. Doherty
*Environmental Communication
Div. Chair*
U of Leeds

Merav Katz-Kimchi
*Environmental Communication
Div. Vice-Chair*
Ben Gurion University of the Negev

Miyase Christensen
*Ethnicity & Race in Communication
Div. Chair*
Stockholm University; Royal
Institute of Technology (KTH)

Federico Subervi
*Ethnicity & Race in Communication
Div. Vice-Chair*
Kent State U

Paula M Gardner
Feminist Scholarship Div. Chair
OCAD University

Natalia Rybas
Feminist Scholarship Div. Vice-Chair
Indiana University East

Amit Pinchevski
Philosophy, Theory and Critique
Div. Chair
Hebrew U

Alison Hearn
Philosophy, Theory and Critique
Div. Vice-Chair
U of Western Ontario

Jesper Stromback
Political Communication Div. Chair
Mid Sweden U

Peter Van Aelst
Political Communication
Div. Vice-Chair
U of Antwerp

Melissa A. Click
Popular Communication Div. Chair
U of Missouri–Columbia

Stephen Harrington
Popular Communication
Div. Vice-Chair
Queensland U of Technology

Jennifer L. Bartlett
Public Relations Div. Chair
Queensland U of Technology

Chiara Valentini
Public Relations Div. Vice-Chair
Aarhus U

Jana Holsanova
Visual Communication Studies
Div. Chair
Lund U

Giorgia Aiello
Visual Communication Studies
Div. Vice-Chair
U of Leeds

SPECIAL INTEREST GROUP CHAIRS

James D. Ivory
Game Studies IG Chair
Virginia Tech

Nicholas David Bowman
Game Studies IG Vice-Chair
West Virginia U

Travers Scott
Gay, Lesbian, Bisexual &
Transgender IG Chair
Clemson U

Adrienne Shaw
Gay, Lesbian, Bisexual &
Transgender IG Chair
Temple U

Howard Giles
Intergroup Communication IG Chair
U of California–Santa Barbara

Janice Krieger
Intergroup Communication IG
Vice-Chair
U of Florida

Andrew C. Billings
Sports Communication IG Chair
U of Alabama

Marie Hardin
Sports Communication IG
Vice-Chair
Pennsylvania State U

Brandi N. Frisby	*University of Kentucky, USA*
Shiv Ganesh	*Massey University, New Zealand*
Howard Giles	*University of California-Santa Barbara, USA*
Nurit Guttman	*Tel Aviv University, Israel*
Lutz Hagen	*Dresden University of Technology, Germany*
Nailah Hamdy	*The American University in Cairo, Egypt*
Jake Harwood	*University of Arizona, USA*
Magne Martin Haug	*Norwegian Business School, Norway*
Evelyn Y. Ho	*University of San Francisco, USA*
Thomas A. Hollihan	*University of Southern California—Annenberg, USA*
Andrea Hollingshead	*University of Southern California, USA*
Gregory G. Holyk	*Langer Research Associates, USA*
Robert Huesca	*Trinity University, USA*
David Huffaker	*Northeastern University, USA*
Dal-Yong Jin	*Simon Fraser University, Canada*
Liz Jones	*Griffith University, Australia*
Amy B. Jordan	*University of Pennsylvania, USA*
Joo-Young Jung	*International Christian University, Japan*
Jennifer A. Kam	*University of California-Santa Barbara, USA*
Vikki Katz	*Rutgers University, USA*
Marj Kibby	*University of Newcastle, Australia*
Youna Kim	*The American University of Paris, France*
Yong Chan Kim	*Yonsei University, South Korea*
Michael Kramer	*University of Oklahoma, USA*
Antonio C. La Pastina	*Texas A&M University, USA*
Ken Lachlan	*University of Massachusetts-Boston, USA*
Chih-Hui Lai	*University of Akron, USA*
Annie Lang	*Indiana University, USA*
Robert LaRose	*Michigan State University, USA*
Chin-Chuan Lee	*City University of Hong Kong, China*
Maria Len-Rios	*University of Missouri, USA*
Xigen Li	*City University of Hong Kong, China*
Maria Löblich	*Ludwig-Maximilians-Universität, Germany*
Robin Mansell	*London School of Economics and Political Science, UK*
Matthew M. Martin	*West Virginia University, USA*
Caryn Medved	*Baruch College, USA*
Rebecca Meisenbach	*University of Missouri, USA*
Vernon Miller	*Michigan State University, USA*
Monique Mitchell Turner	*George Washington University, USA*
Robin Nabi	*University of California-Santa Barbara, USA*
Jeff Niederdeppe	*Cornell University, USA*
Seth M. Noar	*University of North Carolina at Chapel Hill, USA*
Mohammed Zin Nordin	*Universiti Pendidikan Sultan Idris, Malaysia*
Jon F. Nussbaum	*Pennsylvania State University, USA*
Amy O'Connor	*North Dakota State University, USA*

Thomas O'Gorman	*University of Illinois, USA*
Daniel J. O'Keefe	*Northwestern University, USA*
Mary Beth Oliver	*Pennsylvania State University, USA*
Mahuya Pal	*University of South Florida, USA*
Hee Sun Park	*Michigan State University, USA*
Loretta Pecchioni	*Louisiana State University, USA*
Wei Peng	*Michigan State University, USA*
Katie Place	*Saint Louis University, USA*
Marshall Scott Poole	*University of Illinois at Urbana–Champaign, USA*
Linda L. Putnam	*University of California–Santa Barbara, USA*
Jack Linchuan Qiu	*Chinese University of Hong Kong, China*
Brian L. Quick	*University of Illinois at Urbana–Champaign, USA*
Artemio Ramirez, Jr.	*University of South Florida, USA*
Rajiv N. Rimal	*George Washington University, USA*
Gertrude Robinson	*McGill University, Canada*
Clemencia Rodriguez	*University of Oklahoma, USA*
Randall Rogan	*Wake Forest University, USA*
Michael Roloff	*Northwestern University, USA*
Dietram A. Scheufele	*University of Wisconsin–Madison, USA*
Allison M. Scott	*University of Kentucky, USA*
Craig Scott	*Rutgers University, USA*
Timothy Sellnow	*University of Kentucky, USA*
Michelle Shumate	*Northwestern University, USA*
Dave Seibold	*University of California-Santa Barbara, USA*
Kami Silk	*Michigan State University, USA*
Aram Sinnreich	*Rutgers University, USA*
Sandi W. Smith	*Michigan State University, USA*
Jordan Soliz	*University of Nebraska–Lincoln, USA*
Lisa Sparks	*Chapman University, USA*
Krishnamurthy Sriramesh	*Purdue University, USA*
Laura Stafford	*Bowling Green State University, USA*
Michael Stohl	*University of California–Santa Barbara, USA*
Ed Tan	*University of Amsterdam, Netherlands*
David Tewksbury	*University of Illinois at Urbana–Champaign, USA*
C. Erik Timmerman	*University of Wisconsin–Milwaukee, USA*
April R. Trees	*Saint Louis University, USA*
Mina Tsay-Vogel	*Boston University, USA*
Yariv Tsfati	*University of Haifa, Israel*
Sebastián Valenzuela	*Pontificia Universidad Católica, Chile*
Jens Vogelgesang	*University of Muenster, Germany*
Peter Vorderer	*University of Mannheim, Germany*
Steve R. Wilson	*Purdue University, USA*
Werner Wirth	*University of Zurich, Switzerland*
Greg Wise	*Arizona State University, USA*
Saskia Witteborn	*Chinese University of Hong Kong, China*
Y. Connie Yuan	*Cornell University, USA*
Marc Ziegele	*Johannes Gutenberg University Mainz, Germany*

Ad Hoc Reviewers

Editor's Introduction

Elisia L. Cohen

Welcome to the 39th edition of *Communication Yearbook*! This yearbook draws on the work of scholars across the field of communication to present eleven state-of-the-art reviews of communication research. This year's volume offers essays that comment on the conceptual and methodological challenges presented in communication scholarship across the field. Often, the most interesting and exciting research in communication is that which crosses traditional disciplinary boundaries and considers the ways that theoretical and methodological choices affect the answers researchers receive to the questions that we ask. Research that brings disparate theories together presents the opportunity to add conceptual clarity and methodological rigor to the complex, multifaceted problems that we study.

This volume of *Communication Yearbook* brings together essays that seek to inspire researchers to innovate and, in doing so, advance the field of communication as a social science. These essays offer new strategies for examining how communication theories and methods may accelerate our understanding of human communication processes and effects. By reviewing and critiquing prior research, the chapters composing *Communication Yearbook 39* offer productive suggestions for future lines of research that have the potential to make a profound difference in the way that scholars find answers to address complex communication problems.

The first section of the book examines the critical need for attention to message design, context, and relational factors to advance the field of communication research. The first essay offers a methodological review of communication research focused on message design and effects. This chapter, written by Michael D. Slater, Jochen Peter, and Patti M. Valkenburg examines the "defined and operationalized features of messages in a given study" to review how researchers may consider problems of both message variability and heterogeneity in sampling, selecting, and designing appropriate messages to test persuasive effects (p. 3). The authors address the conceptual and methodological challenges of studying messages in an empirically sound manner. The authors conclude by offering seven considerations for how researchers can flexibly and adaptably address message variability and heterogeneity in message design.

The second chapter of the volume, written by Matthew Matsaganis, takes on the question of how place, or the environment in which communication lives, can provide the necessary challenges and practical insights guiding communication research. Matsaganis offers a multidisciplinary overview of the literature on neighborhood effects research on health outcomes and identifies ways that communication-centered theoretical approaches have been applied to address health-related issues in residential communities. In so doing, Matsaganis reviews relevant findings generated from four theoretical traditions—the knowledge gap hypothesis (KGH), the structural influence model of communication (SIM), communication infrastructure theory (CIT), and the culture-centered approach (CCA)—to identify relevant questions yet to be answered. The chapter concludes with Matsaganis's proposal for an integrative communication-centered framework, which highlights the role of communication location-based health outcomes in guiding future research. This framework places communication at the center of neighborhood effects research. Matsaganis argues that studying the influence of place on health from a communication perspective will not only contribute to our understanding of how place influences health but will also challenge "communication researchers to expand existing theoretical frameworks to account for the ecological contexts that shape (and are shaped by) dynamics of individuals' everyday life" (p. 45).

The third chapter of the volume highlights the way that conceptual complexity and rigorous methods of data collection are critical to enhancing established relational dialectics scholarship. In Chapter 3, Danielle Halliwell argues that the potential of relational dialectics theory (RDT), a key theory in interpersonal communication, cannot be realized until scholars expand their methods to include the collection of interactive and longitudinal data. Halliwell details how the field needs to gather interactional data (e.g., in the form of dyadic interviews, focus groups, ethnography, and so forth) and over time (e.g., multiple interviews, diaries, and longitudinal ethnographies) to best explore how relational dialectics emerge over the lifespan of relationships. She also critiques research that provides simplistic applications of RDT (e.g., ones utilizing limited methods and case study approaches) and argues that researchers need to address fully past critiques and attend to the "talk" that guides relationships to advance theorizing.

The second section of *Communication Yearbook 39* includes three essays that consider the challenges of communication research in a ubiquitous media environment, where a torrent of images and tasks affect our lives. In Chapter 4, "Media multitasking: Good, bad, or ugly?" Annie Lang and Jasmin Chzan examine more than 20 years of research on media multitasking to identify how the field of communication (a) theoretically guides and operationally defines multitasking, (b) describes and defines "successful" multitasking, and (c) examines the kinds of perceptual and processing experimental studies in this domain to make recommendations for future research. In so doing, they offer insight on questions related to multitasking's effects on capacity limitations, cognitive overload, and task deficits. Lang and Chzan argue that, instead of using a single definition for multitasking, scholars should instead develop a general theory of multitasking that clearly conceptualizes the important variables that contribute to the success (or lack of success) in multitasking. This type of research, they argue, would allow scholars to move beyond evaluations of multitasking as good or bad and develop a more nuanced understanding of how multitasking influences task completion and when it can be done successfully. These findings offer practical implications for identifying when and how multitasking can be useful.

Next, Robert S. Tokunaga's chapter compares perspectives on Internet addiction, problematic Internet use, and deficient self-regulation as variations in Internet habits, a type of media use. In examining the historical controversy surrounding research examining so-called "maladaptive Internet use," Tokunaga offers historical insight into the tradition of media addiction research. The chapter reviews three perspectives of maladaptive Internet use and proposes several lines of inquiry for researchers seeking to reconcile tensions between these perspectives while refining how to interpret and understand the Internet use and context patterns of diverse populations. Tokunaga argues that this reconciliation would allow scholars to clarify important concepts, both conceptually and operationally, and unify an important area of research that seeks to understand when and how Internet use becomes a problem. Drawing on existing communication research, Tokunaga proposes a research agenda for scholars who seek to further understand how and when people's habits change and their Internet use becomes problematic.

In Chapter 6, Young Ji Kim and Andrea B. Hollingshead present a punctuated history of social influence research, examining three periods—pre-online, the early days of computer-mediated communication in the late 1990s, and the current Web 2.0 environment—to show how the evolution of technology has continually challenged social influence researchers' understanding of source, messages, channels, and audience. Kim and Hollingshead then examine the multidisciplinary field of online social influence and propose that the study of this phenomenon would benefit from a framework that is based on traditional communication concepts, terminology that is more clearly defined, and operating definitions that distinguish between the early Internet (Web 1.0) and the current, interactive version, Web 2.0. By comparing the current research on online social influence to earlier research on social influence, Kim and Hollingshead offer a rich research agenda. The authors recommend that scholars attend to the lack of consensus in online social influence measurement and investigate message and channel variation in influence effect studies. At the same time, they identify the key challenges facing researchers as they continue to examine how and when online social influence occurs.

The third section of *Communication Yearbook 39* includes two chapters theorizing new theoretical and empirical models for examining organizational communication and coordination. In Chapter 7, Eric J. Zackrison, David R. Seibold, and Ronald E. Rice identify four problems in communication scholarship theorizing organizational coordination (pp. 99–100). They argue that (a) organizational coordination research lacks a shared explicit conceptual or operational definition, (b) types of coordination overlap and contradict each other, (c) communication research does not focus on coordination, and (d) research in coordination does not theorize organizational coordination as a distinctly communication phenomenon. As a corrective, Zackrison, Seibold, and Rice propose an integrative model for organizational coordination that addresses these issues by viewing organizational coordination as a phenomenon that is based, fundamentally, in communication. This model, which is based on structuration theory, is more parsimonious than previous modes and, at the same time, comprehensive. The authors then propose an agenda for future research to test and refine the model and identify other areas of communication research that would benefit from application of the organizational coordination model.

Next, Paul M. Leonardi's "Studying work practices in organizations: Theoretical considerations and empirical guidelines" presents an analysis of communication research on work practices. Leonardi argues that communication scholars must attend to the roles that work practices play in the process of organizing. He offers specific recommendations for how organizational communication scholars should conduct research to develop theory, including producing longitudinal studies that examine how work practices develop and dissolve over time. Leonardi argues that the study of work practices is key because it provides a "grammar" for understanding how the process of organizing occurs.

The final section of *Communication Yearbook* offers three systematic reviews focused on important topics relevant to environmental communication, child-targeted endorsement strategies, and instructional communication. In Chapter 9, William J. Kinsella, Dorothy Collins Andreas, and Danielle Endres offer a programmatic argument for the necessity of examining nuclear power as a unique communicative phenomenon. Kinsella, Collins Andreas, and Endres identify nuclear power as simultaneously a material phenomenon, a communicative accomplishment, and a discursive construction. They survey the research on nuclear power within communication and other fields of study and argue that the study of nuclear power poses theoretical and practical problems that, if addressed, will enrich both the study of communication and the study of nuclear power and its influence on the environment, the governance of technology, and the democratic process. They argue that communication scholarship is needed to address (a) the fragmentation of technocratic and public discourse, (b) regulation and governance concerns, (c) waste politics, (d) critical social movements, and (e) research examining the intersections of these concerns.

In Chapter 10, Tim Smits, Heidi Vandebosch, Evy Neyens, and Emma Boyland survey the literature on child-targeted endorsement strategies. They conclude from the existing research that food marketers consistently use endorsing characters, similar to Camel cigarette's use of Joe Camel, to persuade children to consume unhealthy foods. They propose that the endorser effect is strong enough to merit government regulation when companies use endorsing characters to promote unhealthy foods.

Last, Flaviu A. Hodis and Georgeta M. Hodis propose and test a theoretical model that ties the expectations of success and the value of a class to the communication that occurs with their teachers and the students' satisfaction with that communication (SCT). The research clarifies the role of individual differences in students' expectancy and value beliefs in the classroom environment and supports research associating students' strong promotional orientation (when student motivation is driven by personal ideals instead of duties and responsibilities, or a prevention orientation) with communicative self-efficacy in school settings. An important implication is that instructor-related effects on communicative self-efficacy, learning, and engagement may differ for promotion and prevention-oriented students.

The chapters in this volume were selected after a rigorous peer-review process. Starting in May 2013, the International Communication Association solicited manuscripts for this volume. The call for papers requested that authors nominate chapters for consideration that reviewed important scientific and critical insights in communication research, addressing significant theoretical and practical concerns. Copies of the call for manuscripts were sent to all members of the International Communication Association. Members of the editorial board were also asked to identify potential international contributors.

We received 57 complete submissions for *Communication Yearbook 39*, and three papers that began in 2012 for *Communication Yearbook 38* but were not completed. The topics of these manuscripts traversed the breadth of the communication field, including submitters who were members of every ICA division. In selecting essays for this volume, double-blind reviewers were asked to review each manuscript for its "appropriateness" and "fit" for *Communication Yearbook*. In nominating manuscripts for publication, reviewers and editorial staff members examined whether (a) the literature review was comprehensive and current, (b) the method of the review was systematic, (c) the conclusions drawn in the review were clearly related to the evidence presented, and (d) the review advanced theoretical or practical questions to direct future research. The resulting eleven manuscripts contained in this volume survived this rigorous peer-review process, where at least two (and as many as four) reviewers in addition to the editor critiqued each manuscript.

Although manuscripts were solicited from across the ICA membership, manuscripts were accepted for publication solely on the basis of quality and significance to the field. Perhaps unsurprisingly, the manuscripts identified as the most challenging and exciting to reviewers were not singularly focused on specific specializations in the field; a roughly equal number of essays in this volume offer research reviews that span the boundaries of divisions within the International Communication Association.

These eleven chapters have benefited from the constructive criticism offered by members of the editorial board. Producing this volume of *Communication Yearbook* required a team of editorial assistants and the goodwill of reviewers and editorial board members. I acknowledge the critical support of the faculty and staff in supporting my work in the Department of Communication and College of Communication and Information at the University of Kentucky over this past year.

My able and experienced editorial assistants, Laura Young and Sarah C. Vos, shepherded manuscript submissions through the peer-review process. During the months before publication, Rachael Record and Jenna Reno joined the editorial assistant team to help manage the final review, editing and production process. Sarah, Rachael, and Jenna deserve a great deal of credit for the completion of this year's project while I served as department chair. On a practical level, Sarah, Rachael, and Jenna each provided an additional set of eyes for each manuscript and assisted with the copyediting and organization of author correspondence, which is essential given that CY functions as a journal without electronic manuscript management support. As my editorial assistant for a third consecutive year, Sarah was particularly helpful in providing incisive edits to the final copy.

I am particularly grateful to all of the authors who sent in manuscripts for review and with whom I have had the opportunity to correspond over the past year. I agreed to edit CY because I knew that the breadth and depth of the scholarship submitted would be both intriguing and inspiring. *Communication Yearbook* remains an outstanding volume known for publishing only the highest quality work because the editors are able to select outstanding, well-developed manuscripts from an excellent pool of potential submissions.

I am especially appreciative this year of Amy Jordan, Cynthia Stohl, Michael Haley, Michael West, Peter Vorderer, Jake Harwood, other ICA editors, and members of the ICA Publications Committee for their willingness to provide assistance and advice in dealing with editorial challenges. I also want to thank Linda Bathgate and the staff at Taylor and Francis for efficiently moving this volume through the production process.

Finally, I express my gratitude to my husband, Jeff, and my daughter, Addison, for tolerating my late-night editing and periodic inattention to family life when I found myself caught up in the minutiae of putting this volume together.

Elisia L. Cohen

Part I

Advancing Communication Research
Message, Theory, Context, and Method

CHAPTER CONTENTS

1 Message Variability and Heterogeneity

A Core Challenge for Communication Research

Michael D. Slater

The Ohio State University

Jochen Peter and Patti M. Valkenburg

University of Amsterdam

Messages pose fundamental challenges and opportunities for empirical communication research. To address these challenges and opportunities, we distinguish between message variability (the defined and operationalized features of messages in a given study) and message heterogeneity (all message features that are undefined and unmeasured in a given study), and suggest approaches to defining and operationalizing message variability. We also identify alternative message sampling, selection, and research design and analysis strategies responsive to issues of message variability and heterogeneity in experimental and survey research. We conclude with recommendations intended to advance the study of messages in communication research.

Communication researchers share with psychologists, sociologists, and political scientists interest in how mediated and interpersonal communication informs what people believe, who people think they are individually and collectively, and the actions people take as individuals, organizations, and societies. Psychologists are concerned with the manifestations of mental activity (perception, cognition, personality) and their relationship to enacted behaviors. Sociologists study social systems, socialization processes, how they are shaped, and how they in turn shape human attitudes and behaviors. Political scientists do much the same with respect to political systems and processes. Communication researchers, as Paisley (1984) pointed out, are interdisciplinary, exploring the role, function, and impact of communication across each of these levels of analysis. Interdisciplinary approaches have many virtues. However, what are the domains of human activity in which communication researchers offer a clearly distinctive expertise?

We argue that messages represent one such domain. Messages, to adapt Berlo's (1960) classic formulation, are expressions in symbolic form—in verbal language, image, sound, and combinations thereof—from some individual or institutional source, via some mediated or interpersonal channel. Messages are expressions of personal and social meanings, goals, needs, and drives, characterizing humans and their social organizations. Messages have their own distinctive forms, conventions, and constraints. They are extraordinarily heterogeneous, and the task of addressing this heterogeneity is an important enterprise.

There have been various efforts in the communication literature to address some of the conceptual and methodological challenges of studying messages (Bucy & Tao, 2007; O'Keefe, 2003; Jackson, O'Keefe, & Jacobs, 1988). To our knowledge, however, there is no contemporary discussion addressing the range of these challenges. Our aim here is to stimulate greater awareness of the implications of the ways researchers address messages at each step of empirical research. How message variables are defined and operationalized in experiments and survey research, how they are selected for study, how they are analyzed statistically, and how the findings are interpreted impacts the value of individual studies and the communication discipline as a whole. Fundamental knowledge claims in communication depend to a considerable extent on how researchers address the inherent complexity of messages.

In particular, following O'Keefe's (2003) call for objective operationalization of message features, we suggest more frequent use of content analysis in order to identify variables worthy of investigation and to guide the selection of message stimuli for use in experiments. We describe the potential of using random samples of messages from a defined population to facilitate testing of mature theories and policy-relevant claims. In this context, we discuss advantages of multi-level modeling for analyzing data resulting from such designs. We seek to bridge the gap between experimental design and analytic procedures recommended by Jackson (1992) and the research strategies commonly employed in the communication discipline by distinguishing between large and small sample message research, discussing the designs and analysis strategies appropriate to different research objectives and contexts. In addition, we also briefly explore implications of message variability and heterogeneity issues as reflected in operationalizing exposure in survey research. We conclude with a series of suggestions intended to improve conceptual clarity and increase attention to issues of boundary conditions and the nature of generalizability in the study of messages.

Defining Message Variability and Message Heterogeneity

Messages, even within a given genre or message domain, are typically very diverse. For example, movies, television, and video games portraying violence may differ along a variety of dimensions: the personal and physical attractiveness of the heroes, villains, or victims; their gender, age, and race; plot predictability and complexity; justification for the violence or lack thereof; production quality; amount of suspense; extent and type of interactivity; point of view; historical epoch; pacing, length, and use of music; emotional tone during the story; context, severity, and graphicness of violence; nature of subplots; how the story unfolds; and the outcomes for the various protagonists. The list of message variables of potential interest is long, and many more such variables might be identified than are listed here. Any given study will typically conceptually and operationally define a few such variables to manipulate or measure. Media violence researchers might be concerned with distinguishing messages portraying justified violence from those portraying unjustified violence and find reasonable criteria for making this distinction between violence that supports as opposed to undermines a civil society. We refer to message differences that researchers choose to explicitly measure or manipulate in a study as *message variability*. In contrast, we use the term *message heterogeneity* to refer to all the variation amongst messages within the genre or message domain of interest not captured by the variable definitions and operations employed in a given study—the undefined, often idiosyncratic variation among messages.

For example, experiments on the impact of dramas featuring unjustified violence might yield different effects depending on whether the stimuli selected feature attractive or unattractive villains. Moreover, different dramas featuring attractive villains might yield differential effects, as a function of the way plot, character, actor, or performance varies between those dramas. Effects found in survey research assessing exposure to violent media content might be attenuated if distinctions regarding unjustified versus justified violence or attractive versus unattractive villains cannot be made in exposure measures. As soon as variables such as justification of violence or attractiveness of perpetrators are explicated and operationalized, they become message variability (which can serve as a source of explanatory power) rather than heterogeneity (which typically serves as a source of threat to interpretability and generality of findings). Whenever aspects of message heterogeneity (all the possible ways messages may vary in a given domain) are captured via rigorous and replicable conceptualization and operationalization, they become message variables. In the context of research on persuasive messages, O'Keefe (1999) discusses meta-analytic evidence of how message differences affect findings in the literature. He concludes that the influence of message differences on research findings is common and substantial.[1] Message heterogeneity that is not captured through definition and operationalization of message variables introduces a wide range of concerns regarding generalizability of results beyond the specific messages studied, as well as issues regarding appropriate statistical analysis. These issues are addressed in the latter part of this paper. We will begin by discussing some of the challenges in defining and operationalizing message variables, drawing on analyses by O'Keefe (2003) and Bucy and Tao (2007).

Message Variability and Intrinsic Message Features

Communication researchers sometimes define message variability in terms of intrinsic properties of the message. Often, though, they define message variables in terms of the psychological state that the message evokes

(Bucy & Tao, 2007; O'Keefe, 2003). For example, a more or less fear-inducing message will typically be defined by pretests or manipulation checks demonstrating that a given message induced more or less fear than another, typically without specifying the exact features that might give rise to greater fear. O'Keefe (2003) points out that such an approach offers little understanding of the effects of message variables, as researchers do not gain any systematic understanding regarding the intrinsic message features that have led to the psychological state of interest. Consequently, O'Keefe emphasizes the importance of defining the message variable of interest in terms of intrinsic message features.

Take as an example fear appeals in persuasion. Research on risk perception suggests that the extent to which messages emphasize prevalence, severity, and dreadfulness of a given risk will determine responses regarding that risk (Slovic & Fischhoff, 1982). Therefore, following O'Keefe's (2003) recommendations, one might manipulate inclusion of information about the prevalence of a risk in a message to increase or decrease the fear induced by the message. O'Keefe argues that in this way, researchers learn what it is about a message that induces the fear reaction. When the experimenter manipulates the prevalence of a risk as communicated by the message, a subsequent question to participants, such as "How scary did you find this message?" is not a manipulation check but provides a measurement of an intervening psychological response that the researcher expects will influence the outcome (Jensen, King, Carcioppolo, & Davis, 2012). From this perspective, the use of intrinsic message features as variables unravels the various elements involved in the causal process theorized (see also Bucy & Tao, 2007, on advantages for theory-building of incorporating mediating and moderating variables arising from differences in the processing of message content).

However, using intrinsic features to operationalize message differences is often difficult. A study attempting to examine simultaneously each of the many intrinsic message features associated with fear would be cumbersome. Moreover, the distinction between intrinsic features and subjective, psychological responses is not a clean one. What intrinsic features make for a judgment that a risk is particularly dread-inducing or severe? Clearly, a subjective element will remain. O'Keefe acknowledges this problem:

> The separation of intrinsic message features from recipient responses is not an unproblematic undertaking. This is a more complex matter than can be sorted out here . . . Leading researchers to a still more sophisticated understanding of the nature of messages is a very desirable goal. The argument here cannot be more than an initial step toward that end, however, because any easy distinction between message features and recipient responses can be no more than—to invoke Wittgenstein's (1921/1961, 6.54) image—a ladder to be climbed and thrown away.
>
> (O'Keefe, 2003, p. 270)

Content Analysis as a Model for Exploring Message Variability

A likely explanation of why O'Keefe's (2003) proposals about emphasis on intrinsic message features have not been more widely adopted is that the problems and complexities to which he refers are the norm, not the exception. Content analytic approaches may provide a useful conceptual and methodological guidance for addressing some of these problems and complexities. We will discuss scenarios in which content analyses can be conducted to help guide subsequent empirical research through the thickets of message variability and heterogeneity challenges. We are not suggesting that all message-related research should begin with content analysis. However, the mindset with which a content analyst approaches message variable definition, identification of a message domain of interest, and message selection might help guide similar decisions in experiments and survey research that do not follow from a formal content analysis. The identification of intrinsic message features may derive from informal observation, logical inference from theory-based research questions, interpretive analyses of messages, textual analysis, or claims in the press and in public debate. A key task for communication researchers is to consider how to define such message features as variables that can be reliably operationalized and empirically studied.

Content analysis can play a central role in laying the groundwork for theory-development and theory-testing research employing experiment or survey methods (McLeod & Reeves, 1980). Content analysts (a) propose a coding scheme based on their theoretical concerns and their own or others' observations of the messages of interest, (b) refine the scheme empirically in the process of training coders and clarifying coding definitions, and (c) end by identifying reliably replicable and theoretically or substantively useful distinctions amongst messages. In so doing, content analysts seek to transform much of the heterogeneity of a given domain of messages into message variability—that is, operationalized message variables.

Content analysis experts, such as Krippendorff (2013), Riffe, Lacy and Fico (1998), and O'Keefe (2003) agree about the advantages of intrinsic message features: the more objective the message variable to be coded, the more replicable and reliable the coding scheme. Some message variables capture differences that are normally unambiguous, and error in coding is likely to result only from lapses of attention. Other message variables are inherently more subjective. For example, in a content analysis looking at social aggression in children's television programming (Martins & Wilson, 2012), coders assessed clearly objective content such as character's biological sex, and whether they were human, supernatural, anthropomorphized, or other. In another study of violence in YouTube videos (Weaver, Zelenkauskaite, & Samson, 2012), coders coded objective message features including YouTube category, date, length in seconds, rating, number of raters, and number of comments. Other content, in contrast, requires interpretation of a psychological response on the part of a coder regarding the distinction proposed in the coding scheme. Coders in the Martins and Wilson (2012) study had to identify instances of social and physical aggression, character attractiveness, benevolence or malevolence of behavior, rewards or punishments for behavior, and humor—each of which clearly require some measure of subjective assessment. In the Weaver et al. (2012) study, coders also had to assess whether the video was professional or amateur and the valence of on-screen reactions to violence.

The task of content analyses is to develop definitions in the coding scheme that are sufficiently clear and objective so that at least two coders can achieve reasonable agreement, even if as a result some nuance is lost in the process (see Krippendorff, 2013, for a discussion of issues regarding coder selection and implications for intercoder reliability). Sometimes coders cannot come to reliable agreement on a variable that requires subjective judgment even after extensive training and rule refinement efforts. When this happens, the lack of agreement should suggest to the researcher that the desired variable cannot meaningfully be operationalized in the message population. Content analytic coding procedures, then, provide a means to transform subjective, psychological responses (such as attractiveness or moral justification) to operationally defined intrinsic features through creating coding rules and testing them for intercoder reliability.

Use of Content Analyses to Inform Hypotheses and Study Design

The content analysis process normally leads to greater clarity concerning one's construct of interest and possible covariates, moderators, or boundary conditions to address in a study. Consider a researcher wanting to study the impact of media messages modeling social aggression on youth attitudes and behavior. In making sense of the heterogeneity of the portrayals of social aggression through content analysis, researchers would presumably come to consider a variety of factors, including whether aggressive behaviors were rewarded or punished; if they were intended benevolently or malevolently; the attractiveness of the perpetrator and victim; or the humor or lack thereof in the context. Certain of these variables might be included as treatment levels (e.g., behavior rewarded or punished) in an experiment. Some variables might be incorporated as covariates and potential moderators (e.g., character attractiveness). Some variables might identify boundary conditions for the study (e.g., cartoons may be excluded if the focus is on human modeling of aggressive behaviors).

As researchers, we may not want, or realistically be able, to study systematically and rigorously each of these variables. We can, however, spell out what we are studying, what we are not, and why. We can interpret our findings with explicit cautions regarding what we have taken into account in our approach to these message variables and what we have not. We can suggest future research that might be theoretically or substantively interesting regarding unstudied message variables or messages outside the boundaries of the present study.

Developing intrinsic message feature variables and selecting stimuli from content analyses customized for the researchers' own research questions provides some potentially exciting opportunities. The process of developing the content analysis requires the researcher to conceptualize the aspects of message heterogeneity that they want to explicate, define, and code. In so doing, researchers transform part of message heterogeneity in their message population of interest into message variables amenable to empirical investigation. Such immersion in actual messages may facilitate insights into message variation that are theoretically significant. Another advantage of content analysis is that researchers can select messages that have been identified in the content analysis to represent differences on variables of interest in experimentation. Still another advantage is that the process of identifying message variables (in part inductively through examination of the messages themselves) and discovering patterns among variables in the content analysis may lead to insights or hypotheses that can be addressed through further survey or experimental research (Slater, 2013).

Using Pretests and Manipulation Checks to Validate Inherent Message Features

Formal content analyses are time-consuming and presume a specific intellectual interest in a given domain of messages. More often, a research question is more general, and selection of a domain in which to examine the question is irrelevant or, to some extent, a matter of convenience. In such cases, a content analysis is hard to justify. In the absence of formal content analyses, the researcher most likely will provide a conceptual analysis of relevant stimulus variation that parallels the thinking of a content analyst. For example, a researcher might for theoretical reasons propose that effects of unjustified violence are contingent on the attractiveness of the perpetrators, articulate a definition of attractiveness that could permit a reasonable degree of agreement between observers (e.g., age, facial feature regularity, estimated BMI, style of dress), and construct or identify messages to provide a test of this hypothesis without conducting a content analysis that systematically identifies exemplars of these messages. Such a conceptual analysis of message variables would normally be followed up with pretests or other empirical checks to assess the validity of variable distinctions and operationalizations made based on such analysis, including manipulation checks in the experiment itself. These pretests and checks serve an equivalent purpose as intercoder reliability checks in confirming that the distinctions proposed are reliable and valid. In such cases, then, the researcher is doing an informal content analysis based on relevant theoretical message variables assessed through personal observation and study of the literature, followed by pretest of what the researcher considers reasonable exemplars of those message variable differences. Such an informal approach to identifying message variables makes a good deal of sense when the domain of messages is a matter of secondary interest, when the message variables of interest have been determined a priori by the theory being tested, when messages are being created to increase experimental control, or when message research is exploratory. In such studies, researchers may, per O'Keefe (2003), provide definitions of the message variable that strive towards objectivity. In this way, too, manipulation checks (e.g., a rating of the attractiveness of the villain) can more meaningfully be used as mediators or moderators to assess theoretical mechanisms or boundary conditions.

Selecting or Sampling Messages for Study and the Problem of Message Heterogeneity

Our discussion has focused on advantages that can accrue from drawing upon a content-analytic mindset in conceptualizing and operationalizing message variables for the intended empirical study. This approach has other benefits for thinking about message variability and heterogeneity. One such benefit is a focus on clearly defining a message population of interest for a given study. When a researcher plans a content analysis, a key initial step is to define a specific population of messages of interest in a way that is replicable and feasible in terms of obtaining messages to study. Then, the researcher develops a plan to sample or select individual messages from this population.

The utility of defining a workable message population may seem an obvious point but it is central to the problem of constructing a study that permits generalization to a message population. To conduct a content analysis, one must narrow focus from a vaguely conceived domain of messages (e.g., legislative debate) to a clearly identified one in which a population of messages can be accessed in order to draw a random sample (e.g., congressional debates concerning a list of social issues during a given time frame available through the Congressional Record). One can draw conclusions about that specific population from which messages are sampled. Still, the question of how applicable such research is to political debates in other contexts remains open.

Any time a communication researcher selects a message or set of messages to use in an experiment, the researcher has implicitly expressed research interest in a population of messages and made a selection decision of some kind regarding exemplars of that population. Directly testing generality of findings across messages may come, if appropriate, in the later stages of development of a research program and theoretical development. Ambitious research designs that permit testing generality of findings across messages make sense only when a researcher has reason to believe that there are findings likely to hold across populations of messages. However, concern with the question of generality of findings across populations of messages reflects an understanding of the challenges of communication inquiry consistent with maturation of our discipline. Therefore, explicit identification of the range of messages of interest, the reasoning for selecting those messages used in the study, and clear acknowledgements of limitations arising from the selection strategy used are hallmarks of thoughtful research on messages.

Below, we discuss various strategies for selecting messages for study in experiments. We begin by addressing a random selection approach such as those often used in content analysis that may permit statistical generalization across message populations. We then discuss other, more commonly employed approaches to message selection that are appropriate to different experimental research contexts, including using small numbers of messages purposively selected for experimental manipulation, creating messages to be used in an experiment, or manipulating a single message. Our focus is on the trade-offs involved with each choice. We emphasize the importance of providing a clear rationale for the message selection decision and discussion of the theoretical and substantive implications and limitations associated with that decision. We also briefly explore possible implications of message heterogeneity and variability for the conduct of survey research.

Addressing Message Variability and Heterogeneity in Experiments

The methodological issues in selecting messages for experiments in many ways parallel those regarding selection of research participants. In survey research, for example, random selection from a population is the most suitable way to permit generalization of findings. Nonetheless, surveys often use self-selected online panels because of the need to present information on a computer screen or for cost reasons. Sometimes they use systematic convenience or purposive samples for populations that cannot be identified for sampling purposes (e.g., IV drug users or gay men). Experiments typically use relatively homogeneous convenience samples of participants, often undergraduate students. In each case, the compromises required are readily accepted by reviewers and editors if they are appropriate to the research context, are explained and defended, and if resultant limitations to findings are discussed.

The problem of message selection is analogous to that of participant selection. However, for communication researchers, message selection decisions may often be more consequential than decisions about the study population. If the communication researcher is concerned with selection, processing, or effects of some class of messages, how that class is represented becomes a central question.

We will begin by discussing experiments using randomly selected message stimuli. Such experiments throw into clear relief the challenges of message variability and heterogeneity and the possibilities inherent in generalizing more confidently in effects across messages. However, experiments using randomly selected stimuli from a population are worth the time and resource commitment for only certain research contexts, such as attempting to establish definitive findings across messages to influence social policy or testing generality of more mature theories across message populations. As a matter of standard practice, theory development experiments using small numbers of messages as the basis for stimuli, or only single messages where justifiable, have good reason to remain the norm.

Experiments using randomly selected messages as stimuli, though, have the potential to strengthen the contribution of communication research to knowledge of social phenomena. As randomly selected message stimuli have seldom been employed in communication experimentation, they deserve detailed discussion here. Other approaches are relatively familiar, and, in these cases, we will discuss only specific issues relevant to the problems of generalizing across messages.

Sampling Approaches to Message Selection in Communication Experiments

It is rare in message effects research to be interested only in the effects of the specific message or messages studied. Typically, the messages used to create experimental stimuli are exemplars of some kind of message type. Therefore, conceptual and substantive clarity are increased when the researcher explicitly defines the population of messages of interest. One sound approach is to define a message population of interest as a content analyst would—for example, "M" rated video games available in Dutch stores in 2013, speeches made by U.S. senatorial candidates in the 2012 election as available from certain archives, or episodes of the three highest-rated police procedural shows on U.S. television from the past three seasons. Some sampling populations can be based on archived messages that could also be accessed by someone with access to the same archives.

Other approaches to defining message populations are more procedural in nature. In such approaches, the procedure could be replicated at some point in time, but the actual messages obtained would be different. For example, one might specify search terms used on specified search engines that identify relevant blogs or discussion boards and define search terms for relevant postings on those blogs. Messages meeting these criteria become the defined message population. In some cases purposive selection from that population may be more feasible or appropriate to a given research problem. Researchers also have the opportunity to use a systematic method for randomly selecting a subset of those postings for study. Generalization can only be made with confidence to those messages posted at the time of study, but such generalization still represents an advance with respect to the external validity of the experiment. Researchers can address in their discussion of results whether anything distinctive took place in the information environment at the time that might render some findings unreplicable.

Researchers often have the option, then, of identifying a population from which they can randomly select a large enough number of such messages. They can then statistically generalize findings to the population of messages from which the messages were sampled. To do so requires use of appropriate statistical methods (Hayes, 2006; Jackson & Jacobs, 1983; Slater, 1991).

Random effects/multi-level analysis of sampled messages.   Development of multi-level models (MLM), also known as hierarchical linear models (HLM; Raudenbush & Bryk, 2002), provides an efficient and practical way to analyze studies employing large numbers of messages. MLM is comparable to random effects analyses of variance previously recommended in multi-message research (Jackson, O'Keefe & Jacobs, 1988; Jackson, 1992) but is more flexible and is generally to be preferred for such analyses. Multi-level modeling is applicable to any research context in which observations are nested within a larger unit (for introductory discussions related to application of MLM in communication, see Hayes, 2006; Park, Eveland, & Cudeck, 2008). For example, researchers want to set up a model in which they have observations on an individual nested within a school, workplace, or community. In the context of research on messages, they may analyze the responses of different individuals who are responding to (i.e., are nested within) the same message. One may look at the effect tested across messages, or tested across people, while taking into account the statistical effects of being nested within messages or of interactions between person and message characteristics.

While a detailed discussion of MLM is beyond the scope of this paper, it is important to briefly highlight some of the advantages of MLM in the present context. Whenever observations on individual study participants are nested within one of several messages, the variability and heterogeneity associated with that message will influence the overall analysis and should be accounted for in the statistical analysis. One approach, which is most appropriate when a relatively large number of messages are selected from some population to be used as stimuli, is to treat the message as an upper-level random effect in MLM.

Statistically addressing message heterogeneity with MLM.   In the case of research using multiple messages, and any given participant is exposed to one of those messages, MLM can simultaneously model message variable effects while adjusting participant effects for effects of message heterogeneity—the clustering effects of being nested within a message. MLM can also incorporate message variables (e.g., language intensity, sex of protagonist), if they have been coded and identified, in the model, providing statistically appropriate tests of the direct effects of those message variables as well as possible interactions (referred to as "cross-level" interactions) with research participant characteristics or experimental manipulations.

There are two types of effects associated with message heterogeneity that MLM can account for: random slopes and random intercepts (Hayes, 2006; Raudenbush & Bryk, 2002). Random slopes represent the way an independent variable's effects on an outcome measure vary between messages for each participant. The random intercept allows the average response between messages to vary, and provides a means of adjusting for the clustering effects of participants being nested within a message. A typical MLM analysis (Raudenbush & Bryk, 2002) will start by treating all effects as fixed. The next step will ascertain whether adding random intercepts provides a statistically significant improvement to model fit. The third step will test whether incorporating random slopes further improves model fit. MLM thereby permits the researcher an empirical way to assess whether message heterogeneity has sufficient impact on the outcome to require testing treatment effects against this heterogeneity as represented by the random slope and/or intercept (Raudenbush & Bryk, 2002). If the impact of such heterogeneity is small enough to be ignorable, incorporating it will not improve model fit. Often the model will not properly converge due to lack of variance associated with message heterogeneity, which also would usually be reflected in a very small intra-class correlation coefficient.

When messages have been selected randomly from some population, such tests can be used to make possible generalization of effects to that population of messages (Slater, 1991). For at least some research questions, as noted above, being able to generalize findings to populations of messages should be as attractive to communication researchers as being able to generalize from a sample to a human population is for sociologists and political scientists.

How many messages are enough for use in MLM/random effects models?   Models such as MLM require enough upper-level units (here: messages) to meaningfully estimate variability associated with message heterogeneity. How many messages comprise a large enough sample depends on the size of the expected effect and how heterogeneous the messages are (a complex power problem that is beyond the scope of the present paper, see Snijders, 2005). Literature on analysis of MLM or hierarchical models gives varying opinions regarding an appropriate lower bound for the number of exemplars of the random effect (here: the number of messages). Having lots of messages and only a few persons seeing each message is preferable to the reverse, in large-message studies analyzed through procedures such as MLM (Snijders, 2005). A number around 30 is often suggested as a lower bound for upper-level units (here: messages) in MLM (Maas & Hox, 2005). At least one author suggests as few as 10 (Nezlek, 2008), though that seems a rather low minimum relative to recommendations from most statistical experts. So, for heuristic purposes, we will consider experiments using fewer than 10 messages a small number generally ill-suited to such tests, 30 or more a large number reasonably well-suited for such statistical models, and anything between 10 and 30 a grey area subject to statistical and substantive debate. Obviously, larger numbers are needed to adequately represent a relatively heterogeneous population (e.g., all the television dramatic series produced in the U.S. in the first decade of this century) than to represent a more homogeneous population (e.g., all the episodes of a single dramatic series).

Using randomly sampled messages in experiments.   There are two possible approaches to using randomly sampled messages experimentally. One approach is to take a random sample of messages of two or more different types and compare them. For example, the social aggression researcher might employ as experimental stimuli several dozen examples of cartoons from the content analysis sample in which social aggression is rewarded and contrast them with several dozen in which social aggression is punished. The content analysis would have had to address the question of how to define the message population—the distribution outlets, time frames, and other criteria for inclusion of cartoons in the population. The experimenter interested in using a random sample of messages will have to make similar decisions regarding the message population under study from which messages can be sampled. For example, are only television cartoons to be included? What about movie or Internet cartoons? Should cartoons selected be limited to those in time slots typically viewed by children, to avoid inclusion of adult-focused animated programs? Should just cartoons be included that are in production at time of research, or also cartoons that may be decades old and shown on some cable channel?

An attractive part of this sampling approach to operationalizing a variable is external validity and the potential for generalizability if the sample is drawn randomly. It may be that the cartoons in which social aggression is rewarded also differ in other ways from cartoons in which social aggression is punished. Perhaps the former cartoons use more anthropomorphic characters or are less realistic. Nonetheless, if sampling is random and sample size is adequate to reasonably represent variability across the message types of interest, the nature of this confounding represents that confounding as it exists in the actual population of messages under study. In other words, in the real world, cartoons with rewarded social aggression also (in this hypothetical example) have more anthropomorphic characters and less realistic plots. The researcher can therefore draw conclusions about the effects of real-world message populations of cartoons using this design in ways analogous to the survey researcher drawing conclusions about human populations (see Slater, Rouner, Domenech-Rodriguez, Beauvais, Murphy, and Van Leuven, 1997, for an example of such a study looking at types of alcohol advertisements).

The most obvious reason to employ such a design is to be able to generalize conclusions about the impact of real-world messages that can influence social policy. Another possible reason might be to test theoretical claims from more tightly controlled experiments against real-world message populations. For example, consider the elaboration likelihood model (Petty & Cacioppo, 1986), which has demonstrated that people respond to argument quality differences much more in messages that are personally relevant, using messages created by the experimenters. One might randomly select letters to the editor or online comments from some population of newspapers or blogs regarding proposed drinking age enforcement policies (high relevance to undergraduate research participants) or proposed public school closures (low relevance) in their community. The selected letters or posts can be coded and sorted into high, medium, or low argument quality based on a content analysis using formal argumentation standards to make an objective evaluation of argument quality. The experiment can then test the generalizability of predictions regarding message quality and relevance (issue involvement) against these real-world message populations.

The weakness of selecting messages of a given type is that it does not permit unambiguous attribution of effect to a given message variable apart from the various other message characteristics (heterogeneity) with which it might be associated. However, if the combination of traditional experiments, which are internally valid, and the approach sketched here, which is externally valid, elicits homogeneous results across multiple studies, we have obtained causally rigorous and generalizable knowledge.

A second, alternative approach is to experimentally manipulate some random sample of messages obtained from a defined population. Goodall, Slater, and Myers (2013) and Slater, Hayes, Goodall, and Ewoldsen (2012) did this by incorporating or removing alcohol mentions from a random sample of 60 news stories. The exact wording involved in creating the manipulation is unique to each story, producing heterogeneity in the manipulation that reflects real-world news story wordings that should increase validity of the manipulation. Effects are unlikely to be due to some idiosyncratically effective manipulation in a story or two. Still, the manipulations are created by the researcher, and therefore, half of the stories (the ones manipulated into the condition in which they did not originally appear) approximate rather than directly represent real-world differences. Each respondent reads just one story, and each story is read by several respondents, so the effects of message heterogeneity—all the effects associated with the various story differences besides the manipulation—can be statistically estimated and addressed appropriately in the analysis. The advantage here is that one can make relatively confident assertions about the influence of the manipulation, independent of other executional elements which may tend to correspond with the presence of that element (e.g., if stories that actually reported alcohol as a factor also tended to more often involve youthful perpetrators or victims). More important, the effect of the manipulation can be generalized with reasonable confidence to the population from which messages were sampled. This is a resource-intensive approach, and can most readily be justified when generalizability is important in terms of implications for social policy.

This approach also might be used to assess generalizability of previous theoretical claims based on findings obtained from studying only a few messages. Using the previous example about the elaboration likelihood model, one might take a randomly sampled set of online comments or letters about proposed drinking age enforcement changes, and manipulate them, per standard practice in elaboration likelihood research, to be about the students' own community or one far away. Assessing the generalizability of theoretically interesting findings initially obtained from experiments that used a few carefully selected or constructed messages by testing them across messages randomly selected from real-world populations of messages seems a valuable approach for communication scientists to explore more often.

Representing message heterogeneity when random sampling is not possible. There are often circumstances in which one might compare sets of messages, or wish to manipulate a set of base messages, of a type that are impossible to sample randomly. Random sampling from a defined population of messages is primarily relevant to research on mediated messages. Since mediated messages are publicly accessible, defining populations and random sampling is a reasonable option in many cases. Interpersonal communications such as conversations or emails pose distinctive sampling and selection challenges (Bradac, 1986; Jackson & Jacobs, 1983). Nonetheless, in each context researchers should be able to state the population or domain of messages of interest and discuss the compromises in identifying and selecting a message or messages to be used to represent that population. For example, a researcher who wants to compare conversations between romantic partners of the same versus different sex or emails between supervisors and subordinates is unlikely to obtain a random sample. Similarly, if the researcher wanted to experimentally manipulate a set of real-world supervisor–subordinate emails, a random sample would likely not be obtainable. Still, the study of a large group of conversations or emails may be valuable even though random sampling is not possible.

However, the precise nature of that value is a matter of debate. Jackson and Jacobs (1983) and Jackson (1992) argue that when appropriate random-effects statistical analyses are used, one can generalize from purposively selected messages to the "category of messages that could be included given some specified method of locating examples" (Jackson & Jacobs, 1983, p. 176). Their argument can be understood in two ways: first, as a procedural method for identifying a study sample of messages and, second, as a means of claiming generalization to a hypothetical population of messages resembling those sampled. The first interpretation is in line with what we described earlier, in the example of defining a population of blog posts procedurally (with search terms specified for blogs and then for posts). We differ from Jackson and Jacobs (1983) only in pointing out that such a procedure can best be understood as a means of defining a message population procedurally, from which one can then sample randomly, rather than as sampling from a population. The procedural approach to defining a message population, parallel to procedures normally used by content analysts, does solve some of the problems associated with generality and random selection of messages. The message population defined likely will not perfectly represent all the messages in which the researcher is substantively interested. However, advantages and limitations of the population as defined are clear to readers and reviewers. Researchers then also have the option of drawing a random sample of messages from the population and conducting analyses that statistically generalize message effects to that population. Boundary conditions for findings related to how the population has been defined then become subjects for discussion and further research.

The second interpretation of Jackson and Jacobs's (1983) argument implies that researchers can infer the message population to which they generalize from the message exemplars purposively chosen for use in a study. Such an interpretation suggests that a random effects test permits generalization to a population of messages that has not been defined a priori. Inference is instead to some hypothetical population of messages similar to, and represented by, the messages selected for use in the study.

The actual messages that are included in this hypothetical population is, however, impossible to determine. In a sense, to claim statistical generalizability is to claim that the experimental effect is consistent across a population of messages defined as being those messages that are like the set of messages under study. Such a claim of generality to such a hypothetical population does not seem to us especially informative. This argument regarding generalization to a hypothetical population may be based on statistical assumptions in random effects analyses. Distributions in these analyses are assumed to be estimated from some population, a hypothetical one if sampling was not done from an actual population. However, even if a population is assumed for statistical purposes, that population does not necessarily exist. One can attempt to claim generalization from purposively selected messages to a hypothetical population of messages, but one can never know the match of that hypothetical population to actual sets of real-world messages. Substantive interpretation of such claims of statistical generalization is inherently ambiguous.

We would, accordingly, endorse a more qualified version of the Jackson and Jacobs (1983) claims regarding generality of findings when random effects models are used to assess purposively selected messages. As Jackson and Jacobs (1983) urge, a researcher may seek to maximize what they call form-and-content differences when selecting messages for study. In other words, a researcher can make a serious effort to conceptualize and represent the heterogeneous nature of the domain of messages of interest using a large group of purposively selected messages. If significant hypothesized effects emerge from MLM/random effect analysis of a large set of messages purposively selected to represent the heterogeneity of messages within a given domain, researchers have a solid, logical case for arguing the robustness of their findings in comparison with the usual message-based study.

Of course, acceptance of claims of robustness across messages is subject to debate on a variety of fronts. Questions may be raised regarding the theoretical reasoning behind the (a) purposive selection of the messages used, (b) claims made about the relevant dimensions of message variation captured by the selection process, (c) dimensions of message heterogeneity characterizing such messages not captured in the message selection effort, (d) details of the selection process, and (e) specifics of the messages selected. The random effects test, absent random sampling, only provides an unequivocal statistical demonstration that effects generalize across the specific messages used in the study, since researchers do not know what other messages would or would not fall into a hypothetical population represented by those selected messages. In other words, this method provides a logical basis for arguing for the plausibility of claims regarding generalizability but does not permit statistical generalization absent random sampling from a defined population. Providing such evidence of the plausibility of generalization across real-world populations of messages can be an important contribution. If random sampling of messages is not an option, random effects testing across a large set of messages selected to represent a range of relevant form-and-content differences is likely the best option available within a single study for testing robustness of findings across such difficult-to-sample messages.

Studies Purposively Selecting a Small Number
of Messages as Study Stimuli

Use of a large number of experimental stimuli is a resource-intensive strategy. As such, it is hard to justify until late in the process of theoretical development or when there is an effort to contribute to social-policy debate with more generalizable findings. Moreover, often tight experimental manipulations can be readily applied only to a carefully selected or constructed message or set of messages. In such cases, the number of messages that may be realistically employed in an experiment is typically too small to permit meaningfully generalizing to a larger message population. Instead, researchers often select or create several messages to use as stimuli and to decrease the likelihood that the effects found are unique to the particular message selected and then manipulate each of those messages.

Unlike the studies mentioned earlier, with their use of random effects to statistically assess the impact of heterogeneity across sampled or purposively selected messages, studies using a small number of message stimuli typically seek only to replicate the effects of a manipulation across several messages in a single study. Psychologists, to accomplish a similar end, might run an experiment several times with changes in the experimental stimuli to demonstrate that effects are not due to a single stimulus, and may well report the series of experiments in a single research article. Some psychologists argue for greater use of stimulus sampling in psychological experimentation as well (Wells & Windschitl, 1999). However, when several different messages are manipulated as experimental stimuli such replication, in effect, takes place within a single study. Participants, after all, are randomly assigned to each message, and each message usually is separately manipulated. This is one advantage of message research—in many contexts (e.g., using text rather than video stimuli), researchers may find several different message stimuli relatively easy to manipulate within the same study, so findings are not dependent on a single stimulus and manipulation. Therefore, the researcher does not have to rerun the same study multiple times with different message stimuli to reassure readers and reviewers that effects are not dependent on cherry-picking a particular message as a stimulus. Like the researcher in psychology, in such cases the communication researcher is testing theory against a limited number of stimuli and experimental manipulations; further improving external validity and generalizability must be examined via other research endeavors (Slater, 1991).

In a single study using several messages, the reader would want the ability to assess how consistent the effect of experimental manipulations is across messages. There are two primary alternatives for addressing this question, one using random effects analyses and one using fixed effect analyses.

Random effect approaches to addressing message heterogeneity in experiments using a small number of messages. The use of random effects models for studies even with only a few experimentally manipulated messages has been proposed since the 1980s (Jackson et al., 1988; Jackson, 1992) on the basis of the importance of taking message heterogeneity into account statistically. Random effect ANOVAs are similar to MLM. In essence, the degrees of freedom and error term are based on messages and the error variation attributable to those messages, rather than the variability in response to treatment between, and degrees of freedom associated with, the individual participants. The exact way this is set up depends on specifics of the research design (Jackson, 1992). In so doing, the researcher assesses the generalizability of effects across the heterogeneity of, and error variation attributable to, the base messages used in the study (and across a message population if the messages have been selected randomly from some defined population).

However, a random effects approach to analyzing experiments manipulating small numbers of base messages has been contested on grounds of the logic of experimental design (Hunter, Hamilton, & Allen, 1989; Slater, 1991) and researcher intention (Bradac, 1983). When a small number of purposively selected messages is treated as a random effect, a random effect analysis in our view simply tests whether or not the effects of the manipulation are consistent across the specific messages used in the study. No convincing evidence of generality beyond this small set of messages is provided, and such an approach is likely to motivate use of very similar message stimuli to reduce variability and maximize the likelihood of significant results. Even if randomly selected messages were used in an experiment using a small number of messages, it would not be very compelling with respect to generalization. Consider a random effect analysis on an experiment that used four violent films as stimuli. The results of this analysis would be as unconvincing with respect to drawing statistically generalizable conclusions about the population of films containing violence as a random-effect meta-analysis would be that used only four studies of mediated violence, even if randomly sampled, to draw conclusions about the thousands of studies on mediated messages and aggression.

In our view, the primary utility of the random effects test advocated by Jackson and Jacobs (1983) and Jackson (1992) in studies using small numbers of purposively selected messages is to demonstrate the stability of experimental treatment effects across the base messages used to create stimuli. This test has very limited statistical power and little inferential value in assessing generalizability of effects across messages when the number of messages studied is small. Moreover, in studies with only a few messages, the random effects approach is less helpful than a fixed effects approach in identifying what the potentially interesting differences in effects between messages might be.

Fixed effect approaches to addressing message heterogeneity in experiments using a small number of messages.   An alternative approach to random effects analyses is to address effects of message heterogeneity among messages used as experimental stimuli within the traditional fixed effects framework. When only a few variant messages are used as the basis for creating experimental manipulations, differences attributable to the messages used are likely to contribute to variation in results. The researcher and the reader would both want to know how great this contribution is and if there is evidence that experimental effects depend on which message was used as the basis for the stimulus presented. Such information is especially important in the early phases of theoretical development and testing, when small samples of messages are most likely to be used. The simplest way to examine this question within a fixed effect ANOVA or regression model is to look at main effect differences attributable to the individual messages and interactions between the experimental manipulation and the different messages used.

Identifying the size of the main effect attributable to message differences is in itself informative and provides the attentive reader insight into the phenomenon under study. One might also find an interaction pattern indicating that some messages seem to show no effect but some have strong enough effects to generate significance overall. Such a pattern suggests that there are message variables at work that were not identified at the outset responsible for these contingent effects.

The finding that there is a significant interaction with the experimental treatment due to the messages used does not mean the results of the study are problematic. It does mean there are some boundary conditions within the study that demand attention. In the event of a message-by-treatment interaction, a qualitative examination of message content would likely generate ideas regarding message content differences that might explain the pattern of results. In other words, some message variables were lurking among the stimuli selected that had not been anticipated in the initial theorizing and concept explication (Jensen & Hurley, 2012). If the researcher has been careful conceptualizing causal processes and measurement, then the researcher may be able to use post hoc analyses to test such post hoc explanations. The resulting insight should add to, rather than detract from, the scientific value of findings.

Therefore, we generally prefer using a fixed effects approach to assessing the impact of message heterogeneity in an experiment manipulating a small number of base messages. Unlike the random effects approach, the analysis remains focused on the impact of the experimental manipulation across participants rather than on effects across those few messages. Moreover, when base message differences do influence the effects of the experimental manipulation, the nature of this influence can be readily ascertained from the pattern of interaction means, with possible benefit for interpretation and theoretical development regarding boundary conditions for effects.[2]

It is important to note that the lack of an interaction in the fixed effects model does not fully moot concerns regarding evidence for possible effects attributable to message differences. If power is relatively low, non-trivial message-by-treatment interactions may not be statistically significant. Descriptive discussion of possible differences in findings by message is still desirable. Unfortunately, however, it appears to be common practice in communication research with multiple messages to simply average across the impact of the messages used without also assessing message-by-treatment interactions or descriptively characterizing the presence or absence of possible differences in effects across messages.

Of course, the lack of an interaction, or the presence of descriptively similar findings across messages, does not provide statistical evidence for generality of effects across a population of messages in the real world. After all, messages in such studies have not been sampled to accurately represent the message population insofar as possible and then treated as a random effect with a defensible sample size and selection method. The researchers have simply provided evidence, perhaps only descriptive evidence, regarding the replicability of their findings across the several different messages used. The issues of boundary conditions for findings remain important topics for discussion, and limitations must be carefully spelled out.

Summary of our viewpoint vis-à-vis Jackson and Jacobs (1983).   We share with Jackson and Jacobs (1983), then, the belief that communication researchers too seldom attend to generality of findings across messages and share an emphasis on the importance of better representing message heterogeneity in design and analysis of studies when addressing the robustness of findings across messages. We also agree that replication of research results across multiple studies, alone, is less compelling with respect to establishing generality of findings across messages than experiments analyzed with MLM/random effects models using large, appropriately selected messages. We differ from the positions argued by Jackson and Jacobs (1983) in several respects. On the one hand, we acknowledge the research value of experiments with small numbers of messages, even when the ability to make claims about the robustness of effects found across messages is minimal. In contrast to Jackson and Jacobs, we do not recommend use of random effects models to analyze such studies. On the other hand, we place greater emphasis on the potential for use of random sampling of messages in combination with MLM/random effects analyses. We point out that in the tradition of content analysis, researchers often can define message populations from which random sampling is possible, either through sampling from archives of messages or by using a replicable procedure for obtaining a sample in a dynamic communication environment. We do agree with Jackson and Jacobs (1983) that thoughtful purposive sampling when random sampling is impossible, combined with MLM or random effects analysis, can indicate the robustness of findings. In our view, such designs do not permit interpretable claims of statistical generalizability to a population.

Messages Created for or within a Study

A variant of multiple-message studies involves message stimuli that are created for the study or as a function of the study. Such approaches can be very attractive in terms of making possible rigorous manipulations and tests of theory. At the same time, they raise issues of validity (Bradac, 1986); the researcher must grapple with the problem of the extent to which findings might be extended to real-world phenomena and address these questions to the satisfaction of the reviewer and reader.

For example, in a study designed to explore relational factors influencing experience of hurtful messages, relationship partners were recruited, and one partner was trained to be supportive or unsupportive in conversation with their boyfriend or girlfriend (McLaren, Solomon, & Priem, 2012). The study created a "real-time" set of interactions. In other words, the researchers created a situation in which actual messages were generated in manipulated conditions. So, the question becomes to what extent such messages fully represent real-world interactions. The researchers addressed this challenge in two ways. First, they discussed boundary conditions associated with the modest hurtfulness of the conversations that were possible given ethical concerns. Second, they empirically addressed how valid and representative these conversations were of actual conversations of these romantic partners by including measures of the perceived typicality and realism of the conversations.

A study such as this also raises analytic issues. In this study, one partner served as a trained confederate (McLaren et al., 2012). The unit of analysis was the conversation with and responses of, the other conversational partner; the number of conversations and the number of participants were the same, and each participant had participated in one unique conversation. Message and participant variability in effect are necessarily confounded. Message variation in this case is also participant variation, and a separate random effects test assessing impact across messages is not possible or necessary (see Jackson & Jacobs, 1983, for a discussion encouraging greater use of such designs).

Since messages are not crossed with treatments, tests of message-by-treatment interactions are not possible. However, the authors' theoretical insight in measuring the perceived typicality and realism of conversations suggests an alternative avenue for addressing message-related boundary conditions. By including these measures, a theoretically significant aspect of message heterogeneity has been transformed into message variability. The authors have implicitly proposed a hypothesis regarding boundary conditions: that the effect of the experimental treatment on the conversations will be moderated by perceived typicality and perceived realism. Explicitly testing this a priori claim about boundary conditions by statistically assessing moderation would address issues concerning these particular dimensions of message variability within the analysis of the study. Moreover, readers could then assess the strength of the associations found in the study for those conversations deemed highest in typicality and realism; those conversations presumably best represent what might be expected in "real-life" conversations. Such a priori consideration of boundary conditions, and inclusion of moderators to test hypotheses or research questions about boundary conditions, is advisable in many experiments using message stimuli.

Single-Message Studies

Using a single message as a base stimulus for manipulation inherently leaves a greater room for the possibility that study results depend on idiosyncrasies of the message studied and how the manipulation is carried out. Nonetheless, there are circumstances where such research is justified; for example, when narrative film and television programs are studied. Finding a film or program that permits manipulation of a theoretically significant message variable with reasonable plausibility and rigor is often difficult. Sometimes a movie may be structured in such a way that judicious editing permits manipulation of a key variable, making possible the study of an important theoretical or substantive issue that otherwise could not be examined with a comparable, ecologically valid stimulus.

The necessity in some cases of using different dependent measures tailored to the content of specific messages also complicates attempts to do multiple message studies. Responses to such dependent measures might not be readily combined across stimuli into a single analysis. Moreover, single instantiations of messages such as films and television programs may be of substantive interest given their reach, visibility, and potential impact. In such cases, researchers can explain why the single message instantiation is used and can thoughtfully address in discussion the consequent limitations and boundary conditions for findings that might be addressed in future research.

Addressing Message Variability and Heterogeneity in Survey Research

Our discussion to this point has focused on addressing message variability and heterogeneity in communication experiments. Similar issues are faced in survey research, though in different ways than in experimentation. Some strategies are available for contending with questions of message variability and heterogeneity in surveys. An in-depth exploration of these challenging problems of exposure measurement in surveys is beyond the scope of the present discussion, and much empirical work is yet to be done to assess alternative strategies for exposure measurement. Our intention is to raise awareness of these issues in the context of our concern about message variability and to highlight some possible strategies for addressing them.

Specificity of Exposure/Attention Measures

Typically, survey research involving communication asks respondents about exposure and often attention to particular types of media content or interpersonal discussion (Fishbein & Hornik, 2008; Slater, 2004). Questions asking about exposure and attention to some type of communication (let us say news) will usually account for differences in channel—television, newspaper, Internet, magazines, and interpersonal discussion of news. Perhaps this will be broken down further. The researcher may be interested in differences in ideological slant of news used and ask about Fox News, MSNBC, the particular magazines read, the types of Internet news sites viewed, and the ideology of discussion partners. Perhaps use of breaking news versus analysis, opinion, and panel discussion will be distinguished. In our view, the appropriate level of specificity of such questions is critical. News, like many categories of message content, is heterogeneous. Identifying and measuring relevant specifics turns some of this heterogeneity into meaningful variability. The heterogeneity of message content within each category (e.g., variation within Fox News broadcasts), however, does not pose the kind of problem in such survey research as it does in experimentation. The researcher in this case is essentially averaging across the variation in the Fox news broadcasts seen, by using amount of exposure to Fox News as the variable. In a sense, this is equivalent to the experimenter who randomly samples Fox News broadcasts and does not attempt to manipulate them, allowing the natural heterogeneity to represent the message type, which is appropriate to this research context.

At the same time, potential problems arise with a high degree of specificity in recalling exposure. A respondent can likely report with reasonable accuracy on how frequently he or she views Fox News versus MSNBC or CNN. However, if the question asks about specific content exposure—such as pro- versus anti-Obamacare news stories—there may be differences in attention, encoding, and recall as a function of ideological stance which confound the findings. Even recognition of specific messages, a relatively reliable way to assess exposure to specific message content, may vary by demographic factors such as age (Southwell & Langteau, 2008) and possibly as a function of biases in attention and encoding based on sympathy toward the message.

The ability to retrieve such fine-grained data on media use in surveys is often limited, especially when conducting secondary analyses of survey data sets not primarily concerned with communication questions. We grant that some data on media use are better than none and that interesting findings are possible even when there are only a few media-use items available. However, we discourage communication researchers from using measures of exposure to a given medium or broad genre category alone, if they have the opportunity to advocate for or to create more detailed exposure measures that are better suited to assessing their hypotheses.

Assessing Exposure to Campaign Messages

Some survey research is concerned with the possible effects of specific messages present in the social environment. The simplest approach, often used in advertising and public health evaluations of campaigns with relatively small numbers of messages, assesses recognition of the messages via description or sample images. Recognition memory is generally quite good (Shapiro, 1994), and a tendency to falsely report recognition, though commonplace, can be controlled for using recognition of foils or pseudo-messages (Slater & Kelly, 2002; Southwell et al., 2002).

As the number of messages in an advertising or advocacy campaign is relatively small, researchers typically will find it easy to analyze the content of these messages. However, the small number of messages also creates challenges. Message differences of interest are likely confounded with idiosyncratic executional differences. The effects of public health messages that, for example, emphasize social normative concerns compared to personal risk are confounded with how the particular campaign addresses social normative concerns versus personal risk. In such cases, the rationale for such comparison must be made on the basis that the execution of these messages is a substantively important example of how such execution takes place in the social world. In a presidential election, the way character attack ads are constructed may be a function of the personalities involved and the advertising agencies employed; however, how they are executed in that campaign is, in fact, substantively what matters. The confounding of message variable with execution represents the natural confounding present in the social world at the time of the study. Researchers would typically discuss the distinctive approach to the message type taken in the campaign under study when interpreting results and address how that approach might have contributed to findings, and mention possible implications of alternative approaches, in the discussion section.

Combining Surveys and Content Analyses

Linking survey data to content analyses provides another means to examine the impact of exposure to specific message content. For example, researchers interested in effects of popular movies on adolescent smoking and alcohol use content analyzed hundreds of such movies, and by asking teens what movies they have seen (typically by asking specifically about a sample of movies from the list of those analyzed), were able to assess the effects of exposure to various message elements represented in these movies, and to control for other elements also present in these movies (Sargent, Worth, Beach, Gerrard, & Heatherton, 2008). A similar approach has been taken to the impact on adolescents of sexual content in media (Brown, L'Engle, Pardun, Guo, Kenneavy, & Jackson, 2006). Media diaries can be used to assess respondent exposure, and the actual content seen by the respondent can be content analyzed.

Using Geographic Differences to Model Message Variability

Another approach to studying effects of message variables in surveys is based on data regarding the geographic distribution of messages in the social environment. In these studies, differences in content (e.g., as a function of differences in media advertising buying or cable penetration by market) are assessed regionally and the influences of message exposure to a given type of message assessed based on place of residence, using multi-level modeling, with residents of a media market nested within the media-market level data. In this case, content differences are conceptualized as environmental differences and studied as such. These methods can be applied to overcome problems of self-report in campaign evaluations and other effect studies (Snyder, Milici, Slater, Sun, & Strizhakova, 2006). They can also be employed to examine the effect of message variability identified in content analyses that vary by region, such as differences in news coverage associated with the news practices or ideological slant of regional news outlets (Hoffman, 2012).

Summary of Recommendations and Conclusion

We conclude this paper by summarizing our recommendations concerning ways to more thoughtfully and consistently address message variability and heterogeneity in communication research. As noted earlier, we do not advocate a single analytic or design strategy as "the" solution but prefer flexibility and adaptation to the message domain and research question.

1 Researchers can take Daniel O'Keefe's recommendation (2003) as an aspirational goal: When possible, define and operationalize message variables based on intrinsic message features instead of defining message differences based on people's responses to messages.

2 When distinguishing message variables requires some subjective judgment, researchers can accomplish such operationalizations by conducting formal content analyses or by using prior content analyses conducted by others. Alternatively, researchers can challenge their own thinking about message features through careful conceptualization and definition of message differences as they would if creating a content analysis coding scheme, as well as validating these definitions through pretests and manipulation checks.

3 Researchers would increase the value of their research on messages by explicitly identifying the message types of interest and, if possible, formally defining a message population. Researchers can be clear about their approach and rationale used for sampling or selecting messages and why the approach was reasonable given the research question and context. Such definitions involve intentionally excluding some classes of messages. When researchers identify and test theoretically or substantively interesting message boundary conditions—processes or relationships that are dependent on differences in message variables or that are operative for only certain types of messages— they may well make valuable contributions to communication knowledge.

4 When the researcher's objective is to make policy-relevant observations or to demonstrate the robustness of a more mature theory across a range of real-world messages, the researcher would do well to consider defining a message population in a way that permits randomly sampling a large number of messages to use from that population. These messages can then be used as stimuli and analyzed with multi-level models. If defining such a population in a way to permit random sampling is not possible, message stimuli selection to maximize form-and-content differences (Jackson & Jacobs, 1983) characteristic of a message domain may prove a workable alternative suggesting possible generalizability. The ability to generalize to populations of messages has the potential to be as significant to communication scholars as generalizing to human populations for sociologists and political scientists.

5 In experiments focusing on theory development using a single message or small number of messages, researchers need to thoughtfully explain the rationale for message selection. Possible boundary conditions to findings

associated with unstudied message differences deserve discussion. While use of fixed effect models seems appropriate in this research context, analyses showing effects of the different messages used for experimental manipulation may help identify possible boundary conditions for effects. We recommend these be reported. Using manipulation checks and other message response variables not only to assess hypothesized mediating processes (per O'Keefe, 2003), but also to assess boundary conditions of effects through examination of their role as moderators of message effects, also merits greater attention.

6   In survey research, researchers are likely to find it valuable to explore options for operationalizing exposure that increase information about message variability in line with researcher objectives and hypotheses.

By no means do we suggest that communication researchers currently ignore the challenges associated with message variability and heterogeneity. Indeed, as we look at our major journals, typically researchers make a serious effort to address at least some of these issues in each article. However, we find that in many articles, at least some of the research problems associated with message variability and heterogeneity are overlooked or passed over quickly (our own work is not excluded from possible criticism in this regard). This then leads to another recommendation:

7   Reviewers and editors can encourage more explicit discussion of message variability, message selection, and boundary conditions, viewing such acknowledgements as indicators of intellectual rigor rather than of methodological weakness or limitation (unless, of course, the choices made cannot be reasonably justified). Studies testing generalizability of theory across populations of messages, as well as tests of theories and empirical findings in communication and other disciplines to see if they are contingent on theoretically interesting or substantively important message differences, are also worthy of encouragement.

The problems of message variability and heterogeneity, and the resultant limitations and uncertain boundary conditions for findings, deserve the attention of communication researchers. Understanding of message variability and heterogeneity, attention to these challenges in our conceptualizing and theorizing, thoughtful choices in our research design, willingness when appropriate to take on more ambitious and complex message stimuli designs, and careful interpretation of findings in the light of these issues, can increasingly become trademarks of the communication discipline. To the extent communication researchers take on these challenges, the distinctive contributions of the communication discipline to social science are likely to become increasingly evident.

Acknowledgements

The authors thank William "Chip" Eveland of The Ohio State University for comments on a draft of this manuscript. Research on which this paper is in part based was funded by grant AA10377 from the National Institute on Alcohol Abuse and Alcoholism to the first author. The content is solely the responsibility of the authors and does not necessarily represent the official views of the National Institutes of Health.

Notes

1. O'Keefe (1999) uses the term "variability" where we use "heterogeneity." We prefer to call message differences that are operationalized and studied "message variability" given the link of the term variability to the concept of a study variable. The term "heterogeneity" is also used in meta-analysis to describe the many ways studies whose results are being combined may in fact differ methodologically. Some of these methodological differences may be coded and included as variables in the meta-analysis, turning them in our nomenclature from heterogencity to variability.
2. Another option for presenting the effects of individual-based messages, one that has particular potential when a relatively large number of such messages are used as stimuli, is to graph effect sizes attributable to each message in the same way that meta-analysts graph effect sizes across studies (we are indebted to an anonymous reviewer for this suggestion).

References

Berlo, D. K. (1960). *Process of communication: An introduction to theory and practice.* New York: Holt Rinehart and Winston.

Bradac, J. J. (1983). On generalizing cabbages, messages, kings, and several other things: The virtues of multiplicity. *Human Communication Research, 9,* 181–187. doi:10.1111/j.1468-2958.1983.tb00692.x

Bradac, J. J. (1986). Threats to generalization in the use of elicited, purloined, and contrived messages in human communication research. *Communication Quarterly, 34,* 55–65. doi:10.1080/01463378609369620

Brown, J. D., L'Engle, K. L., Pardun, C. J., Guo, G., Kenneavy, K., & Jackson, C. (2006). Sexy media matter: Exposure to sexual content in music, movies, television, and magazines predicts black and white adolescents' sexual behavior. *Pediatrics, 117,* 1018–1027. doi:10.1542/peds.2005-1406

Bucy, E. P., & Tao, C. C. (2007). The mediated moderation model of interactivity. *Media Psychology, 9,* 647–672. doi:10.1080/15213260701283269

Fishbein, M., & Hornik, R. (2008). Measuring media exposure: An introduction to the special issue. *Communication Methods and Measures, 2,* 1–5. doi:10.1080/19312450802095943

Goodall, C. E., Slater, M. D., & Myers, T. A. (2013). Fear and anger responses to local news coverage of alcohol-related crimes, accidents, and injuries: Explaining news effects on policy support using a representative sample of messages and people. *Journal of Communication, 63,* 373–392. doi:10.1111/jcom.12020

Hayes, A. F. (2006). A primer on multilevel modeling. *Human Communication Research, 32,* 385–410. doi:10.1111/j.1468-2958.2006.00281x

Hoffman, L. H. (2012). When the world outside gets inside your head: The effects of media context on perceptions of public opinion. *Communication Research, 40,* 463–485. doi:10.1177/0093650211435938

Hunter, J. E., Hamilton, M. A., & Allen, M. (1989). The design and analysis of language experiments in communication. *Communications Monographs, 56,* 341–363. doi:10.1080/03637758909390269

Jackson, S. (1992). *Message effects research: Principles of design and analysis.* New York: Guilford Press.

Jackson, S., & Jacobs, S. (1983). Generalizing about messages: Suggestions for design and analysis of experiments. *Human Communication Research, 9,* 169–191. doi:10.1111/j.1468-2958.1983.tb00691.x

Jackson, S., O'Keefe, D. J., & Jacobs, S. (1988). The search for reliable generalizations about messages: A comparison of research strategies. *Human Communication Research, 15,* 127–142. doi:10.1111/j.1468-2958.1988.tb00174.x

Jensen, J. D., & Hurley, R. J. (2012). Conflicting stories about public scientific controversies: Effects of news convergence and divergence on scientist's credibility. *Public Understanding of Science, 21,* 659–704. doi:10.1177/0963662510387759

Jensen, J. D., King, A. J., Carcioppolo, N., & Davis, L. A. (2012). Why are tailored messages more effective? A multiple mediation analysis of a breast cancer screening intervention. *Journal of Communication, 62,* 851–868. doi:10.1111/j.1460-2466.2012.01668.x

Krippendorff, K. (2013). *Content analysis: An introduction to its methodology.* Thousand Oaks, CA: Sage.

Maas, C. J. M., & Hox, J. J. (2005) Sufficient sample sizes in multilevel modeling. *Methodology, 1,* 86–92.

Martins, N., & Wilson, B. J. (2012). Mean on the screen: Social aggression in programs popular with children. *Journal of Communication, 62,* 991–1009. doi:10.1111/j.1460-2466.2001.01599.x

McLaren, R. M., Solomon, D. H., & Priem, J. S. (2012). The effect of relationship characteristics and relational communication on experiences of hurt from romantic partners. *Journal of Communication, 62,* 950–971. doi:10.1111/j.1460-2466.2012.01678.x

McLeod, J., & Reeves, B. (1980). On the nature of mass media effects. In S. B. Withey & R. P. Abeles (Eds.), *Television and social behavior: Beyond violence and children* (pp. 17–54). Mahwah, NJ: Erlbaum.

Nezlek, J. B. (2008). An introduction to multilevel modeling for social and personality psychology. *Social and Personality Psychology Compass, 2,* 842–860. doi:10.1111/j.1751-9004.2007.00059.x

O'Keefe, D. J. (1999). Variability of persuasive message effects: Meta-analytic evidence and implications. *Document Design, 1,* 87–97. doi:10.1075/dd.1.2.02oke

O'Keefe, D. J. (2003). Message properties, mediating states, and manipulation checks: Claims, evidence, and data analysis in experimental persuasive message effects research. *Communication Theory, 13,* 251–274. doi:10.1111/j.1468-2885.2003.tb00292.x

Paisley, W. J. (1984). Communication in the communication sciences. In B. Dervin & M. J. Voigt (Eds.), *Progress in communication sciences, Vol. 5.* Norwood, NJ: Ablex.

Park, H. S., Eveland, W. P., & Cudeck, R. (2008). Multi-level modeling: Studying people in contexts. In A. F. Hayes, M. D. Slater, & L. B. Snyder (Eds.), *The Sage Sourcebook of Advanced Data Analysis Methods for Communication Research* (pp. 219–246). Thousand Oaks, CA: Sage.

Petty, R. E., & Cacioppo, J. T. (1986). *Communication and persuasion: Central and peripheral routes to attitude change.* New York: Springer-Verlag.

Raudenbush, S. W., & Bryk, A. S. (2002). *Hierarchical linear models: Applications and data analysis methods* (Vol. 1). Thousand Oaks, CA: Sage Publications, Inc.

Riffe, D., Lacy, S., & Fico, F. (1998). *Analyzing media messages: Quantitative content analysis.* Mahwah, NJ: Lawrence Erlbaum.

Sargent, J. D., Worth, K. A., Beach, M., Gerrard, M., & Heatherton, T. F. (2008). Population-based assessment of exposure to risk behaviors in motion pictures. *Communication Methods and Measures*, 2, 134–151. doi:10.1080/193124508 02063404

Shapiro, M. A. (1994). Signal detection measures of recognition memory. In A. Lang (Ed.) *Measuring psychological responses to the media.* Mahwah, NJ: Erlbaum.

Slater, M. D. (1991). Use of message stimuli in mass communication experiments: A methodological assessment and discussion. *Journalism & Mass Communication Quarterly*, *68* (3), 412–421. doi:10.1177/107769909106800312

Slater, M. D. (2004). Operationalizing and analyzing exposure: The foundation of media effects research. *Journalism & Mass Communication Quarterly*, *81*(1), 168–183. doi:10.1177/107769900408100112

Slater, M. D. (2013). Content analysis as a foundation for programmatic research in communication. *Communication Methods and Measures*, 7, 85–93. doi:10.1080/ 19312458.2013.789836

Slater, M. D., & Kelly, K. J. (2002). Testing alternative explanations for exposure effects in media campaigns: The case of a community-based, in-school media drug prevention project. *Communication Research*, *29*, 367–389. doi:10.1177/009365020 2029004001

Slater, M. D., Hayes, A. F., Goodall, C. E., & Ewoldsen, D. R. (2012). Increasing support for alcohol-control enforcement through news coverage of alcohol's role in injuries and crime. *Journal of Studies on Alcohol and Drugs*, *73*(2), 311–315.

Slater, M.D., Rouner, D., Domenech-Rodriguez, M.M., Beauvais, F., Murphy, K., and Van Leuven, J. (1997) Adolescent responses to TV beer ads and sports content/ context: Gender and ethnic differences. *Journalism and Mass Communication Quarterly*, *74*, 108–122. doi:10.1177/107769909707400109

Slovic, P., & Fishhoff, B. L. S. (1982). Facts versus fears: Understanding perceived risk. In *Judgement under uncertainty: Heuristics and biases*. New York, Plenum Press: 463–489.

Snijders, T. A. B. (2005). Power and sample size in multilevel linear models. In B. S. Everitt and D. C. Howell (Eds.), *Encyclopedia of Statistics in Behavioral Science* (Vol. 3, pp. 1570–1573). Chichester: Wiley.

Snyder, L. B., Milici, F. F., Slater, M., Sun, H., & Strizhakova, Y. (2006). Effects of alcohol advertising exposure on drinking among youth. *Archives of Pediatrics & Adolescent Medicine*, *160*, 18–24. doi:10.1001/archpedi.160.1.18

Southwell, B. G., & Langteau, R. (2008). Age, memory changes, and the varying utility of recognition as a media effects pathway. *Communication Methods and Measures*, 2, 100–114. doi:10.1080/19312450802062380

Southwell, B. G., Barmada, C. H., Hornik, R. C., & Maklan, D. M. (2002). Can we measure encoded exposure? Validation evidence from a national campaign. *Journal of Health Communication*, *7*, 445–453. doi:10.1080/10810730290001800

Weaver, A. J., Zelenkauskaite, A., & Samson, L. (2012). The (non)violent world of YouTube: content trends in web video. *Journal of Communication*, *62*, 1065–1083. doi:10.1111/j.1460-2466.2012.01675.x

Wells, G. L., & Windschitl, P. D. (1999). Stimulus sampling and social psychological experimentation. *Personality and Social Psychology Bulletin*, *25*, 1115–1125. doi:10.1177/01461672992512005

CHAPTER CONTENTS

2 How Do the Places We Live In Impact Our Health?

Challenges for, and Insights from, Communication Research

Matthew D. Matsaganis

University at Albany, State University of New York

Since the 1990s, there has been a resurgence of research on how the places we live in impact our health. I review this interdisciplinary body of work to identify the main factors that explain how residential communities influence individuals' health. In doing so, I highlight unanswered questions which communication research can help address. After surveying communication research that addresses the larger issue of how the places in which we live influence our health, I articulate an integrative, multilevel, communication-centered theoretical framework to guide future work on neighborhood effects on health. Central to this framework is the notion that communication is an elementary social process through which neighborhood life is organized and transformed.

T en years ago, in the preface to their edited volume *Neighborhoods and Health*, Kawachi and Berkman (2003) noted that,

> [t]here are clear signals to indicate that researchers in public health and allied social sciences are converging on the search for place-based influences on health. Even a cursory search of the major professional journals in public health reveals dozens of relevant studies published just in the past few years. Research funding bodies, including the U.S. National Institutes of Health (NIH), have assigned priority to the search for neighborhood effects, especially in the context of explaining social inequalities in health.
>
> (p. v)

Perhaps the most compelling, recent example of the NIH's commitment to research on neighborhood effects and health is to be found in the launching of the National Children's Study (NCS) with the Children's Health Act, passed by the U.S. Congress in 2000. The NCS, which was in pilot phases in 2014, is a massive research endeavor with a 20-year horizon to examine the effects of environmental influences on the health and development of more than 100,000 children across the United States. NCS investigators will follow these children from before birth and until their 21st birthday. In its mission statement, NCS defines the *environment* broadly to include: (a) natural and man-made (or built) environment elements, (b) biological and chemical factors, (c) social conditions, (d) behavioral influences and outcomes, (e) genetics, (f) cultural and family influences and differences, as well as (g) geographic locations. For the NCS to achieve its goals, the National Institute of Child Health and Human Development, the umbrella organization under which NCS is sponsored, has recruited researchers from the biomedical, life, physical, and social sciences (NCS, 2014).

A bird's eye view of the literature through an online citation search revealed over one hundred thousand academic studies on neighborhoods and health published in the decade between 2003 and 2013. For the decade prior, the search returned about half that number (see Figure 2.1). These figures support Kawachi and Berkman's (2003) assertion that evidence confirms the increasing salience of the question: how do the places in which we live impact our health?

Until the 1990s, investigating neighborhood effects on health (NEH) involved primarily the examination of how characteristics of geographical units, such as the poverty rate or ethnic heterogeneity in census tracts, shaped residents' physical and mental well-being. Starting in the 1990s, though, the research agenda on NEH progressively concentrated on the role of social processes (such as social capital), and institutional mechanisms (such as institutional capacity) in health-related outcomes experienced by residential communities (Sampson, Morenoff, & Gannon-Rowley, 2002).

Curiously, and despite the foregoing developments, research outside the discipline itself has largely overlooked communication as a social process through which place impacts people's lives. Even in sociologists' work on neighborhood effects (Sampson, 2012), communication is frequently masked behind terms such as *social interaction* or implied in the examination of social mechanisms

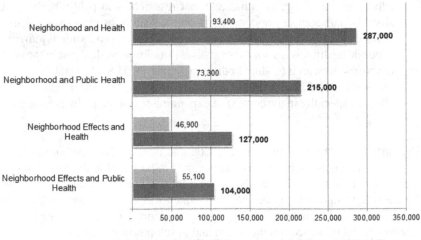

Figure 2.1 Number of citations concerning work on neighborhood effects and health produced by Google Scholar using four combinations of keywords in November 2013.

of neighborhood effects, such as *social ties* or *social networks*. This is curious, because communication featured prominently in the work of early 20th century Chicago School urban sociologists, to which much of the current neighborhood effects literature is genealogically and theoretically related. Theorists like Park, Burgess, and McKenzie argued that communication was one of the critical processes of social organization shaping Chicago and other cities of their time (Park, 1925/1967). Beyond sociology, in the public health literature, communication is discussed in the context of developing public health and social marketing campaigns to shape attitudes and behaviors around health (Daniel, Bernhardt, & Eroğlu, 2009). In this context, the primary focus is on the use of media as conduits of health-related information to diverse audiences. In most health campaign research, scholars and professionals seek to determine what the best combination of communication channels may be to get particular messages to audiences with specific socio-demographic characteristics or health profiles. Place, however, is rarely addressed as a factor that influences, for instance, the availability and choice of communication resources deployed and the success of the campaign. Does it matter, for example, if a campaign is undertaken in smaller versus larger urban communities (see Matsaganis & Golden, in press)?

While communication has been absent from much of the work of other disciplines interested in how place and health are related, relevant research in the communication discipline has been growing steadily. Unsurprisingly perhaps, scholars interested in health communication have played a key role in this trend.

My major goals here are five:

- To introduce and briefly discuss the history of the relationship between communication and neighborhood effects research.
- To review the non-communication literature and identify the main factors and social mechanisms that explain how residential communities shape individuals' lives and particularly their health. In doing so, I also identify questions left unanswered by this literature; I focus on gaps that communication research can help fill.
- To survey communication research that speaks to the larger issue of how the places we live in influence our health and review major, relevant findings of studies based on four communication-centered theoretical approaches; namely, the knowledge gap hypothesis (KGH), the structural influence model of communication (SIM), communication infrastructure theory (CIT), and the culture-centered approach (CCA). These theories have been fruitfully applied to address health-related issues of residential communities in various international contexts.
- To articulate, based on the foregoing four theoretical approaches, an integrative communication-centered framework, which could guide future research on NEH.
- And to suggest directions communication researchers could pursue so as to make visible the field's contribution to this growing body of literature.

Communication in the Ebbs and Flows
of Neighborhood Effects Research

Around the middle of the 19th century, technological innovation in transportation broke the "casement of the walking city" (Melvin, 1987, p. 258). People moved further away from the densely populated and geographically limited urban centers, and they created and settled into neighborhoods. Increasingly, researchers saw cities, counties, states, and the entire country as a quilt made up of distinct neighborhoods (Phillips, 1940). In the early days of the Chicago School of urban community ecology, between 1915 and 1925, Park, Burgess, McKenzie, and others pointed to transportation, but also to communication, as two key mechanisms of social organization that shaped the American urban communities of their time. Park, possibly because of his journalism background, argued that "transportation and communication . . . are primary factors in the ecological organization of the city" (Park, 1925/1967, p. 2).

The Chicago School of the early 20th century carved a path of research focused on understanding how people's lives are impacted by where they live. This work on "neighborhood effects" (Leventhal & Brooks-Gunn, 2003; Sampson, 2012), however, is marked by discontinuity—at least through the first half of the 1990s. The inconsistency in the development of the literature can be attributed to three factors: (a) debates over the perceived salience of the concept of neighborhood, (b) methodological constraints, and (c) the general historical context. A comprehensive historical account of the evolution of this research is outside the scope of this chapter and would require an entire volume (for more, see Jeffres, 2002). Suffice it to say that progress on the methodological front, especially with regard to modeling social processes through which neighborhood effects were thought to be produced, led to a resurgence of interest in this line of inquiry in the 1990s (Sampson et al., 2002). This interest has been sustained to this day.

Despite the growth in the neighborhood effects literature, communication has been largely absent from the repertoire of mechanisms or social processes through which neighborhood effects are thought to manifest. Often, communication is taken for granted, masked behind terms like social ties or social interaction. Communication, however, as conceptualized by the Chicago School sociologists, is more than the interaction between neighbors that share a backyard fence or that meet at the local grocery store.

Park and his colleagues linked social interaction (or interpersonal communication) to the emergence of public opinion, conceptualized as a mechanism of social control in the urban community. They argued that in urban neighborhoods founded on secondary relationships (as opposed to primary relationships among kin), where residents' interactions with one another are "immediate and unreflecting" (Park, 1925/1967, p. 24), it is "public opinion—and not mores—that becomes the dominant force in social control" (p. 38). Park believed that public opinion may be controlled, enlightened, and exploited through the media. "The newspaper," he argued, "is the great medium of communication within the city, and it is on the basis of the information which it supplies that public opinion rests" (Park, 1925/1967, pp. 38–39). Park's reflections on the role of the media illustrate that, for the early community ecology theorists, communication is not just social interaction among individuals, but a process that involves multiple neighborhood actors, including residents and institutional actors (such as media).

That train of thought supports the definition of communication I employ in this chapter. I conceive of *communication* as a social process that takes place at and across multiple levels of analysis within a residential community. The process is set in motion and sustained by a variety of neighborhood actors—ranging from individuals, to community-based organizations and institutions, including media (mainstream, local, and ethnically targeted), but also community-based organizations—who produce and share stories about the neighborhood and about health.[1] Through this process, neighborhood actors co-construct a communication environment, within which residents endeavor to address individual and shared health concerns. The information that is available in this environment (number of communication resources, breadth of issues discussed, quality of information shared) is influenced by the structural and cultural dimensions of the neighborhood. For example, small cities (size as a structural characteristic) typically represent small media markets, in which ownership consolidation is practically absolute (Noam, 2009). Therefore, and all other things being equal (such as individuals' and their residential community's socioeconomic position), people who live in neighborhoods in small cities are likely to have access to fewer media producing stories about health that are relevant to them, than residents of larger city neighborhoods.

A study by Pooley and Katz (2008) offers an intriguing exegesis for why communication has been largely overlooked especially in the sociological literature on neighborhood effects, but, arguably, from the related work of allied sciences, too. Pooley and Katz analyze the historical development of the social sciences from the pre- to the post-World War II era. They argue that the emergence of the field of public opinion was a key factor that led American sociology to depart from the Chicago School tradition, which had clear European roots, and to abandon the study of media. This departure is attributed to: (a) waning interest from government agencies, foundations, and commercial funders who supported this research during the war years; and (b) the new "intellectual coordinates" of the field. Following the war, public opinion research built primarily on attitude psychology, market research, and survey techniques, which focused on individual rather than collective behaviors (e.g., effects of persuasion campaigns). An additional result of these developments was that place was taken out of the study of public opinion.

That said, today, bridging this disconnect between communication and allied social sciences with respect to the impact of place on individuals' health could open new, interesting lines of inquiry. First, however, it is instructive to assess the state of current neighborhood effects research on health and identify gaps that need to be addressed.

Neighborhood Effects and Health

From the mid-1990s to the year 2000, the number of neighborhood effects studies doubled, "to the level of about 100 papers per year" (Sampson et al., 2002, p. 444). The development and application of new methods, such as geographic information systems (GIS)-assisted socio-spatial mapping played an important role in this proliferation. Socio-spatial mapping has allowed researchers to examine, among other things, what difference it makes to conceptualize and operationalize *neighborhood* in different ways. Several studies address whether it makes a difference, for instance, if neighborhoods are operationalized as administrative units (e.g., census tracts in the U.S. or wards in Britain) or in ways that more accurately reflect residents' views of their community (Messer, Vinikoor-Imler, & Laraia, 2012; Sampson, 2012).

In more recent neighborhood effects research, even though neighborhoods are still frequently operationalized as combinations of administrative units, most authors assume that neighborhoods are not merely containers in which individuals live. Places have particular characteristics (e.g., structural, cultural) that shape individuals' attitudes, beliefs, perceptions, and behaviors (such as perceptions regarding the availability of health providers in the local community or behaviors such as not seeking healthcare except in the case of emergencies). The relationship between individuals and neighborhood is defined as dynamic, though. Place enables and constrains human agency, but individuals' actions can also shape the places they inhabit. Neighborhoods are therefore the cause of effects but also are themselves effects (Matsaganis, 2007; Sampson, 2012).

Building on this recent literature as well as relevant communication research (e.g., Ball-Rokeach, Kim, & Matei, 2001), here I conceptualize *neighborhoods* as spatially defined areas that are occupied by individuals and organizations, have particular social characteristics, and are embedded in successively larger ecological units (e.g., within a city). The size, boundaries, and complexity of neighborhoods depend on several factors, including structural, social, and cultural characteristics of the larger ecological unit they are part of (a city's size, location, population diversity), how neighborhoods are socially constructed by local community stakeholders (individuals and organizations), but also the social phenomenon under study (voting behavior versus educational attainment, versus access to healthcare services).

Beyond the conceptual and methodological work that advanced thinking around the definition of neighborhoods, what drove the remarkable growth in the number of studies focused on residential (and usually urban) communities and health in the 1990s and 2000s were new theories and efforts to collect data that allowed for the study of how social processes, such as peer-group influence, collective socialization, or institutional capacity might explain why it matters for the health of a child, for example, where he or she grows up (Sampson et al., 2002). In a recent review of the literature, however, Diez Roux and Mair (2010) point out that our understanding of how neighborhoods' social environment impacts residents' health remains limited. Moving forward, it is important to appreciate, first, the range of health outcomes investigated in this body of work and, second, the neighborhood factors that have been identified as determinants of health.

The Spectrum of Health Outcomes Examined

In the neighborhood effects literature, *health outcomes* are broadly defined to include: (a) accessing, seeking, and utilizing health-enhancing resources (e.g., healthcare, sources of healthier food options, recreation areas); (b) health literacy; (c) attitudes, beliefs, and perceptions around health and healthcare resources; (d) health behaviors (such as consumption of fruits and vegetables, smoking, seeking screening for various types of cancer and sexually trans-mitted infections, compliance with treatment); (e) physical and mental health status; (f) incidence of health conditions (depression, diabetes, hypertension); and (g) population disparities related to a spectrum of health outcomes.

Research on place and health suggests that both structural neighborhood characteristics and several social processes that unfold in a community are related to these health outcomes.

Structural Neighborhood Characteristics

Effects of concentrated disadvantage.   Wilson's (1987) seminal book, *The Truly Disadvantaged* generated new interest and new questions that propelled neighborhood effects research forward in the 1990s. Wilson and others argued that the structural transformation of the American (and arguably the global) economy resulting from de-industrialization, globalization, and technological change (Gephart, 1997), the migration of low-wage jobs from urban centers to the suburbs (Freeman, 1991), and the flight of middle-class families from the inner cities (Gramlich, Laren, & Sealand, 1992) resulted in severe social dislocations in many urban neighborhoods (e.g., higher school dropout rates, proliferation of single-parent families). Gephart (1997) added that, since the 1940s, problems related to concentrated disadvantage have been compounded by increased urban residential segregation attributed to racial discrimination in the housing markets, as well as a number of government policies.

The research spawned by Wilson's work on concentrated disadvantage has focused on a variety of outcomes. Socioeconomic context is the most frequently studied variable in neighborhood effects studies focused on health. And despite some inconsistent results, Ellen, Mijanovich, and Dillman (2001) conclude that the evidence supports the notion that the socioeconomic condition of a com-munity has an independent influence on health behaviors. In one project aiming to uncover predictors of coronary heart disease factors, Hart, Ecob, and Smith (1997) found that area-level socioeconomic status did not predict smoking pat-terns in communities of Scotland, but it did account for significant variation across neighborhoods in terms of alcohol consumption and cholesterol levels;

the variation remained clear, even after controlling for individuals' education level and their occupation.

Several other studies from the U.S., Europe, and elsewhere have reported that residents in poor neighborhoods are more likely than dwellers of more affluent communities to confront, among other things, higher rates of heart disease, respiratory problems, cancer, diabetes, and mental health disorders (Chaix et al., 2008; Cox et al., 2007; Riva, Gauvin, & Barnett, 2007). Moreover, studies indicate that in poorer neighborhoods children are more likely to be hospitalized (Sellström & Bremberg, 2006).

In a review of the literature, Robert (1999) describes eloquently two general pathways through which a neighborhood's socioeconomic status affects health. First, she says, socioeconomic context shapes the socioeconomic position of individuals. This suggests that "the opportunities and constraints present in communities with different socioeconomic contexts can shape the education attainment, job prospects, and income level of individuals" (Robert, 1999, p. 493). Secondly, Robert adds, socioeconomic context directly affects "the social, service, and physical environments of communities shared by residents, which then affect the individual characteristics, conditions, and experiences of individuals that more directly impact health" (p. 493).

Socio-cultural neighborhood characteristics. Beyond socioeconomic status, several studies have found that a neighborhood's ethno-racial composition impacts individuals' access to healthcare services. In a study of all U.S. counties, Haas et al. (2004) found that African Americans and Latinos may perceive fewer barriers to care when they live in a county with a high percentage of people of the same ethno-racial background. In addition, Haas and her colleagues reported that Whites living in an area with a large percentage of Latinos feel that it is more difficult for them to get healthcare. Similarly, the ethnic makeup of a community has been linked to access to "social and material resources that promote health and avoid disease" (Schultz, Williams, Israel, & Lempert, 2002, p. 677), including grocery stores and pharmacies. In Detroit, during the 1960s, ethnic tensions led to the exodus of major grocery stores from poor, predominantly African American neighborhoods. Other studies have demonstrated that in neighborhoods with a prevalence of African Americans and Latinos, residents find it hard to get medications they need (Morrison et al., 2000) and pay more for prescriptions than residents of mostly White neighborhoods (Schultz & Lempert, 2000).

Natural and built environment of the community. Perhaps unsurprisingly, natural environment stressors are among the most commonly studied determinants, along with SES (socio-economic status), of neighborhood effects in the public health literature (Diez Roux & Mair, 2010; Ellen et al., 2001). Proximity to toxic waste sites and polluting factories, as well as air and water quality, are often considered factors that impact individuals' health. These environmental stressors are usually found in poorer neighborhoods (Anderton et al., 1994), signaling that multiple causes of disadvantage and poorer health tend to cluster together.

This clustering is clear in the research that focuses on the health impact of neighborhoods' built environment. Physical decay, land use patterns, transportation infrastructure characteristics, and access to healthier food options and recreation resources are a few of the built environment factors studied in relation to physical activity, diet, related physical health outcomes (such as diabetes and hypertension), and mental health outcomes. In a literature review, Saelens and Handy (2008) found consistent evidence suggesting that greater population density, more mixed land use, and being closer to non-residential destinations were predictors of more walking as a mode of transportation. In two other studies, Lewis et al. (2005) and Zenk et al. (2005) found that African American residents of relatively poor communities in Los Angeles and Detroit, respectively, had fewer options to choose from in terms of restaurants and supermarkets where they could find healthier food choices.

Beyond Structural Characteristics: Social Processes and Mechanisms of Effects

Despite the fact that many studies have produced evidence suggesting that structural neighborhood characteristics matter, frequently they do not fully explain *how* the neighborhood affects the lives of its residents. Is the presence of public parks, for instance, or of markets offering healthier food options sufficient for residents of a community to exercise more or eat more fresh fruits and vegetables? A number of additional social environmental factors, such as perceptions of neighborhood safety or peer influence, are likely to play a role as well. A complementary line of neighborhood effects research focuses on such social environmental determinants of residents' health. This work suggests that there are three types of mechanisms, which are related "yet appear to have independent validity," that help explain how effects are produced (Sampson et al., 2002, p. 457). We find these mechanisms predominantly in the literature that takes a pathway approach to examining factors that impact individuals' health (Diez Roux, 2012). Studies that take this approach aim to elucidate the specific mediating mechanisms through which biological and structural neighborhood factors influence health.

Social disorganization.   Much of the neighborhood effects work on social disorganization has focused on crime and violence as outcomes (Veysey & Messner, 1999). In the health-oriented literature, crime, violence, and social disorganization more generally, are treated as social environmental variables that negatively impact residents' health. Crime and violence can have a direct, short-term impact on residents' physical and mental health and long-term effects, through a process which Geronimus et al. (2006) calls *weathering*. They suggest that accumulated stress caused by violence and crime, over time, weakens individuals' resistance to diseases. Moreover, Ganz (2000) suggests that as violence reduces the expected lifespan of residents in disadvantaged neighborhoods, it also alters individuals' perceptions about how detrimental to their health certain behaviors with long-term effects, like smoking, can be.

Social ties, social interaction, and social capital.   Much of the research on the effects of social ties and interaction in a community has relied on the concept of social capital (Rostila, 2013). Social capital is usually viewed as a resource that is realized through social relationships (Coleman, 1988; Portes, 1998; Putnam, 2000). In communities endowed with rich stores of social capital, Putnam argues, it is easier for residents to get things done. Social capital is thought to impact health by strengthening social support and social cohesion, through social influence, increased civic engagement, and access to resources (Altschuler, Somkin, & Adler, 2004). These social processes, in turn affect health-related behaviors, which eventually impact individuals' health (Dahl & Malmberg-Heimonen, 2010). In a neighborhood rich in social capital, neighbors are more likely to be able to rely on each other for support (e.g., to get a ride to a doctor's office). In a neighborhood with depleted stores of social capital, however, residents' health may suffer.

A number of studies link higher levels of social cohesion among neighbors and social capital to better mental health (lower incidence of depression) and physical health outcomes, such as lower cardiovascular disease incidence or mortality (Kim, Subramanian, & Kawachi, 2006). In a study focused on the Australian city of Adelaide, both questionnaire and in-depth interview data suggested that social cohesion was a protective mechanism for mental health, but had no impact on physical health (Ziersch, Baum, MacDougall, & Putland, 2005). Social capital, however, may have a negative impact on health, too. In a study of Los Angeles communities, Carpiano (2007) showed that higher levels of social capital were associated with increased rates of smoking and drinking (via participation in community social events).

Norms of reciprocity and collective efficacy.   Social ties are important, but the "willingness of residents to intervene on behalf of children may depend . . . on conditions of mutual trust and shared expectations among residents" (Sampson et al., 2002, p. 457). A neighborhood, in which mutual trust and shared willingness to intervene is high, is one with a high level of collective efficacy (Sampson, 2012). The key hypothesis for studies that apply this mechanism of neighborhood effects is that, "neighborhood influences are accounted for by the extent of formal and informal social institutions in the community and the degree to which they monitor and control behavior in accordance with socially accepted practices and the goal of maintaining public order" (Leventhal & Brooks-Gunn, 2003, p. 30).

The research linking collective efficacy and health has been growing. One study conducted in Los Angeles, California, for instance, found that adolescents living in neighborhoods with low levels of collective efficacy (one standard deviation below the mean) exhibited 64 percent higher odds of being at risk for being overweight than those living in neighborhoods with average levels of collective efficacy (Cohen, Finch, Bower, & Sastry, 2006). In other studies, researchers have found that increased collective efficacy is associated with lower local crime rates (Klein & Maxson, 2006; Ahern et al., 2013), and less crime means that fewer people suffer bodily harm. Moreover, collective efficacy can indirectly influence one's mental health, as crime can induce fear, cause increased levels of stress, curb residents' physical activity, and prevent them from utilizing health services in their area (Minkler, 1992). Browning, Soller, Gardner, & Brooks-Gunn (2013) found that girls who lived in Chicago neighborhoods with higher levels of collective efficacy were less likely to internalize symptoms of neighborhood disorder (exhibit depression, anxiety) than those living in residential communities with lower collective efficacy. This was not true, however, for boys. Similar findings are reported in studies conducted in international contexts. Collective efficacy was the second strongest predictor (after education) of reduced mortality among both men and women in Hungary (Odgers et al., 2009), while perceptions of increased collective efficacy among community residents was associated with improvements in health behaviors in the context of an HIV-prevention intervention carried out in the Kilimanjaro region of Tanzania (Kamo, Carlson, Brennan, & Earls, 2008).

Institutional resources. Theoretically speaking, models that focus on institutional resources suggest that neighborhood influences operate by means of the quality, quantity, and diversity of educational (schools, libraries), recreational (sports clubs), social, health (clinics and other medical facilities), family support centers, childcare centers, religious and employment-related institutions available to the community (Leventhal & Brooks-Gunn, 2003). Several studies, for example, have suggested that the availability of high quality childcare in a neighborhood is tied to children's cognitive and socio-emotional health (Benasich, Brooks-Gunn, & Clewell, 1992).

In addition, a number of health disparities (for instance, with respect to diabetes, hypertension, and heart disease) are often associated with access to a variety of health-enhancing resources, such as primary healthcare services (Baldwin et al., 1998), healthful foods and places where one can exercise and play (Edwards, Jilcott, Floyd, & Moore, 2011). Poorer neighborhoods tend to be disadvantaged in terms of the number and quality of medical professionals available (McKnight, 1995). Therefore, residents in poorer communities often have to travel longer distances to find healthcare.

Questions Unanswered, Opportunities for New Research

The literature on neighborhood effects on health (NEH) has been growing at an impressive rate. Several questions, however, have not yet been adequately addressed in this work. I briefly discuss four of these that lend themselves to communication inquiry through theoretical lenses discussed in subsequent sections.

The first question, as eloquently articulated by Sampson et al. (2002) in a review of the broader neighborhood effects literature, is: What produces and can change how social mechanisms, like social capital, collective efficacy, and institutional capacity mediate how the places people live in impact them? Additionally, we might ask: Are there more elementary social processes that, over time, give birth to and sustain more complex social mechanisms?

A review more narrowly focused on health underscores that most research has treated effects of neighborhoods' physical and social environments independently, although "they are clearly closely related" (Diez Roux & Mair, 2010, p. 136). This points to a second major question that needs to be addressed in future research: What are the synergistic effects of physical and social environments on individuals' health?

A third, larger question is: What role does culture play in the production of NEH? Two lines of research could help answer this question: (a) comparative work across neighborhoods, regions, and countries, and (b) studies on how increasing population diversity shapes residential communities. Villarreal and Silva's (2006) work in Brazil and Sampson's (2012) studies in the U.S. and Europe explain why comparative research is necessary. In Brazil concentrated neighborhood poverty was associated with higher levels of collective efficacy, not lower (as expected based on studies conducted in the U.S. and Europe), perhaps, as Sampson asserts, "aiding survival" (p. 167). This finding suggests that although it is a powerful predictor of neighborhood effects, collective efficacy has a cultural component to it. Shared expectations among community members that they can come together to address common concerns are shaped by context, history, and prior experiences. An example of much needed work on how immigration dynamics shape neighborhood environments can be found in public health research. Viruell-Fuentes and Schulz (2009) show that maintaining social ties with co-ethnics in the community of settlement and transnational social relationships had a protective effect on the health of Mexican immigrant women living in Detroit, because these relationships were important sources of emotional, material, but also identity support (as they helped them construct a positive ethnic identity).

Additionally, in much of the NEH research, the relationship of neighborhood context and residents is seemingly unidirectional, with the macro level (community or larger society) ultimately determining the micro (individual). Such an orientation, though, does not allow for answers to another important question: Can residents impact the community context? And, if so, how? Research to address this larger question is warranted by both the definitions of neighborhood and neighborhood effects articulated earlier, in which individuals' agency is key, but also by pressing problems, including but not limited to durable health inequalities that affect many communities and millions of people.

Taken together, this brief discussion of four questions that are under-addressed in the broader literature on NEH underscores a need for more and different ways of thinking about mechanisms through which health and place are related. Building on the early work of Chicago School sociologists, I argue that bringing communication back into the center of the discussion around NEH can help address some of the aforementioned questions. I further develop this argument below by drawing on communication research.

Communication Perspectives on Connecting Place and Health

In a 2010 study on Internet use and concentrated disadvantage in urban communities, Hampton observes that, on one hand, communication research has not explored how individuals' environment influences how they use media and to what effect, while on the other hand sociology work that focuses on collective efficacy tends to reduce social interaction to interpersonal interaction, largely ignoring the role of media in creating and maintaining social ties. Hampton's (2010) study indicates that the Internet supports civic engagement in areas where it is already likely to be high, but that it also creates opportunities for engagement among residents of communities of extreme disadvantage (extreme poverty, unemployment, and racial segregation). These findings suggest that reintegrating media into research on neighborhood effects can provide answers to questions of how place shapes individuals' lives and how intervening social mechanisms like collective efficacy are produced. This is but one example of how communication can contribute to a broader, burgeoning field of study. It also challenges communication researchers to expand existing theoretical frameworks to account for the ecological contexts that shape (and are shaped by) dynamics of individuals' everyday life.

This challenge is particularly pressing given the proliferation of studies on neighborhood effects on health (NEH), but also the increasing interest in health among communication scholars worldwide (Paek, Lee, Jeong, Wang, & Dutta, 2010; Schulz & Hartung, 2010). Although research on health in a variety of neighborhoods is necessary (Matsaganis & Golden, in press), the salience of studies on health in urban community environments, specifically, is underscored by data suggesting that cities are becoming the predominant mode of living. Within the next 30 years, most global population growth is forecasted to occur in cities in poorer parts of the world, and midsize cities are expected to grow faster than the world's megacities (Vlahov et al., 2007). Relatedly, in an examination of the intersections of communication and public health, Kreps and Maibach (2008) identify ecological theoretical perspectives as a key area of transdisciplinary common ground. As noted by Stokols (1996), "a key feature of ecological models is that they incorporate two or more analytic levels (e.g., personal, organizational, community)" (p. 287), in contrast, for example, with behavior change models that focus primarily on individual health behaviors and underlying health-related attitudes and beliefs.

Until now, relatively few health communication studies have adopted an ecological orientation that reflects Stokols's (1996) definition. The majority of those that have, though, are based on four different theoretical approaches: the knowledge gap hypothesis (KGH), the structural influence model of communication (SIM), communication infrastructure theory (CIT), and the culture-centered approach (CCA).

Briefly, KGH and SIM contribute to research on health and place by showing how communication inequalities interact with individual- and neighborhood-level factors identified in the social determinants of health literature to produce health disparities; CIT highlights the role of communication as a multilevel process through which neighborhoods are constituted and health effects may be produced, while CCA emphasizes the role of culture as a fundamental determinant of health disparities. I briefly discuss unique contributions of these theories to NEH research next. In so doing, I discuss how these approaches can help address questions identified earlier and that NEH research has not answered to date. Subsequently, I propose an integrative conceptual framework that enables the study of neighborhood effects from a communication perspective. In this framework, communication becomes an elementary and central social process that explains why and how where we live impacts our health.

Knowledge Gap Hypothesis and the Structural Influence Model of Communication

Two conceptual frameworks, (a) the knowledge gap hypothesis (KGH) and (b) the structural influence model of communication (SIM) have grown out of the structural pluralism (or community structure) tradition. In this context, the driving question is, how macro or structural characteristics of communities (such as city size, demographics, heterogeneity) influence the roles that communication resources (and especially media) perform in residents' lives (Nah & Armstrong, 2011; Pollock, 2011; Tichenor, Donohue, & Olien, 1980). Both theories have been used productively in health communication research. Studies based on the KGH, however, focus largely on individual-level socio-demographic characteristics as determinants of knowledge gaps and not on community-level structural attributes. This research examines how differences in individuals' socioeconomic position will affect how quickly they access available information, with those higher on the socioeconomic ladder benefiting from information quicker, thereby widening the gap between them and individuals of lower socioeconomic status (Hwang & Jeong, 2009; Viswanath & Finnegan, 1996). Shim (2008), for example, found that European-origin and more educated Americans were more likely than Americans of other backgrounds to use the Internet to seek cancer-related information, and this online information enlarged the gaps in cancer knowledge among U.S. subpopulations.

Although most KGH research emphasizes micro-level socioeconomic determinants of health outcomes, there are few KGH studies that account for the role of the ecological context in which they were conducted. Slater, Hayes, Reineke, Long, and Bettinghaus (2009), for example, show that differences in newspaper coverage of cancer-prevention news across 23 regions in the U.S. (defined as areas of similar media market size within four major geographic divisions: northeast, southeast, midwest, and west) moderates the relationship between education and cancer-prevention knowledge. Their approach is novel, as earlier KGH work assessed individual-level differences in news exposure based on self-reports of media use.

The structural influence model of communication (SIM) theoretically complements KGH by highlighting structural (community-level) sources of neighborhood influence and by explicitly connecting communication literature to public health studies on the social determinants of health and neighborhood effects on health. SIM assumes that the structural characteristics of the places individuals live in (for example, rural versus urban, poorer or better off) interact with what are considered mediating or moderating conditions, including individuals' socio-demographic profile and the social resources at their disposal (including social networks they are part of, their social capital, social institutions available in the residential environment, including healthcare providers and media), to shape health communication outcomes (Viswanath & Emmons, 2006). These outcomes include: individuals' health-related media exposure and use, their information-seeking patterns, their attention to health information, and their ability to process health information. Subsequently, communication is linked to a variety of health-related outcomes, ranging from health knowledge and health literacy, to health behaviors (including preventative behaviors), to disease incidence.

Viswanath, Steele, and Finnegan (2006) illustrate the utility of the model through analyses of data from the Minnesota Heart Health Program, a 13-year-long project designed to reduce cardiovascular disease (CVD) incidence in three matched pairs of urban communities in the Midwest of the U.S. The authors examined whether residents' ties to community groups (an indicator of civic engagement) were associated with health message recall, but also whether these correlations differed depending on the community's size (considered as a proxy measure of community pluralism), distance to metropolitan areas, percentage of people employed in agriculture and manufacturing, as well as number of available media outlets. Analyses indicated that even after controlling for gender, education, and other variables, ties to community groups, independently, accounted for recall of CVD-related messages. Community size also explained recall of CVD-related messages, yet community pluralism did not moderate the relationship of civic engagement on message recall.

Although SIM argues that communication and other social processes (such as civic engagement in the study by Viswanath et al., 2006) are related and together they produce effects on health, these relationships have not been adequately elaborated. Likewise, to date, within the SIM framework, the effects of the interplay between a residential community's physical characteristics (e.g., availability of public transportation, recreation areas) and residents' social environment on health remain relatively unexplored. Finally, SIM (as many conceptual frameworks in public health research) assumes a linear path, from distal causes of health outcomes, such as concentrated disadvantage and socio-demographic characteristics of individuals and communities, to social processes considered as intermediate causes of health effects, to health-related behaviors, and ultimately to health outcomes. This assumption of linearity prevents a deeper understanding of complex relationships among factors related to particular effects. For example, as noted earlier in the work of Tichenor et al. (1980), structural neighborhood characteristics, such as poverty and ethnic heterogeneity, might shape the range of media available to community residents (more or fewer, mainstream only or mainstream and ethnically targeted media) and the content they have access to, but extant communication research tells us that media consumption might also influence how residents perceive their neighborhood environment (Gerbner & Gross, 1976; Matei & Ball-Rokeach, 2005). Is it, for example, a place where they can find the healthcare they need? Is it a safe place? Such effects are likely to impact health behaviors and outcomes downstream (less physical activity despite availability of public parks, underutilization of healthcare services).

Communication Infrastructure Theory

As a social ecological theory developed through communication research in urban communities, communication infrastructure theory (CIT) complements SIM-based research. The communication infrastructure of a community comprises a multilevel storytelling network (STN) set in its communication action context (Ball-Rokeach et al., 2001; Kim & Ball-Rokeach, 2006). Residents in their interpersonal networks are micro-level actors, who share stories with each other about their everyday lives in their neighborhoods. Meso-level actors include CBOs and smaller, community-oriented media, whose stories tend to focus on a particular area or population (e.g., an ethnic community). However, macro-level actors, including large-scale, mass media, as well as other large institutions (government agencies, HMOs (health maintenance organizations), food/drug manufacturers, national mainstream media organizations) that tend to tell stories about an entire city, a region, the country or world as a whole also shape communication relationships and content in a neighborhood. Considered together, a community's storytelling network and more macro-level agents make up a community's broader, multilevel storytelling system (Ball-Rokeach et al., 2001). Prior health research employing CIT suggests that the more integrated residents are into their local STN—that is, the more connected they are to their neighbors, local community organizations, and local media—the more likely they are to be knowledgeable about preventing and detecting breast cancer and diabetes (Kim, Moran, Wilkin, & Ball-Rokeach, 2011), actively seek health information (Wilkin & Ball-Rokeach, 2011), perform emergency preparedness behaviors (Kim & Kang, 2010), and to exercise (Wilkin, Katz, Ball-Rokeach, & Hether, in press).

Communication among STN agents is enabled and constrained by the communication action context (CAC). This context includes the community's natural and built environment (presence/absence of organizational resources, technological infrastructure characteristics including the presence and configuration of the public transportation grid), and psychological factors such as residents' perceptions about how safe particular parts of their community are (Ball-Rokeach et al., 2001; Matsaganis, 2007).

Although there is a lack of CIT-based research that employs quantitative methods, typical of neighborhood effects studies, to investigate the impact of CAC factors on health, a small number of studies reporting on intervention research employing mixed-methods designs and guided by community-based participatory research principles (Minkler & Wallerstein, 2008), could inform the design of future, quantitative and multilevel neighborhood effects research on health (Kreuter, Kegler, Joseph, Redwood, & Hooker, 2012; Matsaganis, Golden, & Scott, 2014; Wilkin, Stringer, O'Quin, Montgomery, & Hunt, 2011). In the Accountable Communities Healthy Together (ACHT) project in Atlanta, for example, researchers and community members worked together to address residents' concerns with mental health and depression. Data collected through Photovoice techniques indicated that there were features of the built environment (i.e., CAC) that negatively impacted residents' mental health (Kreuter et al., 2012); the top feature identified was the large number of vacant houses present throughout the community (42 percent of properties). Future work on neighborhood effects using multilevel model ing, could, for instance, investigate the impact of the presence of vacant properties on communication dynamics in this and surrounding communities, and residents' mental health. Vacant properties might become crime hotspots and their presence could discourage communication among neighbors and lead to social isolation. Social isolation could, in turn, negatively impact residents' mental health.

The ACHT project in Atlanta engaged the indigenous STN (interpersonal networks, local media, and community organizations) to mobilize residents to participate in community cleanup efforts and sign petitions. Through the campaign, residents and the academic research team persuaded the city to help local non-profit organizations acquire and reuse vacant properties, beginning with those nearest schools and public parks (Kreuter et al., 2012). The unfolding of ACHT highlights both how the CAC can impact health, but also how the STN can become an engine of community change (Matsaganis, 2007). CIT accounts for the independent and interaction effects of the built and social environment on health (i.e., the interplay of structure and agency). In addition, research based on CIT suggests that communication can be a social process that generates and strengthens other social mechanisms of effects (Kim & Ball-Rokeach, 2006), like civic engagement in the case of ACHT, and lead to changes in structural neighborhood characteristics that influence health.

In an overview of CIT-based research on health disparities, Wilkin (2013) explains how the objectives of ACHT in Atlanta changed from addressing hypertension and diabetes disparities (choices supported by existing health data) to mental health and depression. The shift was driven by the community, which was engaged in all aspects of the research, including the process of defining the project's goals. For residents, mental health and depression were more pressing issues. Residents' choices reflected the community's endogenous culture (values and beliefs around health), which exists often in tension with mainstream culture. The culture-centered approach (Dutta, 2008), discussed next, elaborates, from a communication perspective, the role of culture as a distal determinant of health.

A Culture-Centered Approach to Health Communication

Structure, culture, communication, and agency are key and intertwined concepts in the culture-centered approach (CCA). Structures are defined broadly to include individuals' and communities' material resources, features of the community environment such as the availability of healthcare and transportation services, but also the ways in which the healthcare system is organized (Dutta, 2008). Structures can enable and constrain individuals' capacity to achieve their health-related goals. The impact of structures on individuals acquires significance through communication, conceptualized as the process of "constructing, negotiating, and transforming cultural meanings" (Dutta-Bergman, 2004, p. 260). This process unfolds in individuals' everyday life, as their beliefs, values, and practices around health confront those of their neighbors, those of organizations and institutions they come into contact with in their local communities (including healthcare providers), but also those of media. As an approach with roots in critical theory, CCA emphasizes the need to understand how certain populations (the poor, ethnic and racial minorities, immigrants) become marginalized, and to reveal ways through which these populations can (re-)gain agency and challenge the structures that constrain their efforts to achieve health goals.

CCA-based studies have been conducted primarily in developing countries (e.g., India), but more recently also in the United States. Dutta and Jamil (2013), for instance, show how certain structures act as barriers to undermine low-income Bangladeshi immigrants' efforts to seek healthcare in New York City, while others facilitate immigrants' agency. Having health insurance, for example, depends largely on whether an individual has a job, and insurance is necessary for individuals to seek healthcare (structure as constraint). However, being able to rely on social networks of immigrants with similar backgrounds (a type of enabling structure referred to as community-based social capital) is seen as a way to procure a job faster and thereby also receive necessary insurance benefits. Through in-depth interviews, the researchers illustrate how participants exercise agency by articulating alternative interpretive frames through which taken-for-granted assumptions regarding how the healthcare system of New York operates are challenged. For example, immigrant patients "spoke back" to hospital staff and questioned their practice of letting them wait for hours before getting back to them with something as simple as a "piece a paper" with information about a follow-up appointment (Dutta & Jamil, 2013, p. 177). As one participant recounted telling a health provider, "I told her that because of such reasons we do not come to the hospital because of this behavior, because of their carelessness, we lose one day's job and not able to bring home money to feed the family" (Dutta & Jamil, 2013, p. 179).

In another study, Dutta, Anaele, and Jones (2013) investigated how structure, culture, and communication in two different communities—in Midnapur, West Bengal, India and Tippecanoe County, Indiana, in the U.S.—impacted individuals who suffered from food insecurity. In this case, cultural differences were related to the socioeconomic position of different populations in the communities studied. Dutta et al. (2013) show how the socioeconomic position of the food insecure, the lack of means of transportation, and the location of food pantries (all structural constraints) interacted with the stigma around food insecurity and led to the underutilization of local food pantries. In this case, food insecurity was constructed by members of the dominant culture (individuals of higher socioeconomic status) as the plight of individuals who were lazy. The stigma, an outcome of communication, contributed to the marginalization of this population, and negatively impacted their well-being.

To date, CCA has not been employed as a theoretical approach to study neighborhood effects on health through multilevel statistical analyses (with which neighborhood effects research is frequently associated). This theoretical approach, however, is ecological in nature (Kreps & Maibach, 2008; Stokols, 1996) and it highlights the recursive relationship between communicative practices and the communication environment of residents, which together influence health. Additionally, extant CCA work points to culture as a distal cause of health disparities, and to the need for comparative work across neighborhoods, cities, and countries. Such research, using a variety of methodologies, could enhance our understanding of cultural factors (such as stigma) that reify or reduce health disparities.

Towards an Integrative Communication-Centered Perspective to Neighborhood Effects on Health

Each one of the four communication theories discussed offers insight into how the places we live in impact our health, but it also has blind spots. Viewing them, however, as complementary and integral parts of a broader, ecological, and communication-centered perspective to neighborhood effects on health could contribute answers to questions unaddressed (or under-addressed) in the larger literature on health and place. Such an integrative model:

*   Defines communication—informed by all four theoretical approaches (KGH, SIM, CIT, and CCA)—as a process that takes place at and across multiple levels of analysis within a neighborhood. It involves all residential community actors, ranging from individual residents (micro level), to community-based organizations and local institutions, including local media (meso level). Through communication, neighborhood actors co-construct a communication environment (comprising of health information resources and stories about health), within which residents endeavor to address individual and shared health concerns. This definition allows for the study of interpersonal communication (micro level), but also communication between residents and organizational and institutional actors (micro-meso), and communication among local organizations and institutions (meso-meso) as a determinant of health.

- Understands (again, building on research based on all four approaches) the role of communication in the relationship of place and health as shaped by individual-level socio-demographic differences, but also the features of the natural, built, and social environment of the neighborhood. The proposed integrative perspective assumes that the role of communication is affected by macro-social phenomena and factors, including, for example, mainstream mass media and national- or global-level institutions such as the Centers for Disease Control in the United States or the World Health Organization (as important health information distribution systems and mechanisms of social control), policies (around the allocation of health-related resources or guidelines for health screenings), and immigration and other demographic trends (including urbanization). These macro-level factors can impact communication processes in the community directly (for example, when mainstream mass media highlight certain health issues as being more critical than others, thereby influencing the agenda around health in the local community or making it more difficult for residents to find information about health issues that are important to them) or indirectly by transforming the social, built, and natural environment of the community (as is the case when immigration dynamics change the socio-demographic makeup of a community, thereby introducing new sets of health issues that are salient to new residents).
- Emphasizes (informed primarily by CIT and CCA) that individuals have agency and can, through communication, resist structures that hinder their capacity to address health concerns most salient to them, and transform the environment of their residential community.
- Examines communication (driven primarily by CIT-based research) as a more elementary process through which other social mechanisms that have garnered considerable attention in the neighborhood effects literature focused on health are put into motion and sustained (e.g., social capital, collective efficacy). In other words, the integrative perspective suggests that communication can operate as an antecedent to other social mechanisms considered in the literature as intermediate or proximal mechanisms of effects.
- And foregrounds (based on CCA) the role of culture as a particular structure constituted through communication in local communities. Culture, as illustrated by Dutta and Jamil (2013), interacts with other structures (enabling or constraining) to impact individuals' health.

Moreover, an integrative, communication-centered approach to neighborhood effects on health:

- Encourages researchers to use multiple methods to analyze multilevel phenomena. Studies based on the four aforementioned theoretical frameworks have used a wide variety of quantitative and qualitative methods (including surveys, content analyses, focus groups, in-depth interviews, and Photovoice techniques).

- And lends itself (as indicated in work using each one of the four communication approaches) to the design of place-based communication interventions in a variety of international contexts.

The integrative, communication-centered perspective is not conceptualized as a unified communication theory for the study of neighborhood effects on health (NEH) resulting from a fusion of four distinct theoretical approaches. It acknowledges that these approaches have significant differences, among other things in how they conceptualize communication. It is partly because of these differences, though, that these approaches are complementary and helpful in studying neighborhood effects. The integrative perspective proposed reflects not a fusion, but rather a synthesis of knowledge developed through relevant communication research; a synthesis guided by the notion that a judicious selection and integration of theories may yield more complete answers to complex, multilevel phenomena (Ognyanova & Monge, 2013). Figure 2.2 captures key variables of a communication-centered approach to NEH and relationships among them.

I next discuss two studies; one because it illustrates the potential of applying an integrative communication-centered perspective, and the second because it shows how a communication theory can be fruitfully combined with prominent theories in the broader, non-communication literature on NEH. I conclude this section by discussing how adopting an integrative communication-centered perspective could lead to research extending the studies used here as examples. In the first project, Kim, Moran, Wilkin, and Ball-Rokeach (2011), combined the knowledge gap hypothesis (KGH) and communication infrastructure theory (CIT) and showed that for African American and Latino residents of Los Angeles communities, higher education predicted higher levels of access to community-based communication resources (i.e., neighbors, community organizations, and local media), and better access to such communication resources accounted for higher levels of knowledge around breast cancer and diabetes, but not prostate cancer and hypertension. By integrating KGH and CIT, the authors show how education disparities shape health disparities in a local community through communication. They explain that, individuals "with more education also have the advantage of a network of information (or storytelling) resources to help them access, understand, and apply health information in their daily lives" (pp. 407–408).

In a different study, also focused on disadvantaged communities of South Los Angeles that are predominantly African American and Latino, Matsaganis and Wilkin (2014) investigated how access to local communication resources and civic engagement, independently and in combination, shape residents' access to health-enhancing resources in their communities (i.e., healthcare services, sources of healthier food options, public recreation spaces). Based on CIT, the authors conceptualize individuals' level of integration into their community's storytelling network (comprised of interpersonal communication networks, community-based organizations, and local media)

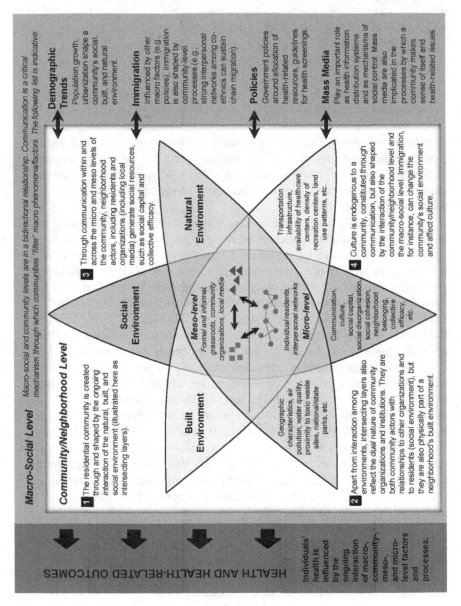

Macro-Social Level *Macro-social and community levels are in a bidirectional relationship. Communication is a critical mechanism through which communities 'filter' macro phenomena/factors. The following list is indicative:*

Demographic Trends
Population growth, urbanization shape a community's social, built, and natural environment.

Immigration
Influenced by other macro factors (e.g., policies), immigration is also shaped by community-level processes (e.g., strong interpersonal networks among co-ethnics can sustain chain migration)

Policies
Government policies around allocation of health-related resources, guidelines for health screenings.

Mass Media
Play an important role as health information distribution systems and as mechanisms of social control. Mass media are also implicated in the processes by which a community makes sense of itself and health-related issues.

Community/Neighborhood Level

1 The residential community is created through and shaped by the *ongoing interaction* of the natural, built, and social environment (illustrated here as intersecting layers).

3 Through *communication* within and across the micro and meso levels of the community, neighborhood actors, including residents and organizations (including local media) generate social resources, such as social capital and collective efficacy.

Natural Environment

Social Environment

Built Environment

Meso-level
Formal and informal, grassroots, community organizations, local media

Micro-level
Individual residents, interpersonal networks

Communication, culture, social capital, social disorganization social cohesion, neighborhood belonging, collective efficacy etc.

Transportation infrastructure, availability of healthcare centers, density of recreation centers, land use patterns, etc.

Geographic characteristics, air pollution, water quality, proximity to toxic waste sites, national/state parks, etc.

4 *Culture* is endogenous to a community, constituted through communication, but also shaped by the interaction of the community/neighborhood level and the macro-social level. Immigration, for instance, can change the community's social environment and affect culture.

2 Apart from interaction among environments, intersecting layers also reflect the *dual nature* of community organizations and institutions. They are both community actors with relationships to other organizations and to residents (social environment), but they are also physically part of a neighborhood's built environment.

HEALTH AND HEALTH-RELATED OUTCOMES

Individuals' health is influenced by the ongoing interaction of macro-, community-, meso-, and micro-level factors and processes.

Figure 2.2 A model of an integrated, communication-centered approach to neighborhood health effects.

as an indicator of communicative social capital; a source not only of social control and social support, but, as Rojas, Shah, and Friedland (2011) argue, a source of social integration. Such integration occurs "at the system level via news media, at the community level via formal and informal social ties, and at the individual level via interpersonal discussion" (p. 694). As this argument suggests, integration requires the scaffolding of social and associational ties, but this social structure is built through communication and facilitates communication among community actors. CIT focuses our attention on community-level social capital resources built through everyday communication. In the ideal scenario, residents communicate with community organizations and local media whose activities and stories, respectively, are geared towards addressing neighborhood issues, including health concerns. Conceptualizing integration of a community's storytelling network as an indicator of social capital puts communication research in direct conversation with neighborhood effects literature, in which social capital is treated as an important mechanism of health effects.

Beyond social capital, collective efficacy is also found to be an important determinant of health-related outcomes (Browning et al., 2013) in the neighborhood effects literature. In their study, Matsaganis and Wilkin (2014) extend CIT work by combining it with the theory of collective efficacy (Sampson, 2012). Through their analyses, the authors show that communicative social capital seemingly plays an important, yet complex role in how individuals relate to their local environment of health resources. For individuals who believe their health is relatively poor, the uninsured, and for those who feel they cannot count on neighbors to address shared concerns (low collective efficacy), being more connected to the local storytelling network can accentuate a sense of vulnerability due to a felt lack of health resources. These findings suggest that the role of communicative social capital, as a determinant of disparities around access to health resources, depends on structural constraints (e.g., lack of insurance), but also on social environmental resources that imbue individuals with agency (e.g., collective efficacy).

Taken together, the foregoing studies lend support for a communication-centered approach to neighborhood effects on health, which can also offer answers (at least partial) to the four unanswered questions or challenges identified in the review of non-communication literature on the connection between health and place. In addition, the preceding examples bolster the argument for an approach building on strengths of multiple socio-ecological (à la Stokols) communication theories. The study by Matsaganis and Wilkin (2014), for example, could be extended by drawing on research based on the culture-centered approach to investigate how a community's endogenous culture (or cultures) is implicated in residents' definitions of a health-enhancing neighborhood environment, their understanding of collective efficacy, but also structural constraints on residents' ability to access health resources.

Moving Forward: Expanding a Communication Research Agenda on Health and Place

Beyond the above-mentioned examples, there is significant potential for communication research to contribute to the literature on health and place. I briefly outline four directions for future research that lend themselves to an integrative, communication-centered approach.

Investigating the Dual Role of Organizational Community Resources

Historically, faith-based organizations have acted as mobilizing forces in African American communities (Owens, 2012). Additionally, they may act as subsidiaries of non-profit organizations and as resources for job-seekers (Owens, 2012). Similarly, substantial research has detailed the important roles of hometown associations for neighborhoods with large Mexican-origin immigrant populations. These organizations act as loci of social exchange, but also as engines of development for the towns immigrants come from (Orozco, 2003). Moreover, organizations frequently serve as locations where health interventions take place (Wilkin, 2013). Although organizational resources are theoretically deemed important as mechanisms of neighborhood effects, most studies only account for their density (density of libraries, medical facilities, recreation centers, childcare facilities). As Sampson et al. (2002) note, most neighborhood effects studies, "do not distinguish well between structural dimensions of institutions (e.g., density) and mediating institutional processes" (p. 458).

Through the lenses of an integrative, communication-centered approach and particularly from a CIT perspective institutions can (a) be part of the storytelling network and simultaneously (b) be implicated in the communication action context as structural resources. Community-based organizations, and many healthcare providers, are often led by individuals who are members of a residential community or who invest considerable material resources and effort to build relationships with members of the community. In the course of everyday life, organizational actors communicate with residents and other organizations. Health and social service professionals interact with families about issues they are dealing with, the local Women, Infants, and Children (WIC) office offers counseling to young mothers, local media producers report on stories affecting residents' lives. To the extent that organizational actors serve the local community, they contribute to the stores of social and communication capital available to community members. They become resources residents depend on to accomplish everyday goals.

This would suggest that organizations have to be considered as part of the storytelling network. Yet, it is also true that local organizations' capacity to serve residents may be limited. Hence, variables like the density of organizations in the neighborhood environment (e.g., density of health providers) are also very important. Communication research, in this case, elucidates the dual role of institutions in neighborhoods. Insofar as organizations are part of the community's multilevel communication network of actors, they do not act alone and their influence is conditioned by their relationship to residents and each other. As part of the communication action context, organizations become problem-solving or problem-causing hubs. Sampson (2012), for instance, shows that communities with higher density of community organizations are communities in which more civic actions take place. Future research should explore this dual role of organizations, particularly in addressing place-based health issues and disparities.

The Communicative Construction of Place and Health

With few exceptions (e.g., Kovandžić et al., 2012), neighborhood effects studies on health do not adequately explain how residents attach meaning and develop a sense of belonging to places. From an integrative, communication-centered perspective, residential communities have physical attributes but are also social constructions, products of storytelling across levels of analysis, from micro (residents), to meso (community organizations, local media), to macro (mass media, larger organizations) (Matsaganis & Golden, in press). Stories constructed by residents about their community and other communities include spatial signifiers, references to geophysical neighborhood characteristics, or references to historical, architectural or other landmarks. Such signifiers are also embedded in stories told by organizations and media in reference to particular communities. As storytelling occurs across levels (micro to macro), stories are edited, revised, or discarded. The end result may affect residents in many ways. For instance, stigmatizing a community as a site of violent crime will likely impact how residents see their neighborhood, with a variety of possible outcomes (Cohen, Ball-Rokeach, & Hayden, 2004; Matei & Ball-Rokeach, 2005). It could, for instance, lead to social isolation with implications for mental health and underutilization of local health services. Future research should investigate the processes through which residential communities' identities (a dangerous place, a food desert, a place lacking health resources, a healthy community) emerge, as well as the ways in which such identities impact health disparities.

Immigration and Communication

Globalization, fueled partly by technological innovation, is transforming population dynamics of cities across the world (Scholte, 2005). In the U.S., it is no longer only larger urban centers—historically recognized as "gateway cities" for new immigrants—that are affected but increasingly so midsize and smaller cities (Painter & Zhou, 2010), as well as many suburban communities (Singer, Hardwick, & Brettell, 2008). Similar trends are observed in Europe, where between 2001 and 2008 the level of net immigration was higher than it was in the U.S. (European Urban Knowledge Network, 2012).

To date, communication researchers' attention to immigration-related issues has been limited. In a recent synthesis of the communication and broader literature on immigrant integration, however, Katz (2014) identifies several ways in which communication can contribute to this larger body of research. As discussed, Dutta and Jamil (2013) have illustrated the utility of a culture-centered approach to health disparities in their study of Bangladeshi immigrants in New York. New research, through the lenses of an integrative, communication-centered perspective could expand their work and provide additional insights as to how, for example: (a) lack of access to local and ethnic media for health information can accentuate health disparities in diverse ethnic communities (Matsaganis, Katz, & Ball-Rokeach, 2011); and (b) how fragmented interpersonal communication networks of residents (i.e., fragmented across ethnic backgrounds) and communication disconnects between residents and organizational resources (e.g., health and human service organizations), independently and together, shape health disparities.

Comparative Research on Neighborhood Health Effects Across Cultures

Research based on CIT and CCA illustrates the complex ways in which cultural differences (across countries or subpopulations within a country) influence health. CCA especially sensitizes us to distal determinants of health that often remain invisible. Whether it is between marginalized populations (immigrants, ethnic minorities, the homeless, the food insecure) and the mainstream population of a residential community, or between populations across countries (U.S. versus India), cultural differences can account for different pathways through which neighborhood effects on health manifest. An integrative, communication-centered perspective lends itself to comparative work across multiple contexts.

Conclusion

The literature on neighborhood effects on health continues to grow at a rapid pace. And although communication has not been part of this discussion for some time, it is clear that it should have a position at the table. The Chicago School's premise that communication is one of the critical processes of social organization of urban communities still holds true today. Four ecological communication theories, reviewed here, and especially an integrative, communication-centered approach to health and place, can speak to a host of critical issues identified in the existing and broader literature (that is, beyond Communication). This essay suggests that to claim space at the table, communication researchers need to intensify collaboration across the discipline, but to also connect and engage the broader research community. The recommendations for future research articulated here offer just a place to start the conversation.

Note

1. Institutions are defined as established organizations (often of public character), including media, churches, departments of health and social services (at local, regional, and national levels). Community-based organizations are defined as associations of persons with a common set of goals. Local-level organizations with goals such as improving social justice and expanding access to Medicaid would be examples of community-based organizations. I use the more inclusive term "organizations" in this essay whenever differentiating between institutions and community-based organizations is not meaningful.

References

Ahern, J., Cerdá, M., Lippman, S. A., Tardiff, K. J., Vlahov, D., & Galea, S. (2013). Navigating non-positivity in neighborhood studies: An analysis of collective effi cacy and violence. *Journal of Epidemiology & Community Health, 67*(2), 159–165. doi:10.1136/jech-2012-201317

Altschuler, A., Somkin, C. P., & Adler, N. E. (2004). Local services and amenities, neighborhood social capital, and health. *Social Science & Medicine, 59*, 1219–1229. doi:10.1016/j.socscimed.2004.01.008

Anderton, D. L., Anderson, A., Rossi, P. H., Oakes, J. M., Fraser, M. R., Weber, E. W., & Calabrese, E. J. (1994). Hazardous-waste facilities: "Environment equity" issues in metropolitan areas. *Evaluation Review, 18*, 123–140. doi:10.1177/0193841X9401800201

Baldwin, L. M., Larson, E. H., Connell, F. A., & Nordlund, K. C. (1998). The effect of expanding Medicaid prenatal services on birth outcomes. *American Journal of Public Health, 88*, 1623–1629. doi:10.2105/AJPH.88.11.1623

Ball-Rokeach, S. J., Kim, Y. C., & Matei, S. (2001). Storytelling neighborhood: Paths to belonging in diverse urban environments. *Communication Research, 27*, 392–427. doi:10.1177/009365001028004003

Benasich, A. A., Brooks-Gunn, J., & Clewell, B. C. (1992). How do mothers benefit from early intervention programs? *Journal of Applied Developmental Psychology, 13*, 311–362. doi:10.1016/0193-3973(92)90035-G

Browning, C. R., Soller, B., Gardner, M., & Brooks-Gunn, J. (2013). "Feeling disorder" as a comparative and contingent process: Gender, neighborhood conditions, and adolescent mental health. *Journal of Health & Social Behavior, 54*, 296–314. doi:10.1177/0022146513498510

Carpiano, R. M. (2007). Neighborhood social capital and adult health: An empirical test of a Bourdieu-based model. *Health & Place, 13*, 639–655. doi:10.1016/j.healthplace.2006.09.001

Chaix, B., Ducimetiere, P., Lang, T., Haas, B., Montaye, M., Ruidavets, J. B., . . . & Chauvin, P. (2008). Residential environment and blood pressure in the PRIME Study: Is the association mediated by body mass index and waist circumference? *Journal of Hypertension, 26*, 1078–1084. doi:10.1097/HJH.0b013e3282fd991f

Cohen, D. A., Finch, B. K., Bower, A., & Sastry, N. (2006). Collective efficacy and obesity: The potential influence of social factors on health. *Social Science & Medicine, 62*, 769–778. doi:10.1016/j.socscimed.2005.06.033

Cohen, E. L., Hayden, C., & Ball-Rokeach, S. J. (2004). Floating signifiers of urban community in Los Angeles. Paper presented at the annual meeting of the International Communication Association, New Orleans Sheraton, New Orleans, LA Online. PDF, 2009-05-26 from http://www.allacademic.com/meta/p112843_index.html

Coleman, J. S. (1988). Social capital in the creation of human capital. *American Journal of Sociology, 94* (Supplement), S95–S120. doi:10.1086/228943

Cox, B., Boyle, P. J., Davey, P. G., Fenq, Z., & Morris, A. D. (2007). Locality deprivation and Type 2 diabetes incidence: A local test of relative inequalities. *Social Science & Medicine, 65,* 1953–1964. doi:10.1016/j.socscimed.2007.05.043

Dahl, E., & Malberg-Heimonen, I. (2010). Social equality and health: The role of social capital. *Sociology of Health & Illness, 32,* 1102–1119. doi:10.1111/j.1467-9566.2010.01270.x

Daniel, K. L., Bernhardt, J. M., & Eroğlu, D. (2009). Social marketing and health communication: From people to places. *American Journal of Public Health, 99,* 2120–2122. doi:10.2105/AJPH.2009.182113

Diez Roux, A. V. (2012). Conceptual approaches to the study of health disparities. *Annual Review of Public Health, 33,* 41–58. doi:10.1146/annurev-publhealth-031811-124534

Diez Roux, A. V., & Mair, C. (2010). Neighborhoods and health. *Annals of the New York Academy of Sciences, 1186,* 125–245. doi:10.1111/j.1749-6632.2009.05333.x

Dutta, M. J. (2008). *Communicating health: A culture-centered approach.* Malden, MA: Polity.

Dutta, M. J., & Jamil, R. (2013). Health at the margins of migration: Culture-centered co-constructions among Bangladeshi immigrants. *Health Communication, 28,* 170–182. doi:10.1080/10410236.2012.666956

Dutta, M. J., Anaele, A., & Jones, C. (2013). Voices of hunger: Addressing health disparities through the culture-centered approach. *Journal of Communication, 63,* 159–180. doi:10.1111/jcom.12009

Dutta-Bergman, M. J. (2004). The unheard voices of Santalis: Communicating about health from the margins of India. *Communication Theory, 14,* 237–263. doi:10.1111/j.1468-2885.2004.tb00313.x

Edwards, M. B., Jilcott, S. B., Floyd, M. F., & Moore, J. B. (2011). County-level disparities in access to recreational resources and associations with obesity. *Journal of Park and Recreation Administration, 29*(2), 39–54.

Ellen, I., Mijanovich, T., & Dillman, K.-N. (2001). Neighborhood effects on health: exploring the links and assessing the evidence. *Journal of Urban Affairs, 23,* 391–408. doi:10.1111/0735-2166.00096

European Urban Knowledge Network (2012, October). Immigrant integration in European cities: Background paper, DG Meeting, Nicosia, Cyprus. Retrieved from www.eukn.org/dsresource?objectid=271670

Freeman, R. (1991). Employment and earnings of disadvantaged young men in a labor shortage economy. In C. Jencks & P. Peterson (Eds.), *The urban underclass.* Washington, DC: The Brookings Institution.

Ganz, M. L. (2000). The relationship between external threats and smoking in central Harlem. *American Journal of Public Health, 90,* 367–371. doi:10.2105/AJPH.90.3.367

Gephart, M. A. (1997). Neighborhoods and communities as contexts for development. In J. Brooks-Gunn, G. J. Duncan, & J. L. Aber (Eds.), *Neighborhood poverty: Context and consequences for children (Vol. I),* pp. 1–43. New York: Russell Sage Foundation.

Gerbner, G., & Gross, L. (1976). Living with television: The violence profile. *Journal of Communication, 26,* 173–199. doi:10.1111/j.1460-2466.1976.tb01397.x

Geronimus, A. T., Hicken, M., Keene, D., & Bound, J. (2006). "Weathering" and age patterns of allostatic load scores among Blacks and Whites in the United States. *American Journal of Public Health, 96,* 826–833. doi:10.2105/AJPH.2004.060749

Gramlich, E., Laren, D., & Sealand, N. (1992). Moving in and out of poor urban areas. *Journal of Policy and Management, 11*, 273–287. doi:10.2307/3325368

Haas, J. S., Phillips, K. A., Sonneborn, D., McCulloch, C. E., Baker, L. C., Kaplan, C. P., . . . & Liang, S.-Y. (2004). Variation in access to health care for different racial/ethnic groups by the racial/ethnic composition of an individual's county of residence. *Medical Care, 42*, 707–714. doi:10.1097/01.mlr.0000129906.95881.83

Hampton, K. (2010). Internet use and the concentration of disadvantage: Glocalization and the urban underclass: *American Behavioral Scientist, 53*, 1111–1132. doi:10.1177/0002764209356244

Hart, C., Ecob, R., & Smith, G. D. (1997). People, places and coronary heart disease risk factors: A multilevel analysis of the Scottish heart health study archive. *Social Science Medicine, 45*, 893–902. doi:10.1016/S0277-9536(96)00431-5

Hwang, Y., & Jeong, S.-H. (2009). Revisiting the knowledge gap hypothesis: A meta-analysis of thirty five years of research. *Journalism & Mass Communication Quarterly, 86*, 513–532. doi:10.1177/107769900908600304

Jeffres, L. W. (2002). *Urban communication systems: Neighborhoods and the search for community.* Cresskill, NJ: Hampton Press, Inc.

Kamo, N., Carlson, M., Brennan, R. T., & Earls, F. (2008). Young citizens as health agents: Use of drama in promoting community efficacy for HIV/AIDS. *American Journal of Public Health, 98*, 201–204. doi:10.2105/AJPH.2007.113704

Katz, V. S. (2014). Communication and immigrant integration: A synthesis. In E. L. Cohen (Ed.), *Communication yearbook 38* (pp. 39–60). New York: Routledge.

Kawachi, I., & Berkman, L. F. (Eds.). (2003). *Neighborhoods and health.* New York: Oxford University Press.

Kim, D., Subramanian, S. V., & Kawachi, I. (2006). Bonding versus bridging social capital and their associations with self-rated health: A multilevel analysis of 40 US communities. *Journal of Epidemiology & Community Health, 60*(2), 116–122. doi:10.1136/jech.2005.038281

Kim, Y.-C., & Ball-Rokeach, S. (2006). Community storytelling network, neighborhood context, and civic engagement: A multilevel approach. *Human Communication Research, 32*, 411–439. doi:10.1111/j.1468-2958.2006.00282.x

Kim, Y.-C., & Kang, J. (2010). Communication, neighborhood engagement, and household hurricane preparedness. *Disasters: The Journal of Disaster Studies, Policy & Management 34*, 470–488. doi:10.1111/j.1467-7717.2009.01138.x

Kim, Y.-C., Moran, M. B., Wilkin, H. A., & Ball-Rokeach, S. J. (2011). Integrated connection to a neighborhood storytelling network (ICSN), education, and chronic disease knowledge among African Americans and Latinos in Los Angeles. *Journal of Health Communication, 16*, 393–415. doi:10.1080/10810730.2010.546483

Klein, M. W., & Maxson, C. L. (2006). *Street gang patterns and policies.* New York: Oxford University Press.

Kovandžić, M., Funnell, E., Hammond, J., Ahmed, A., Edwards, S., Clarke, P., . . . Dowrik, C. (2012). The space of access to primary mental health care: A qualitative case study. *Health & Place, 18*, 536–551. doi:10.1016/j.healthplace.2012.01.011

Kreps, G. L., & Maibach, E. W. (2008). Transdisciplinary science: The nexus between communication and public health. *Journal of Communication, 58*, 732–748. doi:10.1111/j.1460-2466.2008.00411.x

Kreuter, M. W., Kegler, M. C., Joseph, K. T., Redwood, Y. A., & Hooker, M. (2012). The impact of implementing selected CBPR strategies to address disparities in urban Atlanta: A retrospective case study. *Health Education Research, 27*, 729–741. doi:10.1093/her/cys053

Leventhal, T., & Brooks-Gunn, J. (2003). Children and youth in neighborhood contexts. *Current Directions in Psychological Science, 12*, 27–31, doi:10.1111/1467-8721.01216

Lewis, L. B., Sloane, D. C., Nascimento, L. M., Diamant, A. L., Guinyard, J. J., Yancey, A. K., & Flynn, G. (2005). African Americans' access to healthy food options in South Los Angeles restaurants. *American Journal of Public Health, 95*, 668–673. doi:10.2105/AJPH.2004.050260

Matei, S, A., & Ball-Rokeach, S. J. (2005). Watts, the 1965 Los Angeles riots, and the communicative construction of the fear epicenter of Los Angeles. *Communication Monographs, 72*, 301–323. doi:10.1080/03637750500206557

Matsaganis, M. D. (2007). Neighborhood effects and the invisible motor of community change. In G. Burd, S. J. Drucker, & G. Gumpert (Eds.), *The urban communication reader* (pp. 73–104). Cresskill, NJ: Hampton Press.

Matsaganis, M. D., & Golden, A. G. (in press). The communicative construction of a field of health action: Interventions to address reproductive health disparities among African American women in a smaller urban community. *Journal of Applied Communication Research.*

Matsaganis, M. D., & Wilkin, H. A. (2014). Communicative social capital and collective efficacy as determinants of access to health-enhancing resources in residential communities. *Journal of Health Communication.* Advanced online publication doi: 10.1080/10810730.2014.927037

Matsaganis, M. D., Golden, A. G., & Scott, M. (2014). Communication infrastructure theory and reproductive health disparities: Enhancing storytelling network integration by developing interstitial actors. *International Journal of Communication, 8*, 1495–1515.

Matsaganis, M. D., Katz, V. S., & Ball-Rokeach, S. J. (2011). *Understanding ethnic media: Producers, consumers, and societies.* Thousand Oaks, CA: SAGE.

McKnight, J. (1995). *The careless society.* New York: Basic Books.

Melvin, P. M. (1987). *The organic city: Urban definition and community organization, 1880–1920.* Lexington: University Press of Kentucky.

Messer, L. C., Vinikoor-Imler, L. C., & Laraia, B. A. (2012). Conceptualizing neighborhood space: Consistency and variation of associations for neighborhood factors and pregnancy health across multiple neighborhood units. *Health & Place, 18*, 805–813. doi:10.1016/j.healthplace.2012.03.012

Minkler, M. (1992). Community organizing among elderly poor in the United States: A case study. *International Journal of Health Services, 22*, 303–316. doi:10.2190/6KFL-N1WY-NPDG-RXP5

Minkler, M., & Wallerstein, N. (Eds.). (2008). *Community-based participatory research for health: From process to outcomes* (2nd ed.). San Francisco, CA: Jossey-Bass.

Morrison, R. S., Wallenstein, S., Natale, D. K., Senzel, R. S., & Huang, L.-L. (2000). "We don't carry that" – Failure of pharmacies in predominantly nonwhite neighborhoods to stock opioid analgesics. *New England Journal of Medicine, 342*, 1023–1026. doi:10.1056/NEJM200004063421406

Nah, S., & Armstrong, C. L. (2011). Structural pluralism in journalism and media studies: A conceptual explication and theory construction. *Mass Communication & Society, 14*, 857–878. doi:10.1080/15205436.2011.615446

National Children's Study (2014). Retrieved from http://www.nationalchildrensstudy.gov/Pages/default.aspx

Noam, E. M. (2009). *Media ownership and concentration in America.* New York, NY: Oxford University Press.

Odgers, C. L., Moffitt, T. E., Tach, L. M., Sampson, R. J., Taylor, A., Matthews, C. L., & Avshalom, C. (2009). The protective effects of neighborhood collective efficacy on British children growing up in deprivation: A developmental analysis. *Developmental Psychology, 45,* 942–957. doi:10.1037/a0016162

Ognyanova, K., & Monge, P. (2013). A multitheoretical, multilevel, multidimensional network model of the media system: Production, content, and audiences. *Communication yearbook 37,* 67–94.

Orozco, M. (2003, September). Hometown associations and their present and future partnerships: New development opportunities? *Inter-American Dialogue.* Washington, DC: USAID.

Owens, M. L. (2012). Capacity-building: The case for faith-based organizations. In J. DeFilippis & S. Saegert (Eds.), *The community development reader* (2nd ed., pp. 140–149). New York: Routledge.

Paek, H-J., Lee, A. L., Jeong, S.-H., Wang, J., & Dutta, M. J. (2010) The emerging landscape of health communication in Asia: Theoretical contributions, methodological questions, and applied collaborations. *Health Communication, 25,* 552–559. doi: 10.1080/10410236.2010.496705

Painter, G., & Zhou, Y. (2010). Immigrants and housing markets in midsize metropolitan areas. *International Migration Review, 44,* 442–476. doi:10.1111/j.1747-7379.2009.00787.x

Park, R. E. (1925/1967). The city: Suggestions for the investigation of human behavior in the urban environment. In R. E. Park & E. Burgess (Eds.), *The city* (pp. 1–46). Chicago: University of Chicago Press.

Phillips, W. C. (1940). *Adventuring democracy.* New York: Social Unit Press.

Pollock, J. C. (2011). *Media and social inequality: Innovation in community structure research.* New York: Routledge.

Pooley, J., & Katz, E. (2008). Further notes on why American sociology abandoned mass communication research. *Journal of Communication, 58,* 767–786. doi:10.1111/j.1460-2466.2008.00413.x

Portes, A. (1998). Social capital: Origins and applications. *Annual Review of Sociology, 24,* 1–24. doi:10.1146/annurev.soc.24.1.1

Putnam, R. (2000). *Bowling alone: The collapse and revival of American community.* New York: Simon & Schuster.

Riva, M., Gauvin, L., & Barnett, T. A. (2007). Toward the next generation of research into small area effects on health: A synthesis of multilevel investigations published since July 1998. *Journal of Epidemiology and Community Health, 61,* 853–861. doi:10.1136/jech.2006.050740

Robert, S. A. (1999). Socioeconomic position and health: The independent contribution of socioeconomic context. *Annual Review of Sociology, 25,* 489–516. doi:10.1146/annurev.soc.25.1.489

Rojas, H., Shah, D. V., & Friedland, L. (2011). A communicative approach to social capital: A test in an urban context within a society in crisis. *Journal of Communication, 61,* 689–712. doi:10.1111/j.1460-2466.2011.01571.x

Rostila, M. (2013). *Social capital and health inequality in European welfare states.* Basingstoke, United Kingdom: Palgrave Macmillan.

Saelens, B. E., & Handy, S. L. (2008). Built environment correlates of walking: A review. *Medicine and Science in Sports and Exercise, 40,* S550–S566. doi:10.1249/MSS.0b013e31817c67a4

Sampson, R. J. (2012). *Great American city: Chicago and the enduring neighborhood effect.* Chicago, IL: Chicago University Press.

Sampson, R., Morenoff, J., & Gannon-Rowley, T. (2002). Assessing "neighborhood effects": Social processes and new directions in research. *Annual Review of Sociology, 27,* 443–477. doi:10.1146/annurev.soc.28.110601.141114

Scholte, J. A. (2005). *Globalization: A critical introduction.* Basingstoke, United Kingdom: Palgrave.

Schultz, A. J., & Lempert, L. B. (2000, August). "Being part of the world": Detroit women's perceptions of health and the social environment. Paper presented at the annual meeting of the American Sociological Association, Anaheim, California.

Schultz, A. J., Williams, D. R., Israel, B. A., & Lempert, L. B. (2002). Racial and spatial relations as fundamental determinants of health in Detroit. *The Milbank Quarterly, 80* (4), 677–707. doi:10.1111/1468-0009.00028

Schulz, P. J., & Hartung, U. (2010). Health communication research in Europe: An emerging field. *Health Communication, 25,* 548–551. doi:10.1080/10410236.2010.496720

Sellström, E., & Bremberg, S. (2006). The significance of neighborhood context to child and adolescent health and well-being: A systematic review of multilevel studies. *Scandinavian Journal of Public Health, 34,* 544–554. doi:10.1080/14034940600551251

Shim, M. (2008). Connecting Internet use with gaps in cancer knowledge. *Health Communication, 23,* 448–461. doi:10.1080/10410230802342143

Singer, A., Hardwick, S. W., & Brettell, C. B. (2008). *Twenty-first century gateways: Immigrant incorporation in suburban America.* Washington, DC: The Brookings Institution.

Slater, M. D., Hayes, A. F., Reineke, J. B., Long, M., & Bettinghaus, E. P. (2009). Newspaper coverage of cancer prevention: Multilevel evidence for knowledge-gap effects. *Journal of Communication, 59,* 514–433. doi:10.1111/j.1460-2466.2009.01433.x

Stokols, D. (1996). Translating social ecological theory into guidelines for community health promotion. *American Journal of Health Promotion, 10,* 282–298. doi:10.4278/0890-1171-10.4.282

Tichenor, P. J., Donohue, G. A., & Olien, C. N. (1980). *Community conflict and the press.* Beverly Hills, CA: Sage Publications.

Veysey, B. M., & Messner, S. F. (1999). Further testing of social disorganization theory: An elaboration of Sampson and Groves's "community structure and crime," *Journal of Research in Crime and Delinquency, 36,* 156–174. doi:10.1177/002242789903600200

Villarreal, A., & Silva, B. F. A. (2006). Social cohesion, criminal victimization, and perceived risk of crime in Brazilian neighborhoods. *Social Forces, 84,* 1725–1753. doi:10.1353/sof.2006.0073

Viruell-Fuentes, E. A., & Schulz, A. J. (2009). Toward a dynamic conceptualization of social ties and context: Implications for understanding immigrant and Latino health. *American Journal of Public Health, 99,* 2167–2175. doi:10.2105/AJPH.2008.158956

Viswanath, K., & Emmons, K. M. (2006). Message effects and social determinants of health: Its application to cancer disparities. *Journal of Communication, 56* (Suppl. 1), 239–264. doi:10.1111/j.1460-2466.2006.00292.x

Viswanath, K. & Finnegan, J. R. (1996). The knowledge gap hypothesis: Twenty five years later. In B. Burleson (Ed.), *Communication yearbook 19* (pp. 187–227). Thousand Oaks: Sage.

Viswanath, K., Steele, W. R., & Finnegan, J. R. (2006). Social capital and health: Civic engagement, community size, and recall of health messages. *American Journal of Public Health, 96,* 1456–1461. doi:10.2105/AJPH.2003.029793

Vlahov, D., Fraudenberg, N., Proietti, F., Ompad, D., Quinn, A., Nandi, V., & Galea, S. (2007). Urban as determinant of health. *Journal of Urban Health, 84*(Suppl), 16–26. doi:10.1007/s11524-007-9169-3

Wilkin, H. A. (2013). Exploring the potential of communication infrastructure theory for informing efforts to reduce health disparities. *Journal of Communication, 63*, 181–200. doi:10.1111/jcom.12006

Wilkin, H. A., & Ball-Rokeach, S. J. (2011). Hard to reach? Using health access status as a way to more effectively target segments of the Latino audience. *Health Education Research, 26*, 239–253. doi:10.1093/her/cyq090

Wilkin, H. A., Katz, V. S., Ball-Rokeach, S. J., & Hether, H. J. (in press). Community and family support for obesity prevention behaviors among Latinos and African Americans. *Journal of Health Communication.*

Wilkin, H. A., Stringer, K. A., O'Quin, K., Montgomery, S. A., & Hunt, K. (2011). Using communication infrastructure theory to formulate a strategy to locate "hard-to-reach" research participants. *Journal of Applied Communication Research, 39*, 201–213. doi:10.1080/00909882.2011.556140

Wilson, W. J. (1987). *The truly disadvantaged: The inner city, the underclass, and public policy.* Chicago, IL: University of Chicago Press.

Zenk, S. N., Schultz, A. J., Israel, B. A., James, S. A., Bao, S., & Wilson, M. L. (2005). Neighborhood racial composition, neighborhood poverty, and the spatial accessibility of supermarkets in metropolitan Detroit. *American Journal of Public Health, 95*, 660–667. doi:10.2105/AJPH.2004.042150

Ziersch, A. M., Baum, F. E., MacDougall, & Putland, C. (2005). Neighborhood life and social capital: The implications for health. *Social Science & Medicine, 60*, 71–86. doi:10.1016/j.socscimed.2004.04.027

CHAPTER CONTENTS

3 Extending Relational Dialectics Theory

Exploring New Avenues of Research

Danielle Halliwell

University of Missouri

Over the years, relational dialectics theory (RDT) has emerged as a prominent theory in the Communication field. Applied primarily in interpersonal and family contexts, RDT has generated valuable insights into the communicative challenges that characterize relational life. However, despite the impressive body of RDT-informed research, researchers have yet to tap into the theory's full potential. To fully utilize RDT's core premises, I argue that communication researchers must take on two research "tasks": (a) expand their methods of data collection; and (b) respect conceptual complexity. Addressing these tasks will enhance the theory and extend important knowledge about interpersonal and family communication.

Since its inception nearly two decades ago, relational dialectics theory (RDT; Baxter & Montgomery, 1996) has advanced interpersonal and family communication scholarship in new and exciting directions. Defined as a theory of relational meaning-making in which "meanings are wrought from the struggle of competing, often contradictory, discourses" (Baxter, 2011, p. 2), RDT is well-suited to capture the complexities of relational life. With this in mind, RDT has generated rich insights into the communicative processes surrounding numerous relational experiences including marriage (Baxter, 2010; Hoppe-Nagao & Ting-Toomey, 2002), stepfamily life (Baxter, Braithwaite, Bryant, & Wagner, 2004; Braithwaite & Baxter, 2006), adoption (Harrigan & Braithwaite, 2010; Norwood & Baxter, 2011), and illness and death (Baxter, Braithwaite, Golish, & Olson, 2002; Toller & Braithwaite, 2009). As an additional testament to the theory's heuristic value, a recent examination of family communication research published in communication journals from 1990–2009 revealed that RDT was one of the two most commonly used relationship theories (tied with family communication patterns; see Stamp & Shue, 2013). Given its widespread use in diverse communicative contexts, RDT has clearly made significant contributions to interpersonal and family communication scholarship over the past two decades.

As with many theories, RDT has evolved and taken many forms since its initial articulation. Also true of other theories, RDT's journey has not been without obstacles and limitations. In particular, previous studies informed by RDT have often been critiqued for focusing primarily on identifying discursive oppositions in communicative texts without highlighting how the struggle of competing discourses constructs meaning (see Baxter & Braithwaite, 2008, 2010). Along these lines, Baxter and Braithwaite (2008) noted that RDT studies that simply list discursive struggles sometimes fail to offer new insights or address the question of, "So what?" (p. 359). Despite the theory's many strengths, this important limitation in the research created the space and the need for RDT to grow and advance in a new direction. Not surprisingly, no one has been more invested in refining RDT and moving it forward than one of its originators, Leslie Baxter. In 2011, she articulated an updated version of RDT (often referred to as "RDT 2.0") in her book *Voicing Relationships,* which expanded on the original conceptualization of the theory and clearly outlined its purpose and scope. Highly anticipated and well-received among interpersonal and family communication scholars, *Voicing Relationships* has breathed new life into relational dialectics theory and inspired a new wave of research.

Without a doubt, Baxter's (2011) newest iteration of RDT is well-developed and full of promise. Recent research studies engaging RDT 2.0 have demonstrated the theory's utility and generated insightful knowledge on how meaning is constructed through the interplay of competing discourses (Baxter, Scharp, Asbury, Jannusch, & Norwood, 2012; Norwood, 2013; Norwood & Baxter, 2011; Scharp, 2013). However, despite the significant contributions these studies make, many of RDT 2.0's important concepts and assumptions remain underexplored in current work. Although RDT 2.0 is in its early stages of development, the fact that the theory is not being fully engaged is problematic and somewhat reminiscent of earlier struggles to go beyond simply listing discursive tensions in study after study. All theories face the danger of becoming stagnant and—despite the eager reception it has received thus far—RDT 2.0 is not immune to this fate.

To ensure that the theory continues to prosper and does not fall short of Baxter's (2011) vision, it is important to take a step back and examine the strengths and limitations of emerging RDT research. Thus, in this chapter, I argue that there are two important research "tasks" scholars must take on to advance RDT 2.0 in its intended direction. First, in order to fully tap into the theory's vast potential for knowledge production, researchers applying RDT in their work must expand their methods of data collection. Second, if researchers are to demonstrate the value of RDT 2.0 and avoid earlier critiques of the theory, they must respect the theory's conceptual complexity more so than is reflected in current work. To lay the groundwork for my argument, I first briefly review RDT 2.0's core assumptions. Next, I discuss the two research tasks in need of exploration, and provide recommendations for conducting future studies. Finally, I highlight the practical implications of following the research paths outlined in this chapter, and conclude with a discussion of the potential contributions to interpersonal and family communication scholarship.

Relational Dialectics Theory

Rooted in Mikhail Bakhtin's theory of dialogism, relational dialectic theory's central premise is that meaning in the moment emerges from the interplay of multiple opposing discourses, or systems of meaning (Baxter, 2011). According to Bakhtin (1981), every utterance enters a struggle between "two embattled tendencies in the life of language" (p. 272), which he referred to as *centripetal* and *centrifugal* forces. Centripetal discourses are systems of meaning that move toward the center and are thus legitimated; centrifugal discourses, on the other hand, are de-centered and marginalized (Baxter, 2011). Relational dialectics theory assumes that centripetal-centrifugal forces are at play in all interactions, thereby highlighting the multivocality and indeterminacy of social life (Baxter, 2006).

The Utterance Chain

Central to an understanding of RDT is the concept of the utterance chain, which draws from Bakhtin's (1986) assertion that an utterance is not an isolated, autonomous act. Rather, he argued that an individual utterance is a point on the utterance chain that interacts with both prior and anticipated speech acts. Building on Bakhtin's work, Baxter and Montgomery (1996) articulated a typology that presents four utterance "links" that interact with any individual speech act: distal already-spokens, proximal already-spokens, proximal not-yet-spokens, and distal not-yet-spokens. The distal already-spoken link reflects the cultural meanings and discourses that cultural members give voice to in their talk. The proximal already-spoken link, on the other hand, refers to the past meanings and discourses within a given relationship. Finally, the distal not-yet-spoken focuses on the anticipated response from generalized others within the culture, while the proximal not-yet-spoken concerns the immediate response from the hearer in an interaction.

The concept of the utterance chain implies that every utterance has both an author and an addressee (Bakhtin, 1986). Specifically, speakers construct utterances in anticipation of the immediate addressee's (the fellow participant in an interaction) or the superaddressee's (a distant addressee) response (Baxter, 2011). Bakhtin (1986) referred to an utterance's potential to be oriented to an anticipated listener as its *addressivity*. An utterance, then, is constructed both by the speaker and the anticipated listener, which denies the individual speaker sole ownership of the speech act (Baxter, 2011). Viewing an utterance as "jointly owned" by a speaker and an addressee aligns with RDT's premise that meaning does not reside in the individual. Rather, true to its focus on the social aspect of relational communication, RDT posits that meaning is located in the interplay between competing discourses (Baxter, 2011). Given that discursive interplay is of primary interest to RDT scholars, it is important to understand what is meant by the concept of *interplay*.

The Interplay of Discourses

According to Baxter (2011), interpenetration is essential to dialogue because competing discourses "must of necessity come into semantic contact with one another" (p. 127). In RDT literature, the interpenetration of discourses is described in terms of various praxis processes, which are characterized by either *diachronic separation* or *synchronic interplay* (Baxter & Montgomery, 1996; Baxter, 2011). Diachronic practices are marked by a change over time regarding which discourse is privileged and which discourse is marginalized (Baxter, 2011). Thus, rather than highlighting the interpenetration of opposing voices, diachronic praxis processes involve isolating competing discourses from one another (Baxter, 1988). Baxter and Montgomery (1996) identified two praxis processes characterized by diachronic separation: *spiraling inversion* and *segmentation* (see Baxter, 2011, pp. 127–130).

While diachronic practices serve to evade discursive struggles, synchronic processes involve the mixture, or co-occurrence, of competing discourses (Baxter & Braithwaite, 2008). Characterized by the interpenetration of voices at a given point in time (Baxter, 2006), synchronic processes are enacted at each of the utterance chain's four discursive sites (Baxter, 2011). To illustrate synchronic interplay, Baxter (2011) outlined four discursive struggles that interpenetrate across the utterance chain: *antagonistic-nonantagonistic, direct-indirect, serious-playful,* and *polemical-transformative* (see pp. 131–142).

The above review of RDT highlights the theory's assumptions and purpose, as well as its possibilities for knowledge production. To date, however, RDT-based research has yet to utilize the theory to its full potential and therefore fails to live up to Baxter's (2011) vision. I now turn to a discussion of two promising research tasks researchers must engage in for RDT's potential to be fully realized.

Task #1: Expand Methods of Data Collection

Overall, RDT researchers have relied extensively on collecting data via qualitative, in-depth interviews with one member of a relational dyad (Baxter & Braithwaite, 2010). With Baxter (2011) urging against an over-reliance on self-report data gleaned from individual interviews and surveys, scholars have begun to explore different methods of data collection in their RDT-based research. In particular, several recent applications of RDT 2.0 have collected data in the form of narratives and postings from various online forums (Norwood & Baxter, 2011; Norwood, 2012; Scharp, 2013). Given that online data is ideal for examining how posters draw on shared meaning systems or respond to generalized others in their communication, these studies contribute valuable knowledge about the distal sites of the utterance chain. However, aside from this recent work utilizing online data, there have been very few attempts to collect different forms of data in RDT-based research. In the following section,

I argue that an increased focus on collecting dyadic and longitudinal data is particularly important to adequately explore many of the theory's concepts and assumptions.

The Need for Dyadic Data

With the primary goal of understanding how relationships are constructed and given meaning in the communication between relationship parties, RDT demands that researchers study interactions' as they occur. However, what researchers often use instead are interview or survey studies that examine one person in a dyad's perceptions of his or her communication with a relational partner. Even leading RDT scholars Leslie Baxter and Dawn Braithwaite acknowledge their reliance on individual interviews and cite the lack of dyadic data in their own work as a weakness that they need to address (see Baxter & Braithwaite, 2010, pp. 55–57). In an earlier study, Baxter, Braithwaite, and their colleagues (2002) interviewed wives whose husbands suffered from adult dementia to understand how they managed contradictions surrounding their "married widow" status in interactions with their spouses. Their research on stepfamilies also primarily utilizes individual interviews to explore, for example, the contradictions that animate stepchildren's communication with both their stepparents (Baxter et al., 2004) and nonresidential parents (Braithwaite & Baxter, 2006).

By pointing out the focus on analyzing individuals' perceptions of their relational communication in Baxter and Braithwaite's work, I do not mean to imply that such research is not valuable. To be sure, their expert insights and combined program of research have been essential in refining RDT and developing it into the prominent theory it is today. However, their work reflects the general reliance on collecting individual data in the larger body of RDT-based research (Golish & Powell, 2003; Graham, 2003; Prentice, 2009; Sahlstein, Maguire, & Timmerman, 2009). Even recent work applying RDT 2.0 has relied on interview data to examine how individuals construct meaning of challenging family experiences, such as a loved one's gender transition (Norwood, 2013), a parent coming out as lesbian or gay (Breshears & Braithwaite, 2014), or becoming dependent on one's adult child(ren) in old age (Wenzel & Poynter, 2014). While these studies make important contributions to communication scholarship, their reliance on individual interviews leaves readers with interviewees' perceptions of their relational communication rather than actual talk between relationship parties.

A reliance on individual interviews in current RDT-informed research is also a major limitation because it does not allow for an examination of all four sites of the utterance chain. As Baxter (2011) noted, the interviewer (not the participant's relational partner) becomes the "proximal other" in an interview (p. 90). With data from an individual interview, then, researchers cannot truly study how both parties in a dyad give voice to past meanings in their relationship (proximal already-spokens) or how they orient their utterances in anticipation of the other's response (proximal not-yet spokens). At best, individual interviews provide researchers with participants' self-reports of their relational communication at the two proximal links. The recent use of online data in RDT-informed research also neglects the proximal sites in the utterance chain, focusing instead on the cultural discourses implicated in online postings. In order to correct the lack of attention given the proximal already-spoken and proximal not-yet-spoken links in existing RDT-based research, there needs to be a greater effort among scholars to examine the interactions between relationship partners in future work (Baxter, 2011).

RDT work examining the talk between relational partners is also needed because most existing research utilizing dyadic data relies on outdated assumptions about the theory. Therefore, rather than focusing on how relationship parties co-construct meaning or the ways they draw on the various links of the utterance chain in their talk, the analyses highlighted how the couples managed particular contradictions in their relationships (Sahlstein, 2006; Sahlstein & Dun, 2008; Suter, Bergen, Daas, & Durham, 2006). These earlier studies show the value of collecting dyadic data and provide valuable insights into the communicative experiences of relationship parties. However, because they were conducted prior to the introduction of RDT 2.0, they do not address the concepts and assumptions outlined in Baxter's (2011) new iteration of the theory. With RDT 2.0's primary goal being to understand how relational identities are constructed in talk, studying the interactions between relationship parties must be a priority in future work.

Ways to Study Interactions

Collecting dyadic data can be both challenging and time consuming, but it is a task RDT scholars need to tackle in their research. Researchers can study interactions and enhance RDT scholarship through the following methods of data collection: (a) conducting joint interviews, (b) employing ethnographic methods, (c) utilizing focus groups, and (d) examining mediated communication between relational partners.

Joint interviews.   Perhaps the most obvious way to examine actual interactions is to conduct joint interviews with relational partners. In *Voicing Relationships,* Baxter (2011) opens her discussion of RDT 2.0 with an excerpt from a communicative exchange between two friends and demonstrates how to analyze the text in a manner consistent with her updated articulation of the theory (pp. 3–4). Her brief analysis of the conversation reveals how the two friends draw on cultural discourses of friendship to communicatively construct their relational identity. As the excerpt illustrates, joint interviews are a useful method for conducting RDT 2.0-based research because they can capture how meanings and relationships are constituted in communication.

Let me expand on the value of using joint interviews to examine interactions with a personal observation. For my Master's thesis, I interviewed two siblings separately about their experiences of separation in emerging adulthood. After the interviews, I took both of them out to lunch as a "thank you." During our meal, they told me about their mom's obsession with her three cats. The sister, who still lived at home, expressed that the cats were a huge annoyance and that she could not wait to move out to get away from them. Her brother, on the other hand, revealed that he missed having cats around now that he no longer lived at home. By the end of their conversational exchange, the sister reluctantly admitted that she will also miss the cats when she moves out. As they were talking, I came to realize that their discussion of their mom's cats exposed competing discourses of autonomy and connection. Initially, the siblings centered the discourse of autonomy in the interaction by aligning with different perspectives (i.e., the cats as an annoyance versus the cats as something to be missed). However, they ultimately privileged a discourse of connection by agreeing that the cats were an important part of their family and will be missed upon moving away from home. Overall, talking with one another about their experiences with their mom's cats created a way for the siblings to enact connectedness despite their separation. Through the siblings' process of telling a story together, I learned more about how they discursively make meaning of their relationship than I did in the separate interviews.

The rich meanings these siblings constructed "off record" over lunch demonstrates not only the value of joint interviews, but also how creating an environment where relational partners feel comfortable engaging in a conversation can enhance the quality of interview data. While it is convenient to conduct interviews in a campus office or meeting room, these locations may create a professional or intimidating atmosphere that discourages participants from opening up about their relational experiences. Relational partners may even have difficulty talking naturally with one another in a more relaxed and neutral location, like a coffee shop, if it is an unfamiliar place where they do not typically interact. Thus, whenever possible, researchers should ask relationship partners to select an interview location that has special significance for their relationship or where they often spend time together. A couple may be more inclined to share important details about their relationship at the restaurant where they first met than they would in a coffee shop they rarely visit. Similarly, a researcher may learn more about the relationship between two friends by joining them on their weekly walk in a park than by interviewing them in a campus office. By conducting interviews in familiar environments where relational partners are accustomed to interacting with one another, researchers can increase their chances of capturing participants' natural meaning-making processes.

Of course, as is often lamented by researchers, getting two relational partners together for an interview can be quite a challenge. In fact, due to busy schedules, geographic distance, and time constraints for conducting the research, it can be nearly impossible. For these reasons, researchers should take advantage of technological advances such as Skype and FaceTime in order to conduct dyadic interviews. As Hanna (2012) points out, not only do Internet technologies still capture the synchrony of real-time interaction, they also easily record both the audio and video of the interview. A video of an interview "preserves" the interaction between the relationship parties under study, giving researchers the opportunity to check for important details and nonverbal cues they may have missed during the interview. Furthermore, without the researcher invading their personal space, some participants may feel more comfortable opening up and discussing their relationships in a telemediated interview than they would in a face-to-face interview (Hanna, 2012). Thus, although researchers lose out on observing the subtle nuances between relational partners in a physical interaction, telemediated interviews are a viable alternative to face-to-face interviews in qualitative research (Evans, Elford, & Wiggins, 2008; Hanna, 2012).

Ethnography.   Employing ethnographic methods is another way that researchers can study the interactions between relationship parties. Ethnography is the study of the meaning of language, behaviors, and interactions in culture-sharing groups (Creswell, 2007), and is typically applied in organizational research. With RDT's focus on how meanings are constructed in the communication between people, much can be learned from extending the theory to examine interpersonal relationships in organizations. For instance, Kramer (2004) applied RDT in an ethnographic study of a community theater group to understand the dialectical tensions that organizational members experience in their interactions. His analysis revealed that group members' communication about their experiences in the theater group were animated by four tensions: (a) a commitment to the group and a commitment to other life activities, (b) ordered activities and emergent activities, (c) inclusion and exclusion, and (d) acceptable behaviors and unacceptable behaviors. These findings demonstrate RDT's potential to illuminate the discursive struggles surrounding day-to-day interactions between organizational members.

RDT researchers should build on Kramer's (2004) research and use ethnographic methods to examine the communication between relational partners in different contexts. Greek organizations are a particularly fruitful context for conducting ethnographic research using RDT. For example, by attending public events and observing interactions in chapter houses, RDT researchers can explore how relationships change when a friend transitions into a leadership role. Given that college students join Greek organizations for both personal relationships and leadership opportunities (Kelley, 2008), members who take on officer positions can find themselves "in charge" of their friends. Friendships are generally based on equality in U.S. culture (Rawlins, 1992), and that equality can be disrupted when one friend achieves a higher status than the other. Thus, in their daily interactions with other members, leaders of Greek organizations may face a conflict between their identity as leader and their identity as a friend.

Ethnographic methods can also be used in RDT-based research to examine how meanings and identities are constituted in the communication between family members. Despite the challenges associated with using ethnography in family research, Descartes (2007) expressed, "Ethnographic participation gives a researcher the unique opportunity to experience events as they unfold, seeing activities take place in their everyday surroundings and observing the nuances and subtleties of the interactions that provide the backdrop for family life" (p. 35). Clearly, RDT researchers could gain much insight from observing the subtle details of family members' everyday interactions. In an insightful family ethnographic study, Tillmann (2010) followed her friend Gordon on a trip to his parents' home to explore the opportunities and challenges associated with his coming out as gay. Through participant observations and interviews with Gordon's relatives, Tillman uncovered how family members made meaning of Gordon's sexuality within a family system characterized by avoidant communication and hegemonic masculinity. Applying RDT in a similar ethnography could expose how family members give voice to multiple and competing discourses as they construct meaning of their experiences and their family's identity.

Tannen, Kendall, and Gordon's (2007) work is another excellent example of research that captures natural, day-to-day interactions between family members. To examine how adults in dual-earner families construct their identities as both parents and professionals through language use, they asked couples from four different families to tape record themselves for seven days from morning until night. The researchers also shadowed each couple for at least one day to learn more about the family dynamics and the parents' work life. Although the tape-recorded conversations, not participant observations, served as the main source of data, RDT scholars can use this research as a model for engaging in ethnography in their own work. In particular, observing families during dinner or while they hang out at home over the weekend can provide a glimpse into how they construct their familial identity in everyday interactions. According to Baxter (2011), all communicative acts hold dialogical potential; therefore, RDT researchers should not feel confined to studying only the most significant relational transitions and challenges. Because relational meanings are always in flux and renegotiated from one interactional moment to the next, ethnographic methods have the potential to capture how family members constitute their identities in ordinary, everyday interactions.

Focus groups. Conducting focus groups is another method that can be used to collect dyadic data in RDT-based research. Puig, Koro-Ljungberg, and Echevarria-Doan (2008) argued that family researchers should utilize focus groups to examine family communication from a social constructionist perspective. In particular, they emphasized that focus group methods are useful for capturing how collective and interactive meaning-making processes among group members shape individual identities. Researchers have also emphasized that focus groups are an ideal site for exploring how members negotiate group norms and meanings as they construct a collective social reality (Bloor, Frankland, Thomas, & Robson, 2001; Puig et al., 2008). Accordingly, Puig and colleagues

(2008) argue that the "energy and depth of human interactions established during focus group process can produce thick, meaningful cultural data" (p. 142). Whereas joint interviews generally focus on meaning-making at the level of the dyad, focus groups can provide an understanding of how multiple people construct a group identity (e.g., a family identity) or how various cultural members construct meaning of a particular phenomenon (e.g., the meaning of "adoption"). Thus, RDT researchers may find the interactions in focus groups to be rich with both relational and cultural meanings.

One area of research that RDT scholars can explore using focus groups is shared parental caregiving among adult siblings. As the elderly population continues to grow, adult children are increasingly serving as informal caregivers for their aging parents. Because the majority of older individuals have at least two children (Rogerson & Kim, 2005), adult children are often able to share caregiving responsibilities with siblings. In large families, for example, several siblings may be involved in negotiating caregiving tasks for their elderly parent(s). Siblings' relationships with one another inevitably change as they transition into their caretaker roles and attempt to make meaning of their transformed family identity. Given that adult children caregivers also face the challenge of both respecting their parents' desire for autonomy and helping them in their time of need (Hummert & Morgan, 2001), siblings may voice competing views regarding how to properly care for their parents. Thus, conducting focus groups with adult siblings about their experiences with shared parental caregiving has the potential to expose how they draw on multiple and competing discourses to construct meaning of the changes in their family system.

Focus groups can also be used to make significant contributions to the emerging body of RDT-informed adoption research (Baxter et al., 2012; Norwood & Baxter, 2011; Scharp, 2013). Over the past few decades, adoption practices have seen a move toward "open" adoptions, which involve direct and ongoing communication between the adoptive parents, the adopted child, and the birth family (McRoy, Grotevant, Ayers-Lopez, & Henney, 2007). In order to understand the implications of open adoptions, RDT researchers can conduct focus groups with adopted individuals and members of both their adoptive and birth families. Such research can investigate the ways different parties involved construct meaning of the open adoption experience, and how individual and family identities are negotiated in talk. For example, Von Korff and Grotevant (2011) found that individuals develop an *adoptive identity* as they reflect on who they are as an adopted person and as they attempt to make sense of their connection with both their adoptive and birth families. Therefore, using focus groups to examine adopted individuals' interactions with members of both their adopted and birth families may shed light on their development of an adoptive identity.

RDT scholars should also consider using focus groups in research focusing on the reunions between adopted individuals and their birth families. Scharp (2013) recently investigated adoptees' online stories of being reunited with their birth families to understand how they constructed meaning of adoption reconnection. Her analysis revealed that some adoptees privileged a discourse of romanticized reconnection, while others voiced both romantic and pragmatic discourses in their narratives. After highlighting the important contributions of the study, Scharp suggests that future work should also focus on how meanings of adoption reconnection are constructed by members of adoptive and birth families. RDT scholars could answer this call by conducting focus groups with adoptees, members of their adoptive families, and members of their birth families with whom they have been reconnected. In doing so, researchers can examine how meanings of adoption reconnection are constituted in the talk between adoptees' and their adoptive and birth family members.

Mediated interactions. Finally, a creative way researchers can examine the dialogue between relational partners is by examining their communication on social network sites and other mediated contexts. In particular, Facebook allows users to view the "friendship" between two people, including their written conversations back and forth, pictures together, and any other content they post on one another's page. A promising area of research using this method would be to examine the written communication on Facebook between newly dating partners. When a romantic relationship is in its early stages, relationship parties may rely on online forms of communication to "test the waters" and avoid the pressure of face-to-face interactions. Further, given that *dating* is an ambiguous term in our culture (Chornet Roses, 2006), romantic partners in a new relationship may assign different meanings to their relationship status. Along these lines, the Facebook communication between newly dating couples might reveal how they draw on competing discourses about dating to construct meaning of their relationship.

By highlighting the importance of examining interactions, I am not suggesting that RDT-informed research utilizing self-report methods of data collection are neither enlightening nor valuable. To the contrary, I strongly believe that interpersonal and family communication scholarship has been greatly enhanced by the contributions of RDT scholars. However, I agree with Baxter (2011) that methods relying on self-reports of interactions are limited because they cannot address some of RDT's important concepts and assumptions. Therefore, conducting more research that focuses on interactions between relational partners is necessary to realize the theory's full potential. Next, I discuss why longitudinal data is also needed in RDT-based research.

The Need for Longitudinal Data

Without longitudinal data, many of RDT's central premises are not sufficiently explored. In particular, dialogism's (and therefore RDT's) notion of the unfinalizability of centripetal-centrifugal flux (Baxter, 2004) cannot be gleaned from a single interview. A central assumption of RDT is that individuals and relationships are not finalizable; rather, their meanings are always open and emerging anew (Baxter & Braithwaite, 2009). Further emphasizing the unfinalizability of meaning, Baxter (2011) argued that relational partners move their relationship to a new and different state with every utterance. In this sense, examining the meanings that are wrought from relationship partners' communication at one time point does not recognize the unfinalizability of discursive struggles. Simply put, RDT's focus on how meanings are altered from one moment to the next requires that researchers examine communicative processes over time. In fact, given how central the concepts of unfinalizability and flux are to RDT, the lack of longitudinal research is relatively surprising. Although data gathered at a single time point can be fraught with meanings and rich insights into the communicative experiences of relational partners, they cannot truly speak to how relationships change over time.

The diachronic praxis patterns of *spiraling inversion* and *segmentation* also cannot be fully understood without longitudinal data. Spiraling inversion reflects a back and forth separation of discourses based on time, such that prominence is first given to one discourse and then shifted to another (Baxter, 2011). The diachronic practice of segmentation also involves a shift over time regarding which discourse is centered; however, the separation of competing discourses is not based on time specifically, but rather on a topical or activity domain (Baxter, 2011). To the extent that the passage of time is necessary for diachronic processes to emerge in relational talk, a one-time interview is not sufficient. For instance, two emerging adult siblings may center a discourse of autonomy in an interview about their experiences of moving out of the family home. While a researcher may interpret this emphasis on autonomy as an act of single-voiced monologue, the praxis pattern of spiraling inversion might actually be at play. For example, the siblings' communication may shift to privilege a discourse of connection at a later point in their relationship, perhaps once the excitement of establishing independence from the natal family wears off. However, without interviewing these siblings at another point in time, the researcher cannot analyze how they shift back and forth between autonomy and connection via spiraling inversion.

Finally, longitudinal methods of data collection will allow for a more thorough examination of the utterance chain than is reflected in most RDT-informed research to date. Baxter and Braithwaite (2008) highlight the need for researchers to situate utterances more deeply into the utterance chain, which involves moving beyond isolated utterances or a single conversation. Longitudinal data is especially important for exploring how relational partners construct meaning at the proximal already-spoken and proximal not-yet-spoken discursive sites. Although participants can draw on the proximal sites of the utterance chain in a single interview, such data can only capture their perceptions about past relational meanings (proximal already-spokens) and how their relationship will unfold in the future (proximal not-yet-spokens). By collecting data from multiple points in time, however, researchers can examine the ways relationship parties respond to past meanings and utterances from prior interviews to (re)construct their relational identities in the present. Therefore, longitudinal data can shed important light on how relationship partners' meaning systems interact at the proximal sites of the utterance chain across time.

Two concepts related to the utterance chain that can also be fruitfully explored with longitudinal methods are the distal not-yet-spokens and the superaddressee. Recall that the distal not-yet-spoken discursive site refers to the anticipated response of generalized others in the culture, while the super-addressee *is* the generalized other. Speakers often frame their utterances based on the anticipated response from a superaddressee, a "distal imagined listener" who at some point may hear and evaluate a particular utterance (Baxter, 2011, p. 114). Therefore, data collected at a single point in time cannot show how superaddressees respond to and evaluate utterances. By collecting longitudinal data, however, researchers can investigate how meaning is constructed between speakers and superaddressees. In the next section, I discuss techniques for conducting RDT-informed research from a longitudinal perspective.

Ways to Study Relationships over Time

There are various methods RDT researchers can employ in order to examine how relational meanings are constructed and reconstructed over time. I highlight three specific ways RDT scholars can answer the call for longitudinal research: (a) conducting multiple interviews, (b) engaging in ethnography, and (c) utilizing diary methods.

Conducting multiple interviews. One way researchers can collect longitudinal data is by interviewing relationship parties at multiple points in time. As Baxter noted (2006), data must be gathered from *at least* two points in time for researchers to gain insight into the unfinalizable nature of relational and individual meanings. Therefore, conducting follow-up interviews is a relatively easy way for researchers to incorporate longitudinal data into their work.

Relationship transitions are an important area of research that RDT scholars can explore by conducting multiple interviews at different points in time. For example, researchers can interview couples both before and after their weddings to examine how their individual and relational identities change as they transition from being engaged to being married. During the engagement period, couples may evoke cultural discourses about marriage (distal already-spokens) as they make meaning of their "engaged" status (their relational identity) and anticipate their future as a married couple (proximal not-yet-spokens). Once they are married, then, they might draw on both cultural discourses and their own prior utterances to communicatively (re)construct their relational identity as a married couple and attempt to reconcile the loss of their "old" relationship. While interviewing couples at only one point in time can provide insight into their perceptions about the changes in their relationship, collecting longitudinal data can capture the process of how they (re)construct their relationship over time.

RDT researchers can also use follow-up interviews to explore relational change as couples transition into parenthood. For example, Stamp (1994) interviewed couples before and after the birth of their first child to examine the management of the parental role during the transition to parenthood. He found that couples' expectations of parenthood have an important influence on how they navigate and make sense of both the transition into parenthood and their new identities as parents. These findings suggest that couples may rely on cultural discourses surrounding parenthood and what it means to be a "good" mother or father in their communication both before and after the birth of their child. Furthermore, their talk at different points in time might reveal how their identity as a couple competes with, encompasses, or is shaped by their new identity as parents. Therefore, scholars can add to Stamp's (1994) research by utilizing follow-up interviews to examine how couples construct meaning of parenthood and their relational identity before and after the birth of their first child.

In addition to conducting interviews at two (or more) points in time, researchers should explore the potential of combining different methods of data collection in longitudinal work. For instance, a focus group with several siblings who are sharing caregiving responsibilities for an elderly parent can be followed up with interviews with individual siblings and/or different sibling pairs. After engaging in an ethnographic study of a Greek organization to explore the discursive struggles surrounding leadership roles, a researcher might conduct a focus group with all of the officers or with a group of non-officers. Researchers interested in examining how newly dating pairs construct meaning of their relationship over time could first examine their Facebook communication early in the relationship and then interview couples after they have been dating for a few months. Without a doubt, there are a number of creative ways researchers can combine interviews with other methods of data collection to explore how individual and relational identities change from one interactional moment to the next.

With the recent focus on analyzing online texts in RDT-based studies, researchers should also consider using follow-up interviews to build on previously collected online data. For example, Norwood and Baxter (2011) examined how parents seeking to adopt a child framed their messages in "Dear Birth Mom" letters in anticipation of the birth mother's (the superaddressee) response. While the study shed valuable light on the underexplored concept of addressivity, the authors noted that longitudinal data would enhance their findings. Specifically, by interviewing the birth mothers at a later point in time, the researchers could examine how the women responded to the letters and whether the way parents framed their messages was successful. Likewise, Scharp (2013) cited the lack of longitudinal data as a limitation in her research analyzing adoptees' online stories of reconnection. By conducting follow-up interviews with the adoptees, she would be able to assess how their meanings about adoption change over time. For example, as time passes, some adoptees may shift from centering a discourse of "romanticized reconnection" to constructing a discourse of "pragmatic reconnection" when making meaning of their reunion with their birth families. As illustrated by these two examples, the recent wave of RDT-informed research utilizing online data provides fertile ground for future longitudinal research.

Ethnography RDT researchers can also utilize ethnographic methods to study the discourses that animate relational talk over time. Given that ethnographic research is typically characterized by a prolonged time in the "field," it is aptly designed for gathering longitudinal data. By observing relational partners' interactions in their natural environments over an extended period of time, researchers can understand how their relationship is shaped by "ongoing dialogic flux" (Baxter, 2004, p. 18). Along these lines, ethnographic methods are ideal for capturing the change and flux associated with relationship transitions, such as the transition into a stepfamily. In a study examining the enactment of rituals during stepfamily development, Braithwaite, Baxter, and Harper (1998) found that stepfamily members experience ongoing tensions between holding on to rituals from their "old" family and embracing rituals in their "new" family. This research suggests that the transition into a stepfamily introduces a struggle between old and new family identities, but these particular findings can only speak to how stepfamily members constructed meaning at a single point in time. Because relationship transitions are processes and not one-time events (Conville, 1998), a single interview cannot capture how relationships and identities are negotiated and transformed during stepfamily development. The ways that stepfamily members construct a sense of "family" likely changes over time as they interact with other family members and attempt to reconcile the loss of their old family identity. Therefore, observing stepfamily members' communication with one another during stepfamily development can reveal how they make meaning of their "new" family identity and interact in ways that either promote or hinder a successful transition.

Using my previous example of adult sibling caregivers, RDT researchers could also observe siblings' interactions with one another and with their parents over the span of several months by attending family meetings and accompanying siblings when they visit their parent(s). By observing siblings' communication about their caregiving responsibilities at multiple points in time, researchers can analyze how meanings and utterances from previous interactions (i.e., proximal already-spokens) are evoked to construct meaning in the moment. For example, a researcher may observe several conversations between a sister and her brother about the brother's lack of involvement in caring for their parent, which prompts the sister to say, "I can't count on you anymore." The sister's use of "anymore" suggests that she could count on her brother at one point in their relationship, but that recent experiences and interactions with him have shown that he can no longer be counted on. Observing the interactions between these siblings over time can illustrate how the sister draws on previous communicative experiences with her brother to construct meaning in the moment—specifically, that her brother is someone she can no longer rely on. To that end, ethnographic methods have the potential to capture how siblings' relationships and the meanings they construct of their shared caregiving experience change over time.

Diary methods   Another way RDT researchers can collect longitudinal data is through diary methods, which can allow participants to reflect on their relationships at multiple time points. In their qualitative diary entries, participants should be encouraged to write about specific interactions with their relationship partner. Although such data would not be dyadic, it could approximate interactions between individuals in a relationship. Therefore, diary methods may be useful for understanding how relational meanings change from one point in time to another. For example, a researcher might ask young adults to record their experiences as they move out of their childhood home and transition into adulthood. Participants could be instructed to write about their conversations with parents and siblings before, during, and after moving out of the family home. By examining how young adults describe their interactions with family members during this transitional period, RDT researchers can explore how they (re)construct their individual and relational identities in light of the changes they are experiencing. Unlike interviews, which can only provide insight into how participants make meaning of their relationships at a single point in time, diary methods can expose the process of relational change from one entry to the next.

Diary methods also have the potential to capture how multiple family members or relationship parties construct meaning of a particular experience or transition. For instance, diary methods can be used to explore how family members reflect on and make sense of the experience of another family member coming out as lesbian or gay. Having both the individual who came out and his or her family members record their thoughts and conversations at different points in time can reveal how individual and relational identities are constructed throughout the "coming out" process. Furthermore, by examining diary entries from multiple family members about the same experience, researchers can investigate whether they converge or diverge in how they construct meaning of homosexuality and how those meanings change and are negotiated over time.

By conducting research from a longitudinal perspective, RDT researchers can make important contributions to interpersonal and family communication scholarship. In addition to the methods discussed above, I urge scholars to employ other creative techniques to explore how meanings are constructed in the communication between relationship partners over time. In the next section, I highlight the second research task that requires attention from RDT scholars.

Task #2: Respect Conceptual Complexity

In many ways, respecting RDT's conceptual complexity encompasses the first research task discussed above. Conducting research that fails to examine interactions between relational partners and how their relationships change over time reflects a simplistic application of the theory. If dyadic and/or longitudinal data are not collected, even the most interesting and insightful research can be critiqued for not adequately attending to some of the theory's central concepts and assumptions. However, making sufficient use of RDT's concepts requires researchers to go beyond expanding the methods of data collection used in their research; it also involves conducting careful and detailed data analyses that explore the theory's full potential. Below, I discuss why it is important for future researchers to respect RDT's conceptual complexity in their work.

The Need to Respect Conceptual Complexity

First and foremost, respecting RDT's conceptual complexity will ensure that researchers are applying the theory correctly. Baxter (2011) expressed that previous studies using RDT have not appropriately applied the praxis patterns of diachronic separation (i.e., spiraling inversion and segmentation) and synchronic interplay (i.e., antagonistic-nonantagonistic, direct-indirect, serious-playful, and polemical-transformative discursive struggles). Specifically, a perusal of the RDT literature reveals a widespread misconception that these various praxis processes are strategies that relational partners engage in to manage discursive struggles in their relationships (Sahlstein, 2006; Sahlstein & Dun, 2008; Suter et al., 2006; Toller & Braithwaite, 2009). For example, Suter and colleagues (2006) reported that lesbian couples actively engage in integration to simultaneously meet their needs for inclusion (maintaining some privacy) and seclusion (publicizing their relationship to others). Although this research helps us understand the support and challenges lesbian couples experience in their social networks, it is not consistent with the concepts and assumptions outlined in the new iteration of relational dialectics theory.

Having an appreciation for RDT's conceptual complexity will also help researchers avoid simplistic applications of the theory. In the past, many RDT-informed studies simply identified the three basic contradictions—autonomy-connection, certainty uncertainty, and openness-closedness—without detailing how individual and relational meanings are constructed in their interplay (Graham, 2003; Hoppe-Nagao & Ting-Toomey, 2002; Sahlstein et al., 2009; Wozniak, Lollis, & Marshall, 2013). Although the competing discourses of autonomy-connection, certainty-uncertainty, and openness-closedness are certainly prominent in the communication between relationship parties, focusing only on these three discursive tensions ignores the multivocality of relational communication (Baxter, 2004). This critique does not mean that such research is unimportant; rather, it draws attention to the need for a reinvigorated program of RDT-based research. Thus, Baxter (2004) has cautioned against using the primary discursive tensions as "an exhaustive cookie-cutter template" (p. 9), and her new articulation of RDT in *Voicing Relationships* underscores the importance of focusing more closely on some of the theory's central premises. In particular, she urges researchers to go beyond merely identifying competing discourses to examining the meaning that is constructed in their interplay. In doing so, researchers can achieve RDT's primary goal—an understanding of how meanings are wrought from the interpenetration of competing discourses—and avoid producing simplistic, "cookie-cutter" studies.

Overall, it is important for scholars to make better use of RDT's concepts so that the theory continues to evolve and move forward as Baxter (2011) envisioned. If RDT scholars do not stop every now and then to assess whether the theory is being utilized to its full potential, they run the risk of becoming complacent and conducting similar studies time and again. For example, although the emerging body of RDT-based research analyzing online forums has taken the theory in new directions (Norwood & Baxter, 2011; Norwood, 2012; Scharp, 2013), researchers should be cautioned against an over-reliance on online data. In other words, RDT researchers must avoid succumbing to prior pitfalls by collecting the same type of data and exploring the same concepts in study after study. In the following section, I describe how scholars can respect RDT's conceptual complexity in their research.

Ways to Respect Conceptual Complexity

In short, respecting RDT's conceptual complexity comes down to how researchers engage with and analyze their data. To be certain they are making use of RDT's central concepts, I argue that researchers must strive to do the following in future work: (a) attend more closely to language use and the "details of talk" and (b) respond to prior critiques.

Attend to the "details of talk." Making sufficient use of the theory's concepts will require researchers to attend more closely to language use and the "details of talk" (Baxter, 2011, p. 131) than has been done in existing research. As Baxter (2011) emphasizes, RDT researchers must go beyond identifying the competition among discourses to examine how meaning(s) are constructed in the interplay. In her updated articulation of relational dialectics theory, she introduced *contrapuntal analysis,* a type of discourse analysis that provides researchers with the methodological tools to conduct RDT 2.0-based work. According to Baxter (2011), contrapuntal analysis involves three steps: (a) identifying discourses in the text, (b) identifying competition among discourses in the text, and (c) identifying how the interplay of competing discourses constructs meaning in the text (see pp. 121–150). In order to apply RDT 2.0 correctly and utilize the theory to its full potential, researchers must have a strong understanding of contrapuntal analysis.

Recently, numerous RDT scholars have used contrapuntal analysis in their research to closely analyze utterances and draw attention to many of the theory's important concepts (Baxter et al., 2012; Breshears & Braithwaite, 2014; Norwood, 2013; Scharp, 2013; Wenzel & Poynter, 2014). However, other recent work continues to gloss over language use, the "details of talk," and the construction of meaning, relying instead on outdated assumptions about the theory (Amati & Hannawa, 2013; Wozniak et al., 2013). For example, in a recent study examining competing discourses in parent-adolescent communication during the transition to high school, Wozniak and colleagues (2013) focused on the participants' desires for one dialectical pole or another rather than on the discourses themselves. Furthermore, the researchers mostly pointed out that certain competing discourses animated the communication between parents and adolescents without analyzing the meaning constructed in the interplay. Thus, despite the study's potential, it reflects a simplistic application of RDT and fails to focus on how meanings are constituted in talk. Take, for example, the following conversational exchange between a mother and her adolescent daughter:

> Parent: Um, so how do you think high school might affect our relationship?
> Adolescent: Ah, I hope it will be bringing it stronger, but I don't know.
> Parent: What's your worry?
> Adolescent: That it, it will bring it the opposite of stronger.
> Parent: What makes you think it would do that?
> Adolescent: I don't know. It's just like . . ., because you judge everything I tell you.
> Parent: I'm not supposed to do that. I forgot. I'm, I'm your mother. I'm a judge, that's my job.
> Adolescent: Yeah, but I told you if you keep judging, I won't tell you anything.
> Parent: Yeah, that's true. Yeah, I don't blame you.
>
> (Wozniak et al., 2013, pp. 12–13)

Although this excerpt is rich with dialogic undertones, the authors simply categorize it as an example of autonomy-connection/openness-closedness and move on with their analysis. Let me briefly highlight, then, how the parent and adolescent evoke multiple discourses as they construct the meaning of their changing relationship. In particular, a discourse of connection is privileged, indicated by their joint effort to figure out how they can prevent their relationship from becoming the "opposite of stronger." Further, a struggle between certainty and uncertainty is at play as they attempt to make sense of what their future relational identity will be like. The excerpt also demonstrates how the parent and adolescent construct meaning at the proximal already-spoken site of the utterance chain by drawing on previous interactions (e.g., "you judge everything I tell you"). Along these lines, there are also hints of an antagonistic struggle; that is, the parent and child align with different meanings about a mother's "job" (i.e., judging the child vs. not judging the child). As this brief analysis shows, attending more closely to the interplay of discourses is necessary to advance RDT-based research that is consistent with the new articulation of the theory.

Another way that researchers can focus closely on language use and draw out important concepts of the theory is by employing an analytic strategy Bakhtin (1984) referred to as *unfolding*. When researchers unfold an utterance, they imagine that it is a part of a larger conversation; in other words, they consider what prior utterances (already-spokens) the utterance might be responding to, as well as the anticipated responses (not-yet-spokens) that are invited by the utterance (Baxter, 2011). In their analysis of birth mothers' online stories, Baxter and colleagues (2012) found that the narratives seemed to respond with "No!" to the prior utterance, "You are a bad mother" (p. 63). By attending closely to the "details of talk," the researchers were able to expose how the birth mothers resisted the dominant discourse to construct an identity as a good mother. Without focusing explicitly on language use, the researchers could have interpreted the birth mothers' stories as ways they managed the good mother-bad mother discursive tension. Through the process of unfolding, researchers can make better use of the concept of the utterance chain and demonstrate how participants' utterances are embedded in larger systems of meaning.

RDT researchers should also engage more concepts as they attend to the "details of talk" during their analyses. Engaging in contrapuntal analysis has allowed for the examination of previously underexplored concepts, such as addressivity (Norwood & Baxter, 2011), discursive hybridity (Scharp, 2013), and the aesthetic moment (Norwood, 2013). However, despite the advancements in RDT-based research, many of the theory's important concepts continue to be ignored or overlooked in current work. For instance, of the four synchronic praxis patterns Baxter (2011) discusses, the antagonistic-nonantagonistic and serious-playful discursive struggles are relatively neglected in existing RDT-based research. Applying the lens of the antagonistic-nonantagonistic struggle to examine communicative texts might generate valuable insight about various complex issues relational partners face. An *antagonistic struggle,* for example, arises when two speakers privilege different discourses such as when one relational partner assigns prominence to a discourse of openness and the other aligns with a discourse of privacy (Baxter, 2011). Therefore, given the competing discourses regarding homosexuality in our culture (e.g., homosexuality as innate vs. homosexuality as a choice), researchers could examine whether and how multiple family members align with different systems of meaning regarding homosexuality when an individual comes out as lesbian or gay or undergoes a gender transition. Such research could explore the following two research questions: What antagonistic struggles, if any, animate family members' daily conversations surrounding the experience of a family member coming out as lesbian or gay? How do family members construct meaning of this experience through the interplay of competing systems of meaning? If researchers are not familiar with RDT's wide range of concepts and/or are not attuned to the "details of talk," they might miss out on interesting and insightful ways to analyze the communication between relational partners.

Another overlooked concept that RDT researchers should explore is the serious-playful discursive struggle. With a focus on the tone of an utterance, the serious-playful struggle is a synchronic practice that highlights the role of playfulness in communication (Baxter, 2011, pp. 136–138). Bakhtin (1981) claimed that competing discourses can be challenged through the use of three different playful devices: the *rouge,* the *fool,* and the *clown.* Using the serious-playful discursive struggle as a lens, researchers could examine how relational partners use humor, sarcasm, and mockery to construct meaning of their experiences and identities. The rouge, which is employed to parody or ridicule a competing discourse for the purposes of mocking a specific person or group who aligns with it (Baxter, 2011), might play a role in the communication between relationship partners who are at odds with one another (e.g., fighting spouses, rival siblings, unfriendly co-workers, etc.). For example, a husband may enact a parody of the "ideal, romanticized marriage" to mock his wife and her idea of what marriage should be. Rather than focusing solely on the competing discourses of marriage (e.g., Baxter, 2010), researchers could analyze the way the tone of an utterance influences how marital partners construct meaning of marriage and their identity as a married couple. Incorporating the serious-playful discursive struggle in future work and examining how relational partners enact playfulness will shed light on an important, yet understudied, aspect of relating.

Respond to prior critiques. Researchers can also respect RDT's conceptual complexity by addressing prior critiques of the theory in their work. As already noted, RDT-informed research has been criticized for following a predetermined script that simply identifies the three primary tensions in relationships. Underlying this criticism is the assumption that research studies using RDT generate no new findings or insights into relational life (Baxter & Braithwaite, 2008). Although any devoted RDT scholar would disagree, there is some truth to the observation that many RDT-based research studies bear a striking resemblance. Until a "shift" in the research takes place, those unfamiliar with or critical of RDT may continue to be unimpressed with the theory. It is up to researchers to take on exciting and innovative research projects that engage RDT's underexplored concepts and propel the theory in new directions. In doing so, other scholars may develop a greater appreciation for RDT and apply it in their own work.

In the past, scholars have also suggested that the dialectical approach lacks the necessary elements of a theory, such as the ability to predict and causally explain phenomena (Miller, 2005). Baxter (2011) counters this critique by arguing that RDT is not a positivistic theory with the goals of prediction and explanation, but a descriptive/sensitizing theory that "functions as a heuristic device to render the communicative social world intelligible" (p. 7). Indeed, relational dialectics theory has been praised for how well it has stimulated new research in a variety of contexts (West & Turner, 2014). However, RDT's capacity for heurism and ability to help people understand communicative phenomena does little good if the theory is still being evaluated against postpositivist assumptions. If RDT is to be truly appreciated as a heuristic theory, future researchers must expand their methodological horizons and explore different ways to study how relationships are constructed in talk. Addressing prior critiques, then, will not only demonstrate RDT's value as a theory, it will also encourage researchers to conduct studies that respect the theory's conceptual complexity.

Along with questioning RDT's status as a theory, Segrin and Flora (2011) claim that many of the theory's concepts are vague, difficult to understand, and cannot be easily applied in practical settings. Likewise, Miller (2005) argues that some of the terms and processes outlined in dialectical theory are messy and not well-defined. Baxter's (2011) *Voicing Relationships* clears up many misconceptions about RDT's concepts and assumptions, but the full scope and utility of a theory cannot be conveyed in a single book. The extent to which other scholars, practitioners, and members of the public understand RDT's concepts and see them as relevant depends on the ability of researchers to respect the conceptual complexity of the theory and communicate their findings in meaningful ways. While applied research was relatively common among earlier RDT-informed studies (Baxter et al., 2002; Braithwaite & Baxter, 2006; Toller & Braithwaite, 2009), recent work engaging RDT 2.0 focuses less on applying findings to practical settings. In order to extend RDT in important and useful directions, scholars must strive to highlight the practical applications of the theory's concepts and assumptions in future work.

In an example of applied RDT-informed research, Toller and Braithwaite (2009) used their findings related to parents' bereavement processes to create written materials that can be placed in funeral homes and hospitals. In other work, RDT researchers translated their results into communication tips and strategies that can help professionals working with stepfamilies (Braithwaite & Baxter, 2006) and families impacted by adult dementia (Baxter et al., 2002). Similarly, RDT researchers should consider ways they can communicate their findings in blogs, magazines, newspapers, and other outlets beyond academic journals. In addition to developing accessible written materials, scholars can reach a larger audience by seeking opportunities to present their work in contexts other than professional and academic conferences. For instance, a stepfamily researcher might ask to speak at a support group for stepmothers. Likewise, RDT scholars studying transgender identity or gay and lesbian families could present their findings at an LGBTQ event on their campus. Unless there is a stronger effort to make RDT-based research accessible and relevant to other scholars, members of the public, and the populations under study, the theory and its concepts may continue to be critiqued for being too complex and difficult to use in practical settings. Thus, by responding to prior critiques and engaging in more applied work, RDT researchers will make better use of the theory's central concepts.

The present chapter calls for researchers to engage in two research tasks that will move relational dialectics theory forward. First, RDT scholars must expand their methods of data collection in order to explore how relational partners jointly construct meaning both in the moment and over time. Second, more research is needed that respects the theory's conceptual complexity and utilizes underexplored concepts and assumptions. In the future, scholars should take on both of these tasks together to capitalize on RDT's vast potential and ensure that research is keeping up with the complexity of the theory.

Practical Implications

Addressing the gaps in RDT literature has important implications for interpersonal and family communication scholarship. As a prominent and frequently used theory in the communication discipline, RDT is in the position to make significant contributions to existing research on the communicative processes that characterize relational life. Therefore, it is essential that researchers utilize RDT to its full potential in order to maximize the possibilities for knowledge production. The more willing RDT researchers are to take the theory down new avenues, the more valuable insights they will uncover about interpersonal and family communication. Below, I argue that expanding the ways RDT is applied will also allow researchers to advance research on diverse family forms and highlight the theory's critical turn.

Advance Research on Family Diversity

Broadening the horizons of RDT-informed research is important because the theory has the potential to capture the complexity of relational communication in diverse family forms. As Baxter (2011) argued, relationship transitions are prime sites for discursive struggles to emerge in intense fashion. Given the increasing prevalence of family diversity (Galvin, 2006), more families are experiencing transitions and changes that can pose communication challenges for family members. In recent discussions of family diversity, scholars have painted a picture of family life that is chaotic, stressed, and ever-changing (Galvin, 2006; Walsh, 2012). While the mayhem characterizing contemporary family life is sometimes exaggerated, and many families are relatively simple in terms of structure and lifestyle, there is still a long way to go to fully understand how families "do family" in the 21st century. Family scholars, professionals, and practitioners are faced with the arduous task of helping today's families thrive and overcome adversity, but it is important to first understand their experiences and learn what their challenges are. To the extent that all families—no matter their form or their challenges—draw on cultural discourses to communicatively make meaning of their experiences, RDT can make important contributions to research on family diversity.

An excellent recent example of how RDT-informed research can help people understand the communicative experiences of diverse family forms is Kristen Norwood's work on transgender identities (Norwood, 2012, 2013). Using RDT 2.0 as a framework, Norwood (2013) demonstrates how family members attempt to construct meaning of a loved one's new gender identity in light of dominant discourses surrounding sex and gender. In particular, participants expressed that a loved one's gender transition challenged gendered expectations that circulate in mainstream U.S. culture, such as the expectation that a father will walk his daughter down the aisle on her wedding day. Along these lines, family members described feelings of grief following a loved one's gender transition, likening the experience to "losing a daughter" or "losing a husband." Many participants also grieved the loss of their own identities, such as the identity of being a father to a daughter, or the identity of being a wife to a husband.

The experience of undergoing a gender transition is challenging for both transgendered individuals and their loved ones. Further, as Norwood (2013) emphasized, people may not consider how closely connected gender and personhood are until they or a loved one experiences a gender transition (p. 40). Many families are likely not prepared for the changes and challenges associated with trans-identity, and could benefit from the knowledge and insights gained from research on transgendered families. Norwood's research not only has the potential to help families and relationship partners navigate a loved one's gender transition, it also demonstrates RDT's potential to generate important knowledge about diverse family forms.

Highlight RDT's Critical Turn

In her articulation of RDT 2.0, Baxter (2011) notes the theory's potential to conduct interpersonal and family communication research from a critical lens. The critical stance of RDT 2.0 is rooted in its conceptualization of power. From the perspective of RDT, power is not something people have (or a variable to be measured) but a characteristic of discourse (Baxter, 2011). In other words, power is a matter of discursive inequality: some discourses are centered and dominant (the centripetal), and others are marginalized (the centrifugal). In cases of totalizing monologue, all but one authoritative discourse is silenced.

By examining which discourses are centered (i.e., are more powerful) and which discourses are dismissed or altogether silenced in talk, RDT researchers can raise awareness about the systems of meaning and perspectives that are dominant in U.S. culture. Understanding these dominant discourses is important because they define what is accepted as reality by members of society; centripetal discourses are more powerful than centrifugal discourses because their systems of meaning are centered or legitimated as social reality (Baxter, 2011). Thus, centripetal/dominant discourses influence how individuals view the world around them, which ultimately influences how they act and go about their lives.

In terms of family research, the critical lens of RDT can expose the way dominant discourses of the "traditional" family are privileged and alternative views of family are marginalized or dismissed. Although there appears to be growing acceptance of family diversity, members of U.S. culture still largely privilege a nuclear family ideology that stigmatizes diverse family forms, such as stepfamilies (Ganong & Coleman, 2004). In addition, dominant perspectives of what it means to be a "normal" (Walsh, 2012) or "real" (Baxter, 2011) family continue to marginalize certain family forms. If dominant discourses define social reality (Baxter, 2011), then dominant discourses about family define which family forms are legitimated and which are marginalized in mainstream culture. Failing to examine these dominant discourses of family from a critical perspective allows them to be reproduced by cultural members, which further pushes alternative views of family to the margins. However, an RDT-informed critical approach to family research can give voice to marginalized views of family and interrogate dominant discourses that reinforce the nuclear family ideology or the "normal" family.

For example, Suter's research on lesbian families (Suter et al., 2006; Suter & Daas, 2007) found that lesbian couples both embrace and resist heteronormative ideals. Both practices—adhering to conventional standards of family and rejecting them—challenge dominant discourses of family. On the one hand, lesbian couples who embraced heteronormative ideals demonstrated that conventional standards of family are not limited to heterosexual married couples. On the other hand, lesbian couples who rejected heteronormative ideals indicated that they do not need to adhere to conventional standards of family to be a legitimate family. Either way, Suter's research forces readers to think about what it means to be family and whether heteronormative/conventional ideals are appropriate standards against which to compare all families. Although these studies were not presented as critical approaches, they illustrate the important work RDT researchers can do from a critical perspective.

Engaging in more critical family research holds several advantages for both the field of family communication and the families under study. In addition to challenging and dismantling dominant discourses of family that marginalize certain families, critical work from an RDT perspective can shed light on taken-for-granted aspects of relating. In particular, mainstream views of interpersonal communication privilege discourses of connection, openness, and certainty in relationships over the competing discourses of autonomy, closedness, and uncertainty (Baxter, 2011). Thus, the "ideal" relationship consists of partners who focus more on the relationship than their individual goals and needs, are completely open with one another, and are highly certain of one another and the relationship. RDT, however, argues that centering these dominant discourses to the point of silencing autonomy, closedness, and uncertainty stifles dialogic creativity and calcifies meaning (Baxter, 2011). In other words, by denying the interplay of competing discourses, individual and relational identities are restricted by the totalizing voice of monologue. Therefore, according to Baxter (2011), discursive struggles in relationships should not be viewed as a sign of trouble but the opportunity for new meanings to emerge. For example, uncertainty is generally viewed as an aversive state that needs to be reduced (Berger & Calabrese, 1975) or managed (Brashers, 2001), but Baxter and Braithwaite (2009) argue that uncertainty allows individual and relational identities to emerge in unanticipated ways in interaction. Through the critical lens of RDT, interpersonal and family communication researchers can expand how communication and relationships are viewed in U.S. culture.

Conclusion

In publishing *Voicing Relationships* and advancing a revised version of RDT, Baxter (2011) invited scholars to join her in moving the theory forward. Many scholars have accepted her invitation and incorporated RDT 2.0 into their work, producing exciting new knowledge about interpersonal and family communication processes. However, as I have argued, there are important areas that

RDT scholars have yet to explore. The need for researchers to tackle the two "tasks" I have outlined in this chapter—utilizing different methods of data collection and making better use of the theory's concepts—has been long noted by RDT scholars. Indeed, I readily acknowledge that I am not the first to argue for a revitalized research agenda for relational dialectics theory. The problem is that these important research avenues remain underexplored *despite* the persistent call to pursue them. Consistently acknowledging limitations in research with no effort to address them in future work is simply not productive.

A theory's potential rests in the hands of those willing to test its limits and explore new avenues. As Baxter (2011) expressed, "A useful theory, after all, doesn't live off of its past. Theories are not static things. To stay alive, a theory must continue to develop and evolve" (p. 1). If new and creative areas of research are not explored, RDT will, in a sense, be stuck in its past. Although RDT-informed research has generated rich and meaningful insights into relational life thus far, the full potential of the theory has not been fully realized. Communication researchers must rise to the challenge and explore all of the promising avenues relational dialectics theory has to offer.

References

Amati, R., & Hannawa, A. F. (2013). Relational dialectics theory: Disentangling physician-perceived tensions of end-of-life communication. *Health Communication, 29*(10), 1–12. doi:10.1080/10410236.2013.815533

Bakhtin, M. M. (1981). Discourse in the novel. In M. Holquist (Ed.), *The dialogic imagination: Four essays by M. M. Bakhtin.* (C. Emerson & M. Holquist, trans. pp. 259–422). Austin, TX: University of Texas Press. (Original work published in 1975.)

Bakhtin, M. M. (1984). *Problems of Dostoevsky's poetics* (C. Emerson, ed. & trans.). Minneapolis, MN: University of Minnesota Press. (Original work published in 1929.)

Bakhtin, M. M. (1986). The problem of speech genres. In C. Emerson & M. Holquist (Eds.), *Speech genres and other late essays* (V. W. McGee, trans. pp. 132–158). Austin, TX: University of Texas Press. (Original work published in 1979.)

Baxter, L. A. (1988). A dialectical perspective on communication strategies in relationship development. In S. Duck (Ed.), *Handbook of personal relationships* (pp. 257–274). London: Wiley.

Baxter, L. A. (2004). Distinguished scholar article: Relationships as dialogues. *Personal Relationships, 11*(1), 1–22. doi:10.1111/j.1475-6811.2004.00068.x

Baxter, L. A. (2006). Relational dialectics theory: Multivocal dialogues of family communication. In D. O. Braithwaite & L. A. Baxter (Eds.), *Engaging theories in family communication: Multiple perspectives* (pp. 130–145). Thousand Oaks, CA: Sage.

Baxter, L. A. (2010). The dialogue of marriage. *Journal of Family Theory & Review, 2*(4), 370–387. doi:10.1111/j.1756-2589.2010.00067.x

Baxter, L. A. (2011). *Voicing relationships: A dialogic perspective.* Thousand Oaks, CA: Sage.

Baxter, L. A., & Braithwaite, D. O. (2008). Relational dialectics theory: Crafting meaning from competing discourses. In L. A. Baxter & D. O. Braithwaite (Eds.), *Engaging theories in interpersonal communication: Multiple perspectives* (pp. 349–361). Thousand Oaks, CA: Sage.

Baxter, L. A., & Braithwaite, D. O. (2009). Reclaiming uncertainty: The formation of new meanings. In T. D. Afifi & W. A. Afifi (Eds.), *Uncertainty information management and disclosure decisions: Theories and applications* (pp. 26–44). New York, NY: Routledge.

Baxter, L. A., & Braithwaite, D. O. (2010). Relational dialectics theory, applied. In S. W. Smith & S. R. Wilson (Eds.), *New directions in interpersonal communication research* (pp. 48–66). Los Angeles, CA: Sage.

Baxter, L. A., & Montgomery, B. M. (1996). *Relating: Dialogues and dialectics.* New York, NY: The Guilford Press.

Baxter, L. A., Braithwaite, D. O., Bryant, L., & Wagner, A. (2004). Stepchildren's perceptions of the contradictions in communication with stepparents. *Journal of Social and Personal Relationships, 21*(4), 447–467. doi:10.1177/0265407504044841

Baxter, L. A., Braithwaite, D. O., Golish, T. D., & Olson, L. N. (2002). Contradictions of interactions for wives of elderly husbands with adult dementia. *Journal of Applied Communication Research, 30*(1), 1–26. doi:00909880216576

Baxter, L. A., Scharp, K. M., Asbury, B., Jannusch, A., & Norwood, K. M. (2012). "Birth mothers are not bad people": A dialogic analysis of online birth mother stories. *Qualitative Communication Research, 1*(1), 53–82. doi:10.1525/qcr.2012.1.1.53

Berger, C. R., & Calabrese, R. J. (1975). Some explorations in initial interaction and beyond: Toward a developmental theory of interpersonal communication. *Human Communication Research, 1*(2), 99–112. doi: 10.1111/j.1468-2958.1975.tb00258

Bloor, M., Frankland, J., Thomas, M., & Robson, K. (2001). *Focus groups in social research.* London: Sage.

Braithwaite, D. O., & Baxter, L. A. (2006). "You're my parent but you're not": Dialectical tensions in stepchildren's perceptions about communicating with the nonresidential parent. *Journal of Applied Communication Research, 34*(1), 30–48. doi:10.1080/00909880500420200

Braithwaite, D. O., Baxter, L. A., & Harper, A. M. (1998). The role of rituals in the management of the dialectical tensions of "old" and "new" in blended families. *Communication Studies, 49*(2), 101–121. doi:10.1080/10510979809368523

Brashers, D. E. (2001). Communication and uncertainty management. *Journal of Communication, 51*(3), 477–497. doi:10.1111/j.1460-2466.2001.tb02892.x

Breshears, D., & Braithwaite, D. O. (2014). Discursive struggles animating individuals' talk about their parents' coming out as lesbian or gay. *Journal of Family Communication, 14*(3), 189–207. doi:10.1080/15267431.2014.908197

Chornet Roses, D. (2006). "*I could say I am 'dating,' but that could mean lots of different things": "Dating" in the U.S. as a dialogic relational process.* Unpublished doctoral dissertation, University of Iowa, Iowa City.

Conville, R. (1998). Telling stories: Dialectics of relational transition. In B. M. Montgomery & L. A. Baxter (Eds.), *Dialectical approaches to studying personal relationships* (pp. 17–40). Mahwah, NJ: Lawrence Erlbaum Associates.

Creswell, J. W. (2007). *Qualitative inquiry and research design: Choosing among five approaches.* Thousand Oaks, CA: Sage.

Descartes, L. (2007). Rewards and challenges of using ethnography in family research. *Family and Computer Sciences Research Journal, 36*(1), 22–39. doi:10.1177/1077727X07303488

Evans, A., Elford, J., & Wiggins, D. (2008). Using the Internet for qualitative research. In C. Willig & W. Stainton-Rogers (Eds.), *The SAGE handbook of qualitative research in psychology* (pp. 315–333). Thousand Oaks, CA: Sage.

Galvin, K. (2006). Diversity's impact on defining the family. In L. H. Turner & R. West (Eds.), *The family communication sourcebook* (pp. 3–19). Thousand Oaks, CA: Sage.

Ganong, L., & Coleman, M. (2004). *Stepfamily relationships: Development, dynamics and interventions*. New York, NY: Kluwer Academic/Plenum.

Golish, T. D., & Powell, K. A. (2003). "Ambiguous loss": Managing the dialectics of grief associated with premature birth. *Journal of Social and Personal Relationships, 20*(3), 309–334. doi:10.1177/0265407503020003003

Graham, E. E. (2003). Dialectic contradictions in postmarital relationships. *Journal of Family Communication, 3*(4), 193–214. doi:10.1207/S15327698JFC0304_3

Hanna, P. (2012). Using internet technologies (such as Skype) as a research medium: A research note. *Qualitative Research, 12*(2), 239–242. doi:10.1177/1468794111426607

Harrigan, M. M., & Braithwaite, D. O. (2010). Discursive struggles in families formed through visible adoption: An exploration of dialectical unity. *Journal of Applied Communication Research, 3*(2), 127–144. doi:10.1080/00909881003639536

Hoppe-Nagao, A., & Ting-Toomey, S. (2002). Relational dialectics and management strategies in marital couples. *Southern Journal of Communication, 67*(2), 142–159. doi:10.1080/10417940209373226

Hummert, M. L., & Morgan, M. (2001). Negotiating decisions in the aging family. In M. L. Hummert & J. F. Nussbaum (Eds.), *Aging communication, and health: Linking research and practice for successful aging* (pp. 177–202). Mahwah, NJ: Lawrence Erlbaum.

Kelley, D. R. (2008). Leadership development through the fraternity experience and the relationship to career success after graduation. *Oracle: The Research Journal of the Association of Fraternity Advisors, 3*(1), 1–12.

Kramer, M. W. (2004). Toward a communication theory of group dialectics: An ethnographic study of a community theater group. *Communication Monographs, 71*(3), 311–332. doi:10.1080/0363452042000288292

McRoy, R. G., Grotevant, H. D., Ayers-Lopez, S., & Henney, S. M. (2007). Open adoptions: Longitudinal outcomes for the adoption triad. In R. A. Javier, L. A. Baden, F. A. Biafora & A. Camacho-Gingerich (Eds.), *Handbook of adoption: Implications for researchers, practitioners, and families* (pp. 175–190). Thousand Oaks: Sage.

Miller, K. (2005). *Communication theories: Perspectives, processes, and contexts* (2nd ed.). New York: McGraw Hill.

Norwood, K. (2012). Transitioning meanings? Family members' communicative struggles surrounding transgender identity. *Journal of Family Communication, 12*(1), 75–92. doi:10.1080/15267431.2010.509283

Norwood, K. (2013). Grieving gender: Trans-identities, transition, and ambiguous loss. *Communication Monographs, 80*(1), 24–45. doi:10.1080/03637751.2012.739705

Norwood, K. M., & Baxter, L. A. (2011). "Dear birth mother": Addressivity and meaning-making in online adoption-seeking letters. *Journal of Family Communication, 11*(3), 198–217. doi:10.1080/15267431.2011.554751

Prentice, C. (2009). Relational dialectics among in-laws. *Journal of Family Communication, 9*(2), 67–89. doi:10.1080/15267430802561667

Puig, A., Koro-Ljungberg, M., & Echevarria-Doan, S. (2008). Social constructionist family systems research: Conceptual considerations. *The Family Journal, 16*(2), 139–146. doi:10.1177/1066480707313785

Rawlins, W. K. (1992). *Friendship matters: Communication, dialectics, and the life course*. New York, NY: Aldine de Gruyter.

Rogerson, P. A., & Kim, D. (2005). Population distribution and redistribution of the baby-boom cohort in the United States: Recent trends and implications. *Proceedings* of the National Academy of Sciences of the United States of America, *102*(43), 15319–15324. doi:10.1073/pnas.0507318102

Sahlstein, E. M. (2006). Making plans: Praxis strategies for negotiating uncertainty-certainty in long-distance relationships. *Western Journal of Communication, 70(2),* 147–165. doi:10.1080/10570310600710042

Sahlstein, E., & Dun, T. (2008). "I wanted time to myself and he wanted to be together all the time": Constructing breakups as managing autonomy-connection. *Qualitative Research Reports in Communication, 9*(1), 37–45. doi:10.1080/17459430802400340

Sahlstein, E., Maguire, K. C., & Timmerman, L. (2009). Contradictions and praxis contextualized by wartime deployment: Wives' perspectives revealed through relational dialectics. *Communication Monographs, 76*(4), 421–442. doi:10.1080/03637750903300239

Scharp, K. M. (2013). Making meaning of domestic adoption reunion in online narratives: A dialogic perspective. *Qualitative Communication Research, 2*(3), 301–325. doi:10.1525/qcr.2013.2.3.301

Segrin, C., & Flora, J. (2011). *Family communication.* New York, NY: Routledge.

Stamp, G. H. (1994). The appropriation of the parental role through communication during the transition to parenthood. *Communications Monographs, 61*(2), 89–112. doi:10.1080/03637759409376327

Stamp, G. H., & Shue, C. K. (2013). Twenty years of family research published in communication journals: A review of the perspectives, theories, concepts, and contexts. In A. L. Vangelisiti (Ed.), *The Routledge handbook of family communication* (pp. 11–28). New York, NY: Routledge.

Suter, E. A., & Daas, K. L. (2007). Negotiating heteronormativity dialectically: Lesbian couples' display of symbols in culture. *Western Journal of Communication, 71*(3), 177–195. doi:10.1177/0265407506064201

Suter, E. A., Bergen, K. M., Daas, K. L., & Durham, W. T. (2006). Lesbian couples' management of public-private dialectical contradictions. *Journal of Social and Personal Relationships, 23*(3), 349–365. doi:10.1177/0265407506064201

Tannen, D., Kendall, S., & Gordon, C. (2007). *Family talk: Discourse and identity in four American families.* Oxford University Press, USA.

Tillmann, L. M. (2010). Coming out and going home: A family ethnography. *Qualitative Inquiry, 16*(2), 116–129. doi:10.1177/1077800409350697

Toller, P. W., & Braithwaite, D. O. (2009). Grieving together and apart: Bereaved parents' contradictions of marital interaction. *Journal of Applied Communication Research, 37*(3), 257–277. doi:10.1080/00909880903025887

Von Korff, L., & Grotevant, H. D. (2011). Contact in adoption and adoptive identity formation: The mediating role of family conversation. *Journal of Family Psychology, 25*(3), 393–401. doi:10.1037/a0023388

Walsh, F. (2012). The new normal: Diversity and complexity in 21st-century families. In F. Walsh (Ed.), *Normal family processes: Growing diversity and complexity* (pp. 3–27). New York: Guilford Press.

Wenzel, K. A., & Poynter, D. (2014). "I'm mother! I can take care of myself!": A contrapuntal analysis of older parents' relational talk with their adult children. *Southern Communication Journal, 79*(2), 147–170. doi:1080/1041794X.2014.881540

West, R., & Turner, L. H. (2014). *Introducing communication theory: Analysis and application* (5th ed.). New York: McGraw-Hill.

Wozniak, A., Lollis, S., & Marshall, S. K. (2013). Competing discourses in parent-adolescent conversations. *Journal of Personal and Social Relationships, 31*(6), 1–21. doi:10.1177/0265407513508726

Part II

Communication in a Changing, Ubiquitous Media Environment

CHAPTER CONTENTS

4 Media Multitasking

Good, Bad, or Ugly?

Annie Lang and Jasmin Chrzan

Indiana University

In this study we analyze studies published since 1990 which tested task performance in a single and multitasking environment where at least one of the tasks was a media use task; we identify theoretical approaches, conceptual, and operational definitions of multitasking research; we critique definitions of successful multitasking; and we analyze published results in terms of task-related complexity and cognitive and perceptual system overlaps. We conclude that complexity and overlaps appear to be important variables underlying multitasking research results and provide recommendations for future research in the area.

The past decade has shown a sharp increase in research examining people's ability to multitask. A fair amount of that research is focused on a specific type of multitasking called media multitasking. Some studies in this area have received widespread media attention and the most commonly promulgated findings are that people are poor multitaskers, that people are unable to multitask, or that multitasking actively damages cognition and concentration (Ophir, Nass, & Wagner, 2009; Pea et al., 2012; Srivastava, 2013; Wang & Tchernev, 2012). In this paper we seek to examine empirical studies which explicitly measure task performance during media multitasking to assess the extent to which they support this conclusion. Other goals include: (a) describing the range and variation in theoretical approaches that have guided the conceptual and operational definitions used in the experiments, (b) describing and critiquing the definitions of successful multitasking, (c) systematically examining the kinds of perceptual and processing system overlaps in the various task combinations, and (d) analyzing the extent to which these things may play a major role in determining the results. Following this analysis, we make suggestions for future research.

In order to perform this analysis, we searched for studies published since 1990 which included results from an empirical test of media multitasking and met the following three criteria: (a) the study had to include at least one condition where participants completed two tasks simultaneously, (b) one of the tasks had to be a media use task (e.g., watching television, reading print publications, using the computer, listening to radio, etc.), and (c) performance measures on at least one of the two tasks in both the media multitasking condition and a non-multitasking condition had to be included. Initially we used electronic database searches using Web of Science and Communication Abstracts to locate appropriate articles. Search terms included multitasking, dual task, and various media terms including computer, internet, television, radio, media, etc. Following this search, the bibliographies of all papers found were examined for additional papers. Many excellent papers on multitasking were not included here because they did not meet the three criteria. For example, a number of papers used online surveys to ascertain how often people multitask or to examine people's perceptions and thoughts about multitasking (e.g., Wang & Tchernev, 2012; Zhang & Zhang, 2012). Others discussed theoretical models of multitasking (e.g., Salvucci & Beltowska, 2008) and another group examined multitasking as an individual difference variable (Alzahabi & Becker, 2013). The criteria used in this study were chosen in order to be able to compare theories, definitions, and results from a group of experiments that all shared the goal of attempting to measure the extent to which multitasking (when one of the tasks involved media use) altered task performance. By requiring similarity in experimental design (that is a multitask and a single task condition with comparisons of success in the two conditions) outcomes can be directly compared and an analysis of similarities and differences in the various task combinations can be undertaken to uncover trends in the results. A total of 20 papers were deemed appropriate and are included in this analysis.

The first section of this chapter analyzes the range of conceptual definitions found for multitasking. The second section examines the various theoretical approaches taken by those studies, researcher definitions of successful multitasking and offers a critique of these definitions. The third section describes and critiques definitions of successful multitasking. The fourth section examines multitasking manipulations and the cognitive and perceptual system overlaps in both the tasks being combined and responses being required of the participants. The fifth section describes the range of results and provides an analysis of how those results may be related to variations in task overlaps, theoretical approaches, and operational and conceptual definitions. Finally, the sixth section suggests directions for future research in this area.

Conceptual Definitions of (Media) Multitasking

This chapter includes data only from studies that included a media multitasking condition. Media multitasking is defined here as doing two tasks simultaneously, one of which involves media use. Occasionally the definition of media may seem to be somewhat stretched. For example, in the Pratt, Willoughby, and Swick (2011) study, both tasks are completed on a computer (which is a medium), though neither task involves a standard type of media message. The study was included because it involved media use—though it does not include a media message. In general, the studies used here include a broad definition of multitasking and a specific definition of media multitasking. This section reviews both these definitions. The range of definitions and the studies that use them are provided in Table 4.1.

Table 4.1 Conceptual Definition of Multitasking: Definitions and Studies

Definition	Study
Multitasking is when two tasks are completed concurrently	Stephens, 2012 Hembrooke & Gay, 2003 Pratt, Willoughby, & Swick, 2011 Wang & Tchernev, 2012
Multitasking is switching from one task to another in rapid succession	Fox, Rosen, & Crawford, 2009 Law, Logie, & Pearson, 2006
Multitasking is when two tasks are completed concurrently or by switching from one task to another in rapid succession	Lui & Wong, 2012
Multitasking is using media for one task while concurrently completing another, non-mediated task	Ophir, Nass, & Wagner, 2009 Wang, David, Srivastava, Powers, Brady, D'Angelo, & Moreland, 2012 Zhang, Jeong, & Fishbein, 2010 Jeong & Fishbein, 2007
Multitasking is when two media tasks are completed concurrently	Lee, Lin, & Robertson, 2012 Voorveld, 2011 Wang & Tchernev, 2012 Srivastava, 2013 Bowman, Levine, Waite, & Gendron, 2010

Two broad classes of definitions were found in this literature. The first class defines multitasking as two tasks being completed concurrently (Hembrooke & Gay, 2003). The second class defines multitasking as switching from one task to another in rapid succession (Fox, Rosen, & Crawford, 2009). One paper reviewed, though it is not included in this analysis because it did not meet the criteria, defined multitasking in both ways—that is as two tasks being completed concurrently or as switching from one task to another in rapid succession (Lui & Wong, 2012). Within these two broad classes, we find a range of specific definitions of media multitasking.

The most common definition of media multitasking is doing two tasks at once, one of which is a media use task and the other of which is a non-media use task (Wang et al., 2012). Two studies defined media multitasking as when two media tasks are completed concurrently (Lee, Lin, & Robertson, 2012; Voorveld, 2011).

Of interest here is whether the combination of tasks used in the studies can be done simultaneously or if one must switch back and forth between tasks to perform the tasks. For example, some combinations like doing homework with background media (which occurs several times in this group of studies) have both tasks going on all the time. Others, like reading and instant messaging, require you to switch back and forth. For example, Wang et al. (2012) used threaded cognition theory that assumes people have to switch to multitask. In their study, they have participants doing a visual matching task and instant messaging using either voice or text. Thus one condition clearly requires switching and the other does not. Similarly, among studies that use a non-switching theoretical approach (like limited capacity models) combinations which require and combinations which do not require switching occur. This paper will not explicitly separate papers on the basis of the authors' theoretical position on switching but will, instead, consider the extent to which each combination of tasks requires the same perceptual, output, or processing systems. If both tasks require the same system, then this paper will call that an overlap which means, from this point of view, the task requires switching.

Theoretical Approaches to Multitasking Research

A variety of theoretical approaches, summarized in Table 4.2, are used in the studies included in this analysis. The most common theoretical approach is to use some form of limited capacity theory, though this is frequently combined with additional theoretical approaches. Four studies use cognitive load theory. Lee, Lin, and Robertson (2012) use Paas and van Merrienboer's (1994) cognitive load theory which defines cognitive load as "a multidimensional construct representing the load that performing a particular task imposes on learners' cognitive systems" (p. 122). This theory suggests that as tasks are learned, knowledge is stored in schemas and the creation of schemas reduces cognitive load. Thus, newer tasks put a heavier load on the system and familiarity reduces load. In addition, complex tasks are thought to put a heavier load on the system than do simple tasks. Increases in cognitive load are thought to lead to decreases in task performance.

Table 4.2 Conceptual Definition of Multitasking: Theories and Studies

Theoretical Approach	Study
Cognitive Load Theory	Lee, Lin, & Robertson, 2012 Armstrong, Boiarsky, & Mares, 1991 Armstrong & Greenberg, 1990
Threaded Cognition	Wang, David, Srivastava, Powers, Brady, D'Angelo, & Moreland, 2012
Limited Capacity Model (LCM)	Hembrooke & Gay, 2003 Pool, Koolstra, & Van der Voort, 2003 Zhang, Jeong, & Fishbein, 2010 Srivastava, 2013
Multiple component model of working memory	Law, Logie, & Pearson, 2006 Pratt, Willoughby, & Swick, 2011
LCM & Elaboration Likelihood Model	Voorveld, 2011
Capacity Interference and Structural Interference	Armstrong & Chung, 2000
Capacity Interference, Processing interference, Orienting Responses, and Physiological Arousal	Pool, Van der Voort, Beentjes, & Koolstra, 2000
No theory	Fox, Rosen & Crawford, 2009

Other studies use some version of limited capacity model (Kahneman, 1973; Lang, 2000, 2009) which considers humans to be limited capacity information processors who independently allocate resources to various processing tasks. These models assume that many tasks can be performed automatically, requiring very few limited resources while other tasks require controlled processing, and therefore require many processing resources. With practice, many tasks can be automated and become relatively cost free. Complex tasks are defined as requiring more resources than simple tasks and when resources become scarce or are exhausted, performance on these tasks suffers.

Voorveld (2011) combines a limited capacity approach with the elaboration likelihood model (ELM). The ELM proposes two processing routes: the central route and the peripheral route. Central route processing is more thorough while peripheral route processing is more heuristic and less thorough. According to the ELM, people are more likely to process peripherally when they are distracted. Thus, according to Voorveld, messages encountered while multitasking are more likely to be processed peripherally, and therefore less thoroughly, because of the distraction of the second task.

Two studies (Armstrong & Chung, 2000; Pool, Van der Voort, Beentjes, & Koolstra 2000) use interference models suggesting that tasks cannot be performed concurrently when they need to use the same resources or the same cognitive, perceptual, or capacity structures or systems.

Two studies use some version of a working memory capacity model (Law, Logie, & Pearson, 2006; Pratt, Willoughby, & Swick, 2011). Law, Logie, and Pearson (2006) use the multiple component model of memory which conceptualizes working memory as a series of processes and structures. Among these are the phonological loop and the central executive, both considered to be important components of working memory. This approach suggests that problems in multitasking may stem from an overburdened central executive. Law, Logie, and Pearson (2006) increased load on memory processing by engaging the phonological loop, the prediction being that this additional working memory load would result in breakdowns in executive functioning and lower task performance.

Similarly, Pratt, Willoughby, and Swick (2011) suggest that when working memory load is high it specifically reduces our ability to inhibit our attention to irrelevant cues. In this study, they presented both behavioral and electrophysiological data supporting the notion that when working memory is high, irrelevant cues are more likely to capture attention and reduce focal task performance. Increasing both the level of load on working memory and/or the difficulty of the focal task increases the effect.

Finally there is one study which uses the threaded cognition model (Salvucci & Beltowska, 2008; Wang et al. 2012). Wang et al. (2012) state that the key feature of threaded cognition "is the instantiation of multitasking goals as different goal threads" (p. 969). This model defines several types of resource pools (e.g., motor, cognitive-declarative, perceptual, etc.). All these subresource pools can operate in parallel but are presided over by a serial processing pool called the cognitive-procedural resource. When the tasks being performed simultaneously require this uber-resource pool, a bottleneck occurs. If a task thread has control of a resource pool through the cognitive-procedural resource it is not available to other task threads. Hence, parts of tasks may operate in parallel while other parts may operate serially.

There is great variability across these papers as to the extent to which the theory was being used either: (a) to design the experimental conditions and measures, or (b) to test the theory. For example, Wang et al. (2012) chose two tasks which had more or less overlap in the resource pools that would be required by the tasks and predicted that when two threads required access to the same resource pools they would be performed more slowly than when they did not. Thus, threaded cognition both provided guidance in the task selection model and was tested by the experiment. Similarly, Armstrong, Boiarsky and Mares (1991) and Armstrong and Greenberg (1990) designed studies to test cognitive load theories. Armstrong and Chung (2000) and Pool, Van der Voort, Beentjes, and Koolstra (2000) designed studies to examine specific locations of interference (structural, orienting, processing). In general, studies designed to test a theory do generally support the theory but tend to have mixed conclusions about multitasking. However, because none of them include conditions which test one theory against another—it is not at all clear how strong the support is for any given theory. Later in this paper we will analyze the results based on operational rather than theoretical or conceptual definitions in an attempt to discover whether commonalities in manipulations (regardless of concept being manipulated) produce similar results across studies regardless of theoretical approach.

What is successful multitasking?

Of particular interest when drawing conclusions about whether people can multitask or the extent to which people are good at multitasking is the metric one uses to define successful multitasking. In other words, what kind of data do these researchers require before they declare people to be successful multi-taskers? A number of operational definitions of successful multitasking can be found in the studies included in this paper and they are described in Table 4.3. Any definition of successful multitasking requires two things: (a) performance measures on at least one of the two tasks during a multitasking condition, and (b) performance measures on that same task in something considered to be a control or single task condition. Given these two elements, the authors can then define success by achieving some level of performance in the multitasking condition with respect to the control condition. In order to be able to compare results across studies and theoretical approaches, all of the studies selected for this analysis and reported here use a single task condition as the control condition. All of these studies define successful multitasking as *no* decrease in performance for a given task in its single condition compared to its multitasking condition. Thus, no matter what the tasks, manipulations, or theories, all these studies share a common definition of successful multitasking.

Table 4.3 Operational Definition of Multitasking: Successful Multitasking

Definition of Successful Multitasking	Study
Equal **Memory Accuracy** during single and multitask conditions	Hembrooke & Gay, 2003 Voorveld, 2011 Armstrong & Chung, 2000 Armstrong, Boiarsky, & Mares, 1991 Zhang, Jeong, & Fishbein, 2010 Lin, Lee, & Robertson, 2011 Srivastava, 2013
Equal **Task Accuracy** during single and multitask conditions	Pratt, Willoughby, & Swick, 2011 Lee, Lin, & Robertson, 2012 Wang, David, Srivastava, Powers, Brady, D'Angelo, & Moreland, 2012 Armstrong & Greenburg, 1990
Equal **Time to Completion** in single and multitask conditions	None
Equal **Memory Accuracy** and **Task Accuracy** in single and multitask conditions	Furnham & Bradley, 1997
Equal **Memory Accuracy** and **Time to Completion** in single and multitask conditions	Bowman, Levine, Waite, & Gendron, 2010
Equal **Task Accuracy** and **Time to Completion** in single and multitask conditions	Law, Logie, & Pearson, 2006 Pool, Van der Voort, Beentjes & Koolstra 2000 Fox, Rosen, & Crawford, 2009
Equal **Memory Accuracy**, **Task Accuracy** and **Time to Completion** in single and multitask conditions	Pool, Koolstra, & Van der Voort, 2003

A variety of performance measures are used across the studies. To group the studies in this paper we considered two dimensions of the performance measures. First, did the measure occur during or after the multitasking period, and second, was it a time to completion measure or an accuracy measure. The three major types of measures used were memory accuracy, task accuracy, and time to completion. Memory accuracy tests were completed after the multitasking or single task condition and reflected participants' ability to remember content from (usually) the primary task. Task accuracy measures were collected during the single or multitask condition and reflected how well the focal task was performed. Finally, time to completion measures assessed how long it took to do the focal task in both the single and multitask conditions. As can be seen in Table 4.3, various combinations of these three types of measures were used in different studies. Six studies measured only memory accuracy. Four measured only task accuracy. There were no studies that measured only time to completion and only one study that measured the combination of memory accuracy and time to completion. One study measured both memory accuracy and task accuracy while three studies measured task accuracy and time to completion. A single study measured all three.

As mentioned above, based on the presentation and discussion of results it was clear that in all cases successful multitasking was defined as occurring only if these measures did not differ between the single and multitask conditions. While at first glance these may seem like reasonable metrics for success in multitasking, there are grounds to argue that this is an extremely stringent definition of multitasking and that this stringency may be the primary reason that so many studies come to the conclusion that people are not good at or cannot multitask. We know, from decades of dual task research that, without practice, it is rare indeed for two tasks to be done simultaneously without interfering at all with one another (Shiffrin & Schneider, 1977). Given that in most of these experiments the participants have no practice with the experimental task combinations and that when the task combinations are thought to be common (such as watching TV and doing homework) the extent to which the participants routinely perform these tasks is not controlled, it is not surprising that they almost always show at least some slight performance deficits on one or more of these measures.

An equally reasonable approach, therefore, would be to suggest that successful multitasking is to do two tasks concurrently so as to have no decrease in performance and/or accuracy while taking no more time to complete the two concurrent tasks than it would take to do the two tasks serially. In other words, people's real-life choices about multitasking involve whether to do two tasks simultaneously, two tasks serially, or to choose which task to do given the time available. It seems reasonable to suggest that successful multitasking might be defined as completing two tasks without significant loss in performance (e.g., accuracy or memory) in a period of time shorter than the period of time it would take to complete the two tasks serially.

Further, all of the definitions of successful multitasking provided in the studies whose results are analyzed in this paper focus on purely cognitive theoretical approaches and purely cognitive measures and outcomes. Yet, it is reasonable to think that people may multitask not only to increase the amount of work they can do but also in order to alter their motivational or emotional states during work. For example, a person may not enjoy cleaning the house but finds the job much less onerous if they listen to music or watch television while doing the job. While it may be the case that by multitasking they take a bit longer to clean house, the increase in pleasure experienced as a result of multitasking may render this a successful combination on emotional grounds and it likely takes less time to combine the tasks than to clean the house and then watch your favorite show. Indeed, just recently Wang and Tchernov (2012) have proposed and tested a model where both motivational and cognitive needs and gratifications are used to predict multitasking. They find that while cognitive needs may drive multitasking, motivational and emotional needs are satisfied by multitasking.

Examples of this may be found in two of the studies reported here. Pool and colleagues (2000, 2003) examined homework accuracy in conditions where students did homework with or without various types of background television.

Several conditions existed in which there was no difference in accuracy on the homework, though it took participants somewhat longer to complete the homework in the background television condition compared to the no background television condition. These studies concluded that television interfered with homework because it took longer. If, however, the student found it more pleasurable to do the homework with the television on, they might be more likely to engage in homework, and feel better while they are doing it, which might lead to more homework completion. Similarly, if the student had to choose between homework and television, they might choose television which would be a less positive outcome than the combination. Given that, for some multitasking combinations, only time to completion and not accuracy is harmed, this might be considered to be successful multitasking.

In any case, it seems that future research should consider both motivational and emotional factors in defining successful multitasking and seriously consider whether the time comparisons should be between multitask and single task conditions or between multitasking and the time it would take to complete the two tasks in a serial manner.

In addition, the size of the deficits—not just the significance of the difference between conditions—should be considered. If accuracy declines very slightly (though statistically significantly), one might want to consider the actual size of the decline in percentage terms. Many of the results reported in these studies are effects of only two or three percentage points, though they are statistically significant. Depending on the tasks combined, improvement in the emotional experience with only a very small dip in performance might be considered to be successful multitasking. For example, if one combines watching television for entertainment and using Facebook for fun, neither the decrease in memory of the TV show or the taking longer to post on Facebook is very consequential. On the other hand, if one is performing more important tasks, even a small decrease may matter. In any case, it may make sense when drawing conclusions about people's ability to successfully multitask to take note of the size of the deficit, not just its significance.

Empirical Manipulations of Multitasking and Perceptual and Processing Task Overlaps

In this section we consider the extent to which there are system overlaps between the tasks combined in the multitasking conditions found in these studies. A description of the tasks can be found in Table 4.4 and an analysis of the systems required by the tasks and the overlaps that exist is presented in Table 4.5. A wide range of tasks and task combinations exist across this set of studies. In most studies there is a focal task (that is the task whose performance is measured in the single and multitask conditions) and a secondary or background task for which the level of performance is only sometimes assessed (n=5). The focal tasks included browsing a website (one study), reading (two studies), reading and answering questions about the reading (eight studies), a

Table 4.4 Operational Definitions and Results

Study	Operational Definitions	Results
Law, Logie, and Pearson, 2006	Participants completed a virtual errands test (VET) alone (ST) or while repeating the word "December" (MT Dec.) in time with a metronome, or randomly generating months of the year (MT months) in time with the metronome. Accuracy and time to complete VET were measured.	In both MT conditions participants completed the task more slowly and less accurately than in the single task condition. ST>MT – time to completion ST >MT – task accuracy
Pratt, Willoughby, & Swick, 2011	Participants completed a visual flanker task with two difficulty levels (congruent and incongruent) lone and simultaneously with a Sternberg consonant memory task (MT) with two levels (4/7). Accuracy of flanker task was measured as well as size of P1 and P3.	Accuracy was better in the single-task compared to the MT condition at the 7 consonant Sternberg condition only. P1 and P3 were smaller in the same condition. ST>MT – complex task accuracy ST=MT – simple task accuracy
Bowman, Levine, Waite, & Gendron, 2010	Participants read from a textbook (alone, ST) or while instant messaging IM (MT). Memory and time to completion were measured.	ST=MT – task accuracy ST<MT – time to completion
Srivastava, 2013	Participants either read an online article and then listened to a podcast (ST) or read and listened simultaneously (MT). Recall, cued recall, and recognition for online article were measured.	MT<ST – recognition MT<ST – cued recall MT<ST – recall
Furnham & Bradley, 1997	Introverts and extroverts were in one of two groups—Music On (MT) or Off. In the Music Off condition, participants read a passage and then answered questions over it. They were then given a memory test. In the MT condition, participants did the same thing, but with a radio playing.	Memory was worse in the MT compared to music off condition. Task accuracy was worse in the MT condition for introverts only. ST>MT – memory accuracy ST>MT – introverts task accuracy ST=MT – extroverts task accuracy
Voorveld, 2011	Participants browsed a website while listening to radio. Visual banners were presented on the computer and verbal ads on the radio. There were three conditions—same product ad on both media, ad on radio only, and ad on computer only. Memory for target ad was measured.	Memory for the product ad was best on both media, followed by banner only, followed by radio only. MT redundant >ST – memory accuracy

Study	Method	Findings
Wang, David, Srivastava, Powers, Brady, D'Angelo, & Moreland, 2012	Participants in the Control condition completed a Match/mismatch test. In the MT IM condition, participants completed the same task while IMing a confederate. In the MT Voice condition, participants completed the task while talking with a confederate. Task accuracy was measured.	Both multitasking groups showed a decrease in accuracy on the Pattern Matching task, but the IM condition was worse than the Voice condition. ST>MT IM condition – task accuracy MT voice >MT IM – task accuracy.
Lee, Lin, & Robertson, 2012	Three conditions, Control, Background, & Multitasking (MT). In the Control condition, participants read and answered questions about an article in silence. In the Background condition, participants read and answered questions about an article while the television was playing. In the MT condition, participants were instructed to pay attention to the TV while they read the article and answered questions. Afterwards, Background and MT participants answered questions about TV content.	Participants in the Control and Background conditions scored better in accuracy on the reading comprehension test than those in the MT condition. ST>MT – task accuracy
Hembrooke & Gay, 2003	There were two conditions—Closed and Open Laptop (MT). In the Closed condition, participants attended a lecture w/o laptops. In the MT condition, students attended the same lecture, but were encouraged to use their laptops. Both groups were tested over the content of the lecture afterwards.	Memory recognition and recall was poorer in the MT condition compared to the Closed Laptop condition. ST>MT – memory accuracy
Armstrong & Chung, 2000	Participants did a reading homework assignment with (MT during) or without background TV. Then they completed a memory test for the reading with (MT post) or without background TV.	Background TV during reading interfered with memory for the reading. Background TV during memory had no effect. ST>MT during reading/TV – memory accuracy ST=MT during memory/TV – memory accuracy
Armstrong, Boiarsky, & Mares, 1991	Participants were put into a Control condition, a Drama (MT) condition, or a Commercial (MT) condition. In Control, they read a passage in silence, in the Drama condition, they read a passage while a drama played in the background and in Commercial, they read while TV commercials played in the background. Afterwards, all participants took a reading recall test directly or five minutes later.	MT Drama and MT commercial had worse memory than the reading alone condition. ST>MT – memory accuracy

(Continued)

Table 4.4 (Continued)

Study	Operational Definitions	Results
Zhang, Jeong, & Fishbein, 2010	Participants were placed in a TV group, where they paid attention to a TV; a homework group, where they just did a homework assignment; or a Multitasking group where they paid attention to the TV and did the homework assignment. Memory for TV content was compared.	The Multitasking group's recognition of television content decreased compared to the TV condition. ST>MT – memory accuracy
Fox, Rosen, & Crawford, 2009	In the Control condition, participants read a passage and then IMed a confederate. In the MT condition, participants read a passage and completed a comprehension test while simultaneously IMing a confederate. Both groups were timed.	The Multitasking condition took longer to complete both tasks. MT did not affect reading comprehension ST>MT – time to completion ST=MT – task accuracy
Pool, Van der Voort, Beentjes, & Koolstra, 2000	Experiment 1: Participants completed a homework assignment with (1) no background media, (2) TV soap opera in background (native language) (MT-NL), 3) music videos in background – (non-native Language) MT-NNL. Accuracy and time to completion on homework task. were measured.	Accuracy was lower in MT-NL condition than in the other two conditions. Time to completion was not affected. ST>MT-NL, ST=MT-NNL – task accuracy ST=MT – time to completion
	Experiment 2: Same three conditions as experiment 1 crossed by an ignore or attend TV Instruction. Task accuracy and time to completion and TV recognition were measured.	Accuracy was lower in the MT-NL condition (p<.10) No effect of ignore attend TV instruction on accuracy. Time to completion was slower in the MT-NL condition. No effect of ignore attend TV instruction. Recognition for TV was better in attend MT-NNL condition not in MT-NL. ST>MT-NL, ST=MT-NNL – task accuracy ST>MT-NL, ST=MT-NNL – time to completion
Pool, Koolstra & Van der Voort, 2003	There were four groups—Control, Radio, Music Videos (non-native language) and Soap Opera (native language). Participants completed assignments in a booklet either in silence, or with one of the media types in the background. They then completed a memory test in silence. Accuracy on task and memory and time to completion were measured.	Task and memory accuracy decreased for participants in the MT-NL condition. There were no effects on time to completion. ST>MT-NL – task accuracy and memory accuracy ST=MT (NL and NNL) – time to completion

Lin, Lee, & Robertson, 2011	There were four conditions. In the Background conditions, participants completed a reading assignment while a TV played news/comedy, but they were told they could ignore the TV. In the MT conditions, participants completed the same reading while the TV played news or comedy but they were told they would be tested over the material on the TV. Afterwards, all participants completed questions over the reading and the TV content.	Reading memory accuracy was higher in background compared to attend MT conditions. TV accuracy was higher in the attend compared to ignore condition. ST>MT – memory accuracy
Armstrong & Greenburg, 1990	Participants were shown either a high action/low talk TV (MT action) show or a high talk/low action TV show (MT talk) condition or no show for the ST condition. In the MT conditions, there was a Background condition where participants were told to ignore the TV, and a MT condition where participants were told to pay attention to the TV. Participants completed tests on short-term memory, linguistic processing speed, reading comprehension, spatial problem solving, and mental flexibility. Memory for TV was also measured.	Reading comprehension decreased for all MT conditions compared to no TV condition. Mental flexibility lower in all MT compared to no show conditions. Problem solving lower in all MT compared to no show conditions. ST>MT complex – task accuracy (3 tasks) ST=MT simple – task accuracy (3 tasks)

Table 4.5 Perceptual and Cognitive Overlaps

Studies	Task Input		Task Output		Systems Required		System Overlaps
	Task 1	Task 2	Task 1	Task 2	Task 1	Task 2	
Law, Logie, & Pearson, 2006	Visual virtual errands task	Language word generation	VET choices	Word vocalization	Visual perceptual Visual processing	Language	None
Pratt, Willoughby, & Swick, 2011	Congruent & incongruent visual flanker task	Sternberg consonant memory task—4 or 7 consonants	Speed and accuracy	Memory	Visual perceptual Visual processing	Memory	None
Furnham & Bradley, 1997	Reading text	Radio listening	Answering questions about the reading	None	Visual perceptual Language	Audio perceptual Language	Language
Voorveld, 2011	Browse website	Listen to audio Commercials	Memory for ads on website	Memory for audio ads	Visual perceptual Language	Language Audio	Language
Wang, David, Srivastava, Powers, Brady, D'Angelo, & Moreland, 2012	Computer information task	Reading text	Response to computer task	Instant messaged	Visual perceptual Language	Visual perceptual Language	Visual perceptual Language
Lee, Lin, & Robertson, 2012	Reading text	TV viewing & listening	Answered questions about the reading	Visual	Visual perceptual Language	Visual perceptual Language Audio Visual processing	Visual perceptual Language
Hembrooke & Gay, 2003	In-class lecture	Computer use	None	None	Visual perceptual Language Audio	Visual perceptual Language	Visual perceptual Language
Armstrong & Chung, 2000	Reading text	Background TV	Memory for material read	Background TV	Visual perceptual Language Memory	Visual perceptual Language Audio perceptual Audio visual	Visual perceptual Language

Armstrong, Bolarsky, & Mares, 1991	Reading text	TV viewing & listening	Memory of reading	None	Visual Language	Visual perceptual Language Audio visual Audio perceptual	Visual perceptual Language
Zhang, Jeong & Fishbein, 2010	Reading text	TV viewing & listening	Answered questions about the reading	None	Visual perceptual Language	Visual perceptual Language Audio visual Audio perceptual	Visual perceptual Language
Fox, Rosen, & Crawford, 2009	Reading text	Reading text	None	Instant messaged	Visual perceptual Language	Visual perceptual Language	Visual perceptual Language
Pool, Van der Voort, Beentjes, & Koolstra, 2000 Expt. 1	Homework Reading & math	Background TV Native language Non-native language	Homework accuracy & time to complete	None	Visual perceptual Language Math	Visual perceptual Language (NL condition only) Audio perceptual Audio visual	Visual perceptual Language (NL condition only)
Expt. 2	Homework Reading & math	Background TV (native and non-native language) Attend/ignore Instruction	Homework accuracy & time to complete	TV recognition	Visual perceptual Language (NL)	Visual perceptual Language (NL condition only) Audio perceptual Audio visual	Visual perceptual Language (NL condition only)
Pool, Koolstra, & Van der Voort, 2003	Homework tasks paper & pencil memory	Background TVNL—soap opera NNL—music videos Radio music	Homework accuracy, time to complete & memory	None	Visual perceptual Language (NL)	Visual perceptual Language (NL) Audio (music) Language (NNL) Visual	Visual perceptual Language (NL)

(Continued)

Table 4.5 (Continued)

Studies	Task Input		Task Output		Systems Required		System Overlaps
	Task 1	Task 2	Task 1	Task 2	Task 1	Task 2	
Lin, Lee, & Robertson, 2011	Reading text	Background TV Attend TV	Answered questions about the reading	Memory of television content	Visual perceptual Language	Visual perceptual Language Audio perceptual Audio visual	Visual perceptual Language
Armstrong & Greenburg, 1990	Reading compreh. Mental flexibility Problem solving Linguistic processing Short-term memory	TV viewing & listening	Answered questions over text, completed puzzles, memory over memorization tasks, & completed creative thinking task	TV recognition	Visual perceptual Language Visual	Visual perceptual Language Audio visual	Visual perceptual Language
Srivastava, 2013	Reading online story	Listening to podcast	Recognition, cued & free recall of story	Cued and free recall of podcast	Visual perceptual Language	Audio perceptual Language	Language
Bowman, Levine, Waite, & Gendron, 2010	Reading textbook	Instant messaging	Memory for text	None	Visual perceptual Language	Visual perceptual Language	Visual perceptual Language

visual flanker task (one study), watching television (four studies), a memory test for something previously read (one study), a pattern matching task (one study), a virtual errands task (one study), a set of complex and simple cognitive tasks (two studies), and attending a lecture (one study). The non-focal tasks included listening to the radio (one study), background TV (five studies with TV unattended, four with TV attended), using a laptop (one study), background music (two studies), instant messaging (two studies), background music videos (two studies). Perusing the combinations reveals that some multitasking conditions are in fact dual task conditions—that is, performance on both tasks is measured (five studies). Most, however, include a focal and a background task and performance on only the focal task is measured.

The definition of perceptual and processing systems used in this analysis was rather general. First, for each of the tasks the input and output tasks (if any) were described and the system required to take in or put out information during the task was identified. All the tasks required either the visual or the audio perceptual systems to take in information. Second, the type of processing system required was coded into four broad categories: audio, visual, math, and language. The language category was chosen when the task information was in some language (either presented visually as text or as auditory spoken language). The audio category meant the information was audio but not language (usually music but sometimes a beep or a tone). The visual category meant that the information was visual but not language (pictures, spatial relationships, arrows, puzzles, etc.). As can be seen in the last column in Table 4.5, of the 18 task combinations only two had no system overlaps. One had only a visual perceptual system overlap. Three had only a language system overlap. The most common condition (13 studies) had a visual perceptual and a language overlap, and one study had visual perceptual, language, and visual processing overlap in some conditions. This means that there were only two studies where the tasks being combined in the multitasking condition did not require the same processing and/or perceptual system. By far the most common perceptual overlap was visual, and since the eyes cannot be pointed in multiple directions simultaneously and these studies did not present the visual information in the same location, it is virtually impossible for visual information to be taken in from both tasks simultaneously. In most (but not all) of these conditions, starting and stopping one of the visual tasks was under the control of the user (usually a reading, browsing, or question answering task) while the other visual task (usually TV watching and listening) was not under the user's control. Thus, the participant could choose when to look at one of the tasks—but when they made that choice they, by definition, could not take in visual information from the other task. In most of these conditions, the unstoppable task was considered to be the background task and performance was measured on the controlled task. However, in some cases performance was also measured on the uncontrolled task (Bowman et al., 2010; Pool et al., 2000, 2003).

The most common processing overlap (occurring in all but three studies) was a language overlap. In most cases, both tasks required the participant to process language information from both tasks, sometimes from the same perceptual channel and sometimes from different perceptual channels and often simultaneously. Yet we know from years of shadowing experiments that people cannot generally process multiple streams of language information (Broadbent, 1952, 1962).

In the next section we will summarize the results of this analysis and examine the extent to which the number and type of overlap influences the direction of the multitasking effect in these experiments for each of the performance measures (memory, task, and time to completion).

Analysis of the Results of the Studies

Table 4.6 is presented to begin the exploration into how different perceptual overlaps alter the direction of the multitasking effect. Table 4.6 combines the perceptual overlap information (from Table 4.5) with the results information (from Table 4.4) to present a list of studies and results based on shared perceptual overlaps. As can be seen in Table 4.6, there are 41 reported tests of single compared to multitask conditions. Table 4.7 provides a summary of the number of tests for each performance measure (memory, task, time to completion) and the percentage that found the single task condition to be better than the multitask condition. Of the 41 tests, 25 (61%), found better performance in the single task condition compared to the multitask condition. However, an examination of the column and line totals suggests that both the type of performance measure and the number of overlaps seem to influence the percentage of results reporting better performance in the single task compared to the multitask condition.

From the column totals we can see that the participants perform better in the single task compared to the multitask condition most frequently when memory accuracy tests are used (76.92%), followed by task accuracy tests (57.9%), and then by time to completion tests (44.44%). Looking at the row totals, one can see that participants perform better in the single task compared to the multitask condition most often when there are visual perceptual and native-language overlaps (77.27%), followed, interestingly enough, by no overlaps (75%), followed by language only (50%) and visual perceptual, native-language and visual overlaps (50%), and finally by visual perceptual, non-native-language overlaps (0%). In the next section, these summative findings are analyzed by dependent variable.

Memory Accuracy Measures

When task performance is measured using a post-multitasking memory test for information presented during the multitasking condition 76.92% (10 out of 13) of tests find the single task condition to be better. Of the three

Table 4.6 Results by Studies, Overlaps and Performance Measure

Studies	Overlaps	Memory Accuracy	Task Accuracy	Time to Completion
Law, Logie, & Pearson, 2006	None		ST > MT	ST > MT
Pratt, Willoughby, & Swick, 2011	None		ST > MT$_{complex}$ ST = MT$_{simple}$	
Furnham & Bradley, 1997	Language	ST > MT	ST > M$_{introverts}$ ST = MT$_{extroverts}$	
Voorveld, 2011	Language	MT$_{redundant}$ > ST		
Pool, Van der Voort, Beentjes, & Koolstra, 2000 Experiment 1	Visual perception/ Non-native language		ST = MT	ST = MT
Pool, Van der Voort, Beentjes, & Koolstra, 2000 Experiment 2	Visual perception/ Non-native language		ST = MT	ST = MT
Pool, Koolstra, & Van der Voort, 2003	Visual perception/ Non-native language			ST = MT
Pool, Van der Voort, Beentjes, & Koolstra, 2000 Experiment 1	Visual perception/ Native language		ST > MT	ST > MT
Pool, Van der Voort, Beentjes, & Koolstra, 2000 Experiment 2	Visual perception/ Native language		ST > MT	ST = MT
Pool, Koolstra, & Van der Voort, 2003	Visual perception/ Native language	ST > MT	ST > MT	ST = MT
Wang, David, Srivastava, Powers, Brady, D'Angelo, & Moreland, 2012	Visual perception/ Native language		ST > MT	
Lee, Lin, & Robertson, 2012	Visual perception/ Native language		ST > MT	
Hembrooke & Gay, 2003	Visual perception/ Native language	ST > MT		

(Continued)

Table 4.6 (Continued)

Studies	Overlaps	Memory Accuracy	Task Accuracy	Time to Completion
Armstrong & Chung, 2000	Visual perception/ Native language	ST > MT [TV during task] ST = MT [TV during memory accuracy task]		
Armstrong, Boiarsky, & Mares, 1991	Visual perception/ Native language	ST > MT		
Zhang, Jeong, & Fishbein, 2010	Visual perception/ Native language	ST > MT		
Fox, Rosen, & Crawford, 2009	Visual perception/ Native language		ST = MT	ST > MT
Lin, Lee, & Robertson, 2011	Visual perception/ Native language	ST > MT		
Bowman, Levine, Waite, & Gendron, 2010	Visual perception/ Native language	ST = MT		ST > MT
Srivastava, 2013	Visual perception/ Native language	ST > MT ST > MT ST > MT		
Armstrong & Greenburg, 1990	Visual perception/ Native language/ Visual		ST > MT [complex] ST > MT [complex] ST > MT [complex] ST = MT [simple] ST = MT [simple] ST = MT [simple]	

Table 4.7 Summary Results by Overlaps and Performance Measure

System Overlaps	Memory Accuracy			Task Accuracy			Time to Completion			Totals		
	(ST>MT)	(# of Tests)	(%)	(ST>MT)	(# of Tests)	(%)	(ST>MT)	(# of Tests)	(%)	(ST>MT)	(# of Tests)	(%)
None	0	0		2	3		1	1		3	4	75
Language	1	2		1	2		0	0		2	4	50
Visual perceptual/ Non-native language	0	0		0	2		3	3		0	5	0
Visual perceptual/ Non-native language	9	11		5	6		3	5		17	22	77.27
Visual perceptual/ Non-native language/visual	0	0		3	6		0	0		3	6	50
Totals	10	13	76.92	11	19	57.9	4	9	44.44	25	41	61

performance measures, memory accuracy has the most results where single tasking is better than multitasking (10 out of 13). The 10 which find memory accuracy in single tasking to be better than during multitasking are all post-tests given to participants about information presented previously in a single or multitasking condition. The three tests which find multitasking to be as good as single tasking are qualitatively different tests. In one of them, the reported test compares doing the memory accuracy test with or without background television for information previously learned in either a single or multitask condition (Armstrong & Chung, 2000). Hence, this is actually a test of whether multitasking during test taking harms the recall of previously learned information, and it did not. In the second qualitatively different test, multitasking is combined with content redundancy (Voorveld, 2011). Participants performed better in the multitasking condition when the information presented in the two tasks was redundant, but not if it was not redundant. In the third case (Bowman et al., 2010), participants read an online story and listened to a podcast serially or simultaneously. Post memory tests for the reading task did find the single task condition to be better than the multitask condition. But recall of the podcast (the non-focal task) did not vary by condition, it was always poor. If we removed these three tests from consideration, then it appears that in all tests where people are exposed to non-redundant information in a multitasking situation their ability to later remember the information from the focal task they were exposed to is reduced. However, multitasking at the time of memory task completion does not seem to influence the memory task and between task redundancy of information eliminates the multitasking difference.

Task accuracy measures.   When task accuracy of the focal task during the multitasking condition is used as the performance measure, 57.9% (11 out of 19) tests find the single task condition to be better than the multitask condition. Interestingly, when the multitask condition performs as well as the single task condition, there appear to be good reasons for this occurrence. In four of the tests (Armstrong & Greenberg, 1990; Pratt, Willoughby, & Swick, 2011) the no difference finding occurs in the simple condition of a complexity manipulation (complex vs. simple). In both cases, the simple tasks (four tests) showed no detriment in the multitasking condition while the complex tasks (four tests) showed better single task performance. In two cases the non-focal task was not in the participants native language (these studies had an English-language background music video condition and the participants were Dutch; Pool et al., 2000, 2003). In one case extroverts were compared to introverts and the introverts showed a multitasking deficit while the extroverts did not (Furnham & Bradley, 1997). For tests where both tasks were in the native language, no task was designed to be less complex, and no individual differences were tested 11 of 12 tests (91.67%) showed a multitasking deficit.

Task completion measures   Finally, of the nine studies that used task completion as a measure of performance four of them (44.44%) found the single task condition to be better than the multitask condition and five found no difference between the two. The five that found no difference all involved homework as the primary task with some kind of background media (Pool et al., 2000, 2003). Of the four that found faster completion in the single task condition three had simultaneous tasks of equal importance (Bowman et al., 2010; Fox, Rosen, & Crawford, 2009; Law, Logie, & Pearson, 2006) and one was a homework task with native language background media (Pool et al., 2000, experiment 1). Thus, it may be that simultaneous tasks are most likely to slow time to completion and background tasks are less likely to slow down a focal task.

Based on the above discussion, Table 4.8 produces a different organization of studies. The new categories are low complexity, moderate complexity, and high complexity. The one test with no overlap and no complexity manipulation, the five tests with non-native language background media, and the four tests with overlap and a simple condition are combined to create the low complexity manipulation. All the rest of the tests with overlaps and no complexity manipulation are combined to create the moderate complexity group. The remaining tests with overlaps and high complexity manipulation are combined to create the high complexity group. Overall, this produces a combined result of 25 out of 37 (67.57%) tests showing a multitasking decrement, demonstrating that multitasking decreases task performance in one way or another.

However, examining the rows suggests that difficulty (arising either from perceptual or processing overlaps or task complexity) is a major determinate of successful multitasking. When difficulty is low, only 37.5% of tests produce significantly better performance in the single task condition. At moderate levels, 72% demonstrate better single task performance and at high levels 100% have better single task performance. Taken altogether, the analysis strongly suggests that task accuracy during multitasking is influenced by system overlaps and by the difficulty of the focal task. When there are no processing overlaps or when tasks are simple, multitasking rarely influences test performance. However, when tasks are complex and there is overlap, multitasking always impairs task performance.

It is also useful to examine how the different performance measures fare across the three difficulty groups. It is worth noting that post-multitasking memory performance measures only exist in the moderate difficulty condition. This means that there are processing or perceptual system overlaps and the difficulty of the task is not manipulated. Therefore, we do not know if memory for information learned in a multitasking situation would be impaired if the tasks were simple or if there were no cognitive or perceptual overlaps. Nor do we know how memory would fare if complexity were high—though it seems likely that it would be worse.

Table 4.8 Summary Results by Overlaps and Performance Measure

System Overlaps	Memory Accuracy			Task Accuracy			Time to Completion			Totals		
	(ST>MT)	(# of Tests)	(%)	(ST>MT)	(# of Tests)	(%)	(ST>MT)	(# of Tests)	(%)	(ST>MT)	(# of Tests)	(%)
Low difficulty(no overlap or some overlap, simple tasks)	0	0	0	2	7	28.57	1	1	100	3	8	37.5
Moderate difficulty(some overlap, unspecified difficulty)	10	11	90.9	5	6	83.33	3	8	37.5	18	25	72
High difficulty(some overlap, complex task)	0	0	0	4	4	100	0	0	0	4	4	100
Totals	10	11	90.9	11	17	64.7	4	9	44.44	25	37	67.57

Task accuracy, that is how well tasks are being done during the multitasking condition, also declines with difficulty (low = 28.57%, moderate = 83.33%, high =100%). It is more difficult to draw conclusions about time to completion as there is only one test in the low difficulty condition and none in the high difficulty condition. At moderate levels of difficulty time to completion is faster during the single tasking condition only 37.5% of the time.

Conclusions and Recommendations

It seems clear from this review of the recent multitasking literature that there is a multiplicity of definitions of multitasking, theoretical approaches, operationalizations of multitasking, and measures of multitasking success. Future research should be designed in such a way as to carefully manipulate the important underlying variables (e.g., overlaps and complexity) and theoretically explicate how these differences influence specific outcomes. Further, future research might be designed so as to test various theories against one another rather than simply to test single theories.

Must we switch or is simultaneous task completion possible? First, can people perform tasks simultaneously or does multitasking always involve switching? Both viewpoints are represented in the studies reviewed here. However, studies which consider multitasking to be switching, perhaps very quickly, from one task to another, tend to operationalize their multitasking conditions in such a way that the tasks cannot be performed without switching. Either the tasks are performed on the same machine and participants must switch from one task to another, or the tasks require the same perceptual system or the same processing system, and therefore must be perceived or processed sequentially.

Future research should aim to design studies in which the tasks to be done do not share perceptual or processing system overlaps and attempt to determine if the tasks are being done sequentially or simultaneously. It seems likely that the answer to this question may not be a simple yes or no. Perhaps, some combinations of tasks can indeed be done simultaneously without task decrement. For example, physical tasks, such as walking, may easily be combined with auditory verbal comprehension tasks. In other words, an audiobook might be understood and remembered equally well when a person is walking or cleaning the house as when the person is sitting still. Indeed, some of the theories referenced here would suggest that the accompanying physical activity would increase physiological arousal and thereby improve the auditory processing task.

Other tasks, for example watching television and surfing the web, which clearly have a visual perceptual overlap and at times a language overlap, might alternate between task switching and simultaneous completion, depending on the contents of the incoming streams of information.

At times when the two incoming streams of information do not demand similar processing systems, simultaneous processing may occur; at other times, when the same system is required, the user may switch back and forth. In addition, if the two streams are redundant—for example watching a sporting event and following a twitter stream about the sporting event—the redundancy in the information streams may eliminate the multitasking deficit (Voorveld, 2011).

Do some theoretical approaches fare better than others?   Within the studies that involve simultaneous task completion, some version of the cognitive load, cognitive capacity model is almost always included in the theoretical rationale. Some also include distraction and interference type mechanisms as part of the theoretical explanation. In general, a fairly simple limited capacity model can easily explain the findings presented in Table 4.8. Basically, there are two things driving the extent to which multitasking reduces performance. One is the extent to which perceptual or processing systems are shared, and the other is task difficulty. Both of these are basic predictions of a limited capacity model.

To the extent that other models and theories are used to predict multitasking, it seems that it would be logical to include tasks in those studies which are designed to differentiate between a limited capacity explanation and some other explanation, such as threaded cognition (Wang et al., 2012) or structural versus content interference (Armstrong & Chung, 2000) rather than simply testing a single theoretical model by itself.

Operational Definitions of Multitasking

This chapter began with a very specific definition of media multitasking. Only papers which have people doing two tasks simultaneously, where one of the tasks was a media task, and where some measure of performance success was used, were included in the study. This was done to allow results to be compared across studies even though they had very different theoretical, conceptual and operational approaches to the problem. In the process of selecting studies for inclusion, it became clear that people use the word multitasking to describe many other situations. For example, in a recent paper, Yeykelis, Cummings, and Reeves (2014) also undertook a review of the multitasking literature. However, they defined multitasking as doing two or more tasks simultaneously on the same computer. They called this "multitasking on a computer." Many people consider media multitasking to be a subcategory of multitasking. In these cases, multitasking is usually defined as doing two tasks at the same time, either by switching or simultaneously, and it is media multitasking when one of the tasks is a media use task.

Obviously, all of these kinds of multitasking are of interest and can shed light both on how people engage in simultaneous activities at the cognitive, perceptual, or behavioral level and on questions about whether engaging in multiple tasks simultaneously causes neurological change or cognitive impairment (Pea et al., 2012). On the other hand, all types of multitasking and all combination of tasks do not produce the same results. Thus, rather than a single definition of multitasking we need to move towards a general theory of multitasking which strives to explain multiple outcomes (e.g., memory, performance, time to completion) for all combinations of tasks. Based on the analysis presented here, important variables in such a theory would be the perceptual, processing, and behavioral systems required by each of the tasks, the difficulty of each task, and what kind of behavior (memory, task accuracy, or time to completion) is being influenced by multitasking. This would allow different studies to add to scholars' knowledge of how different types of overlaps and different levels of complexity influence the various outcome measures. We hope that this would, eventually, increase understanding of the underlying mechanisms that both limit and enable our ability to engage in multiple activities simultaneously.

What about emotion?   While one study included in this group of papers considered arousal to be an important contributor to multitasking success (Zhang, Jeong, & Fishbein, 2010), the vast majority of studies and papers on multitasking pay no attention to either the emotional content of the tasks being performed or the emotional state of the user. One of the studies reviewed here suggested that arousal as a result of motivation to process would lead to maximum success in multitasking situations (Wang et al., 2012). Another study reviewed here manipulated the extent to which sexual content was included in the background television that was part of the media multitasking condition and theorized that this type of content might elicit attention and arousal and thereby increase or alter performance. While that study did not find an effect of sexual content on the multitasking performance, it is also the case that the multitasking condition involved a visual perceptual overlap and the sexual content was carried in the visual channel.

While people often engage in multitasking in order to save time, it is likely that they also engage in multitasking in order to make less pleasant tasks more pleasant. It would be interesting, in the future, to design experiments to examine the extent to which multitasking not only results in focal task performance changes, but also the extent to which it changes the multitaskers' emotional state and satisfaction.

Some recent studies have begun to actively examine how people's needs and gratifications influence both the decision to multitask and the outcomes of multitasking (Wang & Tchernev, 2012; Zhang & Zhang, 2012). These studies suggest that the primary gratification gained from multitasking may not be more efficient task performance but rather more enjoyable task performance. If this is the case, then it might be useful for future multitasking research to stop asking if various combinations of tasks decrease performance and to start asking what aspects of performance (better memory, time to completion, or task accuracy) are damaged, how much they are damaged, and if the increase in enjoyment is sufficient to make the loss in performance reasonable. So, if studying for a test while watching television is more fun, and it takes the same amount of time, but memory for what was studied is worse then maybe this is a bad idea if one's goal is to do well on the test.

Memory Versus Real-Time Accuracy

Finally, the findings from this analysis suggest that when there are system overlaps and the focal task is relatively complex, multitasking seems to interfere with our ability to store the information being learned in the multitasking condition. It would be useful if future research could determine which overlaps and which combinations of tasks are most likely to interfere with information storage and later memory retrieval as well as which combinations interfere less with memory processing. In other words, do students who study with background silence, radio, and TV have equal performance accuracy during multitasking and memory accuracy at a later time? The results of the analysis reported here suggest that the student who studies with music in the background and the student who studies in silence should perform equally well during the task and at a later time. However, the student who studies with the television in the background may or may not perform equally well in real time, but might have a deficit in memory for the information studied.

Concluding Remarks

Clearly people are concerned about the extent to which people multitask with media in modern America. A better understanding of the types of tasks and the types of processes which are and are not interfered with by multitasking seems to be an important goal. The results of this analysis suggest that our focus should be on the extent to which tasks have perceptual or processing system overlaps and the individual and combined difficulty of the two tasks. Clear definitions of what is meant by multitasking and a differentiation of the combinations of activities which do and do not lead to capacity limitations, cognitive overload, and task deficits, might also allow us to better understand the extent to which different types of multitasking, as opposed to multitasking in general, may play a role in task performance and enjoyment. In addition, future research should move beyond simple questions as to whether multitasking is bad and begin to tackle questions about exactly which combinations are bad for which particular outcome, whether multitasking leads to neurological change, whether decisions to engage in multitasking and/or performance outcomes differ as a function of individual differences, and the extent to which needs and gratifications drive multitasking.

References

Alzahabi, R., & Becker, M. W. (2013). The association between media multitasking, task-switching, and dual-task performance. *Journal of Experimental Psychology: Human Perception and Performance, 39*(5), 1485–1495. doi:10.1037/a0031208

Armstrong, G. B., & Chung, L. (2000). Background television and reading memory in context: Assessing TV interference and facilitative context effects on encoding versus retrieval processes. *Communication Research, 27*(3), 327–352. doi:10.1177/009365000027003003

Armstrong, G. B., & Greenberg, B. S. (1990). Background television as an inhibitor of cognitive processing. *Human Communication Research, 16*(3), 355–386. doi:10.1111/j.1468-2958.1990.tb00215.x

Armstrong, G. B., Boiarsky, G. A., & Mares, M. L. (1991). Background television and reading performance. *Communication Monographs, 58*(3), 235–253. doi:10.1177/009365000027003003

Bowman, L. L., Levine, L. E., Waite, B. M., & Gendron, M. (2010). Can students really multitask? An experimental study of instant messaging while reading. *Computers & Education, 54*(4), 927–931. doi:10.1016/j.compedu.2009.09.024.

Broadbent, D. E. (1952). Failures of attention in selective listening. *Journal of Experimental Psychology, 44*(6), 428–433. doi:10.1037/h0057163

Broadbent, D. E. (1962). Attention and perception of speech. *Scientific American, 206*(4), 143–151. doi:10.1038/scientificamerican0462-143

Fox, A. B., Rosen, J., & Crawford, M. (2009). Distractions, distractions: Does instant messaging affect college students' performance on a concurrent reading comprehension task? *Cyberpsychology & Behavior, 12*(1), 51–53. doi:10.1089/cpb.2008.0107

Furnham, A., & Bradley, A. (1997). Music while you work: The differential distraction of background music on the cognitive test performance of introverts and extraverts. *Applied Cognitive Psychology, 11*(5), 445–455. doi:10.1002/(sici)1099-0720(199710)11:5<445::aid-acp472>3.0.co;2-r

Hembrooke, H. G., & Gay, G. (2003). The laptop and the lecture: The effects of multitasking in learning environments. *Computing in Higher Education, 15*.

Jeong, S.-H., & Fishbein, M. (2007). Predictors of multitasking with media: Media factors and audience factors. *Media Psychology, 10*(3), 364–384. doi:10.1080.15213260701532948

Kahneman, D. (1973). *Attention and effort.* Englewood Cliffs, NJ: Prentice Hall.

Lang, A. (2000). The limited capacity model of mediated message processing. *Journal of Communication, 50*(1), 46–70. doi:10.1111/j.1460-2466.2006.00283.x

Lang, A. (2009). The limited capacity model of motivated mediated message processing. In R. L. Nabi. & M. B. Oliver (Eds.), *The Sage handbook of media processes and effects* (pp. 193–204). Los Angeles: Sage.

Law, A. S., Logie, R. H., & Pearson, D. G. (2006). The impact of secondary tasks on multitasking in a virtual environment. *Acta Psychologica, 122*(1), 27–44. doi:10.1016/j.actpsy.2005.09.002

Lee, J., Lin, L., & Robertson, T. (2012). The impact of media multitasking on learning. *Learning Media and Technology, 37*(1), 94–104. doi:10.1080/17439884.2010.537664

Lin, L., Lee, J., & Robertson, T. (2011). Reading while watching video: The effect of video content on reading comprehension and media multitasking ability. *Journal of Educational Computing Research, 45*(2), 183–201. doi:10.2190/EC.45.2.d

Lui, K. F. H., & Wong, A. C. N. (2012). Does media multitasking always hurt? A positive correlation between multitasking and multisensory integration. *Psychonomic Bulletin & Review, 19*(4), 647–653. doi:10.3758/s13423-012-0245-7

Ophir, E., Nass, C., & Wagner, A. D. (2009). Cognitive control in media multitaskers. *Proceedings of the National Academy of Sciences of the United States of America, 106*(37), 15583–15587. doi:10.1073/pnas.0903620106

Paas, F. G. W. C., & Van Merrienboer, J. J. G. (1994). Variability of worked examples and transfer of geometrical problem-solving skills—a cognitive-load approach. *Journal of Educational Psychology, 86*(1), 122–133. doi:10.1037/0022-0663.86.1.122

Pea, R., Nass, C., Meheula, L., Rance, M., Kumar, A., Bamford, H., & Zhou, M. (2012). Media use, face-to-face communication, media multitasking, and social well-being among 8- to 12-year-old girls. *Developmental Psychology, 48*(2), 327–336. doi:10.1037/a0027030

Pool, M. M., Koolstra, C. M., & Van der Voort, T. H. A. (2003). The impact of background radio and television on high school students, homework performance. *Journal of Communication, 53*(1), 74–87. doi:10.1093/joc/53.1.74

Pool, M. M., Van der Voort, T. H. A., Beentjes, J. W. J., & Koolstra, C. M. (2000). Background television as an inhibitor of performance on easy and difficult homework assignments. *Communication Research, 27*(3), 293–326. doi:10.1177/009365000027003002

Pratt, N., Willoughby, A., & Swick, D. (2011). Effects of working memory load on visual selective attention: Behavioral and electrophysiological evidence. *Frontiers in Human Neuroscience, 5*. doi:10.3389/fnhum.2011.00057

Salvucci, D. D., & Beltowska, J. (2008). Effects of memory rehearsal on driver performance: Experiment and theoretical account. *Human Factors, 50*(5), 834–844. doi:10.1518/001872008x354200

Shiffrin, R. M., & Schneider, W. (1977). Controlled and automatic human information processing: II Perceptual learning, automatic attending and a general theory. *Psychological Review, 84*, 127–189. doi:10.1037/0033-295x.84.2.127

Srivastava, J. (2013). Media multitasking performance: Role of message relevance and formatting cues in online environments. *Computers in Human Behavior, 29*, 888–895. doi:10.1016/j.chb.2011.06.016

Stephens, K. K., Cho, J. K., & Ballard, D. I. (2012). Simultaneity, sequentiality, and speed: Organizational messages about multiple-task completion. *Human Communication Research, 38*(1), 23–58. doi:10.1111/j.1468-2958.2011.01420.x

Voorveld, H. A. M. (2011). Media multitasking and the effectiveness of combining online and radio advertising. *Computers in Human Behavior, 27*(6), 2200–2206. doi:10.1016/j.chb.2011.06.016

Wang, Z., & Tchernev, J. M. (2012). The "myth" of media multitasking: Reciprocal dynamics of media multitasking, personal needs and gratifications. *Journal of Communication, 62*, 493–513. doi:10.1111/j.1460-2466.2012.01641.x

Wang, Z., David, P., Srivastava, J., Powers, S., Brady, C., D'Angelo, J., & Moreland, J. (2012). Behavioral performance and visual attention in communication multitasking: A comparison between instant messaging and online voice chat. *Computers in Human Behavior, 28*(3), 968–975. doi:10.1016/j.chb.2011.12.018

Yeykelis, L., Cummings, J. J., & Reeves, B. (2014). Multitasking on a single device: Arousal and the frequency, anticipation, and prediction of switching between media content on a computer. *Journal of Communication, 64*(1), 167–192.

Zhang, W., & Zhang, L. (2012). Explicating multitasking with computers: Gratifications and Situations. *Computers in Human Behavior, 28*(5), 1883–1891. doi:10.1016/j.chb.2012.05.006

Zhang, W., Jeong, S.-H., & Fishbein, M. (2010). Situational factors competing for attention. *Journal of Media Psychology, 22*. doi:10.1027/1864-1105/a000002

CHAPTER CONTENTS

5 Perspectives on Internet Addiction, Problematic Internet Use, and Deficient Self-Regulation

Contributions of Communication Research

Robert S. Tokunaga

University of Hawai'i at Mānoa

This chapter reviews the contributions of communication research in the study of Internet addiction, problematic Internet use, and deficient self-regulation. A history of media addictions is presented, with Internet addiction and its later refinements situated in their appropriate historical context. The study of Internet addiction, problematic Internet use, and deficient self-regulation originated from different perspectives, each with its unique implications for research. These perspectives can be understood in the context of Internet habits. This chapter closes with a discussion of key areas for future investigation. Recognizing gaps in the literature forecasts exciting new areas in the study of media habits.

Public concern about the social implications of Internet technologies has been ongoing since the inception of the Internet. Widespread debate about the dissocializing qualities of the Internet grew in scale on the public agenda after a number of seminal research projects, including the HomeNet Study (Kraut et al., 1998) and those conducted by Nie and his colleagues (Nie, Hillygus, & Erbring, 2002), reported data on impoverished social relationships associated with increased Internet use. Follow-up studies of Kraut and his associates (2002), however, demonstrated that the ill effects reported by participants in the initial HomeNet Study all but disappeared over time. Internet use instead fostered stronger social bonds and civic engagement. These findings together presented a diffuse, heterogeneous narrative of Internet participation. The Internet was at first vilified for its antisocial effects but later heralded for its prosocial values. The lack of consonance in the findings of HomeNet and other similar studies pointed to a complex media selection process users undergo during initial engagement with the Internet (Tokunaga, 2013).

The findings were reported almost contemporaneously with an area of research on maladaptive[1] Internet use that, at the time, provided a tenable theoretical framework for contextualizing these mixed results. The proliferation of this research was rapid and drew notice worldwide following Young's (1996) initial treatise on the topic (Young, Yue, & Ying, 2011). Over the next two decades, Internet researchers debated how best to situate and understand results from the HomeNet Study and this so-called maladaptive Internet use.

Over 350 theoretical and empirical articles were dedicated to supporting various perspectives of maladaptive Internet use (Byun et al., 2009; Tokunaga & Rains, 2010). Although this phenomenon has enjoyed considerable attention in scholarly writing, conceptual ambiguity still surrounds its definition and interpretation. Communication researchers have even questioned whether it is appropriate to use the label "maladaptive" and argue that these seemingly problematic forms of Internet use lie within the parameters of normal Internet habits. LaRose (2009, 2010, 2011), for instance, views the inability to regulate media use as a normal condition for Internet users and disagrees with those who describe uncontrolled Internet use as inherently problematic, malignant, or maladaptive.

Much of the disagreement among the labels and descriptions reflects the different theoretical perspectives from which the phenomenon under discussion was conceptualized. This pattern of Internet use has been interpreted as an addiction or pathology (Brenner, 1997; Scherer, 1997; Young, 1996, 1998), a cognitive-behavioral problem (Caplan, 2002, 2003, 2005; Davis, 2001), or a deficiency in self-regulation or habit (LaRose, 2010; LaRose & Eastin, 2004; LaRose, Lin, & Eastin, 2003; Tokunaga, 2013). The confusion generated by these inconsistent interpretations has somewhat delegitimized the construct and opened its body of research to critical reception (Ha et al., 2006; Tokunaga, 2014).

Media selection processes and media effects have been important items on the agenda of communication research. Media researchers have long been interested in how consumers select their media and the effects media use has on them (Slater, 2007). Media habits and deficient self-regulation (DSR) offer alternative explanations of consumptions patterns to the dominant rational selection models of media use (e.g., uses and gratifications, media dependency theory, media richness theory) that have long prevailed. Habits explain the sometimes nonconscious choices that consumers make when selecting media, which is fundamentally incompatible with theories maintaining that media use involves thoughtful selections. Problematic Internet use (PIU) can also explain the transitory ill effects of Internet consumption (e.g., failed relationships, poor academic performance) when it falls out of one's control (Caplan, 2002, 2005). The hypothesized reciprocal relationship between the effects and selection of Internet use reflects the reinforcing spiral framework (Slater, 2007). Maladaptive Internet use is therefore unmistakably a communication research problem.

Research on maladaptive Internet use at this stage would benefit from a critical reflection on and reconciliation of the pervasive differences in terminology and conceptual definitions of Internet addiction, PIU, and DSR. Future areas of inquiry that require attention can be inferred by identifying gaps in knowledge or methodological shortcomings. The following sections provide a general overview of the history of media addiction research and a description of three perspectives from which the idea of maladaptive Internet use has been interpreted.

Tradition of Studying Media Addictions

The study of media addictions grew in prevalence following the large-scale adoption of televisions in households, but general interest in media addictions dates back to the 1940s. Cartoons and news stories commonly depicted men falling prey to the "addictive" qualities of radios, but addiction in the earliest form was characterized as the almost obsessive attention males devoted to maintaining quality broadcast signals so that programs or music could be heard without impediment (Butsch, 1998). Although the idea of radio addiction seemed no more than a source of satire at first (Levinson, 2010), the empirical study of radio addiction emerged in response to the supposed deleterious effects of radio programs on their listeners.

Preston (1941) was among the first to write about the addictive qualities of media. She described media addiction as "giving oneself over to a habit-forming practice very difficult to overcome, no matter how the aftereffects are dreaded" (p. 147–148). Interest in media addictions flourished as children and adolescents were observed developing habitual media consumption practices, interpreted then as addiction, to radio programs and movie films. From the outset of media addiction research, the imprecise term "addiction" involved value judgments about the set of behaviors it comprised, which persists today. Media addiction was operationalized as the number of horror movies or radio crime programs that children were exposed to in a given week. In theorizing about radio addiction, it was proposed that listeners became addicted to the content transmitted through the media (e.g., crime stories), not the medium itself (Rowland, 1944). The effects of movies and radio programs on children identified as addicts included sleeplessness, nervousness, and general health problems (Preston, 1941).

The study of media addictions subsided until anecdotal reports of individuals with television addiction appeared in mainstream media (Goleman, 1990; Winn, 1977). Marshall McLuhan (1964, 1978) seminally discussed the addictive qualities of the television, referring to it as a drug. People in the public, including parents, teachers, and professionals, came to recognize television addiction as a legitimate and genuine disorder that warranted critical attention (Winn, 1977). This addiction was described as a dependency, similar to pathological gambling, marked by prolonged involuntary exposure to the television (Kubey, 1996; McIlwraith, 1998).

Television addiction was conceptualized as a multidimensional phenomenon consisting of three key elements: (a) a loss of control that results in too much time spent watching television, (b) unsuccessful attempts to reduce excessive television use, and (c) functional impairment (i.e., mild difficulties in social and professional life) that grows out of exposure (Kubey, 1990). Several measures of television addiction, some using adapted items from instruments of substance dependence found in the *Diagnostic and Statistical Manual of Mental Disorders* (3rd ed., rev.; DSM-III-R; American Psychiatric Association, 1987), were developed and used in research (Horvath, 2004; Kubey,

1990; McIlwraith, 1990; Smith, 1986). The proportion of individuals who self-identified as television addicts or were determined to suffer from addiction through a measure's predetermined cut-off points was relatively small (McIlwraith, 1990; Smith, 1986).

Research on television addiction provided a better understanding of the broader construct of media addiction. Self-labeled television addicts were more likely than nonaddicted viewers to spend time watching television, watch television to pass the time and relieve boredom, and use television viewing to escape from unpleasant or aversive moods often caused by psychosocial problems, such as loneliness and depression (Schallow & McIlwraith, 1986–1987; Steiner, 1963). Television programs offered viewers moments of relaxation and relief from stress, which provided initial gratification and precipitated later addiction (Kubey, 1990; Kubey & Csikszentmihalyi, 1990). The content aired through the television was not proposed as the source of the addiction; instead, individuals were said to form dependency to the television itself (McIlwraith, Jacobvitz, Kubey, & Alexander, 1991). This meant that addiction could emerge no matter what content was aired.

The study of video game addiction had begun to receive attention at about the same time research brought awareness to television addiction. The criteria for detecting video game addiction were largely informed by early work on television addiction (Greenfield, 1984). Characteristics of video game addiction include spending excessive time playing video games, sacrificing important possessions, and being acutely aware of a video game problem but having little capacity to regain control (Fisher, 1994). Various measures of video game addiction, often based on diagnostic criteria for pathological gambling, were proposed (Fisher, 1994; Griffiths, 1992; Griffiths & Dancaster, 1995; Phillips, Rolls, Rouse, & Griffiths, 1995). The content of the video game (e.g., character development, absorption) and the characteristics of the medium (e.g., quality graphics and sound, complex skill development) were together viewed as contributing factors in the development of the addiction (Phillips et al., 1995; Wood, Griffiths, Chappell, & Davies, 2004). The proportion of children and adolescents with video game addiction ranged from 6% to 20% (Egli & Meyers, 1984; Fisher, 1994; Griffiths & Hunt, 1998; Hauge & Gentile, 2003; Phillips et al., 1995). Impairment in the form of declining academic grades (Egli & Meyers, 1984) and poorer social skills (Zimbardo, 1982) were related to this addiction.

The tradition of studying media addictions persisted as concerns surfaced about the addictive qualities of many new media adopted on a large scale. For this reason, it was not unexpected that the Internet, in its many forms, was targeted for its addictive potential. Dystopian views of the Internet had been raised since its inception and critical adoption (Lea, O'Shea, Fung, & Spears, 1992; Katz & Rice, 2002; Wellman, 1997), but specific characterizations of the Internet as an addictive medium had begun to appear in the early to mid-1990s. Personal accounts of individuals with signs of addiction to Internet use began to emerge, which captured the attention of clinicians and scientists (Moore, 1995;

O'Neill, 1995; Rheingold, 1993). Healthcare practitioners reported growing numbers of patients with psychological and behavioral symptoms consistent with an Internet addiction (Orzack, 1999). Anecdotal cases and increasing fears of Internet addiction appearing in popular press generated considerable awareness on this topic (Payne, 2006).

The public's concerns about Internet addiction paralleled rising interest in the phenomenon within the scientific community. A large body of research that attempted to understand the conditions fostering Internet addiction and its implications on Internet users was amassed in the relatively short period of time. Prevalence estimates from this research suggest that somewhere between 1% and 5% of Internet users suffer from this type of addiction (Morahan-Martin, 2008; Tokunaga & Rains, 2010). The signs of Internet addiction include growing investment in Internet activities, experiencing aversive moods when away from the Internet, increasing tolerance for Internet use, and denying a problem exists (Kandell, 1998).

Legitimacy of an Internet Addiction

The emergence of systematic research on Internet addiction, initially interpreted as a clinical disorder, was soon met with critics who altogether dismissed the idea of a psychological dependence to the Internet (Grohol, 1999; Shaffer, Hall, & Vander Bilt, 2000). These critical evaluations were not surprising given that similar questions about the legitimacy of other media addictions preceded them. For instance, concerns about the validity of instruments that measured media addictions had previously been raised (Charlton & Danforth, 2007). Several items used to diagnose video game addiction instead purportedly measured high levels of engagement. In other words, these instruments captured time management problems or underlying disorders rather than an addiction. Wood (2007) also contended that media addiction research was fueled more by anecdotal experiences and public hysteria than legitimate empirical investigation. Livingstone (1999) summarized confusion about the notion of a media addiction by questioning whether it should be interpreted as a "pattern of media use, a psychological condition, the outcome of social deprivation, or a scapegoat constructed by a moral majority" (p. 67).

Questions have likewise been raised about whether Internet addiction should be considered a unique disorder or a condition indicative of other primary problems in one's life (Shaffer et al., 2000). Ha et al. (2006) echoed these sentiments in explaining that Internet addiction has been interpreted as "a genuine diagnosis, a new symptom manifestation of underlying disorders or psychosocial problems in adjusting to a new medium" (p. 821–822). This central issue has been neither reconciled nor exhaustively tested in research. It is nevertheless an important one to consider because validity of the accumulated research on Internet addiction, problematic Internet use (PIU), and the deficient self-regulation of Internet use (DSR) rests on whether some kind of maladaptive consumption pattern involving the Internet truly exists.

Research in the communication field has attempted to answer some of the formative questions about the legitimacy of this pattern of media use. This work was done on PIU, which refers to a mild, emergent, possible form of, phase of, indication of, or approximation of what is regarded as Internet addiction in other research camps. Caplan (2007) discovered that PIU could explain functional impairment, or difficulties in one's personal and professional life, beyond what was uniquely predicted by psychosocial problems. In other words, the variance in outcomes explained by "underlying disorders" could be disentangled from the proportion of variance accounted for by PIU. Another study conducted almost a decade later provided additional evidence for inferring the existence of PIU. A longitudinal study of incoming college freshmen found that PIU predicts difficulties in familial relationships, friendships, and academics or occupational responsibilities while controlling for underlying problems, such as social anxiety, loneliness, and depression (Tokunaga, 2014). This mediation provided further support for viewing PIU as a legitimate construct that could be distinguished from underlying disorders.

Research has not yet substantively tackled all existential and ontological issues of this so-called Internet addiction. LaRose (2010) theorized that media habits and DSR, or a loss of conscious self-control over Internet use, exist in that they have real-world implications on Internet users but argues that habitual media consumption patterns and even the mild life difficulties resulting from them fall within the parameters of ordinary Internet use, not something interpretably malignant. It could also be argued that a predisposition to think of one's own Internet use as maladaptive or disordered is responsible for self-reported levels of Internet addiction. That is, Internet addiction may be capturing the propensity of individuals with psychosocial problems to think of their own Internet use or self as pathological, a product of underlying vulnerabilities, which would still explain the reliable relationship between Internet addiction and psychosocial problems. Future empirical work on Internet addiction should continue to address the important formative questions.

Despite the large collection of research accumulated on Internet addiction, still relatively little is known about this phenomenon. LaRose et al. (2003) argued that even the label "Internet addiction" is inappropriate because the way it is characterized in the literature is at odds with the disease model. They instead suggest that symptoms of Internet addiction should be interpreted as indicators of nonconscious media habits or conscious failures of self-regulation. The term might also be confused with alternative constructions of addiction as something highly enjoyable and involving. In the literature, Internet addiction has been called pathological Internet use, PIU, and DSR among other labels. These labels vary by theoretical perspectives, which have important implications for phenomenal understanding. There is endemic agreement across these perspectives in that all include an element of uncontrollability, but beyond this consistency lies considerable disparity in how this phenomenon is interpreted.

Three Perspectives of Maladaptive Internet Use

Several strands of research on media addictions (e.g., television, video games) provide the foundation for discussing maladaptive Internet use. This concept originated from three independent intellectual camps: the addiction perspective, the cognitive-behavioral perspective, and the social cognitive perspective. These three positions generally reference the same phenomenon but respectively refer to it as Internet addiction, PIU, and DSR. The addiction perspective treats Internet addiction as a pathology or disease that shares common traits with substance dependencies, such as drug abuse, and impulse control disorders, such as pathological gambling (Brenner, 1997; Scherer, 1997; Young, 1998, 1999). The cognitive-behavioral perspective interprets PIU as a set of maladaptive thoughts and actions involving Internet use (Caplan, 2002; Davis, 2001). The social cognitive perspective understands DSR as lapses in the successful management of Internet use caused by a deficiency in observation, judgment, and self-reaction (LaRose & Eastin, 2004; LaRose et al., 2003). Although the three perspectives have independently received empirical support, no one perspective is solely able to explain the process of this media consumption pattern in its entirety. More recently, noteworthy attempts have been made to integrate the varied approaches for better explanatory and predictive utility (e.g., LaRose, Kim, & Peng, 2011; Tong, Vitak, & LaRose, 2010). The next sections offer a historical background of the three perspectives to make sense of the often disparate ways that researchers describe maladaptive Internet use.

"Maladaptive" Internet Use from an Addiction Perspective

The earliest approach to understanding maladaptive Internet use was equating it to a disease or pathology and labeling it Internet addiction (Beard & Wolf, 2001; Griffiths, 1997, 1998; Pratarelli, Browne, & Johnson, 1999; Shaffer et al., 2000; Shotton, 1991). Addiction refers to the persistent use of a stimulus accompanied by compulsive urges, a perceptual loss of control over a behavior, and undesirable personal problems traced to the behavior (Bozarth, 1990; Koob & Bloom, 1998). From this perspective, Internet addiction is characterized as a pathology akin to substance dependence or an impulse control disorder.

Tolerance and withdrawal are important components of substance dependencies (Nathan, 1991). Tolerance is identified by a need for larger doses of a chemical substance to obtain previously-achieved levels of pleasure or euphoria (Babor, 1992). Withdrawal occurs when a substance is abruptly discontinued in an addiction, resulting in anxiety, depression, or cravings (Koob & Moal, 1997). Behavioral addictions, however, can occur in the absence of a chemical substance. Addictive behaviors emerge when a repetitive habit transitions to a loss of control despite efforts to abstain from or moderate the behavior (Marlatt, Baer, Donovan, & Kivlahan, 1988). The same loss of control is said to be subjectively experienced by individuals self-identified or diagnosed with

Internet addiction. Internet addicts require larger amounts of Internet exposure to achieve previously experienced levels of pleasure, underscoring the tolerance component, and feel withdrawal while away from the Internet (Kandell, 1998; Young, 1998). Using functional magnetic resonance images, recent studies observed structural neurological differences and neurochemical changes in dopamine, which satisfies pleasure centers of the brain, between Internet addicts and nonaddicts (Kuss & Griffiths, 2012). In some instances, self-identified Internet addicts may be able to recognize the uncontrollability but not see the loss of control as pathological. Uncontrollability may even be trivialized or embraced in cases where Internet users desire temporal distortions and losses of self-consciousness (Chou & Ting, 2003; Thatcher, Wretschko, & Fridjhon, 2008).

The impulse control disorder perspective is able to inform part of the Internet addiction process. Impulsivity, a personality trait marked by risk taking and hasty choices, originates from a decision to engage in an activity that seeks short-term gains at the expense of long-term losses (Lesieur & Rosenthal, 1991; Marlatt et al., 1988). Control over these impulses relies on successful emotional self-regulation, which those who suffer from impulse control disorders often lack (Tice, Bratslavsky, & Baumeister, 2001). Impulse control disorders, such as pathological gambling, are identified by preoccupation to and compulsive uses of a stimulus, similar to symptoms found in substance dependencies.

Several models and theories have been proposed in the Internet addiction framework. Internet addiction in later adulthood may grow out of weak parent-child attachments (Lei & Wu, 2007) and other problems originating in the family unit (Yen, Yen, Chen, Chen, & Ko, 2007). Young (1998) suggested that a lack of experience on the Internet may be a principal cause of Internet addiction; addicts have very little experience using the Internet, whereas nonaddicts possess greater Internet expertise. Accordingly, Internet addiction may be the manifestation of adjustment issues at the early stages of Internet use. In the ACE model (Young, Griffin-Shelley, Cooper, O'Mara, & Buchanan, 2000), it is proposed that functions of the Internet, Internet affordances, accessibility to others, and escape from the offline world serve as gratifying external cues that hasten addiction. A high degree of control over social interactions is an important affordance provided to Internet users (Leung, 2004).

Serious functional impairment is a necessary condition for a behavior to be classified as an addiction (Grant, Levine, Kim, & Potenza, 2005; Moreyra, Ibanez, Saiz-Ruiz, & Blanco, 2004). Internet addicts encounter acute difficulties managing vital aspects of their lives, including professional performance (Kubey, Lavin, & Barrows, 2001; Nalwa & Anand, 2003; Thatcher, Wretschko, & Fisher, 2008; Young & Rogers, 1998) and interpersonal relationships (Young, 1998). Irregular sleep patterns from late-night Internet sessions explain these growing academic or occupational problems. Internet addicts can also experience health issues, such as increased vulnerability to disease, from fatigue and subsequent weakened immune systems (Young, 1999).

Several conceptual issues emerge with applying the mental disease or pathology metaphor to maladaptive Internet use (see Warden, Phillips, & Ogloff, 2004, for discussion). One problem with using the term addiction is that it trivializes "real" or medically recognized addictions, such as substance dependence (Jaffe, 1990). Pies (2009) argued that the term addiction loses its meaning if every craving represents a symptom of addiction, yet researchers continue to pathologize these developmentally normal behaviors. In fact, the more general failure of researchers to consent to a uniform definition of Internet addiction reduces the legitimacy of the addiction model approach (Warden et al., 2004). The second issue is that the preponderance of evidence on the negative consequences of Internet addiction is derived from scales that have yet to be substantively validated (Shaffer et al., 2000). In the absence of validated screening procedures, a trained clinician, not the self-administered scales currently in use, must evaluate these negative consequences and determine whether a behavioral addiction or impulse control disorder exists. The third concern of the addiction perspective is that mania is not eliminated as a plausible explanation. Mania is described in the *DSM* (4th ed., text rev.; *DSM-IV-TR*; American Psychiatric Association, 2000) as a period of defined irritable, elevated, or unrestrained mood. Pathological gambling, for example, can be diagnosed only in the absence of a manic episode. The failure of empirical research to ensure that mania is not comorbid with the behavioral pathology weakens the addiction perspective (Shaffer et al., 2000). Decisive evidence that disentangles the behavioral addiction from psychopathologies is necessary to put Internet addiction in the company of substance dependencies and impulse control disorders (Ha et al., 2006; Wallace, 1999). Finally, cases of spontaneous remission without clinical intervention for supposed Internet addicts, reported in various studies, challenge this addiction or pathology characterization (Ko, Yen, Chen, Chen, & Yen, 2007; van Rooij, Schoenmakers, Vermulst, van den Eijnden, & van de Mheen, 2011). Despite these conceptual problems, the mental disease metaphor has been the predominant approach used in developing measures and diagnostic criteria (LaRose et al., 2003).

The unsystematic nature of research on Internet addiction was recently exposed in deliberations on whether to include Internet use disorder in the most recent *DSM* (5th ed.; *DSM-5*; American Psychiatric Association [APA], 2013). Members and advisors serving on a behavioral addictions workgroup for the *DSM-5* reviewed hundreds of articles on Internet addiction. The workgroup noted a lack of standardized diagnostic criteria, conceptual inconsistencies, unclear etiology, and an absence of underlying theory in the body of research on Internet addiction (Petry & O'Brien, 2013). Despite considerable pressure from clinicians to add Internet addiction to the list of behavioral addictions, Internet use disorder was excluded from the manual altogether. However, a specific form of Internet addiction, Internet gaming disorder, was included in Section III as a recommended area for future study aside other conditions, such as caffeine use disorder (APA, 2013). The workgroup recognized that more programmatic research on Internet addiction and Internet gaming disorder is necessary before it will entertain their inclusion in the main text of future revisions.

"Maladaptive" Internet Use from a Cognitive-Behavioral Perspective

PIU, discussed from a cognitive-behavioral perspective, exists in the middle range of the maladaptive Internet use continuum. Cognitive distortions and deficiencies in behavioral control over Internet use are markers of PIU (Caplan, 2002, 2010; Davis, 2001; Davis, Flett, & Besser, 2002). The cognitive approach understands human behavior as a function of cognitions (Newell & Simon, 1976), whereas behavioral theorists assert that human behaviors are a reflection of people's personalities (Maultsby & Wirga, 1998). This perspective departs from the addiction approach because cognitive-behavioral models focus on cognitions as a main source of maladaptive behaviors. Various perspectives on human agency preceding cognitive-behavioral models were concerned with only emotional or behavioral responses to stimuli and ignored the role of cognitions altogether. The cognitive-behavioral perspective also accepts the position that PIU coexists with and even stems from mania and attendant psychopathologies (Davis, 2001), moving PIU out of the domain of an addiction or impulse control disorder. Maladaptive cognitions, including rumination, self-distortions, and low self-efficacy in social interactions, impair self-control (Caplan, 2010).

An important distinction between specific and generalized PIU is made in this approach. In specific PIU, people develop maladaptive cognitions and behaviors to content found on the Internet, including gaming, shopping, and social interactions with online others (Davis, 2001; Whang, Lee, & Chang, 2003). Because specific PIU is bound to content, some argue that the Internet merely acts as a conduit to the content that people are using problematically (Davis, 2001). Conversely, generalized PIU is described as a multidimensional overuse of the Internet wherein certain broader characteristics of the medium (e.g., anonymity, asynchronicity) instigate maladaptive uses. Caplan (2002) suggested that individuals with generalized PIU are "drawn to the experience of being online, in and of itself" (p. 556). Generalized PIU has been criticized because it "overlooks the potentially important role played by the uses of specific Internet technologies in the development of PIU" (Tokunaga & Rains, 2010, p. 532). Nevertheless, the conceptual distinction between specific and generalized PIU is important because it lends insight into the exact Internet stimuli to which people develop problematic uses.

The cognitive-behavioral model (Caplan, 2002, 2003, 2005; Davis, 2001; Davis et al., 2002) provides structure and organization to the discussion of causal factors of PIU. The model was founded on a diathesis-stress framework, where preexisting psychosocial problems act as the diathesis and life stressors operate as the stress. PIU is the product of collaboration between psychosocial problems and stress. Social isolation and a lack of social support also make individuals vulnerable to problematic uses of the Internet. Davis

(2001) explained that social isolation and social support deficiency are proximal causes (i.e., central factors) of PIU, whereas psychological problems are distal predictors (i.e., noncentral but important factors).

PIU models have been empirically investigated in communication research. Caplan (2003) tested the cognitive-behavioral model by treating social anxiety, loneliness, and depression as preexisting diatheses. Individuals with these problems are highly motivated to seek Internet-based communication, considering it a minimal-risk activity, and eventually develop PIU (Caplan, 2006). Deficiency in social skills, which indicates an inability to communicate with others in an appropriate and effective manner (Spitzberg & Cupach, 1989; Segrin & Givertz, 2003), also predicts PIU (Caplan, 2005). The relationships between PIU and psychosocial problems or social skills deficiencies are mediated by what Caplan (2003, 2005, 2010) calls a preference for online social interactions, described as "beliefs that one is safer, more efficacious, more confident, and more comfortable with online interpersonal interactions and relationship than with traditional face-to-face social activities" (Caplan, 2003, p. 629). PIU is succeeded by social and professional impairment, which is interpretably milder than the serious negative consequences discussed in the addiction perspective. These empirical tests, however, are often conducted using cross-sectional data, with some notable exceptions (e.g., Tokunaga, 2014). Path models of PIU provide initial support for assumptions of causality, but temporal precedence and other necessary conditions for inferring causation have not been conclusively established.

"Maladaptive" Internet Use from Social Cognitive and Habit Perspectives

Social cognitive theory (Bandura, 1986, 1989) has been used to explain DSR, a transitory state in which conscious self-control over a behavior that typically lies under one's volitional control is lost (LaRose, Mastro, & Eastin, 2001). Human behaviors are controlled by an internal balance between external and self-generated sources of influence (Bandura, 1991). People rely on self-observation to audit or regulate their behaviors and the effects of their behaviors on others. A judgment is made by weighing self-observed behaviors against personal standards and social norms. Self-reactive incentives in the form of rewards are applied to behaviors deemed appropriate, and punishment is used to modify inappropriate behaviors.

Behavioral regulation relies on accurate observations of one's behavior and determining whether its frequency lies within the boundaries of normal performance (Bandura, 1999). People can be confronted, however, with a loss of conscious self-control over a behavior when a disruption occurs in the observation, judgment, or incentive application stages (LaRose et al., 2001). Inaccurate observations of one's Internet use, distorted judgments of normative Internet use, or absences in reward or punishment application represent process malfunctions that undermine Internet self-control (LaRose, 2010).

Self-regulation often fails when profound cognitive immersion in an activity overwhelms the subprocesses necessary to control active media selection (Tokunaga, 2013).

Theorists have invoked outcome expectations as a possible explanation for the loss of conscious self-regulation over Internet use. Prior experiences with a stimulus inform expectations of future interactions through a process of enactive learning. Enactive learning occurs when individuals forecast outcomes of exposure to a stimulus using previous direct or vicarious experiences with it (LaRose & Eastin, 2004). Observational learning through shared codes also informs anticipated expectations of media use (LaRose et al., 2011). The valence of direct or indirect encounters with media shapes one's anticipation of future media use. Prospective positive or negative evaluations of media use are intimately associated with the likelihood of DSR development (LaRose et al., 2001).

Normal Internet use falls out of control when cognitive links are made between Internet use and certain enticing incentives that users are motivated to pursue. These rewards may be behavioral or psychological in nature (LaRose et al., 2001, 2003). Many different expectations can be forecasted for Internet use, including improved self-esteem, enhanced social relationships, and mood regulation (LaRose & Eastin, 2004; LaRose et al., 2003; Song, LaRose, Eastin, & Lin, 2004). The anticipated reward of escaping life stressors through media, for example, is a strong predictor of DSR (LaRose & Eastin, 2004; LaRose et al., 2003; Lin, 1999).

Social cognitive theory has been used to explain why Internet use falls out of one's control when certain vulnerabilities impair the operation of the self-regulatory subfunctions (LaRose et al., 2001, 2003). Personal vulnerabilities, such as psychosocial problems, elicit inner conflicts that serve as a barrier to the successful self-regulation of certain behaviors (Bandura, 1991; Emmons & King, 1988; van Hook & Higgins, 1988). Internet use is one of those behaviors that may spiral out of control when depressed. Depression generates negative cognitive biases that hinder self-regulatory processes (LaRose et al., 2003). These biases prejudice beliefs about one's efficacy to self-regulate personal behaviors and inhibit accurate observation, judgment, or incentive application.

The strength model explanation for self-regulatory failures provides a final explanation for the loss of conscious self-regulation over Internet use. Inadequate strength to override impulsive thoughts of performing a behavior is responsible for self-regulatory failures (Baumeister, Heatherton, & Tice, 1994). The strength of self-regulation can be interpreted as a finite or limited resource. Because generalized self-control is a limited resource, the strength of regulating one behavior comes at the cost of regulating all other behaviors (Baumeister & Heatherton, 1996). The regulation of emotional distress, for instance, weakens the self-regulation of behaviors otherwise under one's volitional control (Tice et al., 2001). In the case of Internet use, the limited resources necessary to regulate or modify unpleasant moods would be redirected from the resources already in place to self-regulate Internet consumption. Internet use would be placed on a so-called automatic mode, being performed without conscious attention to the outcomes of its performance, during moments of ego depletion and ensuing emotional regulation. The strength model thus accounts for the robust relationship between psychosocial problems and DSR but offers an alternative framework for understanding deregulation by underscoring one's limited resources for simultaneously regulating multiple behaviors. These rational-based explanations for media attendance, however, ignore consumption patterns that occur without conscious intention.

More recently, the notion of media habits has been used to refine social cognitive explanations for losses of conscious self-control over Internet use. Habits rival the prevailing theories and perspectives of media selection, such as uses and gratifications (Lin, 1999; Papacharissi & Rubin, 2000). The uses and gratifications approach explains that media consumers rationally select media that satisfy specific needs (Katz, Blumler, & Gurevitch, 1974). Alternatively, media habits are automatic and do not involve conscious intentions (Verplanken & Wood, 2006; Yin & Knowlton, 2006). Habits are learned actions that may be performed without awareness, attention, intention, or cortical control (LaRose, 2010). Individuals who repeatedly perform a rewarding behavior under stable circumstances undergo cognitive reorganization to make future performance of the behavior less effortful, thereby making the learned actions more automatic.

Habitual media use works in concert with conscious intentions to influence one's overall media consumption patterns (LaRose, 2010; LaRose & Eastin, 2004; LaRose et al., 2003). Conscious intentions stem from the immediate outcomes individuals anticipate from their Internet use, whereas habits are sustained by long-term average outcome expectations (LaRose, 2010; LaRose & Eastin, 2004; Wood & Neal, 2007). These habits are not inherently bad but can transition into problematic behaviors under certain conditions. Bad habits emerge when individuals are unable to modify behaviors that begin to fall out of their control (LaRose et al., 2011). That is, the incapacity to reward normative Internet use or sanction negative behaviors leads to uncontrollability (LaRose, 2011). It is also possible for individuals to lose control over their Internet use without ever developing Internet habits.

The addiction, cognitive-behavioral, and social cognitive perspectives hold different assumptions about Internet addiction, PIU, and DSR, and come to different conclusions about its impact on Internet users. Recent efforts to reconcile some of the differences in interpretation through empirical investigations have helped to distinguish these explanations; yet, more of this type of research is necessary to evaluate the merits of the heterogeneous arguments advanced in the various perspectives. Tokunaga and Rains (2010), for instance, tested competing assumptions about the nature of the relationships between psychosocial problems, time spent using the Internet, and unregulated Internet use presented in the addiction and social cognitive perspectives. The findings, using estimates drawn from meta-analyses, revealed that the data were consistent with social cognitive explanations and inconsistent with the addiction perspective. This and other studies (e.g., Caplan, 2010) find consistent support for social cognitive and cognitive-behavioral explanations when evaluated against alternative positions.

Findings from studies that compare conceptual perspectives are not meant to discredit research and theory on Internet addiction. Although evidence from Tokunaga and Rains's (2010) meta-analytic study provides support for social cognitive explanations over competing addiction explanations, the studies analyzed used samples taken from the normal population of Internet users. The results might look different if the studies meta-analyzed were conducted exclusively on the small population of Internet addicts (Tokunaga & Rains, 2010). In fact, some have questioned whether Internet addiction exists among the college students who are mainly under observation in nearly all empirical investigations (LaRose et al., 2003; Song et al., 2004). The comparison between the various perspectives may be unfair because tests of Internet addiction are rarely conducted on genuine pathological Internet users.

Integrating the Addiction, Cognitive-Behavioral, and Social Cognitive Perspectives

Work on habit formation and strength across multiple disciplines, including the communication field, shows promise for integrating the three positions. In interpreting the phenomenon under discussion, some suggest that previous studies of Internet addiction, PIU, and DSR uncover variations of habit strength in the population of normal Internet users (LaRose, 2010). Internet activities can range in form from good habits (e.g., enjoying a favorite Internet game, digitally communicating with a friend for a couple hours per night) to bad habits (e.g., losing control over an online game). This is why appropriating the terms "deficient" or "maladaptive" may be premature in describing these generalized habits. Cognitive-behavioral researchers situate PIU in the middle range of the continuum and emphasize the mild, benign nature of related negative outcomes (e.g., missing class, foregoing a social event). Addiction researchers place Internet addiction at the upper end of the continuum, requiring the experience of serious life consequences (e.g., divorce, dropping out of school, dismissal from a job).

Internet habits are actions performed initially with conscious intention that transition under stable circumstances to nonconscious behaviors (LaRose, 2010). Active selection processes are governed by cortical control, whereas habits emerge when control is transferred to subcortical regions of the brain, such as the basal ganglia (Ashby, Turner, & Horvitz, 2010). Habit learning in the initial stages involves goal-driven behaviors not automatically performed. Training and rewards obtained in consistent intervals over time encourage the performance of automatic behaviors on cue (Balleine & Dickinson, 1998).

Habit research offers valuable new insights into the overlap of the Internet addiction, PIU, and DSR perspectives. Habits involve a tight cyclical loop of cues, routines, and rewards. The repetition of Internet use under stable conditions evolves into Internet routines, triggered by environmental (e.g., the sight of a computer, time, space) and/or internal (e.g., mood) cues. Reward is an important element in the habit loop because it tells the brain a cue is worth remembering in the future. Immediate rewards or gratifications associated with an Internet behavior at first initiate goal-directed actions, but long-term average expected rewards catalyze habits in later stages (LaRose, 2011). Cues, routines, and rewards become intertwined as habits gain strength to such an extent that exposure to a cue relevant to the reward activates pleasurable responses in the brain through dopamine release (Graybiel, 2008; Pessiglione, Seymour, Flandin, Dolan, & Frith, 2006). As habits become ingrained in neural circuitry, reward centers of the brain become activated in anticipation of the reward, called cravings in addiction parlance. In other words, the expectation of a reward precedes its reception in later stages of a habit.

Cognitive-behavioral and social cognitive researchers have made considerable efforts identify internal and external cues that stimulate routinized Internet behaviors. Caplan's (2003, 2005, 2007) work on modeling predictors of PIU demonstrated that social skills deficits and psychosocial problems (e.g., loneliness, social anxiety) serve as important internal cues that catalyze the habit process. Social cognitive approaches to deficient self-regulation and habit identified depression and attendant aversive moods as cues that hasten one's loss of control over Internet use (LaRose et al., 2003; LaRose & Eastin, 2004; Tokunaga & Rains, 2010; Tokunaga, 2014). Tokunaga (2013) also found that appraising novelty in Internet content is a situational cue that can inhibit awareness, attention, intention, and control through the development of flow, a state of deep cognitive immersion in an activity.

The rewards of Internet participation, at least in the early stages of Internet habit, come in myriad forms. Meeting new people online and developing rich, low-risk relationships fall under a gratification Papacharissi and Rubin (2000) call interpersonal utility. Control over immediate feedback, the ability to edit messages, and potential for anonymity online can build confidence for those who doubt their efficacy in offline social interactions (Morahan-Martin, 2008). Some Internet users feel more effective in online social interactions than offline ones on account of these affordances (Caplan, 2003). Other rewards include passing time, seeking information, and keeping in touch with existing friends (Papacharissi & Rubin, 2000). Likewise, the deeply immersive and pleasurable state of flow may be an escapism reward in itself (Tokunaga, 2013). LaRose and Eastin (2004) explained that avoiding or diminishing aversive mood states serves as an important reward for habitual Internet use. Depressive moods (i.e., the cue), engaging in the various functions of Internet use (i.e., the routine), and relieving aversive moods (i.e., the reward) become entangled to such an extent that the habit loop is activated on cue. As Internet habits grow in strength, anticipation of the reward precedes the experience of the reward. The anticipated reward cued by aversive moods is the projected regulation of one's internal state, called self-reactive outcome expectation (LaRose et al., 2003). It is this and other expected outcomes (e.g., status, social, novel) that sustain Internet habits over time.

The element that distinguishes a good from a bad Internet habit is the experience of negative consequences. Missing class or social activities because of one's engagement in online activities represents mild negative outcomes that regularly happen in the population of normal Internet users (Caplan, 2005). LaRose (2011), however, explained that normal Internet habits can spiral downward and produce serious life consequences when the Internet becomes the primary means of coping with dysphoric moods. The emergence of these serious consequences can in turn exacerbate existing dysphoria, generating a vicious cycle. Negative outcomes of this magnitude affect a diminutive proportion of Internet users not considered part of the "normal" population.

Proposed Directions of Internet Habit Work in Communication Research

The social cognitive and cognitive-behavioral perspectives provide fertile grounds for future exploration because they offer a logical calculus for conceptual and operational consistency. The perspectives may also have broader implications on other disciplines that address difficult issues associated with habits (e.g., psychology, information sciences, and computer sciences). The initial step communication researchers must take is holding conviction in the idea that the study of Internet habits is squarely a communication problem. Three arguments can be made in support of this position. The first argument for why habitual Internet use is a communication problem rests in explanations of media selection. The dominant theories of media use assume that making decisions about consumption involves rational, thoughtful selections. Timmerman (2002), however, pointed out that mindless or "overlearned" behaviors sometimes guide decisions about media use, indicating that nonconscious processes are sometimes responsible for some media choices. Media habits therefore complement traditional explanations for media selection processes, a central concern of mass communication research. The second is viewing Internet habits as effects akin to other outcomes of media exposure, such as knowledge acquisition, aggression, and enjoyment. Individuals sometimes strategically expose themselves to the Internet to fulfill certain internal needs. The conscious use of the Internet to obtain needs fulfillment evolves over time into learned habits, the effect of Internet consumption patterns. Other more observable media effects that originate from PIU include mild social and professional difficulties (Caplan, 2003; Liu & Peng, 2009; Tokunaga, 2014). The third pathway for situating Internet habit research in communication is by examining its theoretical antecedents. Routinized Internet use is cued by, among other things, internal factors, such as psychosocial problems, poor social skills, and the anticipation that future Internet use will regulate unpleasant moods (Caplan, 2005; LaRose et al., 2003; LaRose & Eastin, 2004). The theoretical antecedents recognize communication deficits and interpersonal failures as the kernel out of which these habits grow. Communication researchers are thus well-positioned to make significant contributions to the literature on this phenomenon.

Communication research has already moved the literature forward by incorporating theory to explain Internet addiction, PIU, and DSR. However, some lingering conceptual and methodological issues in research can be ascertained by reviewing the body of literature. These areas include unpacking the exact stimulus to which individuals form and maintain habits, the cognitive sub-functions involved with habit, measurement issues, the proposed "negative outcomes" of habit, and the sampling frame for empirical studies. The following sections address the various interpretive and methodological shortcomings in studying media habits, thereby signaling a roadmap for future investigations.

Reconciling the Question of Content and Context

The common approach of research has been to look at the Internet as a nebu-lous, homogeneous technology comprised of "parts" to which people develop and maintain habits. The notion of people losing control over their use of a technical infrastructure that connects computers to each other, however, does not seem intuitive. Although Davis (2001) theorized about the possibility of users forming a multidimensional overuse of the Internet, few hold the posi-tion that habits develop out of generalized Internet use. It is instead likely that habits are born from specific Internet technology use (Tokunaga & Rains, 2010). Internet technologies are not easily understood given that, like any media, they confound content with their affordances. Whether self-control is lost on account of the content delivered through the Internet (e.g., conversa-tions, games, gambling) or to the technology itself (e.g., instant messenger, Facebook) is not readily understood. LaRose (2010) suggested that the antici-pation of a reward and Internet consumption must be cognitively associated under stable circumstances during early stages of a habit; however, a routine may be triggered by a cue despite shifting contexts after habits are learned. The recurrent process of cognitive restructuring is responsible for the malleability of habits in different contexts. The context independent nature of habits indi-cate that Internet users may seek rewarding content not necessarily through the specific technology in which it was originally delivered. Alternatively, it could be argued that a specific technology provides the stable circumstance needed to activate habits and its content is immaterial. For greater explanatory preci-sion, future investigations should examine whether Internet habits depend on specific Internet content, context, or a merger of the two.

Another related issue to consider is whether some Internet media hasten habit formation more than others. Although it may be possible for habits to emerge from any form or function of the Internet, it is unlikely that all types of Internet use elicit them in the same way. Davis (2001) suggested that people lose control over leisure and social-based Internet content more often than other types of Internet use because they provide immediate reinforcement. Interpersonal communication mediated by the Internet, for instance, fulfills social needs in much the same way as in-person social interactions (Flanagin & Metzger, 2001). Preliminary evidence suggests that the nature of the Internet activity is salient in habit development. LaRose et al. (2011), for example, found that habits are strongest in Internet users who designate social networking sites and messaging (i.e., chats, instant messenger, and email) as their favorite leisure activities over those who list Internet gaming or shopping as their favorite Internet activity. This is not to say that Internet habits develop exclusively through leisure and social-based activities over the Internet. Diddi and LaRose (2006) demonstrated that habits of seeking news information over the Internet can grow among college students. Internet and conventional "news junkies," or habitual consumers of news information, are fueled by the desire to escape life challenges. Indeed, Internet users commonly develop Internet habits of using technologies that provide escapism rewards.

A goal of prospective investigations should be to clarify whether the relationships of habit change as a function of Internet technology use. Well-crafted experimental designs may be able to unravel this question. For example, an investigator can assign participants to different conditions, ask them to use unfamiliar Internet media that are inherently tied to specific rewards or gratifications (e.g., asocial Internet games [pass time], chat rooms [social]), and compare their rate of habit growth by taking scores at short intervals (i.e., time series). Results from these investigations are likely to expose the exceedingly complex relationships among internal cues (e.g., boredom, social skills deficits), anticipated rewards, and functions of Internet media.

Reconciling the Question of Subfunctions of Self-Regulation

Successful self-regulation of any behavior relies on three cognitive processes that lie within the executive function (LaRose, 2010). The first process involves the ability to monitor one's own behavior in an effort to obtain diagnostic information about its influence on self and others. The second process, known as self-judgment, relates to the capacity of individuals to compare, with accuracy, their behaviors against personal and social norms. Deficiency in either the observation or judgment subfunctions of behavioral regulation is precipitated by a lack of awareness, attention, and intention to self (Bargh, Gollwitzer, Lee-Chai, Barndollar, & Trötschel, 2001). The third mechanism responsible for self-control is self-reaction, or the ability to apply measures for correcting self-observed behaviors that fail to meet personal or referential standards. Failures of self-reaction are marked by feelings of uncontrollability over the behavior of focal interest.

The way temporal ordering among the subprocesses of self-regulation is described in the literature has invited some confusion. LaRose (2009) originally associated deficient self-observation and self-judgment with media habits, and deficient self-reaction was related to feelings of uncontrollability. The sequencing of the three subprocesses of self-regulation, however, is neither wholly understood nor derived from theory. In early studies, deficient self-reaction, then called DSR, was modeled as a predictor of deficient self-observation and self-judgment (LaRose et al., 2003; LaRose & Eastin, 2004). Longitudinal data also supports the path from deficient self-reaction to deficient self-observation while controlling for psychosocial problems and outcome expectations (Tokunaga, 2013).

The idea that Internet use must initially fall out of one's control before habits can form seems to defy conventional wisdom. Impairments must first occur in the self-observation or self-judgment circuitry for feelings of uncontrollability to exist, implying that deficient self-observation must precede deficient self-reaction in the causal chain. Self-reaction is only made salient when other process malfunctions occur prior and incentives are applied to correct the self-regulatory failure. Alternatively, it may be argued that minor losses of self-control, indicative of low levels of deficient self-reaction, initiate the repetition of Internet use and serve as the stable context in which Internet habits are formed. Future investigations can begin to unpack the complexities of time ordering among self-observation, self-judgment, and self-reaction using fine-grained time-series analyses at shorter intervals, which some investigations are now doing (see Tokunaga, 2013). Conceptual uncertainty about these processes led LaRose (2010) to reorganize the three process malfunctions under one label called DSR and later positioned the malfunctions under the generic umbrella of media habits (see LaRose et al., 2011).

Future research must also label the various subprocesses with a high degree of precision. The jingle-jangle fallacy will otherwise exist in research on media habits wherein people refer to the same concepts by different names and discrepant concepts by the same name. The inconsistent conceptualization of the three process malfunctions ushers in new possibilities for exploring the dimensionality and sequencing of these micro-level mechanisms. The dimensionality question might subsume the sequencing question if it is discovered that a second-order latent factor exerts influence on all three subprocesses. The higher-order latent factor would suggest that the processes are intertwined to such an extent that they are unable to be disentangled from each other. The three subprocesses may instead be measured by discrete latent variables, which would then allow researchers to explore their sequencing. Preliminary data support the position that the three subprocesses of self-regulation are independent, empirically distinguishable functions (LaRose, 2011; Saling & Phillips, 2007). Choi, LaRose, and Lee (2003), for instance, found acceptable model fit for their measurement model that individuated the three process malfunctions. Caplan (2010) and Tokunaga (2014), on the other hand, found that the loss of awareness, attention, intention, and conscious control was measured by a single second-order latent factor.

Reconciling Possible Measurement Differences in Research

Instruments can provide additional clarity to an indefinite construct that is new or has been plagued by the application of inconsistent definitions (Kirsch, 1995). Regularities in themes among the items used to measure a construct offer indirect, implicit suggestions about how the phenomenon under investigation has been interpreted by researchers. The importance of measurement consistency is emphasized in research on almost every concept (Clark & Watson, 1995). Davis et al. (2002) argued that a systematic line of research on this Internet consumption pattern cannot emerge in the absence of refined, well-validated measures. Measurement inconsistency is a particular problem when making cross-study comparisons because measurement differences act as a confounding third variable, which can explain both stability and change. Inconsistencies can thus undermine efforts to construct a cohesive and progressive program of research.

Despite growing conceptual clarity in how to characterize Internet addiction, PIU, DSR, and Internet habits over the last decade, the three perspectives exerted influence on, and led to differences in, operational measurement. At least 29 unique measures have been devised and used in research (Tokunaga & Rains, 2010), and more continue to be proposed. These measures, in accordance with the different perspectives from which they were conceived, vary considerably. Internet addiction measures, for instance, include negative social and professional consequences as part of the construct, whereas PIU, DSR, and media habit measures do not (cf. Widyanto & McMurran, 2004; Caplan, 2010). Items of habit measures, such as "Behavior X is something that would require effort not do it," imply a lack of controllability but do not confront the issue in the same way as compulsive use scales (Meerkerk, van den Eijnden, Vermulst, & Garretsen, 2009). The self-report index of habit strength (Verplanken & Orbell, 2003) instead focuses on the failure of awareness, attention, and intention, indicative of a deficiency in self-observation. Some PIU and DSR measures use persistent thoughts and feelings of unease while away from the technology as proxies for deficient self-observation.

Some instruments are based on items adapted from existing measures of substance abuse and pathological gambling found in the *Diagnostic and Statistical Manual of Mental Disorders*. Indicators indigenous to these measures include "I feel preoccupied with the Internet (think about previous online activity or anticipate next online session)," which represents a preoccupation component of addiction, and "I feel restless, moody, depressed, or irritable when attempting to cut down or stop using the Internet," which reflects withdrawal (Young, 1998). Communication researchers took a different approach to measurement construction. Caplan (2002), for example, focused on the interpersonal or relational deficiencies of users. Items such as "I use the Internet to talk with others when I feel isolated" and "I seek others online when I feel isolated" underscore the view of DSR and Internet habits as outcomes of relationship and relationship-building resource deficits.

A cursory analysis of the scales used to measure Internet habits suggests that they vary as a function of the perspectives from which they originated. Because researchers have not converged on a central measure and continue to select instruments idiosyncratically, it is imperative that prospective research investigates whether results are tied to the instrument employed. If it were determined that findings change as a function of measurement, it would catalyze a transformation in this research landscape by compelling investigators to rally around a small group of reliable and valid instruments. Continuing the trajectory of producing new scales of Internet addiction, PIU, and DSR undermines the cumulative function of research.

Reconciling the "Negative Consequences"

Early research exhaustively tested whether perceptible negative outcomes surfaced when individuals lost control over their Internet use (Caplan, 2003). Investigations on the tangible outcomes of Internet habits resembled the tradition of research on the dissocializing qualities of Internet, initiated by the HomeNet Study and work by Nie and his colleagues (Nie et al., 2002). Internet habits can interfere with "normal life activities, producing negative real world consequences (e.g., faltering relationships, failing grades) that in turn lead to deeper negative effects and a spiral of mounting media usage" (LaRose, Lai, Longe, Love, & Wu, 2005, p. 6).

The terms "outcome" and "consequence" were frequently used in the literature in spite of the large majority of evidence on these outcomes coming from cross-sectional studies, which produces correlational data insufficient for inferring causality. Recent longitudinal investigations, however, find support for the causal ordering of self-control failures and functional impairment. Kerkhof, Finkenauer, and Muusses (2011), for instance, discovered that marital problems can originate from what they call compulsive Internet use. They found that distrust surfaces when spouses believe their partner has lost the ability to regulate his or her Internet use (Muusses, Finkenauer, Kerkhof, & Righetti, 2013). Interpersonal problems between spouses are not the only consequences of this failure of self-regulation. Tokunaga (2014) found that DSR interfered with the maintenance of relationships with friends and other family members. Difficulties in professional work, such as academics and occupation performance, are also outcomes of self-control failures.

Empirical support for "negative outcomes" in the population of normal Internet users indicates that those who lose awareness, attention, intention, or control over their Internet use experience modest ill effects on their offline social involvement. The desire of researchers to locate these negative outcomes, however, may have led them to overlook possible positive outcomes. Shaw and Gant (2002), for instance, discovered that repeated participation in structured Internet chats reduces psychosocial problems, such as depression and loneliness, and results in modest improvements in self-esteem. This oversight could be the byproduct of an endemic bias in thinking about losses of offline social contact as inherently problematic. In measuring negative outcomes of PIU, Liu and Peng (2009) used the item "Online gaming has reduced my offline contact with people" (p. 1308). Caplan's (2010) GPIUS-2 includes the item "I have missed social engagements or activities because of my Internet use" (p. 1093), and Tokunaga (2014) measured social impairment with "I have noticed that my relationships with offline friends have declined."

The current construction of "negative outcomes" represents a predisposition to think of offline social encounters as intrinsically healthier and more adaptive than online social interactions. This prejudice in viewing losses of offline social contact as a malignant impairment may need to be revisited if offline social contact is being supplemented by meaningful online social interactions, particularly for those who lack the self-confidence to be effective offline communicators (Grohol, 1999). Media enjoyment, even as a product of habitual Internet use, could also be considered a positive outcome. Internet users, for example, might at times forego offline social contact to enjoy an online game. These cases should not be necessarily labeled as negative or problematic unless Internet media are being used as the main resource for managing dysphoric moods. Future research should reconsider the biases in current conceptual and operational definitions of these negative outcomes.

Reconciling Questions about Manifestation

Validity and legitimacy of the Internet habit concepts hinge on whether researchers are able to articulate what they are studying and indeed study what they intended. Questions, however, remain about whether variations of Internet habit are substantively being studied in research, considering the low reported means in the samples under investigation. The prevalence of DSR and Internet habits can be examined through a cursory analysis of descriptive statistics published in communication journals. Measures of DSR that used a 5-point Likert scale reported means of 1.49 ($SD = 0.49$) to 1.95 ($SD = 0.94$) (Caplan, 2002, 2005; Caplan & High, 2006; Kerkhof et al., 2011; Kim & LaRose, 2004; Muusses et al., 2013), while instruments based on a 7-point scale presented means ranging from 1.21 ($SD = 0.35$) to 2.60 ($SD = 1.82$) (LaRose & Eastin, 2004; Lee & LaRose, 2007; Tokunaga, 2013, 2014). These means demonstrate only modest levels of DSR and Internet habits among normal Internet users.

Caplan and High (2006) attempted to address this concern by stating that the focal interest of their study is not a comparison of individuals who met or fell short of a predetermined diagnostic cut-off score for deficiency; instead, their interest is the associations between PIU and other variables. Most who study variations of Internet habits agree with LaRose et al.'s (2003) contention that habits should be treated as continuous variables, not as all-or-nothing benchmarks discriminating problematic from benign cases. Nevertheless, the issue is whether Internet habits are even being studied. The problem is analogous to research on depression that uses a sample of non-depressed individuals. It would be expected that mean depression scores of a sample taken from the normal population of those without clinical depression would be slightly higher than the lower limit of the scale given measurement error. But still, the research would be so far removed from the phenomenon of interest that the data lack insight into true clinical depression. A greater effort should therefore be made to include individuals with higher levels of Internet habits in future investigations.

Conclusion

In closing, communication research has made meaningful contributions in refining how to interpret and understand Internet habits in the normal population of Internet users. Positioning Internet addiction, PIU, and DSR as variations in habit strength and articulating how each perspective enriches the explanation of habit formation brings greater conceptual clarity to this research area. As theory on Internet addiction, PIU, and DSR continues to mature, future efforts must be directed at integrating these positions into a cohesive narrative about the complex process of habit formation and maintenance.

Considerable work must still be done to close existing conceptual and methodological gaps in habit research. For instance, research on Internet habits has not yet disentangled important questions about what stimulus (i.e., context or content) individuals form habits to and whether cognitive reorganization happens more rapidly with certain Internet contexts or content. Having greater consistency in habit measurement, reassessing the negative outcomes of media habits, and determining whether these habits are being substantively studied in the corpus of research on this topic also requires further attention. Media habits offer a valuable starting point for communication researchers interested in multidisciplinary investigations with researchers in allied areas, such as social psychology and behavioral neurosciences. The work being done in these disciplines can inform habitual communication patterns, which may be of particular interest to health communication and mass communication researchers.

Note

1. The term maladaptive is used throughout this chapter, but it does not represent the full constellation of views on this phenomenon. Some media habit researchers hold the position that it might be incorrect to label patterns of Internet use that fall within the boundaries of normal behaviors as maladaptive.

References

American Psychiatric Association. (1987). *Diagnostic and statistical manual of mental disorders* (3rd ed., text rev.). Washington, DC: Author.

American Psychiatric Association. (2000). *Diagnostic and statistical manual of mental disorders* (4th ed., text rev.). Washington, DC: Author.

American Psychiatric Association. (2013). *Diagnostic and statistical manual of mental disorders* (5th ed.). Arlington, VA: American Psychiatric Publishing.

Ashby, F. G., Turner, B. O., & Horvitz, J. C. (2010) Cortical and basal ganglia contributions to habit learning and automaticity. *Trends in Cognitive Sciences, 14*, 208–215. doi:10.1016/j.tics.2010.02.001

Babor, T. F. (1992). Substance-related problems in the context of international classificatory systems. In M. Laders, G. Edwards, & D. C. Drummond (Eds.), *The nature of alcohol and drug related problems* (pp. 83–97). New York, NY: Oxford University Press.

Balleine, B. W., & Dickinson, A. (1998). Goal-directed instrumental action: contingency and incentive learning and their cortical substrates. *Neuropharmacology, 37*, 407–419. doi:10.1016/S0028-3908(98)00033-1

Bandura, A. (1986). *Social foundations of thought and action: A social cognitive theory.* Englewood-Cliffs, NJ: Prentice-Hall.

Bandura, A. (1989). Self-regulation of motivation and action through internal standards and goal systems. In L. Pervin (Ed.), *Goal concepts in personality and social psychology* (pp. 19–85). Hillsdale, NJ: Erlbaum.

Bandura, A. (1991). Social cognitive theory of self-regulation. *Organizational Behavior and Human Decision Processes, 50*, 248–287. doi:10.1016/0749-5978(91)90022-L

Bandura, A. (1999). A sociocognitive analysis of substance abuse: An agentic perspective. *Psychological Science, 10*, 214–217. doi:10.1111/1467-9280.00138

Bargh, J. A., Gollwitzer, P. M., Lee-Chai, A., Barndollar, K., & Trötschel, R. (2001). The automated will: Nonconscious activation and pursuit of behavioral goals. *Journal of Personality and Social Psychology, 81*, 1014–1027. doi:10.1037/0022-3514.81.6.1014

Baumeister, R. F., & Heatherton, T. F. (1996). Self-regulation failure: An overview. *Psychological Inquiry, 7*, 1–15. doi:10.1207/s15327965pli0701_1

Baumeister, R. F., Heatherton, T. F., & Tice, D. M. (1994). *Losing control: How and why people fail at self-regulation.* San Diego, CA: Academic Press.

Beard, K. W., & Wolf, E. M. (2001). Modification in the proposed diagnostic criteria for Internet addiction. *CyberPsychology & Behavior, 4*, 377–383. doi:10.1089/109493101300210286

Bozarth, M. A. (1990). Drug addiction as a psychobiological process. In D. M. Warburton (Ed.), *Addiction controversies* (pp. 112–113). London, UK: Harwood Academic Publishers.

Brenner, V. (1997). Parameters of Internet use, abuse, and addiction: The first 90 days of the Internet usage survey. *Psychological Reports, 80*, 879–882. doi:10.2466/pr0.1997.80.3.879

Butsch, R. (1998). Crystal sets and scarf-pin radios: gender, technology and the construction of American radio listening in the 1920s. *Media, Culture & Society, 20*, 557–572. doi:10.1177/016344398020004003

Byun, S., Ruffini, C., Mills, J. E., Douglas, A. C., Niang, M., Stepchenkova, S., et al. (2009). Internet addiction: Metasynthesis of 1996–2006 quantitative research. *CyberPsychology & Behavior, 12*, 203–207. doi:10.1089/cpb.2008.0102.

Caplan, S. E. (2002). Problematic Internet use and psychosocial well-being: Development of a theory-based cognitive-behavioral measurement instrument. *Computers in Human Behavior, 18*, 553–575. doi:10.1016/S0747-5632(02)00004-3

Caplan, S. E. (2003). Preference for online social interaction: A theory of problematic Internet use and psychosocial well-being. *Communication Research, 30*, 625–648. doi:10.1177/0093650203257842

Caplan, S. E. (2005). A social skill account of problematic Internet use. *Journal of Communication, 55*, 721–736. doi:10.1111/j.1460-2466.2005.tb03019.x

Caplan, S. E. (2006). Problematic Internet use in the workplace. In M. Andandarajan, T. S. H. Teo, & C. A. Simmers (Eds.), *The Internet and workplace transformation* (pp. 63–79). Armonk, NY: M. S. Sharpe.

Caplan, S. E. (2007). Relations among loneliness, social anxiety, and problematic Internet use. *CyberPsychology & Behavior, 10*, 234–242. doi:10.1089/cpb.2006.9963

Caplan, S. E. (2010). Theory and measurement of generalized problematic Internet use: A two-step approach. *Computers in Human Behavior, 26*, 1089–1097. doi:10.1016/j.chb.2010.03.012

Caplan, S. E., & High, A. C. (2006). Beyond excessive use: The interaction between cognitive and behavioral symptoms of problematic Internet use. *Communication Research Reports, 23*, 265–271. doi:10.1080/08824090600962516

Charlton J. P., & Danforth I. D. W. (2007). Distinguishing addiction and high engagement in the context of online game playing. *Computers in Human Behavior, 23*, 1531–1548. doi:10.1016/j.chb.2005.07.002

Choi, E.-J., LaRose, R., & Lee, D.-H. (2003). A cross-cultural comparison of Internet usage: Media habits, gratifications, and addictions in Korea and the U.S. *Proceedings of the International Conference of the World Wide Web and Internet, Portugal*, 963–966.

Chou, T. J., & Ting, C. C. (2003). The role of flow experience in cyber-game addiction. *CyberPsychology & Behavior, 6*, 663–675. doi:10.1089/109493103322725469

Clark, L. A., & Watson, D. (1995). Constructing validity: Basic issues in objective scale development. *Psychological Assessment, 7*, 309–319. doi:10.1037/1040-3590.7.3.309

Davis, R. A. (2001). A cognitive-behavioral model of pathological Internet use. *Computers in Human Behavior, 17*, 187–195. doi:10.1016/S0747-5632(00)00041-8

Davis, R. A., Flett, G. L., & Besser, A. (2002). Validation of a new scale for measuring problematic Internet use: Implications for pre-employment screening. *CyberPsychology & Behavior, 5*, 331–345. doi:10.1089/109493102760275581

Diddi, A., & LaRose, R. (2006). Getting hooked on news: Uses and gratifications and the formation of news habits among college students in an Internet environment. *Journal of Broadcasting & Electronic Media, 50*, 193–210. doi:10.1207/s15506878jobem5002_2

Egli, E. A., & Meyers, L. S. (1984). The role of video-game playing in adolescent life: Is there a reason to be concerned? *Bulletin of the Psychonomic Society, 22*, 309–312. doi:10.3758/BF03333828

Emmons, R. A., & King, L. A. (1988). Conflict among personal strivings: Immediate and long-term implications for psychological and physical well-being. *Journal of Personality and Social Psychology, 54*, 1040–1048. doi:10.1037/0022-3514.54.6.1040

Fisher, S. E. (1994). Identifying video game addiction in children and adolescents. *Addictive Behaviors, 19*, 545–553. doi:10.1016/0306-4603(94)90010-8

Flanagin, A. J., & Metzger, M. J. (2001). Internet use in the contemporary media environment. *Human Communication Research, 27*, 153–181. doi:10.1111/j.1468-2958.2001.tb00779.x

Goleman, D. (1990, October 16). How viewers grow addicted to television. *New York Times*, p. C1.

Grant, J. E., Levine, L., Kim, D., & Potenza, M. N. (2005). Impulse control disorders in adult psychiatric inpatients. *American Journal of Psychiatry, 162*, 2184–2188. doi:10.1176/appi.ajp.162.11.2184

Graybiel, A. M. (2008). Habits, rituals, and the evaluative brain. *Annual Review of Neuroscience, 31*, 359–387. doi:10.1146/annurev.neuro.29.051605.112851

Greenfield, P. (1984). *Media and the mind of a child: From print to television, video games and computers*. Cambridge, MA: Harvard University Press.

Griffiths, M. D. (1992). Pinball wizard: A case study of a pinball addict. *Psychological Reports, 71*, 160–162. doi:10.2466/pr0.1992.71.1.160

Griffiths, M. D. (1997, August). *Does Internet and computer addiction exist? Some case study evidence*. Paper presented at the meeting of the American Psychological Association, Chicago, IL.

Griffiths, M. D. (1998). Internet addiction: Does it really exist? In J. Gackenbach (Ed.), *Psychology and the Internet: Intrapersonal, interpersonal and transpersonal applications* (pp. 61–75). New York, NY: Academic Press.

Griffiths, M. D., & Dancaster, I. (1995). The effect of type A personality on physiological arousal while playing computer games. *Addictive Behaviors, 20*, 543–548. doi:10.1016/0306-4603(95)00001-S

Griffiths, M. D., & Hunt, N. (1998). Dependence on computer games by adolescents. *Psychological Reports, 82*, 475–480. doi:10.2466/pr0.1998.82.2.475

Grohol, J. (1999). Too much time online: Internet addiction or healthy social interactions. *CyberPsychology and Behavior, 2*, 395–402. doi:10.1089/cpb.1999.2.395

Ha, J. H., Yoo, H. J., Cho, I. H., Chin, B., Shin, D., & Kim, J. H. (2006). Psychiatric comorbidity assessed in Korean children and adolescents who screen positive for Internet addiction. *Journal of Clinical Psychiatry, 67*, 821–826. doi:10.4088/JCP. v67n0517

Hauge, M. R., & Gentile, D. A. (2003, April). *Video game addiction among adolescents: Associations with academic performance and aggression.* Paper presented at the annual meeting of the Society for Research in Child Development, Tampa, FL.

Horvath, C. W. (2004). Measuring television addiction. *Journal of Broadcasting & Electronic Media, 48*, 378–398. doi:10.1207/s15506878jobem4803_3

Jaffe, J. H. (1990). Drug addiction and drug abuse. In A. G. Gilman, T. W. Rall, A. S. Nies, & P. Taylor (Eds.), *Goodman and Gilman's: The pharmacological basis of therapeutics* (8th ed., pp. 522–573). New York, NY: McGraw-Hill.

Kandell, J. (1998). Internet addiction on campus: The vulnerability of college students. *CyberPsychology & Behavior, 1*, 46–59. doi:10.1089/cpb.1998.1.11.

Katz, E., Blumler, J., & Gurevitch, M. (1974). Utilization of mass communication by the individual. In J. Blumler & E. Katz (Eds.), *The uses of mass communication: Current perspectives on gratifications research* (pp. 19–34). Beverly Hills, CA: Sage.

Katz, J. E., & Rice, R. E. (2002). *Social consequences of Internet use: Access, involvement and interaction.* Cambridge, MA: MIT Press.

Kerkhof, P., Finkenauer, C., & Muusses, L. D. (2011). Relational consequences of compulsive Internet use: A longitudinal study among newlyweds. *Human Communication Research, 37*, 147–173. doi:10.1111/j.1468-2958.2010.01397.x

Kim, J., & LaRose, R. (2004). Interactive e-Commerce: Promoting consumer efficiency or impulsivity? *Journal of Computer-Mediated Communication, 10*(1). doi:10.1111/j.1083-6101.2004.tb00234.x

Kirsch, I. (1995). Self-efficacy and outcome expectancy: A concluding comment. In J. E. Maddux (Ed.), *Self-efficacy, adaptation, and adjustment: Theory, research and application* (pp. 377–385). New York, NY: Plenum.

Ko, C. H., Yen, J. Y., Chen, C. C., Chen, S. H., & Yen, C. F. (2007). Factors predictive for incidence and remission of Internet addiction in young adolescents: A prospective study. *Cyberpsychology & Behavior, 10*, 545–551. doi:10.1089/cpb.2007.9992

Koob, G. F., & Bloom, F. E. (1998) Neuroscience of addiction. *Neuron, 21*, 467–476. doi:10.1016/s0896-6273(00)80557-7

Koob, G. F., & Moal, M. (1997). Drug abuse: Hedonic homeostatic dysregulation. *Science, 278*, 52–58. doi:10.1126/science.278.5335.52

Kraut, R., Kiesler, S., Boneva, B., Cummings, J., Helgeson, V., & Crawford, A. (2002). Internet paradox revisited. *Journal of Social Issues, 58*, 49–74. doi:10.1111/1540-4560.00248

Kraut, R., Patterson, M., Lundmark, V., Kiesler, S., Mukopadhyay, T., & Scherlis, W. (1998). Internet paradox: A social technology that reduces social involvement and psychological well-being? *American Psychologist, 53*, 1017–1031. doi:10.1037/0003-066X.53.9.1017

Kubey, R. (1990, August). *Psychological dependence on television: Applications of DSM-III-R and experience sampling methods finding.* Paper presented at the meeting of the American Psychological Association, Boston, MA.

Kubey, R. (1996). Television dependence, diagnosis, and prevention: With commentary on video games, pornography, and media education. In T. MacBeth (Ed.), *Tuning in to young viewers: Social science perspectives on television* (pp. 221–260). Newbury Park, CA: Sage.

Kubey, R., & Csikzentmihalyi, M. (1990). *Television and the quality of life: How viewing shapes everyday experience*. Hillsdale, NJ: Lawrence Erlbaum.

Kubey, R. W., Lavin, M. J., & Barrows, J. R. (2001). Internet use and collegiate academic performance decrements: Early findings. *Journal of Communication, 51*, 366–382. doi:10.1111/j.1460-2466.2001.tb02885.x

Kuss, D. J., & Griffiths, M. D. (2012). Internet gaming addiction: A systematic review of empirical research. *International Journal of Mental Health and Addiction, 10*, 278–296. doi:10.1007/s11469-011-9318-5

LaRose, R. (2009). Social cognitive theories of media selection. In T. Hartmann (Ed.), *Media choice: A theoretical and empirical overview* (pp. 10–31). New York, NY: Routledge.

LaRose, R. (2010). The problem of media habits. *Communication Theory, 20*, 194–222. doi:10.1111/j.1468-2885.2010.01360.x

LaRose, R. (2011). Uses and gratifications of Internet addiction. In K. S. Young & C. Nabuco de Abreu (Eds.), *Internet addiction: A handbook and guide to evaluation and treatment* (pp. 55–72). Hoboken, NJ: Wiley.

LaRose, R., & Eastin, M. S. (2004). A social cognitive theory of Internet uses and gratifications: Toward a new model of media attendance. *Journal of Broadcasting & Electronic Media, 48*, 358–377. doi:10.1207/s15506878jobem4803_2

LaRose, R., Kim, J., & Peng, W. (2011). Social networking: Addictive, compulsive, problematic, or just another media habit? In Z. Papacharissi (Ed.), *A networked self: Identity, community, and culture on social network sites* (pp. 59–81). New York, NY: Routledge.

LaRose, R., Lin, C. A., & Eastin, M. S. (2003). Unregulated Internet usage: Addiction, habit, or deficient self-regulation? *Media Psychology, 5*, 225–253. doi:10.1207/S1532785XMEP0503_01

LaRose, R., Mastro, D. A., & Eastin, M. A. (2001). Understanding Internet usage: A social cognitive approach to uses and gratifications. *Social Science Computer Review, 19*, 395–413. doi:10.1177/089443930101900401

LaRose, R., Lai, Y.-J., Lange, R., Love, B., & Wu, Y. (2005). Sharing or piracy? An exploration of downloading behavior. *Journal of Computer-Mediated Communication, 11*, 1–21. doi:10.1111/j.1083-6101.2006.tb00301.x

Lea, M., O'Shea, T., Fung, P., & Spears, R. (1992). "Flaming" in computer-mediated communication: observations, explanations, implications. In M. Lea (Ed.), *Contexts of computer-mediated communication* (pp. 30–65). Hemel Hempstead, UK: Harvester Wheatsheaf.

Lee, D., & LaRose, R. (2007). A socio-cognitive model of video game usage. *Journal of Broadcasting & Electronic Media, 51*, 632–650. doi:10.1080/08838150701626511

Lei, L., & Wu, Y. (2007). Adolescents' paternal attachment and Internet use. *CyberPsychology & Behavior, 10*, 633–639. doi:10.1089/cpb.2007.9976

Lesieur, H. R., & Rosenthal, R. J. (1991). Pathological gambling: A review of the literature. *Journal of Gambling Studies, 7*, 5–39. doi:10.1007/BF01019763

Leung, L. (2004). Net-generation attributes and seductive properties of the Internet as predictors of online activities and Internet addiction. *CyberPsychology & Behavior, 7*, 333–348. doi:10.1089/1094931041291303

Levinson, M. (2010). *The Levinson report: Cutting edge satire for geniuses like you.* Bloomington, IN: iUniverse.

Lin, C. A. (1999). Online-service adoption likelihood. *Journal of Advertising Research, 39,* 79–89.

Liu, M., & Peng, W. (2009). Cognitive and psychological predictors of the negative outcomes associated with playing MMOGs (massively multiplayer online games). *Computers in Human Behavior, 25,* 1306–1311. doi:10.1016/j.chb.2009.06.002

Livingstone, S. (1999). Young people and the new media: On learning lessons from TV to apply to the PC. *Réseaux, French Journal of Communication, 7,* 59–81. Retrieved from http://www.persee.fr/web/revues/home/prescript/revue/reso

Marlatt, G. A., Baer, J. S., Donovan, D. M., & Kivlahan, D. R. (1988). Addictive behaviors: Etiology and treatment. *Annual Review of Psychology, 39,* 223–252. doi:10.1146/annurev.ps.39.020188.001255

Maultsby, M. C., Jr., & Wirga, M. (1998). Behavior therapy. In H. Friedman (Ed.), *Encyclopedia of mental health* (pp. 221–234). San Diego, CA: Academic Press.

McIlwraith, R. D. (1990, August). *Theories of television addiction.* Paper presented at the meeting of the American Psychological Association, Boston, MA.

McIlwraith, R. D. (1998). "I'm addicted to television": The personality, imagination and TV watching pattern of self-identified TV addicts. *Journal of Broadcasting & Electronic Media, 42,* 371–386. doi:10.1080/08838159809364456

McIlwraith, R., Jacobvitz, R., Kubey, R., & Alexander, A. (1991). Television addiction: Theories and data behind the ubiquitous metaphor. *American Behavioral Scientist, 35,* 104–121. doi:10.1177/0002764291035002003

McLuhan, M. (1964). *Understanding media: The extensions of man.* Toronto: University of Toronto Press.

McLuhan, M. (April 3, 1978). A last look at the tube. *New York Magazine,* p. 45.

Meerkerk, G.-J., van den Eijnden, R. J. J. M., Vermulst, A. A., & Garretsen, H. F. L. (2009). The compulsive Internet use scale (CIUS): Some psychometric properties. *CyberPsychology & Behavior, 12,* 1–6. doi:10.1089/cpb.2008.0181.

Moore, D. (1995). *The emperor's virtual clothes: The naked truth about the Internet culture.* Chapel Hill, NC: Algonquin.

Morahan-Martin, J. (2008). Internet abuse: Emerging trends and lingering questions. In A. Barak (Ed.), *Psychological aspects of Cyberspace. Theory, research and applications* (pp. 32–69). Cambridge, UK: Cambridge University Press.

Moreyra P., Ibanez A., Saiz-Ruiz J., & Blanco, C. (2004). Categorization. In J. E. Grant & M. N. Potenza (Eds.), *Pathological gambling: A clinical guide to treatment* (pp. 55–68). Washington, DC: American Psychiatric Press

Muusses, L. D., Finkenauer, C., Kerkhof, P., & Righetti, F. (2013). Partner effects of compulsive Internet use: A self-control account. *Communication Research.* Advanced online publication. doi:10.1177/0093650212469545

Nalwa, K., & Anand, A. P. (2003). Internet addiction in students: A cause of concern. *CyberPsychology & Behavior, 6,* 653–656. doi:10.1089/109493103322725441

Nathan, P. E. (1991). Substance use disorders in the DSM-IV. *Journal of Abnormal Psychology, 100,* 356–361. doi:10.1037//0021-843X.100.3.356

Newell, A., & Simon, H. A. (1976). Computer science as empirical inquiry: Symbols and search. *Communications of the ACM, 19,* 111–126. doi:10.1145/360018.360022

Nie, N. H., Hillygus, D. S., & Erbring, L. (2002). Internet use, interpersonal relationships, and sociability: A time diary study. In B. Wellman & C. Haythornthwaite (Eds.), *The Internet in everyday life* (pp. 215–244). Oxford, UK: Blackwell.

O'Neill, M. (1995, March 8). The lure and addiction of life on line. *The New York Times,* C1, C6.

Orzack, M. H. (1999). How to recognize and treat computer.com addictions. *Directions in Mental Health Counseling, 9,* 13–20.

Papacharissi, Z., & Rubin, A. M. (2000). Predictors of Internet use. *Journal of Broadcasting & Electronic Media, 44,* 175–196. doi:10.1207/s15506878jobem4402_2

Payne, J. W. (2006, November 14). Caught in the Web. *Washington Post,* p. HE01.

Pessiglione, M., Seymour, B., Flandin, G., Dolan, R. J., & Frith, C. D. (2006). Dopamine-dependent prediction errors underpin reward-seeking behaviour in humans. *Nature, 442,* 1042–1045. doi:10.1038/nature05051

Petry, N. M., & O'Brien, C. P. (2013). Internet gaming disorder and the DSM-5. *Addiction, 108,* 1186–1187. doi:10.1111/add.12162

Phillips, C. A., Rolls, S., Rouse, A., & Griffiths, M. (1995). Home video game playing in school children: A study of incidence and patterns of play. *Journal of Adolescence, 18,* 687–691. doi:10.1006/jado.1995.1049

Pies, R. (2009). Should DSM-V designate "Internet addiction" a mental disorder? *Psychiatry, 6,* 31–37.

Pratarelli, M. E., Browne, B. L., & Johnson, K. (1999). The bits and bytes of computer/Internet addiction: A factor analytic approach. *Behavior Research Methods, Instruments, & Computers, 31,* 305–314. doi:10.3758/BF03207725

Preston, M. I. (1941). Children's reactions to movie horrors and radio crime. *The Journal of Pediatrics, 19,* 147–168. doi:10.1016/S0022-3476(41)80059-6

Rheingold, H. (1993). *The virtual community.* Reading, MA: Addison-Wesley.

Rowland, H. (1944). Radio crime dramas. *Educational Research Bulletin, 23,* 210–217. Retrieved from http://www.jstor.org/stable/1473640

Saling, L., & Phillips, J. G. (2007). Automatic behavior: Efficient not mindless. *Brain Research Bulletin, 73,* 1–20. doi:10.1016/j.brainresbull.2007.02.009

Schallow, J. R., & McIlwraith, R. D. (1986–1987). Is television viewing really bad for your imagination? Content and process of TV viewing and imaginal styles. *Imagination, Cognition, and Personality, 6,* 25–42. doi:10.2190/1L5Y-TNYL-X5QK-NUVT

Scherer, K. (1997). College life on-line: Healthy and unhealthy Internet use. *Journal of College Student Development, 38,* 655–664.

Segrin, C., & Givertz, M. (2003). Methods of social skills training and development. In J. O. Greene & B. R. Burleson (Eds.), *Handbook of communication and social interaction skills* (pp. 135–176). Mahwah, NJ: Lawrence Erlbaum.

Shaffer, H. J., Hall, M. N., & Vander Bilt, J. (2000). "Computer addiction": A critical consideration. *American Journal of Orthopsychiatry, 70,* 162–168. doi:10.1037/h0087741

Shaw, L. A., & Gant, L. M. (2002). In defense of the Internet: The relationship between Internet communication and depression, loneliness, self-esteem, and perceived social support. *CyberPsychology & Behavior, 5,* 157–171. doi:10.1089/109493102753770552.

Shotton, M. A. (1991). The costs and benefits of "computer addiction." *Behavior Information and technology, 10,* 219–230. doi:10.1080/01449299108924284

Slater, M. D. (2007). Reinforcing spirals: The mutual influence of media selectivity and media effects and their impact on individual behavior and social identity. *Communication Theory, 17,* 281–303. doi:10.1111/j.1468-2885.2007.00296.x

Smith, R. (1986). Television addiction. In J. Bryant & D. Anderson (Eds.), *Perspectives on media effects* (pp. 109–128). Hillsdale, NJ: Lawrence Erlbaum.

Song, I., LaRose, R., Eastin, M. S., & Lin, C. A. (2004). Internet gratifications and Internet addiction: On the uses and abuses of new media. *CyberPsychology & Behavior,* *7*, 384–394. doi:10.1089/cpb.2004.7.384.

Spitzberg, B. H., & Cupach, W. R. (1989). *Handbook of interpersonal competence research.* New York, NY: Springer-Verlag.

Steiner, G. (1963). *The people look at television.* New York, NY: Alfred A. Knopf.

Thatcher, A., Wretschko, G., & Fisher, J. (2008). Problematic Internet use among information technology workers in South Africa. *CyberPsychology & Behavior, 11,* 785–787. doi:10.1089/cpb.2007.0223.

Thatcher, A., Wrestchko, G., & Fridjhon, P. (2008). Online flow experiences, problematic Internet use and Internet procrastination. *Computers in Human Behavior, 24,* 2236–2254. doi:10.1016/j.chb.2007.10.008

Tice, D. M., Bratslavsky, E., & Baumeister, R. F. (2001). Emotional distress regulation takes precedence over impulse control: If you feel bad, do it! *Journal of Personality and Social Psychology, 80,* 53–67. doi:10.1037/0022-3514.80.1.53

Timmerman, C. E. (2002). The moderating effect of mindlessness/mindfulness upon media richness and social influence explanations of organizational media use. *Communication Monographs, 69,* 111–131. doi:10.1080/714041708

Tokunaga, R. S. (2013). Engagement with novel virtual environments: The roles of perceived novelty and flow in the development of the deficient self-regulation of Internet use and media habits. *Human Communication Research, 39,* 365–393. doi:10.1111/hcre.12008

Tokunaga, R. S. (2014). A unique problem or the manifestation of a preexisting disorder? The mediating role of problematic Internet use in the relationship between psychosocial problems and functional impairment. *Communication Research, 41,* 531–560. doi:10.1177/0093650212450910

Tokunaga, R. S., & Rains, S. A. (2010). An evaluation of two characterizations of the relationships between problematic Internet use, time spent using the Internet, and psychosocial problems. *Human Communication Research, 36,* 512–545. doi:10.1111/j.1468-2958.2010.01386.x

Tong, S., Vitak, J., & LaRose, R. (2010). *Truly problematic or merely habitual? An integrated model of the negative consequences of social networking.* Paper presented at the meeting of the International Communication Association. Suntec City, Singapore.

van Hook, E., & Higgins, E. T. (1988). Self-related problems beyond the self-concept: The motivational consequences of discrepant self-guides. *Journal of Personality and Social Psychology, 55,* 625–633. doi:10.1037/0022-3514.55.4.625

van Rooij, A. J., Schoenmakers, T. M., Vermulst, A. A., van den Eijnden, R. J. J. M., & van de Mheen, D. (2011). Online video game addiction: Identification of addicted adolescent gamers. *Addiction, 106,* 205–212.

Verplanken, B., & Orbell, S. (2003). Reflections on past behavior: A self-report index of habit strength. *Journal of Applied Social Psychology, 33,* 1313–1330. doi:10.1111/j.1559-1816.2003.tb01951.x

Verplanken, B., & Wood, W. (2006). Interventions to break and create consumer habits. *Journal of Public Policy & Marketing, 25,* 90–103. doi:http://dx.doi.org/10.1509/jppm.25.1.90

Wallace, P. (1999). *The psychology of the Internet.* Cambridge, UK: Cambridge University Press.

Warden, N., Phillips, J. G., & Ogloff, J. R. P. (2004). Internet addiction. *Psychiatry, Psychology and Law, 11,* 280–295. doi:10.1375/pplt.2004.11.2.280

Wellman, B. (1997). An electronic group is virtually a social network. In S. Kiesler (Ed.), *Culture of the Internet* (pp. 179–208). Mahwah, NJ: Lawrence Erlbaum.

Whang, L. S.-M., Lee, S., & Chang, G. (2003) Internet over-users' psychological profiles: A behavior sampling analysis on Internet addiction. *CyberPsychology & Behavior, 6*, 143–150. doi:10.1089/109493103321640338

Widyanto, L., & McMurran, M. (2004). The psychometric properties of the internet addiction test. *CyberPsychology & Behavior, 7*, 443–450. doi:10.1089/cpb.2004.7.443

Winn, M. (1977). *The plug-in drug.* New York, NY: Bantam.

Wood, R. T. A. (2007). Problems with the concept of video game "addiction": Some case study examples. *International Journal of Mental Health and Addiction, 6*, 169–178. doi:10.1007/s11469-007-9118-0

Wood, R. T. A., Griffiths, M. D., Chappell, D., & Davies, M. N. O. (2004). The structural characteristics of video games: A psycho-structural analysis. *CyberPsychology & Behavior, 7*, 1–10. doi:10.1089/109493104322820057

Wood, W., & Neal, D. T. (2007). A new look at habits and the habit-goal interface. *Psychological Review, 114*, 843–863. doi:10.1037/0033-295X.114.4.843

Yen, J., Yen, C., Chen, C., Chen, S., & Ko, C. (2007). Family factors of Internet addiction and substance use experience in Taiwanese adolescents. *CyberPsychology & Behavior, 10*, 323–329. doi:10.1089/cpb.2006.9948.

Yin, H. H., & Knowlton, B. J. (2006). The role of the basal ganglia in habit formation. *Nature Reviews Neuroscience, 7*, 464–476. doi:10.1038/nrn1919

Young, K. S. (1996). Psychology of computer use: XL. Addictive use of the Internet: A case that breaks the stereotype. *Psychological Reports, 79*, 899–902. doi:10.2466/pr0.1996.79.3.899

Young, K. S. (1998). Internet addiction: The emergence of a new clinical disorder. *CyberPsychology & Behavior, 1*, 237–244. doi:10.1089/cpb.1998.1.237

Young, K. S. (1999). Internet addiction: Symptoms, evaluation, and treatment. In L. VandeCreek & T. L. Jackson (Eds.), *Innovations in clinical practice: A source book: Vol. 17* (pp. 19–31). Sarasota, FL: Professional Resource Press.

Young, K. S., & Rogers, R. C. (1998). The relationship between depression and Internet addiction. *CyberPsychology & Behavior, 1*, 25–28. doi:10.1089/cpb.1998.1.25

Young, K. S., Griffin-Shelley, E., Cooper, A., O'Mara, J., & Buchanan, J. (2000). Online infidelity: A new dimension in couple relationships with implications for evaluation and treatment. *Sexual Addiction and Compulsivity, 7*, 59–74. doi:10.1080/10720160008400207

Young, K. S., Yue, X. D., & Ying, L. (2011). Prevalence estimates and etiologic models of Internet addiction. In K. S. Young & C. Nabuco de Abreu (Eds.), *Internet addiction: A handbook and guide to evaluation and treatment* (pp. 1–17). Hoboken, NJ: Wiley.

Zimbardo, P. (1982). Understanding psychological man: A state of the science report. *Psychology Today, 16*, p. 15.

CHAPTER CONTENTS

6 Online Social Influence

Past, Present, and Future

Young Ji Kim

Massachusetts Institute of Technology

Andrea B. Hollingshead

University of Southern California

Social influence research has flourished for more than five decades. This chapter presents a comprehensive yet selective review of social influence research, demarcated by three points in time—pre-online, the early days of computer-mediated communication, and the current Web 2.0 environment. This chapter's main objective is to show how concepts, theories, and models developed in earlier research can enhance understanding of online social influence in today's digital world. We organize our review of online social influence research around the basic components of communication—source, message, channel, and audience. We also provide a critique and directions for future research.

Understanding how individuals influence and are influenced by other people has been a central topic of study for decades across a variety of fields in the social and behavioral sciences including communication, social psychology, marketing, management, education, political science, and health. Social influence plays a vital role in explaining individual behavior across many contexts, including consumer decision making (Katz & Lazarsfeld, 1955), technology diffusion and adoption (Rogers, 1962), businesses' adoption of innovations (Strang & Macy, 2001), the spread of sociocultural fads (Bikhchandani, Hirshleifer, & Welch, 1992), health behaviors (Centola, 2010; Christakis & Fowler, 2007), and social movements (Marwell, Oliver, & Prahl, 1988) to name a few. And nowadays, *socially influenced* attitudes, communication, and behaviors are increasingly mediated through technologies (Bakshy, Rosenn, Marlow, & Adamic, 2012).

Online social influence, as we call it, is social influence that occurs in online spaces, and is supported by a range of devices such as smartphones, computers, and tablets. It is important to note that online spaces have evolved with marked structural changes from the early Internet era (referred to as Web 1.0) to the contemporary digital environment (referred to as Web 2.0) (O'Reilly, 2005). The essential difference between Web 1.0 and Web 2.0 is the availability of social tools and technologies for easy content creation and sharing among lay users (Ackland, 2013; Kaplan & Haenlein, 2010).

While the terms Web 1.0 and 2.0 are sometimes denounced as marketing buzzwords, the contrast between the two can be useful for appreciating how the social, participatory nature of Web 2.0 has paved the way for new, unprecedented forms of social influence (Walther, Liang, Ganster, Wohn, & Emington, 2012). The early Internet enabled individuals to consume but not produce content and have limited interaction with information sources (e.g., website authors). In contrast, Web 2.0 sites such as social network sites and social media have enabled individuals to both produce and consume content easily and have significantly increased the connectivity of individuals, and the visibility of interpersonal, group, and large-scale social interactions.

For instance, the thoughts, interactions, and behaviors of other individuals are increasingly visible and readily accessible through user-generated content and digital traces including online product reviews, blog posts and responses, votes on recommender systems, social media friending, and page views. User-generated content and digital traces can provide quantitative information that serves as a marker for potential influence, for example, the number of followers a person has, the number of users who provided a hotel with an excellent rating, or the number of likes or comments a news story or video received. They also provide more diagnostic, qualitative information such as follower usernames, a given reviewer's most and least favorite features of a hotel, or the aspects readers found most interesting or troubling in a video or news story, all of which can affect readers in one way or another. All in all, there is a multitude of social interactions online, which are explicitly visible to anyone, each potentially serving as either a source or evidence of social influence.

The noted changes in communication process brought by recent technologies can be arranged in terms of the basic components of communication identified in the traditional models of communication (Berlo, 1960; Lasswell, 1948; Schramm, 1954; Shannon & Weaver, 1949). Specifically, technologies have greatly increased the number and variety of potential *sources* of influence; the amount and types of *messages* exchanged between communicators (i.e., sources and receivers); the variety of *channels* (i.e., applications such as blogs, wikis, and social network sites) available in which a message is transmitted, and the potential size and variability of the *audience*.

The number and variety of influence sources (those who initiate the communication) is potentially very large. Sources are generally aware that their communication is public and may be viewed by other users. Their objectives may or may not be to influence other people, and they may not have had any particular audience in mind when creating messages. The amount and types of messages exchanged between individuals and between sites and individuals is potentially very large. There are many different channels or applications that can be chosen by individuals to transmit messages, which vary in credibility and the form in which the message is conveyed (Metzger, Flanagin, Eyal, Lemus, & McCann, 2003). The audience size can be large, and its composition is often unknown to sources. The technological implications for each factor of the communication process greatly increase the complexity of studying social influence, and introduce new issues regarding its conceptualization and measurement.

While research into online social influence is cross-disciplinary and rapidly growing, the technological implications for online social influence are often not systematically presented and discussed in current literature. Instead, in many cases, certain popular social media (e.g., Facebook, Twitter) are examined as a context in which social influence occurs, and the existence and intensity of social influence is extrapolated. In addition, specific features of those sites (e.g., sharing, retweeting) are readily accepted as measures of online social influence without a careful consideration of their limitations. We will discuss these issues of current research in more detail later in the chapter.

The main thesis we advance in this chapter has three interrelated parts. First, current online social influence literature lacks an organizing framework, and would benefit from a communication-based approach. Second, current research lacks clear concepts and definitions. A look back to classical concepts and theories from early research on social influence can provide useful insights that enrich and extend our understanding in the present Web 2.0 environment, and can inform an agenda for future research. Third, Web 2.0 applications are inherently different from the early Internet, which affects the conceptualization and measurement of social influence.

To that end, this chapter presents a review, integration, and agenda for future research on online social influence. We begin by defining the term social influence and then the scope of our review. We then provide a selective review of traditional social influence research before turning to a discussion of online social influence in early Internet, or Web 1.0. We follow with a survey, synthesis, and integration of research on social influence in Web 2.0 as it pertains to online consumption in particular. The research on social influence in Web 2.0 is organized based on traditional models of communication: source, message, channel, and audience. Finally, we discuss how classical research can extend our understanding of social influence in the present Web 2.0 environment, and the special considerations that affect conceptualization and measurement. We also address directions for future research. This topic is of obvious interest to marketers and others in the business of persuasion, but it is also of critical importance for educators and consumers of online content who are the targets of social influence.

Social Influence Defined

We define social influence as the change in an individual's thoughts, feelings, communication or behavior resulting from the thoughts, feelings, communication, or behavior of one or more other people. Social influence comes in many forms. It can be intentional, as in the case of persuasion, which concerns how individuals exercise influence on others via messages (Dillard & Pfau, 2002). However, social influence can also be unintentional or incidental, as in the case of social proof, where individuals observe the behavior of often unaware others to determine how to respond in uncertain situations (Cialdini, 2001).

Social influence has traditionally been measured by comparing individual's pre-existing attitude or behavioral intention, then providing some type of exposure to the attitudes, communication, or behaviors of one or more others, then measuring the individual's post-exposure attitude and/or behavioral intention. The difference between an individual's pre-existing and post-exposure attitude and/or behavioral intention is a direct measure of social influence. Early research on social influence dating before the Internet era tended to use laboratory experiments, where specific features of sources, messages, channels, and audience were manipulated and their impact on social influence was measured.

Defining the Scope of this Review

The chapter presents a review of social influence research, demarcated by three points in time—pre-online, early computer-mediated communication or Web 1.0, and Web 2.0. The body of research on social influence is notably vast, and many scholarly reviews have been produced on this topic across different disciplines over the decades (e.g., Prislin & Crano, 2012). Communication scholars have focused their attention on identifying message-related factors and mechanisms of persuasion, and we direct readers to the seminal handbook on persuasion edited by Dillard and Pfau (2002) and to recent *Communication Yearbook* chapters (Hornikx & O'Keefe, 2009; Noar, Harrington, & Aldrich, 2009; O'Keefe, 2013; O'Keefe & Jensen, 2006) for a comprehensive overview of current theory, research, and topics in this area.

Our review of early research on social influence is selective, and we have chosen concepts, theories and studies that we believe inform understanding of social influence in the Web 2.0 environment; thus, the bulk of our review examines social influence in the Web 2.0 environment. While the body of research on this topic is cross-disciplinary, we focus the scope of our review on online consumption behavior due to space considerations and the vast amount of research findings the field has produced. Much of the research on consumption investigates the influence of online recommendations, reviews, and ratings, which are forms of communication, on consumer perceptions and purchasing behaviors. We believe that many of the insights gained from our review are comprehensive and applicable to other contexts of interest to communication scholars such as health and advocacy.

Early Social Influence Research

Solomon Asch was one of the first researchers to directly measure social influence. In 1951, Asch designed a series of simple experiments to illustrate the influence of other people on a person's own objective judgments. In these experiments, a research participant was asked to make objective judgments of line length while being surrounded by confederates who gave obviously false answers prior to the subject's answers (Asch, 1951). Social influence was measured by the percentage of participants who adopted the incorrect answer after hearing the confederates' incorrect judgments. Facing two opposing forces—"the evidence of his senses and the unanimous opinion of a group of peers" (Asch, 1955, p. 32)—75% of the subjects followed their peers at least once in several experimental sessions. Post-hoc interviews revealed that some took the majority's consensus as proof of truth while others were suspicious but nevertheless abandoned their own judgment.

Deutsch and Gerard (1955) conducted experiments similar to Asch's line experiment with a few variations, including an anonymous situation (vs. face-to-face), and making a judgment from a visual presentation of others' opinions (vs. making a judgment from memory of others' opinions). They found less social influence in the anonymous situation than in the face-to-face situation, suggesting that physical co-presence is conducive to social influence. They also found less social influence when others' answers were visually shown than when retrieved from memory, showing that uncertainty increases social influence.

Festinger (1953) made a distinction between *public conformity* and *private acceptance* to explain different motives underlying conformity behavior. Specifically, public conformity with private acceptance occurs when individuals behave consistently with others and their own attitudes whereas public conformity without private acceptance occurs when they behave consistently with others without internal acceptance (Festinger, 1953). Along the same line of thinking, Kelman (1958) emphasized the importance of motivational processes in understanding and predicting the consequences of attitude change. He argued that attitude change can occur at many different levels, corresponding to the different processes of influence, namely compliance, identification, and internalization. *Compliance* occurs when an individual conforms to others to achieve the approval of others, and not because he or she believes the content of the induced message or behavior. *Identification* refers to the situation when an individual conforms to others in the hopes of building or maintaining a relationship with others or groups that she or he finds desirable. Finally, *internalization* occurs when an individual accepts influence because the content of the proposed message or induced behavior is "intrinsically rewarding" and "congruent with his [or her] value system" (Kelman, 1958, p. 53).

Deutsch and Gerard (1955) postulated that there were two types of social influence, normative and informational. *Normative* social influence is defined as "an influence to conform with the positive expectations of another" and *informational* social influence is "an influence to accept information obtained from another as *evidence* about reality" (p. 629). Put simply, the motivation behind normative social influence is to obtain approval from others whereas informational social influence is to reduce uncertainty about the given situation. Their typology of social influence became "a cornerstone of dual motive approaches to social influence" (Prislin & Crano, 2012, p. 328).

The dual motive approach was corroborated by later research that found motives moderated the role of group size on social influence. Campbell and Fairey (1989) found that the impact of group size on social influence varied depending on whether normative influence or informational influence occurred. Specifically, when the informational need is high, the first source exerted more impact than the second and third sources, contrary to Asch's experiments in which the second and third sources had greater impact than the first. On the other hand, group size was more important when the normative need was higher than the informational need. It may be that informational influence works to the point that cues inferred from others' actions can reduce uncertainty sufficiently to the focal individual.

The idea that accepting social influence is not mindlessly conforming to others is also shared by others (Cialdini & Goldstein, 2004; Cialdini & Trost, 1998; Wood, 2000). After reviewing the extensive literature on social influence, Cialdini and Trost (1998) were prompted to examine why "someone would choose to yield to influence from another" (p. 151). Specifically, Cialdini and his colleagues suggest that accepting influence could be interpreted as purposive to achieve one's own goals, namely—to behave effectively (goal of accuracy), to maintain social relationships (goal of affiliation) and to manage self-concept (Cialdini & Goldstein, 2004; Cialdini & Trost, 1998). For instance, people look to the action of others as a way to identify correct choices in a cognitively efficient way, a principle termed as "social proof" (Cialdini, 2001) or "social validation" (Rhoads & Cialdini, 2002). Thus, when one is motivated to obtain accurate information, the tendency of following others is heightened under uncertain or ambiguous situations (Rhoads & Cialdini, 2002). On the other hand, when one's goal is affiliation, susceptibility to influence varies upon situational (e.g., public vs. private) (Asch, 1951; Deutsch & Gerard, 1955) and cultural factors (e.g., collectivism vs. individualism) (Bond & Smith, 1996).

Summary.   People may have different motives when exposed to the attitudes and behaviors of others. Motives affect the type of influence, whether normative or informational, that will be more dominant in affecting attitude and behavioral change. Although people may demonstrate conformity in attitudes and behaviors publicly, they may not internalize the attitude change. In some cases, the motive for affiliation or belonging may supersede people's desire for expressing their true opinions. Group size makes a bigger difference when an individual's normative need is high.

Models of Social Influence

While the literature discussed above is mainly interested in qualitatively different types and mechanisms of social influence, a few others made attempts to create general models of the social influence process (Latané & Wolf, 1981; Tanford & Penrod, 1984). Departing from the dichotomical or tripartite approaches to social influence, this line of research aims to explain the influence process by considering factors that determine the amount of social influence. First, Latané

(1981) proposed *social impact theory* (SIT), where social impact, or influence, is generally conceptualized as being the result of social forces. SIT posits that the amount of social impact is a multiplicative function of three factors: (a) the strength or intensity of a given source as perceived by the target, (b) the immediacy between the source and the target, and (c) the number of sources present.

Strength refers to "the source's status, age, socioeconomic status, and prior relationship with, or future power over, the target" (Latané & Wolf, 1981, p. 344). Immediacy is "closeness in space or time and absence of intervening barriers or filters" (Latané, 1981, p. 344). In general, the stronger and more immediate the source is to the target, the stronger the social impact. With respect to the number of sources, Latané (1981) argued that the amount of social impact grows in proportion to some root (mostly square root) of the total number of sources; as a result, the first source has the largest impact and each additional source produces less impact than the previous source. The number of targets is also factored into this model such that total social impact is divided as the number of targets increases. As such, SIT incorporates all key factors of social influence into a single theoretical perspective, giving a parsimonious picture of the influence process.

Along a similar line, Tanford and Penrod (1984) proposed the *social influence model* (SIM). While acknowledging the contribution of Latané's SIT to developing a formal model of social influence, Tanford and Penrod criticized the theory for its lack of precision in making predictions and its inability to account for Asch's experimental data which showed that influence positively accelerated with up to three sources, after which the increase leveled off. The biggest difference between Latané's SIT and Tanford and Penrod's SIM is that SIM includes an S-shaped growth curve for the number of sources as opposed to the negatively accelerating function in SIT. This change allows SIM to explain Asch's data and to be consistent with other empirical data. In addition, SIM incorporated other relevant factors of the social influence process such as task type, group type, and individual differences in resistance.

Summary. The number of sources, the attributes of those sources, and the nature of the relationship between source and target are critical variables in models of social influence. Most models predict the social influence exerted by each additional source as the number of sources increases. There is some debate across models about the shape of the curve depicting the relation between number of sources and social influence.

Resistance to Social Influence

Most social influence research has focused on how and why individuals are influenced by others or "choose to yield to influence" from others (Cialdini & Trost, 1998, p. 151). Yet, while a majority of people give in to the power of social influence, some resist it (Wood, Lundgren, Ouelette, Busceme, & Blackstone, 1994). Brehm (1966) called such resistance *psychological reactance.*

The key assumption of psychological reactance theory is that when an individual's behavioral freedom is eliminated or threatened to be eliminated, he or she becomes motivationally aroused to re-establish the reduced or threatened freedom. Threats often involve "attempted interpersonal influence" (Clee & Wicklund, 1980, p. 389) such as persuasive attempts by political campaigners and advertisers. Furthermore, threats can be also self-imposed, independent of external threats such as social influence and product availability because "simply by entering into the process of a decision, the person arrives at a point beyond which there will be an unwanted reduction in freedom" (Clee & Wicklund, 1980, p. 397).

The magnitude of reactance varies with the importance and proportion of the free behaviors lost or threatened. In addition, reactance can be reduced when a justification is present that suggests the threat was emergent, temporary or unavoidable. Therefore, the "workings" of social influence within an individual can not only be explained by the magnitude of social impact as discussed above, but also by how much reactance the person feels, such that one will yield to influence from others to the extent that the magnitude of reactance does not exceed the amount of social influence.

The theory of psychological reactance adds complexity to the process of social influence; as Brehm (1966) argues, "as the pressure to comply increases, the pressure not to comply also increases and the resultant effect on the individual's final response is difficult to predict" (p. 14). The reason why 25% of participants in Asch's line experiments never let the majority affect their judgments even once could be either that their residual reactance was greater than social influence or that the pressure to conform to the majority in fact increased the amount of reactance.

Summary.   Although many people succumb to social influence, others resist it. Any discussion of social influence should consider what makes people resistant to social influence. There are individual differences in people's susceptibility to social influence. Susceptibility to influence also appears to vary depending on the situation (for example, people succumb more to social influence under uncertainty), and the degree to which people feel their freedom to behave as they choose is threatened.

Online Social Influence in Early Computer-Mediated Communication and Web 1.0

Research within the classical social influence paradigm discussed in the previous section involved face-to-face interpersonal or small group contexts with few exceptions. As the Internet became a major part of communication infrastructure, allowing for so-called computer-mediated communication (CMC), social behavior in mediated contexts grew as an area of research. Computer-mediated communication was once narrowly defined as communication mediated by email or computer conferencing (Walther, 1992), but it has continued to broaden with further technological innovations (Walther & Parks, 2002).

What essentially differentiated CMC from face-to-face was anonymity and limited availability of social and nonverbal cues supposedly rendering CMC more immune to social influence. Anonymity is highest when the identity and location of an interacting partner were unknown (Marx, 2001), which was often the case in initial online encounters with strangers. In addition, CMC was said to lack cues important to communication and social interactions such as physical presence and social, nonverbal, and contextual cues, resulting in a reduced sense of social presence (Short, Williams, & Christie, 1976). Such limited access to information about sources was deemed to liberate individuals from influence by those sources.

However, the issue as to whether the lack of cues in CMC necessarily makes it less social was highly contested. On the one hand, early media characteristics theories that categorized media based on their features suggest that communication mediated by technologies "filters out communicative cues found in face-to-face interaction" (Culnan & Markus, 1987, p. 423). For example, social presence theory, categorizing media depending on their capacity for making the communication partner salient in the interaction, stated that the relative absence of cues in CMC presumably leads users to pay less attention to the presence of the partner, inducing less exchange of social and affective content (Short et al., 1976).

Media richness theory by Daft and Lengel (1986), another media characteristics perspective, considered CMC on the low end for media richness, which is determined by "the medium's capacity for immediate feedback, the number of cues and channels utilized, personalization, and language variety" (p. 560). The implication of these theories is that people should exert less influence on one another in a computer-mediated setting where they do not have access to visual cues and feedback is delayed.

The idea that CMC, being anonymous and virtual, may liberate individuals from social influence follows the earlier work on social influence. For example, Deutsch and Gerard (1955) found less social influence in the anonymous as opposed to face-to-face condition. Latané's (1981) social impact theory suggests that social impact decreases as immediacy including physical proximity decreases.

However, findings from studies that compared influence in CMC and face-to-face groups provided mixed support for this hypothesis. For example, Dubrovsky, Kiesler and Sethna (1991) found evidence that the relative influence of high status and low status members on group decisions was more equal in computer-mediated groups as compared to face-to-face groups. In contrast, Weisband, Schneider, and Connolly (1995) and Hollingshead (1996) found that high status members generally had more influence than low status members on group decisions when status differences were known to group members regardless of the communication medium.

Other research also found that people are not so free from social influence in CMC (Lea & Spears, 1992; Postmes, Spears, & Lea, 1998, 2000; Postmes, Spears, Sakhel, & De Groot, 2001). Experimental research supporting the Social Identity Deindividuation Effects model (SIDE) showed that under conditions of deindividuation and the high salience of a common group identity, CMC groups were subject to more interpersonal influence, social attraction, and stereotyping because, in the absence of individuating cues, people used whatever social cues were available, even subtle ones, to form impressions about other people. In contrast, when a common group identity was not salient to members, CMC groups were subject to less interpersonal influence, social attraction and stereotyping than face-to-face groups.

Walther's (1992) social information processing theory, which is an interpersonal communication theory, took a major departure from cues-filtered-out perspective. The central argument is that people have the need to engage in social interactions whether in CMC or not, and thus, over time, they will adapt to the communication medium while finding ways to communicate socioemotional messages such as using textual emoticons or multimedia messages. Therefore, under this theoretical framework, CMC is not inherently inferior to face-to-face in facilitating social interactions although it may take time and effort to build good rapport.

Summary.   Two decades of research and theoretical development have demonstrated that despite its anonymity and lack of social cues, CMC does not necessarily discourage social interactions nor liberate individuals from social influence. This is because, after all, "people need to connect with others" (Barnes, 2008, p. 21) whether online or offline.

The Evolution of the Web and Social Influence

The early literature on online social influence introduced a new understanding about the role of communication media in social influence: that face-to-face communication and physical co-presence were not necessary for supporting the exchange of social meaning and creating a context conducive to social influence. The contemporary digital environment, however, is far from a monolithic system. Web 2.0 is characterized by principles that support individuals' easy participation in content creation and collaboration, whereas the early web only allowed webmasters to create and manage content, as reflected in applications such as Wikipedia (vs. Britannica Online), blogging (vs. personal websites), search engine optimization (vs. domain name speculation), and tagging (vs. directories) (Cormode & Krishnamurthy, 2008; O'Reilly, 2005).

In addition, Web 2.0 is popularly known as the "social web," easily connecting people including friends and strangers to interact with one another. The social nature of Web 2.0 is articulated in the definition of social network sites by Ellison & Boyd (2013). They define a social network site as

> a *networked communication platform* in which participants 1) have *uniquely identifiable profiles* that consist of user-supplied content, content provided by other users, and/or system-level data; 2) can *publicly articulate connections* that can be viewed and traversed by others; and 3) can consume, produce, and/or interact with *streams of user-generated content* provided by their connections on the site.
>
> (p. 158)

The Web 2.0 applications demonstrating the three defining characteristics of social network sites are widespread in many online communities beyond well-known social network sites such as Facebook; for example, members of Yelp, TripAdvisor, and eBay can have their profiles constructed by themselves and others' feedback; publicly display their connections with other members; and engage in user-generated content.

As discussed earlier, the nature of Web 2.0 implies changes in communication by affecting its basic components—source, message, channel and audience. First, as Web 2.0 explicitly promotes social connections and interactions among existing and new relationships, potential sources of social influence are not limited to friends, family, or opinion leaders one sees face-to-face (pre-online) nor confined to anonymous strangers one meets online (early CMC era). Instead, Web 2.0 facilitates all types of sources including close networks, anonymous strangers, and experts to easily produce and share content, thereby increasing both quantity and diversity of sources of social influence.

Sources may differ in the amount of social influence they may generate, depending on their credibility and connections with audience. How one is perceived as credible in the current web environment is much more complicated than before as many cues beyond the source's self-provided credentials, such as others' comments, contribute to constructing one's perceived credibility online (Metzger, Flanagin, & Medders, 2010). It is also extremely easy and common to form a connection with a source by engaging in such activities as subscribing to someone's blog, "friending" in Facebook and "following" in Twitter.

Second, messages produced online that have potential to influence audiences are not limited to messages deliberately drafted by sources, but include "digital traces" of users' behaviors captured and aggregated at the system level such as visits, clicks, likes, recommending, sharing, and "check-ins." Walther and Jang (2012) identified four types of messages common in Web 2.0 sites: proprietor content, user-generated content, deliberate aggregate user representations, and incidental user representations. *Proprietor content* refers to "messages composed and displayed by the primary author or proprietor of a web page" (p. 3) that tend to persist on the site whereas *user-generated content* includes messages that are appended to the proprietor content such as comments and reviews. *Aggregate user representations* refer to "computer-generated descriptive statistics that a web page displays representing accumulations of users' ratings, votes, or other site-related behaviors" (p. 5), which can be deliberate or incidental. *Deliberate aggregate user representations* are created by users' intentional input such as "likes" to provide an expressive or evaluative message. *Incidental aggregate user representations*, on the other hand, include system-generated data that were not originally meant by users to cue anything. Examples include the displayed number of friends on Facebook and view counts on YouTube.

Third, the applications common in the Web 2.0 environment such as blogs, wikis, and social network sites may serve as channels of social influence in varying degrees. In particular, in social network sites, a content-generating user's social connections are publicly articulated, making the user salient as the source with the audience explicitly listed. Design elements of certain sites and applications may increase the visibility and impact of sources.

Lastly, audience plays a crucial role in the dynamics of social influence in the Web 2.0 environment. In particular, the audience affects the impact of a source by publicly giving feedback to the source such as liking, commenting, and sharing. They may also easily denounce the source's reputation as in the case of leaving negative reviews about businesses. Audience behavior can also challenge influence research. It is tempting to interpret audience's activities like following, liking, and retweeting as evidence of being influenced by the source; yet, motivations behind these activities can vary. In addition, with increased awareness of privacy concerns, audience members may deliberately choose not to leave their digital traces, in which case researchers miss out on observing privacy-conscious users' acceptance of social influence.

While current literature on online social influence has directly or indirectly touched upon these issues, organizing the literature using a communication framework of source, message, channel, and audience can help us evaluate the state of the research and identify ways to extend it in the future. For instance, researchers focusing primarily on influential sources (e.g., a Twitter account with a million followers) can either refine their topic of interest by considering other source-related aspects, or turn their attention to factors related to message, channel, and audience to widen understanding of the phenomenon. To that end, our review of the literature and research findings is organized according to source, message, channel, and audience-related factors.

Source Factors

Much research has investigated source-related factors in social influence; that is, what aspects of the source exert influence on targets. This is not surprising given that classical social influence research has given primary attention to this aspect as well. In addition, literature on persuasion has long examined the role of source credibility in the receiver's attitude change, starting with the pioneering work of Hovland, Janis, and Kelley (1953). Source credibility is conceptualized in terms of expertness and trustworthiness by Hovland et al., which suggests that people trust sources that have a known ability to present valid information and have no apparent motivation to present invalid information. Typically, sources with credentials such as government, mass media, academic and professional qualifications have more influence on receivers through their expertise and exclusive access to quality information. Yet, people also trust others whom they know very well, such as family, friends, and colleagues.

Current research on online social influence has also touched upon source credibility, specifically the so-called "influentials" or online leaders, and peers as in the case of online word of mouth. Influentials or online leaders, as Huffaker (2010) defines, are "those who are the most capable of influencing other members of the community" (p. 595). Huffaker specifically focused on online leaders' ability to trigger feedback, stimulate conversations and shape other members' talk and analyzed various Google Groups, which showed communication activity, tenure within a group, network centrality, and reciprocity are positively related to one's ability to influence others. Leaders also tended to write long messages, and used diverse, affective, and assertive words.

The influence of influentials has been measured in various ways. For example, research on Twitter has measured influence by the number of followers, retweets and mentions one receives (Cha, Haddadi, Benevenuto, & Gummadi, 2010), some existing ranking algorithms such as PageRank (Kwak, Lee, Park, & Moon, 2010), and the distance a source's original message travels through a series of retweeting, referred to as cascade size (Bakshy, Hofman, Mason, & Watts, 2011). Different measures of influence shed light on different aspects of influence. For example, the number of followers indicates the size of the audience the source attracts. The number of retweets one receives refers to the ability of the source to "generate content with pass-along value"; the number of mentions represents the ability of the user to "engage others in a conversation" (Cha et al., 2010, p. 12). PageRank, on the other hand, gives more weight to those who are connected with highly connected individuals. The cascade size as a measure of social influence implies that those who create greater diffusion are considered influential (Bakshy et al., 2011).

In addition to locating certain influential individuals, scholars have been interested in how information generated by other users who are considered as peers exerts influence. The pull to follow others also depends on how strongly one associates oneself with the source(s) (Brown & Reingen, 1987). Research has found that social ties in social network sites and online communities exert influence in users' purchase behavior (Iyengar, Han, & Gupta, 2009) and content creation (Shriver, Nair, & Hofstetter, 2013). This is not surprising given the influence social ties have in offline relations.

On the other hand, the tie between the source and audience may not necessarily be strong in online word-of-mouth communication as information can come not only from friends and family but also from a collective of consumers who are loosely connected with the focal consumer via common interest (Chatterjee, 2001). Thus, the influence of online word of mouth may not necessarily be subject to "people like me" as in traditional face-to-face word of mouth. In fact, research found that consumers pay attention to even anonymous posts (Mayzlin, 2004, as cited in Godes & Mayzlin, 2004). In addition, findings from lab experiments suggest that a recommendation from recommender systems was more influential than one from experts or other consumers (Y.-F. Chen, 2008; Senecal & Nantel, 2004). It was also found that non-loyal customers and non-friends had more influence on consumers' awareness of new products especially at the early stage of product life (Godes & Mayzlin, 2009).

Furthermore, in experiments involving Mechanical Turk users, Abbassi et al. (2012) found that recommendations by the anonymous crowd had more impact on the probability of selecting a given item than recommendations by friends. Precisely, while one additional star rating increased the probability by 107%, one additional friend recommendation increased the probability by 22%. Relatedly, Aral and Walker (2011) showed that a friend's marginal influence is greater than an anonymous person's, but friends generate fewer persuasive messages resulting in less total adoption.

There are some unresolved questions in research regarding source-related factors of online social influence. First, what makes influentials so powerful is not clear yet. Cha et al. (2010) provide preliminary insight into this issue. They observed that conversation with others and focusing on a single topic rather than various topics contributes to the largest increase in influence; as they put it, "influence is not gained spontaneously or accidentally, but through concerted effort" (p. 17). Most research has attempted to describe the entire Twitterverse cross-sectionally, but more longitudinal studies may be needed to tease out factors that make the impact of influentials more pronounced.

Second, to what degree does the relationship one has with the source matter in determining the magnitude of influence given the conflicting findings about the influence of close ties? And beyond such actual tie strength, whether a user's sense of psychological identification with the source can affect the amount of influence needs to be examined because users may not actively interact with the source, but can easily assess how similar they are by checking the source's profile information and past activities.

Message Factors

It is essentially the message that determines whether social influence has occurred or not since influence is examined by the degree to which a person has changed their thoughts, feelings, communication, or behavior corresponding to what is reflected in others' message. The literature on persuasion has identified various message variables that can influence the audience's acceptance of persuasive messages such as fear appeals, evidence, one-sidedness, negativity, and so on (O'Keefe, 2013).

Online word of mouth, or the opinions of consumers posted online in the forms of ratings, reviews, and recommendations, have become a major part of consumer routines and have received increased scholarly attention (Duan, Gu, & Whinston, 2008). Although traditional word of mouth has been conceptualized as oral, one-to-one, face-to-face communication about a product or service from noncommercial sources (Chatterjee, 2001; Godes et al., 2005), online or electronic word of mouth is not limited to oral, person-to-person communication, and it is hard to ensure whether the message includes purely noncommercial sources (Chatterjee, 2001). In addition, compared to traditional, interpersonal word-of-mouth communication, online word of mouth is greater in scale and in the range of sources (Chatterjee, 2001; Dellarocas, 2003; Godes et al., 2005).

Previous research has been fairly consistent in finding a positive impact of online word-of-mouth communication on various aspects of consumer behavior. However, different attributes of word of mouth have differential impact. Attributes of word of mouth that are often studied in the literature are valence and volume (Y. Chen, Wang, & Xie, 2011). Valence affects product sales "by changing consumer valuation of the products" whereas volume affects "consumer awareness and the number of informed consumers in the market" (Y. Chen et al., 2011, p. 240).

Volume and valence of word of mouth have generated differential effects as shown in empirical research. Duan et al. (2008) found that the number of reviews for movies was significantly associated with sales while the ratings (valence) were not. Ye, Law, Gu, and Chen (2011) also found a positive association between the number of reviews for a hotel and the number of bookings for the hotel. This volume effect, however, is not consistent. Moe and Trusov (2011) found that ratings of beauty products affect sales through valence but not volume. Similarly, in their research on the relation between online discussion and TV ratings, Godes and Mayzlin (2004) found no significant effect of the volume of discussions on ratings.

Similar results were found in experimental research. For example, M. Chen et al. (2010) didn't find an effect of number of reviews on the intention to purchase books. Flanagin, Metzger, Pure, and Markov (2011) asked participants to evaluate product quality while varying average product ratings and number of reviews. Results revealed that people attend to the average product ratings but not to the number of reviews; evaluations of product quality did not differ when the number of reviews was 4 versus 1002.

Valence of word of mouth, on the other hand, was generally found to influence consumer attitudes and behaviors both in experimental settings (Y.-F. Chen, 2008) and real e-commerce settings (Chevalier & Mayzlin, 2006), with an exception of Duan et al. (2008). There is a positivity bias from the source side, as reviews and ratings are overwhelmingly positive on commercial sites (Chevalier & Mayzlin, 2006; Mackiewicz, 2007). On the other hand, a negativity bias (Mizerski, 1982), or "positive-negative asymmetry effect" (Abbassi et al., 2012, p. 374) was found from the audience side as negative reviews and ratings were more influential than positive ones (Abbassi et al., 2012; M. Chen et al., 2010; Y. Chen et al., 2011; Y.-F. Chen, 2008; Chevalier & Mayzlin, 2006). Zhang, Craciun, and Shin (2010) provided a more nuanced view into the positive-negative asymmetry effect of word of mouth.

Compared to volume and valence, what is lacking in the literature is attention to the distribution or variance of positive and negative sentiments. Valence of word of mouth is typically measured by the average of all ratings for a given object without considering how the ratings are dispersed. Nowadays, many online retailers such as Amazon and review communities such as Yelp provide information on the distribution of ratings in addition to the average ratings. The distribution of ratings may be particularly important to discriminate products with similar ratings when the ratings are in the middle range (e.g., 2–4 star ratings). As an example, with all things held constant, would consumers be likely to choose 4-star products with individual ratings widely distributed or 3.5-star products with consistent ratings? According to Latané and Wolf (1981), a unanimous majority exerts great influence pressure, pulling the target into the same direction.

In general, prior research finds positive effects of rater consensus on conformity (M. Chen et al., 2010). That is, the more agreement among raters, the more likely a reader will follow the direction induced by the ratings. Yet, a unanimous majority can raise a red flag among readers who doubt the trustworthiness of extremely positive messages. Such optimum balance between consensus in message valence and credibility of messages has not been examined, which is a topic for future research.

Popularity is often a proxy for online social influence. That is, the number of times a particular message is shared or talked about with others is used as a measure of social influence. Berger (2013) examined the factors that drive online news articles, videos, political messages and products to become popular, and identified six main factors: social currency, triggers, emotion, public, practical value, and stories. *Social currency* refers to how good something makes the sender look for sharing it. *Triggers* are the number of ideas, products and behaviors that are naturally associated with triggers. The more a piece of content triggers other concepts, the more likely it will be shared. Highly arousing *emotional* content both negative and positive is more likely to be shared than low emotional content. Items that are highly *public* and visible are more likely to be talked about and imitated than those that are private. Sources are more likely to pass on messages that have a *practical* value for the receiver. Messages that are presented as *stories* are more influential than those that are presented as information.

Channel Factors

The impact of channel on communication and outcomes was a central issue in Web 1.0 research. Literature on media characteristics such as social presence theory, media richness theory, and technology affordances suggested that channels could have a significant impact on the potential for social influence. Researchers proposed various communication technology typologies that involved communication channels. Most were organized around the degree to which the technology included various channels (nonverbal, paraverbal, text or graphics) and supported asynchronous or synchronous communication (McGrath & Hollingshead, 1994).

By defining channels as any means through which people communicate, we focus on technological features of Web 2.0 applications to describe how social influence can be shaped and bounded by structural characteristics of the chosen applications. Web 2.0 applications such as social media offer users a variety of features (e.g., video, photos, audio, text and real-time chat) in which to express themselves. These features can affect the dynamics of social influence as they differ in promoting and articulating social relations and interactions (Kaplan & Haenlein, 2010).

Much research on online social influence has involved social media and commerce applications such as Twitter, Facebook, eBay and Amazon. Twitter, besides its popularity and its role as a real-time information sharing medium, has become a common research context for influence scholars in part because the jargon used in the site has direct reference to influence. On Twitter, people can be "following" others (i.e., subscribing to their updates), have "followers" (i.e., subscribers), and "retweet" others' content (i.e., distribute content while giving credit to the original author). This structural characteristic of Twitter helps make a directed network of "who listens to whom" (Bakshy et al., 2011).

Facebook enables users to interact with others in many different ways such as writing a post, liking, commenting, tagging, sharing photos and videos, making it extremely easy to see who says what, what the person has previously said, who else has agreed with the message, and so on. On the other hand, wikis, the collaborative content creation application, do not explicitly show information about writers of a certain page, making it hard for each individual author to affect the reader's thought.

E-commerce sites such as eBay and Amazon provide online product reviews, ratings of buyers and sellers, and recommender systems so researchers are able to look at the differential impacts of opinions, ratings, and the actions of other people on actual purchase behavior. Many users include photos and videos in their reviews, which may be perceived more reliable by other consumers, thereby exerting more influence.

Audience Factors

As scholars have noted in early literature, one's acceptance of social influence tends to be driven by personal goals such as to obtain accurate information, to affiliate with others, or to manage self-impressions (Cialdini & Trost, 1998). Along this line, research has found that audience characteristics play a role in online social influence. For example, Vermeulen and Seegers (2009) found that the effect of online hotel reviews differed by consumers' familiarity with the hotel as consumers' own knowledge about the hotel made them resilient to the impact of word of mouth. Consumers who had low awareness of a new TV program were found to be more receptive of others' messages as shown in the study of a Usenet newsgroup (Godes & Mayzlin, 2004). Similarly, Hung and Li (2007) analyzed postings of a beauty forum and concluded that the effects of online word of mouth depend on consumers' prior product knowledge. Specifically, "to an uninformed consumer, eWOM (electronic word of mouth) may trigger variety-seeking and excessive buying; to an informed consumer, eWOM facilitates selective buying tailored to the consumer's specific needs" (Hung & Li, 2007, p. 493). These findings are also consistent with the general finding from early research that uncertainty is positively associated with social influence.

Another factor moderating the audience's propensity for conformity is reactance (Brehm, 1966). Drawing from Brehm's (1966) theory of reactance, Fitzsimons and Lehmann (2004) expected that unwanted recommendations and advice from others would be perceived as threats to the freedom to individuals, and found support for this hypothesis. When recommendations were contrary to participants' initial impressions, they went against the recommended direction. Although not examined to date, online reviews and recommendations could be potential sources of freedom threats to some degree, especially if readers perceive certain aspects of reviews and recommendations as explicit attempts to pull them in a certain direction (Brehm, 1966).

Last but not least, audience plays an even more active role in the dynamics of online social influence in the Web 2.0 environment. That anyone can be a content creator means that any receiver can publish thoughts by reacting to the original source's content. Such reaction to other's profiles and content, or "metavoicing" as termed by Majchrzak, Faraj, Kane, and Azad (2013), not only signals the evidence of social influence on the receiver side but also contributes to constructing the source's reputation. Essentially, a source's message hardly stays intact but evolves as the audience reacts to it. Such audience reactions to the original message further affect new audience members' perception of the original message (Lee, 2012).

A Look Back to the Classics: Insights from Traditional Research on Social Influence

Our thesis is that concepts, theory, and research derived from early work on social influence can inform understanding of online social influence. In this section, we lay out five insights gained from our look back at classic research and its integration with current research in the Web 2.0 environment. Some insights demonstrate consistency across different communication contexts: face-to-face, Web 1.0, and Web 2.0. Other insights demarcate differences given the additional complexity introduced by the technology capabilities of Web 2.0 applications.

Insight 1: Social influence is most likely to occur when receivers are trying to reduce uncertainty whether online or offline.

This finding was demonstrated consistently in studies across the three contexts of our review.

Insight 2: User motivations are important to consider in the study of online social influence.

Web 2.0 communications and actions are generally public, and users are often more than aware of this fact. As a result, impression management is likely to be an important motivation for many users in their messages and online behaviors. In addition, user motivations are likely to vary across different applications and may affect the weighting of the factors that lead to social influence. For example, the factors that affect which book a user chooses to purchase on a commerce site are likely to be different than those that affect whether a user responds to a friend's post on a social media site. In the latter case, informational influence may be more likely to operate; in the former, normative influence may be more apparent.

Insight 3: User messages and behaviors may or may not be evidence of private acceptance or of social influence.

This insight is closely related to Insight 2. The public context is likely to affect what users say and do regardless of their private opinions.

In addition, purchase behaviors may be based on other factors besides online reviews and the purchase decisions of other users, such as previous product experience. Users share content for reasons other than social influence (Nadkarni & Hofmann, 2012; Papacharissi, 2010). When users share content with other users, receivers may or may not read or be influenced by the content. In any case, researchers should not assume without measuring private attitudes pre and post exposure to messages and/or digital traces in Web 2.0 applications whether private acceptance has actually occurred.

It is also important to keep in mind when conducting research using field data that some users, whether companies or individuals, engage in questionable practices to appear more popular or important. For example, users can purchase large numbers of followers on Twitter, Instagram and other social media inexpensively. Companies (or individuals) can pay individuals or have employees write fake online reviews, retweet content, or contribute other digital traces to create a positive impression (Guynn & Chang, 2012). Users may also try to sabotage competitors by writing negative reviews or by leaving negative digital traces. Distinguishing inauthentic contributions from authentic ones is not easy. For example, Ott, Choi, Cardie, and Hancock (2011) created a pool of "deceptive" reviews and "truthful" reviews from TripAdvisor.com, and found little difference in language use. Contrary to the interpersonal deception literature, deceptive reviews included positive emotion terms and first person singulars as much as truthful reviews did.

Insight 4: The weights of parameters in general models of social influence in Web 2.0 contexts are likely to differ from face-to-face contexts.

Traditional models of social influence proposed that social influence is a function of the number of sources present, the strength or intensity of a given source as perceived by the target, and the immediacy between the source and the target (Latané, 1981; Tanford & Penrod, 1984).

As shown in Web 2.0 research, the immediacy between the source and the target is generally less important in predicting social influence than the number of sources (Abbassi et al., 2012). In addition, the strength and intensity of a source in Web 2.0 applications is in large part determined by search engines and/or other algorithms in the application, which affect users' prioritization in information processing (Pan et al., 2007). Searching algorithms in applications privilege the most current, the most viewed, the most highly ranked, the most connected or paid sources, each of which can bias users' decisions to select, read, and trust sources. In other words, in Web 2.0 contexts, models of social influence can be complicated by interface design and business interests.

Insight 5: Reactance is psychological resistance to unsolicited and unwanted recommendations, advice and influence attempts that can occur in all communication contexts.

Researchers have provided evidence of reactance in traditional and Web 2.0 contexts. Users are generally more likely to be influenced by solicited rather than unsolicited advice and recommendations. In Web 2.0 contexts, users have a public forum in which to express dissatisfaction with unwanted influence attempts, and their responses can have a large impact on other users. Marketers and other individuals whose intentions are to influence other users should ensure their influence tactics do not threaten the freedom of users especially in Web 2.0 contexts. The conditions under which reactance occurs, the behavioral manifestations of reactance and the consequences of reactance in Web 2.0 applications are especially interesting topics for future research, which we discuss next.

An Agenda for Future Research on Online Social Influence

For scholars studying social influence, the current Web 2.0 environment offers both opportunities for future research and additional challenges. One of the primary opportunities lies in the availability of ample data about real interactions and behavior (Ackland, 2013; Aral & Walker, 2011; Bakshy, Karrer, & Adamic, 2009; Cha et al., 2010). While traditional social influence research employed experiments or surveys, by analyzing online opinions, conversations, and even behaviors, researchers can gather data that do not rely on self-reports, which are subject to inaccuracy (Godes & Mayzlin, 2004). Particularly, studying influence using data that capture people's real interaction patterns and behaviors can provide useful insights into how real societies work outside the lab (Cha et al., 2010). As shown in the Twitter studies, researchers can gather data on users and their interactions in situ.

In addition, by partnering with firms that offer social media platforms and applications, researchers can conduct large-scale, randomized field experiments, which allow them to determine causal links between an influence source and the subsequent adoption of the induced behavior or message (Aral & Walker, 2011; Bakshy et al., 2012).

Lack of Consensus in Online Social Influence Measurement

The most striking and problematic issue in current online social influence research is the lack of consensus in what influence means (Cha et al., 2010), resulting in various measures of social influence. The classical conformity research paradigm such as Asch's line experiment measured social influence directly. Influence occurred when people chose to follow confederates' obviously inaccurate judgments. The question that motivated Asch's experiment was, "how, and to what extent, do social forces *constrain* [emphasis added] people's opinions and attitudes?" (Asch, 1955, p. 31). What made such results interesting is that rational individuals can sometimes ignore their own accurate judgments in favor of others.

Measuring social influence is not so clear cut in Web 2.0 settings and the data can be subject to multiple interpretations. In the context of online social influence, what constitutes influence is questionable. Many studies use the link between predecessors' actions or messages and successors' adoption, purchase (often in aggregated sales data or intention to purchase), or information sharing such as retweeting, as evidence of social influence.

Suppose, however, online social influence is defined as the degree to which one's choices are constrained by others' advice or action online. Without knowledge of one's pre-existing alternatives and preferences prior to exposure to the communicative or behavioral actions of others, researchers cannot determine with certainty whether one's reaction that appears to be in the same direction as sources is indeed the outcome of social influence or is simply a reflection of the person's prior attitude, habit, or identity. Decomposing the audience's reaction into source-induced and self-directed effects is difficult when measures use data that can have multiple interpretations. Therefore, researchers must give careful thought to contextual factors affecting their target's behavior to make sure that the best explanation is that of social influence, not something else.

The issue of the validity of online behavioral data as a measure of social influence is even more complicated when we consider possible motivations behind one's behavior online. First, not everyone who "likes" a post may truly like it. The recent debate about "slacktivism," a combination of the words slacker and activism, speaks of the discrepancy between users' participation in online activism and their actual involvement (Christensen, 2011). In Festinger's (1953) terms, one's online behavior can be "public compliance" but not necessarily "private acceptance." This may not be an issue if a researcher defines social influence considering both public compliance and public acceptance, which has not generally been done in current research.

Another user motivation to consider when interpreting an online behavior is maintaining privacy and protecting personal information online. A recent national survey showed that 86% of Internet users have taken some actions to remove or hide their digital traces such as clearing cookies and avoiding using real names (Rainie, Kiesler, Kang, & Madden, 2013). Researchers must take into consideration the potential sampling bias due to privacy concerns such that only a portion of the total audience, particularly socially active users, are publicly visible and included in the study.

The best strategy is to use multiple research methods. Although big data opens up exciting opportunities for studying online social influence, it requires researchers to make strong assumptions about what constitutes evidence of social influence. Traditional research on social influence used laboratory experiments almost exclusively. Precision and control are paramount to operationalizing social influence and determining whether it has in fact occurred. By designing an additional experiment to confirm the findings of a large-scale study that measures pre-exposure and post-exposure opinions or actions, researchers can gain confidence that their earlier observations were indeed evidence of online social influence. A growing number of researchers have been conducting a massive-scale randomized controlled experiments in situ either by working for or collaborating with social network sites like Facebook (Bond et al., 2012; Kramer, Guillory, & Hancock, 2014). However, there are ethical concerns surrounding this practice as informed consent pertaining to these studies has not been obtained by users who were included in the experiments. The issue of ethics in conducting a field experiment without informed consent is beyond the scope of this chapter, but researchers must be wary of possible risks to participants as they try to increase experimental control in natural settings.

Broadening Online Social Influence to Include Words and Actions

Despite the fact that one's behavior online is easily observable, researchers tend to use behavioral data primarily for measuring outcomes of social influence processes (with a few exceptions such as Celen, Kariv, and Schotter (2010) and Y. Chen et al. (2011)). That is, scholars' interest mainly centers on how user behaviors, such as adoption and purchase, are shaped by *persuasive messages* communicated online, commonly termed as word of mouth in the online consumption context.

Godes et al. (2005) argued that the traditional view of online consumer communication has been too narrow given that consumers engage in a wide variety of interactions online and are increasingly influenced by them. Thus, they propose an intentionally general term *social interactions* (SI) to capture the breadth of actions taken by consumers "not actively engaged in selling the product or service" (Godes et al., 2005, p. 416). Their use of the term social interactions acknowledges the importance of both verbal messages like word of mouth and actions taken by others in online social influence.

In a similar vein, Y. Chen et al. (2011) point out that while word of mouth has been often studied, the role of information about others' actions, or *observational learning,* has been largely ignored in online social influence research. Drawing from the theory of herd behavior (Banerjee, 1992) and information cascade theory (Bikhchandani et al., 1992), they argued that people observe others' actions and follow them while ignoring their private information because it takes less time and effort to follow others. Chen et al. thus applied both word of mouth (WOM) and observational learning (OL) as social influence sources to examine their differential effects on product sales on Amazon.com. Info about others' actions that people attend to (OL) was gleaned by people's reactions to the site's feature, "What do customers ultimately buy after viewing this item?" As typically done, WOM was measured by product reviews. A natural experiment was done as Amazon removed this OL feature, and later reintroduced it. The results showed that negative WOM had a greater impact than positive WOM, supporting the negativity bias; however, positive OL (i.e., a large percentage of people who viewed this item bought it) was more effective than negative OL supposedly because positive OL is more diagnostic of product quality and popularity. In contrast, Celen et al. (2010) conducted an experimental study of decision making involving computerized tasks, while giving participants both advice information (similar to WOM) and consumer action information (OL). Although action and advice were equally informative, participants were more likely to follow the advice than the action information.

Given the conflicting findings between the field and lab experiments, the best conclusion yet may be that we do not have enough evidence to understand how exactly words and actions play different roles in online social influence. However, research opportunities are abundant and wide open. In the social media context, the actions of others are automatically documented at the system level or easily communicated by users. For example, Amazon.com, for each product item, shows a list of items that "Customers who viewed this item also viewed."

In addition, many commercial, entertainment, and informational sites enable users to share the content while showing a running tally of retweets, sharing, and clicks. Individual consumers can also choose to share their check-in at physical places like restaurants and their purchase activities after making actual transactions. All of these are powerful, trustworthy signals of consumer actions (Donath, 2007), which can be considered a new type of social influential message. Future research should take the advantage of using such behavioral data available not only as the outcome variable but also as the predictor variable to observe its ability to facilitate the same behavior in others.

Investigating Message and Channel Characteristics

Although there has been extensive research on the characteristics of persuasive messages, with the rise of sharing activities, recent research has also turned its focus to which content goes viral, creating greater and wider circles of social influence. Berger and Milkman (2012) found that content that evokes high-arousal positive emotions such as awe is more viral than content evoking negative, low-arousal emotions. In addition, message format was found to affect its viral capacity. For example, list-type stories, so-called "listicles" are perceived to be of practical value, and get shared more often (Berger, 2013). On a similar note, many forms of messages exist online such as videos, short looping video clips (e.g., Vine), still images, flash images, filtered photos (e.g.,

Instagram), infographic, listicles, and so on. The extent to which packaging or formatting of a message affects its influence has yet to be examined.

The role of channel on social influence, particularly with regard to structural characteristics of sites and applications on the web, should be explored further. A given word or action may have the same or different amounts of influence depending on the channel where it is encountered. For example, does a positive restaurant review from a given individual have the same impact whether it is viewed on a Facebook page or on a trusted restaurant review site? In this example, the source, message and receiver are held constant and only the channel is varied. Research suggests that websites vary in their perceived credibility and that can impact perceivers' views of the quality of information on the site (Metzger et al., 2003), which could in turn affect the influence of that information. It is an empirical question that needs to be tested.

Conclusion

Increased connectivity in Web 2.0 applications has greatly increased the number and variety of potential influence sources; the amount and types of communication messages exchanged between individuals; the variety of channels available to transmit a message, and the potential size and variability of the audience. In this review of online social influence research, we used a communication approach centering on sources, messages, channel, and audience to organize the burgeoning research around this topic. We referred back to classic works in social influence for insights in conceptualizing and measuring social influence in current Web 2.0 and future applications. We advocate this general approach for studying any online phenomenon and conclude our review with a quote attributed to Aristotle, "If you would understand anything, observe its beginning and its development."

References

Abbassi, Z., Aperjis, C., & Huberman, B. (2012). Swayed by friends or by the crowd? In K. Aberer, A. Flache, W. Jager, L. Liu, J. Tang & C. Gueret (Eds.), *Proceedings of the 4th International Conference on Social Informatics* (pp. 365–378). doi:10.1007/978-3-642-35386-4_27

Ackland, R. (2013). *Web social science: Concepts, data and tools for social scientists in the digital age*. Thousand Oaks, CA: Sage.

Aral, S., & Walker, D. (2011). Creating social contagion through viral product design: A randomized trial of peer influence in networks. *Management Science, 57*, 1623–1639. doi:10.1287/mnsc.1110.1421

Asch, S. E. (1951). Effects of group pressure upon the modification and distortion of judgments. In H. Guetzkow (Ed.), *Groups, leadership and men: Research in human relations* (pp. 177–188). Pittsburgh, PA: Carnegie Press.

Asch, S. E. (1955). Opinions and social pressure. *Scientific American, 193*, 31–35. doi:10.1038/scientificamerican1155-31

Bakshy, E., Karrer, B., & Adamic, L. A. (2009). Social influence and the diffusion of user-created content. In *Proceedings of the 10th ACM Conference on Electronic commerce* (pp. 325–334). doi:10.1145/1566374.1566421

Bakshy, E., Hofman, J. M., Mason, W. A., & Watts, D. J. (2011). Everyone's an influencer: Quantifying influence on Twitter. In *Proceedings of the 4th ACM International Conference on Web Search and Data Mining* (pp. 65–74). doi:10.1145/1935826.1935845

Bakshy, E., Rosenn, I., Marlow, C., & Adamic, L. (2012). The role of social networks in information diffusion. In *Proceedings of the 21st International Conference on World Wide Web* (pp. 519–528). doi:10.1145/2187836.2187907

Banerjee, A. V. (1992). A simple model of herd behavior. *The Quarterly Journal of Economics, 107*, 797–817. doi:10.2307/2118364

Barnes, S. B. (2008). Understanding social media from the media ecological perspective. In E. A. Konjin, S. Utz, M. Tanis & S. B. Barnes (Eds.), *Mediated Interpersonal Communication* (pp. 14–33). New York, NY: Routledge.

Berger, J. (2013). *Contagious: Why things catch on.* New York, NY: Simon & Schuster.

Berger, J., & Milkman, K. L. (2012). What makes online content viral? *Journal of Marketing Research, 49*, 192–205. doi:10.1509/jmr.10.0353

Berlo, D. K. (1960). *The process of communication: An introduction to theory and practice.* New York, NY: Holt, Rinehart and Winston.

Bikhchandani, S., Hirshleifer, D., & Welch, I. (1992). A theory of fads, fashion, custom, and cultural change as informational cascades. *Journal of Political Economy, 100*, 992–1026. doi:10.1086/261849

Bond, R., & Smith, P. B. (1996). Culture and conformity: A meta-analysis of studies using Asch's (1952b, 1956) line judgment task. *Psychological Bulletin; Psychological Bulletin, 119*, 111–137. doi:10.1037/0033-2909.119.1.111

Bond, R., Fariss, C. J., Jones, J. J., Kramer, A. D., Marlow, C., Settle, J. E., & Fowler, J. H. (2012). A 61-million-person experiment in social influence and political mobilization. *Nature, 489*, 295–298. doi:10.1038/nature11421

Brehm, J. W. (1966). *A theory of psychological reactance.* New York: Academic Press.

Brown, J. J., & Reingen, P. H. (1987). Social ties and word-of-mouth referral behavior. *Journal of Consumer Research, 14*, 350–362. doi:10.1086/209118

Campbell, J. D., & Fairey, P. J. (1989). Informational and normative routes to conformity: The effect of faction size as a function of norm extremity and attention to the stimulus. *Journal of Personality and Social Psychology, 57*(3), 457–468. doi:10.1037/0022-3514.57.3.457

Celen, B., Kariv, S., & Schotter, A. (2010). An experimental test of advice and social learning. *Management Science, 56*, 1687–1701. doi:10.1287/mnsc.1100.1228

Centola, D. (2010). The spread of behavior in an online social network experiment. *Science, 329*, 1194–1197. doi:10.1126/science.1185231

Cha, M., Haddadi, H., Benevenuto, F., & Gummadi, K. P. (2010). Measuring user influence in Twitter: The million follower fallacy. In *Proceedings of the 4th International AAAI Conference on Weblogs and Social Media* (pp. 10–17). Retrieved from https://www.aaai.org/ocs/index.php/ICWSM/ICWSM10/paper/view/1538

Chatterjee, P. (2001). Online reviews: Do consumers use them? In M. C. Gilly & J. Meyers-Levy (Eds.), *Advances in consumer research* (Vol. 28, pp. 129–133). Valdosta, GA: Association for Consumer Research.

Chen, M., Ma, Q., Li, M., Lai, H., Wang, X., & Shu, L. (2010). Cognitive and emotional conflicts of counter-conformity choice in purchasing books online: An event-related potentials study. *Biological Psychology, 85*, 437–445. doi:10.1016/j.biopsycho.2010.09.006

Chen, Y., Wang, Q., & Xie, J. (2011). Online social interactions: A natural experiment on word of mouth versus observational learning. *Journal of Marketing Research, 48*, 238–254. doi:10.1509/jmkr.48.2.238

Chen, Y.-F. (2008). Herd behavior in purchasing books online. *Computers in Human Behavior, 24*, 1977–1992. doi:10.1016/j.chb.2007.08.004

Chevalier, J. A., & Mayzlin, D. (2006). The effect of word of mouth on sales: Online book reviews. *Journal of Marketing Research, 43*, 345–354. doi:10.1509/jmkr.43.3.345

Christakis, N. A., & Fowler, J. H. (2007). The spread of obesity in a large social network over 32 years. *New England Journal of Medicine, 357*, 370–379. doi:10.1056/NEJMsa066082

Christensen, H. S. (2011). Political activities on the Internet: Slacktivism or political participation by other means? *First Monday, 16*(2). doi:10.5210/fm.v16i2.3336

Cialdini, R. B. (2001). *Influence: Science and practice* (4th ed.). Needham Heights, MA: Allyn & Bacon.

Cialdini, R. B., & Goldstein, N. J. (2004). Social influence: Compliance and conformity. *Annual Review of Psychology, 55*, 591–621. doi:10.1146/annurev.psych.55.090902.142015

Cialdini, R. B., & Trost, M. R. (1998). Social influence: Social norms, conformity, and compliance. In D. T. Gilbert, S. T. Fiske & G. Lindzey (Eds.), *The handbook of social psychology* (4th ed., Vol. 2, pp. 151–192). Boston, MA: McGraw-Hill.

Clee, M. A., & Wicklund, R. A. (1980). Consumer behavior and psychological reactance. *Journal of Consumer Research, 6*, 389–405. doi:10.1086/208782

Cormode, G., & Krishnamurthy, B. (2008). Key differences between Web 1.0 and Web 2.0. *First Monday, 13*(6). doi:10.5210/fm.v13i6.2125

Culnan, M. J., & Markus, M. L. (1987). Information technologies. In F. M. Jablin, L. L. Putnam, K. H. Roberts & L. W. Porter (Eds.), *Handbook of organizational communication: An interdisciplinary perspective* (pp. 420–443). Newbury Park, CA: Sage.

Daft, R. L., & Lengel, R. H. (1986). Organizational information requirements, media richness, and structural design. *Management Science, 32*(5), 554–571. doi:10.1287/mnsc.32.5.554

Dellarocas, C. (2003). The digitization of word of mouth: Promise and challenges of online feedback mechanisms. *Management Science, 49*, 1407–1424. doi:10.1287/mnsc.49.10.1407.17308

Deutsch, M., & Gerard, H. B. (1955). A study of normative and informational social influences upon individual judgment. *Journal of Abnormal and Social Psychology, 51*, 629–636. doi:10.1037/h0046408

Dillard, J. P., & Pfau, M. (2002). *The persuasion handbook: Developments in theory and practice*. Thousand Oaks, CA: Sage.

Donath, J. (2007). Signals in social supernets. *Journal of Computer-Mediated Communication, 13*, 231–251. doi:10.1111/j.1083-6101.2007.00394.x

Duan, W., Gu, B., & Whinston, A. B. (2008). Do online reviews matter? An empirical investigation of panel data. *Decision Support Systems, 45*, 1007–1016. doi:10.1016/j.dss.2008.04.001

Dubrovsky, V. J., Kiesler, S., & Sethna, B. N. (1991). The equalization phenomenon: Status effects in computer-mediated and face-to-face decision-making groups. *Human-Computer Interaction, 6*, 119–146. doi:10.1207/s15327051hci0602_2

Ellison, N. B., & Boyd, D. (2013). Sociality through social network sites. In W. H. Dutton (Ed.), *The Oxford handbook of Internet studies* (pp. 151–172). Oxford, UK: Oxford University Press.

Festinger, L. (1953). An analysis of compliant behavior. In M. Sherif & M. O. Wilson (Eds.), *Group relations at the crossroads* (pp. 232–256). New York: Harper.

Fitzsimons, G. J., & Lehmann, D. R. (2004). Reactance to recommendations: When unsolicited advice yields contrary responses. *Marketing Science, 23*, 82–94. doi:10.1287/mksc.1030.0033

Flanagin, A. J., Metzger, M. J., Pure, R., & Markov, A. (2011). User-generated ratings and the evaluation of credibility and product quality in ecommerce transactions. In *Proceedings of the 44th Hawaii International Conference on System Sciences* (pp. 1–10). doi:10.1109/HICSS.2011.474

Godes, D., & Mayzlin, D. (2004). Using online conversations to study word-of-mouth communication. *Marketing Science, 23*, 545–560. doi:10.1287/mksc.1040.0071

Godes, D., & Mayzlin, D. (2009). Firm-created word-of-mouth communication: Evidence from a field test. *Marketing Science, 28*, 721–739. doi:10.1287/mksc.1080.0444

Godes, D., Mayzlin, D., Chen, Y., Das, S., Dellarocas, C., Pfeiffer, B., . . . Verlegh, P. (2005). The firm's management of social interactions. *Marketing Letters, 16*, 415–428. doi:10.1007/s11002-005-5902-4

Guynn, J., & Chang, A. (2012, July 4). Yelp reviews: Can you trust them? Some firms game the system. *Los Angeles Times.* Retrieved October 29, 2012, from http://articles.latimes.com/2012/jul/04/business/la-fi-yelp-reviews-20120704

Hollingshead, A. B. (1996). Information suppression and status persistence in group decision making the effects of communication media. *Human Communication Research, 23*, 193–219. doi:10.1111/j.1468-2958.1996.tb00392.x

Hornikx, J., & O'Keefe, D. J. (2009). Adapting consumer advertising appeals to cultural values: A meta-analytic review of effects on persuasiveness and ad liking. In C. S. Beck (Ed.), *Communication yearbook 33* (pp. 39–62). New York: Routledge.

Hovland, C. I., Janis, I. L., & Kelley, H. H. (1953). *Communication and persuasion.* New Haven, CT: Yale University Press.

Huffaker, D. A. (2010). Dimensions of leadership and social influence in online communities. *Human Communication Research, 36*, 593–617. doi:10.1111/j.1468-2958.2010.01390.x

Hung, K. H., & Li, S. Y. (2007). The influence of eWOM on virtual consumer communities: Social capital, consumer learning, and behavioral outcomes. *Journal of Advertising Research, 47*, 485–495. doi:10.2501/S002184990707050X

Iyengar, R., Han, S., & Gupta, S. (2009). *Do friends influence purchases in a social network?* (09–123). Marketing Unit Working Papers, Harvard Business School. Retrieved from http://hbswk.hbs.edu/item/6185.html

Kaplan, A. M., & Haenlein, M. (2010). Users of the world, unite! The challenges and opportunities of social media. *Business Horizons 53*, 59–68. doi:10.1016/j.bushor.2009.09.003

Katz, E., & Lazarsfeld, P. F. (1955). *Personal influence.* New York, NY: The Free Press.

Kelman, H. C. (1958). Compliance, identification, and internalization: Three processes of attitude change. *Journal of Conflict Resolution, 2*, 51–60. doi:10.1177/002200275800200106

Kramer, A. D., Guillory, J., & Hancock, J. T. (2014). Experimental evidence of massive-scale emotional contagion through social networks. *Proceedings of the National Academy of Sciences.* doi:10.1073/pnas.1320040111

Kwak, H., Lee, C., Park, H., & Moon, S. (2010). What is Twitter, a social network or a news media? In *Proceedings of the 19th International Conference on World Wide Web* (pp. 591–600). doi:10.1145/1772690.1772751

Lasswell, H. D. (1948). The structure and function of communication in society. In L. Bryson (Ed.), *The communication of ideas* (pp. 37–51). New York, NY: Harper.

Latané, B. (1981). The psychology of social impact. *American Psychologist, 36*, 343–356. doi:10.1037/0003-066X.36.4.343

Latané, B., & Wolf, S. (1981). The social impact of majorities and minorities. *Psychological Review, 88*, 438–453. doi:10.1037/0033-295X.88.5.438

Lea, M., & Spears, R. (1992). Paralanguage and social perception in computer-mediated communication. *Journal of Organizational Computing and Electronic Commerce, 2*, 321–341. doi:10.1080/10919399209540190

Lee, E. J. (2012). That's not the way it is: How user-generated comments on the news affect perceived media bias. *Journal of Computer-Mediated Communication, 18*, 32–45. doi:10.1111/j.1083-6101.2012.01597.x

Mackiewicz, J. (2007). Reviewer bias and credibility in online reviews. In *Proceedings of the 2007 Association for Business Communication Annual Convention*. Retrieved from http://businesscommunication.org/CMS/Resources/proceedings/2007annual/2007annual/06abc07.pdf

Majchrzak, A., Faraj, S., Kane, G. C., & Azad, B. (2013). The contradictory influence of social media affordances on online communal knowledge sharing. *Journal of Computer Mediated Communication, 19*, 38–55. doi:10.1111/jcc4.12030

Marwell, G., Oliver, P. E., & Prahl, R. (1988). Social networks and collective action: A theory of the critical mass III. *The American Journal of Sociology, 94*, 502–534. doi:10.1086/229028

Marx, G. (2001). Identity and anonymity: Some conceptual distinctions and issues for research. In J. Caplan & J. Torpey (Eds.), *Documenting individual identity: The development of state practices in the modern world* (pp. 311–327). Princeton, NJ: Princeton University Press.

McGrath, J. E., & Hollingshead, A. B. (1994). *Groups interacting with technology: Ideas, evidence, issues, and an agenda*. Thousand Oaks, CA: Sage.

Metzger, M. J., Flanagin, A. J., & Medders, R. (2010). Social and heuristic approaches to credibility evaluation. *Journal of Communication, 60*, 413–439. doi:10.1111/j.1460-2466.2010.01488.x

Metzger, M. J., Flanagin, A. J., Eyal, K., Lemus, D. R., & McCann, R. M. (2003). Credibility in the 21st century: Integrating perspectives on source, message, and media credibility in the contemporary media environment. In P. Kalbfleisch (Ed.), *Communication yearbook 27* (pp. 293–335). Mahwah, NJ: Lawrence Erlbaum.

Mizerski, R. W. (1982). An attribution explanation of the disproportionate influence of unfavorable information. *Journal of Consumer Research, 9*, 301–310. doi:10.1086/208925

Moe, W. W., & Trusov, M. (2011). The value of social dynamics in online product ratings forums. *Journal of Marketing Research, 48*, 444–456. doi:10.1509/jmkr.48.3.444

Nadkarni, A., & Hofmann, S. G. (2012). Why do people use Facebook? *Personality and Individual Differences, 52*, 243–249. doi:10.1016/j.paid.2011.11.007

Noar, S. M., Harrington, N. G., & Aldrich, R. S. (2009). The role of message tailoring in the development of persuasive health communication messages. In C. S. Beck (Ed.), *Communication yearbook 33* (pp. 73–133). New York, NY: Routledge.

O'Keefe, D. J. (2013). The relative persuasiveness of different message types does not vary as a function of the persuasive outcome assessed. In E. L. Cohen (Ed.), *Communication yearbook 37* (pp. 221–249). New York, NY: Routledge.

O'Keefe, D. J., & Jensen, J. D. (2006). The advantages of compliance or the disadvantages of noncompliance? A meta-analytic review of the relative persuasive effectiveness of gain-framed and loss-framed messages. In C. S. Beck (Ed.), *Communication yearbook 30* (pp. 1–43). New York, NY: Routledge.

O'Reilly, T. (2005). *What is Web 2.0: Design patterns and business models for the next generation of software*. Retrieved from www.oreillynet.com/pub/a/oreilly/tim/news/2005/09/30/what-is-web-20.html

Ott, M., Choi, Y., Cardie, C., & Hancock, J. T. (2011). Finding deceptive opinion spam by any stretch of the imagination. In *Proceedings of the 49th Annual Meeting of the Association for Computational Linguistics: Human Language Technologies* (pp. 309–319). Stroudsburg, PA: Association for Computational Linguistics.

Pan, B., Hembrooke, H., Joachims, T., Lorigo, L., Gay, G., & Granka, L. A. (2007). In Google we trust: Users' decisions on rank, position, and relevance. *Journal of Computer-Mediated Communication, 12*, 801–823. doi:10.1111/j.1083-6101.2007.00351.x

Papacharissi, Z. (2010). *A networked self: Identity, community, and culture on social network sites*. New York, NY: Routledge.

Postmes, T., Spears, R., & Lea, M. (1998). Breaching or building social boundaries? SIDE-effects of computer-mediated communication. *Communication Research, 25*, 689–715. doi:10.1177/009365098025006006

Postmes, T., Spears, R., & Lea, M. (2000). The formation of group norms in computer-mediated communication. *Human Communication Research, 26*, 341–371. doi:10.1111/j.1468-2958.2000.tb00761.x

Postmes, T., Spears, R., Sakhel, K., & De Groot, D. (2001). Social influence in computer-mediated communication: The effects of anonymity on group behavior. *Personality and Social Psychology Bulletin, 27*, 1243–1254. doi:10.1177/01461672012710001

Prislin, R., & Crano, W. D. (2012). History of social influence research. In A. Kruglanski & W. Stroebe (Eds.), *The Handbook of the History of Social Psychology* (pp. 321–339). New York, NY: Psychology Press.

Rainie, L., Kiesler, S., Kang, R., & Madden, M. (2013). *Anonymity, privacy, and security online*. Retrived from Pew Internet & American Life Project: www.pewinternet.org/2013/09/05/anonymity-privacy-and-security-online/

Rhoads, K. V. L., & Cialdini, R. B. (2002). The business of influence: Principles that lead to success in commercial settings. In J. P. Dillard & M. Pfau (Eds.), *The persuasion handbook: Developments in theory and practice* (pp. 513–542). Thousand Oaks, CA: Sage.

Rogers, E. M. (1962). *Diffusion of innovations*. New York, NY: Free Press.

Schramm, W. (1954). How communication works. In W. Schramm (Ed.), *The process and effects of communication* (pp. 3–26). Urbana, IL: University of Illinois Press.

Senecal, S., & Nantel, J. (2004). The influence of online product recommendations on consumers' online choices. *Journal of Retailing, 80*, 159–169. doi:10.1016/j.jretai.2004.04.001

Shannon, C. E., & Weaver, W. (1949). *The mathematical theory of communication*. Urbana, IL: University of Illinois Press.

Short, J., Williams, E., & Christie, B. (1976). *The social psychology of telecommunications*. Chichester, UK: Wiley.

Shriver, S. K., Nair, H. S., & Hofstetter, R. (2013). Social ties and user-generated content: Evidence from an online social network. *Management Science, 59*, 1425–1443. doi:10.1287/mnsc.1110.1648

Strang, D., & Macy, M. W. (2001). In search of excellence: Fads, success stories, and adaptive emulation. *American Journal of Sociology, 107*, 147–182. doi:10.1086/323039

Tanford, S., & Penrod, S. (1984). Social influence model: A formal integration of research on majority and minority influence process. *Psychological Bulletin, 95*, 189–225. doi:10.1037/0033-2909.95.2.189

Vermeulen, I. E., & Seegers, D. (2009). Tried and tested: The impact of online hotel reviews on consumer consideration. *Tourism Management, 30*, 123–127. doi:10.1016/j.tourman.2008.04.008

Walther, J. B. (1992). Interpersonal effects in computer-mediated interaction: A relational perspective. *Communication Research, 19*, 52–90. doi:10.1177/009365092019001003

Walther, J. B., & Jang, J. (2012). Communication processes in participatory websites. *Journal of Computer-Mediated Communication, 18*, 2–15. doi:10.1111/j.1083-6101.2012.01592.x

Walther, J. B., & Parks, M. R. (2002). Cues filtered out, cues filtered in: Computer-mediated communication and relationships. In M. L. Knapp & J. A. Daly (Eds.), *Handbook of interpersonal communication* (pp. 529–563). Thousand Oaks, CA: Sage.

Walther, J. B., Liang, Y., Ganster, T., Wohn, D. Y., & Emington, J. (2012). Online reviews, helpfulness ratings, and consumer attitudes: An extension of congruity theory to multiple sources in Web 2.0. *Journal of Computer-Mediated Communication, 18*, 97–112. doi:10.1111/j.1083-6101.2012.01595.x

Weisband, S. P., Schneider, S. K., & Connolly, T. (1995). Computer-mediated communication and social information: Status salience and status differences. *Academy of Management Journal, 38*, 1124–1151. doi:10.2307/256623

Wood, W. (2000). Attitude change: Persuasion and social influence. *Annual Review of Psychology, 51*, 539–570. doi:10.1146/annurev.psych.51.1.539

Wood, W., Lundgren, S., Ouelette, J. A., Busceme, S., & Blackstone, T. (1994). Minority influence: A meta-analytic review of social influence processes. *Psychological Bulletin, 115*, 323–345. doi:10.1037/0033-2909.115.3.323

Ye, Q., Law, R., Gu, B., & Chen, W. (2011). The influence of user-generated content on traveler behavior: An empirical investigation on the effects of e-word-of-mouth to hotel online bookings. *Computers in Human Behavior, 27*, 634–639. doi:10.1016/j.chb.2010.04.014

Zhang, J. Q., Craciun, G., & Shin, D. (2010). When does electronic word-of-mouth matter? A study of consumer product reviews. *Journal of Business Research, 63*, 1336–1341. doi:10.1016/j.jbusres.2009.12.011

Part III

Organizational Communication, Coordination, and Work Practices

CHAPTER CONTENTS

7 Organizational Coordination and Communication

A Critical Review and Integrative Model

Eric J. Zackrison, David R. Seibold, and Ronald E. Rice

University of California, Santa Barbara

We identify, and then attempt to redress, four problematic issues in the organizational coordination literature. First, we distinguish *coordinating* as the overarching process, *coordinating mechanisms* as the structures that are brought to bear, and *coordination* as the in situ interaction. Second, we explicate and distinguish coordinating mechanism from coordination, and reframe the myriad mechanisms in past research into three levels of consciousness specified by structuration theory. Third, we propose a model relating structures (mechanisms) that affect practices (coordination) to outcomes—all within organizational members' ongoing streams of activity and interaction. Fourth, we theorize organizational coordination as a distinctly communication phenomenon.

Coordinated activity arguably is the defining characteristic of organizing and organizations. As McPhee and Iverson (2013) note, organizations' "signal power" derives from the coordinated work of members and stakeholders, the coordinated operations of many units, the coordinated delivery of resources and personnel to core processes, and the coordination of organizational products and services with markets and societies (p. 109). Yet we find both that organizational coordination concepts are somewhat muddled, and that the communication aspect is under-emphasized.

Therefore, we discuss, in turn: (a) four particularly problematic issues with the prodigious research on organizational coordination; (b) two prominent theoretical perspectives on coordination; (c) mechanisms of, underlying assumptions about, and influences on organizational coordination; (d) distinctions among coordinating, coordinating mechanisms, and coordination; (e) propositions and a model of organizational coordination; and (f) an agenda for additional organizational coordination research and contributions.

Our thesis, which underlies and unifies these efforts, is that organizational coordination is a distinctly communicative process that is essential to the understanding of how organizations function. In brief, our argument and analysis unfold as follows across the six sections noted above. We urge definitions of *coordinating* as the overarching process, *coordinating mechanisms* as the structures that are brought to bear, and *coordination* as the in situ interaction, thereby bringing precision to constructs that have been conflated. We also seek to resolve problems related to the variety of coordinating mechanisms and types of organizational coordination in the extant literature we review by explicating what a mechanism is and what coordination is, and by reframing the myriad mechanisms in past research using three levels of consciousness specified by structuration theory. This approach clarifies how types of coordination and types of coordinating mechanisms proposed by others interrelate, and it enables a more parsimonious model. The model we introduce and discuss (formalized in propositions and a visual figure) spotlights coordinating in organizations, including initial interdependencies and uncertainty, organizational and knowledge mechanisms, and routines—all influencing coordination, with possible reproduction or reshaping of those mechanisms, as well as intended and unintended organizational outcomes. Hence, we place coordinating at the core of the process through viewing organizational coordination as influenced by and implemented through coordinating mechanisms, and through interaction (re)creating those mechanisms.

Furthermore, instead of confounding coordination with coordinating mechanisms, coordinating, and outcomes, we propose a parsimonious set of relationships from structures (mechanisms) that influence practices (coordination) that lead to outcomes, including reinforcement or reshaping of those mechanisms—all in organizational members' ongoing streams of activity, meaning, and interaction. In this way we theorize organizational coordination as a distinctly communication phenomenon. We provide several examples of opportunities for integrating coordination and communication in relevant communication-based theories, with the potential to benefit organizational coordination and communication scholarship. We end by summarizing our responses to the four problematic issues about conceptualizations of, and research on, organizational coordination and communication.

Problematic Issues in Organizational Coordination Research

Coordination in organizations has been a focus of study since the turn of the last century (Taylor, 1916) and still is today (Okhuysen & Bechky, 2009a). Studies of organizational coordination also can be found across many disciplines, including economics (Berninghaus & Ehrhart, 2001), computer information systems (Bardram, 2000), linguistics (Gazdar, 1980), management (Endstrom & Galbraith, 1977), organizational behavior (Okhuysen & Beckhy, 2009a), psychology (Kraut, Lewis, & Swezy, 1982), sociology (Sutton, 2008), and communication (Ballard & Seibold, 2003, 2004; McPhee & Iverson, 2009). Scholarship on coordination covers a broad range of contexts and levels of analysis. Micro-level interpersonal interactions include how individuals utilize material signals in an attempt to coordinate everyday actions (Clark, 2005), how individuals negotiate conversations in interpersonal interactions (Hubbard, 2000; Vallacher, Nowak, & Zochowski, 2005), role-coordination in teams (Bechky, 2006), and relational and organizing micro-dynamics in teamwork

(Humphrey & Aime, 2014). Increasingly complex meso-level contexts include urban planning (Tornberg, 2012), coordinating regional or international inter-agency relief networks (Miller, Scott, Stage, & Birkholt, 1995), and the coordination of crisis response (Topper & Carley, 1999). And broad macro-level contexts consider multinational and interorganizational coordination (Alter, 1990; Cray, 1984; Endstrom & Galbraith, 1977), as well as market, marketing, and supply chain coordination (Buvik & John, 2000; Celly & Frazier, 1996; Gerstner & Hess, 1995; Kim, Stump, & Oh, 2009; Raju & Zhang, 2005; Zhao, Liu, Yang, & Sadiq, 2009).

With this rich diversity, however, come four problematic issues: (a) much prior work lacks shared explicit conceptual or operational definitions, (b) types of coordination overlap and contradict each other, (c) coordination is often a secondary aspect rather than a central concern, and (d) coordination—as treated in the organizational literature—receives little attention by communication researchers. As we explicate these issues below, we limit our review to work that is specifically related to organizations and that advances our understanding of organizational coordination as distinctly communicative.

Much Prior Work Lacks Shared Explicit Conceptual or Operational Definitions

The first issue in organizational coordination research is a lack of a shared explicit definition. In general, theorists often assume an understanding of what coordination means and may not offer an explicit definition (Endstrom & Galbraith, 1977; Kellogg, Orlikowski, & Yates, 2006; Larsson & Bowen, 1989; Perrow, 1961; Sutton, 2008). Even some of the most prominent coordination scholars do not always explicitly offer a conceptual definition (Bechky, 2006; Gittell & Weiss, 2004).

Even when definitions are provided, they cover a wide range of conceptual definitions, reflecting disagreement in how to define coordination and disagreement about its constitutive elements and functions (as Table 7.1 shows). Definitions range from the very simple conception of Simon (1947) "The adoption of all members of a group of the same decision" (p. 8) to the more complex view of Rico, Sanchez-Manzanares, Gil, and Gibson (2008) that "Coordination in work teams is an emergent phenomenon involving the use of strategies and behavior patterns aimed at integrating and aligning the actions, knowledge, and objectives of interdependent members, with a view to attaining some common ground" (p. 163). There are differences in whether coordination is, as Bailetti, Callahan, and McClusky (1998) contend, a structure that is "a configuration of actors (individuals or groups of individuals—units in an organizational situation) who have interdependent responsibilities to create, modify and use an array of shared work objects" (p. 238), or a process, as Okhuysen and Bechky (2009a) argue, "coordination, the process of interaction that integrates a collective set of interdependent tasks, is a central purpose of the organization" (p. 463). More difficult to reconcile is whether coordination is necessarily

Table 7.1 Conceptual Definitions of Coordination

Definition and Source	Definition Attributes: *Simple/complex Structure/process Accomplishment/attempt*
Coordination is a structure that is "a configuration of actors (individuals or groups of individuals—units in an organizational situation) who have interdependent responsibilities to create, modify and use an array of shared work objects" (Bailetti, Callahan, & McClusky, 1998, p. 238).	Simple Structure Accomplishment
"Coordination entails integrating or linking together different parts of an organization as they work together to accomplish organizational goals" (Bailetti, Calahan, & DiPietro, 1994, p. 395).	Simple Structure/ Process Accomplishment
"Coordination means the activities of work participants are related to one another in certain ways, according to certain organizing principles" (Cheng, 1984, p. 832).	Simple Structure Attempt
"Coordination refers to the extent to which subtasks allocated to different positions need to be sequenced by definite precedence relationships" (O'Brien, 1968, p. 427).	Simple Structure/ Process Attempt
"The integration or linking together of different parts of an organization to accomplish a collective set of tasks" (Van de ven, Delbecq, & Koenig, 1976, p. 322).	Simple Structure/ Process Attempt
"Coordination can be defined as the collective accomplishment of individual goals through a cooperative process" (Ballard & Seibold, 2003, p. 401).	Simple Process Accomplishment
"Coordination in a group of agents concerns maximizing the joint surplus of their productive activities" (Foss & Lorenzen, 2009, p. 1203).	Simple Process Accomplishment
Coordination is "synchronization of interdependent tasks and schedules" (Hoegl, Weinkauf, & Gemuenden, 2004, p. 39).	Simple Process Accomplishment
"Coordination can be seen as a process of managing resources in an organized manner so that a higher degree of operational efficiency can be achieved for a given project" (Hossain, 2009, p. 25).	Simple Process Accomplishment
"Coordinating (is) the process by which teams attempt to manage interdependencies among individuals" (p. 2); "Coordination (is) the degree to which interdependencies are managed well" (Kraut et al., 2005, p. 2).	Simple Process Accomplishment
"Coordination is managing dependencies between activities" (Malone & Crowston, 1994, p. 90).	Simple Process Accomplishment
"Coordination, the process of interaction (members implicit in interaction) that integrates a collective set of interdependent tasks, is a central purpose of the organization" (Okhuysen & Bechky, 2009a, p. 463).	Simple Process Accomplishment
Coordination is "the coming together of actions into a sequence or pattern, regardless of whether the producers of those actions agree on their meaning" (Salmon & Faris, 2006, pp. 285–286).	Simple Process Accomplishment

"The adoption of all members of a group of the same decision" (Simon, 1947, p. 8).	Simple Process Accomplishment
Coordination is "the act of working together harmoniously" (p. 358) and coordination is "the act of managing interdependencies between activities performed to achieve a goal" (Malone & Crowston, 1990, p. 361).	Simple Process Accomplishment/ Attempt
Coordination is ". . . the use of cooperative methods" and they "differentiated between those used by workers and administrators" (Alter, 1990, p. 483).	Simple Process Attempt
"Coordination involves adjusting the work of the group members to fit the goals of the group" (Cumming & Akari, 2005, p. 258).	Simple Process Attempt
"Coordination refers to the team-situated interactions aimed at managing resources and expertise dependencies" (Faraj & Xiao, 2006, p. 1157).	Simple Process Attempt
"Relational coordination is coordination—the management of task interdependencies—carried out in the context of relationships with other group members" (Gittell, 2001, p. 471).	Simple Process Attempt
Coordination is "the conscious activity of assembling and synchronizing differentiated work efforts so that they function harmoniously in the attainment of organizational objectives" (Young et al., 1998, p. 1215).	Simple Process Attempt
"The extent to which the work activities of organizational members are logically consistent and coherent . . . in role-system terms, coordination represents how well the organizational members as a whole perform in accordance with their roles in the system" (Cheng, 1983, pp. 156–157).	Complex Process Accomplishment
Temporal coordination is "an activity with the objective to ensure that the distributed actions realizing a collaborative activity takes place at an appropriate time, both in relation to that activity's other actions and in relation to other relevant sets of neighboring activities" (Bardram, 2000, p. 163).	Complex Process Attempt
"At its core coordination is about the integration of organizational work under conditions of task interdependencies and uncertainty. . . .Coordination is a temporally unfolding and contextualized process of input regulation and interaction articulation to realize collective performance" (Faraj & Sproull, 2000, p. 1155).	Complex Process Attempt
"Coordination in work teams is an emergent phenomenon involving the use of strategies and behavior patterns aimed at integrating and aligning the actions, knowledge, and objectives of interdependent members, with a view to attaining some common ground" (Rico, Sanchez-Manzanares, Gil, & Gibson, 2008, p. 163).	Complex Process Attempt

a measure of something that is successfully accomplished, as Malone and Crowston (1990) indicate: "the act of working together harmoniously" (p. 358), and as Ballard and Seibold (2003) propose—"coordination can be defined as the collective accomplishment of individual goals through a cooperative process" (p. 401)—or whether it is more generally an intention or attempt, as Rico et al. (2008) state: "with a view to attaining some common ground" (p. 163).

Types of Coordination Overlap and Contradict Each Other

A second problem (related to the first) is a conflation and vagueness of terms surrounding coordination. Such terms include integration (Lawrence & Lorsch, 1967), cooperation (O'Brien, 1968), collaboration (Salmon & Faris, 2006), and congruence (Cataldo, Wagstrom, Herbsleb, & Carley, 2006). Also, coordination, cooperation, and collaboration are used interchangeably (Vlaar, van den Bosch, & Volberda, 2007). A vast array of subcomponents also have been presented to deal with specific types of coordination or to present coordination in a particular way. For example, coordination is conceived of as either existing in some aspect of the organization before interaction or as being created in situ—for example, administrative coordination versus expertise or dialogic coordination (Faraj & Sproull, 2000; Faraj & Xiao, 2006). Another difference is whether coordination is considered as being either internal to or external to the group, like Bardram's (2000) intrinsic versus extrinsic coordination. Other conceptualizations examine whether coordination is based in knowledge, in interactions, in routines, or in some other construct. Knowledge-based conceptualizations include cognitive coordination (Foss & Lorenzen, 2009), expertise coordination (Faraj & Sproull, 2000), and the anticipation component of implicit coordination (Rico et al., 2008). Interactive conceptualizations include relational coordination (Gittell, 2001), communicative coordination (Bardram, 2000), the dynamic adjustment component of implicit coordination (Rico et al., 2008), discursive coordination (Minnsen, 2005), and activity coordination (McPhee & Zaug, 2000). Routines have long been understood to be a component of coordination and have a vast literature (see Becker, 2004 for a full review). Other conceptualizations include Bardram's (2000) temporal coordination that examines the role that perceptions of time have on coordination, an idea also addressed by Ballard and Seibold (2003, 2004), and in Bailetti et al.'s (1994) coordination ensembles, or how groups arrange themselves around objects.

Coordination Is Often a Secondary Aspect Rather Than a Central Concern

A third problematic issue in organizational coordination studies is a lack of focus on coordination as the primary concern. Instead, it is examined as a secondary variable, such as affecting leader member relations (Ilgen & O'Brien, 1974), as an intervening variable when examining leadership style on productivity (Hewett et al., 1974), or as control mechanism when analyzing the transfer of managers (Endstrom & Galbraith, 1977). Some of the second problem above, lack of consensus on its meaning, has been a byproduct of many definitions offered in studies in which coordination was of secondary interest.

Coordination Requires Greater Attention by Communication Researchers

Communication is acknowledged in the earliest organizational coordination work either explicitly, noting the importance of feedback and mutual adjustment, or implicitly, through plans and programming, which require communication to establish and maintain (March & Simon, 1993; Thompson, 1967). More recent organizational coordination work continues to recognize the importance of communication. For example, Okhuysen and Bechky (2009a) identify the role of communication in some coordinating mechanisms, such as the monitoring and updating component of roles, and in integrating conditions for coordination. But these works are external to communication and by non-communication researchers.

However, ironically, communication researchers have not paid much attention to coordination in the senses discussed above, nor have they emphasized the communicative aspects specific to organizational coordination. When organizational communication scholars have engaged coordination, their primary focus has been on communication and organizational constitution—that organizations emerge from and are maintained by communication processes. Emphasis in that vast literature is given to the coordination inherent in communication and, by extension but only secondarily, to organizational coordination (Cooren, Taylor, & Van Every, 2006; McPhee & Zaug, 2000). Work in communication also has examined collaboration (see Lewis's 2006 review), including commentary on organizational coordination. Other prominent communication scholarship on coordination has not been much concerned with organizational processes, but rather with coordinating language, interpersonal interaction, or social ties (Fusaroli & Tylen, 2012; Pearce & Pearce, 2000).

In the remaining sections, we respond to these four problematic issues by (a) reviewing relevant theoretical perspectives on organizational coordination with an eye to identifying problems and applying strengths, (b) identifying key assumptions (structuration, crucial related concepts, and conceptualization of coordinating, coordinating mechanisms, and coordination), (c) advancing arguments for three overarching coordinating mechanisms (routines, knowledge, and organizational) that help resolve problems in the literature, (d) emphasizing a communication perspective, and (e) proposing an integrative model and relevant testable propositions.

Two Prominent Theoretical Perspectives on Organizational Coordination

The scholarship on organizational coordination is prodigious. Thus, we selectively discuss two overarching theoretical perspectives—contingency models and organizational design; and coordination paradigms—followed by a detailed discussion of assumptions and definitions. Our intention is to provide the foundations for a framework and model that redresses limitations in, and integrates central concepts from, these previous theoretical approaches to organizational coordination.

Contingency Models and Organizational Design

The work of Malone and colleagues (Crowston, 1997; Crowston & Kammerer, 1998; Malone, 1987; Malone & Crowston, 1990; Malone and Crowston, 1994) and Bailetti, Callahan, and DiPietro (1994) figures prominently in the modern landscape of organizational coordination research. Extending the traditional design/contingency paradigm that was dominant for much of the last century (e.g., March & Simon, 1958; Thompson, 1967; van de Ven, Delbecq, & Koenig, 1976), these scholars develop a rich taxonomy of contingencies and mechanisms affecting coordination effectiveness (with some focus on information/ communication technology). This research acknowledges the complexity of potential interdependencies, but emphasizes distinctions (Malone & Crowston, 1994) and categorizations (Bailetti, Callahan, & McClusky, 1998). Furthermore, much of the work is technology-centric and lacks much focus on the agency of organizational members. Finally, the coordination processes identified acknowledge a wide range of, and levels of, interdependencies but do not distinguish coordinating mechanisms from coordination, a distinction central to the analysis we develop in the assumptions and model sections later in this paper.

More generally, there are three important criticisms of the contingency approach to organizational coordination. The first is that the number of possible interdependencies and contextual differences makes it nearly impossible to develop an exhaustive catalog of matched organizational situations and coordinating mechanisms. A second critique concerns the dearth of discussion about how organizational members might actually identify, access, and implement these mechanisms. For example, what happens when the mechanisms are not used well (van Fenema, Pentland, & Kumar, 2004) or even function counter to group and organizational goals (as analyzed by Rice & Cooper, 2010)? The third criticism focuses on a lack of specificity about how the coordination mechanisms work, especially for specific contexts. Without that knowledge, further theoretical development is hampered (Okhuysen & Bechky, 2009a).

However, the contingency/design approach also offers two benefits for the study of organizational coordination. It identifies possible coordinating mechanisms from which a typology of matches between situation, coordinating mechanisms, and the attainment of positive coordination can be developed. Additionally, even though much of this work has focused on very specific instances and the ways to manage interdependencies, these still allow for broader theoretical implications in extrapolating from the instances studied to broader theoretical concerns. For example, Crowston (1997) examined coordination problems in software design and how specific organizations dealt with them. In interdependencies where task assignment to the proper engineer is important, utilizing a mechanism focused on identifying expertise is more important than other coordinating mechanisms. This benefit of the contingency/design perspective on organizational coordination informs the concept of knowledge mechanisms that are key to the assumptions and model we offer.

Coordination Paradigms

In a major review of the organizational coordination literature, van Fenema et al. (2004) identified three paradigms of coordination theory. The *contingency paradigm* views coordination as processes or structures that can and should be manipulated to increase organizational effectiveness within varying contexts. The *relatedness of structure and process paradigm* recognizes that process and structure are not necessarily mutually exclusive, and includes theories that focus on their interrelationships. These theories conceive of structure much more broadly than does contingency/design and are relevant for the structuration theory assumptions we make in the next section. Structure includes more than just procedures, plans, manuals, and control mechanisms; rules and resources, mental models, collections of knowledge, and shared meanings are included too. These are the internalized aspects of structure that organizational and group members draw on as generative of action. The *crafting inner and outer world paradigm* views coordination as beginning with the individual. Coordination is accomplished through coherence, or forming a unified whole, in the connection between individuals' outer worlds (structures and processes that exist outside the individual) and inner worlds (how individuals interpret and interact differently with those outer worlds).

Distinguishing among the three paradigms yields insights into how the conceptualization of organizational coordination has changed to accommodate deeper understandings than in early contingency/design work, especially the roles of agency and interaction in producing coordination. The relatedness and crafting paradigms identified by van Fenema et al. (2004) also supply a basis for our more communicative focus in coordination research and for a structurational approach. In particular, the relatedness coordination paradigm includes concern with how structures affect interaction and how interaction, discourse, and conversations create structure. The crafting paradigm concentrates heavily on the communicative nature of coordination and embraces the ways that organizations and coordination are created through interaction and communication.

The assumptions and model we offer in subsequent sections are consonant with these two paradigms.

Mechanisms of, Underlying Assumptions about, and Influences on Organizational Coordination

Coordinating Mechanisms and Integrating Conditions

Perhaps the most cogent analysis of the organizational coordination research literature to date is provided by Okhuysen and Bechky (2009a). We review their work in some detail. While we differ from them in important respects, portions of their analysis are extended in our own model as well as in the structuration theory tenets and other assumptions that underlie it.

Okhuysen and Bechky (2009a) first concentrate on five "coordinating mechanisms": *plans and rules, objects and representations, roles, routines,* and *proximity*. They subsequently identify three overarching "integrating conditions" that those coordinating mechanisms must accomplish to bring about coordination: *accountability, predictability,* and *common understanding*. We discuss the five coordinating mechanisms and the three integrating conditions in that order. Okhuysen and Bechky's work moved the current understanding of coordination forward in several ways. First is their separation of the vast collection of mechanisms into several categories that helped inform our argument for organizational mechanisms and routines. Second, the presentation of the three integrating conditions allowed for a clearer understanding of the knowledge mechanisms we present as well as how the mechanisms might interact. Finally, they call attention to the communicative aspect of organizational coordination, even if only implicitly.

Plans and rules are aspects of the formal organization that are required for organizing. They contribute to coordination through defining responsibilities for tasks, allocating resources, and developing agreement. Objects and representations facilitate coordination though direct information sharing, scaffolding (structures established by a group to allow reference for future work), acknowledging and aligning work, and creating a common perspective. Roles are the expected behaviors associated with a social position in the group or organization, and help coordination through monitoring and updating, substituting (as members become more aware of each other's roles they can fill in for each other), and creating common perspective. Routines are established patterns of behavior that members rely on for action, without having to consciously process those behaviors. They help coordination by increasing task completion and stability, allowing for hand-off work, bringing groups together, and creating common perspective.

The final coordination mechanism identified by Okhuysen and Bechky (2009a), proximity, has two components, visibility and familiarity. Visibility depends on physical co-location and aids coordinating through monitoring (by supervisors, as well as of others' behaviors) and updating, which is the increased ability to realign or gauge task progress in high visibility environments (for discussions of the effect of audio and visual co-location on knowledge and coordination, see Archea, 1977; Kraut, Fish, Root, & Chalfonte, 1990). (Clearly, in the contemporary context of ubiquitous organizational ICTs, the notion of visibility takes on a more general, and both more and less constrained, aspect; see Rice & Leonardi, 2013.) The concept of familiarity focuses on the knowledge one person has about another individual or situation. It aids coordination through an increase in the ability of members to anticipate others' actions and respond appropriately, by knowing where the stores of knowledge necessary for coordination lie, and by increasing the levels of trust among members. This conceptualization of familiarity is also central to the theory of transactive memory (Lewis & Herndon, 2011).

Okhuysen and Bechky (2009a) contend that each of the five coordinating mechanisms above can be accomplished through what they call three integrating conditions: accountability, predictability, and common understanding. Integrating conditions are the means through which organizational members jointly perform workplace tasks that are interdependent. Accountability directs members' attention to whomever has responsibility for particular aspects of an interdependent task, and functions to coordinate action formally and in emergent fashion through vertical authority (directives and reporting) as well as lateral structures that may be formal (e.g., status updates) and informal (e.g., interactions). Predictability facilitates coordination to the extent to which members are aware of task parts and timeline—and thus, can predict ensuing task activity. Predictability is enabled through formal mechanisms (scheduling) and emergent means (familiarity with others' knowledge and preferences, as acquired through interactions with them individually or collectively). Common understanding aids coordination by affording organizational members with shared perspectives on whole-part relationships (e.g., parameters for a task and how each member's work is part of it). Common understanding is reflected in task knowledge, knowledge of relevant members, and context knowledge. It can be enhanced through formal and planned methods (e.g., manuals, assembly drawings) and emergent interactions among members.

Okhuysen and Bechky (2009a) hint at the role of communication in some of the five coordinating mechanisms, such as the monitoring and updating component of roles. Curiously, they offer roles as the salient aspect rather than communication even though, as Bechky (2006) argued, communication is the actual process of enacting those roles. Bechky emphasizes that role structures cannot be taken as givens; they are evident in the streams of action of role occupants—actions that prominently include communication and interaction. Okhuysen and Bechky (2009a) more explicitly note the role of communication in the three integrating conditions for coordination, both in formal authority structures (e.g., directives, setting schedules, manuals) and in informal lateral structures (e.g., meetings and conversations). We extend those notions greatly in our model, and before that in the structuration theory tenets and other assumptions underlying it.

In the remainder of this section we explicate assumptions and key concepts in three areas that will be foundational to the model we propose in the following section. The first area incorporates a structuration theory premise concerning organization as constraining and being (re)created by interaction. The second involves the centrality of two key concepts commonly associated with organizational coordination (interdependencies and uncertainty). The third includes distinctions between coordinating, coordinating mechanisms, and coordination.

Underlying Assumptions

Structuration tenets concerning organizational coordination and communication. McPhee and colleagues (McPhee & Iverson, 2009, 2013; McPhee & Poole, 2001; McPhee & Zaug, 2000; Poole & McPhee, 2005; Poole, Seibold, & McPhee, 1985) argue for a conception of organization grounded firmly within Giddens's (1979) concept of structuration. Structuration is an outgrowth of a period of theory that embraced the role of human agency in the creation of our social realities, and was adopted and developed as a communication theory largely by the above group of researchers. Structuration identifies social systems, including organizations, as systems of human practice in which human activities are interrelated in various ways. This interaction is guided by structure that is composed of rules and resources. Rules are any principle or guide that tells people that draw on them the ways in which they can or should act; resources are anything that people use in action, including material like money or tools, or nonmaterial like skills and information.

A core concept of structuration is that as people draw on structural rules and resources in acting within a social system of practices, they perpetuate that system and reproduce the very structures that guide them. This can occur through perpetuating the system as is, or through transformation, which shifts the system, taking it in new directions. Every interaction within a system has two components: it produces the practices of which it is a component and it reproduces the system and structure.

Communication theorists who embrace structuration theory recognize that humans have agency and are not strictly guided by outside forces, and thus assume that humans have distinct levels of consciousness, they are knowledgeable, and they are reflexive (Poole & McPhee, 2005). *Consciousness* has three levels. The first is *discursive* consciousness, which we can put into words and explain to others. The second is *practical* consciousness, which—like riding a bike—is difficult to impart in words, although we can put it into action. The third is the *unconscious*, of which we are not aware but that nonetheless affects actions. This level includes the effects of our past actions, such as unrecognized fears, or attitudes, and beliefs. Knowledge represents the ability of people to know much about their environments and resources available within that environment, allowing them not only to go about their day-to-day existence, but to know who knows what and where needed resources are located. However, humans do not just go through their day-to-day activities; they also reflect on that activity, making adjustments as needed to current action and to future planned actions.

Communication flows in organizations. In a structuration approach, organizations as social systems are both constituted through communication and, in turn, provide contexts for creating communication. One structuration conception distinguishes four types of communication "flows" essential for the constitution of organization (McPhee & Zaug, 2000). First, organizations typically draw a distinction between members and nonmembers through continuous communicative *membership negotiation*. Second, organizations reflexively self-structure through communicative processes, distinguishing them from mobs or neighborhoods. Third, organizations also follow some manifest purpose(s) which guides communicative processes of activity coordination. This third flow is especially relevant for the present analysis. Activity coordination usually entails interactive episodes in which members who are aligned in an organizational unit and/or location adjust to germane acts of others and to situational constraints (McPhee & Iverson, 2013). Fourth, organizations are embedded within a larger context—another organization, community, industry, technological or legal trends, or society at large. Thus organizations generate and are regulated by communicative processes of institutional positioning, such as negotiating through interaction with stakeholders and other institutions to establish status.

It is from this perspective that the current conception of not only organization but organizational coordination is derived. The reconstituting process suggests that the coordinating mechanisms that engender the coordination process are also (re)created in that very process. It is only through looking at the process as continual and iterative that coordination can be fully explored. The three assumptions about humans in organizations (i.e., they are conscious on several levels, knowledgeable, and reflexive) underscore that coordination is a human activity. The levels of consciousness indicate that the coordination of organizational members involves not only discursive knowledge and practical knowledge of the task, but is influenced by aspects not fully recognized consciously by the members. They do not act as parts of a machine with no knowledge or reflexivity as the earliest coordination theorists imagined, but instead reflexively adjust their future behaviors based on current interactions. Finally, the four flows offer two implications. First, they allow us to define what is and is not organization and thus what is and is not organizational coordination. Second, they place organizational coordination within a larger context, whereby it is affected by and affects that context.

Concepts Influencing Organizational Coordination

As Okhuysen and Bechky (2009a) emphasize, interdependencies and uncertainty are central to conceptualizing the need for coordination in organizations.

Interdependencies.   From a systems theory perspective, the actors, tasks, processes and organizations exhibit both weak and strong interdependencies (or tight and loose coupling) based on exchanges of various resources and outputs to accomplish particular goals or tasks (e.g., van de Ven et al., 1976). These resource interdependencies may be based on specific actor and organizational needs, goals, abilities, and processes. They include not only industrial resources like capital, parts, and time, but also less tangible resources such as emotional support, guidance, and information (Gittell, 2001). They also include responsibilities, linking group members with each other and with objects and actors outside the group, like design plans, customer needs, and test results (Bailetti, Callahan, & McClusky, 1998).

In the earliest coordination work, these interdependencies were a measure of the level of complexities of reliance in order to accomplish the goals of the organization. Thompson (1967) identified three types of interdependencies (in order of complexity from least to most): pooled, in which one person's contribution may move the group forward, but the rest of the group does not rely on that person's contribution per se (e.g., harvesting fruit); sequential, in which one member's actions are required for another's to take place (e.g., assembly line); and reciprocal, in which the members rely on each other in a give and take process (e.g., cooks in a kitchen rely on the dishwashers for clean dishes and the dishwashers rely on the cooks for dirty dishes). Van de Ven et al. (1976) added a fourth level, team, which does not include the temporal aspect of sequential or reciprocal interdependencies, but instead refers to those times when components work jointly and simultaneously (e.g., some kinds of sports teams). Crowston (1997) proposed three other kinds of interdependencies. Task to task interdependencies arise when one task is reliant on another being accomplished. Task to resource interdependencies include situations where a resource is required by a task, and resource to resource interdependencies are those situations where one resource depends on another. Other studies add different possibilities, including interdependencies specific to the construction industry (Hossain, 2009), to the customer service industry (Larsson & Bowen, 1989), interdependencies in groupware (Andriessen, 2003) or between components of a system (Crowston & Kammerer, 1998), and peer-to-peer interdependencies (Cumming & Akari, 2005).

Previous literature on coordination recognizes the alignment of interdependencies as a core property of coordination. Although some of this work is overly simplified or unnecessarily complicated, it is important to recognize that in the absence of interdependencies there is nothing to coordinate. Not only are interdependencies different across context, they may change throughout the life cycle of a project (Adler, 1995). Interdependencies also may be sufficiently complex, ambiguous, and temporally lagged to make it difficult to even know what to coordinate, or to coordinate at a large enough level, in order to avoid or resolve dysfunctional processes. Indeed, without appropriate feedback and coordination, these interdependencies and dysfunctionalities become embedded, routinized, and nearly invisible, into unusual routines (Rice & Cooper, 2010).

Uncertainty. With interdependencies comes uncertainty such as, in the communication sense, divergences in meanings, as well as, in the pragmatic sense, who is responsible for what task when. Coordination is necessary to avoid or resolve that uncertainty in order to accomplish goals. Much of the earliest work examining coordination drew its inspiration from finding ways to manage these uncertainties, such as those created by the introduction of large-scale railways by assuring proper time schedules and allowing for the planning of shipping and traveling (Beniger, 1986; Okhuysen & Bechky, 2009a). This interest grew as increased industrialization took hold. Much of this early work concentrated on design: first of work, then of management, and finally of the organization, in attempts to allow for increased management control (van Fenema, Pentland, & Kumar, 2004). Taylor's Scientific Management concentrated on ways that humans and their work actions could be more mechanized and efficient, thus reducing the uncertainty of production (March & Simon, 1993).

Developing at much the same time were theories of departmentalization (often called administrative management theory), including the work of Fayol, Gulick, and Urwick (March & Simon, 1993). This group differs from the scientific management school in their level of analysis. Rather than attempting to guide the specific worker through planning and training, they focused instead on the design of management systems that allowed for little uncertainty and near-complete coordination (or removal of the need for it). Building on early design theorists' attempts to plan formal elements to accomplish coordination, a substantial shift in focus began with March and Simon's book *Organizations* in 1958. Referred to by a number of names including contingency theory (Galbraith, 1973; van Fenema et al., 2004), organizational design theories (Okhuysen & Bechky, 2009a), and administrative theory (Thompson, 1967), this approach assumed that interdependent aspects of an organization could be planned and thus coordinated in order to reduce uncertainty. For example, Yates (1993) showed that new genres of communication, such as the memo, adapted from British Empire administration, were central in improving control and coordination of the rapidly developing form of corporations in the early 1900s.

Contemporary scholars acknowledge that early contingency theory and research was simplistic (in its assumption that all uncertainty within interdependencies could be eliminated, or that interdependencies could be designed down to simple, repeatable processes). However, scholars still focus on uncertainty as a primary concern for coordination research, and examine how levels of uncertainty require, and affect the use of and the effectiveness of, various coordinating mechanisms (e.g., Argote, 1982; Gittell, 2002; van de Ven et al., 1976).

Distinctions: Coordinating, Coordinating Mechanisms, and Coordination

As noted above, the coordination literature conflates similar terms such as collaboration, cooperation, integration, and congruence. The more difficult part of conceptualizing coordination is not the confounding of it with differing terms, but differentiating between words with the same linguistic root, such as coordination, coordinate, and coordinating. Once these conceptual issues are worked out, it becomes easier to establish coordination as conceptually different from other similar concepts.

The difficulty in conceptualizing coordinating and coordination stems in part from how each is defined in the English language. Merriam-Webster.com defines coordinating as the present participle of coordinate, so that coordinating is

> making arrangements so that two or more people or groups of people can work together properly and well, or as acting or working together properly or well, or as causing (two or more things) to be the same or to go together well.

Thus coordinating can be conceived of as both an act done to something else (i.e., making arrangements or causing . . .) or as an in situ process (i.e., acting or working together properly). This definition of coordinate/coordinating does not bring much clarity. Merriam-Webster.com defines coordination as "either the act or state of coordinating or of being coordinated or as a harmonious combination or interaction, as of functions or parts." Again, coordination, like coordinating, can be conceived of as something done to a group, as something a group does, or as something attained; as an act, a process, or a state. This is exacerbated in the literature as the two terms are so often misused and under-conceptualized. So we propose the following definitions, which will be further explored below:

*   *Coordinating* is the organizational process of applying coordinating mechanisms to attain higher extents of coordination, resulting in outcomes (expected and unexpected, intentional and unintentional, positive and negative).
*   *Coordinating mechanisms* are those processes, structures, artifacts, or interactions that exist to facilitate coordination of a group, or of the organization, that generally exist "before" coordination, and that are either intentionally brought to bear or stored for use in situ.
*   *Coordination* is the extent to which the in situ interactive integration of group(s) and/or organizational members' work activities is logical and coherent in managing interdependencies towards some goal.

To support these definitions, two key problems in previous literature must be addressed: coordinating and coordination are distinct concepts, and the process of coordination is conceptually, if not always empirically, distinct from outcomes. We also argue against (a) conceiving of coordination as a dichotomous variable (either attained or not attained), (b) assuming that the use of coordinating mechanisms is automatically successful in attaining appropriate extent and types of coordination, or (c) assuming that coordination necessarily achieves successful or intended outcomes. In other words, no aspect of coordinating, or the internal relationships, is fully deterministic.

Coordinating and Coordination Are Distinct

As noted, the literature is rife with confusion between the meanings of coordination and coordinating. Other than definitional difficulties, there are two additional issues in delineating between coordinating and coordination. First, we need to distinguish between coordinating as external to a group (i.e., the manager is coordinating that group by giving it direction on an upcoming task) or as internal to the group (i.e., the group has a high extent of coordination towards completing a task). This blending of external and internal was a constant issue in the earliest coordination research (e.g., design contingency, Thompson, 1967), and is an error in recent work as evidenced by the identification of both plans and mutual adjustment as coordinating mechanisms (Grote et al., 2008).

Second, we need to distinguish the boundary between the coordinating mechanisms and coordination (i.e., are instructions from supervisors a mechanism even when accessed by group members during a project?). Cheng (1983, 1984) brings some lucidity to this difficulty when he delineates between coordination, which he identifies as a measure of the articulation of unity of effort between contingent parts of an organization or group, and coordinating, which is the process of utilizing coordinating mechanisms to align those divergent parts of the organization or group around a particular task. Cray (1984) recognizes the same differentiation in concepts (though he still confounds the terms) when he writes that "the issue is not so much the type of coordination (coordinating) used, but the amount or degree of coordination. The primary consideration . . . is that the subunits be successfully integrated" (p. 87). Though Cheng called for researchers to more clearly distinguish between coordinating and coordination, the issue has remained (see, for example, Cumming & Akari, 2005; Janick & Bartel, 2003; and Vlaar, van den Bosch, & Volberda, 2007). More recently, Kraut et al. (2005) make the same call for clarification, identifying coordinating as the attempt to manage interdependencies, and coordination as the resultant state of well-managed interdependencies (although note again here the confounding between whether coordination is a state or not). This manifests in the literature in the common use of both coordinating and coordinating mechanisms to mean the application of some structure to attempt to align interdependencies. To reduce this confounding we call for the term coordinating to be used to describe the overarching process and coordinating mechanisms to represent those structures that exist to facilitate the coordination of group and organizational members' interdependencies. (The use of the term "mechanisms" carries some risk of being associated with technological determinism and Taylorism. However, it has been so ingrained in the coordination literature that it is more fitting than alternatives such as processes or structures, which have structurational theory connotations.)

Coordination and Outcomes Are Distinct

The literature often construes coordination and outcomes as the same (Cheng, 1983, 1984). One possible reason is the difficulty in measuring coordination directly. Instead of coordination being measured as a manifest variable, it often has been measured as a latent variable, including such varied concepts as mutual respect, the timeliness of communication, and the frequency of communication (Gittell, 2002). The common conception of coordination as accomplishing some output logically leads scholars to include some aspect of goal achievement into the measure of coordination—such as including the success of the group in attaining some organizationally desired outputs (Cheng, 1984). These outputs can be measured as a level of quality (e.g., customers report Y level of satisfaction) and/ or quantity (e.g., the group serviced X number of customers) (Argote, 1982).

A possible second reason for misconstruing outcomes as part (and thus an indicator) of coordination is the common assumption that the only valid goals for a group are the official organizational goals. Yet the success or failure of a coordinative action is in many instances and contexts a subjective perception (Martinez & Jarillo, 1989). The goals of the organization are not always as clearly defined as group goals. Perrow (1961) notes that whose goals take precedence changes over the life course of an organization, including administrative goals, organization goals, specific group goals, or some other goal. Depending on whose goals are being measured, the success or failure of a coordinated effort could vary drastically (Lehr & Rice, 2002).

Propositions and Model of Organizational Coordination

In the previous section we reconceptualized coordinating, coordinating mechanisms, and coordination as system, structures, and practice. We distinguished between coordinating, coordinating mechanisms, coordination, and outcomes to show how mechanisms (structures) affect coordination (practices) that lead to outcomes within organizational members' ongoing streams of activity and interaction.

As we note below, each of these types of mechanism works to align organizational members' meanings and practices, but this only occurs through the interaction of the members and the alignment of their interdependencies. As structuration theory argues, these structures both enable and constrain the actions and interactions of the organizational members. Moreover, those very coordinating mechanisms are themselves either reproduced or transformed through the ways that the members enact them in the actual coordination.

Further, we simplify the five mechanisms identified by Okhuysen and Bechky (2009a) and the myriad mechanisms identified by Malone and colleagues into the three structuration theory levels of consciousness: discursive, practical, and unconscious. This allows for a comprehensive yet parsimonious categorization of coordinating mechanisms—and in a manner that enables us to understand their impact on coordination. The discursive level of consciousness aligns with organizational coordinating mechanisms, which are those mechanisms that are consciously created and/or brought to bear to attempt coordination. Practical consciousness aligns with knowledge mechanisms that facilitate coordination that organizational members are conscious of, but may not be able to fully explain how they are brought to bear. The final type of coordinating mechanism, unconscious, aligns with routines, as it occurs when the above mechanisms become embedded in organizational members' practices and allows for action without thought or negotiation.

Thus we explicate our proposed model through five components: 1) coordination itself, 2) organizational coordinating as both mechanism and outcome of coordination, 3) knowledge as both mechanism and outcome of coordination, 4) routines as both mechanism and outcome of coordination, and 5) organizational outcomes of coordination. Each is treated in turn next.

Coordination

We see at least five common errors when coordination is defined or operationalized. First, and typical of the older contingency approach, it is conceived of simply as a mathematical representation of the allocation and sequencing of tasks within a group (O'Brien, 1968). Second, coordination is operationalized as an outcome, such as measuring it as attaining quality of product, quantity of product, or efficiency of delivering product (e.g., Argote, 1982; Faraj & Sproull, 2000). Third, coordination is operationalized as a coordinating mechanism, such as asking if planning was wellconceived, schedules were clear and adequate, or if members have a shared cognition (e.g., Cheng, 1983; Gittell, 2002; Kraut et al., 2005).

The next two errors confound conceptions that are peripheral with the coordinating process itself. Fourth, variables that are more descriptive of the context are included rather than those specifically coordinative in nature. For example, Cray (1984) includes how many functions a task group shares with another and how many other tasks the group must interact with. While these certainly influence the coordination process, they do so by increased interdependencies and uncertainties, which are already accounted for in the proposed model. Fifth, other moderators may exist, but there is too little evidence to support them as needing to be included here. These include Gittell's (2001, 2002) concept of mutual respect and Hoegl et al.'s (2004) project commitment; although both may lead to coordination, a group need not like each other or be highly committed to the task to accomplish it.

The operationalizations that seem to best measure coordination as it is conceived here include variables that measure in situ interaction, and the alignment of work. In situ interaction includes variables such as information that is exchanged in a timely manner, differences negotiated quickly, lack of disagreement, helping, and problem solving capabilities (Faraj & Sproull, 2000; Gittell, 2002). Alignment of work includes coherence of work, lack of duplication of work, everyone in the group doing the tasks they were supposed to do, people able to do their jobs without getting in each other's way, no delays in the process, subtasks closely harmonized, and goals understood by the members (Cheng, 1983, 1984; Gittell, 2001, 2002; Hoegl et al., 2004; Kraut et al., 2005).

Organizational Coordinating as Both Mechanism and Outcome of Coordination

Organizational coordinating mechanisms are the broadest category, but are easier to observe than the other mechanisms. They are created based on specific actions of an organization in an attempt to increase coordination. Three categories of such mechanisms include: structural coordinating mechanisms, conscious interaction mechanisms, and stored organizational coordinating mechanisms.

Structural coordinating mechanisms (SCM) include those components of an organization such as rules, roles, and power structures that constrain and enable any interaction, including coordination. SCM are established at two points, through planning by the organization and through the interaction of organizational members. The first, planning, is well established in the coordination literature as both non-physical though observable (e.g., hierarchical arrangements, rules, and departmentalization) as well as physical (e.g., formal information systems, physical space design; see Andriessen, 2003; Archea, 1977; Kraut, Fish, Root, & Chalfonte 1990; March & Simon, 1993; Tushman & Nadler, 1978). These are conscious decisions on the part of the organization to increase the coordination of its members. The second interaction of members, follows from our discussion above of the centrality of communication in both coordinating mechanisms and integrating conditions as well as the structuration of coordination. Through the interaction of members as they enact and experience the planning of the organization, these mechanisms are (re)created—a concept that will be further explored below in outcomes.

Proposition 1a: Uncertainty is positively associated with SCM.
Proposition 1b: Interdependencies are positively associated with SCM.
Proposition 2: SCM are enacted through communication.
Proposition 3: SCM are positively associated with extent of coordination.

Conscious interaction mechanisms (CIM) involve direct interpersonal or group communication to any member of a group by an organizational member external to the group, with the intent to facilitate coordination of the group. Conscious interaction coordinating mechanisms are similar to what March and Simon (1993) called feedback, or what van de Ven et al. (1976) referred to as group or personal mechanisms. However, it is not the same as the concept of mutual adjustment, which is identified by Thompson (1967) as occurring in the process of action. The difference is that mutual adjustment is something that occurs during group interaction or during coordination, whereas feedback, or personal and group mechanisms, like conscious inter-action mechanisms, originate externally from the group. This measure is somewhat muddled in the literature as so much of the literature confounds this with either what is being conceived here as coordination, or adds mea-sures that make it difficult to tell what is really involved. This latter is evident in Gittell's (2001, 2002) investigations of relational coordination. Her relational coordination measure includes aspects of interaction between orga-nizational members external to the group, but it also includes the timeliness and frequency of group interaction, which by the present conceptualization mixes coordinating mechanism with coordination. The same issue occurs in work by Grote et al. (2010) and others (e.g., Hewett, O'Brien, & Hornik, 1974). Though research shows the effectiveness of face-to-face interaction in improving coordination and output (Kraut et al., 2005; Okhuysen & Bechky, 2009b; Young et al., 1998), organizational communication has been increas-ingly well supported with mediated technologies (Rice & Leonardi, 2013), for example in customer support teams (Rathnam, Mahajan, & Whinston, 1995) and construction projects (Hossain, 2009). These organizational struc-tures (as coordinating mechanisms) often function, or are intended, to reduce uncertainty. They have been found not only to be more common, but also more effective, in high uncertainty environments (March & Simon, 1993; van de Ven et al., 1976).

Proposition 4a: Uncertainty is positively associated with CIM.
Proposition 4b: Interdependencies are positively associated with CIM.
Proposition 5: CIM are positively associated with the extent of coordination.

Stored organizational coordinating mechanisms (SOCM) are artifacts created by organizations that do not require direct interpersonal interaction in the facili-tation of coordination, but that still exist for that purpose. These include training manuals, budgets, memos, plans, databases, programming, or other mechanis-tic, formal, or impersonal artifacts (March & Simon, 1993; Thompson, 1967; van de Ven et al., 1976), as well as any information (physical, digital) that the organization has created and stored to increase coordination. These require some agency to access on the part of the group or organizational member, and may have at one point been part of CIM (e.g., during training employees are given an orientation manual), but now there is only interaction with the object if the organizational member seeks it out. These mechanisms interact directly with resource knowledge mechanisms (see below) and are only as effective as organizational members' ability to access, understand, and use them.

Proposition 6a: Uncertainty is positively associated with SOCM.
Proposition 6b: Interdependencies are positively associated with SOCM.
Proposition 7: SOCM are positively associated with the extent of coordination.

Organizational coordination mechanisms as outcomes of coordination.   Early work assumed that these organizational mechanisms were set forth by management, implemented, accepted, and endured until later organizational changes in procedures. It is now understood that these structural components may be more or less appropriated through the organizational members' interactions, and be more or less adjusted in alignment with the intentions of the organization (DeSanctis & Poole, 1994). A prime example is Bechky's (2006) investigation of roles in temporary organizations such as film crews. Members attained a high extent of coordination quickly through the use of roles that were (re)established through the use of joking and other interactions. Other work supporting this conception of organizational mechanisms as created through interaction found that these structural components can be influenced by network relationships, which are more readily established in collocated teams as opposed to distributed teams (Hinds & McGrath, 2006), or conceptions of time that emerge differently depending on group experience and make-up (Ballard & Seibold, 2003), among others.

Proposition 8a: Extent of coordination may reproduce or reshape structural coordinating mechanisms.
Proposition 8b: Extent of coordination may reproduce or reshape conscious interaction mechanisms.
Proposition 8c: Extent of coordination may reproduce or reshape stored organizational coordinating mechanisms.

Knowledge as Both Mechanism and Outcome of Coordination

Based on such diverse concepts as tacit knowledge (Brockman & Anthony, 2007), transactive memory (Hollingshead & Brandon, 2003; Lewis & Herndon, 2011; Ren, Carley, & Argote, 2006), expertise (Stewart, Walker, Hutt, & Kumar, 2010), and implicit coordination (Rico et al., 2008), knowledge as a coordination mechanism includes facets of coordination for which actors utilize modes that are neither completely without thought and based on repeated patterns, such as routines (explained below), nor are fully conscious (like organizational coordination mechanisms). We emphasize two of those knowledge mechanisms, resource knowledge and relational knowledge, as both involve communication.

Resource knowledge includes information, skills, and materials. When group members know who knows what, and how to get that information, they are able to perform better (Faraj & Sproull, 2000; Olivera, 2000). Knowledge about resources allows members of the group to identify the location of needed resources, whether that means knowing whom to approach in order to obtain materials, in what database information is shared, or which group member has information about a given task or decision. This is not only true about knowledge internal to the group but also knowledge of the environment. For example, boundary spanners in a group have knowledge about where to access external resources (Tushman, 1977).

Relational knowledge allows members to better access those resources that require interaction. Knowledge does not have to be about facts, but can be about how others in a team interact (a central aspect of transactive memory; Hollingshead, 1998). As groups interact, they learn more about each other. In subsequent interactions they have a better idea about not only who knows what, but also how others in the group might react. For example, Faraj and Sproull (2000) and Kraut et al. (2005) found evidence for increased performance and increased knowledge as teams spent more time together. This second form of knowledge mechanism functions through either being able to predict the needs of group members in a situation (implicit coordination; Rico et al., 2008), or having awareness of the how group and organizational members will react in a situation (Ren et al., 2006; Weick & Roberts, 1993). Both kinds of relational knowledge reduce task interaction time and errors. Relational knowledge also includes understanding how to "read" and interpret the other group members during interaction (i.e., interpreting nonverbal behaviors, paralinguistics, politics, network roles, and so forth), resulting in better understanding of each other and, ideally, better performance (Hollingshead, 1998). Even in groups with negative dynamics, knowledge of how others will react and interact can improve performance (Xia, Yuan, & Gay, 2009).

> Proposition 9a: Interdependencies are positively associated with use of knowledge mechanisms.
>
> Proposition 9a: Uncertainty is positively associated with greater use of knowledge mechanisms.
>
> Proposition 10a: More resource knowledge is positively associated with greater extent of coordination.
>
> Proposition 10b: More relational knowledge is positively associated with greater extent of coordination.
>
> Proposition 11: Stored organizational coordinating mechanisms interact with resource knowledge such that higher levels of both lead to even higher extent of coordination.

Routines as Both Mechanism and Outcome of Coordination

Conceptualizations of routines are well established (see Becker, 2004). Routines are those patterns of action that emerge from interaction and that allow us to act with little to no conscious thought (Becker, 2004). They develop over time and become more deeply ingrained in minds and unconscious practice, to the point that actors not only enact them without much thought but also implicitly believe that other actors also are enacting them (Becker, 2004). Successful routines embed the knowledge and organizational coordinating mechanisms necessary to accomplish tasks across individuals and organizational units.

Investigations have found that routines are more complex than originally thought, on several levels. Routines act as grammars for action rather than as a concrete guide (Pentland & Rueter, 1994). They function as grammars by specifying a broad range of possible actions within a context from which we unconsciously select parts that work together to enact the routine. In this way the routine enables and constrains action, but by its selection and use in interaction it is further established as routine. Routines also have been found to function at larger organizational levels than just the individual interaction or group interactions. Entire organizations enact routines without conscious member knowledge (Feldman & Pentland, 2003); once established they can promote stability, but also reduce organizational flexibility and innovativeness. Even at the organizational level, routines are (re)established through interaction and formalization into procedures and policies. As small changes occur to routines, they are adjusted and then retained for future enactment (Feldman, 2000). Routines, however, do not always function to improve processes and outcomes; sometimes the routines that are (re)established and reinforced through interaction end up working against some individual, group, or organizational goals, whether intentionally or not. Routines may both embed and reinforce dysfunctional interdependencies and coordination strategies, thus becoming *unusual routines*, leading to short- and long-term group and organizational negative consequences (Rice & Cooper, 2010). Further, unusual routines reinforce the original problem or biases, eventually routinizing those situations and processes. In general, unusual routines can be prevented or resolved by increased feedback, and feedback about the feedback (e.g., double-loop learning; see Rice & Cooper, 2010), involving both organizational mechanisms and knowledge mechanisms. However, CIM and relational knowledge may both be localized within the group generating the unusual routine, thus making it more difficult to identify and resolve the unusual routines. The routine seems locally beneficial, while being dysfunctional for or harming other groups' or the organization's processes and goals, yet without being identified or explained in SCM, SOCM, or resource knowledge.

Contingency/design theorists present routines as facilitating coordinated action by pre-specifying the sequences of tasks and who should perform them, thus reducing the need for workers to interact, and the cost of coordinating work (Tushman & Nadler, 1978). Grote et al. (2008) found that routines function as coordinating mechanisms by reducing the need for interaction (especially interaction about the interactions).

Proposition 12: Routines are established through consistent use of other mechanisms.

However, routines function as a coordinating mechanism through the subsequent reduced need for other coordinating mechanisms; thus:

Proposition 13a: Routines are positively associated with decreased group access to stored organizational coordinating mechanisms.

Proposition 13b: Routines function as a coordinating mechanism through the reduced need for interaction in situ.

Proposition 14: More cross-group interaction is positively associated with fewer unusual routines (presuming the unusual routine does not involve the group interaction itself).

Organizational Outcomes of Coordination

Beyond the three (re)produced outcomes of coordination (organizational mechanisms, knowledge mechanisms, and routines), the general and primary goal of coordination is to accomplish organization outcomes. These actual outcomes may be more or less expected, more or less intentional, and more or less positive. Expected, intentional, and positive goals are often confounded with coordination, with the logical understanding that a higher extent of coordination should result in more successful attainment of organizational goals. Organizational goals and thus expected outcomes can be either official, which are the understood purposes (from the perspective of the organization), or operative, which more closely represents the actual operating policies of the organization (Perrow, 1961). Operative goals do not necessarily align with official goals and may even run counter to them (a central assumption of agency theory; Eisenhardt, 1989). This is particularly salient when operative goals are examined on the group level or individual level. In these cases there may seem to be a high extent of coordination that manifests as alignment towards attaining an unofficial operative goal, but the net result would be unintended or unwanted outcomes (from the perspective of the organization; Perrow, 1961). Organizational goal outcomes also can be conceived of in terms of quality or quantity (Argote, 1982; Cheng, 1983, 1984). In his examination of Belgian academic departments, Cheng (1983) found that coordination was positively correlated with increases in both quality and quantity of outputs, but those correlations were moderated by uncertainty differently for the quality than the quantity relationships. As uncertainty increased, the correlation between coordination and quality became more positive, but the correlation between coordination and quantity became less positive. Finally, as discussed above, unusual routines may be an organizational outcome differentially desired, intended, or positive, depending on the organizational location and actors involved.

Proposition 15a: Extent of coordination may be associated with both quality and quantity of expected, intended, or positive organizational output.

Proposition 15b: Extent of coordination may also be associated with both quality and quantity of unexpected, unintended, or negative organizational output.

Figure 7.1 portrays the broad relationships among interdependencies, uncertainty, coordinating, coordinating mechanisms, coordination, and coordination outcomes, associated with these propositions.

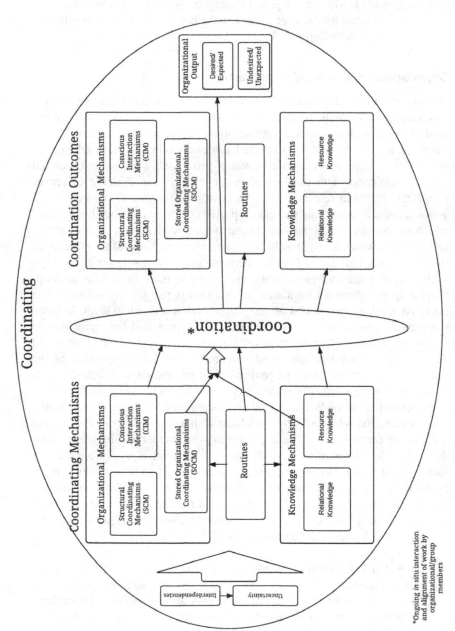

*Ongoing in situ interaction and alignment of work by organizational/group members

Figure 7.1 The relationships between the coordinating mechanisms and outcomes

Discussion

Agenda for Additional Organizational Coordination Research

Although there is an abundance of literature on organizational coordination, we have shown there is still much work to do. An obvious research goal at this time could be testing the current model in Figure 7.1 (a) to determine if the proposed overarching coordinating mechanisms are as inclusive as suggested, (b) to ascertain if the recursive nature of coordinating mechanism to coordination back to coordinating mechanisms is as strong as proposed, and (c) to more fully develop potential mediating variables as well as testing interaction effects.

Beyond testing the proposed model, opportunities abound for utilizing our perspective on organizational communication in other areas of interest to communication scholars in general and to organizational communication researchers in particular. These applications have the potential to advance, for example, coordination as energy-in-conversation (CEC) theory, coordinated management of meaning (CMM) theory, and the high reliability organizations (HRO) perspective. Each of these theories explicitly focuses on the importance, and nature, of coordination, communication, and meaning-making in organizations. Space constraints limit us to only going into detail on these few, but there are many others that could be informed by the current theoretical model, including speech act theories, uncertainty reduction theory, systems theory, and network theories, among others.

Coordination as energy-in-conversation (CEC). Quinn and Dutton (2005) develop a theory of coordination as energy-in-conversation. They identify conversations as the location of coordination in an organization and determine that conversations take energy, so the effort that people invest in a conversation towards coordination depends in part on the amount of energy that they either gain or spend from those conversations. Quinn and Dutton (2005) conceive of energy as texts in that "a person can read his or her own energy as a bodily signal that summarizes how desirable he or she perceives the situation to be and that people can read another person's expressions to interpret how much energy that person feels" (p. 43). With this in mind, they identify energy-in-conversation as a person's energy level (representative of their situational desirability), the interpretation of the energy level of the other participant (represented nonverbally), and a feeling of wanting to act and being capable of acting, all of which leads to the level of effort the person will invest in the conversation and its subsequent coordinative results.

Two obvious aspects of our model of coordination and communication relevant to CEC are *discursive consciousness* (organizational mechanisms) and *practical consciousness* (knowledge mechanisms). Existing SCM such as rules, roles and power structures affect possibilities for conversation and may inhibit or foster appropriate energy-in-conversation, influencing the extent and nature of coordination. In turn, the extent to which people have appropriate energy-in-conversation and share interpretations of that help to create stored organizational coordinating mechanisms and conscious interaction mechanisms through interaction. The relational knowledge mechanism clearly would include organizational members' ability to interpret others' energy levels and whether certain individuals will be accessible for and committed to coordination interaction.

Coordinated management of meaning (CMM).   The premise of CMM is that in interaction people may not have the same intentions for interaction or understandings of how they are attempting to create meaning, but that as "persons-in-conversation" they create bonds of union that co-construct a reality (whether that reality is helpful or not; Pearce & Pearce, 2000). Salmon and Faris (2006) examined professionals from a child and adolescent mental health service as they met with other agencies to coordinate on cases. They utilized a CMM frame to understand the complexity of the discourse involved and discover an understanding or at least work towards a common goal.

CMM can serve a dual role in consideration of our model of coordination and communication. First, CMM can be conceptualized as one of the forms of in-situ interaction that constitute and enable coordination. For example, mis-matched contextual levels or discourse assumptions during coordination interaction may create or reinforce subsequent unusual routines, such as treating certainty as uncertainty or vice versa. This has the effect of disfiguring structural coordinating mechanisms, allowing (un)conscious interaction mechanisms, and inappropriately applying stored organizational coordinating mechanisms, in turn activating inappropriate responses to uncertainties (or masking or creating difficult-to-identify interdependencies), thus weakening or misdirecting conscious interaction mechanisms efforts, and making subsequent successful coordination less likely. Hence, second, CMM itself is one kind of coordination activity (whether conscious or not) influenced by existing organizational and structural resources. Accessibility and relevance of structural coordinating mechanism relational knowledge resources would influence how participants coordinate and shape meaning during coordination.

High reliability organizations (HRO).   Weick and Roberts (1993) offered a conception of the collective mind and heedful interrelating in a study of aircraft carrier flight deck crews. Typical construals of interdependencies and coordination did not seem to fit the context of these types of groups. The standard coordination literature examined groups that were concerned with productivity or efficiency, but did not examine reliability (Weick & Roberts, 1993). Groups such as deck flight crews, nuclear power plant operators, and shuttle crews have as their primary drive not just a task, but an incredibly precise task that requires highly reliable interactions or the consequences could be catastrophic (Weick, Sutcliffe, & Obstfeld, 1999). Weick and Robert's (1993) examination of aircraft carrier flight crews and other high reliability organizations (HRO) unpacked these interactions. They determined that these groups utilize a different type of coordination that they identified as *collective mindfulness*. When a group of individuals working towards common goals enacts mindfulness, their individual interpretations and personal mindfulness combine into a collective mind that allows for a more precise awareness of situations and the environment (Weick & Roberts, 1993). Collective mindfulness includes five processes; a preoccupation with failure, a reluctance to simplify interpretations, sensitivity to operations, a commitment to resilience, and under-specification of structure (Weick et al., 1999).

A preoccupation with failure is unusual, particularly for these types of organizations, because failure is so rarely seen. Alternatively we may argue that it is exactly this preoccupation that generates and maintains a form of coordination that reduces the likelihood of failure. Possibility of failure is attended to in three ways in HROs. First, the expanded emphasis on failures increases the centrality of the maintenance departments of HROs as compared to other organizations, so that they become stronger and more salient structural coordinating mechanisms. The maintenance department has contact with the highest number of failures and maintains a database for learning, increasing stored organizational coordinating mechanisms. Second, HROs encourage the reporting of errors, thus reflexively self-structuring by creating a routine as a resource knowledge mechanism. They note a study by Landau and Chisholm (1995) that refers to a seaman on a nuclear aircraft carrier who loses a tool on deck and reports it. This reporting results in all airborne aircraft being redirected to ground landings until the tool can be located and the commendation of the seaman for reporting it, rather than condemnation. Finally, this preoccupation with failure leads to an attention to the failures inherent in continued success such as complacency, risk aversion, and inattention.

From our perspective, what may be considered as an undesired or unexpected organizational output (the identification and reporting of errors) becomes restructured, through aligning individual communication with HRO goals, and routinization, into a desired/expected output. What is typically seen as a source and form of uncertainty—error—is reconceptualized as a source of reducing future error by understanding interdependencies better. The crucial question here, then, is how both organizational mechanisms and knowledge mechanisms should be restructured to shape interactions and alignments within coordination to accomplish this transformation. For example, Weick et al. (1999) show that HROs redefine coordination through layered systems of checks and balances, adversarial reviews, job re-training and rotation, structural redundancies, and diverse views on their teams. Another approach identified by Weick et al. (1999) is attending to latent epistemic networks that only emerge when expected interdependencies are disrupted or unwanted interdependences are revealed, and then dissipate once the problem has been solved. Before routines are reconstituted, these typically unknown relational knowledge mechanisms should be understood and routinized into conscious interaction mechanisms and stored organizational coordinating mechanisms.

Contributions

We began by identifying four issues in the organizational coordination literature: (a) coordination is typically not explicitly defined, conceptually or operationally, (b) proposed types of coordination overlap or contradict each other, (c) coordination is treated as a secondary aspect rather than as a central concern; and (d) what is arguably a distinctive communicative phenomenon requires more attention by communication researchers. Here we summarize our proposed resolutions of these issues, providing the foundation for our model and propositions.

Coordinating, coordinating mechanisms, and coordination are distinct concepts. Our conceptual definitions of coordinating as the overarching process, coordinating mechanisms as the structures that are brought to bear, and coordination as the in situ interaction, allow for a more precise and distinct view of components of organizational coordinating. In clearly distinguishing between coordinating mechanisms and coordination, many of the terms that were identified as coordination have been reframed as coordinating mechanisms (e.g., expertise, tacit knowledge, implicit coordination).

Distinct coordinating mechanisms represent structurational levels of consciousness. Coordinating mechanisms in the literature were reframed using structuration levels of consciousness as organizational (discursive level), knowledge (practical level), and routines (unconscious level). The conceptual distinctions between coordinating, coordinating mechanisms, and coordination, and among types of coordinating mechanisms enable a specific view of how types of coordination and mechanisms proposed by others interrelate, and provide the basis for a more parsimonious model of organizational coordination and communication.

Coordination is a central concern. Our third task was to highlight the central role of coordination in organizational structuration. By applying a structurational approach toward coordination as influenced both by coordinating mechanisms and through interaction (re)creating those very mechanisms, we place coordination at the core of the process. The proposed model does so in four ways. First, it highlights the distinct levels of consciousness as mechanisms, allows a reframing of them as possessing distinct aspects of organizational structure, and enables tests of the ways that they might interpenetrate in inter-action (coordination). Second, it informs our understanding of structuration via the proposed recursive nature of organizational coordinating. By placing specific mechanisms as the structure (coordinating mechanisms), and offering a conceptual context in which to examine the ways in which practice (re)cre-ates those structures, it encourages further investigation of structuration. Third, it proposes rules and resources as being closely aligned with the distinct levels of consciousness. Fourth, it proposes how coordinating, coordinating mecha-nisms, coordination, and outcomes are interrelated.

Coordination is a communicative phenomenon. We theorize coordination as a fundamentally communicative phenomenon. Without communication, no shared meaning could emerge and no coordinating mechanisms could be created or applied. At the micro level, activity coordination, the third communication flow identified by McPhee and Zaug (2000), underscores the interactive nature of coordination. Activity coordination specifically identifies the interactive nature of organizational members as they adjust to germane acts of others and to the constraints of the situation. At the macro level, a structuration lens underscores the whole of organizational coordination as communicative. As proposed in McPhee and Zaug's (2008) fourth communication flow, institutional positioning, organizations are positioned within a larger context and the relationships between the orga-nization and its context are managed through communication. This framing within a larger context occurs with coordination, but it is nested within the organization, so that coordination occurs as part of the negotiation of positioning. The final point at which organizational coordination is bet-ter elucidated by utilizing an organizational communication lens is at the connection of structure and practice. Much previous work has focused on structures, process, or outcomes. However, by utilizing the concept of the duality of structure we note not only specific aspects of organiza-tional coordination—structures, coordination, or outputs—but also see the ways they interconnect through communication. Coordinating mechanisms (structures) are brought to bear on coordination (practice/process) through communication, and through communicative interaction those very struc-tures can be (re)created.

Conclusion

This work is intended to enrich our understanding of coordination, to expand organizational communication research into an area that is rich with possibili-ties, and to illuminate structuration. Though there has been significant research on organizational coordination, we conceptualize organizational coordina-tion in more concrete and simple ways that should make further progress and understanding easier. And there is a dearth of organizational coordination research from a communication perspective. Our model elucidates not only the ways that the study of coordination can benefit from a communicative lens, but also the depth of material that communication scholars have available to mine. Finally, in linking communication, coordination, and structuration, we have shown ways that our understanding of structuration theory is strengthened through the investigation of coordination.

References

Adler, P. S. (1995). Interdepartmental interdependence and coordination: The case of the design/manufacturing interface. *Organization Science, 6*, 147–167. http://dx.doi.org/10.1287/orsc.6.2.147

Alter, C. (1990). An exploratory study of conflict and coordination in interorganizational service delivery systems. *The Academy of Management Journal, 33*, 478–502. http://dx.doi.org/10.2307/256577

Andriessen, J. H. K. (2003). *Working with groupware: Understanding and evaluating collaboration technology.* Berlin, Germany: Springer-Verlag.

Archea, J. (1977). The place of architectural factors in behavioral theories of privacy. *Journal of Social Issues, 33*(3), 116–137. http://dx.doi.org/10.1111/j.1540-4560.1977.tb01886.x

Argote, L. (1982). Input uncertainty and organizational coordination in hospital emergency units. *Administrative Science Quarterly, 27*, 420–434. http://dx.doi.org/10.2307/2392320

Bailetti, A. J., Callahan, J. R., & DiPietro, P. (1994). A coordination structure approach to the management of projects. *IEEE Transactions on Engineering Management, 41*, 394–403. http://dx.doi.org/10.1109/17.364565

Bailetti, A. J., Callahan, J. R., & McClusky, S. (1998). Coordination at different stages of the product design process. *Research and Development Management, 28*, 237–247. doi:10.1111/1467-9310.00101

Ballard, D. I., & Seibold, D. R. (2003). Communicating and organizing in time: A meso-level model of organizational temporality. *Management Communication Quarterly, 16*, 380–415. doi:10.1177/0893318902238896

Ballard, D. I., & Seibold, D. R. (2004). Communication-related organizational structures and work group temporal experiences: The effects of coordination method, technology type, and feedback cycle on members' construal and enactments of time. *Communication Monographs, 71*, 1–27. doi:10.1080/0363452041000169147

Bardram, J. E. (2000). Temporal coordination: On time coordination of collaborative activities at a surgical department. *Computer Supported Cooperative Work, 9*, 157–187. http://dx.doi.org/10.1023/a:1008748724225

Bechky, B. A. (2006). Gaffers, gofers, and grips: Role-based coordination in temporary organizations. *Organizational Science, 17*, 3–21. doi:10.1287/orsc.1050.0149

Becker, M. C. (2004). Organizational routines: A review of the literature. *Industrial and Corporate Change, 13*, 643–677. doi:10.1093/icc/dth026

Beniger, J. R. (1986). *The control revolution: Technological and economic origins of the information society.* Boston, MA: Harvard University Press.

Berninghaus, S. K., & Ehrhart, K-M. (2001). Coordination and information: Recent experimental evidence. *Economic Letters, 73*, 345–351. http://dx.doi.org/10.1016/s0165-1765(01)00502-x

Brockman, E. N., & Anthony, W. P. (2007). Tacit knowledge and strategic decision making. *Group and Organization Management, 27*, 436–455. doi:10.1177/1059601102238356

Buvik, A., & John, G. (2000). When does vertical coordination improve industrial purchasing relationships? *Journal of Marketing, 64*, 52–64. doi:10.1509/jmkg.64.4.52.18075

Cataldo, M., Wagstrom, P. A., Herbsleb, J. D., & Carley, K. M. (2006). Identification of coordination requirements: Implications for the design of collaboration and awareness tools. In *Proceedings of the Conference on Computer Supported Cooperative Work* (CSCW'06) (pp. 353–362). New York, NY: ACM. doi:10.1145/1180875.1180928

Celly, K. S., & Frazier, G. L. (1996). Outcome-based and behavior-based coordination efforts in channel relationships. *Journal of Marketing Research, 38*, 200–210. http://dx.doi.org/10.2307/3152147

Cheng, J. L. C. (1983). Interdependence and coordination in organizations: A role-systems analysis. *The Academy of Management Journal, 26*, 156–162. http://dx.doi.org/10.2307/256142

Cheng, J. L. C. (1984). Organizational coordination, uncertainty, and performance: An integrative study. *Human Relations, 37*, 829–851. doi:10.1177/001872678403701004

Clark, H. H. (2005). Coordinating with each other in a material world. *Discourse Studies, 7*, 507–525. doi:10.1177/1461445605054404

Cooren, F., Taylor, J. R., & Van Every, E. J. (Eds.), (2006). *Communication as organizing: Empirical and theoretical explorations in the dynamic of text and conversation.* Mahwah, NJ: Lawrence Erlbaum Associates.

Cray, D. (1984). Control and coordination in multinational corporations. *Journal of International Business Studies, 15*, 85–98. http://dx.doi.org/10.1057/palgrave.jibs.8490483

Crowston, K. (1997). A coordination theory approach to organizational process design. *Organizational Science, 8*, 157–175. http://dx.doi.org/10.1287/orsc.8.2.157

Crowston, K., & Kammerer, E. E. (1998). Coordination and collective mind in software requirements development. *IBM Systems Journal, 37*, 227–245. http://dx.doi.org/10.1147/sj.372.0227

Cumming, M., & Akari, E. (2005). Coordinating the complexity of design using P2P groupware. *CoDesign, 1*, 255–265. doi:10.1080/15710880500478361

DeSanctis, G., & Poole, M. S. (1994). Capturing complexity in advanced technology use: Adaptive structuration theory. *Organizational Science, 5*, 121–147. http://dx.doi.org/10.1287/orsc.5.2.121

Eisenhardt, K. M. (1989). Agency theory: An assessment and review. *Academy of Management Review, 14*(1), 57–74.

Endstrom, A., & Galbraith, J. R. (1977). Transfer of managers as a coordination and control strategy in multinational organizations. *Administrative Science Quarterly, 22*, 248–263. http://dx.doi.org/10.2307/2391959

Faraj, S., & Sproull, L. (2000). Coordinating expertise in software development teams. *Management Science, 46,* 1554–1568. http://dx.doi.org/10.1287/mnsc.46.12.1554. 12072

Faraj, S., & Xiao, Y. (2006). Coordination in fast-response organizations. *Management Science, 52,* 1155–1169. doi:10.1287/mnsc/1060.0526

Feldman, M. S. (2000). Organizational routines as a source of continuous change. *Organizational Science, 11,* 611–626. http://dx.doi.org/10.1287/orsc.11.6.611.12529

Feldman, M. S., & Pentland, B. T. (2003). Reconceptualizing organizational routines as a source of flexibility and change. *Administrative Science Quarterly, 48,* 94–118. http://dx.doi.org/10.2307/3556620

Foss, N., & Lorenzen, M. (2009). Towards an understanding of cognitive coordination: Theoretical developments and empirical illustrations. *Organizational Studies, 30,* 1201–1206. doi:10.1177/0170840609337956

Fusaroli, R., & Tylen, K. (2012). Carving language for social coordination: A dynamic approach. *Interactional Studies, 13,* 103–124. doi:10.1075/is.13.1.07fus

Galbraith, J. R. (1973). *Designing complex organizations.* Reading, MA: Addison-Wesley.

Gazdar, G. (1980). A cross-categorical semantics for coordination. *Linguistics and Philosophy, 3,* 407–409. http://dx.doi.org/10.1007/bf00401693

Gerstner, E., & Hess, J. D. (1995). Pull promotions and channel coordination. *Marketing Science, 14,* 43–60. http://dx.doi.org/10.1287/mksc.14.1.43

Giddens, A. (1979). *Central problems in social theory: Action, structure, and contradiction in social analysis.* Berkley, CA: University of California Press.

Gittell, J. H. (2001). Supervisory span, relational coordination, and flight departure performance: A reassessment of post bureaucracy theory. *Organizational Science, 12,* 468–483. doi:1047-7039/01/1204/0468

Gittell, J. H. (2002). Coordinating mechanisms in care provider groups: Relational coordination as mediator and input uncertainty as moderator of performance effects. *Management Science, 48,* 1408–1426. http://dx.doi.org/10.1287/mnsc.48.11.1408.268

Gittell, J. H., & Weiss, L. (2004). Coordination networks within and across organizations: A multi-level framework. *Journal of Management Studies, 41,* 127–152. doi:10.1111/j.1467-6486.2004.00424.x

Grote, G., Kolbe, M., Zla-Mezo, E., Bienefeld-Seall, N., & Kunzle, B. (2010). Adaptive coordination and heedfulness make better cockpit crews. *Ergonomics, 53,* 211–228. doi:10.1080/00140130903248819

Grote, G., Weichbrodt, J. C., Gunter, H., Zala-Mezo, E., & Kunzle, B. (2008). Coordination in high-risk organizations: The need for flexible routines. *Cognition, Technology & Work, 11,* 17–27. doi:10.1007/s10111-008-0119-y

Hewett, T. T., O'Brien, G. E., & Hornik, J. (1974). The effects of work organization, leadership style and member compatibility upon the productivity of small groups working in a manipulative task. *Organizational Behavior, 11,* 283–301. http://dx.doi.org/10.1016/0030-5073(74)90021-x

Hinds, P., & McGrath, C. (2006). Structures that work: Social structure, work structure and coordination ease in geographically distributed teams. In *Proceedings of the Conference on Computer Supported Cooperative Work* (CSCW'06) (pp. 343–352). New York: ACM. doi:10.1145/1180875.1180928

Hoegl, M., Weinkauf, K., & Gemuenden, H. G. (2004). Interteam coordination, project commitment, and team work in multi-team R&D projects: A longitudinal study. *Organization Science, 15,* 38–55. http://dx.doi.org/10.1287/orsc.1030.0053

Hollingshead, A. B. (1998). Retrieval processes in transactive memory systems. *Journal of Personality and Social Psychology, 74,* 659–671. http://dx.doi.org/10.1037//0022-3514.74.3.659

Hollingshead, A. B., & Brandon, D. P. (2003). Potential benefits of communication in transactive memory systems. *Human Communication Research, 29*(4), 607–615. http://dx.doi.org/10.1093/hcr/29.4.607

Hossain, L. (2009). Communications and coordination in construction projects. *Construction Management and Economics, 27,* 25–39. doi:10.1080/01446190802558923

Hubbard, A. S. (2000). Interpersonal coordination in interactions: Evaluations and social skills. *Communication Research Reports, 17,* 95–104. doi:10.1080/08824090009388755

Humphrey, S. E., & Aime, F. (2014). Team microdynamics: Toward an organizing approach to teamwork. *Annals of the Academy of Management 2014, 8*(1), 443–503. doi:10.1080/19416520.2014.904140

Ilgen, D. R., & O'Brien, G. (1974). Leader-member relations in small groups. *Organizational Behavior and Human Performance, 12,* 335–350. http://dx.doi.org/10.1016/0030-5073(74)90056-7

Janicik, G. A., & Bartel, C. A. (2003). Talking about time: Effects of temporal planning and time awareness norms on group coordination and performance. *Group Dynamics, Theory, Research, and Practice, 7,* 122–134. doi:10.1037/1089-2699.7.2.122

Kellogg, K. C., Orlikowski, W. J., & Yates, J. (2006). Life in the trading zone: Structuring coordination across boundaries in postbureaucratic organizations. *Organizational Science, 17,* 22–44. http://dx.doi.org/10.1287/orsc.1050.0157

Kim, S. K., Stump, R. L., & Oh, C. (2009). Driving forces of coordination costs in distributor-supplier relationships: Toward a middle-range theory. *Journal of Academic Marketing Science, 37,* 384–399. doi:10.1007/s11747-008-0126

Kraut, R. E., Fish, R. S., Root, R. W., & Chalfonte, B. L. (1990). Informal communication in organizations: Form, function, and technology. In S. Oskamp & S. Spacapan (Eds.), *Human reactions to technology: The Claremont symposium on applied social psychology* (pp. 145–199). Beverly Hills, CA: Sage.

Kraut, R., Fussell, S., Lurch, E., & Espinosa, A. (2005). Coordination in teams: Evidence from a simulated management game. Human-Computer Interaction Institute. Paper 102. Retrieved from http://repository.cmu.edu/hcii/102.

Kraut, R., Lewis, S. H., & Swezy, L. W. (1982). Listener responsiveness and the coordination of conversation. *Journal of Personality and Social Psychology, 45,* 718–731. http://dx.doi.org/10.1037/0022-3514.43.4.718

Landau, M., & Chisholm, D. (1995). The arrogance of optimism: Notes on failure avoidance management. *Journal of Contingencies and Crisis Management, 3,* 67–80.

Larsson, R., & Bowen, D. E. (1989). Organization and customer: Managing design and coordination of services. *Academy of Management Review, 14,* 213–233. http://dx.doi.org/10.5465/amr.1989.4282099

Lawrence, P. R., & Lorsch, J. W. (1967). *Organization and environment: Managing differentiation and integration.* Boston, MA: Harvard University Press.

Lehr, J. K., & Rice, R. E. (2002). Organizational measures as a form of knowledge management: A multitheoretic, communication-based exploration. *Journal of the*

American Society for Information Science and Technology, 53(12), 1060–1073. http://dx.doi.org/10.1002/asi.10108

Lewis, K., & Herndon, B. (2011). Transactive memory systems: Current issues and future research directions. *Organization Science, 22*(5), 1254–1265.

Lewis, L. K. (2006). Collaboration: Review of communication scholarship and a research agenda. In C. Beck (Ed.), *Communication yearbook 30* (pp. 197–247). Thousand Oaks, CA: Sage. 10.1207/s15567419cy3001_5

Malone, T. W. (1987). Modeling coordination in organizations and markets. *Management Science, 33,* 1317–1332. http://dx.doi.org/10.1287/mnsc.38.12.1819

Malone, T. W., & Crowston, K. (1990). What is coordination theory and how can it help design cooperative work systems? *CSCW '90 Proceedings of the 1990 ACM Conference on Computer-supported Cooperative Work* (pp. 357–370). http://dx.doi. org/10.1145/99332.99367

Malone, T. W., & Crowston, K. (1994). The interdisciplinary study of coordination. *ACM Computing Surveys, 26,* 87–118. http://dx.doi.org/10.1145/174666. 174668

March, J. G., & Simon, H. A. (1993; first published 1958). *Organizations* (2nd ed.). Cambridge, MA: Blackwell Publishers.

Martinez, J. I., & Jarillo, J. C. (1989). The evolution of research on coordination mechanisms in multinational corporations. *Journal of International Business Studies, 20,* 489–514. http://dx.doi.org/10.1145/174666.174668

McPhee, R. D., & Iverson, J. O. (2009). Agents of constitution in Communidad: Constitutive processes of communication in organizations. In L. Putnam & A. Nicotera (Eds.), *Communicative constitution of organization* (pp. 49–88). Mahwah, NJ: Erlbaum.

McPhee, R. D., & Iverson, J. O. (2013). Activity coordination and the Montreal school. In D. Robichaud, & F. Cooren (Eds.), *Organization and organizing: Materiality, agency, discourse* (pp. 109–124). New York, NY: Routledge.

McPhee, R. D., & Poole, M. S. (2001) Organizational structures and configurations. In F. M. Jablin, & L. L. Putnam (Eds.), *The new handbook of organizational communication* (pp. 503–543). London, UK: Sage.

McPhee, R. D., & Zaug, P. (2000). The communicative constitution of organizations: A framework for explanation. *Electronic Journal of Communication/La Revue Electronique de Communication, 10*(1–2), 1–16.

Miller, K., Scott, C. R., Stage, C., & Birkholt, M. (1995). Communication and coordination in an interorganizational system provision for the urban homeless. *Communication Research, 22,* 679–699. doi:10.1177/009365095022006006

Minssen, H. (2005). Challenges of teamwork in production: Demands of communication. *Organizational Studies, 27,* 103–124. doi:10.1177/0170840605056400

O'Brien, G. (1968). The measurement of cooperation. *Organizational Behavior and Human Performance, 3,* 427–439. http://dx.doi.org/10.1016/0030-5073(68) 90019-6

Okhuysen, G. A., & Bechky, B. A. (2009a). Coordination in organizations: An integrative perspective. *The Academy of Management Annals, 3,* 463–502. doi:10.1080/ 19416520903047533

Okhuysen, G. A., & Bechky, B. A. (2009b). Making group process work: Harnessing collective intuition, task conflict, and pacing. In E. A. Locke (ed.), *Handbook of principles of organizational behavior: Indispensable knowledge for evidence based management* (2nd ed., pp. 309–324). Sussex, UK: Wiley and Sons.

Olivera, F. (2000). Memory systems in organizations: An empirical investigation of mechanisms for knowledge collection, storage, and access. *Journal of Management Studies, 37,* 811–832. doi:10.1111/1467-6486.00205

Pearce, W. B., & Pearce, K. A. (2000). Extending the theory of coordinated management of meaning (CMM) through a community dialogue process. *Communication Theory, 10,* 405–423. doi:10.1111/j.1468-2885.2000.tb00200.x

Pentland, B. T., & Rueter, H. H. (1994). Organizational routines as grammars of action. *Administrative Science Quarterly, 39,* 484–510. http://dx.doi.org/10.2307/2393300

Perrow, C. (1961). The analysis of goals in complex organizations. *American Sociological Review, 26,* 854–866. http://dx.doi.org/10.2307/2090570

Poole, M. S., & McPhee, R. D. (2005). Structuration theory. In S. May & D. K. Mumby (Eds.), *Engaging organizational communication, theory, & research: Multiple perspectives* (pp. 171–196). Thousand Oaks, CA: Sage.

Poole, M. S., Seibold, D. R., & McPhee, R. D. (1985). Group decision-making as a structurational process. *Quarterly Journal of Speech, 71,* 74–102. doi:10.1080/00335638509383719

Quinn, R. W., & Dutton, J. E. (2005). Coordination as energy-in-conversation. *Academy of Management, 30,* 36–57. doi:http://dx.doi.org/10.5465/amr.2005.15281422

Raju, J., & Zhang, Z. J. (2005). Channel coordination in the presence of a dominant retailer. *Marketing Science, 24,* 254–262. http://dx.doi.org/10.1287/mnsc.39.10.1281

Rathnam, S., Mahajan, V., & Whinston, A. B. (1995). Facilitating coordination in customer support teams: A framework and its implications for the design of information technology. *Management Science, 41,* 1900–1921. http://dx.doi.org/10.1287/mnsc.41.12.1900

Ren, Y., Carley, K. M., & Argote, L. (2006). The contingent effects of transactive memory: When is it more beneficial to know what others know. *Management Science, 52,* 671–682. doi:10.1287/mnsc.1050.0496

Rice, R. E., & Cooper, S. D. (2010). *Organizations and unusual routines: A systems analysis of dysfunctional feedback processes.* Cambridge, UK: Cambridge University Press.

Rice, R. E., & Leonardi, P. M. (2013). Information and communication technology in organizations, 2000–2011. In L. Putnam, & D. K. Mumby (Eds.), *Sage handbook of organizational communication* (3rd ed., pp. 425–448). Thousand Oaks, CA: Sage.

Rico, R., Sanchez-Manzanares, M., Gil, F., & Gibson, C. (2008). Team implicit coordination processes: A team knowledge-based approach. *Academy of Management Review, 33,* 163–184. http://dx.doi.org/10.5465/amr.2008.27751276

Salmon, G., & Faris, J. (2006). Multi-agency collaboration, multiple levels of meaning: Social constructionism and the CMM model as tools to further our understanding. *Journal of Family Therapy, 28,* 272–292. 10.1111/j.1467-6427.2006.00352.x

Simon, H. A. (1947). *Administrative behavior: A study of decision-making processes in administrative organizations.* New York, NY: The Free Press.

Stewart, M. D., Walker, B. A., Hutt, M. D., & Kumar, A. (2010). The coordination strategies of high-performing salespeople: Internal working relationships that drive success. *Journal of Academic Marketing Science, 38*, 550–566. doi:10.1007/s11747-009-0170-0

Sutton, J. (2008). Between individual and collective memory: Coordination, interaction, distribution. *Social Research, 75*, 23–48. Retrieved from http://www.academia.edu/313908/Between_Individual_and_Collective_Memory_coordination_interaction_distribution

Taylor, F. W. (1916). The principles of scientific management. *Bulletin of the Taylor Society,* December. Reprinted in J. M. Shafritz, & J. S. Ott (Eds.), *Classic organization theory* (pp. 66–79). Belmont, CA: Wadsworth Publishing Company.

Thompson, J. D. (1967). *Organizations in action: Social science bases of administrative theory.* New York, NY: McGraw Hill.

Topper, C. M., & Carley, K. M. (1999). The structural perspective on the emergence of network organizations. *Journal of Mathematical Sociology, 24*, 67–96. doi:10.1080/0022250X.1999.9990229

Tornberg, P. (2012). Committed to coordination? How different forms of commitment complicate the coordination of national and urban planning. *Planning Theory & Practice, 13*, 27–45. doi:10.1080/14649357.1012.649906

Tushman, M. L. (1977). Special boundary roles in the innovation process. *Administrative Quarterly, 22*, 587–605. http://dx.doi.org/10.2307/2392402

Tushman, M. L., & Nadler, D. A. (1978). Information processing as an integrating concept in organizational design. *The Academy of Management Review, 3*, 613–624. http://dx.doi.org/10.5465/amr.1978.4305791

Vallacher, R. R., Nowak, A., & Zochowski, M. (2005). Dynamics of social coordination: The synchronization of internal states in close relationships. *Interaction Studies, 6*, 35–52. http://dx.doi.org/10.1075/bct.4.05val

van de Ven, A. H., Delbecq, A. L., & Koenig, R., Jr. (1976). Determinants of coordination modes within organizations. *American Sociological Review, 41*, 322–338. http://dx.doi.org/10.2307/2094477

van Fenema, P. C., Pentland, B., & Kumar, K. (2004). Paradigm shifts in coordination theory. *Academy of Management Annual Meeting,* New Orleans, LA, August.

Vlaar, P. W. L., van den Bosch, F. A. J., & Volberda, H. W. (2007). On the evolution of trust, distrust, and formal coordination and control in interorganizational relationships: Toward an integrative framework. *Group and Organization Management, 32*, 407–429. doi:10.1177/1059601106294215

Weick, K. E., & Roberts, K. H. (1993). Collective mind in organizations: A heedful interrelating on flight decks. *Administrative Science Quarterly, 38*, 357–381. http://dx.doi.org/10.2307/2393372

Weick, K. E., Sutcliffe, K. M., & Obstfeld, D., (1999). Organizing for high reliability: Process of collective mindfulness. In R. S. Sutton & B. M. Shaw (Eds.) *Research in organizational behavior* (Vol. 1, pp. 81–123). Stanford, CA: JAI Press.

Xia, L., Yuan, C., & Gay, G. (2009). Exploring negative group dynamics: Adversarial network, personality, and performance in project groups. *Management Communication Quarterly, 23*, 32–62. doi:10.1177/083318909335416

Yates, J. (1993). *Control through communication: The rise of system in American management.* Baltimore, MD: Johns Hopkins University Press.

Young, G. J., Charns, M. P., Desai, K., Khuri, S. F., Forbes, M. G., Henderson, W., & Daley, J. (1998). Patterns of coordination and clinical outcomes: A study of surgical services. *Health Services Research, 33,* 1211–1236. http://dx.doi.org/10.2307/2393372

Zhao, X., Liu, C., Yang, Y., & Sadiq, W. (2009). Aligning collaborative business process: An organization-oriented perspective. *IEEE Transactions on Systems, Man, and Cybernetics–Part A: Systems and Humans, 39I,* 1152–1164. http://dx.doi.org/10.1109/tsmca.2009.2027130

CHAPTER CONTENTS

8 Studying Work Practices in Organizations

Theoretical Considerations and Empirical Guidelines

Paul M. Leonardi

University of California, Santa Barbara

A recent practice turn in the communication and organizational sciences has led many researchers to study work in practice. In this chapter I suggest that studies of work practices in organizations would benefit from conceptual clarification. To do so, I organize this review around three central questions: (a) what are work practices? (b) what role do work practices play in the process of organizing? and (c) how can scholars build theory from empirical studies of work practices? I suggest several ways in which the concept of work practice can be clarified to provide coherence for communication researchers.

Over the last several years communication theorists have become interested in collecting data on and theorizing about work in practice (Cheney & Ashcraft, 2007; Cooren, 2010; Gibbs, 2009; Leonardi & Rodriguez-Lluesma, 2013; Treem, 2012). This interest parallels a broader trend in the communication and organizational sciences that focuses on how people's networks (Barley & Kunda, 2001), knowledge (Brown & Duguid, 2001), social skills (Wenger, 1998), and identities (Kuhn, 2006), along with their ability to coordinate (Carlile, 2004), collaborate (Nicolini, Mengis, & Swan, 2012), and develop shared technology use patterns (Orlikowski, 2000), emerge out of the practice of their normal work. Most scholars who are interested in studying practice recognize that social life is an ongoing production and, consequently, emerges through people's everyday actions (Knorr-Cetina, 2001; Nicolini, 2012; Pickering, 2001; Schatzki, 2005). Feldman and Orlikowski (2011) elaborate on this emergent and situated characterization of practice, arguing that by

> focusing on the empirics of practice, we understand organizational phenomena as dynamic and accomplished in ongoing, everyday actions. In focusing on practice theory, we understand the mutually constitutive ways in which agency is shaped by but also produces, reinforces, and changes its structural conditions. In focusing on practice ontology, we understand that it is practices that produce organizational reality.
>
> (p. 1250)

For communication scholars, such a practice turn—and the related focus that it suggests for the activities in which people engage during the practice of their work—seems like a natural fit. Craig (1989, 1999, 2001), for example, has long argued that communication is a practical discipline by claiming that communication theory can and should assist in the cultivation of communication as a social practice. And Deetz (1992, 1994, 2000) has forcefully argued that communication theorists should dispense with studying how communication practices enable people to convey meaning and focus on how the practice of communication produces meaning among individuals. Such admonitions have led communication scholars, broadly, and organizational communication researchers more specifically, to turn to traditions such as the dramaturgical perspective (Goffman, 1959), ethnomethodology (Garfinkel, 1967), negotiated order theory (Strauss, 1978), structuration theory (Giddens, 1984), and practice theory (Bourdieu, 1990), among others to consider how the communicative practice of work is constitutive of the organizing process (e.g., Ashcraft, Kuhn, & Cooren, 2009; McPhee & Zaug, 2000; Putnam & Nicotera, 2010; Taylor et al., 2007). Common to many of these approaches is an interest in understanding what types of practice organizational members routinely perform in the accomplishment of their work roles. Broadly named, the study of *work practices* in organizational settings attempts to understand the recursive relationship between organizations and the actions that give them coherence by focusing on the process of organizing as it happens.

Yet despite the ease with which studies of work in practice and the ontological position that communication is constitutive of organizing seem to fit together, there are, today, at least two related issues that impede communication scholars from developing better theoretical understanding and empirical evidence for how the communicative practice of work can create, sustain, and potentially dissolve the process of organizing. First, although communication and organizational scholars have recently begun to take seriously how work is conducted in practice, they often fail to actually examine and describe people's work practices. If work is seen to be a communicative phenomenon that occurs in practice (Heaton, 1998; Jackson, Poole, & Kuhn, 2002; McPhee & Poole, 2001; Putnam & Stohl, 1990; Taylor et al., 2001), then it would seem to behoove communication scholars to have some theoretical understanding about what work practices actually are. Perhaps the reason that communication scholars who are interested in the practice of work do not routinely describe or analyze people's actual work practices is due to the second issue: That studies that discuss work practices do not always treat the concept similarly. For example, some researchers argue that work practices are situational and are only useful in explaining outcomes in the immediate contexts of their occurrence (Kuhn & Jackson, 2008; Lave & Wenger, 1991; Orr, 1998; Suchman, 1987). Others suggest that types or classes of work practices can be identified across communities of actors (Edmondson, Bohmer, & Pisano, 2001; Feldman & Pentland, 2003; Neff, 2012; Orlikowski, 2002). Some researchers argue that work practices are reformulated due to external pressures exerted on social system (Barley, 1986; Leonardi, 2012; Robey & Sahay, 1996; Vaast & Walsham, 2005), while others claim that they change and adapt in response to internal pressures (Contractor, Monge, & Leonardi, 2011; Knorr-Cetina, 1999; Latour & Woolgar, 1979; Leonardi & Bailey, 2008).

To take some initial steps toward resolving these issues, I argue that studies of work practices in organizations would benefit from some conceptual clarification of their object of inquiry. To do so, I organize this review around three central questions: (a) What are work practices? (b) What role do work practices play in the process of organizing? and (c) How can scholars build theory from empirical studies of work practices? In attempting to answer these questions, I suggest several ways in which the concept of work practice can be clarified to provide conceptual coherence for organizational communication researchers.

What Are Work Practices?

All studies of work practices seem to agree on at least one fundamental point: That understanding *how* people work is part and parcel of the process of organizing. That said, researchers have looked at the practice of work at a variety of empirical levels of analysis. At perhaps the most micro level, scholars have suggested the *gesture* (Murphy, 1998), the *speech act* (Collins, 1981), and the *relay* (Heath & Luff, 2000) are all practices through which work is accomplished. Although exhaustingly microsocial in their detail, each concept defines a fundamental action through which work is carried out. In some senses, such microsocial action is the basic foundation upon which work is accomplished. Without actions that are indexical (they provide knowledge to make sense of the world), accountable (they make people's actions mutually intelligible), and reflexive (commonsensical and intuitive to others), individuals could not meaningfully interact with one another to carry out the tasks of their organization or occupation (Garfinkel, 1967).

Other scholars have suggested that students of organizational communication can learn the most about work when such microsocial actions are viewed collectively (Lammers & Barbour, 2006). That is, shifting the scope of analysis (in terms of time and number of actors) lifts practice out of the minutia of everyday life and defines those microsocial features as resources that organizational members draw upon in the enactment of their work roles. A practice such as an accounting tabulation (which defines a certain class of professional work) would consist of multiple microsocial actions that together constitute a socially recognizable practice (Orlikowski, 2000). Thus, concepts such as the *negotiation* (Strauss, 1978), the *interaction* (Barley, 1986), and the *move* (Pentland, 1992) all represent a more meso-level in which practice can occur.

Moving again up levels of analysis, practices can be conceptualized as the aggregate of these meso-level actions into more macrosocial categories such as *performances* (Pacanowsky & O'Donnell-Trujillo, 1983), *routines* (Feldman & Pentland, 2003), and *patterns* (Perlow, Gittell, & Katz, 2004; Stohl, 2001). For example, the hiring routine can be seen as a combination of meso-level actions such as screening applicants, holding colloquia, and negotiating contracts. When taken together, these macrosocial categories of practice represent the "primary means by which organizations accomplish much of what they do" (Feldman & Pentland, 2003, p. 94).

I have suggested that the concept of work practices can be viewed from a multitude of empirical levels of analysis. I make no attempt to argue for a nested sequence or hierarchy of action, but instead simply suggest that one can look at molar or less molar levels of analysis and encounter what may be broadly termed a work practice. Thus, rather than speculate as to which is the most appropriate level analysis for studies of work practices, I suggest a more fruitful ploy is to examine the similarities uncovered among studies of work practices at various empirical strata. In so doing, I identify five common features of a work practice.

The five characteristics of work practice discussed below should be considered neither exhaustive nor exclusive. They do not operate independently of each other, but overlap and interact at the same time and over time. And as will be apparent, I have tried to emphasize their similarities and interdependences in the discussion. My explication of them as distinct characteristics is for analytic convenience only. That one characteristic cannot exist without another as a feature of work practices should be kept always in mind.

Materially Bound

In his analysis of the work practices of scientists across various laboratories, Pickering (1995) tackled head-on the debate over social vs. material antecedents of practice. Pickering suggested that practice should be considered as a mangle of human and material agency. Criticizing research programs such as the sociology of scientific knowledge (SSK) for casting all discussions of practice generation and maintenance in sociological terms, Pickering advocated for a view of work practices as materially bound. He suggested that the material world itself has "agency"—although not interest—in that it "does things" that cannot be predicted in advance:

> The world, I want to say, is continually *doing things,* things that bear upon us not as observation statements upon disembodied intellects but as forces upon material beings. Think of the weather. Winds, storms, droughts, floods, heat and cold—all of these engage with our bodies as well as our minds, often in life threatening ways. . . . Much of life, I would say, has this character of coping with material agency, agency that comes at us from outside the human realm and that cannot be reduced to anything within that realm.
>
> (Pickering, 1995, p. 6)

In order to explain work practices, researchers need to understand the action of the material properties that those very work practices are aiming to condition.

Within research on organizations, studies of material agency are quite rare. The ontological rejection of technologically deterministic thinking brought about by social constructivist programs of research (DeSanctis & Poole, 1994; Fulk, 1993; Orlikowski, 1992) has tended to downplay notions of material agency in the defense of the constructivist position. However, as Leonardi and Barley (2010) observed, a voluntaristic stance on technological change does not necessarily preclude consideration of material factors in the formation and maintenance of social conduct. Pickering himself attempted such a balanced perspective in his discussion of Giacomo Morpurgo's quest to find evidence for or against the existence of elementary particles called quarks. As Pickering suggested,

> Neither Morpurgo nor anyone else could have foreseen the specific resistance he would encounter in his work. That the first grain to be examined moved in the same direction when the direction of the electric field was reversed just happened in the real time of Morpurgo's practice: likewise the appearance (twice) of a continuum of charges, and of temporally varying changes, in his later measurements.
>
> (1995, p. 91)

Although Morpurgo's practice was directed to a substantial degree by a variety of social factors—access to information, the structure of his laboratory, and interaction with colleagues—the material world also acted upon Morpurgo's practice in ways that shaped and defined it. Similarly, Sims's (1999) discussion of the practice of concrete testing for earthquake analyses shows how the unpredictable character of the shaking earth and of the elasticity of cement meant that work practices of concrete engineers can only be understood by examining the resistances and accommodations made to their encounters with material agency.

Other studies have offered a view of the material agency (inline with Pickering's use of the term) of technologies themselves. Guillemin (2000) described how the work practices of physicians in a menopause clinic could be seen as a set of accommodations to the material demands of the questionnaires they used to diagnose potential patients. In addition to shaping the work of the physicians, the forms also impacted the women's own practices of understanding their conditions:

> Self-assessment charts and preclinic questionnaires performed certain kinds of work in the menopause clinic, resulting in particular kinds of effects. These charts may have been helpful in assisting the quick gathering of information about a woman's symptoms and medical history. However, the charts worked beyond simple information gathering. The charts required women to organize their individual and possibly complex experiences around a discourse of hormonal production and loss. In completing these charts and questionnaires, women's experiences were further shaped into a model of menopause based on hormone deficiency.
>
> (Guillemin, 2000, pp. 460–461)

Without falling into the trap of deterministic thinking, a view of practice as materially bound emphasizes the importance of considering the ongoing negotiation between the material and social elements of practice. As authors who study the relationship between communication and materiality have recently pointed out (see, for example, Ashcraft et al., 2009; Leonardi, Nardi, & Kallinikos, 2012), although the material properties of technologies can indeed manifest themselves as constraints and affordances on the work practices of users, they should not be seen to determine it. Rather, work practices should be seen as Taylor (2001) advocated, as the actions through which the material and social are imbricated—in which material properties are translated into social actions, and vice-versa. Following Taylor's work, Leonardi (2012) has offered one theory about how the social and the material become entangled. This theory suggests that coordinated human agencies (social agency) and the things that the materiality of a technology allow people to do (material agency) become interlocked in sequences that produce the empirical phenomena scholars call technologies, on the one hand, and organizations, on the other. As nonhuman entities, artifacts exercise agency through their performativity; in other words, through the things they do that users cannot completely or directly control. For example, a compiler translates text from a source computer language into a target language without input from its user and a finite element solver calculates nodal displacements in a mathematical model and renders the results of this analysis into a three-dimensional animation without human intervention. Although each of these actions is instigated by a human (presumably to address a particular, local need), the material artifact itself acts (exercises material agency) as humans with goals engage with its materiality.

Both coordinated human (social) and material agencies represent capacities for action, but they differ with respect to intentionality. Pickering (2001) offered a concise and useful empirical definition of human and material agencies that illustrates this difference. For Pickering, social agency is a group's coordinated exercise of forming and realizing its goals. Thus, the practice of forming goals and attempting to realize them is a concrete operationalization of social agency. Material agency, by contrast, is devoid of intention and materiality does not act to realize its own goals because it has none of its own making. In other words, "machine artifacts have no inherent intentionality, independent of their being harnessed to or offering possibilities to humans" (Taylor, Groleau, Heaton, & Van Every, 2001, p. 137). Thus, material agency is operationalized as the actions that a technology takes, which humans do not immediately or directly control. Given this important difference with respect to intentionality, even though social and material agencies might be equally important in shaping one's practice, they do so in qualitatively different ways. The important point, however, is that work practices cannot be fully explained by examining the agency of the people who conduct them. To understand how and why people work as they do, researchers must also pay close attention to the way that their own agency becomes imbricated with the agency of the various materials by and through which they interact in the course of their normal work.

Recurrently Enacted

A second characteristic of work practices is that they are recurrently enacted over time. One feature that makes work practices an important empirical focal point is that they frequently occur in patterns, and, in so doing, have important implications for the process of organizing. As Vaast and Walsham (2005) commented,

> The recurrent dimension of practice is key to the dynamic between agency and structure in practice theory.{. . .}As agents repeatedly and regularly act in certain ways, they contribute to the enactment of social structural properties.

> (p. 67)

Because work practices are continually enacted over time, researchers have suggested that they can be seen to evince structural properties (Collins, 1981; Giddens, 1984; McPhee & Poole, 2001; Strauss, 1978). Here, structural properties are often as patterns of action and interaction, which scholars then assume for organizational structure in the aggregate. In this way, structure is both a medium and outcome of communication. That is, work practices serve as the foundations for social structure inasmuch as they are recurrently enacted. Once their enactment ceases, however, there are no patterns upon which organizational structures can be built. Thus, in considering the nature of work practices it seems that their recurrence plays a pivotal role.

Perhaps no one has taken a more aggressive approach at exploring the implications of recurrent practice than Orlikowski (1992, 1996, 2000). Drawing on Giddens's explication of the structuration process, Orlikowski has suggested that the types of structural features enacted in everyday work practices form the basis for a community's organizing schemata. Orlikowski's theory of enacted practice is illustrated in her empirical cases of technology-centered organizational change. Building a social constructivist framework, Orlikowski (2000) suggested that:

> Human interaction with technologies is typically recurrent, so that even as users constitute a technology-in-practice through their present use of a technology, their actions are at the same time shaped by the previous technologies-in-practice they have enacted in the past.

> (p. 410)

On the one hand, the recurrent nature of practice reminds the reader that work practices are always historically influenced. Thus, in their recurrence, historical patterns accrete into new work practices over time. However, constitution of a particular organizational or occupational structure is dependent upon recurrence of work practices. Barley (1986) made the argument that practices take on a constitutive nature when, through their recurrent enactment, they accumulate temporally emergent responses into recognizable patterns. Latour and Woolgar's (1979) influential look into the production of scientific facts in an endocrinology laboratory at the Salk Institute revealed that the production of scientific facts is made possible only through the recurrent use of a number of rhetorical practices of persuasion in the production of research articles. As the authors suggested, if at any moment scientists abandoned the performance of such rhetorical practices, or varied them slightly, the perceived objectivity of a scientific fact would quickly unravel. Thus, the social world of organizing is produced through the continued perpetuation of work practices.

Orlikowski has also suggested that the recurrence of work practices produces what might be termed a side-effect of their continued enactment: They become institutionalized. In this sense, work practices often reveal a taken-for-granted status. That is, individuals begin to think that because they recur with such frequency, they must continue to recur as such:

> Over time, through repeated reinforcement by the community of users, such technologies in practice may become reified and institutionalized, at which point they become treated as predetermined and firm prescriptions for social action, and as such, may impede change.
>
> (Orlikowski, 2000, p. 411)

The recurrent enactment of work practices produces a stabilizing force (Berg, 1997; Hard, 1994; Kaghan & Bowker, 2001; Knorr-Cetina, 1999; Putnam & Nicotera, 2010). New work practices or the modification of existing ones is subsumed under the logic of the objectivity of existing practice. However, if at any point work practices cease to recur, their stabilizing force is lost. It is the disturbance of such stabilizing forces, the disjuncture from the normal recurrence of practice that is brought about by, for example, the introduction of a new technology that can then lead to the reformation of and realignment of work practices (Leonardi, 2009a). What such exogenous shocks remind us is that work practices become important mediators and outcomes of social action when they serve as "clusters of recurrent human activity informed by shared institutional meanings" (Schultze & Orlikowski, 2004, p. 88).

Temporally Emergent

A longstanding view held by those that study the way individuals in organizations work is that work practices are temporally emergent. What I call here temporal emergence goes by a variety of different names including situated action (Lave & Wenger, 1991; Orr, 1996; Suchman, 1987) and improvisational response (Edmondson et al., 2001; Orlikowski, 1996; Pentland, 1992). The basic point here is that although certain actions toward organizational goals can be planned in advance, the patterns of resistance and accommodation to the demands of a changing world can only be, as Knorr-Cetina (1995) has suggested, unfolded in practice. In other words, work practices themselves have a temporally emergent character. It is only when choices made in the social realm of organizing come into contact with the material constraints and affordances of the practical world that the contours of work practices emerge.

A number of studies take the temporally emergent character of practice as a key empirical focal point. Orlikowski's (1996) detailed study of the implementation of an incident tracking support system into the work of computer technicians demonstrated the situated and temporally emergent character of practice in response to organizational changes. In thinking about the changes in practice occasioned by the new technology, Orlikowski (1996) summarized,

> The transformation, while enabled by the technology, was not caused by it. Rather, it occurred through the ongoing, gradual, and reciprocal adjustments, accommodations, and improvisations enacted by the CSD members{. . .} their action subtly and significantly altered the organizing practices and structures of CSD workplace over time, transforming the texture of work, nature of knowledge, patterns of interaction, distribution of work, forms of accountability and control, and mechanisms of coordination.
>
> (p. 69)

The types of changes to practice that took place after the implementation of the new technology can be seen as a temporally emergent response to the merging of the material features of the technology with the existing demands of the social system. Such meditations of the temporally emergent character of work practices led Orlikowski (2000) to advocate a perspective where the outcomes of a newly implemented technology should be seen as enacted in practice. The finer point to be taken from this suggestion is that the functionality of a technology— its ability to be used to accomplish a particular task—does not exist outside of a situated context of use. In other words, our expectations of what features a technology has, what they are good for, how they should be used, and how they will change the way people work (all of which people draw from their temporally emergent encounters with the technology), buffer our perceptions of the material elements, those elements of the technology that do not change across contexts of use. To this end, Berg (1997) has similarly suggested that, "Only as part of a concrete work practice does a formal tool come to life. By itself, it does not do anything: People must turn on the computer to use the record" (p. 415). Thus, the lesson to take from these studies is that

> To be made useful, these devices needed to be read in relation to each other and to an unfolding situation. Technologies in this view are constituted through an inseparable from the specifically situated practices of their use.
>
> (Suchman et al., 1999, p. 399)

The temporally emergent character of work practice, however, is not confined to interaction with information technology. Hogle's (1995) study of the work of organ procurement coordinators recounted earlier also demonstrates this point. Coordinators consistently worked in a situation in which the guidelines for standard donation procedures meant different things depending on their interpretation of the context surrounding the possible donations:

> Interpreting these guidelines, however, takes place in interaction with brain-dead bodies, and their materials, recipients for those materials and the individuals who have an interest in them, and, finally, knowledge and beliefs brought into the setting from previous experiences.
>
> (Hogle, 1995, p. 494)

As practice unfolded over time, coordinators shaped their actions to respond to their changing ecology of interests. Similarly, Pentland's (1992) study of the "moves" made by call center technicians in response to user problems demonstrates the emergent character of work practices. Technicians could not know in advance the problems users would call about. Therefore, in the practice of responding to their needs, technicians had to make purposeful accommodations to their practice, including decisions about transferring a call, escalating its status, or making a termination. Thus, certain generic practices such as assigning, referring, and transferring could serve as broad guidelines for action, but the actual decision to engage in a practice or modify its content was constructed on the fly by technicians in the temporal course of their work.

Historically Influenced

A basic insight offered by general theorists of practice is that all human action is, to a certain extent, historically bound. Garfinkel's (1967) ethnomethodological approach, for example, described practice as "indexical." Within the ethnomethodological framework, people are seen to make sense of action by indexing it (understanding it, cognitively, through the lens of a prior occurring set of actions) to a particular circumstance that has occurred before. In this way, they can interpret their ongoing and immediate action in light of their previously constructed interactions with the world. Building on this framework, Zucker (1977) showed that work practices are apprehended and perpetuated by linking present action to actions occurring in the past. Thus, practices "persist" over time because individuals who are cognitively limited in their processing ability must index past action (take it for granted) so that they can act consistently while processing new information in the present context (Collins, 1981, p. 992).

Building on Garfinkel's work, Giddens (1984) developed a theory of action, which recognized human beings as knowledgeable agents who reflexively monitor the flow of interaction with one another. In other words,

> Continuity of practices presumes reflexivity, but reflexivity in turn is possible only because of the continuity of practices that makes them distinctively

"the same" across space and time. "Reflexivity" hence should be understood not merely as "self consciousness," but as the monitored character of the ongoing flow of social life.

(Giddens, 1984, p. 3)

For Giddens, the historically influential characteristic of practice is only possible because actors reflexively monitor their present action, and thus link their current understandings of the world to past situations. This approach is similar to the one outlined by Bourdieu (1977) in his explanation of historical influences on action. Bourdieu did not depict practices as reactive in a behaviorist sense or norm-guided in a functionalist sense. Instead, he offered the view of practices as having historical momentum in the *habitus,* "a product of history [that] produces individual and collective practices more history—in accordance with the schemes generated by history" (Bourdieu, 1990, p. 54). In other words, although respective of the role of human agency in constructing new practices and changing practices in line with shifting goal orientations, Bourdieu, like Giddens, recognized that work practices carry with them the history of previous work practices that have proven successful in the accomplishment of organizational life.

A number of studies of work practices show the importance of recognizing the historically influential character of situated action. Blomberg (1988), for example, showed that patterns of interaction among users had a major impact on people's experience of their copiers. Importantly, information about how the machine worked, the sorts of problems it generated, and the advantages of its use were exchanged among users, key operators, and technicians. Thus, past action was made manifest in present practice and carried significant influence for users' perceptions of the copier's reliability and the ways in which they would conceive of using it in their daily work. More dramatic examples can be found in Vallas's (2003) discussion of the failures of introducing teamwork practices into traditional pulp paper manufacturing plant or Edmondson and colleagues' (2001) analysis of the rejection of new minimally invasive surgery practices into a number of cardiology departments at leading hospitals. In both cases, new work practices were rejected because the current practices of workers were so laden with historical values of employment, expertise, and occupational standing that it became impossible for members to think of adopting new work practices that did not align with the practices organizational members had always conducted.

Although the historical influence of practice is essential for the construction of a shared repertoire of action and thus the continued collaboration of a community of actors (Wenger, 1998), the fact that work practices are themselves a historical product of situational encounters can make it difficult for people to change them. Hutchins's (1995) cognitive ethnography of the work practices conducted on the navigation bridges of U.S. Navy ships demonstrated that work practices evolve in response to historical contingencies. For example, the demands of being a quartermaster shift the way that navigation takes place through the use of ship logs, and the evolving practice of discerning ship position and maintaining those logs changes the role of quartermaster. Over time, however, those situated contingencies change but the work practices that were formed in response to them still bear the legacy of past practice. Therefore, work practices run the risk of attempting to impose order on a world whose contours have changed. Sims (1999) demonstrated this issue in his discussion about how graduate students in earthquake engineering learn construction work practices from technicians with many years in the field. Many students, however, find that some work practices do not align with recent theory about quasi-static loads in cement reinforced structures. The consequence is that students' work practices are out of alignment with their perceptions of occupational norms, thus causing role discomfort and, occasionally, innovation in practice. Thus, as several scholars have suggested, work practices can become misaligned from the activities they organize (with both positive and negative consequences) when technologies, innovations, or markets change (Barley & Kunda, 2001; Jackson et al., 2002; Leonardi, 2009b).

Goal Oriented

One cannot understand practice without recognizing its orientation toward individual and organizational goals. Work practices are enacted and perpetuated within the context of organizations that actively pursue their own survival. Evolutionary theorists have for many years convincingly argued that if the practices of a community do not enforce or contribute to the organization's survival, those practices will be selected against (Anderson & Tushman, 1990; Monge, Heiss, & Margolin, 2008; Nelson & Winter, 1982; Sorenson & Stuart, 2000). Thus, one important characteristic of work practice is its goal orientation. Organizational members conduct work practices as they move toward the attainment of certain goals.

Pickering's (1993) analysis of Donald Glaser's work practices in elementary-particle physics demonstrated the importance that goal orientation plays in the construction and perpetuation of work practices. In the early 1950s physicists were having difficulty accumulating data on recently discovered and so-called "strange particles" using common instruments such as cloud chambers. In the midst of such difficulty, Glaser set himself an ambitious goal: "He wanted to construct some new kind of detector{. . .}containing some denser working substance" (Pickering, 1993, p. 569). The issue Glaser faced was that for several years the different configurations he attempted failed to consistently register particle tracks. Despite such slow beginnings, Glaser's practice proceeded along what can be looked at retrospectively as a linear path. Glaser's eventual success at forming small bubbles along particle tracks, however, was anything but linear. The path of resistances he faced when confronted with the unpredictability of the material world were overcome by Glaser's consistent accommodation of his practices to deal with the unanticipated results occurring in his bubble chamber. Thus, the final solution to achieving an operable bubble chamber was one that Glaser himself had not considered at the project's outset. As Pickering (1993) suggested,

> Human agency has an interesting temporal structure that material agency lacks. It seems unnecessary, at best, to think that a bubble chamber has any future end or purpose in view when it produces tracks upon expansion. In contrast, one cannot understand Glaser's practice without recognizing its orientation to future goals.
>
> (p. 577)

Work practices, then, emerge out of actors' orientations toward specific goals.

The important point to be taken here is that explaining the trajectory of work practices requires an understanding of their evolution towards predetermined goals. In his study of scientific work in a biochemical laboratory, Lynch (1985) described the great deal of time scientists spend trying to "make it work," to carry out an experiment in order that the expected outcome is produced (pp. 115–140). To achieve this end they need certain skills that can only be acquired through their involvement in recurrent practice. That is, goals can be laid out in advance, but the work practices that lead toward those goals themselves evolve as actors encounter new material constraints on their work, as they learn new skills to overcome or work around those constraints, and as they adapt their own practices to meet such goals. This is precisely the patterns followed by the organ procurement coordinators studied by Hogle (1995) who were charged with facilitating transplant donations from potential donors. Despite standard criteria for what sorts of individuals counted as acceptable donors, shifting orientations toward the goals of their work meant that, in practice, the notion of acceptability was itself negotiable. In some months coordinators had a donor shortage they needed to make up, other months there were particular patients waiting for certain organs. In these circumstances, the goals of the donation process shifted such as to allow coordinators to reconsider their standard criteria and adapt their work practices.

What Role Do Work Practices Play in the Process of Organizing?

Having spent some time considering the characteristic features of work practices I now turn to the issue of the *work* work practices do in organizations. As Williams (1983) pointed out, work is "our most general word for doing something and for something done." However, as Williams and other have suggested (Barley & Kunda, 2001; Orr, 1998; Wadel, 1979), work is typically defined as a noun—something that is done—as a relationship of employment or as a set of activities that are sold on the market for a price. By contrast, I focus on work as an action and as work practices as primary performances through which organizing is accomplished. From this vantage point, I identify three types of roles that work practices play in the process of organizing: an instrumental role, a communicative role, and a constitutive role.

Instrumental Role

Perhaps the most basic role that work practices play in organizations is one that is often overlooked by researchers: Their instrumental role. Work practices (the way things are done) act as a means to accomplish work (the things that need to be done). Keeping their instrumental role in mind helps researchers to remember the goal-oriented and temporally emergent character of work practices.

The earliest studies of work focused directly in on the instrumental nature of practice. Taylor (1911/1998), Gilbreth (1911/1993) and others were quite concerned with how the practice of work was carried out to improve the performance of routine tasks. Despite the importance of the work organized by work practices, most researchers look to the form rather than the content of work practices. In other words, they focus on the symbolic and performative nature of practice (Henderson, 1998; Orlikowski & Gash, 1994; Prasad, 1993; Trujillo, 1992; Whittle & Spicer, 2008) while overlooking the actual tasks that get done through the enactment of work practices. There are, however, a number of studies that do consider the instrumental role of work practices. Barley (1986), for example, described the work practices of radiologists and technicians around the implementation of a new CT scanner in two hospitals. Members of these two occupational communities came together around the practice of scanner operations and interpretations of results. Although Barley spent a great deal of time discussing the symbolic nature of work practices (the embedded nature of occupational jurisdiction in certain forms of work), his detailed ethnographic approach provided data on the mundane practices that were directed at the operation of the scanner and the interpretation of the results it produced.

Latour and Woolgar's (1979) discussion of the laboratory work practices surrounding the identification and subsequent knowledge generation of a new chemical substance also demonstrated the instrumental nature of practice. Research scientists in two different laboratories engaged in a number of work practices to identify a chemical that could be used in tests to screen for malfunctions of the pituitary. Although Latour and Woolgar detailed the types of practices that helped to produce and reify the discovery of Thyrotropin Releasing Factor (TRF) as a taken-for-granted chemical compound, such work practices must be seen at the most basic level as directed toward the construction of this scientific fact.

Several other studies—such as Pentland's (1992) analysis of call center technician's work, Orr's (1996) discussion of the work practices of copy machine technicians, and Treem's (2013) observations of public relations work practices—are noteworthy for their continued focus on the sorts of tasks that engagement in work practices aims to accomplish. Such studies inadvertently demonstrate that it is easier to focus on the instrumental nature of work if the researcher situates him or herself in only one empirical context. Other studies that have attempted to draw more general characterizations of work practice by comparing work across two or more communities (Barley, 1996; Knorr-Cetina,

1999; Neff, 2012; Orlikowski, 2000) have had a more difficult time staying focused on the instrumental nature of work practices. Instead, in examining practice across empirical sites, researchers often drift away from the historically influenced and temporally emergent characteristics of practice and seek to identify those roles played by work practices that transcend the idiosyncrasies of any particular context (e.g., the communicative and constitutive roles discussed later). I make this observation not to point to the shortcomings or strengths of any particular approach but rather to illustrate the difficulty of explaining all the roles that work practices play in one study. That said, work practices are carried out in order to do work. Understanding what that work is in some detail is important for building a clearer conceptualization of why work practices then take on the communicative and constitutive characters they do.

Communicative Role

In addition to their instrumental role, work practices also play a communicative role in the process of organizing. A basic insight of communication and symbolic interactionist researchers is that the actual enactment of work serves more than an instrumental function, it communicates to other individuals the type of work one should do, how that work should be done, and the value of working in some ways over others (Blumer, 1969; Craig, 1999; Deetz, 1994; Mead, 1934). In other words, work practices are themselves communicative acts shared among members of an occupational or organizational community.

Working in a certain way then becomes the basis for communal membership in that the conduct of certain work practices communicates to others that a person knows how to be a competent cultural member. This is because what is taken to be proper conduct in any occupation or organization stems not from the exigencies of particular tasks but is instead constructed through the social production of meaning amongst individuals (Becker et al., 1961; Hughes, 1958; Reichers, 1987; Van Maanen & Schein, 1979). A view of work practices as communicative in nature coincides with the work of theorists who suggest that the most widely characteristic feature of an occupational culture is the style in which members work (Becker & Carper, 1956; Schein, 1996; Van Maanen & Barley, 1984; Watson, 1958). Nelsen and Barley (1997) suggested that a definition of work practice that represents the particular style in which members engage their work and each other provides an important entry point into the inner-working of occupational communities precisely because: "Behaving consistently within an ideology of practice is necessary for a group to promulgate successfully its perspective on the cultural definition of an activity" (p. 639). Giddens (1984) also suggested that those actions of a community that come to have a "taken-for-granted character" are those "familiar styles and forms of conduct, both supporting and supported by a sense of ontological security" (p. 376). Therefore, it is not necessarily the content of a particular action (like I suggested in the previous section) but the way that action is carried out that defines membership in an occupational or organizational culture (Cheney & Ashcraft, 2007; Eisenberg & Riley, 2001; Kunda, 1992; Pacanowsky & O'Donnell-Trujillo, 1983).

Such a recognition of the communicative role played by work practices helps to replace static notions of social structure with the dynamic concept of performance. As Goffman (1959) indicated more than fifty years ago, performances are the actions through which individuals bring to completion a sense of reality. Because work practices are communicative actions that individuals themselves use to make sense out of their communal membership (Stohl, 1986) and that others use to evaluate whether they are indeed a member or not (Leonardi, Jackson, & Diwan, 2009), they act as affordances, enabling individuals to engage in the instrumental practice of their work, and, at the same time, they act as constraints on human action, delimiting the possible activities in which they believe they can or should engage. Watson (1958) suggested a number of years ago that to understand why occupational members worked in similar ways despite their individual differences, researchers needed a concept that would show how collective orientations were formed with which to interpret the wide variety of tasks workers normally conducted:

> The work style requires segmental presentation of self in which each individual demonstrates his competence and success in a restricted area defined by the job{. . .}the characteristic style is what may be called culture building, in which individuals join together to create and maintain a world of special meanings.{. . .}In this case, the individual dramatizes that part of himself which overlaps with the group culture.
>
> (p. 271)

In this sense, work practices represent a specific "style" of working and are best understood as specific orientations toward tasks and to other workers. In Watson's view, each individual brings his or her own personal attributes to a situation, but those dispositional tendencies are modified, revised, and exert varying degrees of pressure on the situation as the work practices of a community influence the actions of individuals through their communicative power. Orientations become shared amongst individuals as occupational members present their attributes that are most similar to those dominant among their peers and hold in reserve those that are not. This selective presentation of personal attributes is what Watson termed the "segmental presentation of self." These shared orientations then serve as portable filters that are used to interpret and respond to new situations.

Kunda's (1992) analysis of engineering culture in a large computer firm demonstrates this communicative role played by work practice. Engineers who worked late (a work practice) and forwent family events to meet deadlines (another work practice) produced and perpetuated the value of dedicating one's self to the company. Such actions communicated to new and long-tenured employees that Tech valued the commitment of its employees. This culture of commitment at Tech was easily identifiable by Tech's employees, employees at competing firms, vendor firms, and the families and friends of employees.

Thus, the continued conduct of work practices or the creation of new ones can be seen as a response to the reflexive monitoring enabled by their communicative nature.

Constitutive Role

A third role that work practices play in the process of organizing is a constitutive one. During the past quarter century the field of organization studies has seen a turn from fixed and static view of organizational structure to notions of structure as constituted by the micro-practices of organizing. Such views are emphasized in Strauss's (1978) explication of negotiated order theory, Weick's (1979) description of enactment, Collins's (1981) strategy of micro-translation, Giddens's (1984) discussion of the structuration process, and even Bourdieu's (1990) theory of practice. All of these perspectives argue that those abstract forms normally called structures or cultures are really nothing more than an interlocked sequence of repetitive practices. Thus, it is through the continued production and reproduction of micro-level practices that we come to see particular patterns as organizing.

In such models, work practices play a constitutive role. That is, they are the building blocks upon which organizations are constructed. Indeed, most studies of work practices in organizational contexts have focused on their constitutive role (Eisenberg & Riley, 2001). As Barley and Kunda (2001) suggested,

> If one conceives of an organizational structure as the pattern that emerges from real interactions among people, it is possible to link shifts in work practices directly to changes in organizational structure by examining properties of social networks.
>
> (p. 89)

Similarly, Feldman and Pentland (2003, 2005) have discussed the ostensive and performative aspects of work in organizational routines. The authors argue that the work that occurs in organizational routines is performative in the sense that it is historically influenced and temporally emergent practice performed in response to localized exigencies. But in the aggregate, these local performances also have an ostensive aspect: They produce a set of understandings about what the world is and how it works that exists outside of the realm of practice.

This discussion leads to a second important point about the constitutive nature of work practices: the reciprocal relationship they have with the structures, cultures, or ostensive routines they create. The social phenomenological approach outlined by Berger and Luckmann (1967) suggested that certain work practices become institutions—appear objective and external—because individuals come to see actions as seemingly immutable facts imposed on them by the outside. This conceptualization lifted the notion of work practices out of the practical order described by Garfinkel (1967) and argued that although institutions are constituted in the everyday actions of cultural membership (as explicated by the ethnomethodological approach) they also are seen by those members to exist independently of them. An important insight that emerges from this work is that of the dialectic. The authors argued that the products of human action often act back on the very humans who produce them. In such a view, the relationship between institution and action is reciprocal rather than causal: Cultural institutions are constructed and perpetuated through micro-social practices, but culture also influences those practices. The relationship is also transparent such that practices are seen to exist independently of human creation. This creates what Berger and Luckmann (1967) term "objectivated human activity" and the "paradox that man is capable of producing a world that he then experiences as something other than a human product" (pp. 60–61).

Giddens (1984) added to the notion of the dialectical relationship between action and institution the insight that members of a particular culture are aware of the institutions that surround them (their communicative role). Importantly, this awareness prompts individuals to either modify their behavior to coincide with the existing work practices or purposefully alter their behavior to reject them.

In addition to their instrumental and communicative roles, work practices also constitute social structures that appear to exist apart from their perpetuation by work practices. As I have described them, the roles played by work practices in organizational settings do not occur in isolation from one another. In fact, their mutual reinforcement is what allows the multivocality of their role performance. That is, because there are instrumental reasons to use work practices, such practices are recurrently enacted and can serve as communication media for others. Further, because work practices are communicative in nature, members can reflect on them as they produce a certain social structure and thus purposefully chose to align their actions with the cultures their work practices create and perpetuate.

How Do We Build Theory from Empirical Studies of Work Practices?

The foregoing sections have discussed a number of empirical features of work practices. I have described work practices as goal oriented, historically influenced, temporally emergent, materially bound, and recursively enacted. I have also reviewed a number of ways that work practices do work in organizations, namely through their instrumental, communicative, and constitutive functions. Due to their situated, contextually specific and improvisational nature, it seems difficult to build general theory about work practices that transcend the idiosyncrasies of those cultural contexts in which they are enacted and have performative force. Indeed, many studies of situated action have taken an avowedly anti-theoretical stance toward generalizing about work practices (Heath & Luff, 2000; Lave & Wenger, 1991; Suchman, 1987). Instead, these researchers have suggested that the situated nature of work practices means that one can only understand the content of organizational action through detailed ethnographic explorations into specific cultural contexts. I agree wholeheartedly that the ability to specify the form and function of work practices requires tremendous emic insights, but I also submit that a conceptualization of practice as space and action might help to use the empirical insights generated by such research to build more general theory about the role of work practices in the process of organizing.

Practice as Space and Action

As I have discussed above, most extant studies of practice have tended to conceptualize work practices as those actions members take in the accomplishment of organizational goals. Clearly, thinking of work practices as dynamic and active helps to foreground the notion that organizations are produced, perpetuated, and changed through the enactment of work practices. In addition to this view of work practice as action, I offer a view of work practice as space. In other words, practice is a space in which action takes place. This conceptualization gives work practices a dual role: They are generative in the sense that they are actions that produce organizations, but they are also contexts in and of themselves that allow action to occur.

Consider for example, Pickering's (1995) discussion of Glaser's attempt to build a successfully functioning bubble chamber:

> Glaser had to find out, in the real time of practice, what the contours of material agency might be.{. . .}There is not real-time explanation for the particular patterns of resistance that Glaser encountered in his attempts to go beyond the cloud chamber. In his practice, these resistances appeared as if *by chance*—they *just happened*. It just happened that, when Glaser configured his instrument this way (or this, or this), it did not produce tracks, but when he configured it that way, it did.
>
> (pp. 52–53)

Glaser's practice was a space where he attempted to combine the material properties of elementary particles with his own agentic goals of building a device to capture them. Only in this space of practice could the action of combination occur. The copy repair technicians observed in Orr's (1996) study operated in a similar space of practice. They used specific work practices such as conversation with users and replication of problems to elicit the undesired material function of the copiers. In this space of practice technicians could develop the knowledge necessary to provide solutions to common problems. Feeling where certain parts inside the machine had worn down and watching paper jam between layered rollers allowed technicians to develop new knowledge about the problems and to devise solutions to them. We can say that in the space of practice the material functioning of the copier and the theoretical knowledge about how copiers worked came together for technicians. Out of this space of practice they were then able to develop new actions (work practices) that reflected their contextually created knowledge.

Although these two studies illustrate the notion of practice as a space, they are focused on the intertwining of material and social phenomena in the context of machines. Other studies that have dealt with learning and knowledge have shown how the material and social are connected absent any explicit machine behavior. Lave and Wenger (1991) attempted to recast the notion of apprenticeship as a practical action. The authors suggested that knowledge arises in a realm of practice. That is, in the space in which new recruits begin to perform certain actions they create contextually specific knowledge about how and why work is conducted as it is in certain communities. Among the number of empirical cases of apprenticeship they cite, Lave and Wenger discuss how newcomers to Alcoholics Anonymous (AA) learn to construct their identity as a non-drinking alcoholic through their engagement in communal practice. Attending speaker meetings and telling one's story helps newcomers make the eventual transition into old-timers. As the authors describe, newcomers learn what AA is all about and how to see themselves as non-drinking alcoholics through the practices of storytelling, of saying something once and being explicitly or implicitly told not to say it again, or encouraged to elaborate what was once a small part of a story into the main focus:

> Early on, newcomers learn to preface their contributions to A.A. meetings with the simple identifying statement, "I'm a recovering alcoholic," and shortly to introduce themselves and sketch the problem that brought them to A.A. They begin by describing these events in non-A.A. terms. Their accounts meet with the counterexemplary stories by more-experienced members who do not criticize or correct newcomer's accounts directly. They gradually generate a view that matches more closely the A.A. model, eventually producing skilled testimony in public meetings and gaining validation from others as they demonstrate appropriate understanding.
>
> (Lave & Wenger, 1991, p. 106)

In this example, practice is the space in which knowledge and identity are constructed. The space allows for the conduct of certain actions that will then produce a certain organization of knowing in the world.

This discussion of AA members is quite similar to Orlikowski's (2002) exploration of the enactment of performance practices in a successful global product development company. Orlikowski discussed how, in the space of practice, organizational members combined insights they generated through the product development process with the goals of the organization to form certain actions in which knowing can be communicated to others. As Orlikowski framed it, the actions that produce knowing are generated from a space in which individual's real-time experiences with the product development process can be combined with their insights about the functioning of the organization. In other words, in the space of practice, practical action is generated.

Getting Into the Space of Practice to Watch Practical Action

If, as I have discussed thus far, work practice is not only the action by which tasks are accomplished but also a space in which the material demands of the world can be integrated into the realm of human agency, then to build theory about work practice, researchers must enter this practical space. The problem with much contemporary research on work practice is that conceptualizations of work practice as action confines discussion about generative power to localized settings. In other words, by focusing on the content of work practices—what they look like—it is often difficult to build a theory of practice that will allow comparison across diverse contexts. If, however, researchers can begin to think of practice as a space, understanding how and why practices are generated in the first place will take on an important role. Put another way, studies that attempt to answer questions like, "What kinds of work practices develop within a community?" will be limited in their ability to build theory. Instead, researchers must ask, "Why do certain practices develop in a community?" The answer to such a question must involve, at least in some tangential way, the various characteristics of practice I identify above. The more important point here is that answering this question requires that researchers first conceptualize practice as a space in which various material and social phenomena become intertwined and second, that they enter this space to learn how those practices develop in the first place.

After understanding why certain practices develop as they do, researchers can then begin to ask, "What do these practices do?" Again, here I have offered three possibilities for the role practices play in the process of organizing. Thus, thinking about work practice as both space and action may help to lead to insights that are not idiosyncratically based but that produce knowledge about the mechanisms through which organizing is accomplished.

Empirically, this means that researchers must "get inside" the space of practice to understand the action of practice. Ethnographic research provides one avenue for such discovery since the basic epistemology of the method is that knowledge is generated about individual's practices by "getting inside" the interpretations of insiders. To actually get inside the space of work practices will require researchers to focus their efforts in several directions.

Conduct longitudinal research. To understand how work practices are produced, maintained, and dissolve, as well as how their conduct constitutes the organizing process requires observation over time. Consequently, communication researchers must track the conduct of work practices longitudinally. As I have discussed, static studies that map the occurrence of change demonstrate what work practices communities of actors engage in but do not demonstrate the dynamics by which those changes occur. For researchers to be able to demonstrate how the interplay of social and technical forces engender changes in organizational life seems to require a minimum of six to eighteen months of study (Barley, 1986; Latour & Woolgar, 1979; Leonardi, 2012; Orlikowski, 2002). To expand the scope of study and examine the relationship between work practices and organizational change requires even more extended observation—perhaps over three years (Thomas, 1994). For many researchers this commitment to time will surely be off-putting. However, the need to understand not only how but why work practices (a) sometimes become institutions in a community and other times do not; (b) sometimes alter the organization in anticipated ways and other times bring about a number of unanticipated outcomes; and (c) sometimes have positive and other times have detrimental effects on the functioning of an organization is of tremendous concern for both organizational theory and management practice.

This argument for a longitudinal approach to studies of work practice is based on two primary assumptions. The first assumption is that the most trenchant insights about social systems are generated by watching people do things. Although interviews are helpful to explain the progression of events and people's interpretations of their own actions and others, their actual conduct of work is the most revealing source of data that an ethnographer can collect about the contours of a social system. Although individuals' actions produce and perpetuate a social system, they are also influenced by it. Therefore, observing what actions people take to complete their work, when they take those actions, and how those actions are performed not only provides a descriptive understanding of how people work, but it can also help to explain why they work in these ways.

The second assumption is that an informant who is being observed in an organizational context performs certain actions because she believes such actions are necessary to fulfill her work role. In this sense, people's actions don't lie. Although an informant may inadvertently or even purposefully alter his or her actions when under the watch of the ethnographer, people are notoriously bad at maintaining a façade for long. They are bad at it because trying to perform actions in ways that violate a normal routine often proves to be too much a cognitive load for people to handle (Louis & Sutton, 1991) and because, at some point, they have to get their work done, and thus cannot afford to dissimulate their practice for long (Roy, 1959). The upshot, is that even they know they are being watched, people act in ways that they have to get their jobs done. Becker (1996) provides a compelling example:

> When we watch someone as they work in their usual work setting{. . .}we cannot insulate them from the consequences of their actions. On the contrary, they have to take the rap for what they do, just as they ordinarily do in everyday life. An example: when I was observing college undergraduates, I sometimes went to classes with them. On one occasion, an instructor announced a surprise quiz for which the student I was accompanying that day, a goofoff, was totally unprepared. Sitting nearby, I could easily see him leaning over and copying answers from someone he hoped knew more than he did. He was embarrassed by my seeing him, but the embarrassment didn't

stop him copying, because the consequences of failing the test (this was at a time when flunking out of school could lead to being drafted, and maybe being killed in combat) were a lot worse than my potentially lowered opinion of him. He apologized and made excuses later, but he did it.

(p. 62)

In fact, most field researchers seem to agree that when they are in their work setting even those informants who prove most theatrical after meeting the researcher slip back into their normal set of actions after about thirty minutes of observation. Thus, long, repeated stints of observation can reliably capture the normal and routine actions informants conduct co accomplish their work.

Based on these assumptions, Becker and his colleagues (Becker, 1958; Becker et al., 1961) have demonstrated the usefulness of what I term an *action approach* toward longitudinal data collection and analysis. Such an approach takes as its primary unit of analysis the actions that informants take in the conduct of their work. Actions are small but concrete types of behaviors. Reading an error message from a computer screen is an action; calling someone on the phone is an action; placing an accelerometer on a model is an action; and submitting a math-model to a solver is an action. Actions can be observed directly and recorded through the use of field notes. Once they are in written form they can be read, their text can be pointed to, and they can be given a code. Concrete actions can be grouped together into events, or the collection of multiple smaller actions (Becker et al., 1961). Thus, the actions of picking up a piece of paper and calling someone on the phone can be grouped into a trying-to-discover-why-a-model-bombed-out event just as the actions of placing an accelerometer and submitting a model to a solver can be grouped into a pre-processing-a-model event. These events can then be submitted to the types of analysis techniques (e.g. Strauss & Corbin, 1998) that allow the researcher to understand why they occur, what their consequences are, and what other events they connect to.

What is the point of such a detailed coding of actions? Triangulation. Becker (1958) suggested that if observations are coded at the level of actions they can be standardized in a form "capable of being transformed into legitimate statistical data" (p. 656). Counting the number of actions taken by informants in the course of their work can be a simple way to triangulate the findings made through the qualitative interpretations of the data. For example, as he began to sort his data in a qualitative manner, Barley (1990b) noticed a subtle shift in the interactions among his informants. The analysis seemed to suggest that the new computerized imaging modalities he had watched informants use were shifting the power relations among actors in the social order of the two hospitals he observed. By counting identifiable actions from his notes (e.g. "usurping the controls" or "giving someone directions"), Barley was able to verify quantitatively the insights generated by his qualitative sorting of the data (Barley, 1986, 1990a).

Although an action approach to data analysis can allow the analyst to sum qualitative data in quantitative form, which can help to confirm or disconfirm the theories emerging from the analysis, it can also help to reveal more subtle and consistent patterns in the data. By coding specific actions from the data, the analyst can construct data matrices that can be submitted to statistical analyses. For example, using simple tests such as an analysis of variance can help to determine whether actions occurred more frequently in one period than another or whether they were conducted more consistently by one group than another. Thus, by coding actions, longitudinal researchers can triangulate the descriptive and inductive findings of qualitatively coded data with simple quantitative analyses of frequencies that may help to uncover patterns in the data that would otherwise be lost to the analyst due to the data's sheer volume. This is exactly the tactic taken, for example, in Poole and DeSanctis's (1992; DeSanctis & Poole, 1994) brilliant longitudinal work on group decision support system use, which led to their theory of adaptive structuration.

Examine links between macro and micro.   Everyday work practices are both enabled and constrained by the formal structures and procedures of the organization. However, they also produce and perpetuate those very forms that constrain them. What the literature reviewed has consistently demonstrated is that development and change of work practices are associated with micro-level social practices and reinforced or mitigated by macro-level organizational responses to them. Therefore, to understand how and why organizations take the shape they do, future research must alternate between a focus on features of the macro-organizational structure and a focus on the micro-practices that produce and change that structure. This is a difficult task. Several authors have argued for certain pivotal concepts that help researchers look simultaneously at both. Barley (1990a) has argued for roles and networks as such concepts, DeSanctis and Poole (1994) have suggested that norms might fulfill this function, and Feldman and Pentland (2003) have suggested that researchers pay closer attention to routines.

The identification of additional pivotal concepts for explaining how macro-level structures affect micro-level practices, which in turn alter macro-level structures, will help to highlight the constitutive role of work practices in the production of organizations and to demonstrate more effectively how an organization sets its own conditions for the effect that a new work practice will have on it.

The problem with such integration, however, is that scholars who adopt macro-level approaches to the study of work practice often proffer deterministic accounts of how and why people work the way they do, and what effects those ways of working have on organizing, while scholars who adopt micro-level approaches tend to adopt social constructivist views (Leonardi & Barley, 2010). The answer to the question of whether work practices are emergent and idiosyncratic responses to local exigencies, or whether they are shaped by forces outside the control of the people who conduct them may well depend on the level of analysis and the time frame from which researchers choose to work. Historians of science have grappled with this issue in their examinations of the development and use of technologies. Misa, for example, (1994) noted that determinists and social constructivists typically draw evidence from different levels of analysis to construct their arguments:

> machines make history when historians and other analysts adopt a "macro" perspective, whereas a causal role for the machine is not present and is not possible for analysts who adopt a "micro" perspective.{. . .}Besides taking a larger unit of analysis, macro studies tend to abstract from individual cases, to impute rationality on actors' behalfs or posit functionality for their actions.{. . .}Accounts focusing on these "order bestowing principles" lead toward technological, economic or ecological determinism. Conversely, accounts focusing on historical contingency and variety of experience lead away from all determinism. Besides taking a smaller unit of analysis, such micro studies tend to focus solely on case studies, to refute rationality or confute functionality, and to be disorder-respecting.
> (pp. 117–119)

Misa argued that resolving dilemmas of determinism and materialism by privileging one level of analysis over another is not only empirically dissatisfying, it allows analysts to sidestep important issues.

Scholars who champion voluntarism and idealism by insisting on micro-level data are "forced to omit comment on the intriguing question of whether technology has any influence on anything" (Misa, 1994, p. 138). The claim that technology exerts no socially significant material force on the direction of society is not only inconsistent with everyday experience, but, as Misa noted, it "seems especially undesirable in an age of pervasive socio-technical problems" (p. 138). Social constructionists, therefore, risk assigning technology too little role in making history. Determinists, on the other hand, either risk creating the image of an autonomous social process that lies beyond human awareness or imputing motives and intentions without the warrant of evidence. Thus, the worldview of a determinist (whether materialistic or idealistic) too easily reduces humans to cultural and social dupes. Misa argued that a more plausible stance lies in the middle ground between determinism and voluntarism, where constraints and affordances both exist. This middle ground, which Misa called the *meso level*, is populated by institutional actors:

> For historians of technology and business this means analyzing the institutions intermediate between the firm and the market or between the individual and the state. A short list of these include manufacturers' organizations (including cartels and interfirm networks), standard setting bodies (including the engineering profession and public agencies), export-import firms specializing in technology transfer, consulting engineering firms and investment banking houses.
> (p. 139)

Institutions are critical in Misa's view because they represent social mechanisms by which one group's volition can be translated into another group's constraint. As I have shown, most studies of work practices adopt social constructivist orientations and, thus, have concentrated on dynamics at the microsocial level. As a result, this body of work might lead one to conclude that work practices lead to unique and unpredictable forms of organizing. Such a conclusion is problematic because, if taken seriously, social constructionists cannot speak to how the same or similar work practices occasion similar outcomes across organizations.

Misa points to a way out of this dilemma: Look at the varying impact of social and material forces at different levels of analysis. As Misa points out, the relevant actors who move across these levels of analysis are likely to be professionals, consultants, and other occupational members who move across organizations and work contexts. Communication theorists who have begun to focus on how professionals shape and are shaped by practice (Cheney & Ashcraft, 2007; Lammers & Garcia, 2009) may be sowing the seeds for the kind of cross-level analyses that will allow students of work practices to elide distinctions between deterministic and social constructivist views on the antecedents and outcomes of work.

Use alternative theories.   One of the enduring strengths of organizational communication research is that it is populated by a number of theories that illuminate various processes that would remain obscure were it not for a multiplicity of lights shining down upon it (Deetz, 2001; Hatch, 1997; Scott, 1998). The same can be said for research on work practices. Up until this point, the vast majority of studies have used ethnomethodology (Garfinkel, 1967) or structuration theory (Giddens, 1984) as interpretive lenses for understanding work practices in the process of organizing. The use of these perspectives is certainly warranted, as they take as their central task the explanation of the relationship between the micro and the macro through a discussion of agency and structure. However, an over-reliance on one or two theoretical models, or slight variations thereof, runs the risk of generating research that has little value-added. Additional perspectives can help to generate new findings and surface new solutions to old problems.

This point is demonstrated by several of the empirical studies reviewed above. For example, Fulk (1993) combined social information processing theory with social learning theory to show how social influence practices led individuals to perceive the utility of a new technology inline with members of their work groups. Barley (1986) drew on insights from both structuration theory and negotiated order theory to understand how work practices changed in the context of a new technology implementation. Structuration theory's emphasis on cumulative effects and negotiated order theory's emphasis on recurrent social interaction resulted in a more complete understanding of the structuring process. Theories that take both agency and structure seriously in constructing accounts of work practices make good candidates for adoption.

Institutional theory (DiMaggio & Powell, 1983; Lammers & Barbour, 2006), critical-interpretive theory (Alvesson & Deetz, 1999; Mumby, 2005), and critical realism theory (Bhaskar, 1979; Maxwell, 2012) seem most immediately suitable for this purpose.

Institutional theory may help expand studies of work practices in organizations because its specification of institutions that transcend specific practice helps to locate and situate work practices in a broader normative order. Practice theorists have often had difficulty speaking to the entwining of power and practice because most have focused on interaction in the here-and-now to highlight emergence in its various forms (Nicolini, 2012). This strategy enables practice theorists to speak to how local political negotiations shape the development of local routines or what one might call micro-institutions (Powell & Colyvas, 2008) but at the cost of allowing more macro-institutions, such as relations of production and distributions of power, to slip into the background. Powerful actors are generally more interested in maintaining or changing the global institutions of a social order and less concerned with the specific routines by which work is accomplished. Consequently, it is plausible that technologies can significantly alter routines and patterns of interaction, while posing no challenge to the larger institutional order. For example, institutional theorists have long sought to determine why organizations are so similar. Like practice theorists, they have also foregrounded the role that interpretation and symbolism play in the emergence and diffusion of organizational structures and work practices. In fact, Zucker (1977), Meyer and Rowan (1977), and DiMaggio and Powell (1991) specifically turned to Berger and Luckmann's (1967) *Social Construction of Reality* for the microsocial foundations of their institutionalist agenda. Berger and Luckmann were interested in how subjectivity was transformed into objectivity. They rooted the construction process in emergent interactions and interpretations that became habitualized at a local level and then diffused across actors and contexts to become taken-for-granted social forms. Taking Berger and Luckmann's perspective, one can argue that studies of work practices have concentrated on the early phases, while institutionalists have focused on the later phases of social construction. In other words, while practice theory studies of work practices have paid most attention to how similar work practices can occasion distinct cognitive, communicative, and network structures, institutionalists have often concentrated on explaining how structures that have already emerged elsewhere diffuse (e.g. DiMaggio, 1991; Jepperson, 1991; Owen-Smith & Powell, 2004; Scott, 2004; Strang & Macy, 2001). To link these perspectives as Berger and Luckmann might have envisioned would require a theoretically nuanced account of how emergent and heterogeneous work practices conducted in individual organizations become homogeneous, such that they can diffuse across organizational fields.

Critical-interpretive theorists who explore the way that language influences practice often treat organizations as discursive constructions where discourse, which represents the language people use in everyday talk, constructs *discourse,* or an ideological orientation that undergirds the process of organizing (Alvesson & Kärreman, 2000; Fairhurst & Putnam, 2004). Within such a conceptualization, the discourse occurring in everyday interaction produces a *discourse* that shapes individuals' understandings about the relationship between objects in the world and influences their subsequent action (Phillips, Lawrence, & Hardy, 2004). As critical-interpretive theorists argue, *discourse* is always the outcome of some degree of struggle over parties with varying interests (Alvesson & Deetz, 1999). In the realm of work practices, there are at least two important parties with distinct interests: individuals who conduct the work practices in the course of their normal work roles hope to use technology in line with cultural values to maintain cognitive consistency (Waisbord, 1998; Yoon, 2001) and managers, on the other hand, who often wish to standardize and control practices and hope for consistency in the way people work (Tractinsky & Jarvenpaa, 1995). Thus, the conduct of work practices could, from a critical standpoint, be seen as a struggle to establish the *discourse* that will order and naturalize the world in a particular way. If language constructs reality, then in the political process of reality construction leveraging a discourse that renders one's conception of the world as uncontestable will ensure a groups' ability to frame the debate. As Deetz (1996) explained:

> Either explicit or implicit in critical work is a goal to demonstrate and critique forms of domination, asymmetry and distorted communication through showing how social constructions of reality can favor certain interests and alternative constructions can be obscured and misrecognized.
>
> (p. 202)

Whether recognizing the potential outcomes of their actions or not, managers often do use a discourse that enforces a correct way to perceive and relate to the world. Deetz (1992) suggested that such discursive moves work to socially construct reality precisely because perceptual experience is primary. In other words, "on the basis of their perceptions, human beings make judgments, decide courses of action, develop feelings and make claims about the nature of reality" (Deetz, 1992, p. 115). Alvesson (1993) made a similar argument, noting that one of the primary methods through which managers attempt to gain purchase over the meaning-making process is through perceptual control. As Alvesson suggested, perceptual control is quite powerful because it is not targeted at shaping beliefs about what is good and what a person should strive toward (e.g., evaluate claims about a technology) but is aimed at shaping beliefs about what exists and how things are (e.g., the inevitable outcomes of technology). Using *discourse* as a control mechanism at the level of perception is powerful because it influences the social construction process. In other words, instead of waiting until after meaning is formed and attempting to influence meaning through persuasive campaigns, *discourse* often plays on perceptions as the primary experiential interface with the world in a way that makes certain relationships appear natural and uncontestable. In Mumby's (1989) words, creating a *discourse* that shapes individuals' perceptions "invokes a complex system of power structures that inscribe and position individuals in particular ways and with certain constraints and possibilities on their activities" (p. 303). Certain *discourses* about work practices may socially construct people's orientations toward their work precisely because they close off cultural antecedents to the social construction process by making the indeterminate and emergent nature of work somehow formulaic or inevitable.

Critical realism is a philosophical stance that recognizes the potential existence of a reality beyond our knowledge or conscious experience (Bhaskar, 1979). Phillips (1987) summarized this stance as "the view that entities exist independently of being perceived, or independently of our theories about them" (p. 205). That some structures are only experienced through human action does not make these structures any less real—existing apart from humans and their perceptions—and the influence of structure is not dependent on individuals explicitly recognizing it (Fleetwood, 2005). As Ackroyd and Fleetwood (2000) have noted, "Since our knowledge is bound up with our conceptions or even our discourse, it is easy to end up implicitly and illicitly concluding that all that exists are our concepts or our discourse" (p. 6).

One fundamental idea in critical realism that may, at the outset, concern students of work practices, especially those with constructivist leanings, is the critical realist's invocation of the term reality. However, critical realism does not suppose that there is one true reality out there waiting to be found. As Putnam (1999) argued:

> The notion that our words and life are constrained by a reality not of our own invention plays a deep role in our lives and is to be respected. The source of the puzzlement lies in the common philosophical error of supposing that the term "reality" must refer to a single superthing instead of looking at the ways in which we endlessly renegotiate—and are forced to renegotiate—our notion of reality as our language and our life develop.
>
> (p. 9)

This conceptualization of reality has strong parallels to symbolic interactionist thinking. As Herbert Blumer (1969), who combined an ontological realism with an empirical constructivism argued:

> the empirical necessarily exists always in the form of human pictures and conceptions of it. However, this does not shift "reality," as so many conclude, from the empirical world to the realm of imagery and conception.{...} [This] position is untenable because the empirical world can "talk back" to our pictures of it or assertions about it—talk back in the sense of challenging and resisting, or not bending to, our images or conceptions of it.
>
> (p. 22)

Most critical realists hold that mental states and attributes (such as meanings and intentions), although not directly observable, are part of the real world. In other words,

> while critical realism rejects the idea of "multiple realities," in the sense of independent and incommensurable worlds that are socially constructed by different individuals or societies, it is quite compatible with the idea that there are different valid perspectives on reality.
>
> (Maxwell, 2012, p. 9)

Applying this critical realist view to considerations of the study of work practices points communication scholars to consider two analytical assumptions: (a) that structure logically predates the actions that transform it and (b) that structural elaboration logically postdates those actions. Such a position leads to calls for students of work practices to enact an "analytical dualism" that treats the structural and action-based components of work practices as interacting while all the while remaining distinct from one another (Archer, 1995). In other words, structures can be viewed as intransitive, or existing without an identifiable object at which they are directed (Archer, 2000). Within a morphogenetic approach to critical realism, structures can then be analyzed separately from the actions that bring them into existence, and sustain them through elaboration, reproduction, or transformation. Such a view may help to shed light on why certain work practices do emerge, why others do not or cannot, and under what circumstances work practices are likely to sustain or alter the way an organization is structured.

Conclusion

In this paper I have made an attempt at providing some conceptual clarity on the concept of work practices. My review of studies across disciplines as diverse as organization studies, sociology, communication, computer-supported cooperative work, management, information systems, and science studies has surfaced a number of common characteristics that can be said to define a work practice. I have also suggested three overlapping roles that work practices play in the process of organizing—the work that work practices do both for organizational members and for those who research organizations. Finally, I have provided a number of suggestions on how to build theory from empirical studies of work practices. As John Dewey (1934) suggested many years ago, work practices are an intriguing object of study because they form a grammar for understanding organizing as it happens:

> It is no linguistic accident that "building," "construction," "work," designate both a process and its finished product. Without the meaning of the verb that of the noun remains blank.
>
> (p. 51)

Let's begin to fill in the blanks.

Acknowledgements

This chapter was made possible by thanks to generous funding from the National Science Foundation (SES-1057148).

References

Ackroyd, S., & Fleetwood, S. (2000). Realism in contemporary organisation and management studies. In S. Ackroyd & S. Fleetwood (Eds.), *Realist perspective on management and organisations* (pp. 3–25). London: Routledge.

Alvesson, M. (1993). Cultural-ideological modes of management control: A theory and a case study of a professional service company. In S. Deetz (Ed.), *Communication yearbook 16* (pp. 3–42). Newbury Park, CA: Sage.

Alvesson, M., & Deetz, S. (1999). Critical theory and postmodernism: Approaches to organizational studies. In S. Clegg & C. Hardy (Eds.), *Studying organization: Theory and method* (pp. 185–211). London: Sage.

Alvesson, M., & Kärreman, D. (2000). Varieties of discourse: On the study of organizations through discursive analysis. *Human Relations, 53*, 1125–1149. doi: 10.1177/0018726700539002

Anderson, P., & Tushman, M. L. (1990). Technological discontinuities and dominant designs: A cyclical model of technological change. *Administrative Science Quarterly, 35*, 604–633. doi:10.2307/2393511

Archer, M. (1995). *Realist social theory: The morphogenetic approach*. Cambridge, England. Cambridge University Press.

Archer, M. (2000). For structure: Its reality, properties and powers: A reply to Anthony King. *The Sociological Review, 48*, 464–472. doi:10.1111/1467-954X.00226

Ashcraft, K. L., Kuhn, T. R., & Cooren, F. (2009). Constitutional amendments: "Materializing" organizational communication. *Academy of Management Annals, 3*(1), 1–64. doi:10.1080/19416520903047186

Barley, S. R. (1986). Technology as an occasion for structuring: Evidence from observations of CT scanners and the social order of radiology departments. *Administrative Science Quarterly, 31*(1), 78–108. doi:10.2307/2392767

Barley, S. R. (1990a). The alignment of technology and structure through roles and networks. *Administrative Science Quarterly, 35*(1), 61–103. doi:10.2307/2393551

Barley, S. R. (1990b). Images of imaging: Notes on doing longitudinal field work. *Organization Science, 1*(3), 220–247. doi:10.1287/orsc.1.3.220

Barley, S. R. (1996). Technicians in the workplace: Ethnographic evidence for bringing work into organization studies. *Administrative Science Quarterly, 41*(3), 404–441. doi:10.2307/2393937

Barley, S. R., & Kunda, G. (2001). Bringing work back in. *Organization Science, 12*(1), 76–95. doi:10.1287/orsc.12.1.76.10122

Becker, H. S. (1958). Problems of inference and proof in participant observation. *American Sociological Review, 23*(6), 652–660. doi:10.2307/2089053

Becker, H. S. (1996). The epistemology of qualitative research. In R. Jessor, A. Colby & R. Schweder (Eds.), *Essays on ethnography and human development* (pp. 53–71). Chicago: University of Chicago Press.

Becker, H. S., & Carper, J. (1956). The development of identification with an occupation. *American Journal of Sociology, 61*(4), 289–298. doi:10.1086/221759

Becker, H. S., Geer, B., Hughes, E. C., & Strauss, A. L. (1961). *Boys in white: Student culture in medical school*. Chicago: University of Chicago Press.

Berg, M. (1997). Of forms, containers, and the electronic medical record: Some tools for a sociology of the formal. *Science, Technology, and Human Values, 22*(4), 403–433. doi:10.1177/016224399702200401

Berger, P. L., & Luckmann, T. (1967). *The social construction of reality: A treatise in the sociology of knowledge*. Garden City, NY: Anchor Books.

Bhaskar, R. (1979). *The possibility of naturalism*. Hemel Hempstead, UK: Harvester.

Blomberg, J. (1988). Social interaction and office communication: Effects on user's evaluations of new technologies. In R. Kraut (Ed.), *Technology and the transformation of white collar work* (pp. 195–210). Hillsdale, NJ: Lawrence Erlbaum.

Blumer, H. (1969). The methodological position of symbolic interactionism. In H. Blumer (Ed.), *Symbolic interactionism: Perspective and method* (pp. 1–60). Englewood Cliffs, NJ: Prentice-Hall.

Bourdieu, P. (1977). *Outline of a Theory of Practice*. Cambridge: Cambridge University Press.

Bourdieu, P. (1990). *The logic of practice* (R. Nice, trans.). Stanford, CA: Stanford University Press.

Brown, J. S., & Duguid, P. (2001). Knowledge and organization: A social-practice perspective. *Organization Science, 12*(2), 198–213. doi:10.1287/orsc.12.2.198.10116

Carlile, P. R. (2004). Transferring, translating, and transforming: An integrative framework for managing knowledge across boundaries. *Organization Science, 15*, 555–568. doi:10.1287/orsc.1040.0094

Cheney, G., & Ashcraft, K. L. (2007). Considering "the professional" in communication studies: Implications for theory and research within and beyond the boundaries of organizational communication. *Communication Theory, 17*(2), 146–175. doi:10.1111/j.1468-2885.2007.00290.x

Collins, R. (1981). On the microfoundations of macrosociology. *American Journal of Sociology, 86*(5), 984–1014. doi:10.1086/227351

Contractor, N. S., Monge, P. R., & Leonardi, P. M. (2011). Multidimensional networks and the dynamics of sociomateriality: Bringing technology inside the network. *International Journal of Communication, 5*, 682–720.

Cooren, F. (2010). *Action and agency in dialogue: Passion, incarnation and ventriloquism*. Amsterdam: John Benjamins Publishing Company.

Craig, R. T. (1989). Communication as a practical discipline. In B. Dervin, L. Grossberg, B. J. O'Keefe & E. Wanella (Eds.), *Rethinking communication: Vol. 1. Paradigm issues* (pp. 97–122). Newbury Park, CA: Sage.

Craig, R. T. (1999). Communication theory as a field. *Communication Theory, 9*(2), 119–161. doi:10.1111/j.1468-2885.1999.tb00355.x

Craig, R. T. (2001). Minding my metamodel, mending Myers. *Communication Theory, 11*(2), 231–240. doi:10.1111/j.1468-2885.2001.tb00241.x

Deetz, S. (1992). *Democracy in an age of corporate colonization: Developments in communication and the politics of everyday life*. Albany, NY: State University of New York Press.

Deetz, S. (1994). Future of the discipline: The challenges, the research, and the social contribution. In S. Deetz (Ed.), *Communication yearbook 17* (pp. 565–600). Newbury Park, CA: Sage.

Deetz, S. (1996). Describing differences in approaches to organization science: Rethinking Burrell and Morgan and their legacy. *Organization Science, 7*(2), 191–207. doi:10.1287/orsc.7.2.191

Deetz, S. (2000). Putting the community into organizational science: Exploring the construction of knowledge claims. *Organization Science, 11*(6), 732–738. doi:10.1287/orsc.11.6.732.12536

Deetz, S. (2001). Conceptual foundations. In F. M. Jablin & L. L. Putnam (Eds.), *The new handbook of organizational communication: Advances in theory, research, and methods* (pp. 3–46). Thousand Oaks, CA: Sage.

DeSanctis, G., & Poole, M. S. (1994). Capturing the complexity in advanced technology use: Adaptive structuration theory. *Organization Science, 5*(2), 121–147. doi:10.1287/orsc.5.2.121

Dewey, J. (1934). *Art as experience.* New York: Milton Balch.

DiMaggio, P. J. (1991). Constructing an organizational field as a professional project: U.S. Art museums, 1920–1940. In W. W. Powell & P. J. DiMaggio (Eds.), *The new institutionalism in organizational analysis* (pp. 267–292). Chicago: University of Chicago Press.

DiMaggio, P. J., & Powell, W. W. (1983). The iron cage revisited: Institutional isomorphism and collective rationality in organizational fields. *American Sociological Review, 48*, 147–160. doi:10.2307/2095101

DiMaggio, P. J., & Powell, W. W. (1991). Introduction. In W. W. Powell & P. J. DiMaggio (Eds.), *The new institutionalism in organizational analysis* (pp. 1–38). Chicago: University of Chicago Press.

Edmondson, A. C., Bohmer, R. M., & Pisano, G. P. (2001). Disrupted routines: Team learning and new technology implementation in hospitals. *Administrative Science Quarterly, 46*(4), 685–716. doi:10.2307/3094828

Eisenberg, E. M., & Riley, P. (2001). Organizational culture. In F. M. Jablin & L. L. Putnam (Eds.), *The new handbook of organizational communication: Advances in theory, research, and methods* (pp. 291–322). Thousand Oaks, CA: Sage.

Fairhurst, G. T., & Putnam, L. (2004). Organizations as discursive constructions. *Communication Theory, 14*(1), 5–26. doi:10.1111/j.1468-2885.2004.tb00301.x

Feldman, M. S., & Orlikowski, W. J. (2011). Theorizing practice and practicing theory. *Organization Science, 22*(5), 1240–1253. doi:10.1287/orsc.1100.0612

Feldman, M. S., & Pentland, B. T. (2003). Reconceptualizing organizational routines as a source of flexibility and change. *Administrative Science Quarterly, 48*, 94–118. doi:10.2307/3556620

Feldman, M. S., & Pentland, B. T. (2005). Organizational routines and the macro-actor. In B. Czarniawka & T. Hernes (Eds.), *Actor-network theory and organizing* (pp. 91–111). Malmo: Liber.

Fleetwood, S. (2005). Ontology in organization and management studies: A critical realist perspective. *Organization Studies, 12*, 197–222. doi:10.1177/1350508405051188

Fulk, J. (1993). Social construction of communication technology. *Academy of Management Journal, 36*(5), 921–951. doi:10.2307/256641

Garfinkel, H. (1967). *Studies in ethnomethodology.* Englewood Cliffs, NJ: Prentice-Hall.

Gibbs, J. L. (2009). Dialectics in a global software team: Negotiating tensions across time, space, and culture. *Human Relations, 62*(6), 905–935. doi:10.1177/0018726709104547

Giddens, A. (1984). *The constitution of society.* Berkeley, CA: University of California Press.

Gilbreth, F. B. (1911/1993). *Motion study: A method for increasing the efficiency of the workman.* London: Routledge/Thoemmes Press.

Goffman, E. (1959). *The presentation of self in everyday life.* Garden City, NY: Doubleday Anchor.

Guillemin, M. (2000). Working practices of the menopause clinic. *Science, Technology, and Human Values, 25*(4), 449–471. doi:10.1177/016224390002500403

Hard, M. (1994). Technology as practice: Local and global closure processes in diesel-engine design. *Social Studies of Science, 24*(3), 549–585. doi:10.1177/030631 279402400304

Hatch, M. J. (1997). *Organization theory: Modern, symbolic and postmodern perspectives*. Oxford: Oxford University Press.

Heath, C., & Luff, P. (2000). *Technology in action*. Cambridge, England: Cambridge University Press.

Heaton, L. (1998). Preserving communication context: Virtual workspace and interpersonal space in Japanese CSCW. *Electronic Journal of Communication, 8*(3/4), Retrieved September 20, 2002 from http://www.cios.org/getfile/Heaton_V2008N2398.

Henderson, K. (1998). The aura of "high tech" in a world of messy practice. *The Sociological Quarterly, 39*(4), 645–672. doi:10.1111/j.1533-8525.1998.tb00522.x

Hogle, L. F. (1995). Standardization across non-standard domains: The case of organ procurement. *Science, Technology, and Human Values, 20*(4), 482–500. doi:10.1177/ 016224399502000405

Hughes, E. C. (1958). *Men and their work*. Glencoe, IL: Free Press.

Hutchins, E. (1995). *Cognition in the wild*. Cambridge, MA: MIT Press.

Jackson, M. H., Poole, M. S., & Kuhn, T. (2002). The social construction of technology in studies of the workplace. In L. A. Lievrouw & S. Livingstone (Eds.), *Handbook of new media: Social shaping and consequences of icts* (pp. 236–253). London: Sage.

Jepperson, R. L. (1991). Institutions, institutional effects, and institutionalism. In W. W. Powell & P. J. DiMaggio (Eds.), *The new insitutionalism in organizational analysis* (pp. 143–163). Chicago: University of Chicago Press.

Kaghan, W. N., & Bowker, G. C. (2001). Out of machine age?: Complexity, sociotechnical systems and actor network theory. *Journal of Engineering and Technology Management, 18*, 253–269. doi:10.1016/S0923-4748(01)00037-6

Knorr-Cetina, K. (1995). How superorganisms change: Consensus formation and the social ontology of high-energy physics experiments. *Social Studies of Science, 25*(1), 119–147. doi:10.1177/030631295025001006

Knorr-Cetina, K. (1999). *Epistemic cultures: How the sciences make knowledge*. Cambridge, MA: Harvard University Press.

Knorr-Cetina, K. (2001). Objectual practice. In T. R. Schatzki, K. Knorr-Cetina & E. von Savigny (Eds.), *The practice turn in contemporary sociology* (pp. 175–188). London: Routledge.

Kuhn, T. (2006). A "demented work ethic" and a "lifestyle firm": Discourse, identity, and workplace time commitments. *Organization Studies, 27*(9), 1339–1358. doi:10.1177/0170840606067249

Kuhn, T., & Jackson, M. H. (2008). Accomplishing knowledge: A framework for investigating knowing in organizations. *Management Communication Quarterly, 21*(4), 454–485. doi:10.1177/0893318907313710

Kunda, G. (1992). *Engineering culture: Control and commitment in a high-tech corporation*. Philadelphia: Temple University Press.

Lammers, J. C., & Barbour, J. B. (2006). An institutional theory of organizational communication. *Communication Theory, 3*(16), 356–377. doi:10.1111/j.1468-2885. 2006.00274.x

Lammers, J. C., & Garcia, M. (2009). Exploring the concept of "profession" for organizational communication research: Institutional influences in a veterinary organization. *Management Communication Quarterly, 22,* 357–384. doi:10.1177/089331 8908327007

Latour, B., & Woolgar, S. (1979). *Laboratory life: The social construction of scientific facts.* Beverly Hills, CA: Sage.

Lave, J., & Wenger, E. (1991). *Situated learning: Legitimate peripheral participation.* Cambridge: Cambridge University Press.

Leonardi, P. M. (2009a). Crossing the implementation line: The mutual constitution of technology and organizing across development and use activities. *Communication Theory, 19,* 278–310. doi:10.1111/j.1468-2885.2009.01344.x

Leonardi, P. M. (2009b). Why do people reject new technologies and stymie organizational changes of which they are in favor? Exploring misalignments between social interactions and materiality. *Human Communication Research, 35*(3), 407–441. doi:10.1111/j.1468-2958.2009.01357.x

Leonardi, P. M. (2012). *Car crashes without cars: Lessons about simulation technology and organizational change from automotive design.* Cambridge, MA: MIT Press.

Leonardi, P. M., & Bailey, D. E. (2008). Transformational technologies and the creation of new work practices: Making implicit knowledge explicit in task-based offshoring. *MIS Quarterly, 32,* 411–436.

Leonardi, P. M., & Barley, S. R. (2010). What's under construction here: Social action, materiality, and power in constructivist studies of technology and organizing. *Academy of Management Annals, 4,* 1–51. doi:10.1080/19416521003654160

Leonardi, P. M., & Rodriguez-Lluesma, C. (2013). Occupational stereotypes, perceived status differences, and intercultural communication in global organizations. *Communication Monographs, 70*(4), 478–502. doi:10.1080/03637751.2013.828155

Leonardi, P. M., Jackson, M. H., & Diwan, A. (2009). The enactment-externalization dialectic: Rationalization and the persistence of counterproductive technology design practices in student engineering. *Academy of Management Journal, 52,* 400–420. doi:10.5465/AMJ.2009.37315471

Leonardi, P. M., Nardi, B. A., & Kallinikos, J. (Eds.). (2012). *Materiality and organizing: Social interaction in a technological world.* Oxford: Oxford University Press.

Louis, M. R., & Sutton, R. I. (1991). Switching cognitive gears: From habits of mind to active thinking. *Human Relations, 44,* 55–76. doi:10.1177/001872679104400104

Lynch, M. (1985). *Art and artifact in laboratory science: A study of shop talk in a research laboratory.* London: Sage.

Maxwell, J. A. (2012). *A realist approach for qualitative research.* Thousand Oaks, CA: Sage.

McPhee, R. D., & Poole, M. S. (2001). Organizational structures and configurations. In F. M. Jablin & L. L. Putnam (Eds.), *The new handbook of organizational communication: Advances in theory, research, and methods* (pp. 503–543). Thousand Oaks, CA: Sage.

McPhee, R. D., & Zaug, P. (2000). The communicative constitution of organizations: A framework for explanation. *Electronic Journal of Communication, 10*(1–2).

Mead, G. H. (1934). *Mind, self, and society: From the standpoint of a social behaviorist.* Chicago: The University of Chicago Press.

Meyer, J. W., & Rowan, B. (1977). Institutionalized organizations: Formal structure as myth and ceremony. *American Journal of Sociology, 83*(2), 340–363. doi:dx.doi.org/10.1086/226550

Misa, T. J. (1994). Retrieving sociotechnical change from technological determinism. In M. R. Smith & L. Marx (Eds.), *Does technology drive history? The dilemma of technological determinism* (pp. 115–141). Cambridge: The MIT Press.

Monge, P., Heiss, B. M., & Margolin, D. B. (2008). Communication network evolution in organizational communities. *Communication Theory, 18*(4), 449–477. doi:10.1111/j.1468-2885.2008.00330.x

Mumby, D. K. (1989). Ideology and the social construction of meaning: A communication perspective. *Communication Quarterly, 17*(4), 291–304. doi:10.1080/01463378909385551

Mumby, D. K. (2005). Theorizing resistance in organization studies: A dialectical approach. *Management Communication Quarterly, 19*, 1–26. doi:10.1177/08933 18905276558

Murphy, A. G. (1998). Hidden transcipts of flight attendant resistance. *Management Communication Quarterly, 11*(4), 499–535. doi:10.1177/0893318998114001

Neff, G. (2012). *Venture labor: Work and the burden of risk in innovative industries.* Cambridge, MA: MIT Press.

Nelsen, B. J., & Barley, S. R. (1997). For love or money? Commodification and the construction of an occupational mandate. *Administrative Science Quarterly, 42*, 619–653. doi:10.2307/2393652

Nelson, R. R., & Winter, S. G. (1982). *An evolutionary theory of economic change.* Cambridge, MA: Belknap Press.

Nicolini, D. (2012). *Practice theory, work, and organization.* Oxford: Oxford University Press.

Nicolini, D., Mengis, J., & Swan, J. (2012). Understanding the role of objects in cross-disciplinary collaboration. *Organization Science, 23*(3), 612–629. doi:10.1287/orsc.1110.0664

Orlikowski, W. J. (1992). The duality of technology: Rethinking the concept of technology in organizations. *Organization Science, 3*(3), 398–427. doi:10.1287/orsc.3.3.398

Orlikowski, W. J. (1996). Improvising organizational transformation over time: A situated change perspective. *Information Systems Research, 7*(1), 63–92. doi:10.1287/isre.7.1.63

Orlikowski, W. J. (2000). Using technology and constituting structures: A practice lens for studying technology in organizations. *Organization Science, 11*(4), 404–428. doi:10.1287/orsc.11.4.404.14600

Orlikowski, W. J. (2002). Knowing in practice: Enacting a collective capability in distributed organizing. *Organization Science, 13*(3), 249–273. doi:10.1287/orsc.13.3.249.2776

Orlikowski, W. J., & Gash, D. C. (1994). Technological frames: Making sense of information technology in organizations. *ACM Transactions on Information Systems, 12*, 174–207. doi:10.1145/196734.196745

Orr, J. E. (1996). *Talking about machines: An ethnography of a modern job.* Ithaca, NY: ILR Press.

Orr, J. E. (1998). Images of work. *Science, Technology, and Human Values, 23*(4, Special Issue: Humans, Animals, and Machines), 439–455. doi:10.1177/0162243 99802300405

Owen-Smith, J., & Powell, W. W. (2004). Knowledge networks as channels and conduits: The effects of spillovers in the boston biotechnology community. *Organization Science, 15*(1), 5–21. doi:10.1287/orsc.1030.0054

Pacanowsky, M., & O'Donnell-Trujillo, N. (1983). Organizational communication as cultural performance. *Communication Monographs, 50*, 126–147. doi:10.1080/03637758309390158

Pentland, B. T. (1992). Organizing moves in software support hot lines. *Administrative Science Quarterly, 37*(4), 527–548. doi:10.2307/2393471

Perlow, L. A., Gittell, J. H., & Katz, N. (2004). Contextualizing patterns of work group interaction: Toward a nested theory of structuration. *Organization Science, 15*(5), 520–536. doi:10.1287/orsc.1040.0097

Phillips, D. C. (1987). *Philosophy, science, and social inquiry.* Oxford: Pergamon.

Phillips, N., Lawrence, T. B., & Hardy, C. (2004). Discourse and institutions. *Academy of Management Review, 29*(4), 635–652.

Pickering, A. (1993). The mangle of practice: Agency and emergence in the sociology of science. *American Journal of Sociology, 99*(3), 559–589. doi:10.1086/230316

Pickering, A. (1995). *The mangle of practice: Time, agency, and science.* Chicago: University of Chicago Press.

Pickering, A. (2001). Practice and posthumanism: Social theory and a history of agency. In T. R. Schatzki, K. Knorr-Cetina & E. von Savigny (Eds.), *The practice turn in contemporary theory* (pp. 163–174.). London: Routledge.

Poole, M. S., & DeSanctis, G. (1992). Microlevel structuration in computer-supported group decision making. *Human Communication Research, 19*(1), 5–49. doi:10.1111/j.1468-2958.1992.tb00294.x

Powell, W. W., & Colyvas, J. A. (2008). Microfoundations of institutional theory. In R. Greenwood, C. Oliver, R. Suddaby & K. Shalin-Andersson (Eds.), *Handbook of new institutionalism.* Thousand Oaks, CA: Sage.

Prasad, P. (1993). Symbolic processes in the implementation of technological change: A symbolic interactionist study of work computerization. *Academy of Management Journal, 36*(6), 1400–1429. doi:10.2307/256817

Putnam, H. (1999). *The threefold cord: Mind, body, and world* (Vol. 5). New York: Columbia University Press.

Putnam, L. L., & Nicotera, A. M. (2010). Communicative constitution of organization is a question: Critical issues for addressing it. *Management Communication Quarterly, 24*(1), 158–165. doi:10.1177/0893318909351581

Putnam, L. L., & Stohl, C. (1990). Bona fide groups: A reconceptualization of groups in context. *Communication Studies, 41*(3), 248–265. doi:10.1080/10510979009368307

Reichers, A. E. (1987). An interactionist perspective on newcomer socialization rates. *Academy of Management Review, 12*(2), 278–287.

Robey, D., & Sahay, S. (1996). Transforming work through information technology: A comparative case study of geographic information systems in county government. *Information Systems Research, 7*(1), 93–110. doi:10.1287/isre.7.1.93

Roy, D. F. (1959). Banana time: Job satisfaction and informal interaction. *Human Organization, 18*, 158–168.

Schatzki, T. R. (2005). The sites of organizations. *Organization Studies, 26*(3), 465–484. doi:10.1177/0170840605050876

Schein, E. H. (1996). Culture: The missing concept in organization studies. *Administrative Science Quarterly, 41*(2), 229–240. doi:10.2307/2393715

Schultze, U., & Orlikowski, W. J. (2004). A practice perspective on technology-mediated network relations: The use of internet-based self-serve technologies. *Information Systems Research, 15*(1), 87–106. doi:10.1287/isre.1030.0016

Scott, W. R. (1998). *Organizations: Rational, natural, and open systems* (4th ed.). Upper Saddle River, NJ: Prentice Hall.

Scott, W. R. (2004). Reflections on a half-century of organizational sociology. *Annual Review of Sociology, 30*, 1–21. doi:10.1146/annurev.soc.30.012703.110644

Sims, B. (1999). Concrete practices: Testing in an earthquake-engineering laboratory. *Social Studies of Science, 29*(4), 483–518. doi:10.1177/030631299029004002

Sorenson, J. B., & Stuart, T. E. (2000). Aging, obsolescence, and organizational innovation. *Administrative Science Quarterly, 45*, 81–112. doi:10.2307/2666980

Stohl, C. (1986). The role of memorable messages in the process of organizational socialization. *Communication Quarterly, 34*(3), 231–249. doi:10.1080/01463378609369638

Stohl, C. (2001). Globalizing organizational communication. In F. M. Jablin & L. L. Putnam (Eds.), *The new handbook of organizational communication: Advances in theory, research, and methods* (pp. 323–375). Thousand Oaks, CA: Sage.

Strang, D., & Macy, M. W. (2001). In search of excellence: Fads, success stories, and adaptive emulation. *American Journal of Sociology, 107*(1), 147–182. doi:10.1086/323039

Strauss, A. (1978). *Negotiations.* San Francisco: Jossey-Bass.

Strauss, A., & Corbin, J. (1998). *Basics of qualitative research: Techniques and procedures for developing grounded theory* (2nd ed.). Thousand Oaks, CA: Sage.

Suchman, L. (1987). *Plans and situated action.* Cambridge: Cambridge University Press.

Suchman, L., Blomberg, J., Orr, J. E., & Trigg, R. (1999). Reconstructing technologies as social practices. *American Behavioral Scientist, 43*(3), 392–408. doi:10.1177/00027649921955335

Taylor, F. W. (1911/1998). *The principles of scientific management.* New York: Dover.

Taylor, J. R. (2001). Toward a theory of imbrication and organizational communication. *The American Journal of Semiotics, 17*(2), 269–298. doi:10.5840/ajs200117222

Taylor, J. R., Groleau, C., Heaton, L., & Van Every, E. (2001). *The computerization of work: A communication perspective.* Thousand Oaks, CA: Sage.

Taylor, J. R., Groleau, C., Heaton, L., & Van Every, E. (2007). Communication as the modality of structuration. In R. T. Craig & H. L. Mueller (Eds.), *Theorizing communication readings across traditions* (pp. 391–404). Thousand Oaks, CA: Sage.

Thomas, R. J. (1994). *What machines can't do: Politics and technology in the industrial enterprise.* Berkeley: University of California Press.

Tractinsky, N., & Jarvenpaa, S. L. (1995). Information systems design decisions in a global versus domestic context. *MIS Quarterly, 19*(4), 507–534. doi:10.2307/249631

Treem, J. W. (2012). Communicating expertise: Knowledge performances in professional service firms. *Communication Monographs, 79*(1), 23–47. doi:10.1080/03637751.2011.646487

Treem, J. W. (2013). Technology use as a status cue: The influences of mundane and novel communication technologies on assessments of knowledge in organizations. *Journal of Communication, 63*(6), 1032–1053. doi:10.1111/jcom.12061

Trujillo, N. (1992). Interpreting (the work and the talk of) baseball: Perspectives on ballpark culture. *Western Journal of Communication, 56*, 350–371. doi:10.1080/10570319209374423

Vaast, E., & Walsham, G. (2005). Representations and actions: The transformation of work practices with it use. *Information and Organization, 15*, 65–89. doi:10.1016/j.infoandorg.2004.10.001

Vallas, S. P. (2003). Why teamwork fails: Obstacles to workplace change in four manufacturing plants. *American Sociological Review, 68*, 223–250. doi:10.2307/1519767

Van Maanen, J., & Barley, S. R. (1984). Occupational communities: Culture and control in organizations. In L. L. Cummings & B. M. Staw (Eds.), *Research in organizational behavior* (Vol. 6, pp. 287–365). Greenwich, CT: JAI Press.

Van Maanen, J., & Schein, E. H. (1979). Toward a theory of organizational socialization. In B. M. Staw (Ed.), *Research in organizational behavior* (Vol. 1, pp. 209–264). Greenwich, CT: JAI Press.

Wadel, C. (1979). The hidden work of everyday life. In S. Wallman (Ed.), *American sociological association monograph* (Vol. 19). London: Academic Press.

Waisbord, S. (1998). When the cart of media is before the horse of identity: A critique of technology-centered views on globalization. *Communication Research, 25*(4), 377–398. doi:10.1177/009365098025004003

Watson, J. (1958). A formal analysis of sociable interaction. *Sociometry, 21*(4), 269–280. doi:10.2307/2785791

Weick, K. E. (1979). *The social psychology of organizing* (2nd ed.). New York: McGraw-Hill.

Wenger, E. (1998). *Communities of practice: Learning, meaning, and identity.* New York: Cambridge University Press.

Whittle, A., & Spicer, A. (2008). Is actor network theory critique? *Organization Studies, 29*(4), 611–629. doi:10.1177/0170840607082223

Williams, R. (1983). *Keywords: A vocabulary of culture and society* (2nd ed.). London: Fontana.

Yoon, S. (2001). Internet discourse and the habitus of Korea's new generation. In C. Ess & F. Sudweeks (Eds.), *Culture, technology, communication: Towards an intercultural global village* (pp. 241–260). Albany, NY: State University of New York Press.

Zucker, L. G. (1977). The role of institutionalization in cultural persistence. *American Sociological Review, 42*(5), 726–743. doi:10.2307/2094862

Part IV

Focused Systematic Reviews
Adding Insight into Areas for Investigation

CHAPTER CONTENTS

9 Communicating Nuclear Power

A Programmatic Review

William J. Kinsella

North Carolina State University

Dorothy Collins Andreas

Pepperdine University

Danielle Endres

University of Utah

Civil and commercial nuclear power production is a material and discursive phenomenon posing theoretical and practical questions warranting further attention by communication scholars. We provide a brief discursive history of nuclear power, followed by a review of scholarship in communication and related disciplines. We then examine five areas for further research: (a) the fragmentation of technocratic and public discourses; (b) regulation and governance; (c) the politics of nuclear waste; (d) critical social movements; and (e) intersections of communication, rhetoric, and nuclear risk. We provide a rationale and foundation for further work in these and other areas related to nuclear power.

The Fukushima Daiichi nuclear disaster, which began in 2011 but continues to unfold, has brought heightened visibility to a topic deserving close attention from communication scholars. Influential theorists and philosophers (e.g., Beck, 1987, 1992; Giddens, 1990; Heidegger, 1977; Luhmann, 1989, 1993) have identified nuclear technologies, both military and non-military, as paradigmatic features of modernity, late modernity, or contemporary "risk society." Some aspects of those technologies receive regular attention in public and scholarly discourses, while others are often regarded as taken-for-granted, common sense features of the present age. For example, Taylor, Kinsella, Depoe, & Metzler (2005, 2007) note that while the scientific and policy dimensions of nuclear weapons are broadly recognized, the ongoing industrial processes of nuclear weapons production are often considered mundane and unremarkable. We argue here that commercial or civilian applications of nuclear energy—designated *nuclear power* in this chapter—also receive comparatively limited attention. Normalized as inevitable products of technological progress, essential for sustaining a growing, energy-intensive society, more than 400 nuclear power plants operate globally. Those plants are manifestations of a larger system in which material and symbolic power are closely intertwined and in need of closer scrutiny.

"Nuclear power" takes multiple forms; it is simultaneously a material phenomenon, a communicative accomplishment, and a discursive resource (Kinsella, 2004a). Throughout this chapter we use the term to denote a range of activities understood as complex sociotechnical and symbolic systems rather than self-contained technologies. We focus on processes related to commercial/ civilian nuclear electricity production, while recognizing their connections with other commonplace activities such as medical and industrial applications, food irradiation, and smoke detection. Our emphasis is on commercial/civilian rather than military uses, but throughout the chapter we note ways in which that boundary is constructed, permeable, and often problematic.

A body of communication-based scholarship on nuclear power does exist, but necessarily spans a range of focal concerns, methodological approaches, and publication venues. Other relevant scholarship exists outside the field, inviting interdisciplinary engagement. No comprehensive guide to these materials exists; thus, our chapter provides an integrative assessment of such work within and beyond the communication discipline, developing a framework to foster more systematic consideration of this consequential topic. We argue throughout that the institutional, political, and material implications of nuclear power are substantial, as are its implications for communication theory and practice. We incorporate concepts from organizational and institutional communication; environmental communication; science, technology, and risk communication; rhetoric of science and technology; political communication; social movements; communication theory; and related disciplines as appropriate. Our purpose is twofold: to use concepts from those fields to illuminate problems and issues (both theoretical and practical) posed by nuclear power, and conversely, to use the case of nuclear power to inform those fields of study.

Nuclear Power as Theoretical Problematic

Nuclear power presents important theoretical questions regarding relationships among materiality, language, and human agency. Rogers (1998) and Kinsella (2007) have argued that through their strongly recalcitrant materiality, nuclear phenomena challenge core concepts of social, rhetorical, and discursive construction, defying both representational and constitutive models of communication. Nevertheless, nuclear phenomena are in important ways linguistic accomplishments, achieved through processes such as naming, constructing categories, and articulating relationships and boundaries. Much of that discursive work happens in institutional settings including basic science, technology development, policy debate, public discourse, governance, and regulation. Thus relationships among the recalcitrant material world, human institutions, and language, as manifested in nuclear discourses, warrant closer attention by communication scholars and can provide important theoretical insights.

Related to this point are questions of *linguistic representation* involving, for example, technical and technocratic discourses, conceptualizations of nuclear processes, and computer modeling and simulation. These modalities enable and constrain what is said, and what can be said, about nuclear phenomena, with implications for scientific knowledge production as well as for the politics of knowledge (Kinsella, 2005, 2007, 2010, 2012; Kuchinskaya, 2011, 2012). Also related are questions of *political representation*: who gets to speak regarding nuclear topics, in what settings, under what conditions, and with what outcomes (Endres, 2009a, 2009b, 2009c, 2012, 2013). Such questions are often framed in terms of a divide between "expert" and "public" communities (Katz & Miller, 1996; Wynne, 1996) or "technical" and "public" rationalities (Goodnight, 1982), involving fundamental issues of democratic process and social justice.

Latour (2004) argues that although technoscientific discourses seek to establish "objects with clear boundaries," or "matters of fact" to be managed by experts on behalf of society, those objects inevitably entail "risky attachments" among "tangled objects" or "matters of concern" demanding broad democratic engagement (pp. 22–25). More broadly, Beck (1995) theorizes a state of "reflexive modernity" in which society's immersion in self-induced risks demands greater systematic reflection to move beyond current conditions of "organized irresponsibility" (p. 58).[1] Nuclear power exemplifies both of these assessments of prevailing social and political conditions, linking theoretical and practical concerns.

Nuclear Power as Sociopolitical Practice

Before the events at Fukushima, nuclear power was receiving considerable attention in public and policy discourses, viewed as a potential, albeit partial response to problems of climate change and energy security. As early as 1982, commentators and proponents envisioned a "nuclear renaissance" in which issues of safety, regulation, economics, and public support would be resolved and the promises of nuclear energy fulfilled (Hileman, 1982; Weinberg, Spiewak, Phung, & Livingston, 1985). During the 1990s the nuclear industry and its allies began a global promotional effort employing tropes such as "nuclear renaissance," "nuclear renewal," and "nuclear new build." That discourse spread beyond the industry, adopted by politicians and even some environmentalists seeking alternatives to greenhouse gas-emitting energy technologies (Bickerstaff, Lorenzoni, Pidgeon, Poortinga, & Simmons, 2008; Sovacool, 2007). Fukushima has posed new challenges to that narrative, although responses have varied across national contexts and the industry has found ways to discount and deflect nuclear safety concerns. Despite those efforts, longstanding questions remain regarding the economics of nuclear power, the intractable problems posed by long-lived and pernicious nuclear wastes, and links between nuclear power and nuclear weapons proliferation. Climate change has not sealed the case for nuclear power, nor has Fukushima sealed the case against it. The arguments persist, warranting closer analyses of nuclear power as a communicative phenomenon and a topic for democratic debate.

Discursive Civilian/Military Boundaries

Although this chapter focuses on commercial/civilian applications, our discussion is informed by the substantial literature regarding communication and nuclear weapons. Bryan Taylor (1998) has provided a valuable review of work in that area, including the "nuclear criticism" program that emerged in the 1980s in response to the clear political significance and existential threat posed by nuclear weapons, and has pursued a rich program of original analysis comprising works and topics too numerous to summarize here. Brummett (1989) identified important themes of entelechy and perfection evident in nuclear weapons discourses, while Kauffman (1989) and Schiappa (1989) examined linguistic practices that establish and sustain hegemonic nuclear symbolism. Taylor, Kinsella, Depoe, & Metzler (2005, 2007) expanded the focus of this literature to include the implications of nuclear weapons production in the United States for organizational, environmental, and political communication. These and other studies inform our present project.

As we indicate throughout this chapter, nuclear rhetors actively work to construct boundaries between military and civilian/commercial applications. Nevertheless, those fields overlap and interact in important ways. Nuclear waste issues involve materials generated by both military and civilian activities, research laboratories conduct both civilian and military projects, antinuclear protest groups often address both dimensions, nuclear technology choices are driven by both (and sometimes competing) military and civilian priorities, "dual-use" technologies can support nuclear power production while providing paths to weapons proliferation, and emerging terrorism concerns affect both military and civilian nuclear operations.

Preview of the Chapter

In our chapter, we address certain perceptions regarding nuclear power that may have established some traction in public discourse and within the communication discipline. First, we argue that although its discursive and material context has changed as issues of energy and climate evolve, nuclear power has not lost significance as a matter of concern for society or for communication scholars. Nuclear power posed important questions before Fukushima provided a "focusing event" (Birkland, 1998) stimulating public attention, and will continue to do so even if attention wanes until the next prominent nuclear event. The high consequences of nuclear failures, the complexity of nuclear regulation and governance discourses, and the recalcitrant materiality of nuclear processes call for sustained, rather than intermittent, attention. Second, we call not for a return to a topic that has already been examined adequately, but for more systematic focus on this persistently important topic. As nuclear power's rhetorical and political-economic situation changes, its internal discourses and institutional strategies evolve; thus, its historical legacies and new discursive innovations both warrant sustained attention. Within the prevailing space constraints we provide a fairly comprehensive inventory of relevant scholarship, mapping its complex terrain and proposing a framework for future research. We write with multiple audiences in mind, including scholars with established interests in the areas examined below and scholars with broader interests (e.g., technology governance more widely; the role of materiality in communication theory). Professionals in the policy community, regulatory institutions, and industry may also find value in our integrative and interdisciplinary assessment.

We begin with a brief history of nuclear power discourses and then synthesize existing scholarship in communication and related fields. We then pursue some material, social, political, environmental, organizational, and policy dimensions of nuclear power, focusing on particular areas of interest viewed as communication processes. Throughout, we argue that "nuclear power" incorporates not only material, organizational, and institutional phenomena related to the production and use of nuclear energy, but also a range of rhetorical and discursive activities that constitute social and political power. Accordingly, we provide programmatic suggestions regarding how communication scholarship can inform nuclear issues, and how studies of nuclear power can inform the communication discipline, suggesting an agenda for continued research guided by our map of the field. Our analysis draws, as well, on the authors' extended engagements with organizations and institutions including nuclear engineering research programs in the United States and Germany, government agencies involved in promoting (U.S. Department of Energy) and regulating (U.S. Nuclear Regulatory Commission) nuclear power, and critical nongovernmental groups. Although we are U.S.-based scholars and most of our work has addressed U.S. settings, we seek to balance U.S. and global perspectives throughout our analysis. While the United States has played a key role in its history, nuclear power has global origins and is best understood as a globalized system. Most recently, the Fukushima disaster has demonstrated the global consequences of particular nuclear events.

Nuclear Power and Nuclear Discourses

> *All nature, then, as self-sustained, consists*
> *Of twain of things: of bodies and of void*
> *In which they're set, and where they're moved around . . .*
> *Name o'er creation with what names thou wilt,*
> *Thou'lt find but properties of those first twain,*
> *Or see but accidents those twain produce.*
> Lucretius, *De Rerum Natura*

Arguably, "nuclear" discourses are prefigured in the teachings of the atomist philosophers, whose models of the material world established still-unresolved questions regarding causality, agency, and relationships between language and reality. Alternatively, the origin of modern nuclear discourse can be located in late 19th and early 20th century physics, with the identification of phenomena such as x-rays and radioactivity and the theoretical explanations that followed, leading to events of profound historical consequence (Kinsella, 2005). Public awareness of nuclear energy's implications expanded dramatically with the Hiroshima and Nagasaki bombings, entangling military and civilian applications in ways that have generated rhetorical boundary work ever since.[2] The physicist Edward Teller, for example, appears to have viewed the "legacy of Hiroshima" primarily as a public relations problem impeding the advancement of nuclear technologies of all kinds (Teller, 1962). Teller's colleague Alvin Weinberg (1985) argued for the "sanctification of Hiroshima," invoking a moral stricture against further violent uses of nuclear energy. As advocates and agents for the promotion of nuclear technologies, both Teller and Weinberg sought to enact a rhetorical boundary between "military" and "peaceful" uses.

The U.S. "Atoms for Peace" program initiated in 1953 (Chernus, 2002; Medhurst, 1987, 1997) pursued three related objectives: (a) to reframe nuclear energy as a beneficial force; (b) to contrast U.S. nuclear undertakings with those of the Soviet Union, thus helping to enroll developing nations into the U.S. camp; and (c) to establish a global market for nuclear technologies. While some nations looked to the United States and the Soviet Union as suppliers of nuclear energy infrastructures, others such as France sought to develop indigenous capacities (Davis, 1987; Hecht, 1998; Zonabend, 1993). Such efforts do not only address energy needs; they also produce symbolic value for nations striving for status as technologically advanced players on the modern world stage (Jasanoff & Kim, 2009). Other nations have deliberately avoided the nuclear power path; as Felt (2013) argues using Austria as an example, this choice can also constitute an explicit national identity.

Nuclear crises[3] including those at the Chalk River research reactor in Canada in 1952 (Mosey, 1990), the Windscale plutonium production reactor in the United Kingdom in 1957 (Wynne, 1982), a commercial reactor at Three Mile Island in the United States in 1979 (Farrell & Goodnight, 1981), and a dual-use reactor at Chernobyl in the Soviet Union in 1986 challenged the program of global nuclear energy development in varied ways across national settings (Balogh, 1991; Flam, 1994; Giugni, 2004; Goldsteen & Schorr, 1991; Joppke, 1993; McCafferty, 1991; Mehta, 2005; Morone & Woodhouse, 1989; Nelkin & Pollak, 1981; Rüdig, 1990; Walker, 2004; Wills, 2006). In Germany, widespread contamination from Chernobyl enhanced the position of the Green Party and contributed to what may be the strongest national-level movement against nuclear power. In the United States, nuclear advocates attributed the events at Chernobyl to a failure-prone Soviet design and to mismanagement by the plant's operators, while a reactor of related design was quietly shut down at the Hanford plutonium production site. While allegations of design flaws and mismanagement at Chernobyl are accurate, they also exemplify a recurrent form of nuclear rhetorical boundary work: the assertion that technical, geographic, institutional, and/or cultural differences preclude disasters in more advanced or more conscientious nations (Kinsella, 2012, 2013). Controversially, the English-language summary of the Japanese Diet's report on the Fukushima disaster (National Diet of Japan, 2012) sustains such exceptionalist claims, suggesting that the failures there were a product of a distinctively Japanese culture of regulatory deference (Juraku, 2013a).

Safety concerns may provide the most dramatic antinuclear arguments, but in many nations the industry's greatest challenges have been economic ones. Although economic and safety issues are often separated rhetorically and administratively (Kinsella, Kelly, & Kittle Autry, 2013), they are intertwined in practice: enhanced safety measures, regulatory scrutiny, and public opposition following safety failures have contributed to ever-increasing budgets for nuclear operations and construction (Cooper, 2012; Schneider & Froggat, 2013). Nevertheless, even before the events at Three Mile Island, numerous project cancellations in the United States were driven primarily by economic and managerial factors (Birkland, 1998; Pope, 2008; Wellock, 1998). With no new domestic plants licensed from 1978 through 2012, the U.S. industry survived by way of exports, research and development contracts, and corporate investments predicated on the rhetoric of a "second nuclear era" made possible by the development of "inherently safe reactors" (Weinberg & Spiewak, 1984; Weinberg et al., 1985).

According to the International Atomic Energy Agency (IAEA), from 1995 through 2012 the number of power reactors operating globally varied between 430 and 441 without demonstrating a pattern of growth.[4] Schneider and Froggat (2013) report that nuclear power's total electricity production reached its historic peak in 2006, although as a share of total global electricity production the peak occurred in 1993 at 17%, declining steadily through 2010 and then more sharply to reach a 10% share in 2012. These statistics challenge the industry's renaissance narrative, which has nevertheless persisted throughout that same time period and declined little (if at all) since the events at Fukushima. Further challenges to the narrative include a reduced rate of energy demand growth attributable to the 2008 global recession, improved energy conservation and efficiency, new extraction techniques that have lowered the costs of natural gas, and technological advances and policy initiatives that strengthen the competitive position of sustainable energy sources such as wind and solar power.

Accordingly, timely questions for further communication research include how the industry works to sustain a narrative of nuclear power as a "common-sense" response to climate change and energy demand, and how critics contest that narrative (Kinsella, 2015). Other questions follow from the events at Fukushima and their potential to affect nuclear programs and practices in terms of cost, safety, regulation, policies, and public acceptance (Hindmarsh, 2013; Kinsella, 2015a). Additional questions involve the nuclear power discourses of nations such as China (Xu, 2010) and India (Mathai, 2013; Ramana, 2013), where expanding populations, increasing per capita energy consumption, and efforts to reduce dependence on fossil fuels drive ambitious nuclear agendas, and the Republic of Korea, which seeks to become a global nuclear technology provider (Sovacool, 2010).

Research Approaches to Nuclear Power Communication

With this brief and partial discursive history in place, we now identify some approaches that scholars in communication and cognate fields have applied to topics related to nuclear power. Our inventory is selective rather than exhaustive, focusing on examples from within the communication discipline as well as related work of direct significance for the discipline. Our review demonstrates that although there has been communication-focused scholarship on nuclear power, it is broadly distributed and variegated. By identifying and categorizing this work we provide a resource for a more sustained and integrated research program as outlined later in this chapter. Following Latour (2004), we regard the following six areas as comprising a field of tangled objects, risky attachments, and matters of public concern imbricating questions of materiality, discourse, agency, and democratic governance.

Media Representations, Popular Culture, and Public Opinion

Media attention to nuclear power has often been driven by high-profile crises that punctuate its history (Friedman, 1981, 2011; Friedman, Gorney, & Egolf, 1987; Rosa & Dunlap, 1994; Rubin, 1987). Media studies following the Chernobyl disaster highlighted the implications of message content for the safety of local residents (Gale, 1987) and for political debates informed by the event (Young & Launer, 1991). In the U.S. context, Gamson and Modigliani (1989) conducted an influential study of media framings of nuclear power, cited widely by scholars applying framing theory across multiple topical areas. However, Mazur (1990) argued that for both nuclear power and chemical hazards, "intensity and volume of reporting" affect public attitudes more strongly than "what is reported about the topic" (p. 295). Further research can help disentangle the relative effects of quantity and content of reporting, while updating the literature in light of the changing context for nuclear power.

Examining the rhetoric of government and industry proponents, Gwin (1990) argued that systematic understatements of risks and overstatements of the promises of nuclear power fostered a "promotional heritage" that continues to inform public and institutional discourses (cf. Cohn, 1997). Mechling and Mechling (1995) and Nadel (1995) recount how the atom was domesticated and its material and political hazards rhetorically contained through popular culture artifacts such as novels, films, music, and television programs, while Boyer (1985), Henriksen (1997), Lynch (2012), Weart (1988, 2012) and Winkler (1993) highlight the cultural mediation of persistent nuclear anxieties. In the U.K. context, Bickerstaff et al. (2008), Doyle (2011), and Pidgeon, Lorenzoni, and Poortinga (2008) have examined more recent reframings of nuclear power as a response to climate change and their effects on public opinion.

These studies address varied ways in which society makes sense of complex nuclear technologies, while producing the discursive and normative framework for their continued evolution. To extend and contemporize this scholarship, we offer four areas for further research reflecting the changing context for nuclear power. The discursive links between climate change and nuclear power provide a particularly timely exigence for further communication scholarship, including cross-national comparisons. Another exigence is the opportunity to utilize earlier scholarship as a foundation for further longitudinal studies charting changing trends in media reporting, popular culture representations, and public opinion. A third, related exigence involves the still-evolving effects of the Fukushima disaster, and a fourth is the emergence of online media as pervasive communication venues enabling timely but volatile public discussions (Binder, 2012; Friedman, 2011; Ionescu, 2012; Kittle Autry & Kelly, 2012). Together, these four research trajectories can provide valuable insights regarding the intersections among complex technologies, evolving media systems, and public discourses in contemporary risk society.

Social Movements

Social movements provide a counterpoint to the global promotion of nuclear power, and cross-national comparisons are of particular interest (Flam, 1994; Nelkin & Pollak, 1981; Rüdig, 1990). Germany may provide the strongest case of public protest, wherein the influential Green Party has consistently and strategically incorporated opposition to both military and civilian nuclear technologies into its political identity, gaining strength from that emphasis (Hunold, 2001; Joppke, 1993). German protesters often interrupt nuclear fuel and waste shipments, have aggressively blocked efforts to create a permanent waste repository (Hocke & Renn, 2009), and have clashed violently with police on multiple occasions. U.S. opposition to nuclear power has been less widespread and less dramatic, enacted more by groups with particular concerns (including concerns related to specific facilities) in a climate of ambivalent public opinion and limited attention rather than broad national sentiment. U.S. nuclear opponents have also linked concerns about nuclear weapons with concerns about nuclear power, challenging entrenched rhetorical boundaries, but have generally placed less emphasis on those connections.

   Globally, opponents' rhetorical foci include risks of catastrophic plant failures and ongoing low-level emissions (Mehta, 2005, in Canada; Morone & Woodhouse, 1989, in the United States), facility siting (Aldrich, 2008, comparing Japan and the United States), uranium mining (Banjeree, 2000, in India; Falk, Green, & Mudd, 2006, in Australia), nuclear waste disposal (Johnson, 2008, in Canada), environmental justice (Fan, 2006a, 2006b, in Taiwan), regulatory policy and practice (Duffy, 1997, in the United States), nuclear power economics (Cooper, 2012; Pope, 2008, in the United States; Ramana, 2013, in India), and relationships between nuclear power and nuclear weapons proliferation. Focusing events such as those at Three Mile Island, Chernobyl, and Fukushima have highlighted nuclear risks and mobilized opposition (Birkland, 1998; Friedman, 2011; Friedman, Gorney, & Egolf, 1987). Further communication-focused

studies can facilitate more detailed comparisons across national, political, historical, and media contexts.

Nuclear Discourses, Master Themes, and Foundational Premises

A distinctively modern phenomenon, nuclear power articulates discursive
themes including material and social progress, technological creativity and
entelechy, international development, political power, national identity, technocratic rationality, prosperity, consumerism, and the common good (Cohn, 1997;
Felt, 2013, Hecht, 1998; Jasanoff & Kim, 2009; Mathai, 2013; Mechling &
Mechling, 1995; Welsh, 2000). Hecht (2003, 2012) uses the term *nuclearity*
to map the postcolonial geographic and political hegemony of this discursive
constellation, addressing questions of global environmental and social justice.
Kinsella (2005, 2007) has examined four "master themes"—mystery, potency,
secrecy, and entelechy—linked across the military and nuclear power domains,
and the environmental, social, and political consequences of nuclear discourses,
while Kinsella et al. (2013) have explored the role of rhetorical boundary work
in sustaining the nuclear power enterprise.

A related foundational theme is the material and discursive formation
described as *nuclear colonialism* (Endres, 2009a, 2009b; Kuletz, 1998; LaDuke,
1999). This term addresses global patterns of relationship, manifested differently across geographic contexts but similar in their consequences, wherein
indigenous peoples suffer disproportionate negative effects from the development of military and civilian nuclear technologies. Endres (2009a) observes
that discussions about nuclear power often disregard the "cradle" (uranium
mining) and "grave" (waste disposal) of the nuclear fuel cycle, which affect
indigenous people in Australia, Canada, India, Taiwan, the United States, and
several African nations. Communication scholarship has begun to identify
discursive strategies that sustain nuclear colonialism and to reveal linkages
between its material and discursive elements. Future research could investigate
nuclear colonialism as a broader phenomenon affecting not only indigenous
people, but also other marginalized communities including populations living
close to nuclear facilities and temporary workers not protected by radiation
exposure controls (Caulfield, 1989; Jobin, 2012; Parkhill, Henwood, Pidgeon, & Simmons, 2011; Zonabend, 1993). Further, lessons regarding nuclear
colonialism can be brought into conversation with research on other forms of
resource colonialism such as mining practices and oil and gas extraction.

Democratic Discourse, Public Participation, and
Environmental and Social Justice

Communication scholarship also addresses the implications of nuclear power
for democratic institutional practice. One line of research examines public
participation in decision-making about nuclear power and nuclear waste (Besley, 2010, 2012; Clarke, 2010; Endres, 2009c; Johnson, 2008; Kinsella, 2016;

Kinsella et al., 2013; Ratliff; 1997). In most national settings, all phases of nuclear power production are regulated by public agencies; thus, proposals for new plants, nuclear waste storage and disposal facilities, and other changes to the status quo often trigger mandated public engagement processes. Following broader environmental communication research that indicts institutionalized processes for their lack of genuine opportunities for public influence (e.g., Depoe, Delicath, & Elsenbeer, 2004), analyses of the process for the proposed U.S. high-level nuclear waste repository at Yucca Mountain have revealed numerous anti-democratic aspects (Endres, 2009b, 2009c, 2012; Ratliff, 1997). Although these studies have primarily examined official processes, less formal modes of public engagement such as social movement activism, public protest, and performative and visual rhetoric also warrant further attention (Nelkin & Pollak, 1981; Peeples, 2011; Taylor, 1997).

Related research highlights the environmental justice implications of nuclear power including questions of argumentative strategies, rhetorical inclusion and exclusion, and institutional transparency. Nuclear facilities are often located in marginalized spaces (Hevly & Findlay, 1998), as in the case of a plant adjacent to the Prairie Island Indian Community in the United States. Juraku (2013b) argues that the "nuclear village" model in Japan, exemplified by the "concentrated siting" of ten reactors at Fukushima Daichi and Daini, encourages communities with limited economic opportunities to accept risks that more affluent communities can avoid. Fan (2006a, 2006b) examines the controversy surrounding a nuclear waste facility in Taiwan, located in the homeland of the aboriginal Yami tribe. Focusing on the dispute over storing high-level nuclear waste on the Skull Valley Goshute Reservation in the United States, Clarke (2010) examines the mutually constitutive relationship between materialities and discourses, while Fried and Eyles (2011) and Peeples, Krannich, and Weiss (2008) demonstrate the complexity of defining what constitutes environmental injustice in cases where marginalized communities actively seek opportunities to store nuclear and other toxic wastes. Questions of environmental justice in nuclear power contexts present a range of discursive/material practices embroiled with larger discourses of energy, environment, community identity, security, sacrifice, and climate change (Banjeree, 2000; Grinde & Johansen, 1995; Hecht, 2003; Hoffman, 2001; Kuletz, 1998; Sze, 2005). Collectively, these studies illuminate multiple forms of democratic engagement in nuclear power contexts. Further research can move beyond individual case studies to develop comparative and integrative findings of value not only in the nuclear power domain, but across a range of risky technology governance settings.

Communication, Risk, and Expert versus Public Knowledge

Beck (1992) argues that society is now characterized by problems of equitable risk distribution, accompanying and often superseding traditional problems of resource distribution, and that the construct of risk provides "a systematic way of dealing with hazards and insecurities induced and introduced by modernization itself" (p. 21). Nuclear power provides a paradigmatic example: enacted as a solution to problems of energy supply, the technology has generated new risks demanding constant vigilance and democratic decision-making. Nevertheless, democratic discourse is often short-circuited by approaches to defining, assessing, and managing risk that privilege technocratic rationality and disregard broader forms of public engagement.

In the U.S. context, Farrell and Goodnight (1981) examine the role of communication failures at Three Mile Island, identifying implications of technocratic rationality for nuclear safety, crisis management, and public trust, while Goodnight (1982) addresses the fragmentation of "personal, technical, and public" discourse fields and the domination of the technical frame in domains such as nuclear power. Katz and Miller (1996) examine a controversy surrounding a proposed low-level nuclear waste facility, concluding that decision makers maintained a "contemptuous" view of community members' capacities to engage with the issues at stake. Miller (2003) argues that a landmark nuclear safety analysis informing regulatory policy (USNRC, 1975) relied on presumptions of technical authority and tacit professional judgments, emphasizing ethos over logos while purporting to demonstrate the latter.

These rhetorically-grounded critiques resonate with arguments made in the literature on public understanding of science, challenging a "deficit model" of public understanding that presumes "scientific *suf*ficiency and public *de*ficiency" (Gross, 1994, p. 6; cf. Sturgis & Allum, 2004). In the European context, Renn (1992, 2008) provides a typology of approaches to risk, including but extending beyond technocratic frameworks, and offers a more complex model of risk governance aligned with approaches influential in the European Union. Horlick-Jones (2005) emphasizes the role of "informal logics of risk" and practical modes of reasoning as complements to technical rationality. Across national settings but playing out differently in varied political and cultural contexts, vernacular knowledge provided by non-experts can challenge and recontextualize technocratic reasoning (Endres, 2009c; Kinsella, 2004b, 2012; Kinsella & Mullen, 2007; Kinsella et al., 2013; Kuchinskaya, 2011; Wynne, 1991, 1996). Such studies suggest possibilities for new grammars, vocabularies, and forms of democratic engagement for the governance of risky technologies.

Organizational and Institutional Communication

Nuclear power is a complex sociotechnical activity enacted through nongovernmental and governmental organizations and institutions including electric utility providers; equipment vendors; engineering and construction firms; financial, investment, and insurance organizations; regulatory agencies; academic, commercial, and governmental research and development organizations; and myriad technical, legal, and managerial consulting organizations. The roles and relationships among these entities vary across national settings. For example, German nuclear safety regulation emphasizes a partnership of federal and state-level authorities with substantial involvement by independent "technical service organizations," while the U.S. system is more centralized and incorporates a greater degree of industry self-regulation (Kinsella, 2011). Frameworks for nuclear power plant financing, ownership, and management vary from fully privatized, to hybrid, to fully state-controlled. International nongovernmental organizations, particularly the International Atomic Energy Agency and various United Nations working groups, coordinate regulatory standards and organizational practices but are constrained by expectations of national sovereignty. Industry-based groups play important roles facilitating autonomous self-regulation (e.g., World Association of Nuclear Operators, and in the United States, Institute for Nuclear Power Operations) and policy advocacy (e.g., World Nuclear Association, and in the United States, Nuclear Energy Institute). These complex inter-organizational relationships involve blurred boundaries between civilian and military applications, exemplified by the IAEA's dual promotional and regulatory missions and the regular flow of U.S. nuclear naval personnel to the civilian nuclear workforce and U.S. Nuclear Regulatory Commission (USNRC).

The challenges of nuclear safety have provoked much theorizing about organizational practices in high-risk contexts. The Three Mile Island failure inspired two influential streams of thought: normal accident theory and high reliability theory (Rijpma, 1997). Normal accident theory, originated by Charles Perrow (1984/1999), argues that nuclear power plant safety cannot be guaranteed by human organizations, which cannot match the systems' complexity and anticipate all possible failures. Tight subsystem coupling, potential failure combinations, and potentially rapid accident progression led Perrow to conceptualize "normal accidents" as inevitable consequences of complex but pervasive technologies such as nuclear power.

In contrast, high-reliability organizations theory (HRO) proposes that certain organizational practices, such as "collective mindfulness," match organizational and technological complexity, helping to prevent failure and enabling recovery from small failures (Bourrier, 2011; Weick & Sutcliff, 2007). HRO research has examined the "negotiated order" of safe and reliable performance at a nuclear power plant (Schulman, 1993) and organizational learning following non-catastrophic failures (Perin, 2006). Organizational communication scholars have studied how teams of nuclear inspectors make sense of ambiguous information (Barbour & Gill, 2013), and have extended HRO theory to other high-risk domains. Normal accident theory and HRO theory are complementary: one emphasizes the unforgiving demands of nuclear technologies, while the other addresses the organizational and individual vigilance necessary to prevent or minimize failures.

The Chernobyl disaster provoked a "safety culture" discourse that circulates within the nuclear industry and regulatory agencies (Myers, 2005; Silbey, 2009). The IAEA defines safety culture by emphasizing organizational factors and individual attitudes that establish safety as an overriding priority (International Nuclear Safety Advisory Group, 1988), devoting considerable efforts to policies and standards and more recently, questions of "security culture" related to sabotage and terrorism threats. Those efforts inform the regulatory oversight activities of all nations with civilian nuclear power, and have inspired quantitative and qualitative research to assess the safety culture construct at plants in Brazil, Denmark, Finland, Spain, Sweden, and the United States (Branch & Olson, 2011; Carvalho, dos Santos, Gomes, & Borges, 2008; Mariscal, Herrero, & Toca Otero, 2012; Navarro, Garcia Lerín, Tomás, & Pieró Silla, 2013; Reiman, Oedewald, & Rollenhagen, 2005).

Although the organizational communication literature has not focused directly on nuclear power plant safety culture, it offers insights that complicate prevailing practices such as technically-focused safety audits, and challenge approaches to organizational culture that privilege managerial imperatives over other outcomes. This scholarship is especially relevant for the nuclear industry, which perpetually struggles with inherent tensions between profit and safety. For example, a day of lost electricity production can cost a U.S. nuclear utility approximately $1 million; thus, decisions regarding reactor shutdowns in response to ambiguous risk indicators can pit safety culture expectations against production expectations (Hausman, 2013; Perin, 2006). These complex tensions provide rich theoretical terrain for further exploration. Nuclear power poses stark but subtle questions regarding the limits of human agency and control, democratic risk governance, and the co-constitutive relationships among high-risk materialities, political-economic structures, and organizational discourses.

Focal Areas for Further Communication Research

We now revisit some of the topics introduced above and consider additional related topics, identifying areas of particular interest for further communication scholarship. All the areas discussed so far invite further development, and the selections made here partly reflect our own research interests and ongoing projects. These areas, and those outlined above, are best seen as overlapping, mutually constitutive, and particularly suited for interdisciplinary scholarship to which communication and rhetoric can make substantial contributions.

Explicating Material and Discursive Entanglements

Technical and policy discussions regarding nuclear energy often begin with a sketch of the "nuclear fuel cycle," involving uranium mining and milling; chemical conversion; enrichment; another chemical conversion followed by reactor fuel fabrication; irradiation of fuel in reactor cores to produce energy; and removal, cooling, storage, and (ideally) disposal of highly radioactive "used" or "spent" nuclear fuel.[5] Some nations engage in reprocessing, extracting plutonium from used fuel for use in further cycles of energy generation, while others have chosen to avoid reprocessing due to nuclear weapons proliferation risks.

Such discussions may effectively describe the material aspects of nuclear energy production, but they disregard its complex institutional, political, social, and discursive aspects. Although the process is described as a "cycle," suggesting movement through a series of stages and eventual closure, it is actually a set of processes that are rhetorically and institutionally separated but practically intertwined. For example, reactor design decisions affect uranium enrichment requirements and implications for proliferation of weapons-grade materials (plutonium and highly-enriched uranium), choices between permanent disposal and used fuel reprocessing affect reactor design choices and proliferation potentials, and on-site storage of used fuel complicates nuclear plant operations and economics. The social and discursive aspects of nuclear energy production are neither separable nor self-contained; they are complex, interconnected, recursive, and always negotiated. Further, each stage of the fuel cycle involves regular or potential releases of radiological materials into the environment: uranium mill tailings threaten workers and local communities, ongoing reactor operations can involve unintended leaks, reprocessing produces large volumes of high-level liquid nuclear wastes, and catastrophic failures of containment present ongoing risks across the fuel cycle.

We now identify five broad areas in which nuclear power exemplifies those conditions, where approaches grounded in communication, discourse, and rhetoric can contribute to more democratic outcomes by (a) overcoming the fragmentation of technical and public discourses, (b) enhancing the vision of nuclear regulatory institutions, (c) addressing the intractable problems associated with the politics of nuclear waste, (d) illuminating the place of protest and critical social movements in nuclear power debates, and (e) explicating the intersections of rhetoric, communication, and understandings of nuclear risk.

Fragmented Discourses of Nuclear Power

Contrasting with technocratic discourses emphasizing probabilities and cost/benefit calculations, society appears to seek more definitive answers to questions of nuclear risk and safety. The quest for such answers often leads to debates characterized by the rhetorical strategy of extreme case formulation (Pomerantz, 1986), a preference to articulate extreme cases rather than more complex arguments. Such tendencies strip nuclear power issues of the rhetorical richness and technical nuance warranted by such a complex and consequential technology (Weart, 1988). Approaches including issue framing (Lewicki, Gray, & Elliot, 2003), collaborative learning (Daniels & Walker, 2001), and moral conflict (Littlejohn & Cole, 2013; Pearce & Littlejohn, 1997) can help to address the intractability of nuclear debates, reclaiming their potential richness.

Although achieving a richer public debate is challenging, opportunities are seen in the nuanced communication within particular communities concerned with nuclear risks. For example, while promotional industry rhetoric consistently claims that "nuclear power is safe," technical experts can be uncomfortable with such absolute statements. Occupationally obsessed with safety, nuclear professionals often prefer to speak of it as an ongoing process or to use adverbial forms such as "nuclear power can be managed safely." Meanwhile, local communities living with nuclear risks often use discursive strategies such as humor to save face and avoid dwelling unproductively on potential consequences (Parkhill et al., 2011; Zonabend, 1993). Such subtleties of in-group communication rarely appear in public discourses, one marker of the differentiation of personal, technical, and public argument spheres (Goodnight, 1982). Nevertheless the potential exists for overcoming such barriers, and public dialogue scholarship seeks to design communication strategies that embrace differences and address tensions productively (Barge & Andreas, 2013).

Nuclear Regulation: National and Global Challenges

Nuclear power regulation encompasses and engages with multiple discourses including law, administration, politics, engineering, science, risk, economics and finance, probability, cost/benefit analysis, ecology, and antinuclear critique. These discourses are often fragmented, incommensurable, and separated rhetorically by actors for strategic purposes (Kinsella et al., 2013), often operating in tension with the materialities of nuclear safety. National-level regulatory frameworks are informed by diverse historical, cultural, and political influences (Pool, 1997). The legitimacy of regulatory agencies is affected by public evaluations of independence versus "capture" by the regulated industry (Laffont & Tirole, 1991) or "recreancy," understood as " the failure of institutional actors to carry out their responsibilities with the degree of vigor necessary to merit the societal trust they enjoy" (Freudenburg, 1993, p. 909).

Due to its historical precedence and global influence, the U.S. system is of particular interest. The U.S. Atomic Energy Commission was created in 1946 with an emphasis on weapons technologies, accompanied by a statement that "the development and utilization of atomic energy should be directed toward improving the public welfare" (quoted in Pool, 1997, p. 70). Accordingly, the 1954 Atomic Energy Act expanded the institution's activities to include developing, licensing, and regulating reactors for commercial electricity generation. The conflicting mandate to both promote and regulate nuclear technologies ultimately led to a legitimation crisis, and in 1974 the missions were separated, with the USNRC inheriting the regulatory mission and an agency that would become the U.S. Department of Energy inheriting the promotional mission (Walker, 1984, 1992; Walker & Wellock, 2010). The French system, by comparison, does not emphasize boundaries between promotion and regulation and legitimizes more direct cooperation between private industry and government in the development, operation, and oversight of nuclear power systems (Davis, 1987; Hecht, 1998). Most recently, Japan has moved closer to the U.S. model by separating promotional and regulatory activities in response to the events at Fukushima.

In the U.S. case the federal government granted permission, in principle, for nuclear power generation with little public deliberation, enabling the development of technologies and regulatory structures while limiting democratic dialogue. For example, the USNRC's statutory mandate authorizes nuclear safety regulation without encompassing the fundamental question of whether nuclear facilities should exist; thus, the technical-legal discourse constituting licensing and oversight processes provides no basis for denying licenses in response to general objections to nuclear power raised by communities or nongovernmental groups. Nevertheless, several public controversies influenced the evolving shape of U.S. regulations: concerns about fallout from atmospheric weapons tests, debates regarding the cumulative impacts of low radiation doses, uncertainties about the effectiveness of nuclear power plant safety systems, and concerns about the consequences of severe failures (Walker, 1992, 2000). Failures at facilities, including Three Mile Island, Chernobyl, and Fukushima, have periodically forced U.S. and international regulators to reevaluate their policies and processes.

Across national contexts, questions of legitimacy and voice are crucial to the activities of regulatory rule-making, facility licensing, and ongoing oversight (Barbour & Gill, 2013; Besley, 2010, 2012; Perin, 2006). Further research can more fully illuminate processes that build, maintain, and challenge public trust and the legitimacy of regulatory institutions; relations between those institutions and the nuclear industry; and relations between regulators and nuclear critics.

Nuclear Waste and Public Deliberation

The material and discursive aspects of managing nuclear wastes are consequential and intertwined. In the United States, for example, nuclear wastes are classified using categories including "low-level waste," "high-level waste," "waste incidental to reprocessing," and "uranium mill tailings," confounding radiological criteria (low vs. high radioactivity) with criteria based on origin (mill tailings, reprocessing). Critics often challenge these categories and their implications for the institutional status, regulation, and disposition of particular materials. One such critique asserts that the "incidental to reprocessing" category provides an institutional space for dealing with what is, in effect, high level-waste at lower levels of regulatory scrutiny (Makhijani & Saleska, 1992). As in the case of "spent" or "depleted" reactor fuel, which is in fact more hazardous than unused fuel, official terminology often understates risks posed to nuclear workers and communities.[6] Parallel controversies prevail in other national contexts.

Disputes regarding how, and where, to store or dispose of nuclear waste provide some of the most salient topics for further research (Clarke, 2010; Dawson & Darst, 2006; Endres, 2009a, 2009b, 2009c, 2012, 2013; Fan, 2006a, 2006b; Gerrard, 1996; Gowda & Easterling, 1998; Greenberg, 2013; Hoffmann, 2001; Johnson, 2008; Katz & Miller, 1996; Kinsella, 2016; Lidskog & Sundqvist, 2004; Macfarlane, 2011; Peterson, 2001; Ratliff, 1997). These controversies not only highlight interrelationships between discursive and material aspects of nuclear power, but also provide valuable case studies of deliberative democracy, public participation in environmental decision-making, "not-in-my-back-yard" reactions, and environmental justice concerns regarding disproportionately affected communities. In the U.S. context, much interdisciplinary scholarship has addressed the social, political and cultural considerations surrounding siting a proposed high-level waste facility (Easterling & Kunreuther, 1995; Jacob, 1990; Macfarlane & Ewing, 2006; Shrader-Frechette, 1993; Vandenbosch & Vandenbosch, 2007; Walker, 2009). Within communication studies, Endres (2009a, 2009b, 2009c, 2012, 2013) highlights the importance of rhetorical strategies in those controversies.

Waste siting challenges remain problematic for every nation engaged in nuclear power production, posing health and safety risks for communities and international weapons proliferation risks related to plutonium contained in used fuel. In addition to their material risks, nuclear wastes present particular symbolic power as mysterious, potent, and enduring threats that still await solutions. Questions of temporality further complicate problems of equity, democratic process, and divergent cultural understandings of these products of reflexive modernity.

Social Movements and Social Meanings

Activist critics of nuclear power demonstrate classic social movement characteristics including shared identification, moral rhetorics, and long-term commitments to opposition. Nevertheless, the interests, positions, and rhetorical strategies of critics vary within and across national settings, warranting further national-level, comparative, and global studies of opposition to nuclear power. One approach views social movements from a discursive perspective, as evolving systems of meaning interacting with larger social contexts (DeLuca, 1999; Kinsella, 2015; McGee, 1980).

Nuclear power issues have informed the environmental movement's organizational tensions and strategic positions about energy sources. In one U.S. case, in the 1960s the California Sierra Club focused on resisting dam construction and preserving the Pismo Sand Dunes, leading the group to support a nuclear power project at Diablo Canyon. The organization's resulting internal conflict shaped early arguments against nuclear power and split the Sierra Club, with the strongest nuclear opponents forming Friends of the Earth (Wellock, 1998; Wills, 2006). This debate is now echoed as claims regarding the value of nuclear power for addressing climate change complicate oppositional discourses, with a small number of environmental organizations, antinuclear organizations, and opinion leaders reconsidering their opposition.

Another feature of the antinuclear movement is its challenge to the patriarchal foundations of the nuclear power enterprise. Petra Kelly (1994), a much-revered founder of the German Green Party, linked feminist and environmentalist themes that continue to inform a particularly strong national-level antinuclear movement. Markovits and Klaver (2012) cite "ecology, feminism and women, peace and pacifism," and an emphasis on "democracy from below" as the "four pillars defining [German] Green identity" (p. 17). In the United States, the antinuclear organization Mothers for Peace utilized ecofeminist themes to protest the Diablo Canyon reactor project in the late 1960s (Wills, 2006). The group's rhetorical tactics challenged masculinist ideologies characterizing the public hearing practices of the Atomic Energy Commission, and later the USNRC, putting a nurturing face on nuclear power concerns. The influential Australian antinuclear activist Helen Caldicott (2006) has stressed similar themes, articulating them with her professional ethos as a pediatric physician.

Aspects of "public expertise" (Kinsella, 2004b; Kinsella & Mullen, 2007) add another characteristic dimension to antinuclear activism. Groups including Mothers for Peace and Friends of the Earth have developed their own technical and legal proficiencies as needed for engaging with the esoteric details and technocratic policy processes associated with nuclear issues. Nuclear opponents receive further support from organizations that supply both technical capacity and scientific authority, such as the U.S.-based Union of Concerned Scientists and the German-based Öko-Institut. Most recently, new media, open-source, and "do-it-yourself" (DIY) tools have facilitated emerging citizen science initiatives and collaborations linking technical specialists, grassroots activists, and "maker" communities responding to the Fukushima disaster (Kelly & Miller, in press; Kera, Rod, & Peterova, 2013; Morita, Blok, & Kimura, 2013). New media applications constitute an important emerging nexus of democratic engagement, knowledge production, and evolving forms of expertise.

Risk Analysis, Risk Representation, and Risk Communication

Questions of risk circulate prominently both in theories of contemporary society (Beck, 1992, 1995; Luhmann, 1989, 1993) and in public, regulatory, and industry nuclear discourses. In regulatory and industry contexts such questions are largely operationalized through concepts of risk analysis, which simultaneously inform and exist in tension with concepts of risk communication. The practice of risk analysis has ancient roots (Covello & Mumpower, 1985), but has assumed a fundamental role in contemporary technocratic discourses. An approach known as probabilistic risk analysis, widely utilized in nuclear power contexts, seeks to quantify the probability of events such as damage to the core of a distressed reactor, a particularly hazardous scenario for radiological releases. The USNRC's 1975 Reactor Safety Study pioneered this approach, producing the mathematical conclusion that the risk of fatality from a nuclear power plant failure was less than one in a million per reactor per year (USNRC, 1975). The study's controversial executive summary argued that nuclear power plants were safe compared to other risks such as automobile transportation and lightning strikes. Responding to intense objections noting the qualitative differences obscured by such analogies, the USNRC withdrew its support of the executive summary, coincidentally months before the events at Three Mile Island (Keller & Modarres, 2004). This coincidence publicly highlighted the difficulties of assessing theoretical probabilities in contrast with the realities of an event that actually occurred. The events at Fukushima have again demonstrated the limits of representation associated with efforts to reliably quantify nuclear risks (Kinsella, 2012; Paté-Cornell, 2012).

Probabilistic numbers can play a range of roles in sense-making and decision-making about complex reactor systems and other nuclear hazards. Parties making decisions and judgments about risk often focus on the analytical result, a specific numerical probability, either to support or discredit it. Technical specialists often focus instead on the analytical process and operational insights provided by the models and calculations that produce the final number. For example, the U.S. nuclear industry uses probabilistic risk analysis to understand day-to-day plant operations and diagnose risks that need the most attention, while the USNRC uses "risk-informed regulation" principles to guide its oversight activities (Keller & Modarres, 2004; Siu & Collins, 2008). Public understandings of risk often diverge from such institutional understandings, contributing to mutual incomprehension and undermining legitimacy and trust in regulatory processes (Poortinga & Pidgeon, 2003).

Within this larger problematic, scientific and policy questions regarding the concept of "permissible radiation dose" evoke particular issues of communication and rhetoric (Walker, 2000). Technocratic approaches typically assume that some level of radiation exposure beyond "natural background levels" can be considered acceptable, contrasting with the intuitions and embodied narratives of individuals (Kinsella & Mullen, 2007; Lynch, 2012).[7] One example involves the material/discursive tension that nuclear power plant workers face when participating in radiation protection programs. While institutional discourses assert that risks are managed safely, workers' individual dosimeters and safety badges provide direct material evidence of ever-accumulating exposures. Ambiguous workplace exposure standards such as "as low as reasonably achievable," and implicit incentives to under-report doses to retain risky job assignments at higher pay rates, produce paradoxical conditions for many nuclear workers (Jobin, 2012).[8]

More broadly, technical debates regarding setting radiation standards in the face of scientific uncertainty have fundamental communicative dimensions (Walker, 2000). Social scientific research indicates that positions taken in these debates are often informed more by institutional and political factors than by scientific evidence (Silva, Jenkins-Smith, & Barke, 2007). Such findings can be illuminated further by recognizing the multivocality of scientific rhetoric and the complexity of interdisciplinary communication (Thompson, 2009). Public concerns about radiation exposure are especially potent (Weart, 1988), warranting closer examination of the technical and scientific discourses that legitimate policy decisions and institutional practices regarding radiation standards and exposures.

Conclusion: Communication Scholarship and Nuclear Power

The five areas sketched in the previous section represent topics of particular interest for continuing communication scholarship. The research mapped in this chapter provides a strong theoretical and empirical foundation for further work within and beyond the areas we have identified. We expect that communication scholars across a range of methodological traditions and analytical foci can recognize other topics of interest suggested by the map we have provided.

Although the scope of our review has been fairly broad, it remains partial. One topic we have deferred for later attention is a teleological narrative that has persisted throughout the history of nuclear power, promising that "next generation" technologies will overcome the concerns associated with current technologies (e.g., Weinberg & Spiewak, 1984). Rhetorical visions regarding "small modular reactors," "traveling wave reactors," thorium-fueled reactors, nuclear fusion, and other speculative technologies sustain present versions of that narrative. Another topic we have not addressed in detail is the contested rhetorical separation of commercial and military nuclear applications, especially in relation to issues of technology transfer, used fuel reprocessing, and the ambitions of emerging and prospective nuclear power nations. A third area warranting closer examination is the relationship between nuclear power and other nuclear energy applications in industry and medicine, which are less controversial and help to legitimate the larger nuclear power enterprise, but nevertheless pose their own risks and policy challenges. A fourth area concerns the temporality of nuclear phenomena, simultaneously far faster than timescales for human consciousness and action (as in the case of rapid fault progression in reactor systems), and far slower (as in the multi-millennial lifetimes of hazardous nuclear wastes). The relationships among temporality, human agency, and nuclear materialities pose significant challenges for communication theory.

Nuclear power involves a complex discursive terrain encompassing competing promotional and oppositional narratives; ambiguous relationships to problems of climate change and energy security; varied forms of negotiation and rhetorical boundary work; fragmented and often-incommensurable discourses and forms of knowledge; and organizational, institutional, and political challenges related to managing and governing a high-risk technology. All of these areas provide crucial sites for further communication research. Such scholarship can advance communication theory and practice by interrogating relationships among materialities, discourses, and agency, and at the same time, engage across disciplines to address urgent problems of energy, environment, technology governance, and democratic process.

Notes

1. In an interview with a Japanese newspaper (Ohno, 2011), Beck applied the organized irresponsibility concept directly to the Fukushima disaster. Following the onset of the disaster the German government's Ethics Commission for a Safe

Energy Supply (*Ethik-Kommission Sichere Energieversorgung*), on which Beck
served, recommended ending nuclear power production.

2. Regarding sociological and rhetorical boundary work see Gieryn (1983, 1995)
    and Taylor (1996). For boundary work and "discursive containment" in nuclear
    contexts, see Kinsella (2001), Kinsella and Mullen (2007), and Kinsella, Kelly,
    and Kittle Autry (2013).

3. Disagreement exists regarding how to characterize nuclear "crises," "accidents,"
    "incidents," "events," "failures," or "disasters," but recognizing the inherent risks
    of nuclear technologies we choose to avoid the term "accident." One widely-
    used criterion for a serious nuclear failure is reactor "core damage," also known
    as full or partial "meltdown." To date, eleven such instances are generally rec-
    ognized. Broader lists of nuclear failures (e.g., Rogers, 2011) cite more than
    thirty significant events and additional "near-misses." The International Atomic
    Energy Agency's International Nuclear and Radiological Events Scale, widely
    cited since the Fukushima disaster, includes events beyond core damage but
    relies heavily on geographic extent and number of people affected as indicators
    of severity.

4. Statistics from IAEA Power Reactor Information System, www.iaea.org/PRIS/.

5. Critics often challenge the institutional use of the term "spent fuel," arguing that
    it normalizes and downplays the associated radiological hazards.

6. Further compounding terminological confusions, "depleted" reactor fuel differs
    from "depleted uranium," a byproduct of uranium enrichment used controver-
    sially in ordnance. Nuclear insiders internalize such distinctions and find them
    unproblematic, but they pose barriers for other stakeholders.

7. The concept of natural background level is itself problematic, as it ambiguously
    addresses components such as fallout from weapons tests and exposures from
    medical diagnostic procedures.

8. See www.nrc.gov/reading-rm/basic-ref/glossary/alara.html and http://hps.org/
    publicinformation/radterms/radfact1.html

References

Aldrich, D. P. (2008). *Site fights: Divisive facilities and civil society in Japan and the
    West*. Ithaca, NY: Cornell University Press.

Balogh, B. (1991). *Chain reaction: Expert debate and public participation in American
    commercial nuclear power, 1945–1975*. Cambridge, United Kingdom: Cambridge
    University Press.

Banjeree, S. B. (2000). Whose land is it anyway? National interest, indigenous stake-
    holders, and colonial discourse: The case of the Jabiluka uranium mine. *Organiza-
    tion & Environment, 13*(3), 3–38. doi:10.1177/1086026600131001

Barbour, J. B., & Gill, R. (2013). Designing communication for the day-to-day safety
    oversight of nuclear power plants. *Journal of Communication Research, 42*, 168–189.
    doi:10.1080/00909882.2013.859291

Barge, K., & Andreas, D. (2013). Communities, conflict, and the design of dialogic con-
    versation. In J. Oetzel and S. Ting-Toomey (Eds.), *The SAGE handbook of conflict
    communication: Integrating theory, research, and practice* (2nd ed., pp. 609–634).
    Thousand Oaks, CA: Sage.

Beck, U. (1987). The anthropological shock: Chernobyl and the contours of the risk
    society. *Berkeley Journal of Sociology, 32*, 153–165. www.jstor.org/stable/41035363

Beck, U. (1992). *Risk society: Towards a new modernity*. Thousand Oaks, CA: Sage.

Beck, U. (1995). *Ecological politics in an age of risk*. Cambridge, United Kingdom: Polity.

Besley, J. C. (2010). Public engagement and the impact of fairness perceptions on decision favorability and acceptance. *Science Communication, 32*, 256–280. doi:10.1177/1075547009358624

Besley, J. C. (2012). Does fairness matter in the context of anger about nuclear energy decision making? *Risk Analysis, 32*, 25–38. doi:10.1111/j.1539-6924.2011. 01664.x

Bickerstaff, K., Lorenzoni, I., Pidgeon, N., Poortinga, W., & Simmons, P. (2008). Reframing nuclear power in the UK energy debate. *Public Understanding of Science, 17*, 145–169. doi:10.1177/0963662506066719

Binder, A. R. (2012). Figuring out #Fukushima: An initial look at functions and content of U.S. twitter commentary about nuclear risk. *Environmental Communication, 6*, 268–277. doi:10.1080/17524032.2012.672442

Birkland, T. A. (1998). Focusing events, mobilization, and agenda setting. *Journal of Public Policy, 18*, 53–74. www.jstor.org/stable/4007601

Bourrier, M. (2011). *The legacy of the theory of high-reliability organizations*. Geneva, Switzerland: University of Geneva.

Boyer, P. (1985). *By the bomb's early light*. New York: Pantheon.

Branch, K. M., & Olson, J. L. (2011). *Review of the literature pertinent to the evaluation of safety culture interventions*. Richland, WA: Pacific Northwest National Laboratory.

Brummett, B. (1989). Perfection and the bomb: Nuclear weapons, teleology, and motives. *Journal of Communication, 39*, 85–95. doi:10.1111/j.1460-2466.1989. tb01021.x

Caldicott, H. (2006). *Nuclear power is not the answer*. New York: New Press.

Carvalho, P. V. R., dos Santos, I. L., Gomes, J. O., & Borges, M. R. S. (2008). Micro incident analysis framework to assess safety and resilience in the operation of safe critical systems. *Journal of Loss Prevention in the Process Industries, 21*, 277–286. doi:10.1016/j.jlp.2007.04.005

Caulfield, H. (1989). *Multiple exposures: Chronicles of the radiation age*. New York: Perennial.

Chernus, I. (2002). *Eisenhower's Atoms for Peace*. College Station, TX: Texas A&M University Press.

Clarke, T. (2010). Goshute Native American tribe and nuclear waste: Complexities and contradictions of a bounded-constitutive relationship. *Environmental Communication, 4*, 387–405. doi:10.1080/17524032.2010.520724

Cohn, S. M. (1997). *Too cheap to meter: An economic and philosophical analysis of the nuclear dream*. Albany, NY: SUNY Press.

Cooper, M. (2012). *Nuclear safety and nuclear economics*. South Royalton, VT: Vermont Law School.

Covello, V. T., & Mumpower, J. L. (1985). Risk analysis and risk management: A historical perspective. *Risk Analysis, 5*, 103–120. doi:10.1111/j.1539-6924.1985. tb00159.x

Daniels, S. E., & Walker, G. B. (2001). *Working through environmental conflict: The collaborative learning approach*. Westport, CT: Praeger.

Davis, M. D. (1987). *The military-civilian nuclear link: A guide to the French nuclear industry*. Boulder, CO: Westview.

Dawson, J. I., & Darst, R. G. (2006). Meeting the challenge of permanent nuclear waste disposal in the expanding Europe. *Environmental Politics, 15*, 610–627. doi:10.1080/09644010600785226

DeLuca, K. M. (1999). *Image politics: The new rhetoric of environmental activism.* Mahwah, NJ: Erlbaum.

Depoe, S. P., Delicath, J. W., & Elsenbeer, M. A. (Eds.) (2004). *Communication and public participation in environmental decision making.* Albany, NY: SUNY Press.

Doyle, J. (2011). Acclimatizing nuclear? Climate change, nuclear power and the reframing of risk in the UK news media. *International Communication Gazette, 73*(1–2), 107–125. doi:10.1177/1748048510386744

Duffy, R. (1997). *Nuclear politics in America: A history and theory of government regulation.* Lawrence: University Press of Kansas.

Easterling, D., & Kunreuther, H. (1995). *The dilemma of siting a high-level nuclear waste repository.* Dordrecht: Springer.

Endres, D. (2009a). From wasteland to waste site: The role of discourse in nuclear power's environmental injustices. *Local Environment, 14*, 917–937. doi:10.1080/13549830903244409

Endres, D. (2009b). The rhetoric of nuclear colonialism: Rhetorical exclusion of American Indian arguments in the Yucca Mountain nuclear waste siting decision. *Communication and Critical/Cultural Studies, 6*, 39–60. doi:10.1080/147914208 02632103

Endres, D. (2009c). Science and public participation: Public scientific argument in the Yucca Mountain controversy. *Environmental Communication, 3*, 49–75. doi:10.1080/17524030802704369

Endres, D. (2012). Sacred land or national sacrifice zone: Competing values in the Yucca Mountain controversy. *Environmental Communication, 6*, 328–345. doi:10.1 080/17524032.2012.688060

Endres, D. (2013). Animist intersubjectivity as argumentation: Western Shoshone and Southern Paiute arguments against a nuclear waste site at Yucca Mountain. *Argumentation, 27*, 183–200. doi:10.1007/s10503-012-9271-x

Falk, J., Green, J., & Mudd, G. (2006). Australia, uranium and nuclear power. *International Journal of Environmental Studies, 63*, 845–857. doi:10.1080/00207230601047131

Fan, M.-F. (2006a). Environmental justice and nuclear waste conflicts in Taiwan. *Environmental Politics, 15*, 417–434. doi:10.1080/09644010600627683

Fan, M.-F. (2006b). Nuclear waste facilities on Tribal Land: The Yami's struggles for environmental justice. *Local Environment, 11*, 433–444. doi:10.1080/13549830600785589

Farrell, T. B., & Goodnight, G. T. (1981). Accidental rhetoric: The root metaphors of Three Mile Island. *Communication Monographs, 48*, 271–300. doi:10.1080/03637758109376063

Felt, U. (2013). *Keeping technologies out: Sociotechnical imaginaries and the formation of a national technopolitical identity.* Vienna, Austria: University of Vienna.

Flam, H. (Ed.) (1994). *States and antinuclear movements.* Edinburgh, United Kingdom: Edinburgh University Press.

Freudenburg, W. R. (1993). Risk and recreancy: Weber, the division of labor, and the rationality of risk perceptions. *Social Forces, 71*, 909–932. doi:10.2307/2580124

Fried, J., & Eyles, J. (2011). Welcome waste: Interpreting narratives of radioactive waste disposal in two small towns in Ontario, Canada. *Journal of Risk Research, 14*, 1017–1037. doi:10.1080/13669877.2011.571774

Friedman, S. M. (1981). Blueprint for breakdown: Three Mile Island and the media before the accident. *Journal of Communication, 31*, 116–128. doi:10.1111/j.1460-2466.1981. tb01235.x

Friedman, S. M. (2011). Three Mile Island, Chernobyl, and Fukushima: An analysis of traditional and new media coverage. *Bulletin of the Atomic Scientists, 67*(5), 55–65. doi:10.1177/0096340211421587

Friedman, S. M., Gorney, C. M., & Egolf, B. P. (1987). Reporting on radiation: A content analysis of Chernobyl coverage. *Journal of Communication, 37*(3), 58–67. doi:10.1111/j.1460-2466.1987.tb00994.x

Gale, R. P. (1987). Calculating risk: Radiation and Chernobyl. *Journal of Communication, 37*(3), 68–79. doi:10.1111/j.1460-2466.1987.tb00995.x

Gamson, W., & Modigliani, A. (1989). Media discourse and public opinion on nuclear power. *American Journal of Sociology, 95*, 1–37. doi:10.2307/2780405

Gerrard, M. B. (1996). *Whose backyard, whose risk: Fear and fairness in toxic and nuclear waste siting.* Cambridge, MA: MIT Press.

Giddens, A. (1990). *The consequences of modernity.* Stanford, CA: Stanford University Press.

Gieryn, T. F. (1983). Boundary-work and the demarcation of science from non-science. *American Sociological Review, 48*, 781–795. doi:10.2307/2095325

Gieryn, T. F. (1995). Boundaries of science. In S. Jasanoff, G. E. Markle, J. C. Petersen and T. Pinch (Eds.), *Handbook of science and technology studies* (pp. 393–443). Thousand Oaks, CA: Sage.

Giugni, M. (2004). *Social protest and policy change: Ecology, antinuclear, and peace movements in comparative perspective.* Lanham: MD: Rowman & Littlefield.

Goldsteen, R., & Schorr, J. (1991). *Demanding democracy after Three Mile Island.* Gainesville, FL: University of Florida Press.

Goodnight, G. T. (1982). The personal, technical, and public spheres of argument: A speculative inquiry into the art of public deliberation. *Journal of the American Forensic Association, 18*, 214–227.

Gowda, M. V. R., & Easterling, D. (1998). Nuclear waste and Native America. *Risk: Health, Safety & Environment, 9*, 229–258.

Greenberg, M. R. (2013). *Nuclear waste management, nuclear power, and energy choices: Public preferences, perceptions, and trust.* London, United Kingdom: Springer.

Grinde, D. A., & Johansen, B. E. (1995). *Ecocide of Native America.* Santa Fe, NM: Clear Light.

Gross, A.G. (1994). The roles of rhetoric in the public understanding of science. *Public Understanding of Science, 3*, 3–23. doi:10.1088/0963-6625/3/1/001

Gwin, L. (1990). *Speak no evil: The promotional heritage of nuclear risk communication.* New York, NY: Praeger.

Hausman, C. (2013). *Corporate incentives and nuclear safety.* Berkeley, CA: Haas Energy Institute.

Hecht, G. (1998). *The radiance of France: Nuclear power and national identity after World War II.* Cambridge, MA: MIT Press.

Hecht, G. (2003). Globalization meets Frankenstein? Reflections on terrorism, nuclearity, and global technopolitical discourse. *History and Technology, 19*, 1–8. doi:10.1080/0734151022000042243

Hecht, G. (2012). *Being nuclear: Africans and the global uranium trade.* Cambridge, MA: MIT Press.

Heidegger, M. (1977). *The question concerning technology and other essays* (W. Lovitt trans.). New York, NY: Harper & Row.

Henriksen, M. A. (1997). *Dr. Strangelove's America: Society and culture in the atomic age.* Berkeley, CA: University of California Press.

Hevly, B., & Findlay, J. M. (Eds.) (1998). *The atomic west.* Seattle, WA: University of Washington Press.

Hileman, B. (1982). Trends in nuclear power. *Environmental Science and Technology, 16*(7), 373A–378A. doi:10.1021/es00101a718

Hindmarsh, R. (Ed.) (2013). *Nuclear disaster at Fukushima Daiichi: Social, political, and environmental issues.* London: Routledge.

Hocke, P., & Renn, O. (2009) Concerned public and the paralysis of decision-making: Nuclear waste management policy in Germany. *Journal of Risk Research, 12,* 921–940. doi:10.1080/13669870903126382

Hoffmann, S. M. (2001). Negotiating eternity: Energy policy, environmental justice, and the politics of nuclear waste. *Bulletin of Science, Technology & Society, 21,* 456–472. doi:10.1177/027046760102100604

Horlick-Jones, T. (2005). Informal logics of risk. *Journal of Risk Research, 8*(3), 253–272. doi:10.1080/1366987042000270735

Hunold, C. (2001). Environmentalists, nuclear waste, and the politics of passive exclusion in Germany. *German Politics and Society, 19*(4), 43–63. doi:10.3167/104503001782486254

International Nuclear Safety Advisory Group (INSAG) (1988). *Basic safety principles for nuclear power plants.* Vienna: International Atomic Energy Agency.

Ionescu, T. B. (2012). Communicating in Germany about the Fukushima accident. *Environmental Communication, 6,* 260–267. doi:10.1080/17524032.2012.672443

Jacob, G. (1990). *Site unseen: The politics of siting a nuclear waste repository.* Pittsburgh. PA: University of Pittsburgh Press.

Jasanoff, S., & Kim, S. (2009). Containing the atom: Sociotechnical imaginaries and nuclear regulation in the U.S. and South Korea. *Minerva, 47*(2), 119–146. doi:10.1007/s11024-009-9124-4

Jobin, P. (2012). Qui est protégé par la radioprotection? *Ebisu, 47,* 121–131. http://ebisu.revues.org/351

Johnson, G. F. (2008). *Deliberative democracy for the future: The case of nuclear waste management in Canada.* Toronto, Canada: University of Toronto Press.

Joppke, C. (1993). *Mobilizing against nuclear energy: A comparison of Germany and the United States.* Berkeley, CA: University of California Press.

Juraku, K. (2013a). "Made in Japan" Fukushima nuclear accident. STS Forum on Fukushima, http://fukushimaforum.wordpress.com/workshops/sts-forum-on-the-2011-fukushima-east-japan-disaster/manuscripts/session-1/made-in-japan-fukushima-nuclear-accident-a- critical-review-for-accident-investigation-activities-in-japan/

Juraku, K. (2013b). Social structure and nuclear power siting problems revealed. In R. Hindmarsh (Ed.), *Nuclear disaster at Fukushima Daiichi* (pp. 41–56). London, United Kingdom: Routledge.

Katz, S. B., & Miller, C. R. (1996). The low-level radioactive waste-siting controversy in North Carolina. In C. G. Herndl & S. C. Brown (Eds.), *Green culture: Environmental rhetoric in contemporary America* (pp. 111–139). Madison, WI: University of Wisconsin Press.

Kauffman, C. (1989). Names and weapons. *Communication Monographs, 56,* 273–285. doi:10.1080/03637758909390264

Keller, W. & Modarres, M. (2004). A historical overview of probabilistic risk development and its use in the nuclear industry. *Reliability Engineering and System Safety,* *89*, 271–285. doi:10.1016/j.ress.2004.08.022

Kelly, P. K. (1994). *Thinking green! Essays on environmentalism, feminism, and nonviolence.* Berkeley, CA: Parallax Press.

Kelly, A. R., & Miller, C. R. (in press). Intersections: Scientific and parascientific communication on the internet. In A. Gross & J. Buehl (Eds.), *Science and the internet.* Amityville, NY: Baywood.

Kera, D., Rod, J., & Peterova, R. (2013), Post-apocalyptic citizenship and humanitarian hardware. In R. Hindmarsh (Ed.), *Nuclear disaster at Fukushima Daiichi: Social, political, and environmental issues* (pp. 97–115). London, United Kingdom: Routledge.

Kinsella, W. J. (2001). Nuclear boundaries: Material and discursive containment at the Hanford nuclear reservation. *Science as Culture, 10*, 163–194. doi:10.1080/09505430120052284

Kinsella, W. J. (2004a). Fusion power and rhetorical power: A communication perspective on nuclear energy research. In S. Durlabhji (Ed.), *Power in focus: Perspectives from multiple disciplines* (pp. 3–38). Lima, OH: Wyndham Hall Press.

Kinsella, W. J. (2004b). Public expertise: A foundation for citizen participation in energy and environmental decisions. In S. P. Depoe, J. W. Delicath, & M. A. Elsenbeer (Eds.), *Communication and public participation in environmental decision making* (pp. 83–95). Albany, NY: SUNY Press.

Kinsella, W. J. (2005). One hundred years of nuclear discourse: Four master themes and their implications for environmental communication. *Environmental Communication yearbook 2*, 49–72.

Kinsella, W. J. (2007). Heidegger and being at the Hanford reservation: Standing reserve, enframing, and environmental communication theory. *Environmental Communication, 1*, 194–217. doi:10.1080/17524030701642728

Kinsella, W. J. (2010). Risk communication, phenomenology, and the limits of representation. *Catalan Journal of Communication and Cultural Studies, 2*, 267–276. doi:10.1386/cjcs.2.2.267_7

Kinsella, W. J. (2011). Research on nuclear energy in an international context. *Technikfolgenabschätzung: Theorie und Praxis, 20*(2), 84–89. https://www.tatup-journal.de/weiterleitung4300.php

Kinsella, W. J. (2012). Environments, risks, and the limits of representation: Examples from nuclear energy. *Environmental Communication, 6*, 251–259. doi:10.1080/17524032.2012.672928

Kinsella, W. J. (2015). Rearticulating a nuclear renaissance: Energy activism and contested common sense. *Environmental Communication.*

Kinsella, W. J. (2013). Negotiating nuclear safety: Responses to the Fukushima disaster by the US nuclear community. STS Forum on Fukushima, https://fukushimaforum.wordpress.com/workshops/sts-forum-on-the-2011-fukushima-east-japandisaster/manuscripts/session-3-radiation-information-and-control/negotiating-nuclear-safetyresponses-to-the-fukushima-disaster-by-the-u-s-nuclear-community/

Kinsella, W. J. (2016). A question of confidence: Nuclear waste and public trust in the United States after Fukushima. In R. Hindmarsh & R. Priestly (Eds.), *The Fukushima effect: Nuclear histories, representations and debates.* London, United Kingdom: Routledge (forthcoming).

Kinsella, W. J., & Mullen, J. (2007). Becoming Hanford downwinders: Producing community and challenging discursive containment. In B. C. Taylor, W. J. Kinsella,

S. P. Depoe, & M. S. Metzler (Eds.), *Nuclear legacies: Communication, controversy, and the U.S. nuclear weapons complex* (pp. 73–107). Lanham, MD: Lexington Books.

Kinsella, W. J., Kelly, A. R., & Kittle Autry, M. (2013). Risk, regulation, and rhetorical boundaries: Claims and challenges surrounding a purported nuclear renaissance. *Communication Monographs, 80*, 278–301. doi:10.1080/03637751.2013.788253

Kittle Autry, M., & Kelly, A. R. (2012). Merging Duke Energy and Progress Energy: Online public discourse, post-Fukushima reactions, and the absence of environmental communication. *Environmental Communication, 6*, 278–284. doi:10.1080/1752 4032.2012.672444

Kuchinskaya, O. (2011). Articulating the signs of danger: Lay experiences of post-Chernobyl radiation risks and effects. *Public Understanding of Science, 20*, 405–421. doi:10.1177/0963662509348862

Kuchinskaya, O. (2012). Twice invisible: Formal representations of radiation danger. *Social Studies of Science, 43*, 78–96. doi:10.1177/0306312712465356

Kuletz, V. L. (1998). *The tainted desert: Environmental and social ruin in the American west*. New York, NY: Routledge.

LaDuke, W. (1999). *All our relations: Native struggles for land and life*. Boston, MA: South End Press.

Laffont, J.-J. and Tirole, J. (1991). The politics of government decision-making: A theory of regulatory capture. *Quarterly Journal of Economics, 106*, 1089–1127. doi:10.2307/2937958

Latour, B. (2004). *Politics of nature: How to bring the sciences into democracy*. Cambridge, MA: Harvard University Press.

Lewicki, R. J., Gray, B., & Elliot, M. (2003). *Making sense of intractable environmental conflicts*. Washington, D.C: Island Press.

Lidskog, R., & Sundqvist, G. (2004). On the right track? Technology, geology and society in Swedish nuclear waste management. *Journal of Risk Research, 7*, 251–268. doi:10.1080/1366987042000171924

Littlejohn, S., & Cole, K. (2013). Moral conflict and transcendent communication. In J. Oetzel and S. Ting-Toomey *Handbook of Conflict Communication* (2nd ed., pp. 585–608). Thousand Oaks, CA: Sage.

Luhmann, N. (1989). *Ecological communication* (trans. J. Bednarz). Chicago, IL: University of Chicago Press.

Luhmann. N. (1993). *Risk: A sociological theory*. New York, NY: de Gruyter.

Lynch, L. (2012). "We don't wanna be radiated": Documentary film and the evolving rhetoric of nuclear energy activism. *American Literature, 84*, 227–351. doi:10.1215/ 00029831-1587368

Macfarlane, A. M. (2011). The overlooked back end of the nuclear fuel cycle. *Science, 333*(6047), 1225–1226. doi:10.1126/science.1207054

Macfarlane, A. M., & Ewing, R. C. (Eds.) (2006). *Uncertainty underground: Yucca Mountain and the nation's high-level nuclear waste*. Cambridge, MA: MIT Press.

Makhijani, A., & Saleska, S. (1992). *High-level dollars, low-level sense*. New York, NY: Apex.

Mariscal, M. A., Herrero, S. G., & Toca Otero, A. (2012). Assessing safety culture in the Spanish nuclear industry. *Safety Science, 50*, 1237–1246. doi:10.1016/j. ssci.2012.01.008

Markovits, A. S., & Klaver, J. (2012). *Thirty years of Bundestag presence*. Washington, DC: American Institute for Contemporary German Studies.

Mathai, M. V. (2013). *Nuclear power, economic development discourse and the environment: The case of India.* London, United Kingdom: Routledge.

Mazur, A. (1990). Nuclear power, chemical hazards, and the quantity of reporting. *Minerva, 28*(3), 294–323. doi:10.1007/BF01096293

McCafferty, D. P. (1991). *The politics of nuclear power: A history of the Shoreham power plant.* Dordrecht: Kluwer.

McGee, M. C. (1980). "Social movement": Phenomenon or meaning? *Central States Speech Journal, 31*(4), 233–244. doi:10.1080/10510978009368063

Mechling, E. W., & Mechling, J. (1995). The atom according to Disney. *Quarterly Journal of Speech, 81*, 436–453. doi:10.1080/00335639509384128

Medhurst, M. J. (1987). Eisenhower's "Atoms for Peace" speech: A case study in the strategic use of language. *Communication Monographs, 54*, 204–220. doi:10.1080/03637758709390226

Medhurst, M. J. (1997). Atoms for Peace and nuclear hegemony: The rhetorical structure of a Cold War campaign. *Armed Forces & Society, 23*, 571–593. doi:10.1177/0095327X9702300403

Mehta, M. D. (2005). *Risky business: Nuclear power and public protest in Canada.* Lanham, MD: Lexington.

Miller, C. R. (2003). The presumptions of expertise: The role of ethos in risk analysis. *Configurations, 11*, 163–202. doi:10.1353/con.2004.0022

Morita, A., Blok, A., & Kimura, S. (2013). Environmental infrastructures of emergency: The formation of a civic radiation monitoring map during the Fukushima disaster. In R. Hindmarsh (Ed.), *Nuclear disaster at Fukushima Daiichi: Social, political, and environmental issues* (pp. 78–96). London, United Kingdom: Routledge.

Morone, J. G., & Woodhouse, E. J. (1989). *The demise of nuclear energy? Lessons for democratic control of technology.* New Haven, CT: Yale University Press.

Mosey, D. (1990). *Reactor accidents: Nuclear safety and the role of institutional failure.* Surrey, United Kingdom: Nuclear Engineering International.

Myers, G. (2005). Communities of practice, risk, and Sellafield. In D. Barton & K. Tusting (Eds.), *Beyond communities of practice* (pp. 198–213). Cambridge, United Kingdom: Cambridge University Press.

Nadel, A. (1995). *Containment culture: American narratives, postmodernism, and the atomic age.* Durham, NC: Duke University Press.

National Diet of Japan (2012). *The official report of the Fukushima Nuclear Accident Independent Investigation Commission* (English language summary). Tokyo, Japan: National Diet of Japan.

Navarro, M. F. L., Garcia Lerín, F. J., Tomás, I., & Peiró Silla, J. M. (2013). Validation of the group nuclear safety climate questionnaire. *Journal of Safety Research, 46*, 21–30. doi:10.1016/j.jsr.2013.03.005

Nelkin, D., & Pollak, M. (1981). *The atom besieged: Extraparliamentary dissent in France and Germany.* Cambridge, MA: MIT Press.

Ohno, H. (2011, 6 July). Interview/Ulrich Beck: System of organized irresponsibility behind the Fukushima crisis. *Asahi Shimbun*, http://ajw.asahi.com/article/0311disaster/opinion/AJ201107063167

Parkhill, K. A., Henwood, K. L., Pidgeon, N. F., & Simmons, P. (2011). Laughing it off? Humour, affect and emotion work in communities living with nuclear risk. *British Journal of Sociology, 62*, 324–346. doi:10.1111/j.1468-4446.2011.01367.x

Paté-Cornell, E. (2012). On "black swans" and "perfect storms." *Risk Analysis, 32*, 1823–1833. doi:10.1111/j.1539-6924.2011.01787.x

Pearce, W. B. & Littlejohn, S. (1997). *Moral conflict: When social worlds collide.* Thousand Oaks, CA: Sage.

Peeples, J. A. (2011). Downwind: Articulation and appropriation of social movement discourse, *Southern Communication Journal, 76*, 248–263. doi:10.1080/10417 94x.2010.500516

Peeples, J. A., Krannich, R. S., & Weiss, J. (2008). Arguments for what no one wants: Narratives of waste storage proponents. *Environmental Communication, 2*, 40–58. doi:10.1080/17524030701642751

Perin, C. (2006) *Shouldering risks: The culture of control in the nuclear power industry.* Princeton, NJ: Princeton University Press.

Perrow, C. (1984/1999). *Normal accidents.* New York, NY: Basic.

Peterson, T. V. (2001). *Linked arms: A rural community resists nuclear waste.* Albany, NY: SUNY Press.

Pidgeon, N. F., Lorenzoni, I., & Poortinga, W. (2008). Climate change or nuclear power "No thanks!" Public perceptions and risk framing in Britain. *Global Environmental Change, 18*, 69–85. doi:10.1016/j.gloenvcha.2007.09.005

Pomerantz, A. (1986). Extreme case formulations: A way of legitimizing claims. *Human Studies, 9*, 219–229. doi:10.1007/BF00148128

Pool, R. (1997). *Beyond engineering: How society shapes technology.* New York, NY: Oxford.

Poortinga, W., & Pidgeon, N. F. (2003). Exploring the dimensionality of trust in risk regulation. *Risk Analysis, 23*, 961–972. doi:10.1111/1539-6924.00373

Pope, D. (2008). *Nuclear implosions: The rise and fall of the Washington Public Power Supply System.* New York, NY: Cambridge University Press.

Ramana, M. V. (2013). Why India's electricity is likely to remain in short supply: The economics of nuclear power. *Bulletin of the Atomic Scientists, 69*(6), 67–78. doi: 10.1177/0096340213508626

Ratliff, J. N. (1997). The politics of nuclear waste. *Communication Studies, 48*, 359–380. doi:10.1080/10510979709368512

Reiman, T., Oedewald, P., & Rollenhagen, C. (2005). Characteristics of organizational culture at the maintenance units of two Nordic nuclear power plants. *Reliability Engineering and System Safety, 89*, 331–345. doi:10.1016/j.ress.2004.09.004

Renn, O. (1992). Concepts of risk: A classification. In S. Krimsky & D. Golding (Eds.), *Social theories of risk* (pp. 53–79). Westport, CT: Praeger.

Renn, O. (2008). *Risk governance: Coping with uncertainty in a complex world.* London, United Kingdom: Earthscan.

Rijpma, J. A. (1997). Complexity, tight-coupling and reliability: Connecting normal accidents theory and high reliability theory. *Journal of Contingencies and Crisis Management, 5*, 15–23. doi:10.1111/1468-5973.00033

Rogers, R. A. (1998). Overcoming the objectification of nature in constitutive theories: Toward a transhuman, materialist theory of communication. *Western Journal of Communication, 62*, 244–272. doi:10.1111/j.1468-2885.2006.00277.x

Rogers, S. (2011, 18 March). Nuclear power plant accidents: Listed and ranked since 1952. *The Guardian*, www.theguardian.com/news/datablog/2011/mar/14/nuclear-power-plant-accidents-list-rank

Rosa, E. A., & Dunlap, R. E. (1994). Poll trends: Nuclear power. Three decades of public opinion. *Public Opinion Quarterly, 58,* 295–324. doi:10.1086/269425

Rubin, D. M. (1987). How the news media reported on Three Mile Island and Chernobyl. *Journal of Communication, 37*(3), 42–57. doi:10.1111/j.1460-2466.1987.tb00993.x

Rüdig, W. 1990. Antinuclear movements: A world survey of opposition to nuclear energy. Harlow: Longman.

Schiappa, E. (1989). The rhetoric of nukespeak. *Communication Monographs, 56,* 253–272. doi:10.1080/03637758909390263

Schneider, M., & Froggat, A. (2013). *World nuclear industry status report 2013.* Paris: Mycle Schneider Consulting.

Schulman, P. R. (1993). The negotiated order of organizational reliability. *Administration and Society, 25,* 353–372. doi:10.1177/009539979302500305

Shrader-Frechette, S. A. (1993). *Burying uncertainty: Risk and the case against geologic disposal of nuclear waste.* Berkeley, CA: University of California Press.

Silbey, S. S. (2009). Taming Prometheus: Talk about safety and culture. *Annual Review of Sociology, 35,* 341–369. doi:10.1146/annurev.soc.34.040507.134707

Silva, C. L., Jenkins-Smith, H. C., & Barke, R. P. (2007). Reconciling scientists' beliefs about radiation risks and social norms. *Risk Analysis, 27,* 755–774. doi:10.1111/j.1539-6924.2007.00919.x

Siu, N., & Collins, D. (2008). PRA research and the development of risk-informed regulation at the U.S. Nuclear Regulatory Commission. *Nuclear Engineering and Technology, 40,* 349–364. http://143.248.251.66/jknsfile/v40/JK0400349.pdf

Sovacool, B. K. (2007). Coal and nuclear technologies: Creating a false dichotomy for American energy policy. *Policy Sciences, 40*(2), 101–122. doi:10.1007/s11077-007-9038-7

Sovacool, B. K. (2010). A critical evaluation of nuclear power and renewable electricity in Asia. *Journal of Contemporary Asia, 40,* 369–400. doi:10.1080/00472331003798350

Sturgis, P., & Allum, N. (2004). Science in society: Reevaluating the deficit model of public attitudes. *Public Understanding of Science, 13,* 55–74. doi:10.1177/0963662504042690

Sze, J. (2005). Race and power: An introduction to environmental justice energy activism. In D. N. Pellow & R. J. Brulle (Eds.), *Power, justice, and the environment* (pp. 101–115). Cambridge, MA: MIT Press.

Taylor, B. C. (1997). Shooting downwind: Depicting the radiated body in epidemiology and documentary photography. In M. Huspek & G. P. Radford (Eds.), *Transgressing discourses: Communication and the voice of other* (pp. 289–328). Albany, NY: SUNY Press.

Taylor, B. C. (1998). Nuclear weapons and communication studies: A review essay. *Western Journal of Communication, 62,* 300–315. doi:10.1080/10570319809374612

Taylor, B. C., Kinsella, W. J., Depoe, S. P., & Metzler, M. S. (2005). Nuclear legacies: Communication, controversy, and the U.S. nuclear weapons production complex. *Communication yearbook 29,* 363–409.

Taylor, B. C., Kinsella, W. J., Depoe, S. P., & Metzler, M. S. (Eds.) (2007). *Nuclear legacies: Communication, controversy, and the U.S. nuclear weapons complex.* Lanham, MD: Lexington.

Taylor, C. A. (1996). *Defining science: A rhetoric of demarcation.* Madison, WI: University of Wisconsin Press.

Teller, E. (1962). *The legacy of Hiroshima.* New York, NY: Doubleday.

Thompson, J. L. (2009). Building collective communication competence in interdisciplinary research teams. *Journal of Applied Communication Research, 37,* 278–297. doi:10.1080/00909880903025911

U.S. Nuclear Regulatory Commission (USNRC) (1975). *Reactor safety study,* WASH-1400. Washington, DC: USNRC.

Vandenbosch, R., & Vandenbosch, S. E. (2007). *Nuclear waste stalemate: Political and scientific controversies.* Salt Lake City, UT: University of Utah Press.

Walker, J. S. (1984). *Controlling the atom: The beginning of nuclear regulation, 1946–1962.* Berkeley, CA: University of California Press.

Walker, J. S. (1992). *Containing the atom: Nuclear regulation in a changing environment, 1963–1971.* Berkeley, CA: University of California Press.

Walker, J. S. (2000). *Permissible dose: A history of radiation protection in the 20th Century.* Berkeley, CA: University of California Press.

Walker, J. S. (2004). *Three Mile Island: A nuclear crisis in historical perspective.* Berkeley, CA: University of California Press.

Walker, J. S. (2009). *The road to Yucca Mountain: The development of radioactive waste policy in the United States.* Berkeley, CA: University of California Press.

Walker, J. S., & Wellock, T. R. (2010). *A short history of nuclear regulation, 1946–2009.* Washington, DC: U.S. Nuclear Regulatory Commission.

Weart, S. R. (1988). *Nuclear fear: A history of images.* Cambridge, MA: Harvard University Press.

Weart, S. R. (2012). *The rise of nuclear fear.* Cambridge, MA: Harvard University Press.

Weick, K. E., & Sutcliffe, K. M. (2007). *Managing the unexpected: Resilient performance in an age of uncertainty.* San Francisco, CA: John Wiley and Sons.

Weinberg, A. (1985). The sanctification of Hiroshima. *Bulletin of the Atomic Scientists, 34*(11), 34. Available at: http://thebulletin.org/

Weinberg, A. M., & Spiewak, I. (1984). Inherently safe reactors and a second nuclear era. Science, *224*(4656), 1398–1402. doi:10.1126/science.224.4656.1398

Weinberg, A., Spiewak, I., Phung, D. L., & Livingston, R. S. (1985). The second nuclear era: A nuclear renaissance. *Energy, 10,* 661–680. doi:10.1016/0360-5442(85) 90098-2

Wellock, T. R. (Ed.) (1998). *Critical masses: Opposition to nuclear power in California, 1958–1978.* Madison, WI: University of Wisconsin Press.

Welsh I. (2000). *Mobilising modernity: The nuclear moment.* London, United Kingdom: Routledge.

Wills, J. (2006). *Conservation fallout: Nuclear protest at Diablo Canyon.* Reno, NV: University of Nevada Press.

Winkler, A. M. (1993). *Life under a cloud: American anxiety about the atom.* Oxford, United Kingdom: Oxford University Press.

Wynne, B. (1982). *Rationality and ritual: The Windscale inquiry and nuclear decisions in Britain.* Chalfont St. Giles, United Kingdom: British Society for the History of Science.

Wynne, B. (1991). Knowledges in context. *Science, Technology, & Human Values, 16,* 111–121. doi:10.2307/690044

Wynne, B. (1996) May the sheep safely graze? A reflexive view of the expert-lay knowledge divide. In S. Lash, B. Szerszynski & B. Wynne (Eds.) *Risk, environment and modernity: Towards a new ecology* (pp. 44–83). London, United Kingdom: Sage.

Xu, Y. (2010). *The politics of nuclear energy in China*. New York, NY: Palgrave Macmillan.

Young, M. J. & Launer, M. K. (1991). Redefining glasnost in the Soviet media: The recontextualization of Chernobyl. *Journal of Communication, 41*(2), 102–124. doi: 10.1111/j.1460-2466.1991.tb02312.x

Zonabend, F. (1993). *The nuclear peninsula*. Cambridge, United Kingdom: Cambridge University Press.

CHAPTER CONTENTS

10 The Persuasiveness of Child-Targeted Endorsement Strategies

A Systematic Review

Tim Smits

Institute for Media Studies, KULeuven, Leuven, Belgium

Heidi Vandebosch

Department of Communication Studies, University of Antwerp, Belgium

Evy Neyens

Institute for Media Studies, KULeuven, Leuven, Belgium

Emma Boyland

Department of Psychological Sciences, University of Liverpool, UK.

Several European and U.S. reviews have established the link between food marketing and childhood obesity (EU Pledge, 2012; Federal Trade Commission, 2008; Persson, Soroko, Musicus, & Lobstein, 2012), which has stimulated researchers to investigate the effects of the most prevalent child-targeted marketing technique: the use of endorsing characters. This systematic review of these studies (15 identified; participants aged 3–12 years) focuses on three important questions: (a) does a basic endorser effect exist? (b) is the strength of the endorsement effect influenced by endorser type? and (c) does the endorsement strength differ according to the type of food being promoted?

It has been argued that advertising aimed at children (up to age 12) is "fundamentally unfair," because children lack an adult-like understanding of an advertisement's selling intent (Rozendaal, Buijzen, and Valkenburg, 2010, p. 86). However, food marketers employ many techniques in their promotions in order to grab children's attention and persuade them. The use of an endorser to promote products is one of the techniques most often used in food marketing to children (Boyland, Harrold, Kirkham, & Halford, 2011). Friedman and Friedman (1979) discerned three types of endorsers: the celebrity,[1] the expert, or the typical consumer. Although all three are used to target children, this chapter provides an up-to-date systematic review of available insights into celebrity endorsement effects only, as this technique is particularly widely used to promote mainly unhealthy foods to children via TV, packaging and the

Internet (e.g., Elliott, 2008; Boyland et al., 2011; Alvy & Calvert, 2008; Kelly, Chapman, King, & Hebden, 2011).

The current review focuses on research conducted with children between the ages of 3 and 12 years because within these age limits there are large differences in children's susceptibility to (endorsement) advertising. As proposed by Rozendaal, Lapierre, Van Reijmersdal and Buijzen (2011), resisting persuasion not only requires conceptual and attitudinal advertising literacy, but also the ability to apply the former during advertising exposure. For children under 7 years old, their conceptual advertising knowledge is not yet fully developed, which makes them particularly vulnerable. Between 8 and 12 years old, children largely possess conceptual advertising literacy but cannot spontaneously retrieve and apply it while processing the commercial (John, 1999; Brucks, Armstrong, & Goldberg, 1988; Rozendaal, Buijzen, & Valkenburg, 2012; Dixon et al., 2014). Children above 12 years old, on the other hand, are expected to be able to employ their advertising literacy as a defense (Buijzen, Van Reijmersdal, & Owen, 2010).

The aim of this systematic review is to answer a set of specific questions on the effects of endorsement advertising of foods targeted to children. In our reviewed set of studies, authors typically refer to "the endorsement effect" but vary in the control condition to which this term is applied. Some refer to the impact of endorsement relative to a within-participants pre-treatment measure. This interpretation corresponds with an individual effect measuring the reaction to a known food that suddenly gets endorsed. Others use it relative to a between-participants control group, which corresponds with a group effect measuring the actual gain in product liking or consumption attributable to endorsement. Such subtle differences are important and we will explore these, while demonstrating the multitude of effect types documented. A systematic review must also identify yet to be replicated initial findings and hypotheses and corollaries that require further examination. The current article provides such a research agenda.

The use of endorsers as an advertising technique is widespread among marketing targeted at both adults and children. For marketing aimed at adults, Money, Shimp, and Sakano (2006) estimated a worldwide prevalence of endorsements in 17% of commercials, with figures as high as 25% in the United States. For children, the same technique is even more prevalent because advertisers use it to appeal to their fantasy-oriented nature (Rose, Merchant, & Bakir, 2012; cf. Acuff & Reiher, 1997). In Kelly et al.'s (2010) cross-national content analysis of child targeted TV advertising, 9%–49% of all food advertisements (ads) contained promotional characters. The foods these characters promoted were categorized as "non-core" (i.e., high in undesirable nutrients or energy, as defined by dietary standards) in 79% of cases. In their 2011 analysis of 577 TV ads for food targeting children, Castonguay, Kunkel, Wright, and Duff (2013) found that 73% of ads included familiar characters and 72% of these promoted foods of low nutritional quality. In their 2009 systematic review of food marketing to children, Cairns, Angus, Hastings, and Carahar (2013) also identified "animated and other fictional characters [as]{. . .}more likely to be used in food ads than in non-food ads aimed at children" (p. 213). However, it is not just in television advertising that endorsers are used to promote foods to children.

Hebden, King, Kelly, Chapman, and Innes-Hughes (2011) audited three Australian supermarket chains for the use of promotional characters on food packaging. On average, the foods and beverages that were promoted by characters were categorized as less healthful than those without characters on the packaging. Similarly, researchers found endorsers on packaging to be very popular in Dutch supermarkets (Van Assema et al., 2011). In focus groups among elementary school children, Elliott (2009) learned that children derive the healthfulness of foods from the dullness of their packaging. Though little empirical data are available to our knowledge, given the extent to which endorsers appear in online marketing (such as websites or advergames), they are likely to play an important role there as well (Moore & Rideout, 2007). One study in Sweden estimated that 17% (in 2007) to 28% (in 2005) of brand incentives on websites targeting children were mascots (Sandberg, 2011).

Despite their presumed illiteracy with respect to advertising, the literature shows that young children do process advertising cues such as brand logos and characters to a considerable extent. For instance, in a groundbreaking paper in the early 1990s, Fischer, Schwartz, Richards, Goldstein, and Rojas (1991) demonstrated that up to 30% of 3-year-old children could correctly identify such cues. Approximately 30% of 3-year-olds could even match the cartoon character Old Joe with the correct product, Camel cigarettes, the advertising of which was claimed to not be child-targeted. Six-year-olds in the same study could recognize almost 90% of all 10 brands in the study that explicitly targeted children, including food brands such as McDonald's, Burger King, Domino's Pizza, Coca-Cola, Pepsi, Kellogg's, and Cheerios. Given this deep processing of cues, the effects of marketing techniques such as endorsement advertising should not be underestimated. For adults endorsers could be considered mere peripheral cues—except maybe when they are relevant to the product (e.g., a professional model is a more relevant endorser for toothpaste than most sportsmen; see Sengupta, Goodstein, & Boninger, 1997). In contrast, the intimate relationship children often build with characters could result in strong attitudinal effects and associated food preferences.

Food endorsement could be described as an easy strategy to convince the more naive viewers of the purported value and desirability of a product, and therefore, it may be particularly harmful when targeted at children. Recent research shows, however, that even adults can be easily misled. In an online study, Dixon and colleagues (2011) asked parents to choose between a high calorie food item and a healthier option. Most parents did not read the product's nutrition information panel before making their choice. However, when one of the two products was endorsed by a sports celebrity, this increased the odds of the participants choosing the endorsed item. Moreover, the sports endorsement changed their perceptions of the typical consumers buying these items and resulted in participants believing the product to be healthier than the same food item without the endorsement.

Athletes often promote such foods. For instance, Bragg, Yanamalada, Roberto, Harris, and Brownell (2013a) found that from the top 100 endorsing athletes, 24% of their endorsements pertained to food (76% of which were unhealthy) and beverages (93% of which were unhealthy). Bragg et al. (2013b), also found that their sample of athlete or sport endorsed foods and beverages heavily targeted children (34%). Additionally, there were more unhealthy endorsed food and beverage products targeted at children than there were for adults. Similarly, Harris, Brownell, and Bargh (2009) found that endorsement effects are likely to be persuasive for both advertising literate parents and their less literate children because they have an automatic effect on brand and product associations. Such automatic effects are hard to counteract, even for the thoughtful parent making informed consumer decisions. The difference between parents and children might be that adults are better able to discern endorsement marketing when the endorser belongs to the child's environment (e.g., an animated character from a TV program) rather than to the adult's (e.g., a sports celebrity). This demonstrates the important effect endorsers can have, as they are a marketing strategy that often goes unnoticed, even for the more advertising literate consumers.

From an academic perspective, the question of how this endorsement marketing technique actually influences children (and possibly their parents) is a multidisciplinary one. Communication scientists have studied the phenomenon as part of a recent expansion of the literature on advertising literacy, which lacked comprehensive studies demonstrating the impact of advertising techniques (Harris et al., 2009; Institute of Medicine, 2006; Livingstone & Helsper, 2006). Childhood obesity and its relation with marketing communications has also been studied in several other disciplines, therefore in this review we have included studies from the perspectives of psychological consumer behavior and medical pediatrics, as well as from the multidisciplinary field of nutrition research. The journals in which the studies were published are very diverse. The lack of cross-referencing between the different articles further demonstrates that a review combining all available insights is necessary; this should ensure a full understanding of the topic is achieved and that future research is driven to explore gaps in knowledge using a multidisciplinary approach.

Given this diversity of disciplines, it is perhaps unsurprising that the studies reviewed in this chapter approach researching endorsement effects from a number of different perspectives. These differences are apparent both in the dependent measures and the manipulations. In studies originating from a communication perspective, attention has predominantly been given to attitudinal measures such as actual attitudes or parent purchase requests. In other studies, such as those originating within the field of psychology, the focus has been on choice behaviors (e.g., do endorsers influence the choice between a healthy and an unhealthy food item?). In other, more recent studies the focus has been on actual food consumption. With respect to the manipulation, many studies investigated a pure endorsement effect, testing whether the endorsed food was more attractive when compared to a non-endorsed food. Others specifically addressed questions related to types of endorsers (do some endorsers result in stronger effects than others?) or types of food (does the endorsement effect hold for both unhealthy and healthy foods?).

The multidisciplinary nature of academic interest in the topic also seems to have impacted the conceptual design of relevant studies. Each of the design options has its own merits but only portrays part of the persuasive impact of endorsers. Each design also taps into another type of implication, and thus, it is important to sketch the different types of results and their implications.

Therefore, three different research questions will be discussed in the literature review below.

RQ1: Does a basic endorser effect exist?
RQ2: Is the strength of the endorsement effect influenced by endorser type?
RQ3: Does the endorsement strength differ according to the type of food being promoted?

For each of these questions, researchers could use one of a number of different research study designs. Therefore, for each question we will discuss to what extent published studies applied these different design factors:

Factor 1: Is the dependent variable an attitude measure or a choice/behavior measure?
Factor 2: Does the manipulation occur between participants or within participants?
Factor 3: Is it a control-experimental design or an experimental-experimental design?

Research Designs

It is clear that in order to study the above research questions and the underlying causal processes to which they refer, a valid experimental design with appropriate manipulations is necessary. It does not suffice to simply ask children whether they think an endorser would have an effect. Neither is a design without proper randomization sufficient to answer these questions. For instance, Ülger (2008) asked children to choose between an endorsed food item and an item without an endorser, but for each participating child the pairing between endorsement and food item was the same. Effects found in such a design can be attributed to the endorser, the food, or a combination of both, so they do not provide clear evidence for our research questions. Therefore, and because the research on this topic stems from different disciplines each with their own habits of experimentation, it is necessary to first consider the different experimental designs that are acceptable for our purpose.

A few prototypic designs are summarized in Table 10.1, though this is not an exhaustive set. As this table makes clear, a key consideration with any experimental design is whether a between-participants or within-participants format is most appropriate. One benefit of a within-participants design is that there is greater statistical power to detect possible effects, because no intra-individual differences disturb the comparison between conditions. On the other hand, within-participants manipulations in which similar types of outcome measures are repeatedly taken could induce participant awareness of the hypotheses, create answering tendencies or increase the artificiality of the manipulation (e.g., when participants are asked for two ratings of the same food item (not endorsed, then endorsed)).

After considering the manipulation in these designs, the outcome variables must also be considered. As mentioned above, different outcome variables can be deemed relevant to address the question of whether children display endorsement effects with regard to food. Researchers from a communication or psychology background often focus on cognitive measures such as attitudes or preferences. Researchers from a nutrition background are somewhat more prone to test variables such as choice or actual amount of consumption. Again, each of these options are valid and sensible, but the chosen measures qualify the interpretation that can be attached to the results. Of course, cognitive effects are easier to study than behavioral ones that typically involve more researcher time and encoding and accordingly, cognitive effects are more frequently reported in the literature. Moreover, persuasive communication can be expected to have stronger effects on cognitive attitudinal measures than on behavioral measures (Fazio & Roskos-Ewoldson, 2005).

In sum, these designs all have their own merits in answering the three basic research questions outlined above and, of course, variations and combinations of these basic designs exist to answer even more specific questions. In this review we will discuss the extent to which published studies provide answers to these questions, with reference to the particular design factors used in the cited research.

Method

We conducted a systematic review of the published literature concerning the causal impact of endorsement advertising on children's attitudes and behaviors toward food. A systematic review is: "a scientific investigation with pre-planned methods that summarizes, appraises, synthesizes and communicates the results of multiple previous studies" (Jones & Evans, 2000, p. 67). Our goal was to review experimental studies from 2005 to 2014 which measured the impact of

Table 10.1 Research Designs

Design	Manipulation	Uses	Examples of Published Studies
Between-participants control-experimental	Control group views product without endorser. Experimental group views product with endorser.	To explore if an endorsement effect exists.	De Droog, Valkenburg and Buijzen (2011). Dixon et al. (2014). Lapierre, Vaala and Linebarger (2011).
Between-participants experimental-experimental	One group views product with endorser A. Other group views product with endorser B.	To explore the relative endorsement effect: which of the two endorsers is more effective? Does NOT show net endorsement effect.	de Droog, Buijzen and Valkenburg (2014).
Between-participants experimental-experimental food item	One group views product A with endorser. Other group views product B with same endorser.	To explore the relative endorsement effect: for which of the two foods is the endorser more effective? Does NOT show net endorsement effect.	Smits and Vandebosch (2012; mixed design).
Within-participants control-experimental	Participants view product with endorser at one session, and without endorser at another session (order counterbalanced, with suitable time gap to ensure previous response is not readily recalled) OR participants view product without endorser first, then later view product with endorser.	To explore if an endorsement effect exists.	Roberto, Baik, Harris and Brownell (2010). Smits and Vandebosch (2012). Bezbaruah, Stastny and Brunt (2013).
Within-participants experimental-experimental	Participants view product with endorser A at one session, and with endorser B at another session (order counterbalanced, with suitable time gap to ensure previous response is not readily recalled).	To explore the relative endorsement effect: which of the two endorsers is more effective? Does NOT show net endorsement effect.	De Droog, Buijzen and Valkenburg (2012).
Within-participants experimental-experimental food item	Participants view products A and B (or more) with same endorser.	To explore the relative endorsement effect: for which of the two (or more) foods is the endorser more effective? Does NOT show net endorsement effect.	Smits and Vandebosch (2012; mixed design).

endorsers on children's attitudes and food preferences, choices, or consumption. We set 2005 as the starting date because that year can be marked as the starting point of an explicit research focus on child targeted food advertising techniques (see the major review commissioned by the U.S. Federal Trade Commission, 2008).

In this review we have focused on research studies examining endorsement effects for children between 3 and 12 years old, because children notice the perceptual dimension of advertising from this age on, whereas 12-year-old children slowly develop an adult-like understanding of persuasive techniques (John, 1999). Acuff and Reiher (1997) also claim that character-based marketing is most effective for younger children. Older children (from the age of 13) show a stronger appeal towards adult celebrities (such as sports or TV or music celebrities). Furthermore, factors influencing early childhood eating habits are critical because their impact extends to adult health (Owen, 1997).

The literature search was conducted in February 2014. In the first phase, a list of relevant keywords was determined. A few articles were gathered to sample keywords based on a *brief search strategy* and the authors' prior knowledge of the field. The search terms used were combinations of: *endorsement advertising, endorsers, spokes-characters, brand characters, licensed characters, cartoon characters, celebrity endorsement, food promotion, food marketing, children, kids, (un)healthy, (non)celebrity, attitudes toward food, purchase (request) intention, taste, food choice, eating behavior, food intake, food consumption, food preferences, childhood obesity and nutrition.* Next, we used these keywords to scan the following electronic databases: Google Scholar, Psych INFO, and Web of Knowledge. The keyword combinations yielded between 142 and 16800 hits on Google Scholar, between 0 and 40 hits on Web of Knowledge, and 6 articles on Psych INFO. Potentially relevant articles were read and retained only if they matched our a priori inclusion criteria: empirical studies in which manipulation was used to causally verify a basic endorser effect, differences between different types of endorsers, and/or between different types of food, presented to children between 3 and 12 years old. The dependent variables needed to be attitudes, choices, or behavior. The experimental design had to be a between-participants or within-participants control-experimental or experimental-experimental design (see Table 10.1). Finally, we used a snowball search strategy by investigating the references of the suitable articles of the first phase. In total we reviewed 15 articles from 11 journals: *Journal of Health Communication, Appetite, Journal of Communication Science, Journal of the American Academy of Pediatrics, Journal of Pediatrics, Archives of Pediatrics and Adolescent Medicine, Pediatric Obesity, Journal of Consumer Behavior, Journal of Advertising, Journal of Human Nutrition and Food Science,* and *Communications.* The articles were categorized according to our research questions, the design factors, and participants' age. An overview is presented in Table 10.2.

Table 10.2 Overview of All Included Studies and Their Most Important Characteristics

	Year	Author(s)	Research Questions	Participants	Research Design	Type of Measurement	Dependent Variables	Independent Variables	Results
Study 1	2013	Bezbaruah, Stastny and Brunt	Q1	Time 1: 73; Time 2: 92: 9–10 years old	Pre-experimental repeated measures design	Eating behavior	Food selection and consumption	Character presence (time 1–2), gender, ethnicity	Q1: more children consumed endorsed beans in comparison with time 1 regular beans, but average amount per serving decreased
Study 2	2013	Boyland, Harrold, Dovey, Allison, Dobson, Jacobs and Halford	Q1	181: 8–11 years old	Between-subjects mixed control-experimental, post-test only design	Eating behavior	Food intake	Commercial condition, age gender, BMI	Q1: children exposed to endorsed commercial or endorser alone ate more endorsed chips than regular chips than control (no food commercial) condition
Study 3	2011	De Droog, Valkenburg and Buijzen	Q1; Q2; Q3	216: 4–6 years old	Between-subjects control-experimental, post-test only design	Attitudes	Liking, purchase request intent	Character condition (no, (un)familiar), snack condition (((un)healthy), gender, age	Q1: brand characters can increase children's liking of and purchase request intent for fruit up to a level similar to candy. Q2: no different endorser effect between familiar and unfamiliar characters. Q3: only endorsement effect for healthy option

(Continued)

Table 10.2 (Continued)

	Year	Author(s)	Research Questions	Participants	Research Design	Type of Measurement	Dependent Variables	Independent Variables	Results
Study 4	2012	De Droog, Buijzen and Valkenburg	Q2	166: 4–6 years old	Within-subjects experimental-experimental, post-test only design	Attitudes	Automatic and elaborate affective responses toward character-product combinations	Character congruence, character familiarity, perceived congruence, character liking	Q2: more positive elaborate attitudes for the familiar endorser, followed by the conceptual-perceptual congruent character. for automatic affective responses no difference between familiar and unfamiliar conceptually congruent characters
Study 5	2014	De Droog, Buijzen and Valkenburg	Q1; Q2	104: 4–6 years old	Between-subjects control-experimental post-test only design	Attitudes + food intake	Cognitive response/automatic and elaborate affective response to carrots / product consumption	Reading style and character condition, BMI, hunger, time of snacking	Q1: conceptually congruent character did not enhance the impact of the book on carrot consumption, only effect of interactive shared reading. Q2: congruent character induces an automatic positive response toward carrots after a single exposure, after five exposures no difference with incongruent character

Study	Year	Author	RQ	Sample	Design	Measures	Outcome	Variables	Results
Study 6	2014	Dixon et al.	Q1	1302: 10–12 years old	Between-subjects control-experimental, web-based design	Attitudes + food choice	Product ratings, product choice	Promotion condition	Q1: endorser effect only for boys
Study 7	2012	Kotler, Shiffmann and Hanson	Q1; Q2; Q3	343: 2–6 years old 207: 3–6 years old	Between-subjects control-experimental, post-test only design	Attitudes + actual food choice	Food preference + consumption	1: Character condition, age, gender, liking of characters. 2: Food condition, fam condition added	Q1: higher preference for foods endorsed by familiar character relative to the baseline condition. Q2: children preferred and ate more of the familiar character endorsed foods than the unknown character foods. Q3: unhealthy-unfamiliar combination preferred over healthy-familiar combination.

(Continued)

Table 10.2 (Continued)

	Year	Author(s)	Research Questions	Participants	Research Design	Type of Measurement	Dependent Variables	Independent Variables	Results
Study 8	2011	Lapierre, Vaala and Linebarger	Q1; Q3	80: 5–6 years	Between-subjects control-experimental, post-test only design	Attitudes	Taste perception	Character condition (presence), name condition (healthy vs. sugary), character identification and liking, age, gender, parent's education, media-use	Q1: better taste if endorsed, but only for cereals with unhealthy cue. Q3: no endorsement effect for "healthy" cereals
Study 9	2010	Levin and Levin	Q1; Q3	43: 7–8 years old	Within-subjects control-experimental, post-test only	Attitudes	Product good or bad	Product healthiness, brand name familiarity, character presence, gender	Q1-Q3: endorser effect only relevant for unhealthy unfamiliar product. Brand name familiarity more effective than cartoon characters
Study 10	2004	Neeley and Schumann	Q2	1: 682: 37: 2–5 years old	Between-subjects, control-experimental, post-test only design	Attitudes + food choice	Attention, character-product association, recognition and liking, product preference, intention and choice	Commercial condition, age, gender, ethnicity, media-use, food experience	Q2: strongest endorsement effects when endorser interacts with product and without complex auditory communication between the endorsers

	Year	Authors		Sample	Design				Findings
Study 11	2010	Roberto, Baik, Harris and Brownell	Q1; Q3	40: 4–6 years old	Within-subjects control-experimental, post-test only design	Attitudes + actual food choice	Taste preference + food choice	Character and food condition, character identification and liking, age, gender, ethnicity, media-use	Q1: preference for the endorsed food items, positive endorser effect on forced choice between two similar food items. Q3: smaller effect for healthy option
Study 12	2007	Robinson, Borzekowski, Matheson and Kraemer	Q1: branding	63: 3–5 years old	Within-subjects control-experimental, post-test only design	Attitudes	Taste preference	5 food pairs ((un) branded), age ethnicity, media-use	Q1: children preferred branded foods and drinks
Study 13	2012	Smits and Vandebosch	Q1; Q2; Q3	57: 6–7 years old	Mixed design: within-subjects control experimental, pre- and post-test design	Attitudes	Frequency of consumption, appetite, purchase request intention	Food type and set, character distribution and order, age, gender, character identification	Q1: higher attitudes toward endorsed foods versus baseline measure among same participants. Q2: effects for both familiar and unfamiliar characters and stronger effects for familiar characters. Q3: stronger effects for unhealthy food

(Continued)

Table 10.2 (Continued)

	Year	Author(s)	Research Questions	Participants	Research Design	Type of Measurement	Dependent Variables	Independent Variables	Results
Study 14	2012	Wansink, Just and Payne	Q1; Q2; Q3	208: 8–11 years old	Repeated measures control-experimental; pre-post-test design	Food choice + eating behavior	Food choice and consumption	Character condition (presence, (un)familiar), food type	Q1: increased odds of choosing endorsed apple over regular apple. Q2: no effect of unknown character. Q3: only effective with healthy item, no effect for cookie
Study 15	2012	Wansink, Shimizu and Camps	Q2	22: 6–12 years old	Within-subjects, pre-test post-test design	Food choice	Food choice	What would role-model eat? perceived healthiness of food	Q2: children who expected admirable models to eat healthy chose healthy option more often

Results

RQ1: Does a Basic Endorsement Effect Exist?

Attitude studies. A few studies addressed the basic endorser effect using a between-participants design in which at least one group of participants rated foods presented without an endorser and others saw the food endorsed. De Droog, Valkenburg, and Buijzen (2011) asked children ($N = 216$, 4 to 6 years old) to rate a healthy and an unhealthy snack for liking and request intent. Between-participants they manipulated whether the snack was endorsed by a familiar endorser, an unfamiliar endorser, or no endorser. The endorsement did not have an effect on the liking of the unhealthy snack (possibly due to a ceiling effect as all children rated the unhealthy snack very positively), but it did increase the liking of the healthy snack. Similarly, Lapierre, Vaala, and Linebarger (2011) found that supposedly "new" cereals were considered more tasteful by 5- to 6-year-old children ($M_{age} = 5.6$, $SD = 0.96$; $N = 80$) if these were endorsed on the packaging by licensed characters versus when no endorser was present. This effect particularly occurred for those cereals branded as sugary (i.e., unhealthy), whereas it did not occur for the same cereals branded as healthy foods. Here, the lack of an effect for the healthier cereals could be attributed to a ceiling effect because even in the no endorsement condition children already found these supposedly healthy cereals extremely tasteful. However, with only 20 participants per condition in a between-participants design, the study also lacks power.[2]

In Kotler, Shiffman, and Hanson (2012; $N = 343$; 3- to 6-year-old, $M_{age} = 4.08$, $SD = 0.99$) children were asked for relative preference ratings. One third of the participants in their first study rated each of nine food pairs that were not endorsed. The other participants rated the same pairs but each item within the pair was endorsed, either by a familiar endorser or an unfamiliar one. In line with the results discussed above, they found that comparative to the baseline condition, the relative preference increased for the foods endorsed by the familiar character.

Roberto, Baik, Harris, and Brownell (2010) presented children between 4 and 6 years old ($N = 40$; $M_{age} = 5$, $SD = 0.7$) with three different identical food pairs of which one item was endorsed by a licensed character. They found a significant taste preference for the endorsed food items. In fact, this study was an endorsement alternative to an earlier study (Robinson, Borzekowski, Matheson & Kraemer, 2007, $N = 63$, $M_{age} = 4.6$, $SD = 0.5$, ranged 3.5–5.4 year olds) in which identical foods in a pair were either presented in McDonald's branded packaging or in non-branded packaging. Similar to the endorsement effect, the McDonald's brand logo increased the relative taste preference for the branded foods.

Similarly, Levin and Levin (2010) applied a within-participants design, but their 43 participating children (7 to 8 years old) rated eight different foods that were either endorsed or not, healthy or not, and from a known or (artificial) unknown brand. Their measures focused on perceptions of how nutritionally good or bad these children perceived the foods to be, which is strikingly different from the actual attitude and liking measures used in the other studies reviewed here. Their analyses showed no overall endorsement main effect; however, for unhealthy products from an unknown brand, endorsement did have an effect. Though sufficiently powered due to the within-participants design, the simultaneous orthogonal manipulation of three different variables could have disturbed a clear manifestation of an endorsement effect.

Finally, Smits and Vandebosch (2012) demonstrated that when previously non-endorsed foods became endorsed this led to better attitudes towards the items (increased liking, wanting to consume and intentions to request the food from parents) among the same participants ($N = 57$, 6- to 7-year-old, $M_{age} = 6.8$). In sum, these studies clearly demonstrate that the endorsement effect does exist for attitudinal measures, with only Levin and Levin's study (2010) showing no endorsement effect. Interestingly, though, the studies in this category focus on the younger part of our age range (up until 7 years old) with Levin and Levin's being the oldest sample. The basic endorsement effect on attitudinal measures should thus be further confirmed among older children.

Choice/behavior studies.   Some studies also tapped into actual food choice. Comparable to their relative preference questions, Roberto et al. (2010) found that an endorser also positively affected the forced choice between two similar food items such that children were significantly more likely to select the endorsed food item as a snack. Kotler and colleagues (2012) also assessed choices. A subset of their participants in the first study (where they gave relative preference scores) also participated in a second phase of the data collection (Study 2 in the paper). Here, children could eat from each item of three food pairs. Extending the findings of their first study, it was found that the foods endorsed by *Sesame Street's* Elmo were somewhat more likely to be eaten than those endorsed by an unfamiliar character or those not endorsed.

In an Australian web survey (Dixon et al., 2014) 11-year-old children ($N = 1302$, $M_{age} = 11.0$, $SD = 0.7$) chose between an energy-dense nutrient-poor product (EDNP) and a healthier variant; they did so for five food categories. The EDNP product pictures were manipulated to include no specific promotion (control) or front-of-pack promotions such as a male sports celebrity endorser, a premium offer, or a nutrient content claim. Relative to the control condition, the odds of choosing the EDNP rather than the healthier option increased significantly when boys saw the EDNP with the male athlete endorser. For girls, however, the athlete endorser did not have an effect. It is unclear whether this gender difference is indeed attributable to the gender of the endorser, but it seems conceivable. Certainly, the large sample size makes the study well powered to find even a modest effect, should it exist. More research is needed to test whether other endorsers could have an effect on girls of this age (equivalent to the effect of male athlete endorsers on the boys in this study).

Boyland and colleagues (2013) extended the measurement of choice behavior to a measure of the *ad libitum* amount of food intake. In their study, children ages 8 to 11 ($N = 181$, $M_{age} = 10$, $SD = 0.9$) were presented with one of four television clips (three of which were commercials, the other a TV clip of similar duration) and afterwards children could eat from two identical bowls of potato chips that were labeled as a national brand (Walker's Crisps) or a "supermarket" private label. Children generally ate more from the so-called national brand than from its private label alternative. More importantly, children exposed to a commercial for Walker's featuring its longstanding endorser Gary Lineker (a former soccer player and current celebrity) ate more of the Walker's Crisps than those in the control conditions (with a non-related food or non-food commercial). Interestingly, children exposed to a television clip featuring the endorser in his other role as a television presenter also ate more of the Walker's Crisps than the children in the control condition. British children seemingly have such strong mental connections between Lineker and Walker's that exposure to the endorser without reference to the potato chips already works as an implicit ad for those chips.

An intervention study by Bezbaruah, Stastny, and Brunt (2013) on fourth graders (typically 9 to 10 years old, $N_{t1} = 256$, $N_{t2} = 237$) applied a repeated measures design and non-celebrity endorsement of green beans. Three weeks after the initial measurement of typical bean consumption, the same beans were served during school lunch, but accompanied by a graphic of a spokes character (the article does not specify the character). A comparison of consumption at both time points revealed that when beans were endorsed, more children (a 10% increase) chose the beans but that portion sizes were smaller (particularly for boys).

Wansink, Just, and Payne (2012) also studied 8- to 11-year-old ($N = 208$) children and used Elmo as an endorser. They did a five day study with a pretest day, a post-test day and three intermediate intervention days. Though the use of an Elmo sticker increased the odds of an apple being chosen, it did not do so for cookies. Again, the lack of an effect could be attributable to a ceiling effect because even at baseline the cookies had a very high probability of being chosen. Statistical power could not be an issue here given the number of participants. They also found a smaller, but significant positive effect of an unknown endorser for apples.

The previously reported studies mostly used still images, manipulated packaging, or existing TV advertisements to represent the food endorsement. De Droog, Buijzen, and Valkenburg (2014) had a novel approach with an intervention study using picture books. Children, 4 to 6 years old ($N = 160$), participated in a five day intervention study where four different experimental groups had daily reading sessions of a picture book that used a congruent (rabbit) or incongruent (turtle) endorser to promote the consumption of carrots. On the fifth day, the 5 minute free consumption of carrots, cucumber, cheese, and salty sticks was compared between these experimental groups and a control group. Relative to the control group (that did not participate in any study-related activity such as reading a specified non-endorsement book), the children exposed to the picture book (with either endorser) ate more carrots, less cucumber and less cheese. Interestingly, they did not cut down on the salty snacks. In all, the study suggests that there is an endorser effect on carrot consumption though it might be bounded by very appealing consumption alternatives.

To summarize, basic endorsement effects were reported in various ways and on the full age spectrum we consider, so on the basis of this evidence we can answer RQ1 positively—yes, a basic endorser effect does exist. It is important to note the diversity of study designs resulting in similar patterns of findings since this attests to the stability and ecological validity of the effect. Cognitive measures were most often used for younger age ranges, whereas the choice or behavior measures were more spread out over the age continuum from 3 to 12 years.

RQ2: Is the Strength of the Endorsement Effect Influenced by Endorser Type?

Though a number of different dimensions categorizing endorsers could be imagined, attention has largely been dedicated to the difference between familiar and unfamiliar endorsers. At least two (related) reasons can be given for this specific interest. First, from a policy perspective it taps into the question of how harmful the proliferation of celebrity endorsers is when they seem to disproportionately promote unhealthy foods. Second, from a health promoting perspective it is interesting to know the complement: to what extent can an unfamiliar (and thus cheaper) endorser increase the preference for a (healthy) food item?

De Droog, Valkenburg, and Buijzen (2011) presented children (4 to 6 years old, $N = 216$) with both healthy and unhealthy foods (see above) and manipulated between participants whether each food was not endorsed, endorsed by a familiar character (*Dora* for girls and *SpongeBob* for boys), or endorsed by an unfamiliar character (a monkey). In this between-participants design, they did not find differences in the endorsement effect for the familiar versus the unfamiliar endorser. Given the large sample size, the lack of a significant effect should not be attributed to a lack of statistical power.

All other studies addressing RQ2 used a within-participants design. For instance, de Droog, Buijzen, and Valkenburg (2012) presented 4- to 6-year-old children ($N = 166$) with a carrot that was endorsed by a familiar character (*Dora* for girls and *Diego* for boys) and four unfamiliar characters differing in perceptual and conceptual congruence with the product. Contrary to their previous between-participants design, this study revealed more positive attitudes for carrots endorsed by the familiar endorser, followed by the conceptually congruent characters. Note that in their study with the picture books (see above; de Droog, Buijzen, & Valkenburg, 2014), they did not find stronger endorsement effects for the congruent endorser (rabbit endorsing carrots) than for the incongruent one (turtle endorsing carrots). Kotler, Shiff-man, and Hanson (2012) found that children (3 to 6 years old) choosing between food items endorsed by *Sesame Street* characters versus unknown (though professionally designed) "Crumbsnatcher" characters preferred (Study 1, $N = 343$, $M_{age} = 4.08$, $SD = 0.99$) and ate (Study 2, $N = 207$) the former rather than the latter. Wansink, Just, and Payne (2012; children ages 8 to 11) found that *Elmo* was a better endorser to promote the choice of an apple (offered together with a cookie) than an unknown endorser. Still, that unknown endorser had a significant effect compared to a no endorsement condition (see above).

Finally, Smits and Vandebosch (2012; children ages 6 to 7, $N = 57$, $M_{age} = 6.8$) applied a mixed design in which the familiarity of the endorser was both manipulated within-participants and between-participants (cf. a Latin square design). They too found that familiar characters resulted in stronger effects than unfamiliar ones. Interestingly, their design is the only one of the within-partici-pants studies that tests whether the unfamiliar characters are actually persuasive relative to a control condition. Indeed, the other studies used an experimental-experimental design where only the relative effect can be assessed. Smits and Vandebosch (2012) did find endorsement effects (increased liking, wanting to consume and intentions to request the food from parents) for both the familiar and the unfamiliar characters.

Related to the aforementioned study, Neeley and Schumann (2004; chil-dren ages 2 to 5) conducted two studies where they designed TV ads in which endorsers were paired with products. After three exposures to these ads (embedded in a TV show), the attitudinal and choice effects concerning the endorsed cheese crackers were measured. In contrast to the previ-ously mentioned studies, Neeley and Schumann (2004) did not manipulate the endorsers *per se*, but rather manipulated the interaction between the endorser and the product (Study 1, $N = 67$, $M_{age} = 3.83$) and the vocal inter-action between two endorsers (Study 2, $N = 37$, $M_{age} = 3.58$). They found the strongest endorsement effects when the endorser interacted with the product and when the ad did not feature a complex auditory communication between the endorsers.

In sum, unfamiliar characters can produce endorsement effects but the strongest relative effect is to be expected from familiar endorsers. Notably, this evidence stems from within-participants designs, with the only between-participants design (de Droog et al., 2011) unable to detect significant differences between familiar and unfamiliar endorsements. So again, the evidence supports a positive response to RQ2—yes, the strength of the endorsement effect is impacted by the type of endorser used. However, too little is known about the magnitude of the absolute endorsement effect for unfamiliar characters. This is crucial because it applies to the situation of healthy but unprocessed foods where the profits are lower, and thus, relatively cheap characters are the only endorsement possibility.

RQ3: Does the Endorsement Strength Differ According to the Type of Food Being Promoted?

There is an underlying dichotomy in food items typically studied: healthy versus unhealthy products. Again, the focus is dual for good reasons. We do need to know how pervasive endorsement is as a marketing technique used to promote unhealthy foods. We also need to know to what extent the same technique can be applied to promote more healthy foods.

Lapierre, Vaala, and Linebarger (2011; children ages 5 to 6, $N = 80$, $M_{age} = 5.6$, $SD = 0.96$), used a between-participants manipulation to brand the exact same cereals either as "Sugar Bits" or "Healthy Bits" (thus suggesting that the food is unhealthy or healthy rather than using different food items). The children who participated in their study reported liking the so-called healthy option more (4.65 ± 0.84 on a 5 point rating scale) than the "less healthy" version (4.22 ± 1.27). No endorsement effect was found for the "Healthy Bits" (possibly due to a ceiling effect and/or a lack of power). For the unhealthy option, adding an endorser did result in increased liking.

Roberto and colleagues (2010; children ages 4 to 6, $N = 40$; $M_{age} = 5$, $SD = 0.7$) used both unhealthy items and a healthy item (baby carrots) in a within-participants presentation to their participants. Their licensed endorsers (*Scooby Doo, Dora,* and *Shrek*) increased the liking of the foods, but the effect was smaller for the healthy option. De Droog, Valkenburg, and Buijzen (2011; children ages 4 to 6, $N = 216$) also presented each participant with both a healthy option and a less healthy option. Endorsement did have an effect for the healthy option and not for the unhealthy one (again this is a possible ceiling effect; given the sample size it is not likely to be due to a lack of power). The endorsed healthy option was still less liked than the non-endorsed unhealthy option.

Smits and Vandebosch (2012) applied a mixed design where the healthiness of the foods were manipulated both within- and between-participants. They found that endorsement effects were stronger for unhealthy foods than for healthy foods. Although the endorsement effects were smaller for healthy foods, it did occur relative to a pre-test no-endorsement baseline measure among the same participants.

Kotler, Shiffman, and Hanson (2012; children ages 3 to 6) offered an interesting alternative design. For some of their stimuli pairs, one item was healthy and the other unhealthy. As discussed above, children in the Kotler et al., (2012) study saw pairs of food items and in the experimental conditions both items were endorsed (one by a familiar endorser, one by an unfamiliar one). For these pairs, the familiar *Sesame Street* character used to endorse a healthy option did not convince children to like or choose that option above the unhealthy option endorsed by an unknown character. Similarly, Wansink, Just, and Payne (2012) studied 8- to 11-year-old ($N = 208$) children and found that an *Elmo* sticker increased the odds of an apple being chosen, but it did not do so for cookies. This null effect for cookies could be due to a ceiling effect; up to 90% of children chose to have a cookie in the control condition. Given the large sample size, statistical power is not a likely reason for not finding the effect here.

In sum, healthy foods can profit from endorsement effects, although these effects can be expected to be smaller than for a similar endorsement of an unhealthy food option. Again, those endorsement effects were demonstrated across the age range from 3 to 11 and no age-specific pattern of findings seemed to emerge. Similar to RQ2, too few studies reported on actual food choice and consumption, but the evidence supports a positive response to RQ3 also. The strength of the endorsement effect does appear to differ according to the type of food being promoted.

Of course, the strict categorization scheme for endorser effects as outlined above (see Table 10.1) does not represent the full spectrum of possibilities. At least one exception to this scheme should be noted and credited for its demonstration of what could be called an atypical and non-marketing endorsement effect. Wansink, Shimizu, and Camps (2012) conducted a within-participants study (with pre-test and post-test for baseline measures). They asked 22 children, ages 6 to 12 ($N = 22$, $M_{age} = 8.5$), what they expected to be the food choice of real and fictional models (like *Batman*). Asking these children whether the models would prefer apple fries or French fries increased the odds that they would choose the apple fries themselves. This effect was most pronounced for those children who expected the admirable models to choose the apple fries. This study has at least two implications. The first is that endorsement effects could exist even for incidental pairings of the endorsing character and the endorsed foods such that, for instance, parents can adaptively use the endorsement technique to boost their children's healthy preferences. Second, the study also demonstrates that the pairing between food and endorser is not necessarily a top-down given fact, but that it could also work as a bottom-up free association starting from the child's expectations about the endorser.

Conclusion

This review focused on an emerging topic in research: experimental studies measuring the effect endorsers have on attitudes, food preferences, choices and intake in children. Though this taps into a longstanding interest of academics, parents, and policy makers, the empirical evidence is very recent, as demonstrated by the publication dates of the reviewed studies. Studies on this topic mostly emerged after 2005, and the majority were published in the last few years. These studies clearly demonstrate that characters have the persuasive capability of increasing the liking of and preference for foods they endorse, among children aged 3 to 12 years. Together, these studies also suggest that both familiar and unfamiliar characters have the potential to generate these effects, although the evidence up to now suggests that the effects are strongest for familiar characters. Finally, these studies also suggest that both unhealthy and healthy foods can be promoted through endorsement techniques, but that, possibly, the effect is smaller for healthy foods.

Given the potential of endorsement advertising to guide children's food choices, it seems desirable to urge governments to restrict the use of this strategy in the promotion of unhealthy foods to children. One practical implication is that it is important that policy makers realize that the persuasive impact of such endorsements is not constrained to typical mass media advertising such as TV (for example, several studies discussed in this review used characters on packaging as the experimental stimuli). We therefore urge policy makers to restrict endorsement-based marketing strategies for unhealthy foods targeted at children irrespective of the medium in which they are displayed. At the same time, governments could support the use of endorsers to encourage children to eat healthily by using them in public health campaigns, school intervention programs, on healthy food packages and vending machines, and so forth.

Next to active, and possibly subsidized, support, governments could also think of co-branding policies where the use of endorsement strategies is only allowed if the same endorsement campaign also includes balanced promotion of generic healthy options (e.g., in a general health campaign or with promotion of healthy products within the brand's portfolio). Some of the reviewed studies already pertain to this topic. Robinson et al. (2007) already demonstrated the persuasiveness of the McDonald's logo with respect to more healthy options such as milk or carrots. Smits and Vandebosch (2012) showed that their celebrity endorser was effective in endorsing fruits as well as cookies. That same endorser (Kabouter Plop™) has since been used commercially in Belgium and the Netherlands to endorse child-targeted fruits and vegetables as well as cookies. More research is needed, however, to ensure that such dual promotion (on the level of the food brand or the endorser) produces sufficiently positive effects on diet and health.

Notably limited in the published research were studies measuring actual food consumption. Despite the demonstration of persuasiveness by endorsers to promote the liking, choice, and even consumption of healthy foods, it remains unclear whether this technique will lead to additional consumption (next to unhealthy foods) or the replacement of unhealthy consumption with healthy products.

If academic research wants to move on to detecting how to protect children from negative influences of marketing on their food consumption, as suggested by Harris and colleagues (2009), clear insight is needed into which effects occur and how they occur. The present overview tried to systematically shed light on the most widely adopted marketing technique across all marketing communication tools (such as TV advertising, packaging, in-store promotions), namely endorsement marketing. Certainly, endorsement marketing is only part of the marketing spectrum applied to target children; many other techniques exist.

One limitation of this review is that only experimental studies focusing on the effect itself have been studied, while neglecting the equally interesting question of the underpinning cognitive processes. So, while the overview of studies gives a clear insight into the causality of endorsement effects, it does not provide insight as to what is driving these effects. It should be noted that the studies reviewed here did not exist in a theoretical vacuum; however, a general scheme on how to interpret the findings is not apparent. Next to studies demonstrating effects of endorser type and food type on actual food consumption, researchers should also design future studies that can better explain the underlying cognitive processes.

This absence of a clear theoretical process model of childhood persuasion by endorsers is illustrative for the full spectrum of childhood persuasion insights. Whereas adult persuasion literature is clearly covered by many theoretical models and empirical demonstrations of these models (such as elaboration likelihood model, heuristic-systematic model, or transportation theory) only few researchers (e.g., Te'eni-Harari, Lampert, Lehman-Wilzig, 2007; Buijzen, Van Reijmersdal, & Owen, 2010) have empirically studied underlying persuasion processes in childhood. We can only further subscribe to the claim that more research is needed to understand precisely how cognitive processes persuade children. The findings of the current review suggest that endorsement marketing is a powerful persuasion mechanism, but we do not yet know enough to explain how it works.

A second limitation of the current review, and related to the previous limitation, is that too few studies exist to adequately map a developmental path of endorser persuasion. The studies included in this review focused on children aged up to 12 years old. It could be that different processes underlying the endorsement effect co-exist within these age categories. It could equally be possible that these children are all persuaded in a similar cognitive manner and that the only difference is to be found in the type of endorser, which should of course match the child's preferences. Although endorsement is used as an advertising technique for adults as well, it is also worthwhile to study the effects for older children, a focus that is currently missing in the literature. Are endorsers equally persuasive for all age groups? Most studies seem to focus on children between 4 and 8 years old, only some studied children between 8 and 12. But what happens afterwards? And what is the developmental path of the persuasion processes?

A last limitation of the current review is that it singles out endorsement as the most prevalent technique, but it does not take into account possibly relevant medium-specific effects. Most existing studies either present the endorser as an on-pack or similar endorser (e.g., a sticker on a piece of fruit) or as appearing in a TV commercial. Of course, other options exist as well, with website advertising, in-game advertising, apps, books (cf. de Droog et al., 2014), premiums, etc. Does endorsement have a similar effect irrespective of the communication medium? If endorsement works via processes such as fantasy (Rose et al., 2012), it seems likely that a more narrative endorsement (with an endorser actually interacting with the endorsed foods) would work better than rather static depictions of an endorser with a food item. Following Dixon and colleagues (2014) we could also wonder how effective endorsers are compared to other popular persuasive techniques like premiums, humor, nutrient claims, advergames, and so forth. Future research should therefore study the relative effectiveness of different techniques or, rather, the interactive effectiveness of these techniques.

Notes

1. As well as famous people (typically in the field of entertainment or sport), this definition can also include fictional characters. These can either be licensed characters, in which case they are known outside of the endorsed product (e.g., a cartoon character known from a movie or series) or branded characters, which are created specifically to promote the brand and/or product (e.g., Tony the Tiger for Kellogg's Frosted Flakes; or Captain Birdseye, also known as Captain Iglo, for Birds Eye or Iglo frozen seafood products).
2. For inferences about the statistical power of studies in this review, we used the rule of thumb that *n* should reach about 50 per condition, as suggested by Simmons, Nelson, and Simonsohn (2013). We rely on this rule of thumb because the different design approaches in the reviewed literature do not allow the use of a pooled effect size to perform proper power calculations.

References

Acuff, D. S., & Reiher, R. H. (1997). *What kids buy and why: The psychology of marketing to kids.* New York: Free Press.

Alvy, L. M., & Calvert, S. L. (2008). Food marketing on popular children's web sites: A content analysis. *Journal of the American Dietetic Association, 108*(4), 710–713. doi:10.1016/j.jada.2008.01.006

Bezbaruah, N., Stastny, S. N., & Brunt, A. (2013). Does positioning of a spokes-character improve selection and consumption of vegetables among fourth grade school lunch participants? *Journal of Human Nutrition and Food Science, 1,* 1007.

Boyland, E. J., Harrold, J. A., Kirkham, T. C., & Halford, J. C. (2011). The extent of food advertising to children on UK television in 2008. *International Journal of Pediatric Obesity, 6*(5–6), 455–461. doi:10.3109/17477166.2011.608801

Boyland, E. J., Harrold, J. A., Dovey, T. M., Allison, M., Dobson, S., Jacobs, M. C., & Halford, J. C. (2013). Food choice and overconsumption: Effect of a premium sports celebrity endorser. *The Journal of Pediatrics, 163*(2), 339–343. doi:10.1016/j.jpeds.2013.01.059

Bragg, M. A., Yanamadala, S., Roberto, C. A., Harris, J. L., & Brownell, K. D. (2013a). Athlete endorsements in food marketing. *Pediatrics, 132*(5), 805–810. doi:10.1542/peds.2013-0093

Bragg, M. A., Liu, P. J., Roberto, C. A., Sarda, V., Harris, J. L., & Brownell, K. D. (2013b). The use of sports references in marketing of food and beverage products in supermarkets. *Public Health Nutrition, 16,* 738–742. doi:10.1017/S1368980012003163

Brucks, M., Armstrong, G. M., & Goldberg, M. E. (1988). Children's use of cognitive defenses against television advertising: A cognitive response approach. *Journal of Consumer Research, 14,* 471–482.

Buijzen, M., Van Reijmersdal, E. A., & Owen, L. H. (2010) Introducing the PCMC model: An investigative framework for young people's processing of commercialized media content. *Communication Theory, 20*(4), 427–450. doi:10.1111/j.1468-2885.2010.01370.x

Cairns, G., Angus, K., Hastings, G., & Caraher, M. (2013). Systematic review of the evidence on the nature, extent and effects of food marketing to children. A retrospective summary. *Appetite, 62,* 209–215. doi:10.1016/j.appet.2012.04.017

Castonguay, J., Kunkel, D., Wright, P., & Duff, C. (2013). Healthy Characters? An Investigation of Marketing Practices in Children's Food Advertising. *Journal of Nutrition Education and Behavior, 45*(6), 571–577. doi:10.1016/j.jneb.2013.03.007

de Droog, S. M., Buijzen, M., & Valkenburg, P. (2012). Use a rabbit or a rhino to sell a carrot? The effect of character-product congruence on children's liking of healthy foods. *Journal of Health Communication, 17,* 1068–1080. doi:10.1080/10810730.2011.650833

de Droog, S. M., Buijzen, M., & Valkenburg, P. M. (2014). Enhancing children's vegetable consumption using vegetable-promoting picture books. The impact of interactive shared reading and character–product congruence. *Appetite, 73,* 73–80. doi:10.1016/j.appet.2013.10.018

de Droog, S. M., Valkenburg, P., & Buijzen, M. (2011). Using brand characters to promote young children's liking of and purchase requests for fruit. *Journal of Health Communication, 16,* 79–89. doi:10.1080/10810730.2010.529487

Dixon, H., Scully, M., Wakefield, M., Kelly, B., Chapman, K., & Donovan, R. (2011). Parent's responses to nutrient claims and sports celebrity endorsements on energy-dense and nutrient-poor foods. An experimental study. *Public Health Nutrition, 14,* 1071–1079. doi:10.1017/S1368980010003691

Dixon, H., Scully, M., Niven, P., Kelly, B., Chapman, K., Donovan, R., {. . .} & Wakefield, M. (2014). Effects of nutrient content claims, sports celebrity endorsements and premium offers on pre-adolescent children's food preferences: Experimental research. *Pediatric Obesity. 9*(2), 47–57. doi:10.1111/j.2047-6310.2013.00169.x

Elliott, C. D. (2008). Marketing fun foods: A profile and analysis of supermarket food messages targeted at children. *Canadian Public Policy, 34*(2), 259–273.

Elliott, C. D. (2009). Healthy food looks serious: How children interpret packaged food products. *Canadian Journal of Communication, 34,* 359–380.

EU Pledge (2012). *Nutrition criteria white paper.* Retrieved from http://www.eu-pledge.eu

Fazio, R. H., & Roskos-Ewoldson, D. R. (2005). Acting as we feel: When and how attitudes guide behavior. In T. C. Brock & M. C. Green (Eds.), *Persuasion: Psychological insights and perspectives,* 2nd ed., (pp. 41–62). Thousand Oaks, CA, US: Sage Publications.

Federal Trade Commission. (2008). *Marketing food to children and adolescents: A review of industry expenditures, activities, and self-regulation.* Washington, DC: Federal Trade Commission, 149.

Fischer, P. M., Schwartz, M. P., Richards, J. W., Goldstein, A. O., & Rojas, T. H. (1991). Brand logo recognition by children aged 3 to 6 years. Mickey Mouse and Old Joe Camel. *Journal of the American Medical Association, 266,* 3145–3148. doi:10.1001/jama.1991.03470220061027

Friedman, H. H., & Friedman, L. (1979). Endorser effectiveness by product type. *Journal of Advertising Research, 19*(5), 63–71.

Harris, J. L., Brownell, K. D., & Bargh, J. A. (2009). The food marketing defense model: Integrating psychological research to protect youth and inform public policy. *Social Issues and Policy Review, 3,* 211–271. doi:10.1111/j.1751-2409.2009.01015.x

Hebden, L., King, L., Kelly, B., Chapman, K., & Innes-Hughes, C. (2011). A menagerie of promotional characters: Promoting food to children through food packaging. *Journal of Nutrition Education and Behavior, 43*(5), 349–355. doi:10.1016/j.jneb.2010.11.006

Institute of Medicine (IOM) (2006). *Food marketing to children: Threat or opportunity?* Committee on Food Marketing and the Diets of Children and Youth. Washington, DC: National Academies Press.

John, D. R. (1999). Consumer socialization of children: A retrospective look at twenty-five years of research. *Journal of Consumer Research, 26*(3), 183–213. doi: 10.1086/209559

Jones, T., & Evans, D. (2000). Conducting a systematic review. *Australian Critical Care, 13*(2), 66–71. doi:10.1016/S1036-7314(00)70624-2

Kelly, B., Chapman, K., King, L., & Hebden, L. (2011). Trends in food advertising to children on free-to-air television in Australia. *Australian and New Zealand Journal of Public Health, 35*(2), 131–134. doi:10.1111/j.1753-6405.2011.00612.x

Kelly, B., Halford, J. C., Boyland, E. J., Chapman, K., Bautista-Castaño, I., Berg, C., {. . .} & Summerbell, C. (2010). Television food advertising to children: A global perspective. *American Journal of Public Health, 100*, 1730–1736. doi:10.2105/AJPH.2009.179267

Kotler, J. A., Shiffman, J. M., & Hanson K. G. (2012). The influence of media characters on children's food choices. *Journal of Health Communication: International Perspectives*, 17, 886–898. doi:10.1080/10810730.2011.650822

Lapierre, M. A., Vaala, S. E., & Linebarger, D. L. (2011). Influence of licensed spokes characters and health cues on children's ratings of cereal taste. *Archives of Pediatrics & Adolescent Medicine, 165*(3), 229–234. doi:10.1001/archpediatrics.2010.300

Levin, A. M., & Levin, I. P. (2010). Packaging of healthy and unhealthy food products for children and parents: The relative influence of licensed characters and brand names. *Journal of Consumer Behaviour, 9*(5), 393–402. doi: 10.1002/cb.326

Livingstone, S., & Helsper, E. J. (2006). Does advertising literacy mediate the effects of advertising on children? A critical examination of two linked research literatures in relation to obesity and food choice. *Journal of Communication, 56*, 560–584. doi:10.1111/j.1460-2466.2006.00301.x

Money, R. B., Shimp, T. A., & Sakano, T. (2006). Celebrity endorsements in Japan and the United States: Is negative information all that harmful? *Journal of Advertising Research, 46*(1), 113–23. doi:10.2501/S0021849906060120

Moore, E. S., & Rideout, V. J. (2007). The online marketing of food to children: Is it just fun and games? *Journal of Public Policy & Marketing*, 26, 202–220. doi:http://dx.doi.org/10.1509/jppm.26.2.202

Neeley, S. M., & Schumann, D. W. (2004). Using animated spokes-characters in advertising to young children. Does increasing attention to advertising necessarily lead to product preference? *Journal of Advertising, 33*(3), 7–23. doi:10.1080/00913367.2004.10639166

Owen, S. (1997). Food choice: How to assess attitudes of pre-adolescent children. *British Food Journal, 99*(4), 148–153. doi:10.1108/00346659710157240

Persson, M., Soroko, R., Musicus, A., & Lobstein, T. (2012). *A junk-free childhood: The 2012 report of the StanMark Project on standards for marketing food and beverages to children in Europe.* A briefing paper from the International Association for the Study of Obesity. www.worldobesity.org/site_media/uploads/IASO_food_marketing_report_30_June_2011.pdf (accessed May 2014).

Roberto, C. A., Baik, J., Harris, J. L., & Brownell, K. D. (2010). Influence of licensed characters on children's taste and snack preferences. *Pediatrics, 126*, 88–93. doi:10.1542/peds.2009-3433

Robinson, T. N., Borzekowski, D. L. G., Matheson, D. N., & Kraemer, H. C. (2007). Effects of fast food branding on young children's taste preferences. *Archives of Pediatrics & Adolescent Medicine, 161*(8), 792–797. doi:10.1001/archpedi.161.8.792

Rose, G. M., Merchant, A., & Bakir, A. (2012). Fantasy in food advertising targeted at children. *Journal of Advertising, 41*(3), 75–90. doi:10.2753/JOA0091-3367410305

Rozendaal, E., Buijzen, M., & Valkenburg, P. (2010). Comparing children's and adults' cognitive advertising competences in the Netherlands. *Journal of Children and Media, 4*(1), 77–89. doi:10.1080/17482790903407333

Rozendaal, E., Buijzen, M., & Valkenburg, P. M. (2012). Think-aloud process superior to thought-listing in increasing children's critical processing of advertising. *Human Communication Research, 38*(2), 199–221. doi:10.1111/j.1468-2958.2011.01425.x

Rozendaal, E., Lapierre, M. A., Van Reijmersdal, E. A., & Buijzen, M. (2011). Reconsidering advertising literacy as a defense against advertising effects. *Media Psychology, 14*(4), 333–354. doi:10.1080/15213269.2011.620540

Sandberg, H. (2011). Tiger talk and candy king: Marketing unhealthy food and beverages to Swedish children. *Communications, 36*, 217–244. doi:10.1515/comm.2011.011

Sengupta, J., Goodstein, R. C., & Boninger, D. S. (1997). All cues are not created equal: Obtaining attitude persistence under low-involvement conditions. *Journal of Consumer Research, 23*, 351–361. doi:http://www.jstor.org/stable/2489570

Simmons, J. P., Nelson, L. D., & Simonsohn, U. (2013, January). Life after p-hacking. In *Meeting of the Society for Personality and Social Psychology, New Orleans, LA* (pp. 17–19).

Smits, T. & Vandebosch, H. (2012). Endorsing children's appetite for healthy foods: Celebrity versus non-celebrity spokes characters. *Communications: The European Journal of Communication Research, 37*, 371–391. doi: 10.1515/commun-2012-0021

Te'eni-Harari, T., Lampert, S. I., & Lehman-Wilzig, S. (2007). Information processing of advertising among young people: The elaboration likelihood model as applied to youth. *Journal of Advertising, 47*, 326–340. doi: 10.2501/S0021849907070341

Ülger, B. (2008). Packages with cartoon trade characters versus advertising: An empirical examination of preschoolers' food preferences. *Journal of Food Products Marketing, 15*(1), 104–117. doi: 10.1080/10454440802470649

Van Assema, P., Joosten, S., Bessems, K., Raaijmakers, L., de Vries, N., & Kremers, S. (2011). De omvang en aard van verkoopstrategieën gericht op kinderen bij voedingsmiddelen. *Tijdschrift voor Gezondheidswetenschappen, 89*, 108–113. doi: 10.1007/s12508-011-0040-2

Wansink, B., Just, D. R., & Payne, C. R. (2012). Can branding improve school lunches? *Archives of Pediatrics and Adolescent Medicine, 166*(10), 967–968. doi:10.1001/archpediatrics.2012.999

Wansink, B., Shimizu, M., & Camps, G. (2012). What would Batman eat? Priming children to make healthier fast food choices. *Pediatric Obesity, 7*, 121–123. doi: 10.1111/j.2047-6310.2011.00003.x

CHAPTER CONTENTS

11 Expectancy, Value, Promotion, and Prevention

An Integrative Account of Regulatory Fit vs. Non-fit with Student Satisfaction in Communicating with Teachers

Flaviu A. Hodis

Victoria University of Wellington

Georgeta M. Hodis

Massey University

In this study, we report on findings regarding the role that key communication constructs have in mediating the relationships among domain-specific expectancy and value beliefs and general motivation orientations. The results show that when student motivation has a promotion focus, feeling satisfied in communicating with the teacher in a course is a catalyst for heightened levels of expectancy of success and utility value beliefs regarding the course. In contrast, when student motivation has a prevention focus, this orientation is unrelated to expectancy and value beliefs. These findings have pivotal implications for advancing theory development and pedagogical practice.

A growing recognition exists worldwide that mathematics proficiency is required for achieving success and well-being at both individual and societal levels (Martin, Anderson, Bobis, Way, & Vellar, 2012; Mottet et al., 2008). A rich research literature has shown that students' expectancy of success in, and subjective value linked to, a given academic domain (e.g., mathematics) are important determinants of their academic performance, educational aspirations, and key choice behaviors that underlie success in the given domain (e.g., persistence, course enrollment; Conley, 2012; Perez, Cromley, & Kaplan, 2014; Watt et al., 2012; Wigfield, Tonks, & Klauda, 2009). Thus, an in-depth understanding of the nature of the mechanisms linking expectancy and value beliefs regarding mathematics with their antecedents could provide essential new knowledge on why some students achieve better than others.

Sociocommunicative interactions, such as those between student and teacher, are salient factors underlying student learning (Coplan, Hughes, Bosacki, & Rose-Krasnor, 2011; Daly & Korineck, 1980). In particular, communication between a student and her teacher in a class shapes the development of the learner's perceptions of the instructor's attitudes, beliefs, and expectations regarding her class performance. In turn, these perceptions influence a student's expectancies of success in the class and the value she attaches to knowledge and achievement in the given academic subject (Eccles 2005; Eccles (Parsons) et al., 1983; Wigfield & Cambria, 2010a; Wigfield & Eccles, 2000). Thus, factors that influence the nature and outcomes of communication encounters between students and instructors (e.g., students' general and school-related communicative self-efficacy beliefs and their satisfaction in communicating with a teacher) are likely to affect learners' expectancy and value beliefs. Conley (2012) raised a similar point regarding the role of socialization.

Intriguingly, although students' perceptions of teachers' beliefs, attitudes, and expectations are inherently linked to their communicative encounters, we are aware of no investigation of the relationships of expectancy and value that includes relevant communication factors. As a consequence, a key question regarding the role of communication constructs has yet to be answered: How do they mediate relationships among domain-specific expectancy and value constructs and their general motivational precursors? This study will bridge this gap by testing a theoretical model positing that general and school-related communicative self-efficacy beliefs, together with student satisfaction in communicating with their mathematics teachers, provide a mediating mechanism linking pivotal motivational orientations (i.e., promotion and prevention; Higgins, 2012b) to expectancy and value beliefs related to mathematics. This model is titled PRO-PRE-COM-EXP-VAL (promotion-prevention-communication-expectancy-value) and is presented in Figure 11.1.

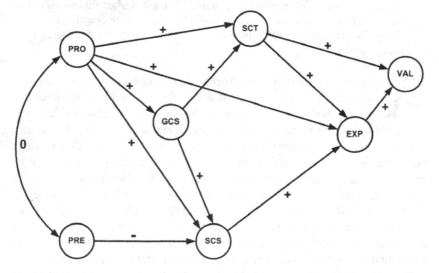

Figure 11.1 Proposed theoretical model: PRO-PRE-COM-EXP-VAL (promotion-prevention-communication-expectancy-value).

Note: PRO = promotion; PRE = prevention; GCS = general communicative self-efficacy; SCT = satisfaction in communicating with teachers; SCS = school-related communicative self-efficacy; EXP = expectancy; VAL = utility value.

Background

Expectancy and Value

Expectancy is a psychological construct that encompasses cognitive beliefs about future events and their likelihood of occurrence (Liberman & Förster, 2012; Roese & Sherman, 2007). Expectancy plays an important role in the self-regulation of behavior, affect, and cognition for it helps individuals employ information revealed by past experiences to shed light on future events and states. In particular, as the expectancy of success influences engagement with tasks, the expectancy construct can be regarded as an antecedent of value (Higgins, 2006, 2012b).

Expectancy-value theory (Eccles (Parsons) et al., 1983; Eccles & Wigfield, 2002) posits that essential student choices that affect their achievement performance (e.g., amount of effort expended toward learning tasks, persistence when facing difficulties, etc.) are influenced by how successful students believe they will be in the given learning domain (activity) and how much they value it (Eccles, 2005). In turn, students' expectancies and values are influenced by their general motivation tendencies and their perceptions/interpretations of other people's (e.g., parents', teachers') behaviors, beliefs, and attitudes regarding them (Eccles, 2005; Wigfield et al., 2009).

In the context of the expectancy-value paradigm, values are defined with regards to the enticing characteristics of tasks and encompass the reasons supporting individuals' desire to engage in a given activity (Eccles & Wigfield, 2002; Wigfield et al., 2009). This conceptualization, which is in line with recent theorizing of value in social psychology (Higgins, 2007), underlines that people's general motivation orientations are key contributors to value judgments (Wigfield et al., 2009). Importantly, unlike more general theories of value (Rokeach, 1973; Schwartz & Bilsky, 1987), the expectancy-value paradigm focuses on values that are task specific (Wigfield & Cambria, 2010a).

The expectancy-value theory distinguishes four components of subjective task values: utility value, intrinsic (interest) value, attainment value (importance), and cost (Eccles, 2005, 2011; Wigfield & Cambria, 2010b; Wigfield & Eccles, 2000). Although these components are theoretically distinct, measuring them empirically does not always result in distinguishable entities. As a consequence, in empirical investigations, researchers either combine two or more dimensions of value into a composite or use only one or two of the four components (e.g., Archambault, Eccles, & Vida, 2010; Chow, Eccles, & Salmela-Aro, 2012). Taking into account all of these aspects, the current investigation focuses only on utility value (usefulness). This construct reflects how a given task is aligned to (matches) a person's future plans (Wigfield et al., 2009); that is, how it supports one's long- and/or short-term goals and/or rewards (Eccles, 2005; Wigfield & Cambria, 2010b).

The Interplay among Communicative Self-Efficacy, Student Satisfaction in Communicating with Teachers, Expectancy, and Value

Self-efficacy beliefs are salient determinants of student learning and performance in academic settings (Bandura, 1997, 2006; Bong, 2001); they provide an important mediation mechanism connecting general motivation orientations to individualized and contextualized expectancies, values, and behavior. Successful navigation of essential aspects of the learning and teaching process (e.g., asking for relevant information, seeking help, class participation, etc.) and important parameters defining the appropriate functioning of this process (e.g., perceived understanding, cognitive learning, motivation, and positive affect toward teacher and class) are affected by how willing students are to engage in communication (Martin, Myers, & Mottet, 1999; Mottet, Martin, & Myers, 2004; Myers, Martin, & Mottet, 2002a, 2002b). In turn, willingness to engage in communication is influenced by students' self-perception of communicative competence (communicative self-efficacy beliefs; G. M. Hodis & Hodis, 2012; MacIntyre, 1994; MacIntyre, Babin, & Clement, 1999). Consistent with Frymier's (2005b) observation that "effective student communication likely consists of students' orientation toward communication *and* communication behaviors in and out of the classroom" (p. 202; emphasis in original), in this research we analyze both general and school-related communicative self-efficacy beliefs.

In line with the findings noted above and with the tenets of the expectancy-value theory, it follows that students' communicative self-efficacy beliefs may be an important mediator linking general motivation orientations and domain specific (e.g., mathematics-related) expectancy and value beliefs. This argument is further supported by findings indicating that: (a) individuals' general self-schemata and goals influence both expectancy and value; and (b) people's expectancies for success are related to their other self-efficacy beliefs (Eccles & Wigfield, 2002; Wigfield & Eccles, 2000). Furthermore, other empirical investigations found positive associations between students' self-reports of communication effectiveness and satisfaction in communicating with their teachers (Frymier, 2005b). Thus, this evidence suggests that communicative self-efficacy beliefs function as antecedents of this specific type of communication satisfaction and we discuss this proposition below.

Students' attitudes toward a course and its teacher, affective learning, and commitment to engage in learning-related practices are positively related to how satisfied learners are with communicating with their class teachers (Prisbell, 1985, 1990). As a case in point, Frymier (2005b) found that undergraduate students' satisfaction in communicating with their instructor had medium to high positive correlations with student motivation, effective learning, and learning indicators. Moreover, student-teacher communication is a key aspect underlying the contextual nature characterizing students' learning environments (Frisby & Martin, 2010; Teven & McCroskey, 1997; Voelkl, 1995). An in-depth understanding of student motivation to succeed in academic settings cannot be separated from the contextual nature and influence of this environment (Eccles & Wigfield, 2002). Hence, how satisfied students are with communicating with their teachers could be an important determinant of their expectancy of success and utility value.

Effective communication between students and teachers underlies positive developments of their relationships and influences student communication satisfaction (Goodboy, Martin, & Bolkan, 2009; Teven & McCroskey, 1997; Voelkl, 1995). In its most general form, communication satisfaction is conceptualized as a valenced affective response associated with attaining goals and expectations related to communication (Hecht, 1978a, 1978b). In classroom settings, the communication between students and teachers is both relational and "content driven" (Frymier & Houser, 2000, p. 215), centers on information access/exchange, exhibits a significant power differential, and functions under certain time constraints (Frymier & Houser, 2000; Goodboy et al., 2009; Martin, Mottet, & Myers, 2000; Martin et al., 1999; Myers et al., 2002a,b; Prisbell, 1985, 1990, 1994). All of these characteristics differentiate student-teacher communication from other types of interpersonal communication in important ways (Goodboy et al., 2009).

Student communication satisfaction with teachers (SCT) reflects the relational quality of student-teacher communication (Goodboy, Bolkan, Myers, & Zhao, 2011). Specifically, SCT is defined as the specific aspect of communication satisfaction associated with communication encounters taking place in instructional settings (Goodboy et al., 2009; for earlier conceptualizations of the construct see Prisbell, 1985, 1990, 1994). Students who are satisfied with their communication with teachers perceive their instructors as supportive (Prisbell, 1994) and are likely to engage more often with them. This increased frequency of student-teacher interactions may contribute to enhancing the rapport between students and their teacher; in turn, rapport relates positively to students' reports of perceived cognitive learning (Frisby & Martin, 2010). Additionally, being satisfied in communicating with teachers may support enhanced student communicative self-efficacy beliefs regarding school; this self-efficacy dimension is positively associated with college GPA (grade point average) (Barry & Finney, 2009).

When students have meaningful and significant communication encounters with their teachers, educators may have extended opportunities to promote shared beliefs about what is considered as desirable and valuable in the given settings (Wigfield et al., 2009; see also Higgins, 2007, 2012b). In turn, students who internalize these shared beliefs are likely to feel satisfied with the communication they have with their teachers and expect to do well in the given school subject. Additionally, students' satisfaction in communicating with teachers may support adaptive information- and help-seeking behaviors in educational contexts. Moreover, when students find their communication with teachers satisfying, they are more likely than not to regard instructors as supportive (Prisbell, 1994); this perception has been shown to be positively associated with student learning and well-being (Ryan & Shim, 2012). Furthermore, the extensive research literature focusing on teacher-student relations (interactions), student engagement, and classroom connectedness (climate) offers additional support for arguing that satisfactory communication between student and teacher is salient for a host of pivotal outcomes pertaining to student learning, motivation, behavior, affect, cognition, and communication skills (Prisbell, 1985; Prisbell, Dwyer, Carlson, Bingham, & Cruz, 2009; Sidelinger, Myers, & McMullen, 2011; Wubbels & Brekelmans, 2005). This body of evidence suggests that satisfaction in communicating with teachers is likely to play a pivotal role in the mediating mechanisms connecting expectancy of success and value with their motivation antecedents.

General Motivation Antecedents of Expectancy and Value: Regulatory Focus Theory; Promotion and Prevention Orientations

Regulatory focus theory (Higgins, 1997), which has at its conceptual core self-discrepancy theory (Higgins, 1987), proposes that the kinds of early socialization encounters of children influence the predominant type of self-guide they adopt, and thus, have readily accessible. In turn, consistent with the principles of accessibility theory (Higgins, 2012a), the predominant self-guide which they embrace influences, in essential ways, children's subsequent behavior and social judgment (Dweck, Higgins, & Grant-Pillow, 2003; Higgins, 1997). In particular, children for whom socialization with care givers revolves around hopes, ideals, aspirations, and personal advancement adopt ideal self-guides and develop strong promotion orientations. Children for whom socialization emphasizes safety and duty are likely to adopt ought self-guides and develop strong prevention orientations (Higgins, 1997). Differences in the strength of individuals' promotion and prevention focuses are consequential and they have been linked to inter-individual variability in people's personality traits, attitudes, cognitions, behaviors, and emotions (e.g., goal representation, choice of strategic approaches employed during goal pursuit, problem solving, decision making, and affective reactions to success and failure; Crowe & Higgins, 1997; Dweck et al., 2003; Higgins, 1997, 2012b; Molden, 2012).

People who have predominant promotion orientations focus on ideals and aspirations, prefer to use enthusiastic and eager strategies, and look for opportunities to advance and grow (Higgins, 2012b). As a result, they are willing to consider a wide range of information that could be relevant to goal accomplishment (Molden, 2012). This attitude shapes their perceptions of personal interactions and underlies the fact that promotion oriented individuals actively seek relevant advice and take it into consideration when available (Righetti, Finkenauer, & Rusbult, 2011). In addition, people exhibiting predominant promotion focus are sensitive to positive feedback and pay close attention to rewards (Förster & Werth, 2009; Lockwood, Jordan, & Kunda, 2002; Lockwood, Sadler, Fyman, & Tuck, 2004).

When prevention orientations are predominant, individuals focus on duty, responsibility, and security and prefer to forsake opportunities to gain rather than risk a loss (Molden, 2012). As a consequence, they tend to concentrate on the task at hand, are reluctant to consider new information, are not receptive to offers of assistance, and are unwilling to request feedback regarding the progress of their goal pursuit (Righetti et al., 2011; see also Förster & Higgins, 2005). In addition, people who have predominant prevention foci are sensitive to negative role models and are affected by negative feedback (Förster & Werth, 2009; Lockwood et al., 2002, 2004).

The interplay between class-related communicative interactions and promotion (vs. prevention) is important for learning and teaching. Specifically, when teachers transmit positive expectations about a students' abilities, these expectations are likely to promote and/or strengthen promotion. In contrast, exposing students regularly to low expectations and communicating some reservations about their abilities is likely to induce and/or strengthen prevention (Molden & Miele, 2008).

Interrelations among Expectancy, Value, Promotion, and Prevention: The Role of Regulatory Engagement and Regulatory Fit Theories

Regulatory engagement theory (Higgins, 2006, 2012b) posits that the extent to which people value the outcomes of goal pursuit is not determined solely by the magnitude of the desired/undesired (anticipatory) feelings associated with attaining the given outcomes. On the contrary, value is also affected by the strength of individuals' engagement with the goal pursuit process and by the confidence they have in their own evaluative judgments regarding its outcomes (Avnet, Laufer, & Higgins, 2013; Higgins, 2012b). Specifically, because regulatory fit is an important antecedent of engagement (Higgins, 2006, 2012b), value is enhanced when the actual manner in which an individual pursues a goal is sustained by (i.e., corresponds to, fits) her strategic manner of goal pursuit (Higgins, 2000, 2012b). Thus, eager pursuits of ideal aspirations (respectively vigilant pursuits of ought responsibilities) fit a promotion (respectively a prevention) orientation (Dweck et al., 2003; Higgins, 2006). Regulatory fit strengthens the intensity with which individuals experience attraction toward, or repulsion from, a target via mechanisms that are orthogonal to the hedonic properties of the outcomes of the goal pursuit. As a consequence, regulatory fit is a key motivational mechanism that enhances the value of a target in important ways (Higgins, 2012b).

Development of the PRO-PRE-COM-EXP-VAL (promotion-prevention-communication-expectancy-value) Mediation Model Linking Promotion, Prevention, Mediators, Expectancy, and Value

Individuals' regulatory foci are rooted in their fundamental needs (nurturance and security; Higgins, 1997), reflect the kinds of self-regulatory socializations they experienced as children, and determine their behavior, cognition, affect, and social judgment (Dweck et al., 2003; Higgins, 2012b). Taking all of these aspects into account, we hypothesize that promotion and prevention are antecedents of domain-specific self-efficacy beliefs (i.e., communicative self-efficacy beliefs), satisfaction in communicating with teachers, expectancy, and value. Because promotion and prevention orientations are independent of each other (Higgins, 1997, 2012b), they do not exert isomorphic influences on mediators and criteria. Thus, promotion is hypothesized to have positive direct relationships with general and school-related communicative self-efficacy, satisfaction in communicating with teachers, and expectancy, and to exert a positive indirect influence on value (see Figure 11.1). On the other hand, prevention is hypothesized to have a negative association with school-related communicative self-efficacy and no significant relationships with the other mediators. Additionally, prevention is hypothesized to exert no direct effects on expectancy and value.

The proposed relationships between promotion, prevention, and communicative self-efficacy beliefs reflect the fact that, in school settings, a focus on promotion (vs. prevention) may be associated with a distinct pattern of internalizing the meaning and significance of learning tasks and assignments. In particular, for the specific context of a basic communication course, G. M. Hodis and Hodis (2013) noted that promotion-oriented students may perceive assignments (e.g., delivering a public speech) as opportunities to gain knowledge and improve performance. In contrast, their prevention-oriented counterparts may regard the same task as an "unavoidable 'chance' to fail" (G. M. Hodis & Hodis, 2013, p. 108). As a consequence, the authors hypothesized that "these marked differences in internalizing the role of learning opportunities . . . can go a long way toward exploring variations in students' change in self-efficacy beliefs and willingness to communicate" (p. 108).

In a similar vein with Weber, Martin, and Myers's (2011) instructional beliefs model (IBM), our PRO-PRE-COM-EXP-VAL model hypothesizes that core self-efficacy beliefs (general and school-related communicative self-efficacy) are influenced by student characteristics (student motivation) and act as mediators between these student characteristics and key factors that affect learning outcomes (expectancy and value). Additionally, in line with regulatory focus theory (Higgins, 1997), we propose that when student characteristics are represented by general motivational orientations, such as promotion and prevention, these characteristics may have both direct and indirect effects on expectancy and value. In this way, our model departs somewhat from the IBM, which hypothesizes that self-efficacy fully mediates motivation effects on learning outcomes (see Weber et al., 2011, Figure 2).

We hypothesize that general and school-related communicative self-efficacy beliefs have positive direct and indirect effects on expectancy and value (see Figure 11.1). This proposition is supported by the fact that: (a) student communicative self-efficacy beliefs are positively related to cognitive and behavioral processes underlying success in school settings (G. M. Hodis & Hodis, 2012; Martin et al., 1999; Mottet et al., 2004; Myers et al., 2002a, 2002b); and (b) people's perceptions of the likelihood of success in goal pursuits are positively associated with their self-efficacy beliefs regarding the ability to perform the actions needed to support their goal strivings (Higgins, 2012b).

Given that communication satisfaction is influenced by self-perceptions of communicative competence (i.e., communicative self-efficacy beliefs) (Spitzberg, 1991), we hypothesize that communicative self-efficacy has a positive influence on satisfaction in communicating with teachers. This hypothesis is consistent with findings from Frymier (2005b) indicating that students' satisfaction with teacher communication is positively related to self-reports of their communication effectiveness.

Being satisfied in communicating with one's teacher affects important drivers of the learning and teaching process that underlie the expectancy of success in these settings (Frisby & Martin, 2010; Goodboy et al., 2009, 2011; Prisbell, 1985). Moreover, having meaningful and significant communication with teachers, which is a prerequisite of being satisfied with this kind of communication, gives students opportunities to co-create and internalize shared beliefs regarding the nature and the significance of success, the expectations for it, and the value associated with being successful (Wigfield et al., 2009; see also Higgins, 2006, 2012b).

Research conducted within regulatory focus, regulatory fit, and regulatory engagement (Higgins, 1997, 2000, 2006, 2012b) theoretical frameworks supports the hypothesized role that satisfaction in communicating with teachers plays in the PRO-PRE-COM-EXP-VAL model. Specifically, regulatory focus theory posits that because promotion and prevention are rooted in different survival needs of individuals (nurturance vs. security), they focus people's attention on different concerns related to task engagement (Higgins, 1997, 2012b). Drawing from this paradigm, Shah (2003) found support for "a connectionist conception of implicit social influence" (p. 436) indicating that perceptions of significant others' achievement expectations influence individuals' own expectancy of success, most likely by affecting their emotional reactions to the task via a mechanism that resembles regulatory fit at an interpersonal level. Importantly, Righetti and associates (2011) found that promotion-oriented individuals (but not prevention-oriented ones) experience certain motivation benefits when obtaining relevant information under interpersonal regulatory fit.

In line with these considerations, and consistent with Förster, Grant, Idson, and Higgins (2001) who argue that "success feedback maintains eagerness but reduces vigilance" (p. 255; see also Idson, Liberman, & Higgins, 2000), we maintain that being satisfied in communicating with one's teacher in a class might be, unconsciously, interpreted as a kind of success feedback by promotion-oriented students. This interpretation supports the eager pursuit of ideals and aspirations characterizing promotion-oriented students and drives a new kind of interpersonal regulatory fit. Hence, consistent with regulatory engagement theory, for students having a strong promotion orientation, the interpersonal regulatory fit associated with high levels of satisfaction in communicating with the class teacher is hypothesized to enhance the strength of their engagement and the expectancy of success and, consequently, to intensify their utility value perceptions. This argument is also in line with Förster et al.'s (2001) point of view, when they noted that "increasing expectancies after promotion success would continue the level of eagerness that fits a promotion focus" (p. 255).

Of importance, being satisfied in communicating with a teacher is a non-fit for prevention focused students because this satisfaction undermines the vigilance that constitutes the core of prevention (Förster et al., 2001; Higgins, 2012b). Taking into account all of these aspects, we argue that the relationships between promotion orientation, satisfaction in communicating with teachers, and expectancy of success are strong and positive. On the other hand, we expect that a prevention focus has neither direct influence nor mediated effects (by means of communication satisfaction) on expectancy.

Our PRO-PRE-COM-EXP-VAL model posits that expectancy is an antecedent of value. This argument is in line with Higgins's (2012b) countenance that subjective likelihood (i.e., expectancy) of success is a powerful "motivational force that affects not only commitment but also value" (p. 224). This hypothesis is further supported by Fishbach's (2009) instrumental view of value, which posits that people's level of expectancy to achieve a goal influences the value estimate they attribute to the given goal. In sum, because "to predict value and subsequent behavior, factors of both the person and the social environment, plus their interaction have to be identified" (Förster, 2009, p. 125), our model is well-suited to facilitate an integrated assessment of expectancy, value, and their antecedents.

Method

Participants

Approval for conducting this study was received from the University's Ethics Committee (the equivalent of the U.S. Institutional Review Board). Each participant gave individual consent for participation; the principals of the schools at which students were enrolled also provided consent for the study. Respondents were secondary school students ($N=463$) recruited from three demographically diverse schools that were selected at random from the list of all New Zealand (NZ) schools. All students in these schools who were enrolled in years 10–13 were invited to take part in the study. They received no incentives for participating in this research.

New Zealand has three official languages: English, Te Reo Māori, and sign language. In the NZ educational system, English is the primary language of instruction; this was the case for all of the three schools participating in this research. However, in numerous institutions, the educational process makes references to, and acknowledges the role of, the Te Reo Māori language or the Māori worldviews and cultural values.

More girls (272) than boys (141) participated in the study, and 50 students did not disclose their gender. In terms of ethnicity, 207 students (44.7%) indicated they were European, 19 (4.1%) Asian, 99 (21.4%) Māori, 36 (7.8%) Pacific, and 102 (22.0%) indicated other ethnicity or did not specify their ethnicity. With respect to year in school, 138 students (29.8%) were enrolled in year 10, 128 (27.7%) in year 11, 145 (31.3%) in year 12, and 52 (11.2%) in year 13 or did not specify the year. The age of the participants was not recorded. However, a typical year 10 student in NZ is approximately 14 years old.

Measures

The measures employed to gauge the seven constructs of interest (see Figure 11.1) were administered to students in the first part of the academic year. Each construct was assessed by several items taken or adapted from standardized instruments that have been shown to offer valid and reliable operationalizations of the respective constructs. Two instruments have been most often employed in social psychology research to gauge regulatory focus, namely the Regulatory Focus Questionnaire (Higgins et al., 2001) and the General Regulatory Focus Measure (Lockwood et al., 2002). Although both measures are grounded in the same theoretical framework, they attend to distinct definitions of regulatory focus (self-guide vs. reference point; Summerville & Roese, 2008). Based on the results of extensive reviews of these instruments (Haws, Dholakia, & Bearden, 2010; Summerville & Roese, 2008) and taking into account the target population for this study, the measure of regulatory focus proposed by Higgins and colleagues (2001) was chosen. This scale has 11 items: six for measuring promotion and five for measuring prevention.

Initially, all of the five prevention items were employed. However, after conducting a confirmatory factor analysis (CFA), we identified that one prevention item had much lower standardized loadings than all of the other prevention items (0.292 vs. 0.705; 0.568; 0.894; 0.647). A careful re-reading of this item revealed that its content overlapped with that of the item having the highest standardized loading; the only difference between the poorly performing item and the other prevention items was that it was worded in a different direction than all of the other prevention items. After removing the problematic item, the CFA, which included all seven constructs, was rerun. The interfactor correlations for the two models (one having five prevention items, the other having four prevention items; all else was identical) were indistinguishable, as the largest difference between corresponding correlations in the two models was 0.01. As a result, all of the analyses in this study employ a four-item prevention construct (see Table 11.1 for a summary of the information regarding all of the measures).

Satisfaction in communicating with teachers (SCT) was measured with six items from Goodboy et al.'s (2009) Student Communication Satisfaction Scale (Short Form). The original instrument contains eight items; however, two items are practically identical (with one being a negatively worded version of the other); in addition, the content of a third item is subsumed by that of a fourth item, with the difference being that they were worded in opposite directions. As a consequence, only six items were used to measure SCT in this study.

Taking into account that decontextualized measures of self-efficacy provide neither insights into behavior nor indications of self-regulatory success or failure (Bledow, 2013; for similar points see Bandura, 1997) this study employs domain

Table 11.1 Description of the Measures Used in the Study

Construct (# of items)	Symbol	Scoring Scale	Source of the Items	Examples of Items
Promotion (6)	PRO	1 (SD) to 7 (SA)	Higgins et al. (2001)	When it comes to achieving things that are important to me, I find that I perform as well as I ideally would like to do.
Prevention (4)	PRE	1 (SD) to 7 (SA)	Higgins et al. (2001)	When I grew up, I often got on my parents' nerves.
Satisfaction with communicating with teacher (6)	SCT	1 (SD) to 7 (SA)	Goodboy, Martin, and Bolkan (2009)	My conversations with my mathematics teacher are worthwhile.
General communicative self-efficacy (3)	GCS	0 (CI) to 100 (CC)	McCroskey and McCroskey (1988)	How competent do you believe you are to talk with an acquaintance?
School-related communicative self-efficacy (4)	SCS	0 (CDA) to 100 (HCCD)	Barry and Finney (2009)	How certain are you that you can participate in class discussions?
Expectancy (3)	EXP	1 to 7, anchors differ	Eccles, Wigfield, Harold, and Blumenfeld (1993)	How successful do you think you would be in a career requiring mathematics skills?
Value (3)	VAL	1 to 7, anchors differ	Wigfield et al. (1997)	In general, how useful is what you learn in mathematics?

Note: SD = Strongly disagree; SA = Strongly agree; CI = Completely incompetent; CC = completely competent; CDA = Cannot do at all; HCCD = Highly certain can do.

specific self-efficacy measures pertaining to communication. General communicative self-efficacy (GCS) was measured with three items from the Acquaintance subscale of McCroskey and McCroskey's (1988) Self-Perceived Communication Competence instrument. The original subscale has four items; one item that pertains to speaking in public was not appropriate for the context of NZ secondary school students and was not employed in this research. School-related communicative self-efficacy (SCS) was measured with four items from the Professor and Class Interaction Efficacy subscale of the College Self-Efficacy Inventory (Barry & Finney, 2009; Solberg, O'Brien, Villareal, Kennel, & Davis, 1993).

Finally, because expectancy and its influence on subsequent relevant behavior are domain-specific (Eccles, 2011), this research involves expectancy and utility values related to mathematics. The measures for expectancy and value used in this study are the ones employed in most of the expectancy-value research (see Table 11.1).

Data Analytic Techniques

In the first step, a CFA was conducted to examine the adequacy of the measurement model linking the measured items to their respective underlying constructs. Because this model fit the data well, in the second step of the analysis, a structural equation model (SEM) was employed to test the proposed theoretical model (see Figure 11.1) and evaluate total, direct, and indirect effects corresponding to expectancy and value. To assess the fit of the CFA and the SEM models to the empirical data, we employed the following fit indices: comparative fit index (CFI) (Bentler, 1990), Tucker-Lewis index (TLI) (Tucker & Lewis, 1973), and root-mean-square-error-of-approximation (RMSEA) (Steiger, 1990). Consistent with widely followed methodological recommendations (Hu & Bentler,1999), values of .95 and higher for CFI and TLI were employed as benchmarks for good fit. For RMSEA, values below .05 were considered to indicate very good fit. All analyses were conducted in Mplus, version 6.11 (Muthen & Muthen, 2010).

To gauge the extent to which the set of intervening variables (i.e., satisfaction in communicating with teachers, general and school-specific communicative self-efficacy beliefs) mediated the relationships among exogenous constructs and criteria, a mediation analysis was conducted. This analysis centered on the disaggregation of the total effects into direct and indirect effects and on the assessment of the role of specific indirect effects. This strategy is consistent with recent calls from methodologists, who have advocated that meaningful mediation analyses should not focus on the statistical significance of structural relations linking independent variables, mediators, and criteria but should instead examine the magnitude and direction of mediated effects (Preacher & Hayes, 2008a; see also Hayes, Preacher, & Myers, 2011). Moreover, in line with extensive methodological evidence indicating that "bootstrapping is the most sensible approach to assessing the size of indirect effects" (Hayes et al., 2011, p. 451; see also Preacher & Hayes, 2008b), we employed bias corrected bootstrap confidence intervals (BCBCI; Efron & Tibshirani, 1993) to assess statistical significance. Specifically, in the mediation analyses, effects were considered statistically significant when their associated 95% BCBCI did not include zero (see Hayes, 2009). This choice was informed by extensive methodological research showing that bootstrapping, in general, and BCBCI, in particular, have a host of desirable properties such as offering a general approach to making inferences in any types of mediation models, providing accurate confidence intervals and Type I error rates, facilitating adequate levels of power for testing given null hypotheses, and not requiring assumptions that are often violated (e.g., normality) (Hayes, 2009; Hayes, et al., 2011; Preacher & Hayes, 2008a; Preacher & Selig, 2012).

Results

Confirmatory Factor Analysis

In the first phase, a CFA model was fit to the data. Consistent with the theoretical conceptualization of the constructs employed in this research, each item was hypothesized to be influenced by a single unobserved factor, namely the latent variable that the item was designed to measure. This CFA model consisted of seven factors: promotion (PRO), prevention (PRE), satisfaction in communicating with teachers (SCT), general communicative self-efficacy beliefs (GCS), school-specific communicative self-efficacy beliefs (SCS), expectancy (EXP), and value (VAL) (see Figure 11.1).

The hypothesized CFA model imposed a highly restrictive structure at the measurement level, as it did not include any cross-loadings or correlated residuals. The fit of the model was excellent: Chi-square (356, $N=463$)=619.327, $p<.001$; CFI=.960; TLI=.954; RMSEA=.040, 90% CI [.035, .045]. This analysis encountered neither estimation problems nor inadmissible solutions (e.g., out-of-bound parameters such as negative variances). All factor loadings were statistically significant and of sizeable magnitude (72.4% of them were larger than .70 in standardized units). Moreover, all of the factors had high and very high values of the construct reliability as measured by the H coefficient (Mueller & Hancock, 2008) (see Table 11.2). Taken together, these results indicate that the observed variables employed measured adequately the hypothesized constructs.

Structural Equation Model

To assess whether or not the proposed model (summarized in Figure 11.1) is consistent with the empirical data, an SEM was employed. This model had a close fit to the data: Chi-square (363, $N=463$)=645.422, $p<.001$; CFI=.957;

Table 11.2 Interfactor Correlations and Construct Reliabilities

	1	2	3	4	5	6	7
1 PRO	1.000	−.103	.364**	.423**	.638**	.440**	.366**
2 PRE		1.000	−.079	−.040	−.120*	−.039	−.039
3 SCT			1.000	.269**	.278**	.505**	.578**
4 GCS				1.000	.537**	.170**	.055
5 SCS					1.000	.320**	.153**
6 EXP						1.000	.806**
7 VAL							1.000
Reliability (H coefficient)	.717	.861	.925	.871	.892	.883	.893

Note: * $p<.05$; ** $p<.01$; PRO = promotion; PRE = prevention; GCS = general communicative self-efficacy; SCT = satisfaction in communicating with teachers; SCS = school-related communicative self-efficacy; EXP = expectancy; VAL = utility value; H = Construct reliability coefficient (Mueller & Hancock, 2008).

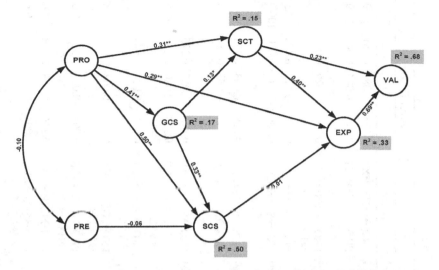

Figure 11.2 Standardized parameter estimates for the PRO-PRE-COM-EXP-VAL model (promotion-prevention-communication-expectancy-value).

Note: *$p<0.05$; **$p<0.01$; PRO = promotion; PRE = prevention; GCS = general communicative self-efficacy; SCT = satisfaction in communicating with teachers; SCS = school-related communicative self-efficacy; EXP = expectancy; VAL = utility value.

TLI=.952; RMSEA=.041, 90% CI [.036, .046]. Hence, it is meaningful to interpret its parameter estimates.

Figure 11.2 summarizes the standardized direct effects associated with this model. Of the proposed paths, all but two (PRE → SCS; SCS → EXP) were statistically significant and in the hypothesized direction. An analysis of the results in Figure 11.2 reveals that most of the significant structural relations among constructs were of medium size. The model accounts for 50% (or more) variability in SCS and VAL, for 33% of variability in EXP, and for smaller percentages in GCS and SCT.

Analysis of Total, Direct, and Indirect Effects

Following, we overview the effects associated with the expectancy construct, focusing on the statistically significant results (see the bolded entries in Table 11.3). Student promotion orientation has significant positive direct and indirect effects on their expectancy of success. Over two-thirds of the total effect is a direct one. About 88% of the total indirect effect from promotion to expectancy is mediated by satisfaction in communicating with teachers; the remainder is transmitted by general communicative self-efficacy beliefs and SCT. The important mediating role of SCT can be attributed to the fact that this construct has strong positive relations with both promotion and expectancy of success. With one exception, prevention, GCS, and SCS have no significant direct or indirect effects on EXP. The exception is a weak positive indirect effect of GCS mediated by SCT.

Table 11.3 Summary of Total, Direct, Total Indirect, and Specific Indirect Effects

	Total Effect			Direct Effect			TE (%)	Total Indirect Effect			Specific Indirect Effects				
	Est.	LB	UB	Est.	LB	UB		Est.	LB	UB	Name	Est.	LB	UB	TI(%)
PRO→EXP	0.529	0.364	0.715	0.355	0.138	0.608	67.1	0.174	0.027	0.324	PRO→SCT→EXP	0.153	0.081	0.251	87.9
											PRO→GCS→SCT→EXP	0.026	0.004	0.061	14.9
											PRO→GCS→SCS→EXP	−0.001	−0.029	0.024	0.5
											PRO→SCS→EXP	−0.004	−0.112	0.086	2.3
PRE→EXP	0.000	−0.010	0.020				0.0	0.000	−0.010	0.020	PRE→SCS→EXP	0.000	−0.010	0.020	100.0
SCS→EXP	−0.005	−0.140	0.123	−0.005	−0.140	0.123	100.0								
GCS→EXP	0.056	−0.025	0.144				0.0	0.056	−0.025	0.144	GCS→SCT→EXP	0.058	0.003	0.124	103.6
											GCS→SCS→EXP	−0.002	−0.063	0.051	3.6
SCT→EXP	0.451	0.311	0.598	0.451	0.311	0.598	100.0								
PRO→VAL	0.677	0.474	0.924				0.0	0.677	0.474	0.924	PRO→SCT→VAL	0.125	0.055	0.226	18.5
											PRO→SCT→EXP→VAL	0.153	0.080	0.264	22.6
											PRO→GCS→SCT→VAL	0.021	0.004	0.048	3.1
											PRO→GCS→SCT→EXP→VAL	0.026	0.004	0.064	3.8
											PRO→GCS→SCS→EXP→VAL	−0.001	−0.031	0.023	0.0
											PRO→EXP→VAL	0.356	0.138	0.646	52.6
											PRO→SCS→EXP→VAL	−0.004	−0.117	0.081	0.6

Path	Est.	LB	UB	Est.	LB	UB	TEC (%)	Indirect effect path	Est.	LB	UB	TIC (%)
PRE→VAL	0.000	−0.010	0.022				0.0	PRE→SCS→EXP→VAL	0.000	−0.010	0.022	100.0
SCS→VAL	−0.005	−0.149	0.118				0.0	SCS→EXP→VAL	−0.005	−0.149	0.118	100.0
GCS→VAL	0.103	−0.011	0.225				0.0	GCS→SCT→VAL	**0.047**	0.004	0.100	45.6
								GCS→SCT→EXP→VAL	**0.058**	0.004	0.127	56.3
								GCS→SCS→EXP→VAL	−0.002	−0.068	0.049	1.9
SCT→VAL	**0.821**	0.608	1.086	**0.370**	0.214	0.538	45.1	SCT→EXP→VAL	**0.452**	0.297	0.656	100.0
EXP→VAL	**1.002**	0.768	1.306	**1.002**	0.768	1.306	100.0					
PRO→SCT	**0.397**	0.270	0.535	**0.339**	0.190	0.499	85.4	PRO→GCS→SCT	**0.058**	0.006	0.124	100.0
GCS→SCT	**0.128**	0.001	0.252	**0.128**	0.001	0.252	100.0					
PRO→GCS	**0.449**	0.285	0.650	**0.449**	0.285	0.650	100.0					
PRO→SCS	**0.895**	0.696	1.129	**0.703**	0.493	0.940	78.5	PRO→GCS→SCS	**0.192**	0.106	0.321	100.0
PRE→SCS	−0.078	−0.206	0.044	−0.078	−0.206	0.044	100.0					
GCS→SCS	**0.428**	0.264	0.598	**0.428**	0.264	0.598	100.0					

Note: The bolded values are significant at the .05 level; TEC (%) = percentage of the total effect; TIC (%) = percentage of the total indirect effect; Est. = estimate; LB = lower band of the 95% confidence interval; UB = upper band of the 95% confidence interval; PRO = promotion; PRE = prevention; GCS = general communicative self-efficacy; SCS = school-related communicative self-efficacy; SCT = satisfaction with communicating with teachers; EXP = expectancy; VAL = utility value.

A similar pattern of results is revealed when analyzing the effects associated with value. Promotion orientation has a strong positive indirect effect on VAL but no direct effect. Virtually all of the total indirect effect is mediated by SCT (18.5% by SCT alone, 22.6% by SCT and EXP, 3.1% by GCS and SCT, and 3.8% by GCS, SCT, and EXP) and EXP (52.6%). PRE, GCS, and SCS have no significant direct or (total) indirect effects on VAL. However, two small positive specific indirect effects of GCS (via SCT and, respectively, via SCT and EXP) differ significantly from zero. SCT has significant direct and indirect effects on value (via EXP), with the direct effect accounting for about 45.1% of the total effect. Finally, as hypothesized, expectancy has a strong direct effect on value.

In terms of the relations between exogenous constructs and mediators, promotion has positive direct effects on SCT, GCS, and SCS. The direct effects of PRO are much higher than the corresponding indirect effects (proportion of direct effect is 85.4% for SCT and 78.5% for SCS). Hence, although GCS has positive direct relations with both SCT and SCS and is positively influenced by PRO (and, thus, it mediates the relationships between PRO and SCT, respectively PRO and SCS), most of these relationships are due to the direct (rather than the indirect) influence of the promotion orientation. Finally, the effects of prevention on SCS (direct) and EXP (mediated) were not significantly different from zero. The following section includes a detailed analysis of the implications of these results.

Discussion

The Role of SCT in Creating an Interpersonal Regulatory Fit for Promotion- but Not Prevention-Oriented Students

Findings from this study suggest that feeling satisfied in communicating with their mathematics teachers (i.e., having a high SCT) acts as a type of interpersonal regulatory fit for promotion-oriented students. This fit enhances students' engagement with, and positive affective feelings about, the class and its content (Higgins, 2000, 2005, 2006, 2012b). In turn, in line with findings from research examining the role of inferences drawn from feelings (Pham, 2004; Schwarz, 1990; Schwarz & Clore, 1988), heightened engagement and the presence of positive affect contribute to increasingly positive evaluations of expectancy of success related to mathematics. Importantly, as previous investigations revealed only negligible differences between students' perceptions of teachers' instruction-related communication behaviors in mathematics and science fields versus non-mathematics and non-science areas (Mottet et al., 2008), we are confident that our findings generalize beyond the context of mathematics.

To fully explicate the role of SCT in this mechanism of interpersonal regulatory fit, it is important to stress that low levels of SCT may not be interpreted as a negative or failure feedback by prevention-oriented students. This is the case because unlike their promotion-oriented counterparts, who take into account and consider diagnostic information from a broad range of sources (Molden, 2012; Righetti et al., 2011), prevention focused individuals attempt to keep to a minimum the possible flows of new information. As a result, they are relatively unwilling to seek help or to request feedback on progress toward their goals (Righetti et al., 2011). Hence, low satisfaction in communicating with a teacher is unlikely to be a fit for prevention-oriented students. This interpretation is supported by empirical data in our study showing that although promotion is strongly related to the expectancy of success (both directly and indirectly), prevention has a non-significant indirect effect on expectancy.

The Interplay among SCT, Regulatory Focus, and Psychological Distance Shapes Students' Expectancy and Value Beliefs

Another key implication of our findings is that students experiencing high levels of SCT might also have enhanced confidence in their own evaluative reactions regarding the given course, such as the expectancy of success. This interpretation is closely aligned to current theoretical conceptualizations of expectancy, which posit that along with information obtained from first-hand experience, information derived from "communicating with others can dictate to a large extent the confidence with which the individual expects a particular outcome" (Roese & Sherman, 2007, p. 94). In addition, the interpretation is consistent with the self-validation hypothesis, which argues that when individuals are confident in their own evaluative reactions of a target their judgments of the target rely heavily on these reactions (Briñol & Petty, 2009). As results from a recent study (Avnet et al., 2013) show, this strong reliance on own evaluative reactions could be responsible for increases in either the positivity or the negativity of how the target is evaluated, depending on whether the target is perceived positively or negatively.

An examination of the significance of our findings from this vantage point suggests that for promotion-oriented students high levels of satisfaction in communicating with teachers can facilitate positive developments of expectancy of success and value. However, these desirable outcomes are contingent on teachers projecting a positive view about the given academic subject or specific class. This interpretation is consistent with recent findings (Amit, Wakslak, & Trope, 2013) that extend construal level theory (CLT; Trope & Liberman, 2010) from the intrapersonal to the interpersonal level.

A review of CLT is beyond the scope of this paper. However, for the purpose of our discussion, we note that, according to CLT, individuals perceive attitude objects as being psychologically distant when they subjectively experience the given object as being removed from the self as it exists *hic et nunc* (Trope & Liberman, 2010). Particularly relevant for the current research, Amit and colleagues (2013) show that "when communicating with others, people take into account the *other person's* [psychological] distance" (p. 53; emphasis in original). Thus, instructors who are not enthusiastic about the class or subject they teach are likely to be perceived by their students as having a heightened psychological distance with respect to it. The opposite is true for teachers who transmit a positive view of the subject. It is noteworthy here that the 'heightened' psychological distance refers to the subject or class and not to the teacher. Amit et al.'s (2013) findings provide support for arguing that learners take instructors' psychological distance into account when making judgments related to this class (e.g., when forming expectations of success in it). As the results of our study suggest, this transfer of psychological distance from teacher to students may be amplified by having a satisfactory communication with the given instructor. Additionally, the transfer of psychological distance is likely to be much stronger for promotion focused students, who are open to considering a broad range of information, than for their prevention-oriented counterparts, who try to limit the amount and type of information they process (Molden, 2012; Righetti et al., 2011).

Promotion Orientation and its Role in Predicting Differences in Students' School-Related Communicative Self-Efficacy Beliefs

This research revealed that being satisfied in communicating with one's teacher in a mathematics class was an important mediator between students' promotion orientation and their subject-specific expectancy of success and value. In addition, the study showed that general and school-related communicative self-efficacy beliefs played a lesser role in the mediation mechanisms connecting regulatory focus orientations, expectancy, and value. While the causes underlying these differences remain to be determined, one of the findings regarding communicative self-efficacy beliefs has pivotal implications for communication, education, and psychology research as well as pedagogy. Specifically, our parsimonious model, involving only promotion, prevention, and general communicative self-efficacy as predictors, accounted for 50% of variability in school-related communicative self-efficacy. In this model, promotion emerged as the strongest predictor, followed by general communicative self-efficacy, while prevention played a non-significant role. This pattern of empirical relationships is consistent with G. M. Hodis and Hodis's (2013) hypotheses that promotion-oriented students regard learning tasks as opportunities to gain knowledge whereas their prevention counterparts perceive these tasks as opportunities to fail.

To our knowledge, this result is the first of its kind, as it reveals that an important communication construct is strongly associated with a general regulatory focus dimension. Hence, our finding could spearhead efforts to analyze how promotion and prevention orientations relate to a wide range of specific communicative self-efficacy beliefs. In addition, this finding has important pedagogical implications, as it suggests that a longer-term perspective on learning and teaching with its associated focus on ideals, aspirations, and gains, is positively associated with confidence in one's ability to communicate effectively in school-related settings. Noting that prevention was not a significant predictor of communicative self-efficacy beliefs, this result also suggests that students could benefit more from learning in environments that emphasize long-term gains associated with effective communication than from studying in settings stressing that effective communication requires avoiding mistakes and performing correctly all pivotal aspects of communicative encounters.

Implications for Future Research and Limitations

Downstream Effects of Prevention

In this study, inter-individual differences in prevention were not associated with significant differences in expectancy or value beliefs. Given the important role that prevention plays in human growth and survival (Higgins, 1997, 2012b), this finding suggests that the effects of having a prevention orientation, unlike those of exhibiting a promotion one, are manifest "downstream" of expectancy and value. Our understanding of the theory of goal systems (Kruglanski et al., 2002) suggests that prevention may influence aspects of motivated behaviors that are not directly linked to expectancy or value. In particular, it may be the case that prevention affects the accessibility of a certain type of goal (e.g., becoming an effective communicator) and its connections with instrumental vs. non-instrumental means to attain it (which influence the choice of means employed in the goal pursuit process). Future research would do well to assess the tenability of these assertions.

Social Distance Theory of Power and Learner Empowerment

Analyzing findings in this study in light of research in social distance theory of power (SDTP) (Magee & Smith, 2013) and learner empowerment (Frymier, Shulman, & Houser, 1996; Houser & Frymier, 2009) presents important opportunities to unearth essential fresh knowledge. In particular, it provides insights on how future research could expand the nomological network of the expectancy and value constructs, inform pedagogical practice, guide the designing of targeted communicational and educational interventions, and advance knowledge of currently unresolved conceptual issues.

Magee and Smith (2013) noted that "abstract mind-sets appear to facilitate behavior congruent with one's values more than concrete mind-sets do" (p. 166). As a result, helping students construe effective communication as something that is pivotal for having a good life (rather than as something that is important for getting a good grade in a communication class) may motivate them to make efforts to acquire communication skills if they value communicating effectively. Additionally, the SDTP suggests that people who feel empowered act in ways that are consistent with their values (Magee & Smith, 2013). Moreover, theoretical principles and empirical results support the idea that regulatory fit increases task engagement (Higgins, 2000, 2012b) and, in some situations (e.g., negative managerial communication) enhances empowerment (Fransen & ter Hoeven, 2013). Furthermore, psychological distance may moderate the relationship between regulatory focus and empowerment (F. A. Hodis & Hodis, 2013). Taking all of these aspects into consideration, we consider that analyzing the interrelations among promotion, prevention, empowerment, engagement, and psychological distance in communication contexts holds promising opportunities.

An important strand of communication research shows that students' feelings of empowerment have positive associations with their (a) engagement (Frymier & Houser, 1999), learning (Frymier et al., 1996; Goodboy et al., 2009), and motivation (Goodboy et al., 2009; Mazer, 2013), which are constructs that are conceptually similar to utility value (Frymier & Houser, 1999; Weber, 2003); and (b) satisfaction in communicating with teachers (Goodboy et al., 2009). Integrating all of these aspects provides support for arguing that helping students feel empowered in their school pursuits could increase their resilience to detrimental peer pressure, strengthen the value of their academic strivings, and enhance their motivation to act in value-congruent ways.

Findings from Frymier et al. (1996) revealed strong positive associations between students' feelings of empowerment in the class and their perceptions of relevance of the content studied. Thus, one potentially promising way to enhance student empowerment is to strengthen their perceptions of the relevance of the course content. Taking into account that "when students perceive a concept or task as relevant, they see it as valuable, as having importance" (Frymier, 2005a, p. 84), this strategy is also likely to increase utility value perceptions (see Frymier et al., 1996; Houser & Frymier, 2009 for in-depth discussions of learner empowerment). Achieving these objectives may require adjusting classroom settings and practices to maximize opportunities for students to be involved in relevant class interactions and feel understood in their communication (Finn & Schrodt, 2012; Frymier & Houser, 1999; Myers & Bryant, 2002). Encouraging teacher communicative behaviors that promote learner empowerment (e.g., clarity and immediacy; Frymier et al., 1996; Houser & Frymier, 2009) is also worth considering. Noting that all three dimensions of learner empowerment are positively related to satisfaction in communicating with teachers (Goodboy et al., 2009) provides support for hypothesizing that the aforementioned strategies could enhance communication satisfaction as well. However, as "scholars have yet to identify the *underlying mechanisms* that could potentially enhance our understanding of *how* students' perceptions of teachers behaviors, such as clarity and immediacy, empower students" (Finn & Schrodt, 2012, p. 112; emphasis in original), these hypotheses need to be tested in future research.

Teacher Immediacy

Waldeck, Kearney, and Plax (2001) noted that "teachers who engage in immediacy behaviors are better able to facilitate student learning and motivation" (p. 224). More recently, Houser and Frymier (2009) argued that teacher immediacy could have a positive impact on student engagement in the classroom. In this light, the fact that promotion, prevention, and regulatory fit are essential drivers shaping engagement (Higgins, 2012b) suggests that these factors could moderate the relationship between teacher immediacy and student learning. Thus, findings from this study could contribute to advancing teacher immediacy research (Allen, Witt, & Wheeless, 2006; Finn & Schrodt, 2012;

Kerssen-Griep & Witt, 2012; Myers & Bryant, 2002; Witt & Kerssen-Griep, 2011; Witt, Wheeless, & Allen, 2004).

Results from our study provide a strong foundation for positing specific hypotheses regarding the relationships among teacher immediacy and student regulatory focus orientations. Regulatory focus theory (Higgins, 2012b) posits that promotion and prevention focused individuals employ different information-seeking strategies. Specifically, promotion focused learners are interested in acquiring information from a variety of sources. As the results of our study show, their expectations of success in, and utility value associated with, mathematics are enhanced when they are satisfied with the communication they have with their mathematics teachers. Noting that "higher levels of immediacy would contribute to a positive reinforcement that creates a motivation for the student to interact with the teacher and . . . a sense of reward or positive valence" (Allen et al., 2006, p. 24), we hypothesize that students having a strong promotion orientation may benefit from interacting with high immediacy teachers.

In contrast, prevention focused learners try to limit the type and amount of information they process and, thus, may regard high levels of teacher immediacy as extraneous or even burdensome for their overarching goals (e.g., meeting their duties and obligations). As a result, these students might be less inclined to seek relevant information from the given instructor. Consequently, high immediacy contexts may not have a beneficial influence on the learning and achievement of students having a strong prevention orientation. This hypothesis is especially plausible if students interpret a teacher's immediacy as signalling enthusiasm (toward the class or the subject taught) that students are expected to share (Allen et al., 2006). As enthusiasm is not a fit for the vigilant outlook that characterizes prevention, these students' engagement with the material, their expectancy of success in the class, and the perceived utility value of the knowledge they learned are not likely to increase in high immediacy classes.

In the teacher immediacy literature, "there is little agreement about *how* immediacy works to enhance learning" (Witt et al., 2004, p. 188; emphasis in original; for a similar point see Allen et al., 2006). However, we consider that our propositions arguing that teacher immediacy effects on engagement and learning differ for promotion- and prevention-oriented students are tenable across various conceptualizations of immediacy. Our confidence is rooted in the fact that the empirical findings supporting our hypotheses are consistent with general theoretical predictions (Higgins, 2012b) that are likely to hold true regardless of the key aspects emphasized in specific conceptualizations of this construct. As a result, we believe that considerations of students' promotion and prevention orientations could reveal some of the underlying causes of the consistent heterogeneity reported in meta-analyses of teacher immediacy effects (see, for example, Allen et al., 2006; Witt et al., 2004).

Limitations

Even though this research has advanced knowledge in important ways, it is not without limitations. First, because the nature of the data in this research is correlational, no causal inferences can be made. Although the pattern of hypothesized relations is firmly rooted in an extensive survey of relevant theoretical and applied communication, education, and social psychology research, no causal claims can be inferred from these findings. Second, although predictors included in the proposed model account for statistically significant and practically important proportions of variability in criteria, the model's explanatory power could be further strengthened. Third, data were collected from a sample of secondary school students from NZ, a country characterized by unique cultural features. We are not aware of any other research that has investigated the linkages among these constructs (in NZ or any other culture), but because theoretical principles governing the relationships among the constructs investigated are not culture specific, we believe that our findings are culture independent. However, empirical data are needed to test this assertion.

Conclusion

Bridging findings from human communication, educational psychology, and social psychology research, this study provides novel and important insights regarding the mechanisms underlying individual differences in students' expectancy and value beliefs. Most importantly, the research advances understanding of how general motivation strivings affect domain-specific expectancy and value via mediation mechanisms that center on key communication variables. In particular, findings from our study suggest that having a long-term perspective on learning that focuses on ideals and personal aspirations—that is, having a strong promotion orientation—is associated with high levels of communicative self-efficacy in school-related settings. Additionally, this research shows that a new type of *inter*personal regulatory fit, facilitated by high levels of satisfaction in communicating with teachers, contributes to enhanced expectancy of success and utility value beliefs for promotion (but not prevention) oriented students. Taking all of these aspects into consideration, underlines that this study advances theory development in important ways.

In addition, findings from this work suggest that effective strategies to enhance student learning and performance may need to include aspects helping them boost their resilience to peer pressure, strengthen the value of academic pursuit, and enhance the motivation to act in value congruent ways. Moreover, this research opens important avenues for promising future explorations that have the potential to continue to advance knowledge related to student expectancy, value, satisfaction in communicating with teachers, communicative self-efficacy beliefs, learner empowerment, and teacher immediacy.

References

Allen, M., Witt, P. L., & Wheeless, L. R. (2006). The role of teacher immediacy as a motivational factor in student learning: Using meta-analysis to test a causal model. *Communication Education, 55*, 21–31. doi:10.1080/03634520500343368

Amit, E., Wakslak, C., & Trope, Y. (2013). The use of visual and verbal means of communication across psychological distance. *Personality and Social Psychology Bulletin, 39,* 43–56. doi:10.1177/0146167212460282

Archambault, I., Eccles, J. S., & Vida, M. N. (2010). Ability self-concepts and subjective value in literacy: Joint trajectories from grades 1 through 12. *Journal of Educational Psychology, 102,* 804–816. doi:10.1037/a0021075

Avnet, T., Laufer, D., & Higgins, E. T. (2013). Are all experiences of fit created equal? Two paths to persuasion. *Journal of Consumer Psychology, 23,* 301–316. doi:10.1016/j.jcps.2012.10.011

Bandura, A. (1997). *Self-efficacy: The exercise of control.* New York, NY: Freeman.

Bandura, A. (2006). Guide for creating self-efficacy scales. In F. Pajares & T. Urdan (Eds.), *Self-efficacy beliefs of adolescents* (pp. 307–338). Greenwich, CT: Information Age.

Barry, C. L., & Finney, S. J. (2009). Can we feel confident in how we measure college confidence? A psychometric investigation of the college self-efficacy inventory. *Measurement and Evaluation in Counseling and Development, 42,* 197–222. doi:10.1177/0748175609344095

Bentler, P. M. (1990). Comparative fit indexes in structural models. *Psychological Bulletin, 107,* 238–246. doi:10.1037//0033-2909.107.2.238

Bledow, R. (2013). Demand perception and self-motivation as opponent processes. A response to Bandura and Vancouver. *Journal of Management, 39,* 14–26. doi:10.1177/0149206312466149

Bong, M. (2001). Role of self-efficacy and task-value in predicting college students' course performance and future enrollment intentions. *Contemporary Educational Psychology, 26,* 553–570. doi:10.1006/ceps.2000.1048

Briñol, P., & Petty, R. E. (2009). Persuasion: Insights from the self-validation hypothesis. In M. P. Zanna (Ed.), *Advances in experimental social psychology,* (Vol. 41, pp. 69–118). Burlington, MA: Academic Press.

Chow, A., Eccles, J. S., & Salmela-Aro, K. (2012). Task value profiles across subjects and aspirations in physical and IT-related sciences in the United States and Finland. *Developmental Psychology, 48,* 1612–1628. doi:10.1037/a0030194

Conley, A. M. (2012). Patterns of motivation beliefs: Combining achievement goal and expectancy-value perspectives. *Journal of Educational Psychology, 104,* 32–47. doi:10.1037/a0026042

Coplan, R. J., Hughes, K., Bosacki, S., & Rose-Krasnor, L. (2011). Is silence golden? Elementary school teachers' strategies and beliefs regarding hypothetical shy/quiet and exuberant/talkative children. *Journal of Educational Psychology, 103,* 939–951. doi:10.1037/a0024551

Crowe, E., & Higgins, E. T. (1997). Regulatory focus and strategic inclinations: Promotion and prevention in decision-making. *Organizational Behavior and Human Decision Processes, 69,* 117–132. doi:10.1006/obhd.1996.2675

Daly, J. A., & Korinek, J. (1980). Instructional communication theory and research: An overview of classroom interaction. In D. Nimmo (Ed.), *Communication yearbook 4* (pp. 515–532). New Brunswick, NJ: Transaction Books.

Daniels, D. H., & Shumow, L. (2003). Child development and classroom teaching: A review of the literature and implications for educating teachers. *Journal of Applied Developmental Psychology, 23,* 495–526. doi:10.1016/S0193-3973(02)00139-9

Dweck, C. S., Higgins, E. T., & Grant-Pillow, H. (2003). Self-systems give unique meaning to self-variables. In M. R. Leary & J. P. Tangney (Eds.), *Handbook of self and identity* (pp. 239–252). New York, NY: Guilford.

Eccles, J. S. (2005). Subjective task value and the Eccles et al. model of achievement-related choices. In A. J. Elliot & C. S. Dweck (Eds.), *Handbook of competence and motivation* (pp. 105–121). New York, NY: Guilford.

Eccles, J. S. (2011). Gendered educational and occupational choices: Applying the Eccles et al. model of achievement-related choices. *International Journal of Behavioral Development, 35,* 195–201. doi:10.1177/0165025411398185

Eccles, J. S., & Wigfield, A. (2002). Motivational beliefs, values, and goals. *Annual Review of Psychology, 53,* 109–132. doi:10.1146/annurev.psych.53.100901.135153

Eccles, J. S., Wigfield, A., Harold, R. D., & Blumenfeld, P. (1993). Age and gender differences in children's self- and task-perceptions during elementary school. *Child Development, 64,* 830–847. doi:10.1111/j.1467-8624.1993.tb02946.x

Eccles (Parsons), J. S., Adler, T. F., Futterman, R., Goff, S. B., Kaczala, C. M., Meece, J. L., & Midgley, C. (1983). Expectancies, values, and academic behaviors. In J. T. Spence (Ed.), *Achievement and achievement motivation: Psychological and sociological approaches* (pp. 75–146). San Francisco, CA: Freeman.

Efron, B., & Tibshirani, R. (1993). *An introduction to the bootstrap.* New York, NY: Chapman & Hall.

Finn, A. N., & Schrodt, P. (2012). Students' perceived understanding mediates the effects of teacher clarity and nonverbal immediacy on learner empowerment. *Communication Education, 61,* 111–130. doi:10.1080/03634523.2012656669

Fishbach, A. (2009). The function of value in self-regulation. *Journal of Consumer Psychology, 19,* 129–133. doi:10.1016/j.jcps.2009.02.005

Förster, J. (2009). Knowing your customer better: The strength of a self-regulatory value approach. *Journal of Consumer Psychology, 19,* 124–128. doi:10.1016/j.jcps.2009.02.004

Förster, J., & Higgins, E. T. (2005). How global versus local perception fits regulatory focus. *Psychological Science, 16,* 631–636. doi:10.1111/j.1467-9280.2005.01586.x

Förster, J., & Werth, L. (2009). Regulatory focus: Classic findings and new directions. In G. B. Moskowitz & H. Grant (Eds.), *The psychology of goals* (pp. 392–420). New York, NY: Guilford.

Förster, J., Grant, H., Idson, C. L., & Higgins, E. T. (2001). Success/failure feedback, expectancies, and approach/avoidance motivation: How regulatory focus moderates classic relations. *Journal of Experimental Social Psychology, 37,* 253–260. doi:10.1006/jesp.2000.1455

Fransen, M. L., & ter Hoeven, C. L. (2013). Matching the message: The role of regulatory fit in negative managerial communication. *Communication Research, 40,* 818–837. doi:10.1177/0093650211427140

Frisby, B. N., & Martin, M. M. (2010). Instructor-student and student-student rapport in the classroom. *Communication Education, 59,* 146–164. doi:10.1080/03634520903564362

Frymier, A. B. (2005a). Making content relevant to students. In J. L. Chesebro & J. C. McCroskey (Eds.), *Communication for teachers* (pp. 83–92). Boston, MA: Allyn & Bacon.

Frymier, A. B. (2005b). Students' classroom communication effectiveness. *Communication Quarterly, 53,* 197–212. doi:10.1080/01463370500089896

Frymier, A. B., & Houser, M. L. (1999). The revised learning indicators scale. *Communication Studies, 50,* 1–12. doi:10.1080/10510979909388466

Frymier, A. B., & Houser, M. L. (2000). The teacher-student relationship as an interpersonal relationship. *Communication Education, 49,* 207–219. doi:10.1080/03634520009379209

Frymier, A. B., Shulman, G., & Houser, M. L. (1996). The development of a learner empowerment measure. *Communication Education, 45,* 181–199. doi:10.1080/03634529609379048

Goodboy, A. K., Martin, M., & Bolkan, S. (2009). The development and validation of the student communication satisfaction scale. *Communication Education, 58,* 372–396. doi:10.1080/03634520902755441

Goodboy, A. K., Bolkan, S., Myers, S. A., & Zhao, X. (2011). Student use of relational and influence messages in response to perceived instructor power use in American and Chinese college classrooms. *Communication Education, 60,* 191–209. doi:10.1080/03634523.2010.502970

Haws, K. L., Dholakia, U. M., & Bearden, W. O. (2010). An assessment of chronic regulatory focus measures. *Journal of Marketing Research, 47,* 967–982. doi:10.1509/jmkr.47.5.967

Hayes, A. F. (2009). Beyond Baron and Kenny: Statistical mediation analysis in the new millennium. *Communication Monographs, 76,* 408–420. doi:10.1080/03637750903310360

Hayes, A. F., Preacher, K. J., & Myers, T. A. (2011). Mediation and the estimation of indirect effects in political communication research. In E. P. Bucy & R. L. Holbert (Eds.), *The sourcebook for political communication research: Methods, measures, and analytical techniques* (pp. 434–465). New York, NY: Routledge.

Hecht, M. L. (1978a). The conceptualization and measurement of interpersonal communication satisfaction. *Human Communication Research, 4,* 253–264. doi:10.1111/j.1468-2958.1978.tb00614.x

Hecht, M. L. (1978b). Measures of communication satisfaction. *Human Communication Research, 4,* 350–368. doi:10.1111/j.1468–2958.1978.tb00721.x

Higgins, E. T. (1987). Self-discrepancy: A theory relating self and affect. *Psychological Review, 94,* 319–340. doi:10.1037/0033-295X.94.3.319

Higgins, E. T. (1997). Beyond pleasure and pain. *American Psychologist, 52,* 1280–1300. doi:10.1037/0003-066X.52.12.1280

Higgins, E. T. (2000). Making a good decision: Value from fit. *American Psychologist, 55,* 1217–1230. doi:10.1037/0003-066X.55.11.1217

Higgins, E. T. (2005). Value from regulatory fit. *Current Directions in Psychological Science, 14,* 209–213. doi:10.1111/j.0963-7214.2005.00366.x

Higgins, E. T. (2006). Value from hedonic experience *and* engagement. *Psychological Review, 113,* 439–460. doi:10.1037/0033-295X.113.3.439

Higgins, E. T. (2007). Value. In A. W. Kruglanski & E. T. Higgins (Eds.), *Social psychology: Handbook of basic principles* (2nd ed., pp. 454–472). New York, NY: Guilford.

Higgins, E. T. (2012a). Accessibility theory. In P. A. M. Van Lange, A. W. Kruglanski, & E. T. Higgins (Eds.), *Handbook of theories of social psychology* (pp. 75–96). Thousand Oaks, CA: Sage.

Higgins, E. T. (2012b). *Beyond pleasure and pain: How motivation works.* New York, NY: Oxford University Press.

Higgins, E. T., Friedman, R. S., Harlow, R. E., Idson, L. C., Ayduk, O. N., & Taylor, A. (2001). Achievement orientations from subjective histories of success: Promotion pride versus prevention pride. *European Journal of Social Psychology, 31,* 3–23. doi:10.1002/ejsp.27

Hodis, F. A., & Hodis, G. M. (2013). Latent growth modeling for communication research: Opportunities and perspectives. In E. L. Cohen (Ed.), *Communication yearbook 37* (pp. 183–218). New York, NY: Routledge.

Hodis, G. M., & Hodis, F. A. (2012). Trends in communicative self-efficacy: A comparative analysis. *Basic Communication Course Annual, 24,* 40–80.

Hodis, G. M., & Hodis, F. A. (2013). Static and dynamic interplay among communication apprehension, communicative self-efficacy, and willingness to communicate in the basic communication course. *Basic Communication Course Annual, 25,* 70–125.

Houser, M. L., & Frymier, A. B. (2009). The role of student characteristics and teacher behaviors in students' learner empowerment. *Communication Education, 58,* 35–53. doi:10.1080/03634520802237383

Hu, L., & Bentler, P. M. (1999). Cutoff criteria for fit indexes in covariance structure analysis: Conventional criteria versus new alternatives. *Structural Equation Modeling: A Multidisciplinary Journal, 6,* 1–55. doi:10.1080/10705519909540118

Idson, L. C., Liberman, N., & Higgins, E. T. (2000). Distinguishing gains from non-losses and losses from non-gains: A regulatory focus perspective on hedonic intensity. *Journal of Experimental Social Psychology, 36,* 252–274. doi:10.1006/jesp.1999.1422

Kerssen-Griep, J., & Witt, P. L. (2012). Instructional feedback II: How do instructor immediacy cues and facework tactics interact to predict student motivation and fairness perceptions? *Communication Studies, 63,* 498–517. doi:10.1080/10510974.2011.632660

Kruglanski, A. W., Shah, J. Y., Fishbach, A., Friedman, R., Chun, W. Y., & Sleeth-Keppler, D. (2002). A theory of goal systems. In M. P. Zanna (Ed.), *Advances in experimental social psychology* (Vol. 34, pp. 331–378). San Diego, CA: Academic Press.

Liberman, N., & Förster, J. (2012). Goal gradients, expectancy, and value. In H. Aarts & A. J. Elliot (Eds.), *Goal-directed behavior* (pp. 151–173). New York, NY: Psychology Press.

Lockwood, P., Jordan, C. H., & Kunda, Z. (2002). Motivation by positive or negative role models: Regulatory focus determines who will best inspire us. *Journal of Personality and Social Psychology, 83,* 854–864. doi:10.1037/0022-3514.83.4.854

Lockwood, P., Sadler, P., Fyman, K., & Tuck, S. (2004). To do or not to do: Using positive or negative role models to harness motivation. *Social Cognition, 22,* 422–450. doi:10.1521/soco.22.4.422.38297

MacIntyre, P. D. (1994). Variables underlying willingness to communicate: A causal analysis. *Communication Research Reports, 11,* 135–142. doi:10.1080/08824099409359951

MacIntyre, P. D., Babin, P. A., & Clement, R. (1999). Willingness to communicate: Antecedents and consequences. *Communication Quarterly, 47,* 215–229. doi:10.1080/01463379909370135

Magee, J. C., & Smith, P. K. (2013). The social distance theory of power. *Personality and Social Psychology Review, 17,* 158–186. doi:10.1177/1088868312472732

Martin, A. J., Anderson, J., Bobis, J., Way, J., & Vellar, R. (2012). Switching on and switching off in mathematics: An ecological study of future intent and disengagement among middle school students. *Journal of Educational Psychology, 104,* 1–18. doi:10.1037/a0025988

Martin, M. M., Mottet, T. P., & Myers, S. A. (2000). Students' motives for communicating with their instructors and affective and cognitive learning. *Psychological Reports, 87,* 830–834. doi:10.2466/pr0.2000.87.3.830

Martin, M. M., Myers, S. A., & Mottet, T. P. (1999). Students' motives for communicating with their instructors. *Communication Education, 48,* 155–164. doi:10.1080/03634529909379163

Mazer, J. P. (2013). Validity of the student interest and engagement scales: Associations with student learning outcomes. *Communication Studies, 64*, 125–140. doi:10.0108 0/10510974.2012.727943

McCroskey, J. C., & McCroskey, L. L. (1988). Self-report as an approach to measuring communication competence. *Communication Research Reports, 5*, 108–113. doi:10.1080/08824098809359810

Molden, D. C. (2012). Motivated strategies for judgment: How preferences for particular judgment process can affect judgment outcomes. *Social and Personality Compass, 6*, 156–169. doi:10.1111/j.1751-9004.2011.00424.x

Molden, D. C., & Miele, D. B. (2008). The origins and influences of promotion-focused and prevention-focused achievement motivations. In M. Maehr, S. Karabenick, & T. Urdan (Eds.), *Advances in motivation and achievement: Social psychological perspectives* (Vol. 15, pp. 81–118). Bingley, Wales: Emerald.

Mottet, T. P., Martin, M. M., & Myers, S. A. (2004). Relationships among perceived instructor verbal approach and avoidance relational strategies and students' motives for communicating with their instructors. *Communication Education, 53*, 116–122. doi:10.1080/0363452032000135814

Mottet, T. P., Garza, R., Beebe, S., Houser, M. L., Jurrells, S., & Furler, L. (2008). Instructional communication predictors of ninth-grade students' affective learning in math and science. *Communication Education, 57*, 333–355. doi:10.1080/03634520801989950

Mueller, R. O., & Hancock, G. R. (2008). Best practices in structural equation modeling. In J. W. Osborne (Ed.), *Best practices in quantitative methods* (pp. 488–508). Thousand Oaks, CA: Sage.

Muthen, L. K., & Muthen, B. O. (2010). *Mplus, user's guide* (6th ed.). Los Angeles, CA: Muthen & Muthen.

Myers, S. A., & Bryant, L. E. (2002). Perceived understanding, interaction involvement, and college student outcomes. *Communication Research Reports, 19*, 146–155. doi:10.1080/08824090209384842

Myers, S. A., Martin, M. M., & Mottet, T. P. (2002a). The relationship between student communication motives and information seeking. *Communication Research Reports, 19*, 352–361. doi:10.1080/08824090209384842

Myers, S. A., Martin, M. M., & Mottet, T. P. (2002b). Students' motives for communicating with their instructors: Considering instructor socio-communicative style, student socio-communicative orientation, and student gender. *Communication Education, 51*, 121–133. doi:10.1080/03634520216511

Perez, T., Cromley, J. G., & Kaplan, A. (2014). The role of identity development, values, and costs in college STEM retention. *Journal of Educational Psychology, 106*, 315–329. doi:10.1037/a0034027

Pham, M. T. (2004). The logic of feeling. *Journal of Consumer Psychology, 14*, 360–369. doi:10.1207/s15327663jcp1404_5

Preacher, K. J., & Hayes, A. F. (2008a). Asymptotic and resampling strategies for assessing and comparing indirect effects in multiple mediator models. *Behavior Research Methods, 40*, 879–891. doi:10.3758/BRM.40.3.879

Preacher, K. J., & Hayes, A. F. (2008b). Contemporary approaches to assessing mediation in communication research. In A. F. Hayes, M. D. Slater, & L. B. Snyder (Eds.), *The Sage sourcebook of advanced data analysis methods for communication research* (pp. 13–54). Thousand Oaks, CA: Sage.

Preacher, K. J., & Selig, J. P. (2012). Advantages of Monte Carlo confidence intervals for indirect effects. *Communication Methods and Measures, 6*, 77–98. doi:10.1080/19312458.2012.679848

Prisbell, M. (1985). Interpersonal perception variables and communication satisfaction in the classroom. *Communication Research Reports, 1*, 90–96.

Prisbell, M. (1990). Classroom communication satisfaction, teacher uncertainty and course certainty over time. *Communication Research Reports, 6*, 20–24. doi:10.1080/08824099009359849

Prisbell, M. (1994). Affinity-seeking strategies associated with students' perceptions of satisfaction with communication in the classroom. *Perceptual and Motor Skills, 79*, 33–34. doi:10.2466/pms.1994.79.1.33

Prisbell, M., Dwyer, K. K., Carlson, R. E., Bingham, S. G., & Cruz, A. M. (2009). Connected classroom climate and communication in the basic course: Associations with learning. *Basic Communication Course Annual, 21*, 145–177.

Righetti, F., Finkenauer, C., & Rusbult, C. (2011). The benefits of interpersonal regulatory fit for individual goal pursuit. *Journal of Personality and Social Psychology, 101*, 720–736. doi:10.1037/a0023592

Roese, N. J., & Sherman, J. W. (2007). Expectancy. In A. W. Kruglanski & E. T. Higgins (Eds.), *Social psychology: Handbook of basic principles* (2nd ed., pp. 91–115). New York, NY: Guilford.

Rokeach, M. (1973). *The nature of human values.* New York, NY: Free Press.

Ryan, A. M., & Patrick, H. (2001). The classroom social environment and changes in adolescents' motivation and engagement during middle school. *American Educational Research Journal, 38*, 437–460. doi:10.3102/00028312038002437

Ryan, A. M., & Shim, S. S. (2012). Changes in help-seeking from peers during early adolescence: Associations with changes in achievement and perceptions of teachers. *Journal of Educational Psychology, 104*, 1122–1134. doi:10.1037/a0027696

Schwartz, S. H., & Bilsky, W. (1987). Toward a universal psychological structure of human values. *Journal of Personality and Social Psychology, 53*, 550–562. doi:10.1037/0022-3514.53.3.550

Schwarz, N. (1990). Feelings as information: Informational and motivational functions of affective states. In E. T. Higgins & R. M. Sorrentino (Eds.), *Handbook of motivation and cognition: Foundations of social behavior* (Vol. 2, pp. 527–561). New York, NY: Guilford.

Schwarz, N., & Clore, G. L. (1988). How do I feel about it? The informative function of affective states. In K. Fiedler & J. Forgas (Eds.), *Affect, cognition and social behavior* (pp. 44–62). Toronto, Canada: Hogrefe.

Shah, J. Y. (2003). The motivational looking glass: How significant others implicitly affect goal appraisals. *Journal of Personality and Social Psychology, 85*, 424–439. doi:10.1037/0022-3514.85.3.424

Sidelinger, R. J., Myers, S. A., & McMullen, A. L. (2011). Students' communication predispositions: An examination of classroom connectedness in public speaking courses. *Basic Communication Course Annual, 23*, 248–278.

Solberg, V. S., O'Brien, K., Villareal, P., Kennel, R., & Davis, B. (1993). Self-efficacy and Hispanic college students: Validation of the College Self-Efficacy Instrument. *Hispanic Journal of Behavioral Sciences, 15*, 80–95. doi:10.1177/07399863930151004

Spitzberg, B. H. (1991). An examination of trait measures of interpersonal competence. *Communication Reports, 4*, 22–29. doi:10.1080/08934219109367517

Steiger, J. H. (1990). Structural model evaluation and modification: An interval estimation approach. *Multivariate Behavioral Research, 25,* 173–180. doi:10.1207/s15327906mbr2502_4

Summerville, A., & Roese, N. J. (2008). Self-report measures of individual differences in regulatory focus: A cautionary note. *Journal of Research in Personality, 42,* 247–254. doi:10.1016/j.jrp.2007.05.005

Teven, J. J., & McCroskey, J. C. (1997). The relationship of perceived teacher caring with student learning and teacher evaluation. *Communication Education, 46,* 1–9. doi:10.1080/03634529709379069

Trope, Y., & Liberman, N. (2010). Construal level theory of psychological distance. *Psychological Review, 117,* 440–463. doi:10.1037/a0018963

Tucker, L. R., & Lewis, C. (1973). A reliability coefficient for maximum likelihood factor analysis. *Psychometrika, 38,* 1–10. doi:10.1007/BF02291170

Voelkl, K. E. (1995). School warmth, student participation, and achievement. *Journal of Experimental Education, 63,* 127–139. doi:10.1080/00220973.1995.9943817

Waldeck, J. H., Kearney, P., & Plax, T. G. (2001). Instructional and developmental communication theory and research in the 1990s: Extending the agenda for the 21st century. In W. Gudykunst (Ed.), *Communication yearbook 24* (pp. 207–229). Thousand Oaks, CA: Sage.

Watt, H. M. G., Shapka, J. D., Morris, Z. A., Durik, A. M., Keating, D. P., & Eccles, J. E. (2012). Gendered motivational processes affecting high school mathematics participation, educational aspirations, and career plans: A comparison of samples from Australia, Canada, and the United States. *Developmental Psychology, 48,* 1594–1611. doi:10.1037/a0027838

Weber, K. (2003). The relationship of interest to internal and external motivation. *Communication Research Reports, 20,* 376–383. doi:10.1080/08824090309388837

Weber, K., Martin, M. M., & Myers, S. A. (2011). The development and testing of the instructional beliefs model. *Communication Education, 60,* 51–74. doi:10.1080/03634523.2010.491122

Wigfield, A., & Cambria, J. (2010a). Expectancy value theory: Retrospective and prospective. In T. C. Urdan & S. A. Karabenick (Eds.), *The decade ahead: Theoretical perspectives on motivation and achievement* (pp. 35–70). Bingley, UK: Emerald.

Wigfield, A., & Cambria, J. (2010b). Students' achievement values, goal orientations, and interest: Definitions, development, and relations to achievement outcomes. *Developmental Review, 30,* 1–35. doi:10.1016/j.dr.2009.12.001

Wigfield, A., & Eccles, J. S. (2000). Expectancy-value theory of motivation. *Contemporary Educational Psychology, 25,* 68–81. doi:10.1006/ceps.1999.1015

Wigfield, A., Tonks, S., & Klauda, S. L. (2009). Expectancy-value theory. In K. A. Wentzel & A. Wigfield (Eds.), *Handbook of motivation at school* (pp. 55–75). New York, NY: Routledge.

Wigfield, A., Eccles, J. S., Yoon, K. S., Harold, R. D., Arbreton, A. J., Freedman-Doan, C., & Blumenfeld, P. C. (1997). Change in children's competence beliefs and subjective task values across the elementary school year: A 3-year study. *Journal of Educational Psychology, 89,* 451–469. doi:10.1037/0022-0663.89.3.451

Witt, P. L., & Kerssen-Griep, J. (2011). Instructional feedback I: The interaction of facework and immediacy on students' perceptions of instructor credibility. *Communication Education, 60,* 75–94. doi:10.1080/03634523.2010.507820

Witt, P. L., Wheeless, L. R., & Allen, M. (2004). A meta-analytical review of the relationship between teacher immediacy and student learning. *Communication Monographs, 71*, 184–207. doi:10.1080/036452042000228054

Wubbels, T., & Brekelmans, M. (2005). Two decades of research on teacher-student relationships in class. *International Journal of Educational Research, 43*, 6–24. doi:10.1016/j.ijer.2006.03.003

About the Editor

Elisia L. Cohen earned her PhD in Communication from the University of Southern California, and is an Associate Professor of Communication and Director of the Health Communication Research Collaborative at the University of Kentucky. Today, she is the Chair of the Department of Communication in the College of Communication and Information at the University of Kentucky. Her research has been supported by the Centers for Disease Control and Prevention, National Institutes of Health, Merck Sharp & Dohme Corporation, and an unrestricted gift from GlaxoSmithKline. She is an investigator with the Rural Cancer Prevention Center, St. Louis Center for Excellence in Cancer Communication Research, and was past media coordinator for the Cervical Cancer-free Kentucky initiative. Her research on public communication, public opinion, and public health has appeared in such journals as: *Health Communication, Health Education and Behavior, Journal of Applied Communication Research, Journal of Broadcasting and Electronic Media, Journal of Communication, Journal of Health Communication, Qualitative Health Research,* and *Prometheus.* She is married and has one daughter, Addison Lydia.

About the Contributors

Dorothy Collins Andreas (PhD, Texas A&M University) is an Assistant Professor in the Communication Division of Seaver College at Pepperdine University. Her research interests address the intersection of organizational, health, environmental, and conflict communication in ways that help explain how individuals, groups, and communities make sense of potential risks, coordinate different views, and determine how to respond. In particular, her expertise focuses on communicating about nuclear power in public contexts and within nuclear-related organizations. She has experience working for and consulting with the U.S. Nuclear Regulatory Commission. Her work is published in *Social Science and Medicine*, *Qualitative Health Research*, and *The Handbook of Conflict Communication*.

Emma Boyland completed her PhD examining food promotion to children in the UK and its potential consequences on their eating behaviors within the Department of Psychological Sciences at the University of Liverpool in 2010. She has since taken up a lectureship position and continued to pursue those research interests. Specifically she is carrying out studies to quantify the extent and nature of food advertising via television, new media and other sources (e.g., supermarket and point of sale promotions) and to elucidate the effects of branding activity (e.g., use of promotional characters) on children's responses to advertising (taste preferences, food choices, and consumption). She is also undertaking research to determine the role of situational factors (e.g., hunger state), and both intrinsic (e.g., tendency to eat in the absence of hunger, cue responsiveness) and extrinsic (e.g., parental control, independent spending power) mediating factors on children's intake and request responses to food marketing.

Jasmin Chrzan (BA, Indiana University) is currently attending the Masters of Addictions Counseling Program at Hazelden.

Danielle Endres (PhD, University of Washington) is an Associate Professor of Communication and faculty member in the Environmental Humanities Masters Program at the University of Utah. She is a rhetorical theorist and critic with expertise in environmental communication, science communication, social movements, and Native American cultures. Her research focuses on the rhetoric of environmental and science controversies and social movements including nuclear waste siting decisions, climate change activism, Native American environmental activism, and low carbon energy policy. Endres is the co-editor of *Social Movement to Address Climate Change: Local Steps for Global Action* (2009) and has published in *Quarterly Journal of Speech*, *Communication and Critical Cultural Studies*, *Western Journal of Communication*, *Environmental Communication*, *Argumentation*, and *Local Environment*. She has also received U.S. Department of Energy and National Science Foundation funding for her research.

Danielle Halliwell (MA, University of Cincinnati) is a doctoral candidate in the Department of Communication at the University of Missouri. Her research focuses on communicative processes during family transitions, with a particular emphasis on how siblings communicatively construct and maintain their relationships as they navigate various changes and challenges in emerging adulthood. She has received top papers at both regional and national conferences and co-authored publications in the *Southern Communication Journal* and *Communication Monographs*.

Flaviu Hodis received his PhD in Educational Psychology (Statistics and Measurement) from Southern Illinois University Carbondale in 2008. He is currently a senior lecturer in the School of Education at Victoria University of Wellington, New Zealand. Flaviu's research programme aims to advance understanding of how individuals' concomitant strivings for value, control, and truth effectiveness shape their self-regulation, performance in work- and school-related settings, communication preferences, and well-being. His methodological interests relate to structural equation modeling and advanced methods for analyzing multidimensional and interactive change processes. Flaviu has co-authored a number of articles, which were published in journals such as the *Journal of Educational Psychology, Communication Yearbook, Journal of Applied Communication Research, Basic Communication Course Annual, Journal of Statistical Software, and Applied Mathematical Sciences*.

Georgeta (Mimi) Hodis is a lecturer in the School of Communication, Journalism, and Marketing at Massey University, New Zealand where she teaches research methods and public relations. She received her PhD in Communication from Southern Illinois University Carbondale in May 2009. Mimi's main research interest centers on class instruction and its effect on communication apprehension, self-perceived communication competence, willingness to communicate, and student satisfaction in communicating with teachers. Her research has been published in the *Communication Yearbook, Journal of Applied Communication Research, International Journal of Communication*, and the *Basic Communication Course Annual*.

Andrea B. Hollingshead (PhD, University of Illinois at Urbana–Champaign) is Professor of Communication, Psychology, and Management and Organizations at the University of Southern California. Her research concerns the factors and processes that lead to effective and ineffective group performance. Her work also addresses how groups collaborate and create community using communication technologies. She has co-authored or co-edited three books, *Research Methods for Studying Groups and Teams, Theories of Small Groups: Interdisciplinary Perspectives*, and *Groups Interacting with Technology* and has published many articles in top tier communication, psychology and management journals.

Young Ji Kim (PhD, University of Southern California) is a Postdoctoral Associate at the MIT Center for Collective Intelligence. Kim studies the ways in which individuals interact with various information sources online especially in the context of credibility assessment and social influence. She is also interested in how groups collaborate and develop collective intelligence both in offline and online settings.

William J. Kinsella (PhD, Rutgers University), is a Professor of Communication at North Carolina State University, where he directed the interdisciplinary program in Science, Technology & Society from 2009–2014. His work addresses topics in organizational communication, environmental communication, rhetoric of science and technology, and rhetoric of public policy. He is a co-editor of *Nuclear Legacies: Communication, Controversy, and the U.S. Nuclear Weapons Complex* (2007), and has published in numerous journals and books in the fields of communication, rhetoric, and science and technology studies. He has served with the citizen advisory board for the U.S. Department of Energy's Hanford nuclear site (2000–2004) and as a U.S. Fulbright Scholar at the Institute for Nuclear Energy and Energy Systems, University of Stuttgart (2010). His publications have examined communication issues in the areas of nuclear fusion, environmental cleanup across the U.S. nuclear weapons complex, and commercial nuclear energy in U.S. and global contexts.

Annie Lang (PhD, University of Wisconsin at Madison) is Distinguished Professor of Telecommunications and Cognitive Science at Indiana University. She is interested in message processing. She is a former editor of Media Psychology, a Fellow of the International Communication Association, and recipient of the Steven H. Chaffee career productivity award.

Paul Leonardi (PhD, Stanford University) is the Reece Duca Professor of Technology Management at the University of California, Santa Barbara. His research focuses on helping companies to create and share knowledge more effectively. He is interested in how implementing new technologies and harnessing the power of informal social networks can help companies take advantage of their knowledge assets to create innovative products and services.

Matthew D. Matsaganis (PhD, University of Southern California) is Assistant Professor in the Communication Department at the University at Albany, State University of New York. His research focuses on communication as determinant of health and health disparities in urban communities, the roles of ethnic media in increasingly diverse communities (from a consumption, production, and policy perspective), and digital inequalities and the social impact of new communication technologies. He is first author of *Understanding Ethnic Media: Producers, Consumers and Societies* (2011) and the co-editor and a contributing author to *Communicative Cities in the 21st Century* (2013). In addition, his research has been published in several journals including the *Journal of Health Communication, Human Communication Research,* the *Journal of Applied Communication Research,* the *International Journal of Communication, Journalism: Theory, Practice and Criticism,* the *Electronic Journal of Communication,* and *Communication Research Reports.*

Evy Neyens obtained her MSc in Communication in 2012 at the University of Leuven. Her dissertation examined the impact of television exposure on young females' body dissatisfaction with romantic experience as a moderator. Subsequently she earned credits in various sociological and statistical courses. In addition, she acquired a postgraduate degree in Marketing Communication at the Ehsal Management School in 2013. Since 2014 she has been a PhD student at the Institute for Media Studies at the Faculty of Social Sciences of the University of Leuven. She investigates children's processing of endorsed food advertising in order to develop and test interventions to bolster children's defenses against the promotion of unhealthy foods and beverages.

Jochen Peter (PhD, University of Amsterdam) is a Full Professor in and Director of the Amsterdam School of Communication Research, ASCoR, at the University of Amsterdam. His research focuses on the consequences of adolescents' media use for their psycho-social development. Specifically, he investigates the effects of teenagers' use of online sexually explicit material on their sexual attitudes and behaviors.

Ronald E. Rice (PhD, Stanford University) is the Arthur N. Rupe Chair in the Social Effects of Mass Communication, and Department Chair, in the Department of Communication, and Co-Director of the Carsey-Wolf Center, at the University of California, Santa Barbara. His co-authored or (co)edited books include *Organizations and Unusual Routines: A Systems Analysis of Dysfunctional Feedback Processes* (2010); *Media Ownership: Research and Regulation* (2008); *The Internet and Healthcare: Theory, Research and Practice* (2006); *Social Consequences of Internet Use: Access, Involvement and Interaction* (2002); *The Internet and Health Communication* (2001); *Accessing and Browsing Information and Communication* (2001); *Public Communication Campaigns* (1981, 1989, 2001, 2012); *Research Methods and the New Media* (1988);

Managing Organizational Innovation (1987); and *The New Media: Communication, Research and Technology* (1984).

David R. Seibold is Professor of Technology Management (and Vice Chair) at the University of California, Santa Barbara, and an Affiliated Faculty member in the Department of Communication. His research interests include innovation and organizational change, group interaction and decision making, temporality, influence processes, and organizational and management communication. He has published two books and nearly 150 articles and chapters. A former editor of the *Journal of Applied Communication Research*, he has been a member of the editorial boards of numerous journals. He has been elected a Distinguished Scholar in the National Communication Association and a Fellow of the International Communication Association.

Michael D. Slater (PhD, Stanford University) is Social and Behavioral Science Distinguished Professor at the School of Communication, Ohio State University. His research includes theory-building efforts in message effects, persuasion, narrative influences, and dynamic processes of media selection, media effects, and maintenance of personal and social identity, with a particular interest in using mediated communication to support positive public health outcomes. Dr. Slater is also a Fellow of the International Communication Association.

Tim Smits is an assistant professor in persuasion and marketing communication at the University of Leuven (Belgium). He completed his PhD on comparative optimism (social psychology, Department of Psychology at Leuven University) in 2005 but also has an MA in Statistics (Leuven University). Since his PhD, he has been involved in interdisciplinary research (psychology, marketing, pharmacy, ethics, sociology) and now he combines these influences to study persuasive communication at the Institute for Media Studies (communication science, University of Leuven), of which he is the current director. His main research interests are the persuasiveness of apparently peripheral communication cues and food marketing targeting children. For both, it is the seemingly implicit nature of the persuasion process Tim wants to quantify, assess its effects, and investigate the possibilities to embed such heuristics in beneficial interventions.

Robert S. Tokunaga is an Assistant Professor in the Department of Communicology at the University of Hawai'i at Mānoa. His research addresses the psychological and relational implications of communication technology use. He is particularly interested in refining the conceptual and measurement issues of interpretably negative communication events over the Internet, such as Internet habits, cyberbullying, cyberstalking, relational transgressions, and interpersonal surveillance. He is also presently completing two experiments on Internet phishing and the sexual solicitation of minors over the Internet. He uses various statistical tools, including mixed modeling and latent growth modeling, to address questions about the so-called negative effects of Internet use.

Patti M. Valkenburg is Distinguished University Professor of Media, Youth, and Society at the University of Amsterdam. Her research interests include the cognitive, emotional, and social effects of media and technologies on children, adolescents, and adults. She is particularly interested in how media users differ in their susceptibility to media effects. Dr. Valkenburg is a Fellow of the International Communication Association.

Heidi Vandebosch is an Associate Professor at the Department of Communication Studies at the University of Antwerp (Belgium), specialising in media sociology and health communication. She has an MA in Communication Studies (K.U.Leuven) and a PhD in Social Sciences (K.U.Leuven). Her research focuses on media/ICT uses and effects. She has published internationally about TV use and obesity amongst children, the use of (celebrity) spokes characters for health promotion, and cyberbullying amongst youngsters.

Eric J. Zackrison is a PhD candidate at the University of California, Santa Barbara. After 20 years in management and as an entrepreneur he went back to school attaining a MBA and a MA in Communication from Missouri State University. His research interests include coordination in complex organizations, leadership, interviewing, small group dynamics, and socialization in complex organizations.

About the Editorial Assistants

Rachael A. Record is a doctoral candidate at the University of Kentucky. Her research interests include methodological and theoretical explorations of message design and campaign efforts aimed at fostering health-related behavior change. Specifically, her research has focused in the area of tobacco, including topics of policy, cessation, air quality, and secondhand smoke. Her published work has appeared in the journals of *Nursing Clinics of North America, Journal of Online Learning and Teaching, Journal of the Kentucky Medical Association,* and *Public Health Nursing.*

Jenna E. Reno is a doctoral candidate at the University of Kentucky. Her interests include the research, development and evaluation of health campaigns, particularly the processes of message design and the application of social marketing techniques. Specifically, she has investigated the development and reification of social norms and the ways in which they inform health beliefs and behaviors through processes of socialization, as well as the use of social media to disseminate and reinforce normative health messages. Her published work appears in the journals of *Health Communication* and *Clinical Journal of Oncology Nursing.*

Sarah C. Vos is a doctoral student at the University of Kentucky. Her research examines the intersection of health and the mass media. Her research has been presented at national and international conferences and has been published in *Health Communication.* Before turning to the study of communication, Sarah worked as a reporter at *The Lexington Herald-Leader* in Kentucky and the *Concord Monitor* in New Hampshire. She was also an assistant editor at *Harper's Magazine* in New York City.

Laura E. Young was an editorial assistant for *Communication Yearbook 39* as a doctoral candidate and is currently an Assistant Professor at Butler University. Her research examines internal and external communication processes in high-risk, high-consequence environments such as fire departments. Specifically, she concentrates on the intersection of public relations and organizational communication by examining how communication during change can affect the organizational culture, satisfaction, structure, and performance as well as the external image and reputation of the organization. Her work has been presented at national and international conferences and published in journals such as *Communication Education* and *Qualitative Health Research*.

Author Index

Subject Index

Please note: page numbers in *italics* followed by an *f* indicate figures and by a *t* indicate tables.